China's 40 Years of Economic Reform and Development

Xinli Zheng

China's 40 Years of Economic Reform and Development

How the Miracle Was Created

商務印書館
创于1897
The Commercial Press

Springer

Xinli Zheng
China Center for International Economic Exchanges
Beijing, China

ISBN 978-981-13-4804-4 ISBN 978-981-13-2727-8 (eBook)
https://doi.org/10.1007/978-981-13-2727-8

Jointly published with The Commercial Press, Ltd., Beijing, China

The print edition is not for sale in China Mainland. Customers from China Mainland please order the print book from: The Commercial Press, Ltd.

This Springer imprint is published by the registered company Springer Nature Singapore Pte Ltd.
The registered company address is: 152 Beach Road, #21-01/04 Gateway East, Singapore 189721, Singapore

Xinli Zheng

Resume

Xinli Zheng was born in a rural family on February 12, 1945, in Chuzhuang Village, Shangtun Township, Tanghe County, Henan Province. In 1964, he graduated from Tanghe No. 1 Secondary School. From 1964 to 1970, he studied in the Mining Department of the University of Science and Technology, formerly known as Beijing Steel and Iron Institute. From 1970 to 1978, he worked at the Handan Metallurgical and Mining Headquarters, Hebei Province, where he worked as a worker, technician, theoretical teacher, deputy chief of the Theoretical Education Department, and deputy director of the Party Committee Office. In 1978, he was admitted to the Graduate School at the Chinese Academy of Social Sciences, majoring in Industrial Economics, and obtained a master's degree in economics in 1981.

From 1981 to 1987, he worked in the Economic Section of the Research Office of the Secretariat of the Central Committee of the Communist Party of China and served as a researcher at the section level and deputy chief of the Economic Section. From 1984 to 1986, he studied at the Training Department of the Party School of the CPC Central Committee for 2 years.

From 1987 to 2000, he worked in the National Planning Commission. He first served as deputy chief economist for the State Information Center for 2 years and then worked in the Policy Research Office for 11 years. He served as deputy director, director, deputy secretary-general, and spokesman.

From 2000 to 2010, he served as Deputy Director of the Policy Research Office of the CPC Central Committee. From 2008 to 2013, he served as Deputy Director of the Committee for Economic Affairs of the Chinese People's Political Consultative Conference.

In 2009, he assisted Mr. Zeng Peiyan to establish the China Center for International Economic Exchanges. From 2009 to 2015, he served as its executive vice chairman. He was concurrently Chairman of the China Federation of Industrial Economics, Executive President of the China Association of Policy Science and Research, and Executive Vice Chairman of the China Urbanization Promotion Association. In 2014, he was named one of China's top ten economists for 2013.

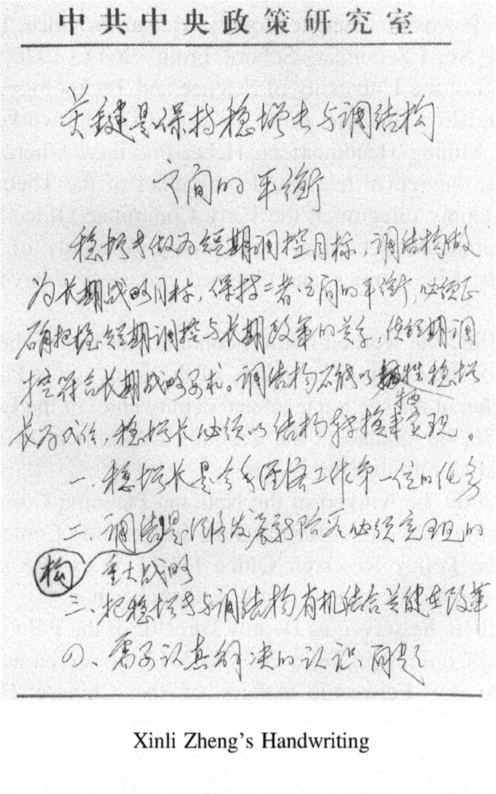

中共中央政策研究室

关键是保持稳增长与调结构之间的平衡

稳增长做为短期调控目标，调结构做为长期战略目标，保持二者之间的平衡，必须正确把握短期调控与长期改革的关系，使短期调控符合长期战略要求。调结构不能以牺牲稳增长为代价，稳增长必须以结构转换来实现。

一、稳增长是今年经济工作第一位的任务

二、调结构是经济发展新阶段必须完成的重大战略

三、把稳增长与调结构有机结合关键在改革

四、需要认真解决的认识问题

Xinli Zheng's Handwriting

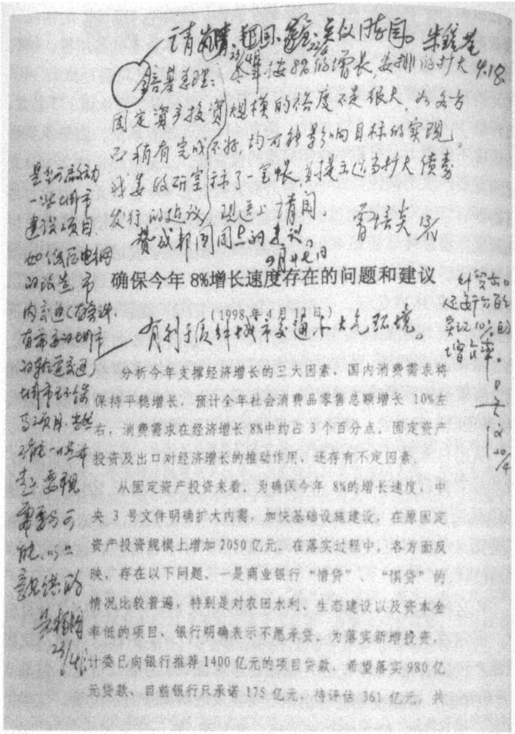

确保今年 8%增长速度存在的问题和建议

（1998 年 4 月 12 日）

分析今年支撑经济增长的三大因素，国内消费需求将保持平稳增长，预计全年社会消费品零售总额增长 10%左右，消费需求在经济增长 8%中约占 3 个百分点。固定资产投资及出口对经济增长的推动作用，还存有不定因素。

从固定资产投资来看，为确保今年 8%的增长速度，中央 3 号文件明确扩大内需，加快基础设施建设，在原固定资产投资规模上增加 2050 亿元。在落实过程中，各方面反映，存在以下问题。一是商业银行“惜贷”、“惧贷”的情况比较普遍，特别是对农田水利、生态建设以及资本金率低的项目，银行明确表示不愿承贷。为落实新增投资，计委已向银行推荐 1400 亿元的项目贷款，希望落实 980 亿元贷款，目前银行只承诺 175 亿元，待评估 361 亿元，共

In April 1998, Xinli Zheng wrote “Ensuring 8 Percent Economic Growth This Year,” in which he proposed issuing government bonds to expand domestic demand. At the time, Zeng Peiyan, Minister of the State Planning Commission, reported this to the Premier of the State Council. This prompted the State Council to decide to issue 10-year bonds worth 100 billion yuan each year for five consecutive years to fund infrastructure construction, such as transportation and communications, successfully turning the challenges posed by the Asian financial crisis into opportunities, supporting current economic growth and laying a solid foundation for the rapid economic growth over the next decade.

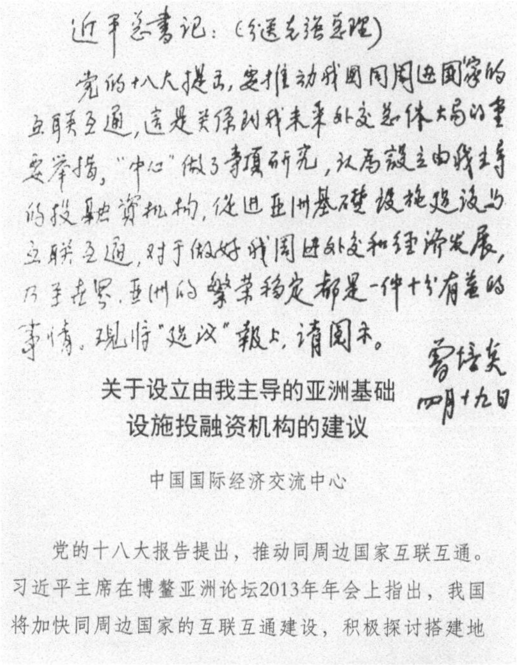
近平总书记：（并送克强总理）

党的十八大提出，要推动我国同周边国家的互联互通，这是关系到我未来外交总体大局的重要举措，"中心"做了专项研究，认为设立由我主导的投融资机构，促进亚洲基础设施建设与互联互通，对于做好我周边外交和经济发展，乃至世界、亚洲的繁荣稳定都是一件十分有益的事情。现将"建议"报上，请阅示。

曾培炎
四月十九日

关于设立由我主导的亚洲基础设施投融资机构的建议

中国国际经济交流中心

党的十八大报告提出，推动同周边国家互联互通。习近平主席在博鳌亚洲论坛2013年年会上指出，我国将加快同周边国家的互联互通建设，积极探讨搭建地

In April 2013, Xinli Zheng wrote "Suggestions on Building an Asian Infrastructure Investment and Financing Institution Led by China." Zeng Peiyan, Chairman of the China Center for International Economic Exchanges, reported these suggestions to General Secretary Xi Jinping and Premier Li Keqiang, and they fully affirmed them. In October of the same year, President Xi Jinping announced the proposal for establishing the Asian Infrastructure Investment Bank in Indonesia. In December 2015, the AIIB was formally established. Some foreign commentators believe that this is China's wisest proposal, making China a major actor on the global financial stage.

Theoretical Breakthroughs in China's Economic Reform

The Chinese economy has made tremendous progress in the past 40 years, mainly thanks to successful reform efforts, which themselves are the result of theoretical breakthroughs and the development of new systems. What have been the main breakthroughs in economic theory? What shifts in understanding have occurred? And which new systems have been established? These are questions of widespread interest in China and abroad, and they are answered broadly in the following six points.

China is still in the primary stage of socialism and will remain so for a considerable time in the future: China established socialism on the foundations of a backward agrarian economy. Before the policy of reform and opening up was introduced, the economic system and policies we implemented exceeded the stage of development of our productive forces. It was believed that high levels of public ownership and even distribution of wealth were the best approaches. But they hindered the economy. They made us realize that we are still in the primary stage of socialism and that we need systems and policies compatible with the development level of our productive forces. With this in mind, we were able to take bold measures to establish new systems and policies conducive to developing the productive forces in the course of reform.

Building a socialist market economy: Prior to reform, we had a planned economy. Practice proved that the system hampered the development of the productive forces. For 40 years, we have adhered to market-oriented reforms, and we have constantly sought to inject economic development with new vitality, as evidenced by the transition from allowing the market to play a basic role in allocating resources to allowing it to play the decisive role in their allocation. Meanwhile, considerable attention has been given to improving and making best use of the government's guidance and managerial role. These two approaches are organically linked and have formed a dynamic and balanced mechanism for economic development and promoted healthy and rapid development of the economy.

Adhering to the approach of developing both the public and non-public sectors of the economy: While adhering to an approach of giving primacy to the public sector, China has allowed the non-public sector, including private companies and self-employed workers, to develop. State-owned enterprises (SOEs) have established modern corporate structures, and private enterprises have been encouraged to become shareholders of SOEs. A mixed-ownership economy has been developed, and a scientific governance structure has been established based on a standardized shareholding system. As such, implementing a mixed-ownership system has become the primary method of realizing a system of public ownership. The private economy has grown rapidly from nothing and played a significant role in developing the national economy.

Adopting a combination of distribution according to work and distribution according to factors of production: Breaking away from the "communal pot" and egalitarianism was an important step in China's reform process. This began with allowing some people and some regions to prosper first, then encouraging them to help those less fortunate, and finally enabling everybody and all regions to prosper together. It began with rewarding performance and considering fairness and evolved to giving equal importance to performance and fairness, to reflect the shift in policy concerning distribution. The government is now concerned with trying to solve the excessive income gap and achieve shared development.

Implementing the rural household contract responsibility system with remuneration linked to output: In the early 1980s, reform began in the countryside with the introduction of the rural household contract responsibility system, which mustered the enthusiasm of farmers for raising production and meaningful agricultural development. The government is currently implementing reform measures to separate rural land ownership rights, contract rights, and management rights, and it is promoting larger-scale farms with more professional management standards in order to accelerate agricultural modernization, promote the integration of various rural industries, and revitalize rural areas.

Continuing to open up in order to promote reform and development: China has opened itself up to the world gradually, starting with establishing special economic zones in the early stages of reform, then opening up coastal cities to foreign trade, and then opening up other coastal and inland areas. In recent years, free-trade zones and free-trade ports have been established to allow more foreign investment in some fields and reduce import tariffs. The economy is increasingly geared toward trade with the outside world, so an open economy is taking shape. The fact is that China has already embarked on the road of opening up to promote reform and development.

Xinli Zheng's new book records China's reform and opening up process as well as its economic development, revealing successful experiences along the way. In the course of drafting documents on reform for the Party Central Committee and State Council over many years, Zheng undertook research on economic theories and policies, participated in and presided over the planning of development projects and conducted frequent investigations in different parts of the country. As a result, his articles shine a light on the background, content, and implementation of central government decisions over the past four decades of reform and opening up, particularly in terms of the six aforementioned major breakthroughs in reform theory, which are elaborated upon in this publication. Reading this book will serve as a shortcut to anyone wishing to understand fully China's reform experience.

Beijing, China
2018

Jiang Zhenghua

A Book Explaining the Secrets Behind the 40-Year Success of the Chinese Economy

This year is the 40th anniversary of the introduction of China's reform and opening up policy. Four decades ago, China's primary motivation for reform was its experience operating a traditional planned economy over the previous 30 years. Practice had proved that the system hindered the development of the productive forces. Actively and consciously reforming a socialist economic system was a great and unprecedented undertaking. It was a victory for the materialist ideological line of seeking truth from facts and a grand awakening for the Communist Party of China.

Instituting economic reform in a country with a population of more than a billion requires theoretical guidance and unified command. It also requires the formulation of clear guidelines and policies, which must be tested before being rolled out. As such, researching reform theory and coming up with reform plans and programs became a major task of the Party. Reform began in the countryside and spread to the cities; it developed from energizing microeconomic entities to making changes to the macroeconomic system; and it started with opening coastal areas to the world and was gradually rolled out across the country. Correct reform theories and policies are derived from practical application and are created by the public at the community level and by government officials. The process leading to China's large-scale social revolution entailed dedication to investigations and research, summing up the reform experiences of communities, elevating practices proven to be effective to the status of theory, and creating national guidelines for smoothly implementing reform methods. A large number of people at all levels of Party and government organs as well as academic research institutions have been involved in exploring and researching reform-related issues, and we have drawn useful lessons from comparative studies of the economic systems of other countries.

The period since the 1980s has been the most active in terms of new economic theories and reform ideas since the founding of the People's Republic of China in 1949 thanks to the emergence of a cohort of reform thinkers, theorists, and pioneers. Despite their divergent views and occasional disputes, they are united by the common objective of reform. Following the promulgation of a reform "Decision" of the Party's Central Committee, for example, everyone's thinking is unified by the guiding principles of the Decision and falls in line with the Central Committee. All parties create a synergy and work together to push forward reform.

At the start of the reform period, Xinli Zheng worked on economic theory and policy at the Research Office of the Secretariat of the Central Committee of the Communist Party of China. He went on to research economic policy at the State Planning Commission before moving to the Central Policy Research Office in 2000. After he retired in 2009, Zheng helped Zeng Peiyan set up the China Center for International Economic Exchanges, where he continued to do research and consultancy work on central government economic decision-making. The focus of Zheng's career was drafting reform documents and national five-year plans and researching important reform issues and interpreting major decisions of the Party Central Committee and the State Council. On the back of his diligent efforts, he wrote a large number of articles on economic theory, many of which were published in newspapers and magazines including *People's Daily*, *Qiushi*, *Economic Daily*, and *Guangming Daily*. He also wrote and edited works that researched and interpreted major economic policies and decisions of the Central Committee.

Zheng was an independent thinker, and he was not afraid to make policy recommendations based on the realities he saw before him. For example, he suggested that China should issue long-term development bonds following the Asian financial crisis in 1997, and he proposed establishing the Asian Infrastructure Investment Bank in 2013, which was later approved by Party and State leaders and worked out very well. Zheng truly deserves praise for his ability to get to the heart of matters and his courage to make policy recommendations and remain steadfast in his opinions. This is a rare but much-needed quality among economic researchers.

There is no shortage of creativity and innovation in Zheng's work. These qualities can be seen in his suggestions to use the final-goods ratio as a major indicator for evaluating macroeconomic benefits, increasing urban and rural residents' income as a proportion of gross national income, increasing the household consumption rate, optimizing the scale of national investment, adopting a mixed-ownership shareholding system to achieve public ownership, and establishing a unified urban–rural real estate market, as well as his efforts to develop the two disciplines of modern policy science and development planning to create a market economy in China. In the course of his career, Zheng made tremendous contributions to thousands of reform theories and policies through his dedicated and tireless efforts.

Reviewing the past four decades of the reform and opening up policy, there are many successes worth mentioning. *How the Miracle Was Created: China's 40 Years of Economic Reform and Development*, the Chinese version of which is being published by the Commercial Press and the English version by Springer, is a collection of Zheng's important articles published over the years. It faithfully documents major breakthroughs in various periods of China's reform and how reform and development have been mutually promotional and closely integrated, answering the question of how China's 40-year miracle was created. Its publication will aid anyone wishing to better understand China's experiences in reform and development.

The 19th National Congress of the Communist Party of China in 2017 established the guiding role of Xi Jinping's Thought on Socialism with Chinese Characteristics for a New Era within the whole Party and set out the Party's new goals. These include creating a moderately prosperous society in all respects by 2020, basically achieving socialist modernization by 2035, and developing China into a great modern socialist country that is prosperous, strong, democratic, culturally advanced, harmonious, and beautiful by the middle of this century. To realize these goals for the next 30 years, China must continue to deepen reforms of its economic, political, cultural, social, ecological, and Party building systems; pursue reforms in a more systematic, holistic, and coordinated manner; and modernize its system and capacity for governance.

Reform continues, and the body of theory that supports it is growing. Theoretical innovations will constantly emerge based on the need to meet new targets. This is a fundamental source of the great vitality of socialism with Chinese characteristics. The theoretical and policy innovations made in the first 40 years of the reform and opening up policy were responses to problems at the time, and new theories and policies will undoubtedly emerge to solve new problems along the way and constantly promote China's sustained and healthy development while resolving contradictions and issues.

Beijing, China
2018

Li Yining

Works Must Be Relevant to Everyday Life

In the autumn of 1981, the Research Office of the Secretariat of the CPC Central Committee selected four comrades from a list of the first students to graduate from the Graduate School of the Chinese Academy of Social Sciences to train as researchers. Xinli Zheng was one of the four chosen. At the time, I was working for the Research Office's theory group, and Zheng was placed in the economics group. In 1987, the Secretariat Research Office was abolished, and I was sent to work for a branch of the Central Advisory Commission, while Zheng was transferred to the State Planning Commission. In 1993, when I was a leader at the Policy Research Office of the CPC Central Committee, I was invited by the US-China Cultural Exchange Association to act as a consultant for a delegation visiting the USA headed by Gui Shiyong, Deputy Director of the State Planning Commission. Zheng was also a member of the delegation, and this led to an unforgettable period of investigation in our lives.

In 2000, Zheng was transferred from the State Planning Commission, where he was director and deputy secretary-general, to take up the post of deputy director of the Policy Research Office of the CPC Central Committee, which meant we worked together again for a number of years. After we retired, we also conducted some research together for the China Association of Policy Science. As such, we worked together on many occasions over the years.

This year marks the 40th anniversary of the policy of reform and opening up. The economics community is, therefore, publishing academic biographies of scholars who have contributed to theoretical and policy research related to the policy. Xinli Zheng, an economic theory and policy researcher, is one such scholar. This is a hugely important matter and a great honor. An academic biography is a record and account of a scholar's unique academic research process and achievements. Producing academic biographies on a specific subject is like creating an "academic garden" that gathers together in one place the achievements and splendors of a host of individuals in a way that enhances the whole, and it can be instructive for statecraft.

Although Zheng worked in many departments and institutions after the policy of reform and opening up was introduced, the majority of his work concerned economic theory and policy research in reform and development, on the back of which he wrote countless research articles and participated in drafting important documents for the Party and State. As such, he was not only personally involved in the research and practice of China's reform and development in the 1980s and 1990s, he was also a historical witness to the creation and development of important theories and policies that shaped China's economic reform.

Each participant and researcher has contributed their own achievements to the course of China's socialist reform, opening up, and modernization epic. Qing painter Zheng Banqiao once said, "Works must be relevant to everyday life," and he believed that "Scholars should make their own mark," in terms of their academic style. Under the banner of developing socialist ideology with Chinese characteristics, Xinli Zheng made great achievements in academic research, but he also developed his own research characteristics and style. His approach combined research, study, investigative research and theoretical thinking, and melded practical experience, cognitive elevation, and the application of results. Zheng adhered to this approach throughout his career, which can be seen in his own works and academic biographies. As a Marxist theoretical worker and academic researcher, it was important that he was consistent in this respect, but it is rare and therefore deserving of praise.

Beijing, China
2018

Teng Wensheng

Xinli Zheng's and My Shared Experience of the Reform Years

I met Xinli Zheng for the first time in 1984 when Song Shaowen, Deputy Director of the State Planning Commission, hosted a seminar on planning system reform in Harbin. I worked in the Policy Research Office of the State Planning Commission, and Zheng worked for the Research Office of the Secretariat of the CPC Central Committee. We were both very interested in planning system reform, and we greatly admired the knowledge and mentorship of Gui Shizyong, Zheng's dissertation advisor at graduate school and head of the Planning Commission's Research Office, so we had things in common.

In 1987, the Secretariat's Research Office was abolished, and Zheng was transferred to the National Information Center under the State Planning Commission. In 1989, under the guidance of Fang Weizhong and Gui Shiyong, I was placed in charge of putting together a team to draft the Eighth Five-Year Plan for National Economic and Social Development of the People's Republic of China. That team included Xinli Zheng. Afterward, until we retired, we worked together on drafts of various documents for the CPC Central Committee, State Council, and State Planning Commission. The following are the three main types of drafts we worked on together:

The first is drafts of national five-year plans and the annual report on the plan for national and economic and social development submitted by the director of the State Planning Commission to the National People's Congress. The main objectives of the Eighth Five-Year Plan were to meet people's basic requirements for food and clothing and to stabilize market prices. The primary tasks of the Ninth Five-Year Plan were to promote the transformation of the economic growth model and economic system and to complete the second stage of strategic goals for development. Once each five-year plan was approved by the National People's Congress, it was our job to write articles and readers explaining their content and publicizing the central government's major strategic decisions and policies.

The second is draft documents for the National Conference on Financial Work. During the mid-1990s, arbitrary charges, fund-raising, quotas, and fines were commonplace and real estate and development zones were booming. Under the direct leadership of the Standing Committee of the Political Bureau of the CPC

Central Committee and Vice-Premier of the State Council Zhu Rongji, these chaotic phenomena were curtailed and the financial system was thoroughly reformed. On the back of in-depth investigations and research, the central government decided to hold a National Conference on Financial Work. At the time, I was Deputy Director of the Office of the Central Leading Group for Financial and Economic Affairs and responsible for preparing documents for meetings. Zheng was also involved in this work. Neither of us was particularly knowledgeable about finance at the time, so it took a lot of effort to write the documents well. We humbly learned from colleagues well versed in business and learned through doing, eventually improving our knowledge of finance by drafting central government documents. I was placed in charge of drafting documents for the National Conference on Financial Work a further three times, and Zheng participated in that work too. Those four conferences and their documents played an important role in financial reform and development as well as promoting stable economic development in China.

The third is drafting the Report on the Work of the Government. When I was transferred from the Office of the Central Leading Group for Financial and Economic Affairs to the State Council Research Office, I was placed in charge of drafting the Report on the Work of the Government each year for most of Zhu Rongji and Wen Jiabao's premierships. Zheng was also involved in this work. The two premiers had exacting standards when it came to the reports, so we had to be extremely focused during the drafting work. We would breathe a sigh of relief each time a report received positive feedback from the National People's Congress.

In retirement, we both went to work for the China Center for International Economic Exchanges to help build a new type of think tank in China under the leadership of Zeng Peiyan.

Reflecting on our more than three decades of cooperation, I feel that Xinli Zheng's greatest attributes are his sincere love for our Party, the country, and socialism and his willingness to work tirelessly for those causes, which produced a work ethos of selflessness. We often worked overtime, yet we never complained. Though the work was difficult and tiring, it did not compare to toiling on the land like our forefathers and farmers. More than that though, we were proud and honored to have the opportunity to participate in such important work. Zheng is always eager to learn new things, focuses on understanding the overall economic situation, and is good at offering constructive opinions. He views things in a unique way and has clear ideas. He likes to discuss problems and is not afraid to propose solutions in difficult situations.

At this juncture of the 40th anniversary of the policy of reform and opening up, I feel excited when I look back at the times we spent together. I would like the above to be used as a foreword to Xinli Zheng's works.

Beijing, China
2018

Wei Liqun

Comments on Xinli Zheng's Academic Thoughts[1]

Academic Contributions of Xinli Zheng

Xinli Zheng graduated from the Institute of Industrial Economics at the Graduate School of the Chinese Academy of Social Sciences in August 1981 and joined the economics team at the Research Office of the Secretariat of the Central Committee of the Communist Party of China. So began a 35-year career dedicated to economic policy and theory. Having helped to draft important documents for the central government concerning reform and development while working for the research offices of the Secretariat and the State Development and Planning Commission as well as the Central Policy Research Office, applying his scholarly diligence, pragmatism, and scientific rigor, Zheng wrote many theoretical papers and academic works throughout his career. These include theoretical explanations of the Party's policies, analyses of economic trends and suggested countermeasures, research on major economic issues, and experience-based comparisons with other countries. The following is a summary of Zheng's academic achievements and research ethos.

Using the Final-Goods Ratio as a Major Indicator for Evaluating Macroeconomic Benefits

In the three decades before the reform and opening up policy were introduced, China's economy was heavily skewed toward heavy industry due to a belief in the need to prioritize growth of the means of production, which led to a cycle of self-perpetuating growth in heavy industry. Each year, transportation and the

[1]This is an abridged version of the "Editor's Notes" from the 16-volume *Collected Works of Xinli Zheng*.

production of coal, electricity, and oil were determined by steel output. Many of the goods being made were at the intermediate stage of production so they could not be used directly by people in their daily lives, resulting in acute shortages of everyday consumer goods. China's product structure was extremely irrational, creating very few economic benefits and preventing the masses from benefitting from economic development. China was, however, a world leader in machining, with output exceeding that of steel. Xinli Zheng studied the steel industry at university and went on to work in the industry for 15 years after he graduated. While pondering issues related to China's steel output, he began to question why China produced such a high quantity of steel and machining products, neither of which affected the lives of ordinary people. He realized that because these products are not final goods, they were irrelevant to people's consumption behavior.

After reflecting on both practical and theoretical issues, he chose to write his master's thesis on "Final Goods and the Final-Goods Ratio." Zheng's thesis analyzed the theory of prioritizing growth of the means of production in the three decades prior to China's reform and opening up policy and the country's focus on heavy industry to the detriment of light industry, which had created a shortage of consumer goods and commodities. In his study, Zheng proposed using the final-goods ratio (final goods are consumer goods, and the final-goods ratio is the proportion of the social product ultimately consumed by final consumers) as the main indicator for evaluating macroeconomic benefits. Zheng suggested that the government should formulate plans to increase final goods and raise the final-goods ratio in order to deliver more practical economic benefits to ordinary people. To this end, he created an empirical method for classifying the social product into primary goods, intermediate goods, and final goods, which provided a scientific basis for formulating plans for increasing the production of final goods. Zheng also proposed the concept of the final-goods ratio, which created an index for evaluating and adjusting the structure of production to reduce the overstock of intermediate goods and increase macroeconomic benefits. He proposed and demonstrated the need to apply his final-goods method and created a semi-dynamic input–output model to make it workable.

His suggestions were instrumental in guiding policies to focus on agriculture and prioritize development of the textile industry in the 1980s, putting an end to the era of the shortage economy. His views also enriched and developed economic theory and provided strong theoretical support for reforms in China.

Limits to Rational Investment

Under the planned economy, a chronic lack of investment and eagerness for success meant that the eventual increase in investment caused inflation and led to cyclical rises and falls in the economy, which turned into a long-term problem. The government's economic departments and the economic community devoted considerable efforts to researching this issue. In 1983, Zheng wrote an article titled "Factors Restricting the Scale of Capital Construction," in which he proposed the idea of minimum and maximum limits to rational investment. At the minimum limit, the scale of social expansion and reproduction should at least ensure that the level of technical equipment for the increasing labor force is not lower than the average level for the existing labor force and that it gradually increases. At the maximum limit, social expansion and reproduction should enable the average consumption levels of the population, including new members of the population, not to fall below the level of the previous year, but to improve to some extent.

Based on these two criteria, Zheng formulated a method for determining optimal investment. He suggested an upper limit on infrastructure investment and recommended that it should be reduced and calculated year by year. In practice, this meant identifying two objective red lines for capital construction investment that would harm the national economy when crossed. Identifying this optimal scale of investment greatly reduces blind investment, thereby avoiding major increases and decreases in investment on the basis of subjective decisions and ensuring steady improvements in people's lives and economic development. The limits to rational investment proposed by Zheng in this paper constituted a pioneering approach to curing China's "investment hunger" at the time as well as determining a scientific scale of investment.

Establishing New Planning Functions to Improve Macro-control

From 1993 to 1998, the main challenge in terms of economic policy in China was to curb inflation. Back then, China was transitioning from a traditional planned economy to a socialist market economy. Xinli Zheng's job was to work out whether the market economy should still have an element of planning and how to switch planning functions. His view was that a market economy required a form of macro-management that differed from the planned economy.

In 1993, Zheng published a study titled "The Socialist Market Economy Requires a Strong Macro-Control System." In it, he stated that due to low productivity, a dual structure, and a focus on both industrialization and modernization, China would need to implement a catch-up strategy if it wished to achieve per capita GDP similar to moderately developed countries by the middle of the twenty-first century. He also suggested that China needed to establish a system of macro-control. The main tasks of this macro-control were, according to Zheng, to balance economic output, optimize the industrial structure and distribution of regional productivity, cultivate internationally competitive conglomerates, and protect the interests of the State and enterprises in international exchanges.

He proposed that a system of macro-control should be a coordinated, efficient, and flexible organic whole. Having sound macro-control is necessary for a modern market economy to operate healthily. The various methods of control should be closely aligned but also check and balance each other's authority. The most important element in this respect is coordination and cooperation between planning, government finances, and monetary tools. The basis of macro-control is initiative and selectivity in macroeconomic activities. Indeed, the key to the vitality of a market economy is the ability to unleash the full initiative and creativity of producers and business operators through material interest and market competition, allowing them to choose their own business approaches and methods according to market demand and the principle of efficiency. In this way, every factor of production is used where it is most needed and to the greatest benefit based on price. Zheng stated that macro-control must unleash this initiative and selectivity and must be conducive to the normal operation of market mechanisms. It is worth pointing out that enterprises are the main market entities in macro-control, and maintaining market order and fair competition are important functions of that control.

The transition from a planned economy to a socialist market economy was a fundamental change in China's economic system. In 1994, Zheng published an essay titled "Reforming the Planning System and Transforming Planning Functions." That same year, in response to China's worsening inflation, Zheng also published "Setting Up New Planning Functions in the Course of Strengthening and Improving Macro-control." The latter study also looked at the question of how to transform planning functions and proposed that plans should rationally determine the system of macro-control, formulate policies to achieve those objectives, coordinate the use of economic levers, and use resources directly controlled by the State to maintain market stability.

Establishing an Investment System Compatible with the Market

In the course of adapting China's method of allocating resources from direct allocation by the government to using the basic role of the market under State macro-control, China's investment mechanisms underwent fundamental reform. In his 1995 work titled "Establishing an Investment System Adapted to the Requirements of the Market Economy," Zheng stated that to create investment incentives through market competition and industrial policy guidance and leverage the basic role of the market in allocating resources, it is necessary to have mechanisms that will allow the free flow of capital and other factors of production between enterprises in the same and different industries according to the laws of value and of supply and demand. He also pointed out the guiding role of national plans and industrial policies in guiding resource allocation in addition to the basic role of the market. Zheng suggested implementing industrial policies that clearly define the economic scale, product quality standards, technical processes, and overall arrangements for key national industries in specific periods, as well as stipulating corresponding preferential fiscal, tax, credit, and export policies. According to Zheng, the State also needed to support a number of large-scale conglomerates that combine trade, scientific research, and production to expand market share and solve the issue of low-level redundant development. Moreover, as the domestic and international markets became more connected, Zheng noted the need to protect the domestic market while gradually entering the international market.

Zheng proposed constraining investment risk by implementing the "project legal person responsibility system." This involved implementing different management methods for different types of investment projects: strengthening market regulation of investment and financing for competitive projects; broadening investment channels for basic projects; and improving investment and financing systems for public welfare projects. Zheng suggested improving control of the overall scale of investment by strengthening constraints on investment risks, establishing a sound system of investment controls, and using necessary administrative means and economic and legal means such as capital and scale controls as well as quality testing, to adjust and optimize the investment structure and foster a system of consultation, design, auditing, bidding, project supervision, and other services for investors. These suggestions were instrumental in deepening reform of China's investment system.

Establishing a Sound Macro-control System that Coordinates Planning, Finance and Taxation, and Banking

Having a system of macro-control that is compatible with a market economy is important for a socialist market economy to avoid economic fluctuations. It is also important to have a sound macro-control system that coordinates planning, finance and taxation, and banking, in order to adapt to new situations.

In the mid- and late-1990s, Zheng published a series of articles on the functions, features, and operational mechanisms of macro-control that focused on curbing inflation and expanding domestic demand. Zheng suggested that China's system of macro-control differed from the decentralized market economies of the USA and UK or the coordinated market economies of Germany, Japan, and South Korea. According to Zheng, this was mainly reflected in the three major regulatory levers of planning, finance and taxation, and banking. As such, he argued China needed to create an efficient and flexible regulatory system with Chinese characteristics that focused on developing productivity, China's level of market development, and the need to catch up with developed countries. Zheng pointed out that planning is the fundamental basis of macro-control; government finance is an important tool for structural adjustment; and the role of banking regulation is to balance the macro-economy. These three things must be coordinated to create synergy, and they constitute dynamic and balancing mechanisms of economic operations, creating the conditions for the sustained, rapid, and healthy development of the national economy.

Revitalizing the Four Pillar Industries

When the Ninth Five-Year Plan for National Economic and Social Development was being formulated, having conducted research and drawn up demand forecasts, Zheng suggested that automobile manufacturing, electronic machinery, petrochemical engineering, and construction should be the pillar industries of the Chinese economy. Zheng also organized a special discussion on the revitalization of pillar industries in *People's Daily* newspaper, and he wrote a book titled *Strategies for Revitalizing China's Pillar Industries*. Between 1995 and the 17th National Party Congress in 2007, China made remarkable progress in transforming its mode of economic growth. A notable achievement in that time was the increased share of GDP enjoyed by the four industries of automobile manufacturing, electronic machinery, petrochemical engineering, and construction, which increased from 12 to 20%, thereby confirming their status as pillar industries. The rise of these four pillar industries played a significant role in supporting the sustained and rapid growth of the national economy during that period.

Development Planning and Xinli Zheng's Collected Economic Works

In 1999, Xinli Zheng edited the book *Development Planning*. In this work, he summarized the outcomes of reform from a development perspective. This book completely reinterpreted the concept of planning as well as planning functions and theory, and it helped to popularize planning knowledge. *Development Planning* meant planning thoroughly eliminated the influence of the old planned economy, and it became a brand-new discipline. In 2000, Zheng published *On Suppressing Inflation and Expanding Domestic Demand* (*Zheng Xinli's Collected Economic Works*, Volume I), *On New Economic Growth Points* (*Zheng Xinli's Collected Economic Works*, Volume II), and *Reform is China's Second Revolution* (*Zheng Xinli's Collected Economic Works*, Volume III). These three works totaled over 1.2 million words and contained 178 articles published by Zheng over the space of 20 years. These collections of essays accurately reflect the trajectory of China's economic development and macro-control over 20 years of the reform and opening up policy. The articles in *On Suppressing Inflation and Expanding Domestic Demand* are mainly on economic aggregates and the economic structure. They record the whole process of China's transition from shortage to low-level surplus, the shift in the main objective of macro-control from restraining demand and inflation to expanding domestic demand, and the historic transition from being anti-inflation to being anti-deflation. *On New Economic Growth Points* included articles on pillar industries and guiding industrial cultivation and development. In it, Zheng demonstrated the necessity and effort required to transform the mode of economic growth and analyzed the main tasks and relevant policies of optimizing the industrial structure. Zheng also pointed out the potential to support sustained and rapid economic growth in the long run, as well as the need to satisfy people's housing and educational requirements to stimulate economic growth in the new stage of economic development in the twenty-first century. Development is an absolute principle, and at the heart of *On New Economic Growth Points* is an unerring belief in using development to solve a variety of problems. *Reform is China's Second Revolution* is a collection of essays and investigative reports on the policy of reform and opening up, including enterprise reform, rural reform, fiscal and taxation reform, as well as on the programs of opening up.

A Mixed-Ownership Shareholding System as the Main Way of Achieving Public Ownership

Prior to the 16th National Party Congress in 2002, Zheng led a research team to Zhejiang Province to investigate ownership structures. He concluded the following: The key to Zhejiang's economic rise was its adherence to developing public ownership and developing various forms of ownership simultaneously; having a mixed-ownership shareholding system is compatible with developing productivity and is an extremely dynamic economic form; a shareholding system of public ownership is a new method of achieving public ownership under socialism. In his investigative reports, Zheng proposed that a shareholding system under socialist conditions is the active abandonment of private ownership, and an economy consisting primarily of a combination of labor, technology, and capital of workers should be a public sector economy; employee stock ownership essentially makes workers the owners of companies, thereby creating a direct link between workers and the means of production; employee stock ownership turns workers from producers into property owners, which helps to put people on the road to prosperity; the shareholding system gives workers investment autonomy and is compatible with requirements for developing the socialist market economy.

Guiding Non-government Capital Toward Building a New Countryside and Agricultural Modernization

On the topic of building a new socialist countryside, Zheng thought that developing the rural economy and increasing the incomes of people in rural areas should be the focus, prominence should be given to improving rural infrastructure and public services, and effective mechanisms are needed to deepen rural reform. He felt that by combining the building of a new countryside with industrialization and urbanization, China could create positive interactions that would accelerate industrialization and urbanization and drive the construction of a new countryside.

Zheng proposed deepening rural reform through six systems: first, a stabilized and improved basic rural management system, which would clarify the development direction of household operations and unified operations; second, a strict and standardized rural land management system to encourage, support, and regulate land transfers; third, a system of fiscal support for agriculture and rural development in order to gradually equalize urban and rural public services and guide non-government capital toward rural areas and agriculture; fourth, a modern rural banking system, as the focus of rural reform should be on rural finance; fifth, a system of urban and rural economic and social development that integrates urban and rural planning, industrial distribution, infrastructure, public services, markets for factors of production, and social management; and sixth, an improved rural democratic management system that makes village affairs more transparent, develops village Party branches, uses intra-Party democracy to drive democratic decision-making, thereby leading to the establishment of a comprehensive rural democratic management system for developing community-level political power, among other things.

By the time the 12th Five-Year Plan for National Economic and Social Development was announced in 2011, the conditions for accelerating agricultural modernization in China had already been put in place: surplus non-government capital, a solution for transferring human resources, and demand for quality agricultural products. As such, China needed to seize the opportunity to encourage investment of non-government capital in agricultural modernization and encourage new entities to manage agricultural investment, including family farms, agricultural cooperatives, and agricultural companies, so as to achieve large-scale and intensive management of agriculture and make some agricultural land available for secondary and tertiary industries. To this end, it was necessary to register and certify contracted land and housing land of farmers to ensure usufructuary rights. The experiences of Chengdu, Kunshan, and Xinxiang in terms of urban–rural integration are worthy of consideration in this regard.

Changing the Economic Growth Model and then Changing the Economic Development Model

The Ninth Five-Year Plan published in 1996 proposed transforming China's economic growth model. The report of the 17th National Party Congress in 2007 proposed changing the economic development model. Before and after these two major development strategies were announced, Zheng wrote many articles discussing, rationalizing, and interpreting them.

Zheng proposed the content and primary approach for transforming the economic growth model, and his policy recommendations were ultimately adopted.

Based on the recommendations contained in the Ninth Five-Year Plan, the Fifth Plenary Session of the 14th CPC Central Committee in 1995 proposed transforming the economic growth model, with particular emphasis on transforming China's economic growth from extensive to intensive growth. The session also proposed encouraging a shift in the economic growth model by transforming the economic system. To promote research on transforming the economic growth model, in the summer of 1996, Zheng arranged the National Exchange of Experiences Meeting on Transforming the Economic Growth Model in Nandaihe, Hebei Province, on behalf of the Policy Research Office of the State Planning Commission. Leading members of the State Council, including the Premier and Vice-Premier, met with the participants. After the meeting, Zheng published *A Collection of Papers on Transforming the Economic Growth Model*, *Compilation of Experiences on Transforming the Economic Growth Model*, and *Research Report on Transforming the Economic Growth Model*. He then published an article titled "Macro-Control: Focusing on Structural Adjustments and Transforming the Growth Model" in 2004 and "Independent Innovation: The Key to Transforming the Growth Model" in 2005. In 2007, the salient issues affecting China's economic development concerned the structure of domestic demand and the country's industrial structure. China had excessive investment but insufficient consumption. Economic growth was over-reliant on industrial growth, and the lagging development of the tertiary industry was a growing concern. Zheng, who was by then Deputy Director of the Central Policy Research Office, believed that failing to resolve problems in domestic demand and the industrial structure would inhibit sustained economic growth. Zheng pointed out that transforming the structure of demand, industry, and factors of production would require a change in the development model. After much collective discussion and extensive solicitation of opinions, on the eve of the 17th National Party Congress, transforming the economic development model was proposed.

After the report of the 17th National Party Congress proposed the three transformations of the development model, Zheng wrote a series of publicity and explanatory articles. In 2009, he published "The Correct Orientation That Must be Upheld to Promote China's Economic and Social Development: On the Three Transformations," which proposed a series of measures for implementing the "three transformations." In 2010, he published "Transforming the Development Model is the Fundamental Way to Deal with Crises," which proposed fiscal stimulus policies to expand domestic demand and the need to focus on promoting the transformation of the development model. He pointed out that only by making substantive breakthroughs on the basis of transforming the development model is it possible to lead the global recovery from the financial crisis and lay a foundation for smooth and rapid future growth. It is no exaggeration to say that, from publicity to implementation, Zheng made unparalleled contributions to the topics of transforming the economic growth model and transforming the development model.

Expanding Domestic Demand

In April 1998, Zheng wrote a report titled "Problems and Suggestions for Ensuring a Growth Rate of 8% This Year," which advocated expanding domestic demand. Chinese investment, consumption, and exports had all suffered as a result of the Asian financial crisis. To ensure economic growth, Zheng suggested that China should increase infrastructure investment to drive investment demand and create a material foundation for future economic development. That same year, he also published a paper titled "Expanding Domestic Demand: A Detailed Explanation of China's New Economic Policy," in which he argued that expanding domestic demand was a basic policy that should be implemented over the long term in combination with optimization and upgrading of the industrial structure and with the focus on increasing consumption (the paper also included measures for increasing consumption). In 1999, Zheng published "Expanding Domestic Demand: An Important Strategic Approach," which identified an expansion of domestic demand as the jumping-off point for China's economic development as well as a series of specific measure for achieving such an expansion. In 2003, in "Development Needs New Ideas," Zheng pointed out the need to gradually increase the proportion of GDP accounted for by consumption and to shift the focus from expanding investment to expanding consumption. He argued that increasing incomes of urban and rural residents and cultivating new consumption hotspots would increase non-government investment, and he advocated taking a new industrialization path to create an industrial distribution led by high-tech industries and supported by manufacturing industries and a comprehensively developed service industry.

Proposing Consumption "Engines" Coordinated Development of the Real Estate, Automobile and Stock Markets, and the "Two Increases" Plan

Zheng has long been a proponent of the positive effect of consumption on economic growth. In the 1980s, he wrote a series of articles on correctly handling the relationships between accumulation and consumption and between developing production and people's lives, emphasizing that the basic objective of production is to satisfy growing material and cultural needs. When China was expanding domestic demand in the late-1990s, he wrote an article emphasizing the need to focus on stimulating consumption in order to improve people's living conditions. Later, he again pointed out that food, clothing, housing, cars, and tourism are the "engines" of consumption. From 2003 to 2008, amid a new round of economic growth, investment in China rose to a new historic high, while household consumption fell to a historic low. After analyzing a large volume of data, Zheng suggested adjusting the income distribution structure and greatly increasing domestic consumption. He also suggested coordinating the development of the real estate, automobile, and stock markets (the main engines of the economic development at the time) to expand the domestic market. Zheng made three policy recommendations for coordinating the development of the three markets: using adjustments to real estate policies and institutional reforms to enhance the development of the real estate industry, meet demand in the multilayered housing market, and fully utilize the stimulatory role of the housing industry on the national economy, in order to ensure the continued prosperity of the real estate market; expand car consumer credit, improve the environment for car use, and formulate policies to encourage purchases of hybrid vehicles and small- and medium-sized cars with low emissions, in order to encourage increased car consumption; and promote the stable and healthy development of capital markets and use capital markets to support the continued prosperity of the real estate and automobile markets, and strive to make both those markets important industries for driving the growth of the national economy.

Based on the guiding principles of the 17th National Party Congress, Zheng issued his "two increases" proposal at the National Committee of the Chinese People's Political Consultative Conference, which consisted of increasing urban and rural residents' income as a proportion of gross national income and increasing the household consumption rate. In his proposal, Zheng suggested trying to increase urban and rural residents' income as a proportion of gross national income from 43 to 53% and the household final consumption rate from 35 to 50% in 3 to 5 years. Zheng believed this to be highly achievable and that increasing them by such a large margin would greatly alter the demand structure as ordinary people's income and consumption increased markedly, boosting the effect of consumption on economic growth. For almost three decades, Zheng has repeatedly called for increased consumption and less investment waste as well as more restructuring to allow the masses to benefit from economic development. Nobody has been a greater champion of this viewpoint than Zheng, which gave rise to his nickname, "Mr. Consumption."

Proposing Ways to Achieve Independent Innovation

Zheng looked at the experiences of Chinese enterprises in terms of independent innovation and proposed the following ten ways to increase it: first, introduce, digest, absorb, and re-innovate; second, innovate through system integration; third, conduct original innovation; fourth, integrate technology acquisition with trade and accept tenders from international companies; fifth, acquire intellectual property rights (IPR) through international mergers; sixth, set up R&D institutions abroad or entrust foreign R&D institutions to create independent IPR; seventh, work with foreign countries on R&D and share results; eighth, design in China and manufacture abroad, or import key components and manufacture in China; ninth, make innovation breakthroughs in key components and key links to gradually create independent IPR; tenth, combine production, study, and research. Zheng also pointed out that innovations by tertiary industry are primarily format innovations, i.e., business model innovations.

Proposing to Include the Increased Value of Intangible Assets in Assessments of the Maintenance and Appreciation of the Value of Assets of State-Owned Enterprises

State-owned enterprises (SOEs) contain a large pool of innovative talent, allowing them to take the lead in technological advancement within their industries, and Zheng believes they should become the primary driving force of independent innovation. However, because assessments of the maintenance and appreciation of the value of assets of SOEs only considered tangible assets and not intangible assets, patents and technological achievements resulting from R&D are not included the scope of such assessments, which suppressed enthusiasm for R&D among enterprises and contributed to a short-term approach to business decision-making. In response to this, Zheng conducted investigations and wrote many articles calling for improvements to indicators for assessing SOEs. He even submitted a special proposal to the Chinese People's Political Consultative Conference. In the end, this incident attracted the attention of departments in charge of managing state-owned assets who formulated suggestions to encourage SOEs to increase R&D investment and to play a central and leading role in independent innovation, as well as to include intangible assets, such as technology and patents, when assessing the maintenance and appreciation of assets.

Proposing Increasing Chinese Exports and a Focus for Overseas Investment

Zheng believes that there are two factors constraining China's long-term economic development: the energy and resource bottleneck and the technology bottleneck. China has huge foreign exchange reserves, but to ensure their security and efficient use Zheng argues that China must expand foreign investment and transform some or most of its foreign exchange reserves into resource and material reserves. In response to the 2008 financial crisis, Zheng suggested combining China's substantial foreign exchange reserves and excess production capacity by exporting capital to drive Chinese exports of goods and services, thereby placing China at an advantage in the global economy. Zheng argued that increasing overseas investment would achieve multiple objectives, including creating demand for exports, overcoming the energy and resource bottleneck, improving independent innovation and international operations, and promoting the internationalization of RMB.

He proposed that creating demand for Chinese exports through overseas investment could be achieved in at least five areas. The first is by expanding investment in energy and resources overseas, which will drive exports of Chinese exploration and excavating equipment, as well as meet demand for energy and resources in China. The second is by expanding overseas processing trade, which would drive China's manufacturing exports, especially parts and components. Third is by expanding economic aid to developing countries, thereby driving exports of Chinese equipment and services. Fourth is by increasing consumer credit for exports of Chinese mechanical and electrical products. Fifth is by increasing exchanges of RMB so that countries that would like to buy Chinese goods but lack the ability to pay can buy Chinese goods in RMB and repay loans with energy and resources. Zheng also suggested increasing the international competitiveness of Chinese enterprises by increasing international mergers and acquisitions to access the innovative resources and international marketing networks of international enterprises. These views have strong practical significance.

Three Major Opportunities Presented to China by the Global Financial Crisis

In the second half of 2008, the global financial crisis caused China's export market to shrink, seriously impacting its economic growth. Zheng looked at how to turn the challenge of the crisis into an opportunity and to convert pressure into impetus. In early 2009, he wrote a report in which he suggested that the current crisis presented China with three major opportunities: for international mergers and acquisitions, for expanding domestic demand, especially consumption, and for the internationalization of RMB. His views reflect the dialectical way of thinking, which not only enhances confidence but also translates into macroeconomic policies.

Proposing Policy Recommendations for Transforming Inflationary Pressures into Motivation for Industrial Upgrading

In 2011, the Chinese economy faced inflationary pressures. Guiding excess liquidity to achieve steady and rapid economic growth while maintaining stable overall prices was a severe challenge at the start of the 12th Five-Year Plan period. Zheng analyzed the situation and proposed reducing the price of agricultural products, with the focus on the "vegetable basket" (non-staple food supply) project, reducing house prices by constructing affordable housing, and reducing the price of imported iron ore through overseas investment. Zheng believed that increasing effective supply would suppress commodity prices that were rising excessively. Moreover, he felt that by reasonably guiding capital investment, excess funds could be directed to much-needed industrial upgrading, including capital markets, strategic emerging industries, public services, infrastructure, agricultural modernization, tertiary industry, and overseas investment. Zheng maintained that as long as China worked hard in this direction, it would be possible to maintain rapid economic growth while stabilizing prices.

Establishing the Two Disciplines of Modern Policy Science and Development Planning

As its economy develops, China urgently needs a new theoretical system to support it. It also needs to adapt to the new discipline of market economics to methodically summarize and provide theoretical guidance for China's planned system reforms, policy research and utilizing the fundamental role of the market in allocating resources. In the 1990s, the books *Collected Works of Modern Policy Research* and *Development Planning*, both edited by Zheng, proposed a number of innovative theories that led to two new disciplines in China. Policy has been an important tool of the Communist Party of China for seizing political power and long-term governance, and it has been a key to its success. Although policy is important to the Party, the theoretical system of policy studies has lagged behind practice, and it is still not a complete discipline like law. Based on his practical experience in policy research over more than three decades, Zheng looked at the theory behind policy science and made significant contributions to establishing it as an independent discipline. Zheng led China's policy research community in conducting comprehensive research concerning the basic theories, methodologies, foundations, hierarchy theory, and department theory of policy science as well as descriptions of domestic and international policy research institutions and domestic and international policy research practices. This gave China a complete theoretical system of policy research for the first time and provided a solid theoretical foundation for policy research in China.

The discipline of development planning founded by Zheng refers to development planning under the socialist market economy. As a discipline, it looks at how to improve the organization of society, accelerate economic development, and improve the productivity of the whole of society. It reflects the requirement of developing a socialist market economy, explains the objective laws of economic and social development, and discusses the relationship between planning and the market under the socialist market economy. The discipline has established a complete system of medium- and long-terms plans, annual plans, and special plans. It particularly emphasizes the need for plans to complement market conditions in order to better utilize the functions of government and the role of the market in allocating resources so as to make the visible and invisible hands work together in economic and social development and provide institutional support for realizing the main task of socialism, namely increasing productivity.

Research on the Innovative Huai River Economic Zone Strategy

To support the development of the Huai River Basin and benefit the people, Zheng organized for various parties to research the development strategy of the Huai River Economic Zone. Zheng spent 3 years traveling up and down the Huai River conducting investigations and research and repeatedly demonstrating theories before publishing a research report titled "Accelerating Development of the Huai River Ecological Economic Zone as a Strategic Fulcrum for Expanding China's Domestic Demand," which was well received among leaders of the State Council.

This research led by Zheng created a number of firsts. It was the first research project to focus on the Huai River Basin and propose administrative recommendations. Previous research on the development of the Huai River was conducted by individual departments or localities. This was the first time civil forces from agriculture, water conservancy, industry, transportation, tourism, and other sectors joined forces for the sake of research. This was achieved with the help of the development and reform commissions of Henan, Anhui, and Jiangsu provinces, allowing researchers to overcome departmental or regional restrictions and form effective synergies in a number of areas. Zheng's research was pioneering in that it considered a whole river basin, providing valuable experience for conducting research on other river basins. Previous research on the Huai River concentrated on flood control; this was the first time the Huai River Basin had been researched from the perspective of development.

Zheng's innovative development model for Chinese river basins proposed developing the Huai River into China's third great waterway after the Yangtze and Pearl rivers and to develop the Huai River Economic Zone into the fourth growth pole behind the Pearl River Delta, Yangtze River Delta, and Bohai Sea. His suggestions have provided a wonderful blueprint for the development and utilization of the Huai River Economic Zone, with practical and feasible policy measures. Under Zheng's impetus, the provincial governments of Fujian, Henan, and Jiangsu submitted a joint report on developing the Huai River Economic Zone to the State Council.

Two Recommendations Adopted by the Central Government That Had Significant Economic Benefits and International Impact

The two reports "Problems and Suggestions for Ensuring a Growth Rate of 8% This Year" and "On Setting Up an Asian Infrastructure Investment and Financing Institution Led by China" are prime examples of research results being used in national decision-making.

In response to the 1997 Asian financial crisis, Zheng wrote a report titled "Problems and Suggestions for Ensuring a Growth Rate of 8% This Year" in April 1998, which advocated increasing national debt to build infrastructure and thereby expand domestic demand and solve the problem of deflation in China. The report was submitted to the State Council by the State Planning Commission and was ultimately adopted by the central government. In April of the same year, the State Council decided to issue an additional RMB 100 billion of long-term development bonds and ordered banks to lend a further RMB 100 billion. This policy was implemented for five consecutive years and was instrumental in the following six major events: reconstruction of rural power grids, construction of urban infrastructure, construction of highways, reinforcement of levees along the Yangtze River, construction of a national grain store, and better facilities to allow the enrollment of more college students. This policy not only allowed the completion of dormant projects, it also supported steady and rapid economic development and laid a solid foundation for a period of golden development characterized by high growth and low inflation over the following decade.

In March 2009, Zheng proposed establishing the Asian Infrastructure Investment Bank and the Asian Agricultural Investment Bank at the Boao Forum for Asia. In July 2013, Zheng wrote "Proposal on Establishing an Asian Infrastructure Investment and Financing Agency Led by China," which was submitted to the Party Central Committee and the State Council by the China Center for International Economic Exchanges and was well received by central government leaders. In October 2013, President Xi Jinping held talks with Indonesian President Susilo Bambang Yudhoyono in Jakarta, where he announced China's initiative to establish the Asian Infrastructure Investment Bank (AIIB). The main purpose of establishing the AIIB was to assist the construction of infrastructure in Asian-Pacific countries for the sake of greater interconnectivity and economic development in the region. On October 24, 2014, finance ministers and authorized representatives of 21 founding member countries, including China, India, and Singapore, signed an agreement in Beijing to establish the AIIB. On June 29, 2015, representatives from 57 member countries of the AIIB attended a signing ceremony in Beijing to mark the founding of the bank. China has a shareholding of US$29.78 billion and 26.06% of the voting rights in AIIB, giving it the largest shareholding and voting rights of any member country. Establishing the AIIB was a key step in the internationalization of RMB. It has changed China's position in the world economy, been pivotal in raising China's international profile and is a pragmatic step in changing the pattern of global and international governance. Commentators agree that the founding of the AIIB is a wise move by China. The famous economist Joseph Stiglitz has spoken in positive terms about the AIIB and believes that 2015 will be remembered as the first year of China's financial era.

Proposing a Zhoushan Archipelago Free-Trade Port

After the State Council established the Zhoushan Archipelago New Area, the government considered how to make best use of the islands. Zheng was tasked by the Zhejiang Provincial Government and Zhoushan Municipal Government with organizing a research group to conduct a thorough investigation of the Zhoushan Archipelago. Zheng reported that the establishment of the Zhoushan Archipelago New Area is strategically significant for building a new growth pole of national economic development, for building a new platform for China to expand overseas trade, for providing a demonstration of how to develop national marine economics, and for improving the security of national strategic resources. Zheng proposed developing Zhoushan in three phases. The first phase is making the archipelago a free-trade port, then creating a free zone and then developing a free port area. The Zhoushan Archipelago New Area Development Plan approved by the State Council proposed developing the first free port area in China, echoing Deng Xiaoping's ideas for Hong Kong. Zheng's research report also proposed constructing a second sea bridge across Hangzhou Bay, connecting Fengxian in Shanghai to Ningbo via the Zhoushan islands of Dayangshan, Lushan, and Zhoushan. The crossing would be a dual-purpose highway and railway bridge, providing seamless vehicle and rail connections around Hangzhou Bay. The bridge would allow the Zhoushan deep-water port to be utilized to its full potential and develop Zhoushan into an international logistics hub. The research report also proposed building a large environmentally friendly petrochemical base on Daxiaoyushan Island. After further work, Zheng proposed focusing on the development of petrochemical products, which there are a shortage of in the domestic market, to replace imports and utilizing private capital in Zhejiang to construct a petrochemical base and other projects. These recommendations have been included in the development plans of the State Council, and a number have already been implemented.

Xinli Zheng's Philosophy and Work Style

Realistic, Pragmatic, Rigorous, and Innovative

"Learn earnestly and sufficiently to be able to teach others, and behave in a manner that serves as an example to others." In his research, Zheng adheres to an ethos of being realistic, pragmatic, rigorous, and innovative. He is a prolific reader but is not a slave to theory. Zheng views China's reform and development as an unprecedented undertaking with no ready-made experiences to follow or books to provide simple answers. In this era of huge economic and social change in China, new problems are constantly emerging, so it is necessary to study and resolve issues as they arise. This requires constant emancipation of the mind, bold innovation, and the development of economic theories.

Zheng seeks to emulate the eminent Chinese economist Sun Yefang and be bold enough to hold his own views as well as seek to bring people over to his way of thinking based on thorough research. He insists that research should be based on practice for conclusions to stand up to scrutiny.

"Those who fail to plan for the long term will not be ready in the moment; those who do not adopt a global perspective will miss out on local knowledge." Zheng insists on analyzing problems from a holistic and long-term perspective and observing problems from a dynamic perspective. He tries to understand China's economic situation, but also understand the world economy so as to analyze China within the wider context. For many years, he has dreamed of and struggled to make China rich and strong. His forward-looking perspective, adoration for his country, and concern for its people are reflected in his research results, and he deeply influences those around him.

Connecting Theory and Reality

Zheng believes that the most important quality a policy researcher can have is the ability to connect theory and reality. He believes that faced with complicated and constantly changing problems, effective solutions can only be found by looking first at reality. China's economy is in a catch-up period of rapid growth. There are many complex tasks to overcome in reform and opening up as well as in economic development to achieve the objective of building a moderately prosperous society in all respects by 2020 and basically achieving modernization by the middle of the twenty-first century. Many new economic theories need to be explored, and many problems in reform and development need to be resolved. This requires theoretical thinking and interest, bold innovation, and the development of economic theory. Zheng has long been engaged in economic theory and economic policy research, and he has a broad economic vision. He often says that he would like to improve China's innovation capabilities, the quality of its research and promote the infiltration and integration of research in different fields. He is sensitive to trends in economic operations and has his finger on the pulse of economic development. Zheng has been studying China's economic situation for more than 30 years. His research results are understandable, his methods are rigorous, and his analytical reasoning is clear and concise.

Zheng reaches his own theoretical understanding on the basis of in-depth investigations and independent thinking. His theory of ownership is that an economy with mixed forms of ownership is the most dynamic and fastest growing and that it is compatible with the public ownership model in the primary stage of socialism. Zheng believes China should establish a macroeconomic policy system that is suited to China's national conditions and with Chinese characteristics.

His theory of macro-control is based on his belief that China needs a strong macro-control system, so it needs to establish new planning functions to strengthen and improve macro-control and that emphasize the vital function of enterprises in the market. He proposed that national macroeconomic control policies and macroeconomic plans should be coordinated annually and in the medium and long term and that China should establish sound macroeconomic controls that coordinate planning, finance and taxation, and banking.

In terms of his analysis and research of China's sustainable development practices, he stated that the main problem facing the Chinese economy after 1998 was a lack of demand, especially a lack of domestic demand. He feels that expanding final consumption, that is the consumption requirements of the Chinese people, provides the main impetus for economic development. On top of that, he believes in expanding investment in infrastructure and public services. And he proposes creating demand for exports of Chinese goods and services by expanding overseas investment.

Zheng believes in adhering to a combination of "bringing in" and "going out," paying equal attention to both foreign investment and overseas investment and improving China's ability to utilize two markets and two types of resources. He also believes that it is necessary to take advantage of China's foreign exchange reserves and surplus industrial production capacity to actively implement the "going out" strategy.

In-depth Investigations and Research

Xinli Zheng particularly values field research. From desert slopes to far-flung islands, he has travelled the length and breadth of China. Wherever there is a positive example to be learned from, he works tirelessly to investigate, summarize, and promote that example.

To unleash the potential of the Huai River Basin, Zheng spent 9 days conducting in-depth research in cities and rural areas along the length and breadth of the river. At the end of his research, he suggested establishing the Huai River Economic Zone, which was developed into China's third great waterway and fourth growth pole.

Zheng also led research teams to rural areas of Heilongjiang and Henan provinces to study how to deepen rural reform by promoting agricultural modernization, build a new countryside, and narrow the gap between urban and rural areas. His research led him to suggest that agricultural modernization, building a new countryside, and granting urban residency to migrant workers are the three main approaches for integrating urban and rural areas, but that the focus should be on reforming the rural land system. Zheng believes these to be fundamental measures for overcoming downward pressures on the economy, creating a moderately prosperous society in all respects, avoiding falling into the middle-income trap, and becoming a high-income country. It will also support the sustained and healthy development of the national economy.

Learning from the Economic Systems and Development Models of Other Countries

Zheng looks at the experiences of other countries to make practical recommendations for developing China. By conducting comparative analyses of national macro-control systems and development policies, Zheng learns what works for other countries and then proposes corresponding measures tailored to China's circumstances.

Establishing a New Type of Think Tank in China

In the 1990s, Zheng travelled to the USA to learn more about think tanks. In 1995, he edited a paper titled "The US Technology Market and the Information Consulting Market," which introduced the workings of US think tanks to Chinese readers. It has long been Zheng's wish to establish a world-class think tank. In 2008, he introduced the idea of creating a new type of think tank in China: a non-governmental think tank. The China Center for International Economic Exchanges was set up in March 2009, with Zheng appointed as a permanent vice chairman. In June of the same year, the First Global Think-Tank Summit was held in Beijing. Representatives from famous Chinese and international think tanks attended the summit to discuss global development. It was a great success. Former US Secretary of State Henry Kissinger said at the meeting how simple and important an idea it was but that it had never been done before. From a scholarly official to the head a leader of China's new think tank, Zheng has always been at the forefront of central government decision-making, State governance, and academic research in China. Even in his retirement, Zheng hopes to develop the China Center for International Economic Exchanges into a world-class institution and to make useful contributions to creating a new type of think tank with Chinese characteristics.

Proposing Urgent Monetary Policy Support to Stabilize Growth

Through his analysis of the role of the relationship between the M_2 money supply and GDP growth in the process of industrialization and urbanization in developed countries and emerging economies, and looking at the problems in China's economic development after 2011 within this context, Zheng surmised that lower growth of the M_2 money supply was the fundamental cause of the economic downturn. He wrote the article "Stabilizing Growth Urgently Requires Monetary Policy Support" in response to downward pressures on the Chinese economy, which stated that a proactive fiscal policy and moderately loose monetary policy should be implemented to reduce interest rates and appropriately increase currency in circulation. The article was published on June 12, 2015, and it was quickly shared on a number of Web sites and garnered a strong public reaction. His proposals were soon adopted by relevant departments. On June 27, 2015, the People's Bank of China (PBC) announced that it would cut interest rates and make targeted cuts to required reserve ratios starting on June 28. This was the first time that the central bank had adopted the dual measure of cutting interest rates and reserve ratios at the same time. On August 26, the PBC announced another cut in interest rates to loosen monetary policy and stimulate economic growth.

Proposing Building a New Socialist Countryside

To formulate the 11th Five-Year Plan and to make progress with solving problems in work relating to agriculture, rural areas, and the rural population as well as with the economic and social development of rural areas, personnel from the Central Rural Work Leading Group Office, Ministry of Finance, Ministry of Housing and Urban-Rural Development, PBC and Guizhou Province visited South Korea to learn about the "Saemaul Undong" (New Village Movement). Zheng, the then deputy director of the Central Policy Research Office, was asked to head up the delegation. After returning to China, the delegation submitted their research findings in two papers titled "Investigative Report on South Korea's New Village Movement" and "Suggestions on Building a New Socialist Countryside," which suggested emulating South Korea by making the construction of a new socialist countryside one of China's major strategies to ensure its effective promotion. Zheng later published papers including "Learning from the Experience of the New Village Movement in South Korea and Accelerating Building a New Countryside in China," "Promoting Development of a New Countryside is an Important Way to Achieve a Moderately Prosperous Society in All Respects," "Building a New Countryside Requires System Design," and "Integrating Rural Reforms and Building a New Socialist Countryside," which played a positive role in promoting the new socialist countryside policy and improving rural development.

Focusing on Countermeasure Research and Providing Results for Use in Formulating Central Government Economic Policy

The purpose of Zheng's research is to aid central government decision-making. Zheng's philosophy is that he does it because it is helpful. Over the many years of his policy research, he has constantly developed new ideas and perspectives by studying problems in reform and development that China urgently needs to solve, and he has constantly focused on converting his results into State policies. He has channeled his energy into researching drafts of central government documents and on interpreting, publicizing,s and implementing the guiding principles of central government documents. Zheng's main work consists of helping to draft important documents for the central government. Most of the time he does economic policy research at central government policy research institutions and the Comprehensive Economic Management Department of the State Council, where he has had the opportunity to experience the whole process of China's reform, opening up and economic development as well as to participate directly and indirectly in the generation, introduction, and implementation of major economic decisions in the course of reform and opening up.

Zheng has been involved in macroeconomic theory and economic policy research for many years and has done thorough research and possesses unique insights in areas including reform of planning and investment systems, macroeconomic controls, and medium- and long-term development policies. He always starts from China's realities when suggesting theoretical opinions or policy recommendations. Many of his views and opinions have been made into implemented policies, and some of his predictions have come to pass. His research and policy recommendations on issues such as adjusting the industrial structure, transforming the economic growth model, expanding domestic demand, and transforming the economic development model have played an important role in solving problems in China's economy at various stages. From a new type of think tank to the Asian Infrastructure Investment Bank, from the Zhoushan Archipelago New Area to the Huai River Economic Zone, from proposing perspectives to implementing in practice—all these things reflect Zheng's focus on solving practical problems. He has always insisted that research results and policy recommendations must conform to China's national conditions. Such results are only meaningful if they are used in the country's development plans, strategies, and policies measures.

Most of Zheng's economic papers and published works over the years have focused on macroeconomic control, medium- and long-term development strategies, and major economic policies for reform and opening up. They have included theoretical explorations, proposed policy recommendations, interpreted central government documents, or reflected research results. His views are highly predictive and forward-looking, and they are concerned with the development of China's economy. He has grappled with pertinent and thorny economic issues in each period, which has made his research realistic and policy-oriented. Zheng's thoughts have advanced with the times, and he has always stood at the forefront of his field. His various proposals and suggestions provide strong theoretical guidance and will have great practical value for a long time to come.

Scientific Analysis that Combines Qualitative and Quantitative Elements

Zheng pays significant attention to combining qualitative and quantitative analyses in his research. This is evident from his articles. He believes that economic events are unique and complex, so research should include both types of analysis to grasp accurately the essence of phenomena. He uses this method to try to reveal inherent economic laws in various phenomena and economic data in order to understand their true nature. Zheng strives to reveal the relationships between things. Only when a correct judgment has been made based on scientific analysis does he put forward practical and feasible policy recommendations. It is perhaps his science and engineering background at university that led to his special interest in data and his insistence on using it in his research. When expressing his thoughts, opinions, and research results, he uses a lot of informative data and examples to try to make them more persuasive. This makes his results reliable, his recommendations reasonable, and his measures effective, as well as being more actionable and convincing as intellectual support for economic decision-making.

Contents

Preface

After graduating from the Graduate School of the Chinese Academy of Social Sciences in 1981, I started my career in economic research at the Research Office of the Secretariat of the CPC Central Committee. In 1987, because the Research Office was closed, I was transferred to the National Planning Commission and spent the initial 2 years at the State Information Center, before moving to the National Planning Commission's Research Office. In 2000, I was transferred back to the Central Policy Research Office of the CPC Central Committee, where I remained until my retirement in 2013. In 2009, I assisted Mr. Zeng Peiyan in founding a social think tank—the China Center for International Economic Exchanges (CCIEE)—to continue my dedication to economic research and international exchanges.

As you can see from my experience of the past 40 years of China's reform and opening up, I have always had the honor of studying economic theory and conducting economic policy research at CPC central-level institutions. Since the 1990s, I have been involved in the drafting of CPC central documents. I have participated in the drafting of the eighth through 12th five-year plans and four key CPC reform documents: the Decision on Establishing the Socialist Market Economy at the Third Plenary Session of the 14th CPC Central Committee, the Decision on Improving the Socialist Market Economy at the Third Plenary Session of the 16th CPC Central Committee, the Decision on Rural Economic Reform at the Third Plenary Session of the 17th CPC Central Committee, and the Decision on Comprehensively Deepening Reform at the Third Plenary Session of the 18th CPC Central Committee. Furthermore, I have also taken part in drafting the political report to the 17th National Congress of the CPC. For work reasons, my research has been largely focused on producing and interpreting CPC central documents and addressing problems regarding their implementation. Therefore, the articles in my *Collected Works* truly provide a sideline view of the evolution of China's development strategies, guidelines and policies and systems and mechanisms since reform and opening up began. It also reflects the various difficulties and conflicts in different historical periods and depicts how one by one these problems have been solved. Of course, the vast amount of information in my *Collected Works* also reflects the hard work I have put in over the years, the creative approach I have taken to economic research, and how the research of an individual can be integrated into the tide of our times.

Through my experience in economic policy and theory research work over the previous four decades, I have come to see the following points as being critical:

Economic research must start with China's realities. The purpose of the economy is to help people enjoy a good quality of life and make the country stronger. How China's economy is to catch up with those of the developed countries is the central mission of economic research. China's national conditions—a large population and imbalanced economic development—have determined that we must find a suitable development path which fits our realities. Good solutions come from the people. Therefore, economic researchers must work on the basis of reality and try their best to find and summarize effective approaches to local economic development. They should also strive to see their experience transformed into national policies and theories. In doing so, they can contribute to the growth of the country as a whole. For many years, whenever I heard about some place implementing good practices, I would rush there to conduct field research and surveys. The articles I wrote, the reports I submitted, and the suggestions I raised were all supported by concrete cases. They were by no means empty talk. This is what we call being down to earth. I persist with my points, because they are based on reality.

Economic research must be based on quantitative analysis. Economics is a form of sophisticated science. Interactional parameters in the modern economy can illustrate varied economic performances. Without specific, dynamic economic data, it is impossible to make correct analyses and judgments on the health of the economy. Many economic rules are derived from analyzing massive economic data, so research in this field requires a strong interest in and a high sensitivity to data. I generally ensure there is ample data to support my arguments and points. And this tends to be one of the reasons why they are cogent.

An economic researcher must think independently instead of blindly worshipping authority, because economics is a science that studies objects that are constantly changing. As a large developing country, China has continually faced various conflicts and problems in different historical periods due to rapid economic growth and rapidly changing economic systems. My personal experience is that if you attempt to adopt old methods to solve new problems, it will only throw you off the right track. When I was working at the National Planning Commission, we were continually fighting against inflation between 1993 and 1998. Then after 1998, we had to make a sharp turn to deal with deflation. While we were curbing inflation from 1993 to 1998, we were working to expand domestic demand from 1998 to 2003. If you dwell on established rules, it can lead to huge mistakes. When new problems arise, no one can tell you how to solve them, nor can you follow the usual practices. What you must do is seek truth from facts, think independently, and solve the problems independently. Researchers in think tanks should express their own independent views. They should never just parrot the opinions of others or try to guess what leaders think about a certain topic, because what leaders need most are a researcher's independent views. As long as they are based on independent research, he or she must, regardless of disagreement, stand by these views. For history has repeatedly proven that the truth is always in the hands of the minority.

An economic researcher must have a global vision and endeavor to take inspiration from international comparative studies. Economics as discipline is international in nature. Developed and developing countries have different national conditions, while every country, regardless of size, has its own characteristics. China is a country that has developed later than many others. It should take advantage of this by learning from the experiences of developed countries to accelerate its own development and achieve the goal of seeing the latecomers surpass the old-timers. In the early 1980s, we learned mainly from Japan how to formulate industrial policies and then drew upon Germany and US experiences of macro-regulation. I personally was able to broaden my horizons and gain inspiration as a result of visits to a number of fast-developing small economies. In the Republic of Korea I learned about industrialization, in Ireland about leapfrog development, in Finland and Israel about science, technology, and education development, in the Netherlands about high-efficiency agriculture, in India about the software industry, and in France about rural cooperative development. As part of the drafting of the Law on Tendering and Bidding, I visited a number of relevant international organizations and developed countries. I have visited the USA 15 times for research purposes, during which I conducted fruitful and in-depth studies from various perspectives. China has made tangible progress over the past four decades since reform and opening up began, but there is still a huge development gap compared with developed countries. In order to avoid the middle-income trap and join the ranks of high-income countries, we should act as modest students and study the strengths of all nations and the wisdom of all peoples, with the goal of advancing and maintaining healthy and sustainable economic development.

Economic researchers must be eager to learn and work hard. Economics is a science that requires knowledge and the accumulation of experience. In the Research Office of the Secretariat of the CPC Central Committee, I had the honor to work under the leadership of Mr. Mei Xing. He is a noble-hearted and extraordinarily talented revolutionary. He always told us that the philosophy of the Research Office is to work for no fame or fortune. This has left a deep impression on me; no matter where I go, I always remember this motto. Researchers in think tanks must read, see, think, and write as much as they can to improve their skills, especially when they are young and energetic. At the National Planning Commission, I often worked late into the night. My colleagues also had a great passion for work. Anyone who stayed behind to work overtime did not feel a sense of loss. A document usually needed to be revised many times, the result of which would sometimes be rejection and an order to start all over again. The formulation of the CPC central documents is one of the most democratic processes in the world. Members of the drafting team treat each and every character as a matter of great importance to the Party's undertaking and the People's interests. It could be said that working hard and working meticulously are the basic requirements for an economic researcher in a think tank.

My students used to ask me how I managed to write so many articles while burdened with so much work. I am keenly aware that while I was working hard, my mother devoted so much of herself to my family and my kid. Although she is now 91 years old, she still insists on climbing ladders as a way of exercising. One of the things she passed onto me was tenacity. In addition, my old wife, a Professor at Peking University Health Science Center, did almost all the housework, so I could focus on my research. Zheng Zhe, my son, did not enjoy much company or help from his father while he was growing up. He was usually asleep by the time I had returned home. I feel a sense of shame that I did not fulfill my responsibilities to my mother, wife, or son. These articles are the results of their dedication.

I want to thank my student Xu Wei who scoured so many libraries and Web sites and found and printed out so many articles and papers for me. I also want to thank my editor Xu Lin for her careful correction and refining of the drafts.

Should you read my book and find it useful, it shall give me great satisfaction as I shall know my work has not been without value and I have not been idling away in this great era.

Beijing, China
2018

Xinli Zheng

Preface to the English Edition

Over the past 40 years from 1978 to 2018, China has achieved economic miracles recognized the world over. Its reform and opening up program have been a fundamental reason for these miracles. In the 1980s, we focused on rural reform by implementing the household contract responsibility system with remuneration linked to output and developing rural enterprises. As a result, we ensured adequate clothing and food for people, brought an end to the history of commodity shortages, and kick-started China's economic takeoff. Internationally, we mainly drew upon the experience of Japan and the Four Asian Dragons—Hong Kong (China), Singapore, the Republic of Korea, and Taiwan (China).

In the 1990s, we vitalized the four pillar industries of electronic machinery, petrochemical engineering, auto-manufacturing, and construction by advancing reform of the macro-management system of which SOE reform was the centerpiece. This reform powered vital and rapid economic growth. During this period, we gradually came to see the value in learning from Germany and the USA in terms of macro-regulation.

In the first decade of the twenty-first century, we developed infrastructure construction by issuing long-term construction bonds. This would pave the way for the world's largest highway, high-speed railways, and communications networks and help us achieve a golden decade of growth. During this time, we continued learning from other countries; we drew lessons from Finland's valuable education system, Israel's advanced science and technology, and Ireland's development of the software and biopharmaceuticals sectors by building free-trade zones. We also learned much from India's booming software industry and the highly efficient agriculture of the Netherlands. Therefore, China's success in reform and opening up is a result of learning from other countries, but it is also based on our own realities.

In the second decade of the twenty-first century, the changes in China's development pattern prompted us to promote reforms and adjust the economic structure. In the demand structure, we worked to strike a better balance between investment and consumption and make consumption the greatest driver for economic growth in place of investment. In the industrial structure, we reformed the tax system to encourage the development of the tertiary industry and become a growth area of the economy. In the factor structure, we worked to ensure that technology, management, and the quality of the workforce played their role in growing the economy. Changes in the development pattern brought about progressive improvements in the quality of economic growth.

China's successful experience belongs also to the world and to humanity. Though China does not proactively promote its experience, its economists have a responsibility to review the Chinese development process and the major policy measures it has taken in the past 40 years and to introduce them in foreign languages so that they are available to any country or think tank that is interested in our experience of reform, opening up, and economic development. The content of this book is drawn partly from my 16-volume collected works published last year and also includes six articles written in the second half of last year. These articles are my most recent and are categorized under different subject areas in chronological order in each section. The appendices of the book include the main arguments of my economic research and the original preface as well as the entire catalogue of the original 16-volume collected works as a reference for interested readers.

The Chinese economy now faces a new challenge: overcapacity. How this problem is addressed will determine whether we can avoid the middle-income trap and rise to the ranks of high-income countries. Chinese economists are racking their brains for a solution. Therefore, we still have to study and learn from both positive and negative international experiences and search for inspiration through international comparative studies.

I would like to express my gratitude to all friends and colleagues who have worked on translating and publishing this book. And I very much appreciate the comments and criticisms of you, the reader.

Beijing, China Xinli Zheng
2018

Part I
Reform and Opening Up

Chapter 1
The Mixed-Ownership Joint Stock System Is a Major Way to Realize Public Ownership

The *Decision on Issues concerning the improvement of the Socialist Market Economy* (the *Decision*) adopted at the Third Plenary Session of the 16th CPC Central Committee stated that China will adapt to the trend of continuous development of the economic market, further enhance the vitality of the public sector of the economy, vigorously develop mixed ownership in the form of state-owned capital, collective capital, and non-public capital, realize investment diversification and make the shareholding system the primary platform for realizing public ownership. This important decision represents not only a breakthrough in our understanding of how we should realize public ownership, but also a step forward in the theories of socialist market economic reform. Conscientiously studying and understanding this decision is of vital importance for deepening reform in state-owned enterprises, improving the socialist market economic system, and further fulfilling the development potential of China's economy.

1.1 The Proposal that Mixed Ownership Is the Most Vital Form of Public Ownership Continues and Further Develops the Related Theories of the Communist Party

The shareholding system is the result of the emergence and development of socialized mass production. As a form of capital organization and allocation, the shareholding system has played a major role in promoting the development of mechanized production and modern industry, and has progressively been improved through practice. Under a socialist market economy, adopting a shareholding system to develop socialized mass production is both inevitable and essential. Of course, the environment and conditions for developing such a system in China differ from those in countries with

---

This article originally appeared in *Party Building*, no. 11, 2003.

X. Zheng, *China's 40 Years of Economic Reform and Development*,
https://doi.org/10.1007/978-981-13-2727-8_1

a more developed market economy. The main difference lies in the process of capital accumulation. The five plus decades since the founding of the People's Republic of China is a period that has seen the accumulation of more than ten trillion yuan of fixed assets consisting of more than seven trillion yuan of operational assets. These assets are the common wealth of generations of Chinese people accumulated as a result of hard work, and are where the common benefit of all Chinese people lies. Apart from accumulated assets, there are also publicly owned assets. The sum of these assets must be carefully protected in promoting their appreciation, and under no circumstances can they be subject to any form of embezzlement or erosion. Mixed shareholdings for state-owned capital, collective capital, and non-public capital naturally creates mixed ownership, which is an important characteristic of the ownership structure of China's shareholding economy. In terms of operational mechanism, China will adopt a form of shareholding system in common with that of developed market economies, in order to see that the social-economic mechanism stimulates productivity. Since beginning of reform, we have actively explored the system of mixed ownership and made progress through innovations in theory and practice. The conclusion of the Decision adopted by the 16th CPC Central Committee's Third Plenary Session to develop mixed ownership represents a new development on the basis of the CPC's relevant theories. As early as a decade ago, the *Decision of the CPC Central Committee on Certain Issues concerning the Establishment of a Socialist Market Economy* stated that through the circulation and reorganization of ownership, the number of mixed ownership economic entities will increase, thus giving rise to a new structure of asset ownership. The CPC's 15th National Congress held that share ownership is not exclusively applicable to capitalism. Socialism could also adopt this system because it would be public in nature, whereby assets would be owned and shared by the state and the public, respectively. The 15th CPC Central Committee's Fourth Plenary Session decided that large and medium-sized state-owned enterprises, especially preponderant ones, would reorganize themselves into shareholding enterprises under optimum conditions, thus developing mixed ownership through listings on the stock market according to related regulations, joint ventures, and mixed shareholdings. The CCP's 16th National Congress then required that, with the exception of those enterprises that must be owned by the state, enterprises shall complement the shareholding system by developing mixed ownership. The 16th CPC Central Committee's Third Plenary Session has now further confirmed that actively developing mixed ownership and instituting the shareholding system is the primary way to realize public ownership. This is a new breakthrough in ownership theories, reflecting the party's deeper understanding of how to achieve public ownership.

Making mixed ownership the primary path for realizing public ownership requires various investment resources in order to transform enterprises into shareholding companies. Within an enterprise, all varieties of ownership, including state-owned shares, collective shares, individual shares, foreign shares, and corporate shares, are equal, with benefits varying in proportion to the ownership of stock rights. All forms of shareholding for state-owned capital, including dominant or simple participatory forms, can be considered to be methods for realizing public ownership. Only on the basis of ownership diversification can a board of shareholders be established to create a body with the highest authority within an enterprise. In a policy-making organization, the board of directors should also come from the board of shareholders. And the managers, appointed by the board of directors, should serve as the executive organizers of the enterprise. Only by ensuring checks and balances between these three entities—the board of shareholders, board of directors and the manager—can an appropriate corporate governance structure be formed and a modern corporate system be truly established. If all of our state-owned enterprises were wholly state-owned or controlled by the state as a dominant shareholder, then there would be no necessity for maintaining the board of shareholders and board of directors. Such a situation would make it virtually impossible to form a corporate governance structure with appropriate checks and balances. Without these three entities, the modern enterprise system would nothing more than empty words. The *Decision* requires that mixed ownership be made the primary channel for realizing public ownership, and, in doing so, paves the way for the establishment of a modern corporate system. Thus, the *Decision* essentially guides enterprises along the path of establishing a modern corporate system.

1.2 Taking a Mixed Ownership Model as the Primary Means for Realizing Public Ownership Represents a Scientific Summary of Our Experience in Reform

Implementing a mixed ownership model is conducive to bringing funds together from all social sectors to accumulate capital and meet the large funding demands of large-scale programs and construction projects. It is also of help in separating ownership and management rights and selecting and promoting management talent for leading positions. Further, this system protects the benefits of all and unlocks the enthusiasm of vast numbers of workers for investing in and starting businesses. Implementing such a system also encourages the separation of government and enterprise and the separation of government and funds. Enterprises become entities for market competition while the functions of government will shift to providing public services and carrying out social management. As result of these advantages, mixed ownership has developed in many places, coastal places in particular, to become the most dynamic and the fastest developing component in local economic development. Economically, mixed ownership is playing an ever more important role. For example, in Zhejiang province, the shareholding system, based on a mixed ownership economy, has seen consistently strong growth since the 1990s, with annual rates reaching more than 15%. Presently, mixed ownership entities contribute more than 60% of provincial GDP, and it is estimated that this figure will reach 70% or more by 2005. Enterprise ownership structures are typically composed of three parts, namely, a public share (state-owned or collective), a social share (held by investors in the form listed companies) and an employee share, and these are separately held by core-level members, key-level members, and regular employees. Property rights structures of this kind can not only expand public capital and meet the demands of the public, but also enable enterprises to motivate staff with low productivity and form a relatively strong bond with them. Moreover, enterprises adopting such a structure would also be able to attract capital and receive supervision from investors, both of which are beneficial for developing enterprises. In practice, the property rights structures of various enterprises could differ on the basis their specific development histories and industrial characteristics. Experience has proven that enterprises under this kind of mixed ownership structure enjoy great vitality. Those that reform and adjust in accordance with this kind of a structure can get rid of the defects of egalitarianism, advance quickly and experience unlimited growth and vitality. Collective enterprises that adopt mixed ownership can avoid the influence of political powers in rural places and also develop rapidly. For private enterprises, adopting the shareholding system can evade the restraints of family-run management and upgrade their management models into a more modern corporate system. In conclusion, mixed ownership should be the final destination for all enterprises, regardless of whether they are state-owned, collectively owned, or privately owned. It is clear that developing mixed ownership is consistent with the path of enterprise development and operation in a socialist market economy. Mixed ownership is an effective form of organizing property rights.

On the other hand, we can see clearly that quite a number of state-owned enterprises have not yet realized the advantages of mixed ownership, and although many companies have created a corporate system, such systems are still far from what a proper shareholding structure should look like. By the year 2000, China had 145,000 wholly state-owned enterprises with a single investment resource, accounting for 75.9% of all state-owned enterprises. Of the 520 key national enterprises, 430 have carried out corporate reform, of which only 282 have wholly or partially been reorganized into limited liability companies or limited companies and become entities receiving investment from multiple sources. Even for a large proportion of companies under diversified ownership, their majority shareholdings (equity accounting for more than 50%) are state owned. In 2001, for the 32,000 state-holding companies throughout the country, the average proportion of state-owned shares to overall share capital was a mere 63%. By the end of April 2001, there number of listed companies with the largest shareholder holding more than 50% of the company's total capital was 890, accounting for 79.2% of all listed companies. In terms of the major shareholders, state and corporate shareholders account for an absolute majority, with quite a number of corporate shares being held by the state. When shares are predominantly state owned, the checks and balances between parties, namely, shareholders, the board of shareholders, the board of directors and managers, do not function efficiently, which results in an insider control situation that damages the interests of minority shareholders. If such an ownership structure persists, it becomes difficult to establish a modern corporate system and to create the required concomitant corporate governance structures. This means companies won't be able to develop in the most efficient way possible. It is in old industrial bases, the home of the state-owned enterprise, that ownership reform has run into the greatest difficulty. This is mainly because it is incomplete. Many companies simply changed their names and superficially identified themselves as operating under a mixed ownership system, all the while maintaining their original ownership and corporate governance structures. Instead of solving existing problems, this exacerbated the conflicts and overall situation in these enterprises. To sum up, it is high time that ownership reforms were implemented in their totality.

Experiences, both positive and negative, demonstrate that reforming SOEs in accordance with the *Decision's* requirements on mixed ownership and truly realizing investment diversification represents the way forward in reforming and developing SOEs and the correct path to revitalizing the old industrial bases.

1.3 Taking Mixed Ownership as the Primary Means for Realizing Public Ownership Is an Important Outcome of Explorations on Combining Public Ownership with the Market Economy

Since reform began, whether public ownership could, either theoretically or practically, be combined with the market economy has been the question has needed answering. Many foreign critics have raised doubt about our explorations, and even asserted that the market economy can only be built on the basis of private ownership. They believe that if China wants to have a market economy, the full implementation of private ownership is the only way to do so. After 20 years of reform, we have basically established the fundamental economic system, with public ownership serving as the main component and allowing for the development of all varieties of ownership. At its 16th National Congress the CPC decided to unwaveringly consolidate and develop the public sector of the economy and to unswervingly encourage, support, and guide the development of the non-public sector. Upholding the basic economic system in the primary stage of socialism is a fundamental requirement for establishing and improving the socialist economic system. Adjusting the ownership structure in accordance with the basic economic system is the most important component of reform. Practice has proven that the public sector can be closely combined with the market economy, just as the non-public sector can, by employing the key strategy of utilizing the shareholding system. Through a shareholding system many varieties of ownership can be effectively combined. By forming corporate legal property, this combination can not only leverage the respective advantages of each, but it also functions as a single unit, which represents the successful and effective integration of public ownership and the market economy. The solution to the problem that has troubled many since reform began is to improve the theory of reform and see it is complemented.

Our explorations continue on and further develop Marxist theory on shareholding. In the era when Marx and Engels flourished, the capitalist shareholding system was already fully developed, and they gave a positive evaluation of the shareholding system. In his analysis of the system, Marx stated, the stock-company business "represents the abolition of capitalist private industry on the basis of the capitalist system itself and destroys private industry as it expands and invades new spheres of production."[1] Marx regarded the cooperative factory as a positive abandonment of the capitalist mode of production, but the shareholding system as a negative abandonment of the capitalist mode of production. He also considered the capitalist stock companies and the cooperative factories "as transitional forms from the capitalist mode of production to the associated one."[2] As the shareholding system of today is far more developed than that of more than a century ago, we can assuredly use it to develop the socialist market economy. It should be noted that our equity owners do not just include state-owned and collective enterprises, employees also account for a large proportion. Increasing the proportion of employees holding shares, as well as the number of shareholders, can encourage workers to get involved in the production and operation of enterprises, stimulate their enthusiasm for work, increase their incomes, and, ultimately, accelerate the building of a moderately prosperous society in all respects. In short, developing mixed ownership is not only an essential part of integrating public ownership with the market economy but also the best option for doing so successfully.

1.4 Studying and Implementing the *Decision's* Conclusions on How to Realize Public Ownership Can Have a Significant and Far-Reaching Impact on SOE's Reform and Development

The key to improving the socialist market economy, and to achieving an effective combination between public ownership and the market economy, lies in SOEs. We should boost the developmental potential of SOEs by enabling them to truly become market entities that make their own management decisions. Through years of effort, the management systems and operating mechanisms of China's SOEs have achieved great changes, and market competition has been greatly enhanced. Though there has been much progress, there are, however, some deep-seated problems that have yet to be fully resolved, which means SOE reform is still the centerpiece of the overall reform. At present, deepening SOE reform entails adjusting ownership structures and addressing enterprises' deep-seated contradictions. It also involves speeding up corporate restructuring and optimizing capital structures. This can be achieved through the introduction of strategic investment, which includes investment by outstanding industry enterprises, private capital, and upstream and downstream corporate capital. At present, there are a number of well-run enterprises both in China's private and state-owned sector. These companies should choose partners for cooperation through an open bidding process. To ensure there is no erosion of state capital during corporate reorganization, we should strengthen supervision. We should also encourage foreign

[1] Karl Marx and Frederick Engels, *Collected Works*, Lawrence & Wishart, 2010, vol. 37, p. 436.
[2] Ibid., p. 438.

companies, especially transnational companies, to participate in SOE reorganization and reform. And we should also combine reorganization efforts with technological upgrades and systemic reform. Only when the restructuring of enterprises has been completed should the government consider investment policy support. The design of enterprises' ownership structures should be meticulous, and the interests of all parties should be fully and practically considered. If reform involves reducing the number of employees, the company must actively assist in ensuring laid-off workers can find alternative work and maintain their quality of life.

Transforming how we realize public ownership requires us to change our ideas and thoughts accordingly. We cannot hold onto the belief that only traditionally state-owned enterprises can be counted as entities of the public sector of the economy. State-owned capital distributed among various enterprises should also be considered an element of this sector; such a view is more conducive to the appreciation of state-owned capital. We cannot hold on to the belief that establishing and developing SOEs is the only way to implement a macro-economic policy that safeguards the interests of the people. It crucial that we recognize that ensuring enterprises with mixed ownership operate in accordance with market demand and national law is the best way to implement national macro-economic policy and to safeguard the interests of the people. Only by disposing of administrative influence can enterprises operate independently and continue to become more internationally competitive. In the past, we often made the analogy of likening SOEs to caged tigers. It is only through complete reformation of capital structure that we can change the operational mechanisms of these companies and unleash their huge potential, thereby, so to speak, releasing the tigers into the wild. Shareholder reform will put China's existing 7 trillion yuan of operating state-owned assets to good use, one that sees them making capital flow, appreciating in value, and providing capital the very same way that private capital does. This will see state-owned capital becoming a powerful driving force for the Chinese economy and a means for benefiting all Chinese people. Thus, state-owned capital will come to play an irreplaceable role in building a moderately prosperous society in all respects and realizing the great rejuvenation of the Chinese nation.

Chapter 2
The Mainstay that Successfully Dealt with the International Financial Crisis

In commemoration of the 90th anniversary of the birth of the Communist Party of China, reviewing the process of our victory over the international financial crisis, and analyzing its root causes, while exploring ways of preventing similar future crises is of great practical significance that pertains to improving the Party's ability to govern, maintaining long-term stable and rapid economic development, and leading Chinese people to a rejuvenation of their beloved nation.

2.1 The Root Cause Was that the United States Used State Credit to Create Financial Bubble

The international financial crisis that began in the second half of 2008 hit the global economy particularly hard, leaving people from many national economic circles reflecting on the causes from different perspectives. In summary, there are three relatively popular theories that explain why this financial crisis happened. One is that the world economic imbalance, brought about by excessive exports from developing countries, was the main trigger. Another theory is that, it was due to the over-leveraging of capital, created by excessive financial derivatives. The third belief is that, it happened because of a sovereign debt resulting from a surging government debt. All of these assumptions seem correct, and especially after following the mainstream media's take, many experts therefore believe that any of these theories could be the root cause for the global financial crisis.

Certainly, from the standpoints of certain countries and interest groups, these conclusions appear to make sense, although they are far from the truth.

Why? Developing countries managed to accelerate economic development and, in turn, rapidly increased exports by taking advantage of labor and resources in an

---

This article originally appeared in *Qiushi*, Chinese edition, no. 13, 2011.

X. Zheng, *China's 40 Years of Economic Reform and Development*,
https://doi.org/10.1007/978-981-13-2727-8_2

attempt to attract capital and technological advancements. This was as a result of optimization and allocation of production factors in the world. While exports were increasing, these developing countries had also been expanding their imports, providing a driving force that created jobs and promoted their economic growth. On the other hand, multinational groups in these developed countries utilized cheap labor and simultaneously increased their investment in these developing countries, thus directly providing a profit growth point. This type of economic activity, featuring mutual benefits and win-win outcomes is the inevitable direction for economic globalization as well as historical blueprints for the common progress of nations. Looking at the history of world's development, developmental disparity is absolute, while the balance is relative. Since the beginning of modern times, the United Kingdom and the United States have long been the biggest exporters, maintaining long-term trade surpluses. Today, while the United States is still a major exporter in service trade, Japan, Germany and other developed countries have also continued to be major exporters for technology-intensive and knowledge-intensive products. So in effect, blaming developing countries that have exports of labor-intensive and resource-intensive products for the global economic imbalance and concluding that these imbalances are the root cause of the global financial crisis would completely be missing the point.

It is also evident that the over-leveraging of capital created by excessive financial derivatives was one of the direct causes of the crisis, however the question still remains: What exactly resulted from the proliferation of these financial derivatives? Why were all those investors so keen on pursuing risky financial investments, most notably credit default swaps (CDS)? And why did the United States turn out to be the birthplace of excessive financial derivatives? The fact is, after the Great Depression of the 1930s, the US learned a lesson and adopted a series of laws to strengthen financial regulation. But by the 1980s, these laws had been abolished because it was believed that they inhibited the development of the financial sector. Whenever there were excessive financial derivatives, intellectuals from the country's economic communities and government would propose the strengthening of the legislation pertaining to financial regulation, but these propositions would be turned down the very instant they got submitted to the Congress. Congressmen in America usually claim to represent the interests of voters, but why did they sit on their hands and watch the financial derivatives proliferate? And what were the underlying interests that drove their actions? The truth is, financial over-leveraging is just an over-simplification of the phenomenon. Behind it lie the fundamental causes.

The sovereign debt crisis caused by the overexpansion of government debt also contributed to the crisis, but it cannot be considered as the fundamental cause either. Fiscal deficit and government debt can also create pressure for currency to be issued. Thus the issuance of currency must be kept within a reasonable range, as determined by the fiscal revenue and gross domestic product. When the currency issued has surpassed this range, it means that there is too much money in circulation, which inevitably leads to inflation. In fact, the United States has long relied on a fiscal deficit and government bonds to pay their bills. Following the financial crisis, the US government's fiscal deficit and debt continued to increase. By the end of 2010, its federal government had attracted a deficit of US$1.4 trillion that amounted to 9.4% of its GDP. At this time, the public debt amounted to $9.02 trillion, which during that fiscal year, was 62.1% of GDP; a very high level for a developed country. America's high deficit rate and high debt rate, however, did not trigger inflation. The reason why the country can still maintain a low interest rate is entirely because of its position as the issuing country of the world's major reserve currency, and that it can attract a large inflow of foreign funds and cheap goods. Whether it was before or after the crisis, it should be noted that America's large-scale borrowing only acted as a driving force and ultimately the source of power accumulation of the financial tsunami.

The fundamental cause of this financial crisis lies in the long-term abuse of state credit by the United States. Taking advantage of being the issuing country of the world's major reserve currencies, the country implemented double deficit policies, in form of current account and fiscal budget deficits, in order to maintain the over-consumption of its people and excessive government spending, thus gradually increasing the enormous power of a financial tsunami. Concurrently, exploiting their global monopoly positions, credit rating agencies in the United States concealed state credit risks, reversing the debtor's risk-relationship between the debtor and the creditor nations. Therefore a large amount of international capital was attracted to high risk fields, dismantling the last barrier preventing a financial crisis.

Through market economies acting as credit economies, economic globalization made state credit a major component of its overall national competitiveness and economic strength. A good state credit can lower the financing costs for a country's government and enterprises, attracting more foreign investment and eventually becoming an important driving force in the development of the economy. On the other hand, countries that abuse state credit, especially those that are the issuer of major reserve currencies, can ultimately attract a global catastrophe because of embezzling from the wealth of other countries as a result accumulate and spread financial risks.

The fact that the United States became the source of the global financial crisis has once again clearly demonstrated that the scale of financial products created by state credits must be parallel to the scale of the real economy. The excessive expansion of a virtual economy makes the US economy look like an inverted pyramid built on a beach. Before the financial crisis, subprime mortgages, which were at the bottom of the pyramid, totaled about $2 trillion and ordinary mortgages were approximately $12 trillion. Corporate debt, including the collateralized debt obligation (CDO) and credit default swaps (CDS) stood at about $62 trillion. According to the Bank for International Settlements, financial derivatives held by major US financial institutions were about $300 trillion. Therefore, this giant upside-down financial pyramid would have the potential to collapse at any time if even one of its bricks moved. For that reason, if this historic economic crisis of capitalism was mainly caused by the overproduction of material products, then it should be safe to say that today, against the historical backdrop of a highly developing financial industry, the glut of financial products relentlessly created by state credits is undoubtedly the fundamental root cause for most of the global financial crises of our time.

2.2 The Chinese Economy Has Become the Stabilizer and Engine Driving the World Economy

Following the outbreak of the financial crisis, the Chinese government derived various decisive policies in response. In accordance with the requirement that we act fast and be more forceful, the Chinese government implemented a fiscal investment plan prior to the end of 2008. The volume of planned investments added up to $4 trillion and would be finished within two years. In 2009, because of a shrinking domestic market in the developed economies impacted by this crisis, the volume of Chinese exports fell 16% from the previous year's, and the pull effect of exports that drove economic growth by more than 2% in 2008 also dragged the economy down by 2%. The extraordinary growth for China's investment had effectively offset the negative impact on the economy resulting from the declining exports, thus maintaining the GDP growth in 2009 at 9.2% and striking a relatively steady, yet continuous growth in the year the financial crisis was the most severe. The manufacturing sector was the hardest hit, causing more than 20 million rural migrant workers to lose their jobs. The industry did not recover until the second year after the crisis. Compared with the overall decline of more than 40% of imports in developed countries, Chinese imports only fell 11.2%, thus playing an important part in fending off a further impact from the dwindling international trade and world economy. This not only maintained a steady growth for the Chinese economy, but also drove the economic recovery of the entire world. Since China has shown its ability to be a mainstay in coping with the international financial crisis, it has therefore become the bona fide stabilizer of the global economy.

By 2010, China's economy had undergone its transformation from recovering to regaining momentum and finally to sustaining a fast growth. GDP in 2010 grew to 10.3% and exports also grew 31.3%, higher than the level prior to 2008. The volume of imports also skyrocketed to 38.7%, ranking second only behind the US imports increased by $389.2 billion, leading that of all countries and accounting for 15% of the total increased imports worldwide. Since then, Chinese imports have become the prominent engine for the recovery and growth of the world economy. During this period of the 12th Five-Year Plan, the development model of China's economy is to get away from an investment and export driven model to a consumption-driven model, under which domestic demand, especially consumption demand, still has great potential to increase. At the same time, China will gradually narrow its trade surplus and strike a balance in international payment, which will cause imports to grow to unprecedented levels. Last year, the total Chinese imports reached $1.4 trillion, and are estimated to get to $12 trillion in the next five years. The transformation of China's economic development model has also demonstrated that the contribution China makes to the world's economic growth is ever increasing, and China's economy would definitely become the prominent engine that drives the growth of the world economy in the future.

The key to China's success in dealing with the crisis is to expand domestic demand, especially within the public service sector. The Chinese government has stressed on developing various social undertakings, such as improving the social security system, accelerating infrastructure building, and the ecological environment management, so as to enable new investments to greatly improve the quality of its people's lives and create a more friendly environment for economic development. These undertakings will result in a batch of high-performance assets and would avoid inefficient investments and defaults.

China's success in the crisis also relies on its emphasis on innovation and infrastructure upgrading. The country is also encouraging the establishment of strategic emerging industries, including those in the new generation of information technology, energy-efficient environmental protective technology, new energy, biological, high-end equipment manufacturing, new materials, and new energy vehicles, etc. At the same time, China is paying particular attention to phasing out inefficient capacity, the release of pollutants, and preventing redundant construction projects by setting up mandatory targets for reductions in energy consumption per unit of GDP.

China's success in defusing the crisis therefore hinges on the leadership of the Communist Party of China. The CPC has reached an agreement and led people throughout the country to make joint efforts amid economic hardships. Guided by the strong leadership of the CPC, China has also managed to form a cohesive and consistent effort, and strength through fiscal and financial planning, and appropriate land policies. As a result, the Chinese government has a more efficient coordination and governing mechanism, which many other countries don't.

2.3 Taking Multiple Effective Measures to Fend off International Financial Risks

As the US dollar is in a position of absolute control with regards to the international reserve currency, the instability of the dollar market will inevitably spread to the rest of the world. Since the economies of the United States and China are now closely connected, the crisis emanating from the US dollar will unequivocally be the most problematic financial risk China would have to confront in the near future.

The US dollar acquired its dominant position as one of the major global reserve currencies more than a century after the World War II. Although its dominating power was weakened after the emergence of the Euro, the dollar still takes up 60% of the global currency reserve and accounts for 70% of the reserve currencies in international trade and investment settlements. While there would not be a dramatic change in the short term, the United States has bogged the country down into financial overstretch and forced it to live beyond its means as it recklessly exploits its privilege as the issuing country of a major global reserve currency. If there was any doubt of the US dollar's ability to maintain its position as the major global reserve currency, then no country or enterprise would have any interest in the US dollar or even take the United States' national debt. As a result, the dollar crisis would deteriorate because of this rejection. In this case, the second round of quantitative easing, initiated by the

Federal Reserve regardless of the opposition from many economists, would have just dragged the American people into a far worse situation. Quantitative easing would turn on the money-printing machine and inject excessive amounts of banknotes into the market, causing the devaluation of the US dollar and triggering a global inflation. Not long ago, Standard & Poor's, America's own credit rating company, announced that the US state credit rating was negative. Under tremendous pressure, the Federal Reserve claimed it would not continue to carry out quantitative easing. However, stopping the flood of banknotes meant that the only resort of supporting the deficit was to expand the fiscal deficit. Recently there have been talks and debates concerning whether the deficit's ceiling should be increased to expand the fiscal deficit for government spending. From all perspectives, the degradation and devaluation of the US dollar, as a major global reserve currency, was inevitable and the questions that remained were when and in what form.

Meanwhile, after more than 30 years of fast development, China's economy has seen an accumulation of over $3 trillion in foreign exchange reserves. The major part of this treasure, which was mainly acquired as a result of the toil of all Chinese, is in the form of US dollars, and the national debt of the United States is worth about $1 trillion. The safety of this asset is what all Chinese experts are concerned about. If the US dollar is devalued by even as much as 1%, it means that tens of billions of US dollars held by China would have no value. Therefore, the task of defending China's assets against an international financial crisis is far from over. While China succeeded in the first wave of the financial tsunami, the country still needs to be on the lookout for the next wave, which is characteristic of the devaluation of the US dollar, and we must study when and how to confront it.

Expanding overseas investment and turning part of foreign exchange reserves and US national debt into material reserves, such as energy and mineral resources, is an important measure of preventing an imminent attack due to a devaluation of the US dollar. Other than the essential foreign exchange reserves, we should also take advantage of other aspects, which means that we should also encourage commercial banks and enterprises to use foreign exchange. At present, the only way for these institutions to utilize foreign exchange is to purchase them with RMB, which essentially transfers the exchange-rate risks to them, which in turn actually dampens their enthusiasm to use foreign exchange. So, if the Central Bank can transfer and deposit part of its foreign exchange into commercial banks and lend to those enterprises in need of foreign exchange, then these companies would happily welcome the use of foreign exchange.

Realizing the diversification of a foreign exchange reserve is one way of preventing the associated risks and avoiding the overconcentration of one foreign exchange by modestly adjusting its proportions according to the situation and economic trends of currencies of other countries. Therefore, in trying to prevent a great loss, it's advisable not to put all your eggs in one basket.

Essentially, we can only limit the risks associated with foreign exchange reserves and other financial risks by encouraging the globalization of the renminbi, which, in turn, would cause the renminbi to become a global reserve currency. Of course, this would require time, but regardless, this is a goal we shall strive to achieve. To reach our collective goal, we should therefore extend the bilateral currency swap scale and promote the use of the renminbi as the settlement currency in global trade and investments. We should also promote the liberalization of interest rates and increase capital account convertibility of capital accounts. Also further improving the capital market and providing various renminbi financial products for foreign and domestic investors will make the renminbi a currency that is easy to exchange and a currency that carries the appeal of high return on investment. Therefore we should especially take advantage of a potential renminbi appreciation to promote its globalization. If our wealth can be stored in the form of this Chinese currency, then we could really be at the helm of confronting the waves of international financial risks.

2.4 Upholding China's Legitimate Rights and Interests in the Reform of the International Financial System

As a major economic and financial country, everything within the international financial reform is highly relevant to China. We should therefore actively be a part of the research and debate regarding international financial reforms, and propose constructive guidelines to upholding and protecting legitimate rights and interests of China. In respect to the fundamental causes of this financial crisis, we should also develop a definitive strategy to prevent a crisis like this from ever happening again and take the opportunity in the construction of an efficient and secure global financial system. In order to secure the safety of international finances, I believe the most urgent thing now is to construct three firewalls against any financial risks that include:

1. *Establishing a global monetary system of diverse competition*

The building of the diversified, competitive global monetary system would be the basic approach to the stabilization of the international financial system. The future of the global reserve currency system is very likely to be a diverse system with the US dollar, the Euro, the renminbi, the Japanese yen and the British pound. Competition, checks and balances, and inter-connectivity within these currencies will form a system where people can sell off currencies with devaluation risks and rush to buy currencies of a more stable nature or with an appreciation potential. Therefore, the mechanism of competition and selection will drive issuing countries of the global reserve currencies and their central banks to implement a steadier and more secure monetary policy that will, as a result, stabilize their currencies and maintain their state credit. It's only with a global reserve currency system like this can we reverse the economic environment of over-reliance upon one sovereign currency and prevent the over-concentration of international financial risks upon one currency. After the cancellation of the gold standard by global reserve currencies, the competition mechanism should be in place so as to form a stable monetary system for global reserve currencies. This would be the best option against the backdrop of economic globalization.

2. *Establishing a monitoring and warning system for global reserve currencies*

In the 1970s, the collapse of the Bretton Woods System and the decoupling of international monetary values and gold made the US dollar the world's major reserve currency that relied on the US state credit, allowing America to transfer its debt abroad through a currency devaluation. From 1971 to 2010, the US dollar depreciated by about 97.2% against gold, causing huge losses to countries that had US dollar as a reserve currency. While the devaluation of the dollar caused a relatively slow shrinking of the wealth of dollar asset owners, this financial crisis resulted in some dollar securities assets vanishing overnight. This shows that the issuer of the world's major reserve currency had exceeded its national boundaries and had a direct bearing on the interests of all residents, enterprises and foreign governments holding dollar assets. Therefore, it is necessary to monitor any warnings signs, and observe international regulations on the issuance and circulation of major global reserve currencies. At present, it is entirely feasible for the international financial organization to carry out these functions.

3. *Establishing international cooperation and a relief mechanism for financial security*

Economic ties between countries are becoming increasingly close. In this context, a country's financial problems often spur a chain reaction. In order to maintain an international financial security, countries should join forces in the establishment of the international cooperation relief mechanism for financial security. The Chiang Mai Initiative, signed after the Asian financial crisis, is an example of this joint force. At present, the International Monetary Fund should expand the size of its Special Drawing Rights (SDR) and adjust the proportion of countries within the SDR. This should be relative to each country's strength in economics and trade as a result increasing the voting rights for emerging economies. Therefore in order to maintain the stability of the global monetary system, when a country meets a financial crisis, the International Monetary Fund should give a timely relief and help them find an immediate solution in order to prevent a ripple effect.

Chapter 3
Adhering to the Strong Engine of the Expedited Innovation Reforms

Since 1978, the reform and opening up of the China has stimulated a huge developmental momentum. China's economy has in fact achieved rapid growth for a consecutive 34 years. The country has also gained a comprehensive national strength and living standards have greatly been improved. As a result, experience has proven that the reform and opening up of the country was the correct choice in determining the fate of China. It was also a powerful driving force in the promotion of the country's economic and social development. Therefore it is a critical strategy that we must always adhere to in the primary stages of socialism.

At present, China is at a crucial stage of development. In 2011, China's per capita GDP reached US$5400, even though this number was still $6600 less than the World Bank's recommended threshold of $12,000 for high- and middle-income countries. Therefore, China still faces a steep climb ahead to get itself out of the middle-income trap. Foreign experience has shown that a country can easily raise its average income from a relatively low level to a middle-class level of $4500 per capita by virtue of a low cost of labor and resources, and the introduction of advanced technology. However, we have to admit that it is difficult to raise the income level from $5000 to $12,000. Why is it so? Because at this stage, we must first complete the upgrading of our industrial structure from a mainly labor and resource-intensive structure to a mainly capital, technology, and knowledge-intensive one. To achieve this transformation, we must rely on the improvement of our labor quality, establish independent brands and products with independent intellectual property rights, and set up a number of multinational companies that can drive industrial upgrading and are fully capable of operating a global business. When it comes to South-East Asian and Latin American countries, most are able to reach a level of $4000 or $5000 per capita. But only few countries and regions, such as Japan and the Four Asian Dragons (Taiwan, Singapore, Hong Kong and South Korea) have really gotten into the ranks of high-income countries. If China wants to join this rank of these high-income countries, it is crucial

This article originally appeared in *Qiushi*, Chinese edition, no. 8, 2012.

X. Zheng, *China's 40 Years of Economic Reform and Development*,
https://doi.org/10.1007/978-981-13-2727-8_3

for it to solve its various existing problems hampering development, by eliminating the bottlenecks impacting energy resources and technology and attaining coordinated development among different sectors of its economy and regions of society. It would also be instrumental to strike a balance between economic development and environmental protection as well as strike a balance between domestic and foreign economies. To solve these problems, we therefore need to continue with further reforms in our efforts to exploit the great potential of economic development and achieve a comprehensive, coordinated, and sustainable growth. At the two sessions this spring, deputies of the National People's Congress (NPC) and the Chinese People's Political Consultative Conference (CPPCC) members issued a strong appeal for furthering reforms. They also put forward a large number of proposals, reflecting the people's strong wishes for reforms.

At present, the most important thing is to sort out the macro-level policy reforms. We therefore need to carefully design top-level planning, get to the key links, stress systematic innovations, and continue reforms with gusto, stamina and diligence. Based on experience, we must also engage in reforming our socialist market economy, strengthen the role of market mechanisms, and stimulate the vitality of economic development by taking advantage of the market's fundamental role in the allocation of resources. More than 30 years of reform practices have proven that, if the development of a field is full of vitality, and if its various production factors are functioning perfectly, then the field must have stricken the coordination between the government and the market and must have also taken advantage of the market's fundamental function in the allocation of resources. On the contrary, if a field cannot exploit the market, its development will just be like a pool of stagnant water due to a lack of competition. Therefore, market-oriented reforms should continue to serve as a direction for deepening reforms. At the same time, in fields where it is difficult for the market to play its role, we should leverage the role of government policies and macro regulations. In special stages, defusing the global financial crisis entails a greater role of the government, which should be in line with the law of economic development.

We should also continue pushing forward with the opening up to boost reform, development, and innovation because it is through opening up the country's economy that has helped us broaden our horizons, introduce foreign technology, capital, management experience, and put pressure on reforming domestic enterprises. When drawing up new plans for reforms, we therefore should keep in mind China's competitive edge and adopt successful strategies that are beneficial to our country from the outside world. We should also not forget our successes and failures. We ought to keep learning from especially the lessons drawn from this international financial crisis. We must thus improve this process of opening up, develop an open economic system, and aim for a steady and rapid economic development by actively participating in the ongoing globalization process.

In order to make any breakthroughs, furthering reforms should only focus on crucial areas and key links that hamper economic development. For that to happen, the spotlight should be on reforming existing systematic innovations, standardizing and regulating any mature measures and using legal means to strengthen and promote these reforms. We must therefore insist on continuous practice to test and prove whether these reform measures are actually conducive to developing productivity and whether the laws and regulations could be beneficial for stimulating economic vitality and ensuring market order. Balanced and sustainable development should also be set as the starting point for these reforms and should set the standards for improving people's lives. In recent years, as the influence of China's economy on the world has grown, there has been an ever-increasing concern regarding the country's economic situation. Many domestic and foreign experts have also been keen to give their evaluations and estimations on whether China can actually maintain its economic momentum at a fast, yet steady pace while keeping an eye on how long China can sustain its rapid growth under the impact of the international financial crisis. For example, Nouriel Roubini, an American scholar also known as "Dr. Doom," once predicted that "China's economy would have its hard landing in 2013, and its rapid growth would end then." But apart from these kinds of opinions coming from foreign experts, there also have been domestic concerns that China cannot maintain its pace because of the many constraints it faces.

However, I strongly disagree. Personally, I believe that China's rapid growth will continue for at least another 20 years, mainly due to its economic potential still waiting to be tapped. As long as we further reforms and keep opening up, while encouraging institutional innovations, the economy will continuously gain power and so it will keep moving forward. But if the economy loses its momentum, then there must be problems within our systems and policies. It is therefore vital that we implement a Theory of Balanced and Sustainable Development that puts its people first, stresses comprehensive, coordinated, and sustainable development, while at the same time putting emphasis on viable growth model. By analyzing the current economic situation, I believe we should follow the recommendations from the Report on the Work of the Government and tap the huge potential of our economy from these five angles.

First, deepening the income distribution system reforms and tapping the demand potential in consumption.

We should be able to significantly adjust the demand structure and shift the engine for economic growth from investment and export to consumption. This is a significant measure that can oversee the implementation of a Theory of Balanced and Sustainable Development and its initial task of transforming the development of economic growth. In 2010, China's investment rate set its highest record in history at 48.6% while the final consumption rate dropped to 47.4%. This was the first time that the investment rate was higher than the final consumption rate. At the same time, the household consumption rate fell to its lowest point in history with 33.8%. All these numbers therefore have clearly shown that nearly half of the total value of social goods that were produced throughout the year was used to expand reproduction, but only a third of the total value went into people's consumption. Therefore, this rapid growth, mainly driven by high input, will not only bring about excess capacity, but also increase the pressure on resources and the environment. Hence this kind of growth cannot last long. Reducing the investment rate and raising the consumption rate of the people must be based on the adjustment of the national income distribution structure. The income distribution system must also be reformed. The government's work report in 2012 proposed that we should pay close attention to the overall plan of the income distribution system reforms, strive to improve the proportion of residents' income in the distribution of our national income, and increase the proportion of labor remuneration so as to tackle the crux in the transformation of the developmental model. Since 2011, we have achieved some notable results from reforming the structural tax cuts, although we still need to invest more efforts. For example, increasing the threshold of small low-profit businesses, value-added tax, and business tax from the monthly sales of 5000–20,000 yuan so that the mount paid by more than 9 million business taxpayers will reduce by an average of 40%, while the monthly tax revenue would decrease by only 900 million yuan. Raising the threshold to monthly sales of 0.1 million would be very positive move that would encourage entrepreneurship in turn cultivating financial resources. We should therefore continue to implement policies that cut tax for enterprises and make enterprises transfer benefits to their employees in a bid to exploit the role played by taxes within the national income distribution process. Conditions for transforming the tax system from a dominating indirect tax, to a direct tax are developed enough, and we should hence proceed to study the impact of this direct tax-based tax reform program. We should also expand the proportion of our fiscal overheads within the public service expenditure, and stress the extension of public service consumption. By adjusting the income distribution structure, we should be able to spontaneously increase the wages for those people that fall within the low -middle-income bracket and form an olive-shaped income distribution structure that will enhance the people's purchasing power. It is important to note that, within this 12th Five-Year Plan, every 10% increase in residents' consumption rate is equivalent to about 5 trillion yuan of goods being used from investment and export. This is not only a powerful driving force to stimulate economic growth, but one that also will result in the consumption levels of people increasing greatly.

Second, speeding up the financial system reform and tapping the potential of capital.

China's scale of capital stock has grown immensely. The country's banks' supply of broad money (M_2) amounts to more than 70 trillion yuan while financial assets have reached a staggering 119 trillion yuan. However, as the financial system reform is out of step with the growth of the capital stock, the banking structure does not have enough small financial institutions specializing in service for small and medium enterprises, resulting in an inefficient allocation of capital resources and low turnover rates. Enterprises that are in desperate need of funds aren't able to receive the support needed when there exist large amounts of idle funds. Various research studies have shown that, in the first half of 2011, the average lending rate for enterprises in Wenzhou was 25%, and so some companies had no option but to resort to private lending and usury. Thus the centerpiece of reforming the financial systems should be in accordance with the recommendations given in the State Council's repo Guidelines on Encouraging and Guiding Healthy Development of Private Investment. We should allow private capital to initiate and set up various small financial institutions with a shareholding system, and at the same time, strive to establish local regulatory institutions, introduce a deposit insurance system, and implement the liberalization of interest rates. We should also develop a multi-tiered capital market. Improving the dividend system for listed companies and increasing information transparency will also enhance the attractiveness of the stock market to investors. We should therefore actively develop the bond market and strive to expand the insurance market and fully exploit the value-adding function of capital through deepened reforms. Currently, China's foreign exchange reserves have reached US$3.2 trillion. If we can take advantage of this, then this treasure will become the major driving force for a fast, yet steady economic growth. Reasonable foreign exchange reserves should meanwhile meet the demands of imports within six months. We should also transform any excessive foreign exchange reserves into material reserves by expanding our investment overseas. Reforming this foreign exchange management system and transforming it from a management of settlement and into the management of the use of foreign exchange, would largely encourage commercial banks to operate businesses in foreign exchange loans. We should therefore encourage all kinds of enterprises, especially private businesses, to "go global" and improve the safety and benefit of foreign exchanges. There are four targets for these kinds of enterprises "going global." The first one is to get more exploration rights and development rights for energy and resources. The second one is to expand international mergers and acquisitions (M&A). By making full use of the technology and management experience of the international market, we can improve our capacity for innovation and international businesses. The third one is to launch a processing trade and to create demands for export through capital output. The fourth is to extend overseas project contracting and to drive exports for construction machinery, materials, and labor. We should steadily push forward the internationalization of the renminbi and step-by-step expand its scale as the currency for settlement in international trade. As long as financial reforms exude an enormous potential for capital, then it should be enough in meeting the demands for funds through a rapid economic growth.

Third, improving the mechanism that provides incentives and tapping the potential of technological innovation.

Compared with developed countries, China still has a long way to go before it can catch up on developing industrial technology. Regardless, the potential for China to continue introducing, studying, applying, innovating, and exploiting technologies in the international market is still there. The critical part lies in heavily investing in the development of technology and sciences, through which enterprises can be turned into entities for technological innovation. Currently, investment for developing technology and the application for international patents are rather uneven. In 2011, the Chinese company, ZTE Corporation applied for 2800 international patents and went straight to the top of the list. At the same time, Huawei, another Chinese company, ranked third, obtaining 1800 international patents in the same year. The total patents applied for by both companies added up to more than a quarter of all patents submitted by Chinese companies. If each province can establish several major patent-applying companies like ZTE and Huawei during this 12th Five-Year Plan period, then our country's capacity for innovation could make a giant leap forward. Currently, the crucial thing is to establish an incentive mechanism for technological innovations in state-owned enterprises, which in turn can help turn state-owned enterprises into market leaders and transform them into becoming the mainstays for innovation. Universities and colleges should also become bases for technological innovation and the cradle for innovative talent. In 2009, the number of applications for international patents from the United States was six times that of China, that number however dropped to three times by 2011. If this trend continues, then China could catch up with the United States in applying for international patents by 2015. Therefore by improving incentive mechanisms for technological innovations and the creativity of the Chinese, this great potential of technology will become the engine that drives industrial upgrading and the one that generates a new path for growth.

Fourth, developing rural-urban integration and tapping the potential of the workforce.

There is still an enormous potential within China's workforce. Recently, in the face of a "labor shortage" in some places, some people were quick to jump to the conclusion that the supply of labor force had reached its turning point from a huge surplus to a shortage and that the "Lewis turning point" had finally manifested itself in the Chinese economy. Those who hold this type of assumption, in my opinion, do not see the enormous potential hidden within the agricultural workforce. At present, China boasts 280 million agricultural workers and 1.8 billion mu (120 million ha; 1 mu = 1/15 ha) worth of arable land, which means that the average land for each farmer is only 6.4 mu (0.43 ha). This is in contrast with the United States, where each farmer can possess thousands of mu of land while their European counterparts have hundreds. Although Chinese farmers are considered more diligent and that China's capacity for agricultural equipment production could catch up with that of the US and Europe, the biggest challenge for China is a shortage in land resources. With the development of agricultural modernization, we should therefore direct and encourage the centralization of land and form new types of operating entities, including rural cooperatives, family farms, and agricultural companies. These entities would free part of the workforce from land labor and divert them toward the secondary and tertiary industries in cities, thereby encouraging these employees to bring along their relatives who could also join the labor force in urban centers. In 2010, the agricultural workforce accounted for 36.7% of all working people, while the added value for agriculture only took up 10.1% of its GDP; which means that the value created by each 3.6 agricultural laborers is equivalent to the value created by only one laborer in the secondary and tertiary industries. Diverting part of the agricultural workforce would not only help release this huge capacity of rural workforce and meet the need for industrialization and urbanization for laborers, but will also encourage farmland formula management, increasing agricultural labor productivity and narrowing the income gap between urban and rural residents. Finally after more than three decades worth of efforts, over 200 million workers have been diverted from agriculture. Therefore if this workforce diverted from agriculture increases by another 200 million within the next 20 years, labor productivity in the primary industry is likely to catch up with the average level of the second and third industries, thereby balancing out the income for both urban and rural residents. It's only when the farmers' income exceeds that of migrant workers can a high-quality workforce remain in the countryside. The diversion of the agricultural workforce to other industries can also inject a strong impetus to the process of urbanization. In 2011, China's urbanization rate reached 51.27%, an increase that was seen as being emblematic of a historic shift in the population demographics. However, we still have a long way to go in order to reach the maturity stage for urbanization, which stands at a rate of 70%. In the next two decades, if China is to achieve a historic goal in industrialization and urbanization, the country has to raise its rate of urbanization by at least 1% each year and get to the 70% target by 2030. Experience has proven that for each new urban individual, there is a need to inject an extra 100,000 yuan of additional investment into the urban infrastructure. Therefore, each of the 10 million people added to the urban population would create 1 trillion yuan of investment needed in infrastructure building. Demands for investment in infrastructure therefore, together with an increasing need for other public services plus the rising level of individual consumption, will form an enormous demand for investment and consumption, which will in turn become the basic driving force for a rapid development of the Chinese economy within the next two decades. Tapping into this kind of potential will hence require us to work hard in two areas. We must work hard to construct a new pattern of rural-urban integration, and strive to establish governance systems for land reforms, household registration, and public services. To create a good environmental policy for rural-urban integration, we must also remove all the barriers against a free flow of all kinds of production factors between rural and urban places.

Fifth, reforming land management systems and tapping land potential.

A large population with relatively little arable land is China's basic national challenge. While the shortage of land resources is seriously holding back economic development, waste of land is still rampant. Therefore in reforming the land management system and increasing the efficiency of use there is an enormous potential to be tapped. Other than barren beaches and hills, resources like land for rural construction also have the potential for savings. At present, land for nationwide urban and rural construction is 220,000 km^2 in total, including 50,000 km^2 for city (including county towns and prefectures) construction and 170,000 km^2 for construction in small towns and villages. Meanwhile, land for village construction is 130,000 km^2. Currently, many migrant workers leave their homes vacant for long periods of time, creating a lot of "shell villages" (villages with few strong young men). The disorderly and unauthorized acquisition of farmlands could also be viewed as a wastage of land resources. If anything, experience has also taught us that in the building of a new socialist countryside, rectifying homestead land in villages could save more than 50% in land resources. In other words, we could potentially save over 100 million mu worth of village construction land, and this land could in fact be secured for farming and construction projects. The critical point of reforming the land management system therefore lies in making use of and implementing a farming households usufruct and property rights for contracted land, forest land, and homesteads. By encouraging voluntary and compensated transfers in exchange for land-usage rights, famers could also gain another a source of income through their lands. These lands just need to be turned into tangible wealth that can be seen and felt, for farmers to appreciate the value of their properties and cherish them even more. Therefore, it's only by speeding up the reform of the management system can we greatly improve the utilization and output rates of land, eliminate the land left idle, wasted or abandoned in order to unbind their potential.

Promoting integrated and comprehensive reforms will also unleash the enormous potential in all aspects driving economic growth. Through which we could also completely sustain this momentum for China's rapidly-growing economy for another 2 decades or more. For instance, Japan maintained its economic growth for 20 years, and South Korea kept its economy going up for 30 years. Global records also prove that China can absolutely set a new record for keeping its economic momentum for the longest period of time. If the economy can continue to grow by approximately 8%, then the per capita GDP in 2025 will double that of 2010 and reach $12,000. China can then finally lift itself from the dreaded middle-income trap and step onto the much revered members only list of high-income countries. It could even reclaim its position at the top of the list for boasting the largest economic aggregate. However, it's crucial to remember that even though this period for rapid economic growth has not yet ended, the experiences of Japanese and Korean economies have shown that economic growth will slow down significantly when the per capita GDP reaches $17,000. However, considering the country's vast territory, its giant population, and uneven development across its regions, it is very likely that growth will not slow down at least up until 2030. Therefore, furthering reforms and grasping a strong impetus for innovation reforms could be the key to realizing the rejuvenation of the Chinese nation.

Chapter 4
Balancing the Government-Market Relationship Is Instrumental for Economic Structural Reform

The political report to the 18th CPC National Congress pointed out that the underlying issue China faces in economic structural reform is how to balance the government-market relationship. Letting the market regulate the economy is essential to ensuring economic vitality. If the government performs its well defined functions, it will safeguard macroeconomic stability. If the government and the market work together and complement each other, it will provide a fundamental guarantee for sustained and sound economic development. This is what China has learned from its reform over the past more than 30 years, and it is also the orientation and a priority of China's future reform.

4.1 Streamlining Administration and Delegating Powers to Boost the Vitality of Enterprises: The Key to Success in China's Reform

China's reform over the last 34 years has transformed China from a highly concentrated planned economy to a socialist market economy. This transformation has released the massive potential that was locked away amongst China's population of over one billion, giving rise to China's miracle development.

The entire reform has been focused on adjusting and changing the government-market relationship. A major characteristic of the old system was the fact that the government took responsibility for everything. Under that system, the government was solely in charge of the purchase and sale of goods and materials, the distribution and management of manpower, and the collection and allocation of funds. Moreover, all authority to make investments rested with the central government. This policy repudiated the production and exchange of commodities, had a suffocating

This article originally appeared in *Qiushi*, Chinese edition, no. 2, 2013.

X. Zheng, *China's 40 Years of Economic Reform and Development*,
https://doi.org/10.1007/978-981-13-2727-8_4

effect on microeconomic vitality, and the result was that economic development was hampered.

China's reform began with a push to streamline administration, delegate powers, and foster market forces. The household contracting system for farmland, which links remuneration to output, was implemented in rural areas. This allowed farmers to become independent producers and sellers of commodities. This represented the first step in breaking away from the constraints of the old system. Shortly afterwards, industrial and commercial reform were carried out, leading to the rapid development of township and village enterprises.

China's urban reform began by breaking the "iron rice bowls" of SOE employees, and by dismantling the "big pot" system of egalitarianism. This prompted reform in regard to planning, investment, personnel, wages, taxation, and other aspects of macroeconomic management. In 1992, the CPC stated at its 14th National Congress its goal of reform was to establish a socialist market economy. At the Third Plenary Session of its 14th Central Committee, the CPC decided to develop market entities, a market system, a macro regulation system, and a framework of laws, which were referred to as the four pillars of the market economy. This ushered in a new phase of rapid and steady reform.

SOEs implemented a modern corporate system and thus became entities for market competition like collective, private, and overseas-funded enterprises. In addition, a unified, open, competitive, and orderly market system began to take shape. A macro regulation system integrating planning, taxation, and banking as complementary but mutually restraining policy tools was quickly formed and made a major contribution to regulating the actions of market entities and the government and maintaining market order.

After the basic framework of the market economy was formed, the CPC decided to improve the socialist market economy at the Third Plenary Session of its 17th Central Committee in 2008, setting new requirements for better balancing the government-market relationship. During China's response to the international financial crisis, close collaboration between the government and the corporate sector enabled the market economy to withstand the test posed by the crisis and the government to gain new knowledge in macro regulation.

Experience demonstrates that the key to success in China's reform has been keeping reform market-oriented. Market-oriented reform is the correct choice for China in this primary stage of socialism. To put it in nutshell, the defect of the old planned system is that this basic context of China was ignored, the socialist principle of material interest was violated, and the market economy, a stage of development humanity must go through, was skipped.

In a market economy, enterprises' interests are determined by their performance, and individuals' incomes are decided by their work. The market economy allows enterprises and workers to retain material interests, which makes them more enthusiastic for production. Also in the market economy, factors of production are allocated mainly by the market, which improves social benefits and economic performance. By making use of the law of value as an invisible hand in regulating the economy, China has significantly boosted the vitality of its economy and built up a strong source of momentum that will drive its economic development forward. In the space of just ten-odd years, China has put an end to the economy of scarcity that was there for decades. In the meantime, the government has played a role as a visible hand by formulating rules and exercising macro regulation to ensure that the market forces function normally, and keep the regulation by the market from being rash and behind developments. This has gradually eliminated drastic periodic economic fluctuations. Experience shows that both the market and the government should be allowed to play a role, and combining their roles is an important principle for balancing the government-market relationship.

4.2 Expanding the Fundamental Role of the Market in Allocating Resources

The government-market relationship must be balanced in accordance with the requirements of the 18th CPC National Congress. It is essential to expand the fundamental role of the market in allocating resources to the fullest possible extent and scope. The ongoing global financial crisis has cut external demand's contribution to China's economic growth. To halt the economic downturn, bring China's economy back to healthy development, and ensure that GDP and both urban and rural incomes double those of 2010 by 2020, and complete a moderately prosperous society in all respects, China must further release its potential for economic growth.

The market is the source of economic vitality. Through more than 30 years of reform, China has learned that the fastest growing sectors are always those which are more oriented toward the market and allow factors of production to enter freely; while sectors that experience slow growth are always those which are relatively closed to external participation and restrict the entry of factors of production.

At present, a large surplus of factors of production is found in many sectors, but acute shortages in others owing to restrictions on the entry of factors of production into those sectors. As a result, the demand for factors of production in these sectors is unable to be met. Therefore, only by expanding the fundamental role of the market in allocating resources will China be able to create better conditions for the free flow of factors of production and further release its potential for economic growth, thus providing support for achieving the goals set at the 18th CPC National Congress.

To expand the regulatory role of the market, China should now take the following four actions.

1. *Deepening the reform of the financial system to unlock the potential of capital*

The market is important in allocating resources, primarily capital. Wherever capital goes, physical resources follow. China has a huge stock of financial capital. However, this capital has poor liquidity and a low rate of utilization, tending to converge toward SOEs, key projects, cities, and coastal areas whereas rural areas, small low-profit businesses, and central and western regions experience fund shortages. This has created and exacerbated unbalanced economic development in the country. Therefore, China needs to identify financial structural reform as the breakthrough point for the next step in its overall reform and see this as a means of increasing the ability of the market to allocate resources over a wider scope. At the National Financial Work Conference in early 2012, the orientation and priorities of financial structural reform were defined. These include relaxing access to the financial market, creating local regulatory authorities, establishing a deposit insurance system, and liberalizing interest rates, establishing a foreign exchange management system with the focus on foreign exchange usage and developing a multi-tiered capital market. These ideas are constructive and measures should be worked out as soon as possible to carry them out each step of the way. Among these ideas, allowing the development of private financial institutions should be made a priority and should be promoted on the basis of a review of the experience gained in the Wenzhou pilot project. The reform of the financial system will unleash potential for capital and further liberate productive forces.

2. *Reforming the urban and rural management system to unlock the potential of China's labor force*

This labor force still boasts huge potential for development. The reason why China is said be suffering from a labor shortage is that the enormous potential for the agricultural workforce has gone unnoticed. At present, there are still 280 million agricultural laborers working 1.8 billion mu of land, which is 6.4 mu per capita. Agricultural labor productivity is only 28% of that in secondary and tertiary industries, and the per capita net income of farmers is only 31% of that for urban residents. Small-scale land operation is the fundamental cause of low agricultural labor productivity and of the large gap between urban and rural incomes.

If we can accelerate the pace of agricultural modernization and realize the intensive use of land, the area farmed by each rural laborer in China will have the potential to be increased by several 10-fold, and maybe even by 100-fold.

Over the next 20 years, another 200 million rural workers will be liberated from their land and move into secondary and tertiary sectors. Some of them, together with their families, will move to the cities. The transfer of agricultural workers to non-farming sectors will give us significant leverage for promoting industrialization, urbanization, and agricultural modernization, becoming the fundamental means by which we will narrow the gap between urban and rural incomes.

Such efforts hold the key to whether China can succeed in raising its GDP per capita from US$5400 to US$12,000 over the next 12 years, thereby avoiding the middle income trap and establishing itself as a high-income country.

Therefore, China must set up a new system for rural-urban integration, encourage paid transfers of land-use rights, and develop family farms, agricultural cooperative, agribusiness, and other new agricultural investment entities. China should also attract private investment to agricultural modernization and cultivate new types of farmers. Permanent certificates should be issued to farmers for their contracted land-use rights. China should accelerate the establishment of a system for transferring social security accounts to make the free movement of labor possible.

3. *Reforming the management system for science and technology to unlock our potential for technological innovation*

To implement the innovation-driven development strategy, China must improve its allocation of scientific and technological resources and enhance its capacity for innovation. China has increased its spending on scientific research by significant margins over recent years. This has resulted in a constant succession of new advances in science and technology, with China now filing more domestic patent applications than any other country in the world. The ratio of China's international patent applications to that of the United States was 1:6 in 2010, and became 1:3.6 in 2011. It is very likely that China will catch up with or even surpass the United States in this regard by the end of the 12th Five-Year Plan. Private enterprises have become a major force for innovation, accounting for 67% of the country's patent applications.

However, there are still two major sectors whose potential for innovation desperately needs to be tapped: One is SOEs, and the other is universities.

SOEs boast a large amount of talent and other scientific and technological resources. The State-owned Assets Supervision and Administration Commission has formulated regulations on encourage SOEs to lead in innovation. The Commission also decided to count technological achievements as intangible assets in assessing companies' ability to preserve and increase the value of state-owned assets. This should encourage enterprises to increase investment in research and development. I believe this decision will be implemented and make enterprises more enthusiastic for innovation.

With regard to universities, at present, no Chinese university has become one of the top 50 in terms of the number of patent applications. Universities should become the centers for creating technology patents and exert more influence over industrial development. Universities should select innovative teachers to train innovative talents.

China should seize take advantage of the global economic crisis to increase international mergers and acquisitions and attract scientists and engineers. Relevant experience shows that using the scientific and technological resources from the international market is an important way for promoting innovation. To develop its strategic emerging industries, China must have its own technology. Many areas list the seven strategic emerging industries as development priorities and suffer from inefficient and redundant construction.

Placing the focus on key generic technologies, government departments should organize collaborative innovation between enterprises through the formation of industrial alliances. All government policies that encourage innovation should be implemented. The government should increase fiscal incentives to encourage enterprises to invest more in scientific research, thereby creating a social atmosphere in which technological innovation is encouraged.

4. *Reforming mechanisms for the pricing of resource products to promote resource conservation and environmental protection*

Prices of mineral, land and water resources should reflect the scarcity of the resources and environmental costs. The low prices of certain resources at present have encouraged the irrational and even wasteful use of resources. By making use of pricing mechanisms, China needs to promote keener public awareness with regard to resource conservation and environmental protection, and make efforts to achieve higher efficiency in the utilization of resources, so that ecological progress can be secured.

Given its large population and its shortage of arable land, China must establish a stringent system for the protection of farmland in order to secure the supply of food and meet the need of land for industrialization and urbanization. We must also depend on market forces to ensure that land for urban and rural construction projects can be developed more intensively.

Northern China faces serious water shortages. But despite this, the amount of water that goes to waste in these areas is still considerable. Therefore, while implementing the South-to-North Water Diversion Project, spending on water-saving projects should be increased, and mechanisms for the pricing of water resources need to be reformed in order to promote water conservation. Projects for the recovery of mineral resources from waste, which have been launched in some cities, represent an important means of turning waste into a valuable resource. Such projects should be expanded to more cities.

4.3 Deepening the Reform of the Administrative System and Building a Service-Oriented Government with Carefully Defined Functions

The key to balancing the government-market relationship lies in the government. According to the political report to the 18th National Congress of the CPC, China should deepen reforms aimed at separating government administration from the management of enterprises, state assets, public institutions, and social organizations and building a well-structured, clean, efficient and service-oriented government that has scientifically defined functions and that the people are satisfied with, as is required by our goal of establishing a socialist administrative system with Chinese characteristics. At present, China should focus on deepening reform in the following areas:

1. *Making improvements to the macro regulatory system and institutionalizing regulatory goals and policy measures*

A macro-economic regulatory system whereby planning, taxation, and finance supplement and condition each other should be established in order to improve the economic structure and maintain economic stability. China should improve its framework of plans, which includes mid- and long-term plans, annual plans, and dedicated plans, and strive to formulate plans that are better conceived, more feasible, and more tailored to future needs. Doing so will ensure that the plans China makes are able to serve as a basis for its macro regulation.

In addition, the reform of the fiscal and taxation systems should be accelerated. China should establish a sound public finance system under which the financial resources of the central government and local governments accord to their respective responsibilities, access to basic public services is made available to more people, and the building of development priority zones is promoted. China should form a taxation system that is conducive to improving the economic structure and promoting social equity.

In addition, the reform of the financial system needs to be deepened. China should establish a modern financial system in which the money market, the capital market, and the insurance market develop in a coordinated fashion. Under this system, China should strive to maintain a basic equilibrium in total supply and demand, promote macroeconomic stability, and support the development of the real economy.

It is commonplace China does not have the necessary means to achieve its macro regulatory goals. For example, the central government has long decided to increase consumer spending and the proportion of tertiary industry in the economy. But little progress has been made, and in some cases the situation is even worse than before. The fundamental cause of this is the lack of effective regulatory means. To address this situation, it has been decided at the 18th CPC National Congress to strengthen institutional procedures for setting macro regulation targets and employing policy tools.

2. *Streamlining administrative reviews and reduce government intervention in the management and operation of enterprises*

Many enterprises complain that new projects are subject to too many administrative reviews and are required to go through superfluous formalities. There are also complaints that some industries are not accessible owing to stringent entry criteria and "invisible walls," and that problems that the market can address are still being habitually addressed via administrative means.

To address these concerns, China should streamline administrative reviews, and leave matters that can be regulated by the market and decided by enterprises to the market and enterprises.

3. *Regulating market practices and creating an environment in which all types of enterprise can compete fairly*

The market economy is the rule of law economy encouraging fair competition for all enterprises, and consumer interests must be protected. People dislike unfair competition, especially the sale of fake and inferior commodities that harm consumers' interests. Bearing in mind that the government is there to serve the people, the related government departments should crack down on illegal behavior so that people can shop with peace of mind. China should formulate strict and scientific standards for product quality, intensify market oversight, leverage the role of the public in monitoring the quality of commodities, and raise public awareness with regard to the importance of honesty and trustworthiness. Enterprises under all forms of ownership should be given equal treatment with regard to taxation, financing, land use, and market access, and should enjoy equal access to factors of production. In so doing, China will ensure that advanced enterprises develop to their full potential while backward ones are eliminated.

4.4 Principles for Balancing the Government-Market Relationship

All countries face the problem of how best to balance the government-market relationship. Different economists have different approaches and answers to this issue. Having built up a wealth of experience during more than 30 years of reform and development, China has formulated several tried and tested principles with regard to addressing this problem, and these have become an important the policy for the socialist market economy.

1. *In balancing the government-market relationship, due consideration should be given to the extent to which productive forces are developed*

At different stages of development in different countries, productive forces have different levels of development and the market demonstrates different levels of maturity. For this reason, in setting out to handle the government-market relationship, China must take actual market conditions into consideration and display flexibility in adopting measures that can effectively develop productive forces, as opposed to following any one theory or model. Proceeding from reality, keeping pace with the times, and being realistic and pragmatic—these are the important principles that China must follow in balancing the government-market relationship.

2. *Significant efforts should be devoted to fostering market entities, a market system, industrial associations, and social organizations, so as to put society in a better position to develop and regulate itself*

The government cannot stretch itself too far. The more dynamic enterprises China has, the more wealth it will be able to create. A sound market system will allow China to bring potential of factors of production into play and allocate them based on the needs of the market. A good range of social organizations will be able to exert a role that the government cannot in rating, arbitrating, maintaining order in the market, and coordinating the interests of all related parties. China lags far behind developed countries in this regard, and so more must be done to encourage the development of social organizations.

3. *Provided that a unified national market is maintained, local governments should be given appropriate administrative powers*

The free flow of commodities and factors of production in a unified nationwide market constitutes a prerequisite for sustainable economic development. Therefore, China should do more to remove barriers in regional markets, and encourage different regions to draw on each other's strengths and develop side by side. Meanwhile, powers need to be appropriately split between the central government and provincial, prefectural, and county governments, so as to address the overconcentration of financial resources at the central level, which has led to the overuse of transfer payments and fund shortages in local governments, particularly at the county level. A local tax system also needs to be established. County finances should be placed directly under the management of provincial governments in areas where conditions permit. Local governments should be given greater powers in economic management.

China should develop a global strategic vision, and seek the optimal allocation of global resources in developing an open economy. It should improve its import and export mix and make better use of international markets and resources. China should use its wealth of foreign exchange reserve to expand overseas investments and secure more right to explore and develop energy and resources overseas so as to remove the bottleneck for its economic development in the future. China should obtain intellectual property rights and international marketing networks through international mergers and acquisitions so as to improve its enterprises' abilities to make scientific and technological innovations and operate internationally. China should create export demand and maintain stable growth of exports through developing overseas processing trade, and drive the export of labor services, construction materials, and construction machinery by contracting overseas projects. Expanding overseas investment also helps to defuse the risk of dollar depreciation. Therefore, it is necessary to cultivate multinational corporations and encourage qualified enterprises to operate internationally.

Chapter 5
Building Consensus on Reform by Changing the Growth Model

My topic today is *Building consensus on reform by changing the growth model*. This is a controversial issue at the moment.

In the current economic situation, the focus of this year's macro regulation is to maintain the trend of economic recovery from the fourth quarter of last year. Prior to that quarter, economic growth had been slowing for seven straight quarters and fell below 7.5% in the third quarter of last year. Last July, the Political Bureau of the CPC Central Committee held meetings to analyze the economic situation in the first half of the year. Responding to the severe downturn of the economy, the Political Bureau decided to make steady economic growth a priority in macro regulation. A number of measures were taken in the second half of the year, including the modest easing of the money supply and the restarting of some projects, including high-speed rail projects, which had been suspended a year ago. The National Development and Reform Commission has approved a batch of subway construction projects in a dozen cities worth about 800 billion yuan. As a result, the economy showed signs of recovery in the second half of last year, and the turning point finally appeared in the fourth quarter. Seven consecutive quarters of downturn finally came to an end.

The biggest challenge for macro regulation this year is to maintain this recovery. We may face many challenges this year, and there will be inflationary pressure. The latest figures show that the CPI rose by 3.2% in February, causing concern that an increase of CPI will tighten money supply. Which one should we choose—curbing inflation or stabilizing growth? I think steady growth should come first, for it is the main problem we are facing this year. This year, we may face a dilemma regarding macro regulation. We need to strike a balance between expanding demand and avoiding inflation. While we should encourage investment, we should also avoid the old path of high investment, high consumption, and high pollution. On the one hand we should expand domestic demand, while we continue to encourage exports on the

---

This article originally appeared in *Globalization*, no. 3, 2013.

X. Zheng, *China's 40 Years of Economic Reform and Development*,
https://doi.org/10.1007/978-981-13-2727-8_5

other. The right direction for our policies relies on changing the growth model to solve the economic growth problems we have been facing recently.

At its 18th National Congress the CPC set a long-term objective of doubling China's 2010 GDP and per capita income for both urban and rural residents by 2020. Last year, the total GDP of China reached US$8.2 trillion, and the per capita GDP reached US$6086. If we set the 18th National Congress of the CPC in 2012 as the base period, then the GDP will have doubled by 2022 when the 20th National Congress of the CPC is held. By then, the incomes of urban and rural residents will have doubled and the per capita GDP will have doubled to reach more than US$12,000. What is the significance of this figure of US$12,000? The World Bank regards this as the watershed between middle income and high income countries. In another decade, China, with a population of 1.3 billion, will enter the ranks of high-income countries and will have a profound impact on the world economic landscape. It will be of huge significance in the history of human society.

With a large population and a per capita GDP of US$12,000, it is possible that the economic aggregate of China could catch up with or even surpass the United States. So for China, the next decade will be a challenging stage in its development effort. According to the World Bank's international experience and research, it is easy for a country to jump from US$3000 to US$5000, but it is very difficult to climb to US$12,000. The discovery of this economic phenomenon led to the concept of the "middle-income trap." While some challenge the idea of the middle-income trap, it does exist. In the 1950s and 1960s, dozens of countries had reached the per capita GDP of 4000 or 5000 dollars, but only a few of them were able to step into the ranks of the high-income countries, leaving the others stuck in the middle-income bracket. Brazil, for example, achieved per capita GDP of US$12,000 the year before last, and it was already in the ranks of high-income countries, but last year its currency devalued, so it fell back into the middle-income bracket. Countries and regions in East Asia, such as Japan and the "Four Dragons" have succeeded in emerging from the middle-income trap and have become high-income countries. In this case, the next decade will be the decade in which we fight our way through the middle income range and step into the ranks of the high-income countries. The new leadership team elected by the 18th CPC National Congress is the team that will lead the people of China into the high income bracket.

In the next decade, we are likely to encounter stresses and problems that are completely different from those of the last three decades. We must use new ideas and new methods to solve them. I worked in the National Planning Commission for more than a decade, and my experience is that we must not try to solve new problems with old thinking and old methods. China's economy is growing too fast, and the system is changing rapidly. Anyone who says that they have the experience to solve new problems using old methods will surely achieve the opposite of their aim. The new problems we encounter must be solved through reform and through changing the growth model. In addition, after more than three decades of development, we have accumulated many stresses and problems: Unfair distribution of income, lagging provision of utilities, and other problems that disrupt social stability. We did not encounter these problems in the past; we will face many challenges in achieving sustainable and sound development, realizing the development goals set out by the 18th CPC National Congress, and joining the ranks of high-income countries within a decade.

If we take favorable conditions into account, we will find that it is entirely possible for China to achieve steady yet rapid growth in the next decade or two. There now seems to be a public view that rapid growth has ended and China has entered a stage of medium-paced growth, and that a slowdown in economic growth is inevitable. This view has considerable support. I strongly disagree with this opinion, and I wrote many articles to argue my case last year. I heard similar viewpoints in the 1980s and 1990s, and I contested those views and challenged those who held them. In the 1980s and 1990s it was said that the most reasonable growth rate for China was 7%. At the time of the 14th CPC National Congress, President Jiang Zemin addressed the Party School of the Central Committee of the CPC and suggested that we should strive for economic growth of around 9%. Many people disagreed with this at the time, but as a result we embraced a golden decade of high-growth, low-inflation, and high-efficiency as we entered the 21st century.

In the 21st century, our economy grew considerably, though many people said that it would be more difficult to maintain rapid growth. They were wrong; the pace of growth was even faster. And we achieved double-digit growth in the decade from 2000 to 2010. So according to my own experience of the last three decades of reform and opening up, most of our forecasts, including some economists' predictions, lagged behind the reality. People tend to underestimate the power of reform in China. For now, China's per capita GDP is US$6000, which is still less than the world average. There is a view that the benefits of low-cost labor, reform, and the impact of global industrial chains have faded, and therefore China's development has slowed. This opinion was encouraged in particular by the 1.4 million km^2 of territory that was afflicted by smog around Spring Festival this year. Some people suggest that we cannot succeed in tackling smog unless we first slow down China's development. I do not agree with this.

Achieving steady yet rapid growth in the next one or two decades can be achieved through changing the growth model. The experiences of Japan, South Korea and Taiwan show that rapid growth need not stop until per capita GDP reaches US$17,000. Since they have achieved this, China will also be able to achieve this goal. Japan, South Korea and Taiwan have succeeded in their own development. With Chinese socialism, the socialist market economy, and the leadership of the CPC, how can China prove the strength of its model of socialism if we cannot succeed like them? We are able to succeed, and we are confident in our ability. The key is to change the growth model, or to achieve the industrial upgrade and economic transformation that was proposed at the 17th National Congress of the CPC. However, five years have gone by, and change in some crucial areas has not turned out successful; some indices have even deteriorated. The primary task of changing the growth model lies in adjusting the contributions of investment and consumption, and expanding the role of consumption in driving economic growth.

However, it is clear that in the five years from the 17th CPC National Congress to the 18th CPC National Congress, the investment rate was higher, the consumption rate decreased, and the imbalance between investment and consumption got even worse. The investment rate rose to a record high of 49% in the first two years, and the final consumption rate fell to a record low of 48%. The final consumption rate included government consumption and consumer spending. Government consumption generally accounted for about 14% of the whole, while consumer spending fell to a record low of 34.9%. The data did not turn out for the better. On the contrary, it showed that the situation had become worse.

Why were there few substantial changes during the five years following the 17th CPC National Congress decision to change the growth model? Now the calls for comprehensive reform have become enthusiastic, and there are many who want reform. But what should we do to bring about reform? What will be the focus of the reform? People hold different ideas. The 18th CPC National Congress reintroduced this issue, and emphasized pursuing balanced and sustainable development as the underlying guideline and accelerating the change of the growth model as a critical task. Now, the key to changing the growth model is to advance reform, although how to build consensus on reform has become a conspicuous issue. At its 18th National Congress the CPC decided to "build consensus." I think that we should build consensus by focusing on changing the growth model.

The reason why the reform of the first three decades succeeded, and why the Chinese economic miracle could be achieved, is that we focused on reforming the old system which hindered the development of productive forces. Deng Xiaoping said that we should cross the river by feeling the stones, and the only criterion to check whether reform was sound was to ask whether it was conducive to the development of productive forces and to removing any obstacles hindering the development of productive forces. In this way all the rules of the past were broken, and some taboos were broken, too. The breakthrough in reform resulted in a great liberation of productive forces and in the Chinese miracle. Over the three decades of development, many stresses and problems accumulated. In my opinion, to cope with these new problems, we should continue to focus on whether reform can release the productive forces, and remove systematic barriers that hinder reform. In other words, we should center on changing the growth model to push forward reform.

Here I will talk about ways to build consensus on reform from six perspectives.

5.1 Promote Income Distribution Reform that Centers on Changing the Driver of Economic Growth from Investments and Exports to Consumption

The rapid growth of the past three decades has been largely driven by high rates of investment and consumption, with investments growing at twice the rate of overall economic growth. Our GDP is the second largest in the world, but our material consumption tops the world. China's crude steel output exceeds 700 million tons, and our production capacity is 900 million tons, accounting for more than half of the world

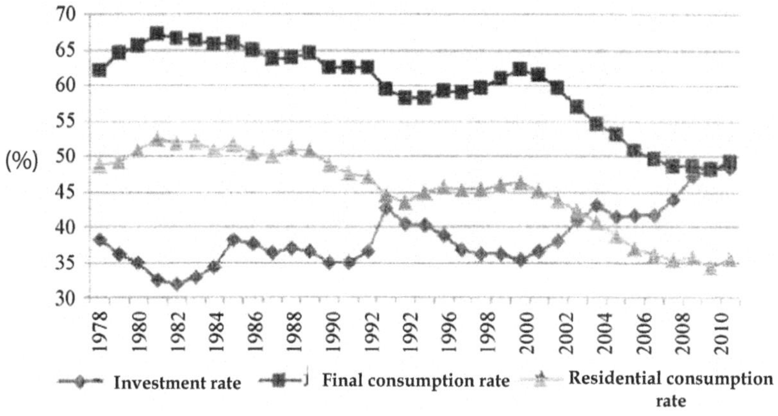

Fig. 5.1 Chinese residential consumption rate, final consumption rate and investment rate from 1978 to 2011. *Source* National Bureau of Statistics

total; we host half of the world's production capacity in cement, aluminum, flat glass, and household appliances. Our shipbuilding capacity exceeds the total global market demand. Our production capacity in home appliances, power generation equipment, and automobiles accounts for more than 30% of the world's capacity. Even some strategic emerging industries have huge production capacity. For example, wind power equipment production is more than twice that of domestic demand. Therefore, overcapacity is the most prominent problem in our current economic operations.

The global financial crisis struck the markets in developed countries and has weakened demand for Chinese goods, exacerbating the strain of domestic overcapacity. To solve this problem, we must encourage consumption and significantly adjust the economic contribution of investment and consumption (Fig. 5.1).

As seen from this table, the household consumption rate declined over the three-plus decades of China's reform and opening up. The household consumption rate hit 52% in the early 1980s and fell to 34%, down by 18% while investment rates gradually rose. In 2011, the investment rate was as high as 49.2%, and the consumption rate fell to 48.2%. It was the first time in history that the investment rate was 1% higher than the final consumption rate, a very rare phenomenon anywhere in the world.

The highest final consumption rate of the United States was 91.7%, and the highest consumption rate was 72%. The latter was over twice that of China (Fig. 5.2).

To address overcapacity, we need to identify the fundamental cause. For a long time in the past, we lived with a planned economy. The distinguishing feature of the planned economy was shortage of goods. To put it more specifically, insufficient supply could not keep up with growing demand. In comparison, the market economy is characterized with inadequate demand and excessive supply, which conforms to Marx's analysis of capitalism in his book *Capital*. In *Capital*, Marx concluded from the analysis of the dual character of products and the production of surplus value that the fundamental contradiction of capitalism is the contradiction between unlimited

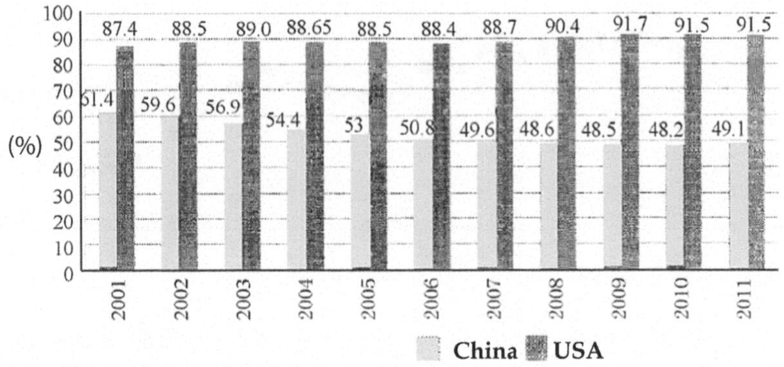

Fig. 5.2 The consumption rates of China and the United States from 2001 to 2011. *Source* National Bureau of Statistics

expansion of production capacity and the limit on demand of what consumers are able to pay. Since the right of distribution is in the hands of the capitalists, these capitalists will pay workers as little as possible. C symbols material consumption, M represents profit, V signifies wages. Lowering V and increasing M as much as possible can produce more profits. Profits can be reinvested to further increase profits by expanding the scale of production. But the ability of people to pay is limited by their income growth. This fundamental contradiction leads to the crisis of cyclical overproduction. The analysis of Marx is profound and worth pondering deeply. Western capitalist countries learned this lesson, and attempted to avoid an overcapacity crisis by establishing a welfare society, forecasting economic situations, and engaging in macro regulation, which significantly eased the contradiction of overcapacity. But now they have gone too far and are beginning to swallow the pain of these measures. Since the burden of social security is too heavy and beyond their financial capacity, it is now their turn to struggle. It is easy to give people more social welfare, but it is difficult to withdraw such welfare. People will take to the streets if the social welfare budget is reduced.

We currently lack a deep understanding of the fundamental causes of overcapacity. We say that the Theory of Balanced and Sustainable Development puts people first. Its very essence entails that development is for the people and the fruits of development should be shared by the people. But in real economic life, the growth of people's incomes and their ability to pay cannot keep up with the expansion of production, giving rise to serious overcapacity. Now that minor adjustments are no longer an option to solve the problem, it is imperative to make big changes. We need to figure out the root causes of our problems and ensure that the whole party understands them clearly. Only by achieving unity in ideology and understanding can we make big adjustments to investment and consumption.

At the beginning of reform, we summarized the experiences and lessons we had learned in the economic development of the previous three decades. All these experiences and lessons from our failures or setbacks can be summed up in one, and that is the anxious pursuit of quick results. We used high investment rates to push high economic growth, but we forgot that more haste results in less speed. During the Sixth Five-Year Plan period, we greatly reduced investment rates and increased consumption rates, so that people would gain real benefit from economic growth. But after this, the investment rate continued to climb from 25 to 30%, and surpassed 45% and finally reached the historical high of 49.2%.

The primary form of distribution nowadays lies in allowing businesses to determine the wages of their employees. Enterprises naturally would like to keep wages down and retain more profit, thus the growth of personal incomes is slower than the growth of GDP. The 18th National Congress of the CPC proposed the "two synchronous steps," which was designed to increase individual incomes in step with economic development as well as to increase work remuneration in step with improvements in labor productivity. Last year we successfully achieved income growth that was higher than GDP growth. We should, through major adjustments, strive to grow personal incomes faster, and enable more people—especially those on low to middle incomes—become wealthy enough to buy houses and cars, to travel and spend more on culture, and to give their children a better education. This is the primary task of changing the growth model, or rather, we must reform the income distribution system to transform the main economic driver from investment and exports to consumption.

Recently, three ministries of the State Council combined to issue *Several Guidelines to Adjust the Distribution of National Income*, in which the government put forward certain principles and guidelines to this end, and required all ministries and commissions of the State Council to set detailed rules and regulations. We hope these rules and regulations will come out as early as possible and make a major change in the distribution of income so that we can finally reverse the problem of high investment rates and low consumption rates, and realize the first transformation of the growth model.

5.2 Promoting Reform of the Tax System to Replace Business Taxes with VAT While Accelerating the Development of the Tertiary Industry

The lagging tertiary industry is a longstanding problem in our economy. In the 1990s, the State Council formulated guidelines and convened a national meeting to encourage the development of the tertiary industry. However, 20 years on, the tertiary industry is still lagging behind.

In 2011, the added value of the tertiary industry accounted for 43.1% of the GDP, and employed only 35.7% of the total work force. Both figures are too low. The world average of the proportion of tertiary industry employees is 62%, and for developing countries, the number is 50%. There is no excuse for China to be 14% lower than the average of developing countries. I have been to India. India's per capita GDP is less than half of ours, but both the output and the workforce of the

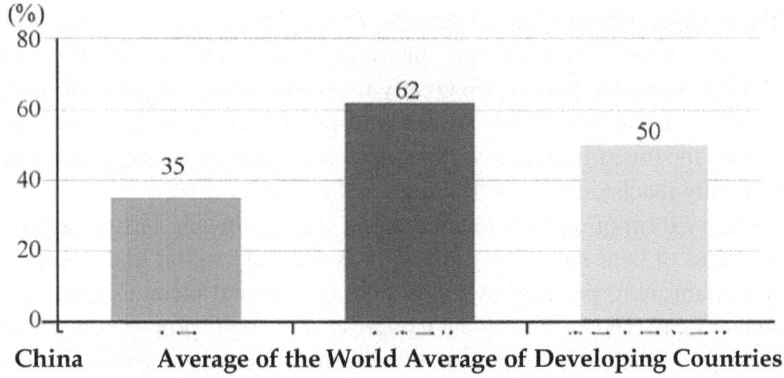

Fig. 5.3 2011 Employment proportions in the tertiary industry. *Source* National Bureau of Statistics

tertiary industry account for more than half of the three industries. India attaches great importance to the tertiary industry. You can see small shops everywhere in New Delhi, while big shopping malls are not so common. Considering the tertiary industry is more profitable, the Indian government leaves this sector to its people, and so a small shop can support an entire family. The fundamental reason for the long-term lag of China's tertiary industry lies in its inequitable tax system. The tertiary industry attracts business taxes, while the secondary industry applies value-added tax (VAT). In contrast, the sales tax burden averages about a third more than value-added tax. Traditional economic theory shares the blame for our backward tertiary industry. In the past, political and economics textbooks classified the manufacturing, agricultural, construction, transportation and postal service industries in the material production sector, and the national economic statistics only recorded statistics for these five sectors and recognized them as society's total economic output, while the tertiary industry was not considered value-creating. This traditional theory still has its repercussions even today. Local governments in some areas will first choose to develop industrial projects and will often neglect the tertiary industry. The price of water, land and electricity applied to tertiary industries is higher than secondary industries. Currently, some cities still apply different electricity pricing methods between businesses and secondary industries. In conclusion, the development of the tertiary industry is suppressed in all respects (Fig. 5.3).

The tertiary industry consists of a large number of small businesses, micro-enterprises and individual household enterprises. The taxation threshold for small low-profit enterprises was originally 5000 yuan of monthly turnover. Since the year before last, it has risen to 20,000 yuan. It seems that the change is significant, for the threshold is now four times what it was initially. But when we calculate and compare, we find that if we estimate the profit margin at 10%, then net income is only 2000 yuan if turnover is 20,000 yuan a month. The net income is still 1500 yuan lower than the threshold of individual income tax (3500 yuan). Heavy taxation drains the vitality of the tertiary industry and dampens its development. I suggest a further increase in the taxation threshold for businesses in the tertiary industry. Statistics show that if we

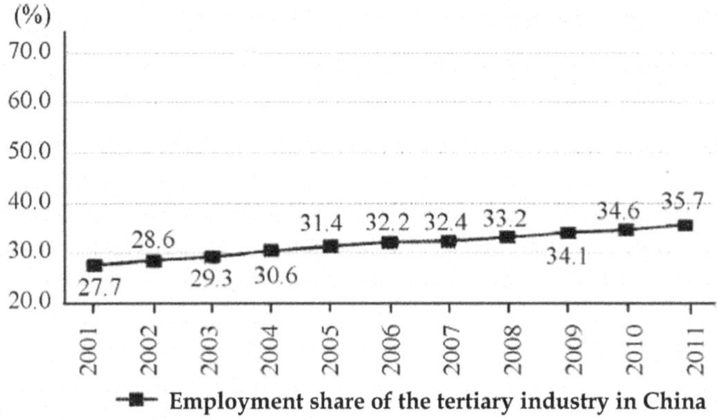

Fig. 5.4 Percentage of employees in China's tertiary industry (2001–2011). *Source* National Bureau of Statistics

raise the threshold from 5000 to 20,000 yuan, then more than 20 million small and micro businesses can benefit from this. As their tax burden is reduced by 40%, tax revenues fall by only 900 million. We should continue to promote such a good thing. I submitted a proposal to the CPPCC and suggested that we should raise the threshold from the perspective of cultivating financial resources, or as we say, releasing more water to raise the fish in the pond. That is to say, when enthusiasm for starting businesses is high, there will be more small and micro businesses. These businesses can grow into bigger enterprises in the future, thus tax revenues will also increase (Fig. 5.4).

In 2012 we piloted a tax reform that replaced business tax with value-added tax (VAT) for the tertiary industry in 11 cities, in sectors that are mainly production-oriented service industries such as transport, logistics and research and development. The effect of the reform was very successful, as the numbers of newly established businesses and small and medium-sized businesses significantly increased by more than 20%. I believe that there will be an explosive growth of businesses in the tertiary industry if this reform can be carried out throughout the entire country and other sectors of the tertiary industry as soon as possible. The reform of the tax system in the tertiary industry could help increase the proportion of workers in the tertiary industry from the present 35 to 50% and reach the average proportion of developing countries in 5 years. The increase of 15 percent points would create 100 million jobs. Currently, the risk for comprehensive reform is low as the conditions are all favorable. Tax revenues may not be as high as before, but they will definitely increase in parallel with the tax sources. The growth in employment will drive personal incomes, and consumption will correspondingly increase.

5.3 Reform the Technology and Education System While Centering on Industrial Upgrades

The report of the 17th National Congress of the CPC proposed that we should place this at the core of our national development strategy to improve the capacity of innovation and build an innovative country. During the five years from the 17th to the 18th National Congress, research funds for all levels of governments, enterprises, schools and research institutes increased substantially, and investment in R&D accounted for 1.97% of GDP. Sweden has the highest proportion of R&D investment in the world, reaching 4%, and Finland is second with 3.9%. For developed countries, it is generally above 3%. China is second only to the United States with regard to total investment in scientific research. After years of effort, scientific research began to bear fruit, and the number of patents applied in China increased dramatically. In 2012, the number of patent applications in China surpassed that of the United States, ranking first in the world. Of course, the quality of China's domestic patent applications is inferior, and the number of invention patents is low, and so is the utilization rate of the patents. Therefore, I deem applying for international patents to be of more significance. In 2010, we filed 8000 international patent applications while the United States filed 40,000. In 2011, the number of applications filed in the United States was basically the same as in 2010, but in China this number grew by more than 20%, making the ratio 3.6:1. If this trend continues, China could catch up with the United States by 2015 or 2016 in international patent applications. Although we still have a lot to do to catch up with the United States in certain high-tech areas, it is likely that our ability to innovate can catch up with or even surpass the United States in general industrial technology. Huawei applied for the most patents in the world in 2009, and ZTE took over as number one in 2011. The applications filed by these two companies made up a quarter of the total applications from China. If each province can cultivate several major patent-developing companies like ZTE and Huawei, then our capacity for innovation can surely catch up with the United States.

Currently, two areas with innovation potential are still waiting to be tapped. One is state-owned enterprises. Currently, private enterprises have become a vital source of innovation, and the number of patent applications amounts to 67% of the total applications in China. In comparison, the mechanism for innovation in state-owned enterprises is yet to be formed. The State-owned Assets Supervision and Administration Commission issued a guideline last year and set several rules on encourage state-owned enterprises to lead and become the driver of innovation. This guideline is commendable. Its biggest breakthrough is that it requires that the value of technological achievements created by state-owned enterprises be incorporated into the assessment of the corporation's ability to preserve and increase the value of state-owned assets.

Marx predicted that with the advance of technology, the organic composition of production materials will continue to improve, and its technical content will also increase gradually. In the past, when we assessed the ability of state-owned enterprises to preserve and increase state property values, we only took the value of tangible assets into account, and excluded intangible assets. No matter how many technological achievements were created, they were kept outside the brackets of assessment. It took eight years for Datang Telecom Technology & Industry Group to create a 3G standard of TD-SCDMA with an investment of over a billion yuan. But as technical achievements are not within the brackets of the assessment, and as the telecom group is a listed company, this resulted in a loss in the books. Finally Zhou Huan, president of the company and the person who led the initiative, stepped down.

Zhou Huan once said to me that Americans were willing to spend billions of dollars to buy his standards. If sold, his researchers would receive considerable bonuses, all the losses would be made up, and the books would show good performance because of the considerable profits. But he couldn't sell it, because it is China's sole standard of innovation in the high-tech field. It is obvious that something is wrong with the assessment standards. Now we have a new assessment standard that includes the value of technological achievements in the assessment of an SOE's ability to preserve and increase state property values. This is a breakthrough in the state-owned enterprise management system. We should establish a mechanism that encourages innovation of state-owned enterprises so as to encourage these enterprises to increase investment in research and development. I believe that the results from innovation of state-owned enterprises will mushroom in the near future. Only state-owned enterprises have the critical mass to innovate in some high technology fields and major technology industries, such as aerospace, aircraft, and high-speed rail. The power of state-owned enterprises would be great if all state-owned enterprises would commit themselves to innovation and let that become their main driving force.

The other area with innovation potential is our colleges and universities. The current situation of these institutions is less than satisfactory. I remember the statistics I saw the year before last. All the colleges and universities in the world are listed according to the number of patent applications and there is not a single Chinese university or college in the top 50, while 30 of the top 50 are American universities and colleges. We can see from this that Chinese colleges and universities still have much to do to catch up with American universities with regard to innovation capacity. An important assessment standard for American universities regarding the quality of their departments is their influence on the technological progress of relevant industries. This means the extent to which the department is capable of driving technological progress in the industry. Many Chinese universities lag far behind the companies from which they learn technology. Professors go to these companies, sum up the technical achievements and then return to write textbooks to teach students.

The Shenhua Group currently has the most advanced technology in China's coal mining industry. The annual output of one of their mines is more than 10 million tons of coal. One of the group's branch managers returned to his university to give lectures, and when he flipped through the textbook, he found that more than 30 concepts were already out of date in relation to the company's contemporary production practices. But professors at the school are still teaching students such outdated knowledge. How do schools cultivate creative talent? Colleges and universities boast enormous potential for innovation. There are so many professors, doctors, and postgraduates at the peak of their potential for innovation. Last year, American universities enrolled more than 200,000 Chinese high school students. Education in the United States has become its sixth biggest industry. A key source of their education funding is actually Chinese students. Reform of the education system is the key in making our colleges and universities excellent schools and keeping our students or even attracting American and European students to study in China. We need to have a mechanism for competition in our colleges and universities, as competition is the very thing they lack.

Currently, there is a good sign: It is estimated that colleges and universities will transform from 'sellers' to 'buyers' in 2015. By that time, colleges and universities will be able to choose the applicants they want to recruit, rather than having to recruit students. Some schools might shut down because they cannot enroll enough students. Taiwan is now in a similar situation. Good schools have a lot of candidates, which enables them to choose excellent students. Inferior schools that cannot attract students will eventually shut down or be downgraded into technical schools. When our universities and colleges become buyers in 2015 or 2016, they might have the opportunity to become competitive in China's education. Once such competition is in place, Chinese universities and colleges can truly become innovative schools and a base for scientific research and technical patents. With a competitive system, Chinese universities and colleges can have the same impact on technical innovation as American universities.

Therefore, we are in desperate need to further reform the technology system in state-owned enterprises and the education system in colleges, so as to stimulate their innovative potential. We should drive industrial upgrading with our own technology achievements that have intellectual property rights, and realize the transformation from resource and labor-intensive industries to technology-and knowledge-intensive industries through innovation.

5.4 Accelerate the System for Rural-Urban Integration While Narrowing the Rural-Urban Gap

In the next decade, we will have to cross the middle income range and join the ranks of high-income countries. One of the biggest problems we are facing now is how to raise the income level of the 700 million people who make up the rural population, and narrow the widening urban-rural income gap as soon as possible. Solving the problems of agriculture, rural areas and farmers is the key that determines whether China can become a high-income country. Currently, the urban-rural income ratio is 3.2:1. According to research, all countries and regions listed in the ranks of high-income countries generally meet three criteria. The first criterion is that the urbanization rate reaches about 70%. The second criterion is that agricultural productivity is close to or exceeds labor productivity in the secondary and tertiary industries. The third criterion is that the per capita income of farmers is close to or exceeds the income of urban residents. It is difficult for a country or a region to join the ranks of high-income countries without meeting these three criteria. Currently, agricultural productivity in China is only 28% of the secondary and tertiary industries, and the per capita income of farmers is just 31% of the income of urban residents. It is difficult to raise farmers' incomes without narrowing the huge gap in productivity. This entails agricultural modernization and agricultural intensification. Currently, many people say that China's labor benefits are gone, and that the labor shortage is the biggest obstacle to development in the next decade. The World Bank has a research report called China 2030, in which it points out four problems that will restrict China's economic development in the future. The first problem is the shortage of labor, which, in my opinion, does not actually exist. It is still too early to say that China has a labor shortage, and perhaps we should talk about this in 20 years. The World Bank fails to see the giant surplus of labor in agriculture. At present, there are 280 million in the agricultural workforce planting 1.8 billion mu of land, which means the average allotment for each farmer is only 6.4 mu. In contrast, a farmer can have thousands of acres of land in the United States and hundreds in Europe. While Chinese farmers are more diligent, the critical problem for China is the shortage of land.

Currently, China's agriculture has excellent prospects for modernization. The first opportunity is that the workforce has many possible urban locations, as many cities in the Yangtze River Delta and the Pearl River Delta find it difficult to recruit workers. I went to a meeting last year in Mumbai, India, and then went to Bangladesh to attend seminars given by some Chinese enterprises. At a symposium in Dhaka, there was a manager of a clothing company in Fujian, China. He arrived in Bangladesh and opened factories in the 1990s. The manager from Fujian said that the wage for an employee in Fujian is 2000 or 3000 yuan a month, while the wage in Bangladesh is only 700 yuan a month. There was no tariff for exporting clothing from Bangladesh to developed countries in Europe and to the United States, and there was no quota restricting the volume of exports. Moreover, Bangladesh's tax was only 18% and there was no other tax. So for businessmen, Bangladesh's tax burden is much lower than that of China's, and therefore you would find it so easy to make money by opening factories in Bangladesh. Now China's labor-intensive industries and companies in the processing industry are moving to Southeast Asia. A worker in Cambodia, Laos, India, Bangladesh and Vietnam only costs 500–800 yuan per month. If we cannot seize the opportunity to accelerate the transfer of the agricultural workforce we will lose it, as labor-intensive industries and companies in the processing industry move to Southeast Asia. I believe there will be nothing we can do to digest the surplus of agricultural workforce after that point.

The second opportunity is that plenty of private capital is available. Agricultural modernization requires a lot of money. It is impossible to just rely on government funds, as governmental investment can only play a guiding role. Nor can low-income farmers be expected to provide capital. Therefore, it is essential to introduce private funds. More than three decades of reform has proven that fields that are open to private capital will gain vitality. In contrast, fields that exclude private capital will dry out and wither. Agriculture is no different. Agricultural modernization will be a difficult task without the input of private funds.

The third opportunity is the ever-growing demand for high-quality and pollution-free agricultural products. As long as a product brand proves to be good, and the quality proves to be trustworthy, then urban people will be willing to pay more. It is a shame that we Chinese rush to buy milk powder in foreign countries and cause a global shortage of milk sources. Here is an example of how things should be. A manager from Wenzhou, China, who did business in Urumqi, Xinjiang, sold all his shops and went to Kashi to run a modern dairy farm in the Gobi Desert. His milk powder is now sold in areas as distant as the Yangtze River delta. His slogan is one single sentence: "All my milk powder comes from the milk of my own dairy farm, and not from other dairy farmers." This slogan has won the confidence of the Yangtze River delta, and although the price is high, people are still willing to buy his milk powder. It is impossible to guarantee the quality of products from the small-scale production of thousands of households, and only modern scale agriculture, including cooperatives, agricultural companies, and family farms, can build their own brands. Only by cherishing brands can we guarantee the quality of products. There are countless business opportunities in producing high-quality products and building brands.

The fourth opportunity is that our production capacity in agricultural machinery can meet the needs of agricultural modernization, and we can import any machinery that we cannot produce. We should seize this opportunity to promote agricultural modernization and accelerate the transfer of the agricultural workforce to non-agricultural industries. Farmer's rights to land should be confirmed by issuing land management right certificates to them. The certificates must be issued at the household level, and the usufructuary rights of farmer households should be guaranteed so that farmers can transfer their land rights and receive compensation for the transfer of the land.

When I went to Dongting Lake several months ago, I saw an example in Huarong county of Yueyang City which left me very excited. There is a village in Huarong County with more than 70 families and 800 mu of rice paddy fields. Now the 800 mu fields have been subcontracted by the party branch secretary, who has become a tenant farmer of the whole village. He bought a full set of agricultural machinery that could increase the yield per acre by 5% and he utilized the entire workforce of the village. The transfer fee for each mu of land is 700 yuan, and the workers who are willing to work on the fields are paid 130 yuan a day. If they were willing to work in the city, they could earn more than 70,000 yuan a year, including their land transfer income of 7000 or 8000 yuan.

What does 70,000 yuan mean? It means that the couple can be regarded as a middle-income household. According to the National Bureau of Statistics, the yearly income of a middle-income household is 60,000–200,000 yuan. For a household whose members work in cities and do not farm at home, the total income of the family can also reach the level of middle-income households. Such simple subcontracting needs policy encouragement, and would also entail reform. Before the Two Sessions this year, I read a headline article published by Xinhua News Agency. The news said that before the Spring Festival Xiaogang Village in Anhui Province had prepared several thousand mu of land for a tender after the Festival. Whoever offers the highest price can farm the land. Those who participated in the bidding, including those who parceled out their land to others by fingerprint confirmation, can make more money by letting others farm their own land than farming it on their own. I think this is a historic turning point that marks the moment when agricultural modernization starts to gain speed in China.

The establishment of a system for rural-urban integration can solve China's economic problem of labor demand within the next two decades The United States' agricultural workforce accounts for less than 1% of the entire county's workforce, but the agricultural products produced not only meet the needs of its own people, but are also exported to other countries. In the next 2 decades, we will move more than two hundred million people from agriculture, and the remaining 80 million farmers will be more than sufficient for the 1.8 billion mu of arable land.

Let me give you another example. There are actually two and a half pig-farming companies in the United States. The output of one company is more than 30 million pigs and that of the other company is over 20 million. A single company's output is that of several Chinese provinces. Therefore, the breeding industry can fully scale up and utilize mechanized production to ensure the quality of products. This example shows how we need to change our perceptions in order to solve problems and accelerate reform.

5.5 Further Reform the Financial System While Leveraging the Basic Role of the Market in Allocating Resources

The 18th National Congress of the CPC decided that we should leverage the basic role of the market in allocating resources to a greater extent and with a broader scope. At the National Financial Work Conference at the beginning of last year, Premier Wen Jiabao put forward six tasks for reforming the financial system. The first was to expand market access. The second was to establish local regulatory institutions. The third was to establish deposit insurance and a loan guarantee system. The fourth was to implement interest rate liberalization. The fifth was to reform the foreign exchange management system from focusing on foreign exchange settlement to foreign exchange usage. The sixth was to establish a multi-tiered capital market. These six reforms are very good, but they do not constitute a comprehensive reform plan. Because of the advantages of capital, the first breakthrough has been made in interest rate liberalization. In the absence proper competition and a regulatory system, there could be some dormant risks in opening interest rates before expanding access. Therefore, we are in urgent need of a comprehensive reform plan to advance reform.

5.6 Reform the Land Management System While Unleashing the Potential of Land

Currently, some say that land resources in China are severely constrained and that there is little land left for industrialization and urbanization. In fact, such people fail to see the great potential of the land. In addition to the barren slopes, barren hills, and beaches that can be used, the total land area used in urban and rural construction is only 230,000 km^2, of which village construction take up 170,000 km^2. Nowadays, many villages are "shell villages" (villages with few fit young men), as people have gone to other places to work. The doors of their houses are always locked, and as they are not authorized to sell them, they have no choice but to leave their houses vacant.

Through reforming the rural land system, owners of these houses could to transfer their houses and move to other places, which will increase their property income. Farmers could sell their home and buy a new one in the city. Homestead reclamation in rural areas could reclaim more than half of the land occupied by houses. Reforming the land system is an important measure to unleash the potential of land resources and to meet the demand for urban land. The central government also allows for requisition-compensation balance within provinces. The balance between requisition and compensation can be adjusted for different areas across the entire country. We also need to make the best use of overseas resources. For example, the Mekong river basin in Southeast Asia is ideally suited to agriculture. Rice in the basin can be harvested three times a year, but people there do not cultivate many paddy fields, and even if they do, the local market is not capable of absorbing such a large amount of rice. Southeast Asia can be a production base for China; we can connect China with this area by rail when we achieve connectivity in the future. We can also rent land in Africa and South America, so that we could produce soybeans there and therefore meet our import demands.

In conclusion, if we can fully tap into our consumption potential, our tertiary industry, our technology and education sectors, our workforce, our capital and our land, then the driving force we will gain from this could be big enough to support sustained and rapid development for the next two decades. Reform is the key.

Chapter 6
Suggestions on Building an Asian Infrastructure Investment and Financing Institution Led by China

The Political Report to the 18th National Congress of the CPC called for pushing forward connectivity between China and its neighboring countries. At the 2013 Annual Conference of the Boao Forum for Asia, President Xi Jinping stated that China would seek to increase connectivity with its neighbors and explore building a regional financing platform, in order to advance economic integration within the region and thus boost its competitiveness. This issue was the focus of a special study conference hosted by the China Center for International Economic Exchanges. To discuss the matter, it invited officials and experts from the Ministry of Foreign Affairs, the National Development and Reform Commission, the China Banking Regulatory Commission, the State Administration of Foreign Exchange, the National Council for Social Security Funds, China Development Bank and China Investment Corporation and other relevant departments. By the end of the conference, those in attendance had all come to hold a relatively consistent opinion. We believe that infrastructure

---

This article, authored by Zheng Xinli in July 2013, is a proposal to found the Asian Infrastructure Investment Bank (AIIB). Zeng Peiyan, chairman of the China Center for International Economic Exchanges, sent the proposal to President Xi Jinping and Premier Li Keqiang, which was highly endorsed by the two leaders. In October 2013, during a meeting with Indonesian President Susilo Bambang Yudhoyono in Jakarta, President Xi announced China's initiative to found the AIIB. The main purpose of the AIIB is to assist countries in the Asia-Pacific with infrastructure development and promote connectivity and economic integration in the region. On October 24, 2014, the finance ministers and representatives of the first group of the 21 Prospective Founding Members, including China, India and Singapore, signed an agreement in Beijing to found the AIIB. On June 29, 2015, representatives of the 57 Prospective Founding Members of the AIIB attended a ceremony to sign the Bank's Articles of Agreement in Beijing. With a total capital stock subscription of US$29.7804 billion and 26.06% of the voting shares, China is currently the AIIB member with the largest number of shares and votes. The establishment of the AIIB is a crucial step in the internationalization of the RMB. It will alter China's position in the world economy, and it represents both an important achievement in raising China's international standing and a practical step in reforming the global governance system. Some commentators have classed the AIIB's establishment as China's most intelligent move yet. Renowned economist Joseph Eugene Stiglitz also commented positively on the move, stating his belief that 2015 would be the first year of the Chinese financial era.

X. Zheng, *China's 40 Years of Economic Reform and Development*,
https://doi.org/10.1007/978-981-13-2727-8_6

and connectivity represent new growth areas for Asia's economy and constitute the very foundations of Asian economic integration. Promoting the establishment of a Chinese-led regional investment and financing institution and accelerating infrastructure cooperation amongst Asian countries will strengthen China's influence among its neighbors and enable China to play a proactive role in Asian economic integration and in the establishment of a China-centered regional economic system. In the current international and domestic context, it is necessary and feasible to establish such an institution. The conditions for doing so are now basically favorable, and this initiative should be actively promoted.

6.1 Establishing a Chinese-Led Asian Infrastructure Investment and Financing Institution Serves China's Strategic Interests

1. *Implementing a strategy of facilitating political development by promoting economic progress and cultivating and exercising China's soft power would help build a peaceful and stable neighboring environment and protect China's political and security interests.*

The United States tried to influence the economic and security landscape of the Asia Pacific by emphasizing smart power and proposing the "Return to Asia" and "Asia-Pacific Rebalancing" strategies. As disputes over Asian territories and maritime rights and interests have intensified, some countries have become ambivalent toward China as their doubt and wariness about China's intentions are intertwined with a reliance and dependence upon it. In the face of this situation, China should attach equal emphasis to soft and hard power. In terms of soft power, a strategy of facilitating political development by promoting economic progress is an effective tool, and one which should serve as both the focus and lever of China's neighborhood diplomacy. First, promoting mutually beneficial economic initiatives and taking the lead on Asian infrastructure connectivity would be conducive to strengthening the ties between China's and its neighbors' interests, to enhancing China's ability to manage and plan in neighboring areas and to easing current geopolitical tensions. Moreover, promoting the construction of Asian connectivity networks with China at the center would help open up its maritime and air passageways in important directions and put in place more secure and stable transportation lines for resources and energy. Furthermore, it would also consolidate the strategic support of neighboring countries and expand the space for implementing China's security strategy.

After World War II, the United States initiated the World Bank and the International Monetary Fund, while in the 1960s Japan pushed forward the establishment of the Asian Development Bank (ADB) and the Overseas Economic Cooperation Fund just as its economy was taking off. The establishment of these international and regional financial institutions significantly expanded the international and regional impact of the dollar and the yen, and allowed the United States and Japan to obtain a large amount of international resources in a more efficient way, thus helping them attain the international status they enjoy today. In the same way, setting up a regional investment and financing institution led by China can help convert China's economic strength into political and diplomatic influence and give it a greater presence worldwide. It is also of benefit to establishing an image of China as a responsible major country that supports its neighbors, thereby further enhancing its international influence.

2. *The demand for Asian infrastructure investment is strong, and there are currently great opportunities for boosting connectivity. Therefore, infrastructure and connectivity are important areas in which China can deepen economic cooperation with neighboring countries.*

Most Asian countries are in the primary stage of industrialization and urbanization, and inadequate infrastructure represents a bottleneck restricting their development. As a result of the international financial crisis of recent years, Asian countries have generally tended to regard investment in infrastructure as an opportunity and a driver for economic growth and structural adjustment. And most Asian countries have launched their own programs in this regard. For example, the government of Thailand has made plans focusing on the construction of ports, rail systems and highway networks so as to improve the infrastructure for logistics, which has been a weak link for the country. The Philippine government has targeted a 19% increase in infrastructure expenditures based on 2013 levels. ASEAN countries have also put forward a "Master Plan on ASEAN Connectivity." According to the Asian Development Bank, between 2010 and 2020, domestic infrastructure investment in various Asian countries will total about US$8 trillion, and another US$300 billion will be spent on regional infrastructure construction.

Countries such as Japan and South Korea have long been actively committed to the development of infrastructure and connectivity in Asia. Japan boosted its investment in Asian infrastructure through institutions such as the Asian Development Bank and Official Development Assistance (ODA). By doing so, Japan has tried to expand its global market, ease the pressure brought on by a persistently sluggish domestic economy, take the initiative in the development of Asian infrastructure connectivity and ultimately expand its regional influence. Asian infrastructure connectivity represents a huge market with strong demand for investment and great potential for cooperation. In this regard, China enjoys obvious geographical advantages as it is located at the center of Asia, which implies that, in general, Asian connectivity means connectivity with China. For this reason, China should take the lead and commit itself to playing a more expansive role in Asian infrastructure investment. It is believed that doing so would represent another important step for China in strengthening economic and trade cooperation with other Asian countries following the establishment of the China-ASEAN Free Trade Area (CAFTA). This will consequently give shape to the twin drivers of trade and investment which can facilitate more comprehensive and stronger economic relations between China and its neighbors.

3. *Encouraging industries to go global through financial cooperation will help leverage China's advantages in terms capital, absorb surplus domestic production capacity, and create greater potential for China's economic development.*

As the balance of China's foreign exchange reserves has grown over recent years, most of its assets have been used to buy treasury bonds from developed countries, such as the United States. However the yields from these bonds have been relatively low. Recently, China's foreign exchange reserves have been further eroded by widespread quantitative easing (QE) in western countries. If we could earmark some of these assets to establish regional investment and financing institutions and invest in infrastructure projects that ensure stable returns, we would put our foreign exchange reserves to better use and enhance the security of our money. At the same time, these institutions would facilitate RMB regionalization and internationalization, and strengthen China's status as a major country in the regional financial cooperation framework.

With China now going through a stage of structural adjustment, some industries have been plagued by overcapacity. According to statistics, China's steel production capacity was 1 billion tons in 2012, with more than 200 million tons of surplus capacity. The production capacity of cement was 3 billion tons, of which 800 million tons were surplus. Establishing a China-led investment and financing institution and expanding investment in Asian infrastructure construction will help promote the export of raw materials and foreign investment in related industries and provide a new way to digest and transfer domestic production overcapacity.

In recent years, Chinese enterprises have repeatedly encountered various national barriers that have hindered investment and mergers and acquisitions (M&A). In particular, there are more and more cases of countries rejecting investment cooperation with our enterprises on national security grounds. Promoting the participation of Chinese enterprises in connectivity construction projects, through a Chinese-led multilateral commercial financing platform, would help dispel the doubts of neighboring countries and the international community at large and avoid sensitive issues and differences in bilateral cooperation. In this way, we can create favorable conditions for domestic enterprises to go global.

6.2 It Is Possible and Feasible to Build a Chinese-Led Asian Infrastructure Investment and Financing Institution

First, China enjoys favorable conditions in terms of labor, financial and material resources. With growing economic strength, China's economic aggregate is now the second largest in the world. Its financial situation is healthy: Household saving rates are high and foreign exchange reserves have reached US$3.4 trillion. Thanks to its efforts in developing the domestic economy, China has also accumulated a great deal of experience and developed approaches in planning formulation, project construction and management. We have a number of senior management skilled personnel who are familiar with international affairs and who have worked with the World Bank, Asian Development Bank (ADB) and other international financial institutions and transnational companies. China has a number of outstanding enterprises in the fields of architecture, highway and railway construction, electric power, telecommunications and water conservancy whose engineering technology, construction teams and mechanized equipment are cost-effective. These enterprises boast international competitive advantages and are eager to go global.

Second, developing countries in Asia seek assistance from China because they themselves do not have adequate economic strength. Infrastructure construction demands large investment and a long-term commitment, and governments of developing Asian countries are limited particularly in terms of their financial resources. The World Bank and the Asian Development Bank are unable to provide much assistance because their focus is more on poverty alleviation. In addition, private capital is not so confident of getting a return on infrastructure investment. In short, many projects cannot get started because current regional financing channels fail to meet the demand for infrastructure investment. That means developing countries in Asia are looking to cooperate more closely with China. Last August, at the 44th ASEAN economic ministerial meetings in Cambodia, the ASEAN countries proposed to visit China in 2013 to promote connectivity in hopes of encouraging more Chinese enterprises to participate in infrastructure construction.

Third, as the United States and European countries are preoccupied with their own internal affairs, there are currently great opportunities for China. Asia—especially Southeast Asia, South Asia and West Asia—is an important source of energy and resources for European and American countries. Historically, countries in these areas have long been influenced, or even infiltrated, by the United States and European countries. Thus, these countries have relied heavily on the United States and European countries and received a significant amount of investment for infrastructure from them. But now, in the face of debt predicaments and a relative decline in financial resources, governments, financial institutions and businesses in these countries are tightening their finances. The United States and European countries don't have any excess zeal for investing in other countries because domestically they are faced with an extensive amount of renovation work which is as yet unfinished. Moreover, in infrastructure, because construction costs for western enterprises are high, they lack competitiveness, thus giving rise to a valuable opportunity for China to engage in the field of Asian infrastructure connectivity development.

Fourth, our proposed institution is compatible with the Asian Development Bank and other relevant institutions, as the priorities of the ADB are utilities, poverty alleviation and development, though its available funds are relatively limited. Our proposed institution would primarily invest in infrastructure and fund construction. This institution can serve to supplement the shortcomings of the ADB, given that the ADB's priorities are very narrow in terms of regional investment and it has limited funds. In addition, compared with the BRICS states' New Development Bank and the Shanghai Cooperation Organization Development Bank, this institution differs greatly in terms of the regions it covers, its geographical relationships and its economic connectivity. These financial institutions are complementary and cooperative, and do not constitute competition or overlap.

There are, of course, some disadvantages to setting up such a financial institution. In recent years, the United States and Japan have been defensive about China's activities in neighboring areas; this could potentially become a check on China regarding investment and financing in Asian infrastructure development. Disputes over territorial and maritime rights and interests in the region have also been intensifying of late, which may affect neighboring countries' acceptance of a China-led institution. Various risk factors, such as political situations, economic cycles, legal systems, and government policies and interests, may also create challenges for the international operation of such an institution.

This year's Annual Conference for the Boao Forum for Asia put forward the Asia Infrastructure Cooperation Initiative and proposed to expand interaction and cooperation in infrastructure planning between countries in the region and to establish special multilateral financial institutions or funds. On this issue, various parties responded positively and reached consensus in certain aspects. Goh Chok Tong, the Minister Mentor of Singapore and member of the Board of Directors of the BFA, and Sachin Pilot, the Minister of Corporate Affairs of India, along with others, remarked that Asia had a practical need for such an institution and that they were willing to promote its establishment. Stephen Groff, Vice-President of the ADB, also agreed that this initiative was essential, as it could provide funds for the construction of infrastructure, which is a weak link in Asia. Overall, the establishment of a new Asian infrastructure investment and financing institution is in line with the will and interests of most Asian countries. It is also in line with the long-term strategic intentions of China and the overall arrangements of the country's foreign policies. It is time for China to seize this opportunity and answer the call of the times, for it has both the need and the ability to set up such an institution.

6.3 Considerations for the Establishment of a Chinese-Led Asian Infrastructure Investment and Financing Institution

Establishing an Asian infrastructure investment and financing institution is a major step for our foreign affairs work and has far-reaching implications. But it is also a sensitive issue. In the process of implementation, not only should we cater to the strategic considerations of China and pursue substantive progress in this regard, but we should also operate in line with international practices so that the international community and relevant countries accept and approve of our plans.

First, we should operate in an open and transparent manner and adapt to international approaches. The institution should, on the condition that China's dominant position is ensured, be open and allow various governments, international institutions, as well as social and private capital to participate and invest, including countries and regions such as the United States, Europe and Japan. Promoting it as an international institution, we should draw on the experience of the World Bank and the Asian Development Bank to bring it in line with international market rules, adopt international practices and accept the supervision of the international community.

Second, the institution should be run commercially and take public welfare into consideration. The institution should be of a commercial nature, so returns and interests are taken into account in its investments. This is both a requirement to attract investment and a good way of avoiding the institution being co-opted for political ends. Its commercial nature will also differentiate it from the ADB and the World Bank. In reality, infrastructure projects have considerable medium to long-term returns, in which case the yields produced by such a commercial operation would be at least higher than those on US national debt. At the same time, it is necessary for the institution to take into account public-interest projects that are important to destinations where investment is going.

Third, we should cooperate with ASEAN countries and work to win over the United States and Japan. China and its neighboring countries, including ASEAN countries, need each other most in the area of interconnectivity. These countries are also the political foundation for China's foreign diplomacy. Therefore, establishing this institution first requires enthusiastic support and participation from these countries. At the same time, we should try to get along with the United States and Japan by building mutual trust and removing doubts between the two sides. We need to win their understanding and support so that we can create a positive environment in which Asia can develop together; or at the very least, we should avoid their rejecting or disrupting this initiative.

Fourth, we should not hesitate to play a leading role and to shoulder the concomitant responsibilities. The institution must be initiated by China so that it can play a leading role. In terms of capital composition, China should resolve to invest enough to surpass Japan and become the largest shareholder. China should be proactive in initiating the institution, drafting regulations and recruiting staff. It should also actively increase the presence of the RMB in the institution's capital and future financing operations. Given the economic strength and influence of China, member parties should accept these conditions as long as we advocate and stand firm on our propositions.

6.4 Suggestions for Establishing a Chinese-Led Asian Infrastructure Investment and Financing Institution

1. *Positioning and name*

This institution is to be positioned as a commercial and financial bank. Its primary function is to provide medium and long-term financing services for Asian infrastructure construction in the fields of transportation, telecommunication, energy, municipal services and water conservancy, agriculture, and ecological and environmental protection. Name suggestions include the Asian Infrastructure Cooperation Bank, Asian Industrial Bank, Asian Construction Bank, or Asian Bank of Communication.

2. *Location of headquarters*

Considering the international nature of the institution, we can establish headquarters in any countries with sound political and economic environments that have good relations with China, such as Thailand, Malaysia or Indonesia. Hong Kong is also an option. Establishing headquarters in Hong Kong is conducive to strengthening the region's status as an international financial center and to promoting its long-term prosperity and stability.

3. *Selection of senior executives and managers*

To ensure China's effective control and influence over the development and operations of the institution, we should appoint our senior financial experts as heads of the institution. There should also be considerable Chinese representation within the core and on the front lines of the institution. Likewise, to demonstrate the international nature of the institution, we should hire the best international talents possible.

4. *The scale and source of the capital*

The institution should adopt a shareholding system. The capital base should be approximately US$100 billion, and should be put in place gradually as operations develop. The capital adequacy ratio should be slightly higher than that of commercial banks. Considering that infrastructure projects generally last a long time and some are in the public interest, institutional lending rates should be slightly lower than market rates. Similar to what Japan did when it initiated the ADB, China should take up a 49% shareholding in the institution to ensure its dominant position. This shareholding would also guarantee that China can still play a decisive role when shares are diluted in the future. China's main capital contributor could be a Chinese bank. The government could set aside a portion of financial aid as an interest subsidy for the contributor, and at the same time encourage other domestic institutions and enterprises to contribute their capital.

5. *Roadmap for promoting the institution*

Domestically, it is recommended that a leading official of the State Council or of the Office of Central Leading Group for Financial and Economic Affairs lead the establishment of steering and working groups. These groups are to be responsible for preparatory work for establishing the institution, including demonstrating the program, formulating implementation plans and relevant policies, etc. On the International front, domestic and Asian bilateral and multilateral non-governmental groups should play a role in introducing and promoting the institution. These groups should use communications and discussions to see that foreign countries reach a relative consensus. China's leaders should promote the institution officially and properly when the time is right. Official promotion could be carried out on important occasions at which Chinese leaders are present, such as relevant Asian conferences.

Chapter 7
The Roadmap for the Reform of the Financial System

The Political Report to the 18th National Congress of the Communist Party of China decides that we should leverage, to a greater extent and in a wider scope, the basic role of the market in allocating resources. Capital leads and guides factors of production. The allocation of resources by the market mainly refers to the allocation of capital, and other factors of production would follow and gather where financial institutions allocate capital. At present, the scale of China's capital stock is huge. By the end of March, the balance of the broad money supply had reached 103.6 trillion yuan, and the financial assets of China's banks had exceeded 160 trillion yuan. Nonetheless, because financial system reform has lagged behind and poor capital liquidity, enterprises and investment projects that desperately need funds are unable to obtain financial support and have to seek high-interest loans. A lot of idle private capital can be invested where there is demand for it. The fact that the interest rate of private lending is three times higher than that of bank loans is strong evidence. Accelerating the reform of the financial system has already become the starting point for breakthrough in deepening the reform of economic system. On May 6, 2013, Premier Li Keqiang chaired an executive meeting of the State Council, at which the State Council discussed and prioritized the tasks of deepening economic reform in 2013, offered to formulate reform measures for interest rate liberalization and the exchange rate, and put forward an implementation plan for capital account convertibility of the renminbi. Our goal should be to standardize various forms of investment and financing, such as bonds, equities, and trusts.

Our goal should be to actively yet prudently proceed with the reform of the financial system, and we must develop a comprehensive and thorough implementation plan with a clear roadmap. At the beginning of last year, in his speech at the National Financial Work Conference, Premier Wen Jiabao, noted the direction of reform and put forward major tasks for reform. Nonetheless, because of the lack of detailed

This article originally appeared in the *Journal of the China Executive Leadership Academy, Jinggangshan*, no. 4, 2013.

X. Zheng, *China's 40 Years of Economic Reform and Development*,
https://doi.org/10.1007/978-981-13-2727-8_7

implementation rules, it was interest rate liberalization that became the first breakthrough of reform. High interest rates triggered a sharp increase of various non-bank loans. In the first quarter of this year, private financing reached 6.16 trillion yuan, an increase of 36.9% on a year-on-year basis, but the proportion of renminbi loans fell to 44.8%. In the absence of effective regulation and market risk prevention, the rapid expansion of non-bank loans as a business financing option could breed certain financial risks. As a result, studying and designing a roadmap of financial reform has become an urgent task of the current reforms to the financial system.

7.1 Make Expanding Access to Finance the Priority of Financial System Reform

At the Fourth National Financial Work Conference held at the beginning of last year, Premier Wen Jiabao, put forward six reform tasks in his speech, which put expanding access to finance at the first place. This was addressed to problems existing in the financial system. In the current banking structure, there is a glut of state-owned banks but a scarcity of small and medium-sized regional banks. In particular, financial institutions providing services for small and micro enterprises and farmer households are severely inadequate. There are historical reasons for this, but the structural defects lead to insufficient competition, which is the main reason why the financing cost of private enterprises is too high while small and low-profit enterprises and farmer households cannot get enough loans. The United States, which has built a highly developed financial market, has only 7000 more banks nationwide, but most of them are small and medium-sized regional banks. China's 2000 or so banks are far from sufficient to meet the funding demands for regional economic growth and small and micro economic entities. Although commercial banks have increased their proportion of loans for small and micro businesses in recent years, it was out of moral consideration rather than consideration of interests. It is impossible to rely on the existing big banks to meet the demand for loans from small and micro economic entities.

The later 36 provisions of *Guidelines on Encouraging and Guiding Healthy Development of Private Investment* issued by the State Council explicitly allow private capital to set up small financial institutions, including village banks, finance companies, financial cooperatives, and other institutions. Nonetheless, the detailed implementation rules formulated by relevant departments still stipulate that the condition to set up small financial institutions is that 15% of their shares must be held by a bank as the legal person and principal sponsor, which is clearly inconsistent with the above Opinions. Given that the state-owned commercial banks have control over the vast majority of China's financial market and a large amount of foreign capital has been allowed to enter the domestic financial market, why not allow private money to enter the financial market too? The authorities repeatedly set up barriers against the entry of private money into the financial market, mainly with the concern that private funds could bring about financial risk. In fact, it is the barring of private capital that could actually bring about real risk. Opening the door for private capital can help reduce risk and improve our financial security, which has been proven by the experience of reform. The entry of private funds into the financial sector can form a sufficiently competitive environment, which could eliminate monopoly profit and reduce the financing costs of enterprises, so that we can truly leverage, to a greater extent and in a wider scope, the basic role of the market in allocating resources. The equalization of capital profit can effectively protect against the inflow of hot money and reduce the impact on China's domestic financial market, and maintain the nation's financial security.

7.2 Establish Local Financial Regulators to Improve Accountability of Local Governments

Establishing local financial regulators as soon as possible is the second task of deepening financial system reforms. This is a new requirement for regulatory work in consideration of the situation after expanded access to finance. We will work to allow private funds to enter the financial sector. These funds are mainly for building financial institutions that provide services in local economies. These institutions would only be allowed to absorb deposits and offer loans within their respective region, while trans-regional operations would be prohibited. This is an important principle. We will work to set up local regulatory institutions that are guided by state-led businesses. These authorities will shoulder the responsibility of regulating local small financial institutions. If there is anything wrong with these institutions, the local government would be responsible for them. This will effectively prevent possible risks after expanding access to finance. In order to develop our local economies, local governments are sure to be very concerned about the operations of local financial institutions. Thus, local governments will conscientiously fulfill their regulatory responsibilities. Central regulatory authorities also save the trouble of regulating domestic markets beyond their reach. As central authorities do not regulate local financial institutions directly any more, their barriers against private capital into the financial sector are therefore easily removed. In the worst scenario, even if something did go wrong, any problem would be local in scale and would not cause a lot of trouble for the whole environment. As a result, the establishment of local financial regulatory institutions is an indispensable part of the comprehensive reform plan to expand access to finance.

7.3 Establish Deposit Insurance and Loan Guarantee Systems and Resolve Risk Through Market Mechanisms

China's banking system, which is based on state-owned banks, has gained high credit amongst the majority of people and enterprises by relying on state credit. In fact, the government also takes on huge risk for these banks. In the past, Chinese banks shed trillions of dollars of bad assets by enabling the government to pay for it. In fact, due to the devaluation of the currency, it was the entire country that bore the loss. The result was that some enterprises, which defaulted on their loans, essentially embezzled the wealth of people. It would be intolerable if this kind of occasional occurrence happened under the old system. Nonetheless, after the establishment of the socialist market economy, especially after the diversification of business entities, such embezzlement could never happen again. As a result, it is essential to establish the deposit insurance system and loan guarantee system through which we can use market-based mechanisms to prevent and defuse risk. The establishment of this new system has long been suggested in the circle of economic theories, but it has never been put into practice. Now, it is time to act. The establishment of the deposit insurance system and loan guarantee system and local regulatory institutions are both preconditions for expanding access to finance. The three reforms are indispensable and must be implemented in tandem.

During inflation, some developed countries implement the policy of inflation-protected fixed deposits in order to protect the basic benefits of people. France, for example, stipulates that every citizen can deposit 20,000 euros in a designated bank, and the actual deposit rate will not be less than 3%. When the difference between the inflation rate and the interest rate is lower than 3%, the French government subsidizes. This type of deposit is used as a special fund in central banks for the development of public services such as infrastructure. Central banks play an important role in maintaining social stability. During the period of inflation in the 1990s, China also adopted the policy of offering inflation-protected fixed deposits. In view of the phenomenon of negative interest rates on deposits in China in recent years, we should study foreign experiences and continue to improve the practice. The approximate amount of inflation-protected deposits for each person could be in the vicinity of 50,000 which can then be handed over to central banks and be used for the construction of infrastructure and for public services.

The loan guarantee system, like the mortgage loan system and credit loan system, is an important measure to prevent loan risk. Since the beginning of reforms, there have been attempts in some places for the loan guarantee system, from which we gained some experience. Our goal should be to further improve and promote the system. In regard to micro-credit loans, establishing the guarantee system is more necessary and adaptable. This is because these loan-borrowers generally lack necessary assets as collateral, as their businesses are too small to have a credit score. The establishment of the loan guarantee system is conducive to expanding credit coverage, being an entrepreneur and starting a small business, and driving development and improvements in rural and poverty-stricken areas.

7.4 Promoting Interest Rate Liberalization Is the Centerpiece of Deepening Reforms in the Financial System

Capital is an important factor of production and must be selected and allocated by market-forces to places where profits are the highest. Interest rate liberalization can optimize capital allocation. Projects and enterprises that can attract capital flows with higher interest rates are those with higher returns on investment and stronger competitiveness. In the pricing mechanism of factors of production, capital price liberalization lagged far away behind. As a result, the key to leveraging, to a greater extent and in a wider scope, the basic role of market in allocating resources is to accelerate interest rate liberalization in order to achieve the optimal allocation of capital.

Since 2012, inspired by the spirit of the National Financial Work Conference, we have made major breakthroughs in interest rate liberalization and the liquidity of capital has been significantly enhanced. On the whole, when looking at total social financing, the proportion of bank loans dropped sharply from about 70% in previous years to 45%. More than half of the capital was allocated through a variety of direct financing means at market prices, marking a significant step forward. Similarly, we should also see that while the market access was expanded, the reform of establishing local regulators and deposit insurance and loan guarantee systems has not yet been launched, so it is possible that interest rate liberalization may breed new financial risk. The risk comes from the fact that direct loan interest rates are usually above 15%, which is untenable for projects and enterprises in the real economy. Projects and businesses that dare to risk the high interest rates to borrow are now in the predicament of servicing their debts. We must remain alert and pay more attention to this problem. There is no turning back from interest rate liberalization. The only option is to accelerate the three reforms in expanding access to finance, establishing local regulating institutions, and setting up deposit insurance and loan guarantee systems in order to support the interest rate liberalization in a coordinated and comprehensive manner. It is urgent to draw up rules that include the four items mentioned above for reform of the financial system.

Just like the rule of price when price controls were lifted at the beginning of reform and opening up: At that time, the price of fish in southern China entered a cycle: when the price control was lifted, the price of fish increased, and when the price was higher, the fish market prospered. When the fish market was booming, the number of fish farmers grew, and when there were more fish farmers and thus more fish, the price of fish fell back down. The key to this phenomenon was allowing farmers to raise and sell as many fish as they wanted. When the price of fish was high, their enthusiasm to raise fish grew. When the production and sales of fish grew, the price fell back. Similarly, the current high interest rates are the result of long-term price control. Unless we expand access to finance, capital markets will not be a buyer's market, and high interest rates will persist for a long time. To say that the accumulation of financial bubbles heralds crisis is by no means an exaggeration. As a result, we should waste no time in implementing the Guidelines on Encouraging and Guiding Healthy Development of Private Investment, allowing the establishment of small financial institutions with various shareholding systems (just like allowing farmers to raise and sell as many fish as they want), and carrying out comprehensive reforms to prevent risk. Expanding access to finance would bring private loans to the surface, and legalize and regularize private lending. It would encourage the free flow of private funds as a kind of commodity, which would enable needing enterprises to receive financial support and reduce the financing costs in their competitions in the buyer's market. The cycle in the fish market will definitely happen again in the capital market. To cope with that, the top priority should be to abandon the stipulation that the bank must be the legal person and control 15% of the shares as main sponsor when allowing qualified private capital to set up small financial institutions.

7.5 Develop a Multi-tiered Capital Market System

The development of China's capital market is still lagging and the proportion of direct financing is relatively low. Corporate financing relies heavily on bank loans, pooling financial risk for the banking system. Developing the capital market and expanding the scale of direct financing can both reduce the financing cost of enterprises and reduce financial risk, which should be the goal of the reform of the financial system and the development of the financial industry.

The main problems in the current capital market are the high proportion of stocks trading and underdevelopment of the bond market. As a result, the focus of expanding direct financing should be on improving the multi-tiered capital market system and creating non-equity financing forms, such as bonds, funds, and finance leasing.

After years of development, China now has a relatively complete stock market system, which is composed of three boards: main, small and medium-sized enterprises (SMEs), and growth enterprises (such as the ChiNext, a NASDAQ-style board of the Shenzhen Stock Exchange, which listing requirements are less stringent than those of the main and SME boards). The stock market system has played an important role in evaluating enterprises and gathering funds, allowing a number of listed enterprises to develop rapidly. Nonetheless, China's stock market has not achieved the expected results. Compared with mature markets in developed countries, there remain defects in our stock market. The trickiest problems are as follows:

First, the market is not well established and there are many illegal trading activities. Second, a number of listed companies just want to seize money from the market, so they do not make increasing the value of the enterprise their highest goal in business. Third, high-quality institutional investors are relatively rare, while individual investors often make irrational and haphazard investments. Lastly, market intermediaries are incomplete, and have to resort to administrative approval systems in terms of enterprise listing.

Since the stock market does not perform its basic functions, including enhancing the value of enterprises and providing returns for investors, it has become less attractive to shareholders. As a result, the stock market has, to some extent, lost its credibility as a barometer of the economy. To revitalize it, we should start from the basics.

Our goal should be to strengthen legal and institutional regulations, crack down on malicious hype, fraud, and insider trading, enhance the transparency of listed enterprises, establish the concept of being responsible for shareholders, and rebuild confidence in the stock market. Our goal should be to improve the quality of market intermediaries, establish market mechanisms for determining market listing and withdrawal, and reduce administrative intervention. Our goal should be to vigorously develop institutional investors, and gradually replace malicious hyping and haphazard investment with expert financing and rational investment. Our goal should be to give full play to the functions of venture investment in growth enterprises, and moderately lower the threshold of listing in order to cultivate innovative enterprises. Our goal should be to properly develop the Counter Bulletin Board to provide services for the financing of small and medium-sized enterprises. Our goal should be to expand information exchange and cooperation with Hong Kong and Taiwan stock markets, and facilitate stock trading for people in Hong Kong, Macao, and Taiwan.

Our goal should be to actively develop the bond market, and to encourage qualified enterprises and construction projects to issue short-term and long-term bonds in areas such as high-speed railway, intercity rail transit, subway, and large-scale hydropower stations. Our goal should be to allow special construction bonds to be issued for the construction of public service facilities in utilities such as water, gas, and garbage disposal. Our goal should be to encourage the development of all kinds of investment funds, such as ecological and environmental protection industry fund, old-age care industry fund, green energy fund, ocean industry fund, emerging industries fund, green agriculture fund, science and technology development fund, education development fund, and so on. Our goal should be to encourage the development of public offerings as well as private equity. Our goal should be to develop financial leasing, trust loans, and other investment and financing businesses.

In short, by encouraging the development of all kinds of direct investment and financing activities, we should make full use of the huge amount of private capital accumulated since the start of reforms and opening up. Similarly, we should speed up capital turnover and deal with the fact that a large number of projects face a severe shortage of funds while there remain large quantities of idle funds.

7.6 Push for Progress in Renminbi Internationalization in an Orderly Manner

Currently, the US dollar, the euro, and the Japanese yen are all depreciating, while the renminbi remains strong. China has significant foreign exchange reserves and its economy is in a critical period of transformation and upgrading, which provides a rare historical opportunity for renminbi internationalization. If handled properly, internationalization of the renminbi can create new economic advantages and a powerful driving force for the transformation and upgrading of the economy, as well as sustainable development. The result would increase China's economic strength while securing its finance and economy.

Our goal should be to integrate renminbi internationalization with overseas investment expansion and promote it with the help of overseas investment. Implementing the "Go Global" strategy with overseas investment expansion is a major strategic imperative. Expanding overseas investment has the effect of hitting three birds with one stone. The first is it enables us to create export demand through overseas investment, which can still maintain the sustainable growth of our country's exports when the markets of developed countries are weak. Second, by seeking natural resources and scientific and technological resources abroad, expanding overseas investment will enable more sustainable development and independent innovation. Third, by translating some of the foreign exchange reserves into material reserves, overseas investment could be an effective way to avoid the risk of US dollar depreciation.

There are four priorities of overseas investment: (1) Gaining more energy resource exploration and development rights; (2) Buying some enterprises with better technology resources and international marketing networks; (3) Developing processing trade and transferring domestic industrial overcapacity; and (4) Contracting construction projects and expanding labor export.

In order to expand the volume of renminbi circulating overseas, we should give priority of overseas investment to countries willing to accept renminbi as an investment settlement currency and to countries that have bilateral currency swap agreements with China. In addition to making Hong Kong an offshore renminbi clearing center, we should also encourage the establishment of offshore renminbi clearing centers in Singapore, London, and other appropriate places. We will work to encourage more countries, regions, and businesses to use renminbi as a settlement instrument in trade. We will work to liberalize the capital account convertibility of the renminbi in due course. In order to accommodate the gradual increase of renminbi circulating overseas, we should expand the scale of renminbi bonds issued overseas, allow companies to raise renminbi finance overseas, and provide more renminbi financial products for overseas investors holding renminbi. We will work to encourage domestic banks to set up branches abroad and expand overseas businesses. The services of domestic banks should follow domestic businesses.

We will work to gradually allow more foreign investment in the domestic financial industry in order to promote reform of the financial system and development of the financial industry. Foreign investment in the domestic financial industry is conducive to building up competition at home and improving the competitiveness of domestic financial enterprises, thereby facilitating the security of the domestic financial sector. In regard to the inflow and outflow of hot money, we need to strengthen regulation and, when necessary, levy special taxes to curb speculation.

Renminbi internationalization is an inevitable trend. Our goal should be to ride along with this trend, and take active and effective measures to seek the largest national interest in the process of promoting renminbi internationalization.

Financial system reform is a systemic project. We must study carefully and organize thoughtfully, manage the top-level planning, and formulate a roadmap and timetable for reform. General calls will not guarantee its success, because specific implementation guidelines are needed to keep confusion and chaos in the reform at bay, so as not to badly influence financial security and social stability as well as economic development.

Chapter 8
Keeping Reform Oriented Toward a Socialist Market Economy

The *Decision of the CPC Central Committee on Certain Major Issues concerning Comprehensively Deepening Reform* (hereinafter "the *Decision*") adopted at the 18th CPC Central Committee's Third Plenary Session, states, "We will uphold the direction of reform toward the socialist market economy, take the promotion of social fairness, justice and improvement of livelihoods as the starting point and ultimate goal, further free our minds, continue to release and develop the productive forces, unlock and enhance the vitality of the society, remove deficiencies in various systems and mechanisms, and strive to open up broader prospects for socialism with Chinese characteristics." This statement sums up both the direction and the requirements for comprehensively deepening reform and constitutes the guiding thinking to be followed during reform. To keep reform oriented toward a socialist market economy, we should focus on and stick to the following guidelines.

8.1 Leveraging the Decisive Role of the Market in Allocating Resources Represents a New Leap in the Party's Understanding of the Laws of the Market Economy

At the 14th CPC National Congress, the reform objective of establishing a socialist market economy was set, and it was made clear that the basic role of the market in allocating resources should be leveraged to a greater extent and depth under the macro regulation of government. Over the past 21 years, as market-oriented reforms have been deepened, the market has come to play an increasingly important role in allocating resources. Practice has proven that, in sectors where the market is well utilized toward this end, not only does the efficiency of allocation improve signif-

---

This article originally appeared in *Economic Daily*, November 20, 2013.

X. Zheng, *China's 40 Years of Economic Reform and Development*,
https://doi.org/10.1007/978-981-13-2727-8_8

icantly, but these sectors are also infused with greater vitality. Conversely, sectors with market restrictions and weak demand for resources have shown to be inert, much like a pool of stagnant water. Furthermore, experience has shown that what is referred to as "the market allocation of resources" is essentially allocation that is determined by market entities with independent economic interests according to national macro policies and market signals. In other words, enterprises make investments independently, raise funds in financial markets independently and are fully responsible for the production and operation of their business. Such economic activities, as pure market behavior, fully embody the function of the law of value—the basic law underlying the market economy. In a market economy, this law plays the decisive role. It exerts its influence over industries of all types by determining the proportion of labor distribution in them. Industries where demand exceeds supply provide higher profit margins than the average social profit margin, and, therefore, attract a greater flow of funds, thus resulting in a balance between supply and demand. Conversely, in industries with overcapacity, funds will exit and flow into other industries because the profit margin is lower than the average social profit margin. Thus, the function of the law of value is to enable a general balance between supply and demand among various industries. Within each specific industry, it also automatically decides the flow of funds between advanced and less-developed enterprises. Advanced enterprises can develop fully thanks to adequate financial support, while less-developed ones are phased out due to a lack of funds. This is the reason why the market system maintains vitality, and the root reason why the market is more efficient than the government in allocating resources.

On the basis of a summary of China's experience in reform, the *Decision* explicitly emphasizes "the decisive role of the market in allocating resources." This is a continuation of and further development on the principle of "basic role of the market in allocating resources" which was set at the 14th CPC National Congress. Compared with the government's role as the allocator of resources under the planned economy, it could be said that noting "the basic role of the market in allocating resources" represented the Party's first leap in its understanding of objective economic rules, especially those underlying the market economy. Now, after 21 years, underlining the "decisive role of the market in allocating resources" is another leap in the Party's understanding of those rules. These two leaps are a reflection of the spirit of seeking truth from facts, exploration and endeavor embraced by Communists. History has proven and will continue to prove that the decision of the 14th CPC National Congress to establish a socialist market economy was a great liberation of the productive forces, and as is that of the 18th CPC Central Committee's Third Plenary Session on the decisive role of the market in allocating resources.

Regarding the next task of the reform, the *Decision* states that "we must deepen economic reform by centering on the decisive role of the market in allocating resources." This essentially means that "we must actively and prudently push forward the market-oriented reform both in breadth and depth, significantly reduce the government's direct allocation of resources and strive to maximize the benefits and efficiency of the allocation of resources in accordance with the rules, price and competition of the market." As per the requirements of the *Decision*, in future, further economic restructuring should be oriented toward expanding market resource allocation. The reason for this is to deal with existing problems in the way resources are allocated at present. Although years of reform have seen historic progress being made in giving play to the market's role in allocating resources, we have still yet to fully manage and leverage this role. This is down to a relatively low degree of liberalization for factors of production and an underdeveloped market, which have dampened the benefits and efficiency arising from allocation by the market. Specifically, because social system reform lags behind, factors of production, like capital, are still shut out of the utilities and public services sectors, which has caused an imbalance between economic and social development. Traffic jams, the difficulty of getting a place in a nursing home or kindergarten, problems with parking, and other similar issues are all the result of a refusal of private capital.

Because the pace of urban-rural integration reform is slow, barriers between urban and rural markets have formed, impeding the two-way free flow of factors of production between urban and rural areas. On the urban side, there is a large quantity of idle factors of production, such as funds, technology and talent that are barred from the rural market. On the rural side, there are abundant resources that cannot attract investment because they have yet to be liberalized. This leads to a situation where farmers hold treasures but are still poor, much like begging with a golden bowl. The result has been a severe hampering of agricultural modernization and rural development and a growing disparity between urban and rural areas.

Due to administrative division of regions, the allocation of factors of production within regions has been seriously distorted, resulting in a huge gap in the development levels of cities and surrounding areas. In cities, people and industries are highly concentrated while land, fresh water and other resources are in serious short supply. Also, housing prices are constantly climbing. In comparison, the economies of surrounding areas are underdeveloped, investment is severely lacking, and resources are largely idle. Within the distance of half an hour's drive, the difference in house prices can be ten-fold or more. The situation where prosperous cities are surrounded by poor hinterlands undermines the role that cities should play in driving the development of surrounding areas.

As reform to build an ecological civilization system is lagging, factors of production have been locked out of the environmental protection sector, directly resulting in massive smog and serious contamination of water resources. The core problem is that we have yet to find a value compensation mechanism for the sharing of public goods. Thus, appeals for environmental protection cannot receive a substantive response, and while protectors go unrewarded, polluters make a fortune. Tasks such as desulfurization, denitration and dust elimination have not been assigned to enterprises that have franchise rights and that are independent of polluters. As a result, the polluter pays principle is reduced to nothing more than a slogan. We need to establish an incentive investment mechanism for the environmental protection sector as quickly as possible in order to attract social funds and make the sector popular for investment and a new economic growth point. All these pressing tasks can be solved through the market-oriented reforms.

The market exchange value of cultural products is difficult realize, again because of lagging reform, but this time in relation to the cultural system. This impedes the inflow of social funds into the cultural industry and restricts people's wisdom and potential for cultural innovation. China is a nation of cultural creativity. Our cultural prosperity is sure to come in the near future once we promote core socialist values, and as long as we deepen cultural reform, introduce market concepts, make people more aware of the value of cultural commodities, and ensure investments in the cultural industry receive reasonable returns.

The market in the decisive role of resource allocation constitutes the "engine" for deepening economic reform. As long as we hold on to this key link, reforms in other aspects will come naturally, thereby allowing us to continuously develop and make new achievements in reform.

8.2 Deepening Reform to Promote Public Ownership and More Efficiently Integrate It with the Market Economy

Whether the market economy can be linked smoothly with a publicly owned economy is a key question to be answered in establishing the socialist market economy. A full 21 years ago, when we set the reform goal of creating a socialist market economy, some western economists asserted that such an economy could only be built on the basis of private ownership, and that it would be impossible for a market economy to operate in China until full privatization was realized. Nonetheless, by exploring ways of ensuring public ownership, China has separated ownership and management rights for state-owned assets. On this basis, state-owned enterprises have established a modern corporate system based on a shareholding mechanism and have thus integrated themselves into the market economy. In rural areas, the implementation of the household contract responsibility system confirmed that the ownership of land belongs to the collective and the management rights to the farmer. This has turned agricultural households into independent commodity producers and operators, thus unlocking their enthusiasm and realizing the integration of the collective ownership approach for rural land into the market economy. During reform, Chinese farmers also created a joint stock cooperative system. This system allows for the organization of property rights and combines mergers of capital and mergers of labor, and is also a form of collective ownership. Establishing and operating rural township enterprises on the basis of the joint stock cooperative system makes farmers both owners and employees of these enterprises. Such enterprises not only bring together the scattered funds of agricultural households to do things they cannot do separately, but also increases the property income of farmers. Experience has shown that our approach to realizing public ownership, including ownership by the people as a whole and ownership by a collective, is a success. The harmonization of public ownership and the market economy is not only conducive to tapping the strength of the publicly owned economy, but also helps leverage the market mechanism.

In regard to deepening reforms for the realization of public ownership, the *Decision* puts forward new requirements from the perspective of developing the public-owned economy.

It states that our goal should be to see that state-owned enterprises "strengthen the regulation of state-owned assets with capital management at the core. Other aims are to reform the mechanism of authorized operation for state-owned capital, to establish a number of operating companies for state-owned capital and support qualified SOEs to reorganize themselves into state-owned capital investment companies." These are new tasks in SOE reform arising from the establishment of the modern corporate system. Switching the focus from "cooperate management" to "capital management" is beneficial for prioritizing and adjusting distribution in relation to the state-owned economy and for expanding SOEs' right to operate independently. A "capital management" focus will also help SOEs boost their operating and innovative abilities, as they engage in fair competition with all forms of enterprises, and to expand their control and influence over the state-owned economy by holding and controlling shares. These reforms represent innovations and improvements to our approach for ensuring a state-owned economy; they will ensure better harmony between it and the market economy.

In relation to reforming China's approach to realizing collective ownership of rural land, the *Decision* makes it clear that rural land-contracting relationships will remain stable over the long-term, and states that "we will endow farmers with the rights to land tenure, land use, land revenue, land transfer, mortgage and guarantee of land contract management right, and allow farmers to become shareholders in agriculture-industrialization via their land-contracting rights." It also proposes to establish a development-land market that unifies urban and rural areas, reform and improve the rural residential la system in rural areas and "steadily and prudently push forward the mortgage, guarantee and transfer of rural residential property rights, and expand the channels for rural residents to increase their property income." These reforms to the rural land system will ensure the smooth transfer of land and see the development of intensified and large-scale agriculture. They are also of significance in that they will fully unlock the potential of land, ensure the demand for land for economic development and rural and urban construction is met, and simultaneously promote urbanization and agriculture modernization. Land is a resource in short supply. In accordance with market exchange, land prices reflect this scarcity. It is only through market exchange that people can become aware of land conservation, and that rural residents' usufructuary right to land can become a source of income for them. The separation of land ownership and management rights not only preserves the public nature of land and avoids purchase and annexation, but also reflects the commercial characteristics of land, once more helping to further integrate public ownership with the market economy.

The *Decision* calls for the proactive development of a mixed ownership economy, noting that "the mixed ownership economy, featuring cross-shareholding of state-owned capital, collective capital and non-public capital, is an important way to realize the basic economic system of China." The *Decision* also requires that the economy based on state ownership and the private economy based on various forms of ownership be further developed so as to form a mixed ownership economy. It also encourages employees to hold shares in their companies in order to "form a vested community of capital owners and workers." This kind of mixed ownership economy featuring a shareholding system represents a form of organizing property rights that is highly integrated with the market economy. Employee stock ownership can make employees owners of their enterprises, a move which is crucial for motivating employees, making enterprises more cohesive and ensuring common prosperity.

8.3 Distribution System Reforms Will Allow for a Stronger Incentive Mechanism for Promoting Economic Development

The socialist distribution system with Chinese characteristics is predominantly based on distribution according to work with multiple forms of distribution existing alongside each other. The system is underpinned by the principle that factors of production, including labor, capital, technology and management, should be allocated according to their contribution to the system, thereby motivating workers to study technology and improve management, boosting the potential of factors of production and creating an incentive mechanism for promoting economic development.

In addressing the widening income gap which has arisen between industries, regions and individuals under the present distribution system, the *Decision* determines the direction and measures for furthering reform from three aspects: primary distribution, secondary distribution and the order of distribution. It sets out requirements for "raising the proportion of labor remuneration in primary distribution," and "facilitating employment of young people, especially college graduates, and rural migrant workers, urban residents who have difficulty finding jobs as well as former soldiers." It states that work will be carried out to reasonably determine and strictly regulate the wage levels, position benefits, position expenditure and business spending of SOE executives. We should work to "improve the compensation system in which the returns for capital, knowledge, technology, managerial expertise and other factors of production would be determined by the market." We should work to "open up channels for investment and lease services," "improve the investment return system for listed companies," and "increase residents' property income by diversifying channels." For secondary distribution, we should "improve regulatory mechanisms… mainly by means of taxation, social security and transfer payments and put more effort into adjusting taxation." The *Decision* also confirms that moves will be made to standardize income distribution, establish information systems for individual income and property, increase the income of low-income groups and expand middle-income groups. These are steps that will see us working toward narrowing the income gap and gradually creating an olive-shaped distribution structure.

In terms of the reform of the allocation system, the *Decision* sets down three specific requirements. First, national income distribution should be slanted toward residents as much as possible, and the ratio of residential income to Gross National Income (GNI) should be increased. This reflects the need to raise the consumption rate of individuals and the priority of transforming the development mode. By employing diverse channels to raise resident's income levels and increase their purchasing power, we can establish a long-term mechanism for consumption growth. Second, the income distribution structure should be adjusted with a focus on increasing the incomes of low- and middle-income groups and regulating excessively high incomes. The point of this is to work toward prosperity for all by narrowing the income distribution gap. One important way to realize an increase in the incomes of low- and middle-income groups is to expand employment. Third, income distribution should be better regulated to ensure the transparency of income and prevent the generation of illicit income. By working to further reforms to the income distribution system and establish a reasonable and orderly structure of income distribution, an endless supply of dynamic support can be ensured for China's economic development.

8.4 Improving the Macro Regulatory System Is Intrinsically Important for Harnessing the Strengths of the Socialist Market Economy

An important feature of the socialist market economy is the government's sound macro regulation and effective management. China needs to quickly catch up with the levels of economic development in developed countries and promote the transformation of its economy, which means that the government must play its appropriate role. Under the planned system, the government interfered too much in microeconomic activities, and did many things it should not have, thus hindering economic development. Over 35 years of reform, although it has streamlined administration, delegated powers and expanded the role of the market, the government has not taken the simple view that the less it interferes, the better things would be. Rather, it has been continuously changing its role to effectively take on problems that the market cannot solve. Through macro regulation, it can maintain a balance in economic aggregates, coordinate major economic structures, optimize the distribution of the productive forces, mitigate the impact of periodic economic fluctuations, prevent regional and systemic risk, stabilize market expectations, and realize sustainable and sound economic development. This makes macro regulation a crucial function that the government must strengthen and spare no effort to fulfill.

The *Decision* puts forward a series of reform measures for the transformation of government functions and the improvement of the macro regulatory system. It notes that "we should improve the macro regulatory system which is guided by the national development strategy and plans, and that is supported by fiscal and monetary policies as the primary means of regulation, and institutionalize the formulation of macro regulatory targets and the implementation of relevant policies." We must work to improve the system for evaluating development achievements, and take steps to correct the inappropriate tendency of evaluating official accomplishments merely on the basis of economic growth rates. We should also see work being stepped up to streamline administration and delegate powers, and to abolish all administrative approval procedures for economic activities that can be effectively regulated by the market. The government will also strengthen the formulation and implementation of development strategies, plans, policies and standards, and other aspects in order to enhance market regulation and increase the supply of various public services.

The reform plans put forward by the *Decision* regarding the role of market, the basic economic system, the income distribution system, and government macro regulation, as well as others issues, ensure that keep reform oriented toward a socialist market economy. They should be carefully and thoroughly studied and implemented. If we can comprehensively deepen reform, then we are sure to realize the goal set at the 18th CCP National Congress of building a moderately prosperous society in all respects by 2020.

Chapter 9
Establishing an International Reserve Currency System with Checks and Balances

The current US dollar-based international monetary system was formed after the US's departure from the gold standard caused the collapse of the Bretton Woods System. The US dollar, as a sovereign currency, is issued in accordance with the needs of the domestic economy of the United States. The US dollar is a major international reserve currency. From the perspective of achieving robust growth of the global economy, the supply of US dollars should not only satisfy the demand of international economic activities for the currency, but also avoid excessive virtualization—the conversion of physical and tangible things into virtual things, that could trigger fluctuations in international markets. Thus, the role of the US dollar in the global economy inevitably contradicts with the sovereign nature of its monetary policies. How can this contradiction be resolved? A return to the gold standard is surely out of the question, and the creation of a super-sovereign currency presents its own set of unique challenges. However, one feasible and good option is to establish a multiple currency system with built-in restraint mechanisms resting on three main pillars—the US dollar, the euro, and the yuan, and consisting of several other major currencies.

This essay proposes some ideas in this regard.

9.1 Replacing the Single Reserve Currency with Multiple Reserve Currencies Is a Historical Inevitability

In 2008, the global financial crisis, which was triggered by the US dollar, resulted in a heavy blow to the global economy. Conscientious economists are struggling to understand the causes of this crisis and are trying to figure out ways to prevent it from happening again. The crisis can be explained from many perspectives, but something undeniable is that the main cause was the excessive virtualization of the

This article originally appeared in *Globalization*, no. 8, 2014.

X. Zheng, *China's 40 Years of Economic Reform and Development*,
https://doi.org/10.1007/978-981-13-2727-8_9

economy, which resulted from the proliferation of derivatives for the US dollar. The United States has long taken advantage of its status as a major reserve currency to abuse sovereign credit and to have "twin deficits,"—which means having both a current account deficit and a fiscal budget deficit, to maintain excessive levels of consumption and excessive government spending. That is what led to the financial crisis. In 2010, the US federal government's fiscal deficit reached US$1.4 trillion, accounting for 9.4% of the GDP. Public debt was US$9.02 trillion, taking up 62.1% of the GDP of the country. The reason why high budget deficits and high debt as well as years of easy monetary policies did not trigger higher inflation and interest rates in the United States is due to its position as the world's most dominant reserve currency. This position of dominance allows the United States to attract foreign funds and also allows cheap goods to flow into the country.

The fact that the United States became the wellspring of the global financial crisis in 2008 has once again demonstrated that the scale of financial products created by sovereign credit must fit the demand and the scale of its real economy. The excessive expansion of the virtual economy has made the US economy like an inverted pyramid built on sand. Before the crisis, there were about US$2 trillion in subprime mortgages at the bottom of the pyramid. The balance of ordinary mortgages was approximately US$12 trillion, and corporate debt, including collateralized debt obligation (CDO) and credit default swaps (CDS), was about US$62 trillion. The value of financial derivatives held by major US financial institutions were approximately US$300 trillion, according to the Bank for International Settlements. As can be imagined, this giant inverted pyramid could collapse at any time if there was a problem. If the Great Depression in the United States was mainly caused by the overproduction of material products, then history would tell us that the glut of financial products relentlessly created by sovereign credit caused the global financial crisis.

The lesson of the financial crisis is that a stable international monetary system is not possible until an oversight mechanism is created to keep US dollar financial derivatives in check. As there will never be enough gold to keep up with the demands of economic growth, there is no way to turn back to the gold standard. The decision of US President Richard Nixon to end international convertibility of the US dollar to gold was also due to this fact. The establishment of a super-sovereign international reserve currency is an option, but there are many difficulties to overcome in realizing this idea. Acting as a special drawing right (SDR), we must ask how a super-sovereign reserve currency can be used for international settlements. We must also ask how the weight on different countries in a unified international reserve currency should be determined, as well as how this SDR can adapt to imbalances in development. Problems like these are all extremely difficult to properly resolve.

Replacing the single international reserve system based on a single currency with one that is based on multiple international reserve currencies might be the best way to achieve a check on the excessive virtualization of international finance. Three conditions are needed for a currency to become an international reserve currency:

One is that the scale of the currency must be global in reach.

Second is that the weight of the currency must be relatively high in international trade.

And third is that the currency must he backed by a government or administrative organization.

At present, the only countries that can satisfy these three conditions are the United States, the European Union, and China. Unfortunately, however, the current weight of the European Union and China in the composition of international reserve currencies is too low. This is especially true of China, as China's financial market reform is still under way and the internationalization of the renminbi is just getting started. In 2012, the renminbi share as an international payment currency was almost negligible, accounting for just 0.2%. If the three aforementioned currencies could all take up a reasonable proportion in the overall composition, then the system of checks and balances would create a situation in which governments, enterprises, and individuals will sell off currencies at risk of devaluation and rush to buy currencies that are likely to appreciate in value. Such a mechanism would put pressure on issuing countries to ensure a stable value. This mechanism would operate much like the gold standard by impelling issuing countries to strengthen financial regulation to protect national interests, which would avoid the excess printing of currencies and help keep financial derivatives in check. From the perspectives of geometry and mechanics, three points determine a plane, and a triangle is stable in any position. Likewise, three major reserve currencies would serve as the main reserve currencies and meet countries' demands for global economic development and financial stability.

It would be counterproductive for any country to undervalue its currency in order to strengthen the competitiveness of its exports. The exchange rate, as they say, is a double-edged sword. An undervalued currency would suppress imports, but in today's globalized world, the decline in the currency value would also shrink personal wealth and reduce purchasing power, which would reduce people's willingness to hold their own currency. And when the people of a country abandon the currency of their own country and rush to hold foreign currencies, it is likely that big problems will follow.

9.2 Establishing an International Reserve Currency System with Checks and Balances Could Help Solve the Triffin Dilemma

How to strike a balance between meeting demands for liquidity of global economic activities and avoiding excessive issuance to maintain global financial and economic stability is a problem for the supply of reserve currencies. This problem is called the Triffin Dilemma. The goal should be to establish a diversified international reserve currency system with checks and balances, and seigniorage should be used to form incentives, which could impel issuing countries to increase the money supply in order to meet the needs for international liquidity. Similarly, there should be a risk-prevention mechanism t to control the issuance of sovereign currency and maintain the overall stability of currency values. A combination of an international reserve monetary system with checks and balances and a super-sovereign currency, or SDR, just might be the best way to address the Triffin Dilemma and ensure the stability of the international reserve currency system.

If a country's sovereign currency becomes an international reserve currency, then both its international payment capacity and its economic strength would be strengthened. In this case, it is in that country's interest to export its currency through trade deficits and a deficit in the capital account, and also relinquish part of the domestic market. Clearly, there are both advantages and disadvantages to this approach, but overall, the benefits are weightier. This is especially true when the country is creating "catch-up" growth or is facing a standstill on official debt. As an international reserve currency issuer, it makes better use of global resources to accelerate national development and alleviate or even eliminate its debt crisis through deficit financing. This is undoubtedly an incentive for the issuing countries of international reserve currencies. The government of a currency-issuing sovereign nation is encouraged to increase the amount of its currency circulating overseas. In addition, replacing the single-currency reserve system with one anchored to multiple reserve currencies would make it easier to export currency and disperse risk.

An international reserve currency system would help restrain issuers of a currency, such as central banks, thus avoiding the proliferation of reserve currencies and the derivatives that follow. As a result of the need to preserve their own currencies, countries that accept the reserve currency system must prefer the currencies that trend toward appreciation or are stable. If a currency is considered a "hot potato" by governments, enterprises, and individuals, the economy of the issuing country will suffer strong external shocks, forcing the government to take measures to stabilize the value of its currency. Following the 2008 financial crisis, for instance, the US Federal Reserve has pursued quantitative easing (QE). By vigorously printing currency and thus depreciating the dollar, the United States has, essentially, spread its crisis to other countries. As a result, foreign US dollar-holders bore the brunt of the losses. When the US economy fought off the doldrums, the US Federal Reserve, considering the domestic situation, announced that it would slow or stop buying US debt. As a result, US interest rates recovered, attracting US dollars flowing overseas to flow back into the United Sates, weakening the foreign exchange markets of some developing countries. This has created potential risk for financial fluctuations.

Of course, the US Federal Reserve should consider the domestic economy first, and this US institution does not function to attend to any possible impacts on the intereconomy. The US government, Congress, and Federal Reserve are elected by the American people or appointed by the US government. In other words, they all represent the interests of the American people, and as we all know, the interests of the American people do not always line with the interests of the world. In order to resolve this contradiction, an international reserve currency system with checks and balances should be established. By giving governments, enterprises, and individuals the right to replace the US dollar as a reserve currency, a mechanism to restrain the currency supply can be put in place to maintain the stability of the international monetary system.

The goal should be to, under the management of the International Monetary Fund (IMF), expand the scale of the SDR basket, and adjust the respective weightings of countries according to the proportion of countries engaged in international trade and aggregate figures. This could give play to the role of SDR in stabilizing the international monetary system. SDR is like a basket of international currencies, and it will play a different role in maintaining stability of the international monetary system in a system with built-in checks and balances.

9.3 China's Financial System Reform Will Set the Stage for the Renminbi to Become an International Reserve Currency

The Chinese financial system is undergoing extensive and profound reforms in accordance with the plans of the Third Plenary Session of the 18th CPC Central Committee. This reform will not only influence and determine the future of China's economy, but it will have a significant impact on the global monetary system. With the current financial system, China's financial system reforms will make four major breakthroughs.

The first breakthrough will be allowing private capital to be used to set up small and medium-sized commercial banks and other financial institutions. For a long time, the financial industry has become a monopoly. This is because private capital has been kept out of the industry, resulting in poor liquidity and finance mismatch. Bank lending has been concentrated in big companies, key projects, major cities, and coastal areas, while small and micro-sized businesses, private enterprises, rural areas, and the central and western regions of the country have struggled to get loans. Interest rates are twice as high as that of the US and developed countries in Europe, and the financial industry's return on net assets was double that of the real economy. The biggest breakthrough of this reform is allowing private capital to be used to set up small and medium-sized commercial banks and other financial institutions. By intensifying competition and reducing financing costs for enterprises, the financial industry's profits will be reduced to a more reasonable level. The *Decision* adopted at the Third Plenary Session of the 18th CPC Central Committee acknowledged the market's "decisive" role in allocating resources, for which it is required to expand access to and increase competition in financial markets. Only through full competition can the interest rate of the renminbi, or capital price, be reduced to roughly that of the same levels as the United States and developed countries in Europe. The falling interest rate of renminbi will not only help support the development of the domestic real economy, but also encourage the outflow of funds, thereby creating favorable conditions for increasing the volume of renminbi circulation overseas. Expanding access to financial markets will strengthen domestic financial market competition, and also enhance the competitiveness of domestic financial institutions.

The second breakthrough will be promoting interest rate liberalization. Interest rate liberalization is essential for the allocation of financial resources. China has already liberalized the interest rate floor. The next step for China is to liberalize the deposit rate ceiling in order to gradually realize interest rate liberalization. Interest rates may rise shortly after the liberalization, but they will surely fall to normal levels when the forces of supply and demand are fully brought into play. No doubt, the full liberalization of interest rates will have some impact on existing commercial banks. For a long time now, China's commercial banks have been accustomed to risk-free fixed interest rates and the market has lacked competitiveness. The reforms will push them to the forefront of international competition. Competition is the biggest test for domestic commercial banks. If Chinese commercial banks can pass this test, then they will become an integral part of the international monetary system and have influence on the supply and demand of international currencies and the corresponding stability of those currencies.

The third breakthrough will be to develop a multi-tiered capital market system. A major disadvantage of the old financial system in China is that most of the financing was indirect while direct financing played only a subsidiary role. This led to an excessive concentration risk, making it difficult for enterprises to raise capital funds. The excessively high debt ratio raised the operating costs for enterprises, weakening their international competitiveness. Developing a multi-tiered capital market system will make it easier for enterprises to increase equity financing. Although China's capital market has more than two decades of history already, it is not a mature open market yet. The past three-plus decades of experience in China has shown that opening up is a catalyst and impetus for reforms, and China's capital market must grow into the opening process. The recent reform to allow stock purchases in different places and to connect the Shanghai and Hong Kong stock markets (known as the Shanghai-Hong Kong Stock Connect) is a major step forward in opening up of capital markets. For the next step, China will need to push forward the integration of the Taipei stock market into greater China and allow overseas companies to be listed in the mainland, just as mainland companies have already listed overseas. China's integration with international capital markets will not only help improve its own regulatory system and strengthen enterprises' performance evaluations, fund raising strategies, and distribution of profits, but also inject vitality into the global stock market and act as a new source of stability.

The fourth breakthrough will be pushing forward the renminbi's capital account convertibility. With the development of China's foreign trade and investment, the scale of bilateral renminbi swaps is expanding, and the proportion of renminbi as an instrument in international trade and investment settlements is increasing. Naturally, the full convertibility of the renminbi is coming as a result. But the main concern right now is the adverse impacts caused by short-term hot money flows. Experience abroad has shown that the Tobin Tax can be levied to prevent the large-scale influx and outflow of short-term funds. The increase of the renminbi circulating overseas will make the currency more internationalized. And the inclusion of the renminbi as an international reserve currency will make an important contribution to the establishment of a new and stable international reserve currency system.

9.4 The Position, Role, and Strategic Choice of the Euro in Maintaining the Stability of the International Monetary System

The euro plays a unique and important role in the reconstruction of the Bretton Woods System. The euro has only a short history, but it accounts for 24% of a currency in which foreign countries held in reserves, and its record proportion was 26%. From the perspectives of Europe's international trade, economic aggregate, and area of coverage, as well as its proportion of the world's population, the share of the euro in the mix of international reserves still has the potential to increase. As a result, Europe should contribute much to the stability of the international monetary system.

If we compare the international financial system to a company, this company would need an internal mechanism of checks and balances. In order to accomplish this goal and also prevent substantial shareholders from encroaching on the interests of minority shareholders, the total equity of the two minority shareholders must be greater than the proportion of substantial shareholders. This is the way forward for a listed company. The entry of the euro and renminbi into the international reserve currency system will inevitably require the US dollar to make some room by modestly reducing its share in global reserves. In 2012, the US dollar accounted for 62.2% of global reserve currencies, demonstrating its predominance. The formation of a multiple reserve currency system should be a peaceful process of fair market competition as well as a process wherein shareholders can independently choose the currency they would like to hold, in which case countries' financial institutions have to improve their services. The IMF would play a crucial role as coordinator. A stable international monetary system cannot form until the euro and the renminbi together account for more than the proportion of the US dollar in the international reserve currency system.

If the euro and renminbi are to form a three-currency reserve system with the US dollar, both must do their "homework" and increase their internal strength. As the second-largest international reserve currency after the US dollar, at least at present, the euro must solve its debt problem as soon as possible. Europe needs to strengthen the unity and coordination of its monetary policy and enhance the euro's capacity to resist risk and external shocks.

The position and role of the euro in the international reserve currency basket should be strengthened. Policy makers in Europe should partner with China to increase support for renminbi internationalization and to promote bilateral trade and investment settlements with the renminbi. This is necessary because competition against the US dollar by the euro alone would inevitably fail. Europe and China should support each other in this effort, and the two currencies should be compatible with the US dollar. It is an absolute requirement to establish a long-term stable international reserve currency system, but such a system is also needed to protect the interests of humanity, including the American people. Economists should seek to understand and respect the fundamental laws of economics, and avoid becoming emotionally involved or clinging to outdated thinking.

Chapter 10
Giving Play to New Development Engines Through Reform and New Breakthroughs

For the first half of the year, China's domestic economy has generally performed well. However, various economic indicators suggest that downward pressure, which has lasted for over two consecutive years, remains unabated. The source of this pressure not only comes from the short-term effects of the global financial crisis, but also from long-term factors affecting the domestic economic cycle. In the 21st century, China's economy experienced a decade of rapid growth, which was supported partly by high investment, high consumption, and high pollution. Although the 17th CPC National Congress in 2007 provided a strategy for transforming the model of economic development, major economic structures, including investment and consumption structures, did not improve and, in fact, became even worse due to the international financial crisis and reform setbacks. The current economic downward pressure is the result of various factors, including under-consumption, overcapacity, slow industrial upgrading, overstretched resources, too much strain on the environment, the widening urban-rural divide, and imbalances in regional development. The 18th CPC National Congress reiterated the central importance of transforming the development model for reform, and the Third Plenary Session of the 18th CPC Central Committee decided to comprehensively deepen reform. Both decisions provide an opportunity to transform the development model through reform as well as new driving forces for further development. Reform is necessary to alleviate the current downward pressure on the economy. This means breakthroughs must be made in removing the institutional defects that impede transformation of the development model, but also so enable the breakthroughs to unleash new driving forces for development. Only in this way can the country achieve a new round of continuous and sound development.

This article originally appeared in in *Qiushi*, Chinese edition, no. 15, 2014.

X. Zheng, *China's 40 Years of Economic Reform and Development*,
https://doi.org/10.1007/978-981-13-2727-8_10

10.1 Reform the Household Registration System and Unleash the Potential of Urbanization

For at least the next decade, urbanization will be the most powerful driving force for China's economic development. Each additional urbanite requires 100,000 yuan of additional investment in urban infrastructure. With the addition of 10 million urbanites, therefore, 1 trillion yuan of investment will be generated for infrastructure construction. The household registration system is the important link in pushing forward urbanization. The central government has pointed out that the general requirement for household registration system reform is to completely lift restrictions on new residence registrations in administrative townships and small cities, lift restrictions on new residence registrations in medium-sized cities in an orderly manner, lay down appropriate conditions for new residence registrations in large cities, and strictly control the population size of mega cities. This means China must spread distribution of productivity to small towns and medium-sized cities in order to create more jobs. As a result, the State Council has made it a requirement to fulfill three pressing tasks—tasks that affect 100 million people each.

The first task is to help 100 million rural migrants enjoy resident status in cities and towns in eastern China.

The second task is to accommodate 100 million rural people as local residents in cities and towns in central and western China.

The third task is to provide 100 million people living in rundown areas in cities with decent housing.

Fulfilling these three tasks will not only offer much-needed policy support to rural migrant workers and low-income urban residents, but also accelerate urbanization and immediately facilitate steady growth.

The future urbanization of China will progress synchronously on three levels: city clusters, sub-regional clusters of cities, and the landscape-urbanization relationship.

The first level is the three core city clusters; that is the Beijing-Tianjin-Hebei city cluster centered on Beijing, the Yangtze-River-Delta city cluster centered on Shanghai, and the Pearl-River-Delta city cluster centered on Guangzhou. After a decade or so, the economic aggregate of these three city clusters will be among the top in the world, and the clusters will be the three major engines for China's economic growth.

The second level is the group of sub-regional clusters of cities that respectively take their provincial capitals as the center and link with surrounding prefecture-level cities. This group of provincial city clusters will play an important role in driving the economic growth of provinces.

The third level is the physical changes to the rural landscape of in situ urbanization supported by counties, small towns, and new communities. This kind of urbanization has already appeared in developed regions at the county level.

The aforementioned three levels of urbanization all require modern transportation, such as high-speed railways and highways, to connect cities of all sizes and ultimately form a half-hour radius for daily life and an hour radius for business life. Thus, China could see acceleration in the construction of high-speed railways, highways, airlines, cruise lines, and Internet networks, as they form the basis for urbanization and provide an excellent opportunity to expand domestic markets and drive economic growth.

10.2 Reform the Rural Land System and Unleash the Potential of Agricultural Modernization

Based on the experience of rural reform, the *Decision* adopted at the Third Plenary Session of the 18th CPC Central Committee put forward three groundbreaking measures for reforming the rural land system. The three breakthroughs are recognizing farmers' land contract rights, the management rights over contracted land, and the marketization of collective-owned rural land. This is another major adjustment in the rural transition since the household contract system. As long as the Chinese government steadily and prudently pushes forward the right reforms in accordance with the requirements of the *Decision*, it is possible to further unleash the potential of China's agricultural workforce and land and accelerate agricultural modernization. This will not only increase arable land and satisfy municipal demand for construction land, but also narrow the income gap between urban and rural residents, which will make the country's agricultural workers even more productive. Last year, China's GDP per capita reached US$6750. If the momentum of healthy development can be sustained, then by 2021—the centenary of the founding of the Communist Party of China, GDP per capita could amount to more than US$12,000. If it does, this would put China in the ranks of high-income countries. Leading China out of the semi-feudal and semi-colonial era and into a prosperous, democratic, culturally advanced, and harmonious new era over the past century is the ruling party's great contribution to human society. But the key to achieving this was to increase agricultural productivity and increase farmers' incomes. And the fundamental way this target was achieved was to implement the plans of the Third Plenary Session of the 18th CPC Central Committee on reforming the rural land system to the letter.

Therefore, China must carry out the following tasks:

First, farmer households should be allowed to mortgage land to banks and guarantee and transfer land contract rights. According to President Xi Jinping's address at the Central Conference on Rural Work held at the end of last year, revealed plans to carry out a three-pronged reform featuring separation of ownership rights, contract rights, and management rights of arable land, forests, and grassland. Specifically, it made clear that ownership rights are allocated under collective rights, contract rights belong to farmer households, and management rights would be liberalized.

With regard to the latter, the government will maintain land ownership rights, implement contract rights, and lift restrictions against management rights; issue certificates to confirm land-use rights as soon as possible; and encourage a system of compensation for the occupation and use of land. The transfer of land-use rights can provide farmer households with property income. Once that income reaches or even exceeds farm income, there will be even more land-use transfers, which in turn will help more farmers enter non-agricultural industries. Big farming households and cooperatives can take full advantage of the benefits of the scale effect in economics. Experience has proven that removing ridge and furrow can increase the area of arable land by 5%, and the unified application of deep plowing, irrigation, fertilization, and soil disinfestation can increase agricultural output by over 30%, and the return on investment can reach 30%. If one agricultural workforce in the northern single-crop region of the country can plant 100–120 mu of land, and one agricultural workforce in the southern double-crop region can plant 50–60 mu of land, then labor productivity can reach or even exceed the level of the secondary or tertiary industries, which would make farming a much more decent occupation. Reform of the land contracting system will help speed up agricultural modernization, which in turn will turn agriculture into an internationally competitive industry and facilitate the development of the agro-industry.

Second, farmers should be allowed to borrow against the value of homesteads, the government should guarantee homestead property rights, and farmers should have the right to transfer homestead property rights. This will provide important support for the urbanization of rural migrant workers. At present, China's rural homestead system is not effectively protected and utilized. Currently, the area of land for construction in urban and rural areas totals 220,000 km^2, of which 50,000 km^2 is land for urban construction and 170,000 km^2 is for rural construction. Over the past 30 years since reform, China's rural population has shrunk by over 200 million, while the area of homesteads has swelled. China should respect the will of urban and rural residents to independently decide where to settle and properly guide the expectations and decisions of rural residents to settle down in cities and towns. In addition, China should protect farmers' rights to use and transfer their homesteads.

Third, the rights and prices of profitable collective-owned land for construction should be equal to that of state-owned land. The government should reform the system to requisition land, establish a unified market for land for construction in urban and rural areas, and share more of the revenue from the transfer of land-use rights with farmers. Rural collectives should also be allowed to use the profitable collective-owned land for construction of profit-oriented projects after legal approval.

The significance of the above three reforms is they concentrate on enabling farmers—and not just urbanites, to benefit from land appreciation during the process of urbanization. And, at least according to international experience, this is the key to avoiding the so-called middle-income trap.

Of course, reform of the rural land system must first conform to land-use regulations and urban-rural planning principles. Under this premise, efforts should be made to carry out reform in a steady and prudent manner and with a detailed and accurate plan. Doing so will profoundly change the urban-rural dual economic structure, effectively narrow the urban-rural development gap, and unleash great potential for development.

10.3 Implement Reform of the Financial System and Unleash the Potential of Capital

China's capital stock is very large in scale. The supply of banks' money (M_2) equals 116 trillion yuan, and foreign exchange reserves have reached nearly US$4 trillion. However, because less attention had been paid to financial system reform and due to poor capital liquidity, capital allocation is not optimal, and financing costs for enterprises are too high. In terms of fund prices, the price of the capital in China is more than double that of developed countries. In 2013, the one-year lending rate for Chinese enterprises was 6.15%, while rates in the United States, Japan, and Germany were about 2.25, 1, and 3.5%, respectively. The profits from net assets in China's financial industry were more than double that of the real economy. High interest rates and high profits in the financial sector mainly came from monopolies and industrial barriers that impeded the free flow of production factors among various industries. It this situation continues, it will be detrimental to the development of the real economy.

Targeting this problem, in the *Decision* adopted by the Third Plenary Session of the 18th CPC Central Committee, the CPC decided to expand access to finance and allow "qualified private capital" to establish financial institutions, such as small or medium-sized banks. Only by expanding access and competition can the financing costs of enterprises be reduced. Likewise, in order to solve the problem of increasing regulatory difficulties, in the *Decision* the CPC specifically decided to improve the mechanism for regulation and coordination and clarify central and local responsibilities for financial regulation and risk management, as well as to build a deposit insurance system and improve the market exit mechanism for financial institutions. In other words, China will delegate the supervision of small financial institutions at the local level to respective local governments and establish market mechanisms for resolving risks. There are more than 8000 banks in the United States, but only hundreds in China. Thus, it is the primary task of China's financial system reform to allow private capital to enter the market, increase competition, and break monopolies.

It is generally believed that the debt ratio should remain between 40 and 60%. However, because enterprises' financing channels is impeded, the debt ratio of Chinese enterprises has been rising—from about 70% a decade ago to more than 80% now, and in some enterprises, it has even exceeded the international warning line. Therefore, scaling up direct finance and raising the proportion of the total amount of capital in enterprises will not only reduce the costs of business operations, but also increase residents' property income. Therefore, to advance financial system reform, China will need to increase the proportion of direct financing by improving the multi-tiered capital market system. In addition, China will need to take steps to strengthen how the country's stock market is regulated, push forward the registration system for initial public offerings (IPOs), boost investor confidence, and give full play to the role of the stock market in raising funds, evaluating the performance of enterprises, and wealth distribution. At the same time, enterprises should be encouraged to accept private equity from citizens and various types of funds from investors, and to expand equity through multiple channels. In the current capital market structure, the bond market lags behind the stock market. Thus, the corporate bond market should be developed and a variety of financing instruments for enterprises should be provided.

Reforming the foreign exchange management system and improving the benefits of using foreign exchange reserves are also an important direction for reform of the financial system. China should continue to expand overseas investment, make better use of global resources and markets to break development bottlenecks, enhance innovation capabilities, create demand for exports, and transfer overcapacity to overseas. The government should make effective use of the nation's foreign exchange reserves to help ease downward pressure on the economy and support the sound economic development. Furthermore, the government should expand use of renminbi for international trade and investment settlements, accelerate the renminbi's convertibility in capital accounts, and continue its efforts to internalize the renminbi. In order to prevent the adverse impact of footloose international capital on the domestic market—at least in the short term, China can explore the Tobin tax option.

10.4 Reform Investment and Financing Mechanisms and Unleash the Potential of Private Investment

In the long run, the answer to the problem of inadequate demand is to increase consumption, while the short-term solution is to increase investment. In order to avoid returning to the old approach of supporting high growth by encouraging high investment and high consumption, the government must guide the direction of investment and prioritize the investment structure. In particular, private investment should be encouraged, which involves deepening reform of investment and financing mechanisms.

In order to adjust the investment structure while focusing on changing the development model, funds should be attracted into the following fields and sectors: construction projects, services, infrastructure and public services, environmental protection, import substitution industrialization, and regional economic growth pillars.

The first is construction projects that focus on upgrading the industrial structure, which includes new energy, new material, electric vehicles, new-generation mobile internet technology, biotechnology, advanced manufacturing, the marine economy, and other projects related to strategic emerging industries.

The second is the service industry, which includes research and development (R&D), design, finance, logistics, information, consulting, accounting, auditing, legal services, culture, and creative services.

The third is the infrastructure and public services in severe shortage, including inter-city high-speed railways, subways, parking lots, facilities for the elderly, medical care and health services, and vocational education and preschool education.

The fourth is environmental protection, which, among other things, includes flue-gas desulfurization, denitrization, and dedusting technologies, sewage treatment, garbage disposal, promotion of low-emission vehicles and high-quality fuel standards, and greening.

The fifth is import substitution industrialization. China imports over US$200 billion of chemical products and chips every year, many of which can be developed and produced in China. For example, the import of the chemical paraxylene (PX) accounts for 64% of the domestic market, and foreign investors have been taking advantage of this situation to raise prices, causing great profit losses for the Chinese people. To end this situation, China should concentrate more attention on building large and advanced petrochemical projects on isolated islands that are far away from residents. For another example, China imports more than 50 million tons of soybeans each year. Therefore, the government should support domestic woody oil plantations, which will not only afforest barren mountains, but also increase the income of farmers.

The sixth is the new regional economic growth pillars, including the Yangtze River Economic Belt, the Huai River Economic Belt, and the Beijing-Tianjin-Hebei coordinated development plan. In particular, the Huai River Economic Belt is rich in natural resources, but it remains an underdeveloped region in the provinces of Henan, Anhui, and Jiangsu, mainly because of the lack of an overall long-term development plan for the whole river basin, but also because of insufficient investment. If the government can draw up a comprehensive development plan, coordinate relevant parties, and unify management to transform the floodwaters into resources, then this area of the country will become a large river reservoir that covers thousands of miles. This reservoir, once finished, would connect the "third golden corridor" to the sea, and become a fourth growth pillar after the Pearl River Delta, Yangtze River Delta, and Beijing-Tianjin-Hebei growth pillars.

After more than three decades of reform and development, China's private investment capacity has grown dramatically, and a large number of enterprises with strong investment capacity have mushroomed. By deepening reform of investment and financing mechanisms, the country can reduce administrative approval procedures to the max; and at the same time, more decision-making power will be given to enterprises so as to better tap the huge potential of private investment.

First, China should promote a franchise management system in public sector construction projects. The current insufficient supply of public goods and services is a result of inadequate financial support. As public sector construction projects mainly depend on government investment, the development of public utilities is sensitive to the amount of financial resources available. The way to solve this problem is to give enterprises greater investment options by implementing a franchise management system. Generally speaking, it is difficult to receive considerable return on public sector construction projects, so tax subsidies and other suitable approaches are needed to help support such projects. For projects in need of funding, such as high-speed inter-city railway and urban rail transit, construction enterprises should be allowed to develop commercial real estate around the construction sites to enhance their ability to receive returns on these projects and avoid long-term losses from operations or long-term financial burdens. The subway in Hong Kong is a great example of using commercial benefits to offset operational losses. For other projects, such as nursing homes, kindergartens, and parking lots, as long as there is some policy support to allow reasonable returns on investment, then these projects will attract a large amount of private funds, and the problem of insufficient supply will be solved.

Second, China should establish a market mechanism to attract investment in the environmental protection industry. The "war against pollution" declaration in this year's government work report is a demonstration of the determination of the State Council and the strong desire of the Chinese people. In order to attain remarkable achievements in managing air pollution, water pollution, and other environmental problems within a short period of time, it is important to focus on the principle of "whoever causes pollution shall be responsible for it" and implement a third-party management system. The government should set consistent emission standards and environmental standards, and strictly supervise implementation to ensure that those standards are met. At the same time, enterprises should be charged for their emissions, and government or intermediary organizations should explore a bidding system for public pollution. In this way, pollution control can be highly effective, as the enterprises that invest in environmental protection industry can have reasonable returns.

Third, China should support changes to the investment structure with positive fiscal policies and flexible monetary policies. The liability ratio of the Chinese government is only 39.4%, which is the lowest in the world. Therefore, there is a lot of space for the expansion of domestic demand via fiscal policies. Likewise, deflation has become a major threat, as the price of commodities is falling. China should adopt active fiscal policies and flexible monetary policies to encourage investment in construction projects that are supported by the government through tax cuts, discounts, and capital subsidies. At the same time, China's central bank should expand domestic demand, enact quantitative easing, and approve loans for key construction projects if necessary. By effectively driving investment, the investment pattern will, through necessitating change in the development model and improving the economic and social benefits of investment, become more consistent over time.

Chapter 11
Getting Rid of Misconceptions on the Deepening of SOE Reform

On August 24 2017, the Central Committee of the Communist Party of China together with the State Council issued a *Guideline to Deepen the Reform of State-owned Enterprises (SOEs)* (hereinafter referred to as the *Guideline*), marking the start of another round of reforms that were sorely needed. Since the Third Plenary Session of the 18th CPC Central Committee was held in November 2013, the implementation of the reform plan has been in provision for over two years during which key stakeholders from various facets of society have also articulated their thoughts on these reforms through various channels. As a result, many of their objective and most practical proposals have been included in the *guideline*, while those deemed factually inaccurate amended or simplified to match the core principle of this G*uideline* in order to reach a consensus, which would help steer forward the envisioned reforms.

11.1 Rectifying False Perceptions of SOE Reform

The first false perception lies in whether the transformation from "asset management at the core" to "equity management at the core" would weaken the state's mandated regulatory role. Since its establishment, the State-owned Assets Supervision and Administration Commission of the State Council (SASAC) has on behalf of the government been responsible for employee recruitment and management, any business ventures and the consolidation of assets for state-owned enterprises, a crucial role played in preserving and increasing the value of SOEs thereby accruing some great achievements. However, as SOEs are deemed independent entities, this kind of regulatory mechanism is increasingly becoming incompatible with various businesses that want to strengthen their decision-making autonomy as well as boost their competitiveness in both domestic and foreign markets. According to the laws of the

This article originally appeared in *People's Daily* on October 31, 2016.

X. Zheng, *China's 40 Years of Economic Reform and Development*,
https://doi.org/10.1007/978-981-13-2727-8_11

current system of property rights, SOEs have legal individual rights of assets they possess, including the right of use, the right of usufruct, and the right of disposal. Along with that, state-owned enterprises must also have the autonomy to invest. In particular, if their operating assets have been growing rapidly; their types of operating assets increasing, and the range of their business coverage broadly expanding. In order to boost revenue from their assets, enterprises are required to dispose of any idle or low-yielding property in time, purchase new assets that can return higher long-term profits for the business and optimize their global resource allocation through international mergers and acquisitions. Operational autonomy of state-owned enterprises is therefore a key target required to enhance their international competitiveness and improve the basic conditions in which SOEs can easily grow and expand their operations. On the other hand, SOEs cannot be given the autonomy to independently venture into the markets unless they have been evaluated based on value rather than substance. Only in this way can we really enable them to grow into independent, large and robust international corporations that can become the backbone of and play a leading role in enhancing China's overall competitiveness in the global arena. Therefore, it is necessary to adapt productivity, change from "asset management at the core" to "capital management at the core," and switch from regulating physical assets to managing capital appreciation and revenue. This should rather be viewed as optimizing and not weakening the regulatory mandate because it will not result in the loss of state-owned assets, but will instead help these enterprises grow.

The second false perception is that developing a mixed ownership economy might lead to state assets retreating and help private assets in advancing or cause state assets to advance and private assets to retreat. It should clearly be understood that developing a mixed ownership economy and encouraging cross-shareholding of state-owned capital, collective capital as well as non-public capital to form a company with diversified shareholding systems, can in fact be complementary and help achieve capital concentration, which would consequently meet the demands of different forces for business development. Equity diversification helps in forming an excellent corporate governance structure with checks and balances. In this regard, contributors have different voting rights depending on their equity while different contributors enjoy equal rights as well as a democratic decision-making process, which can facilitate scientific decision-making processes and help avoid total internal control. Internationally, equity diversification is a general developmental trend. Many large multinational corporations have both domestic shareholders and foreign shareholders and allow individuals, as well as various funds and organizations to hold shares. Many domestic firms, including listed companies, concurrently hold both state-owned or collective shares as well as private shares. Just like what the theory of hybrid vigor in Biology stands for, mixed ownership is the embodiment of this "biological" law in the economics field. Experience proves that an economy with a single ownership is to some extent fragile, and the pursuit of sole ownership is often detrimental to businesses. In comparison, a mixed ownership economy encourages all sectors to take the initiative and helps facilitate a mutual growth and development in all forms of ownership, which in turn is the fastest and most dynamic economic way to develop. The theory that "state assets will advance and private assets will retreat or state assets will retreat and private assets advance" is nothing but subject to speculation and has no credible ground. Some people even say that the development of mixed ownership is privatization in disguise, which is more confusing and unworthy of an argument.

The third false perception is that salary cuts for SOE executives means reverting back to the old path. At present, administrators of state-owned enterprises are appointed by the central administration, and the conditions for recruiting executives from the entrepreneurial market are not yet in place. Therefore, it is necessary to control the wage gap between SOE executives, civil servants and corporate employees. With the development of the entrepreneurial sector, the proportion of executives in state-owned enterprises recruited from the external market will increase. For the time being, it is mutually acceptable that the remunerations for senior administrators recruited from the external market be higher. At the same time, as state-owned businesses are morphed into mixed ownership entities, allowing these enterprises to adopt the employee shareholding system enables the technical backbone as well as management to obtain earnings from future stocks, in which case equity returns will be the main source of revenue. The employee stock ownership would enable workers to be both employees and shareholders. This in turn will not only increase their personal wages, but will also stimulate their sense of ownership thereby establishing a mid- to long-term incentives mechanism.

The fourth false perception is that the reform of state-owned enterprises might indicate another wave of lay-offs. In the 1990s, a large number of employees were retrenched during the reform process. Unfortunately, this was a price that had to be paid as a consequent of the longstanding "equal distribution" and "iron rice bowl" policies that had resulted in many redundant employees at state-owned enterprises, and so there was no better alternative than to lay them off. It should be noted that in addition to a few monopolistic industries, increased efficiency through downsizing and tackling any other challenges have in fact previously been accomplished in various competitive industries. This time however, reforms involve only monopolistic industries and a small number of industries with severe overcapacity. Amending the current industrial structure is essential and the pain that comes with it must be withstood if increased efficiency is to be achieved even if it requires downsizing as there are more jobs today than there were in the 1990s. It therefore would be easier for the government to reemploy personnel through the state reemployment and skill training program. It in fact may well be a great opportunity for the downsized employees to challenge themselves and take advantage of the acquired skills from their experience working at state-owned enterprises to establish their own businesses. Previously Chinese Premier Li Keqiang also announced that the central government will particularly allocate 100 billion yuan to aid laid-off individuals start over.

11.2 Highlighting the Importance and Urgency of Deepening SOE Reform

In recent years, President Xi Jinping has given a series of major speeches about SOE reform. In these speeches he pointed out why "state-owned enterprises, especially those owned by the central government, are in a dominant position in major industries and key areas that affect national security and economics. That is because they are the backbone of the country's economy on whose basis the Communist Party of China and the socialist system of China govern. We must therefore ensure excellency from these enterprises." In his visit to Jilin last July, President Xi Jinping also stressed that, "We should unswervingly uphold the significant position of state-owned enterprises in the development of the state, and we should also unswervingly cultivate state-owned enterprises and help them grow even stronger." These remarks underscored the importance of SOEs as well as the significance of the reforms. The term "unswervingly" was mentioned twice which highly demonstrates the Party Central Committee's determination to advance SOEs. State-owned assets are a precious treasure that many generations have been accumulating for more than 60 years, since the establishment of the People's Republic of China. These assets are thus a wealth that belongs to the 1.3 billion Chinese people. In order to improve the welfare for all Chinese citizens, state-owned assets must only increase and not decrease and it's only by running these state-owned enterprises well and acquiring more assets, can we increase their value and better serve our people.

At present, state-owned enterprises are facing stiff rivalry from both private domestic enterprises as well as rivalry from foreign multinationals that have got an upper hand when it comes to capital and technology. Hence, if state-owned enterprises are to develop and grow while facing internal and external pressures, they must deepen institutional reforms and enhance their internal capabilities. President Xi also pointed out that "promoting SOE reform should be conducive to ensure the preservation of and value increase of capital, be conducive to raising competitiveness of state-owned businesses and be conducive enough to amplify the role of state-owned capital." The three mentions of the word "conducive" emphasize the ultimate goal of the reforms. If we analyze the current state of SOEs according to these requirements, we can see that there are pressing issues and flaws that can be solved by reforms. The first issue is that some enterprises have yet to be transformed into market oriented entities, thus the efficiency of their state-owned capital is low. The second problem is that because the management of some businesses is not standardized or regulated, issues such as insider control, bribery, and loss of state-owned assets are rampant. At the same time it's a challenge to try and relieve SOEs of their obligations to operate social programs and resolve their longstanding issues. The third problem is that the organization's Party policies to govern and manage members have not been well implemented in some enterprises, thus weakening the core role of the Party regarding enterprises. These challenges have therefore seriously hindered the development of these SOEs and are thus unsuitable for the crucial role mandated to state-owned enterprises. Hence, we must strengthen a sense of urgency, accelerate the reform process and adopt targeted measures with a problem-oriented approach.

In comparison with the challenges previously encountered, it's evident that today we have access to many favorable conditions through which we can deepen reforms and cultivate state-owned enterprises. Clearly after more than three decades, most SOEs have accumulated a lot of experience, resulting in the mushrooming number of successful state-owned businesses. Accordingly we should sum up and replicate these success stories in the current process not forgetting the lessons learned from past reforms to avoid repeating the same mistakes. Looking at the external environment, the growth of the private sector has so far been the biggest transformation. Throughout the reforms and reorganization of enterprises, SOEs must therefore treat private businesses as equals and should not take a condescending attitude toward them. The shareholding structure of transformed enterprises shall thus be determined after consultations amongst relevant stakeholders as per specific scenarios. They can also moderate or simply participate in these consultations, but they cannot demand full control or consolidated financial statements. Past experiences have proven that the integration of the state-owned sector and the private sector can be beneficial because SOEs can boost their capabilities when they absorb the private economy. At the same time, the private sector can grow rapidly with the help of the platforms provided by the state-owned economy. However, let's not forget that the combination of the two sectors is not as easy as a one-plus-one equation. This round of reforms only involves the transformation and upgrading of the economy. The implementation of supply-side structural reform will require state-owned enterprises to play a key and leading role, especially in the fields of the strategic emerging industries, including those in electronic information, aerospace, biotechnology, advanced manufacturing, new energy and new materials. It's therefore crucial to cultivate a number of leading enterprises with strong innovative abilities in these fields, so that they are capable of being at the forefront of the global technological progress and draw all other industries toward the middle to high-level global industrial chain. In China, state-owned enterprises are duty-bound to take on this significant role. For a long time, central government owned enterprises have already been playing an important role in the fields of aerospace, high-speed railway, and electric power and so we should further strengthen other key areas in technology, design and assembly, global marketing, as well as expand the supply chain and logistics services to form closely related industrial clusters, through which we can reduce costs, improve quality and enhance our overall competitiveness. It is also important to note that, an advanced manufacturing industry represents a country's technological prowess and industrial capacity, most notably the capability to produce large commercial aircrafts, medium to high-end cars, space ships, CNC machining centers, engines and other high-end equipment, as well as key components and innovative materials such as chips, displays and carbon fiber. For these sectors, we need to achieve independent manufacturing and invest a lot of research and development funds and personnel into the implementation of systematic integrated and collaborative innovation. We can therefore only count on the central government-owned enterprises to accomplish such a demanding task. We need to also establish some technological innovation incentive mechanisms for SOEs, thereby impelling them to consciously adopt major technological innovations and lead their industry's technological progress. In fields such as those dealing with steel production, nonferrous metals, and building materials, SOEs just like private enterprises have a similar level of capacity, resulting in these industries being too fragmented. Through these reforms we therefore need to increase industrial concentration and create a group of large enterprises with an international edge to enhance their capacity for technological research and development as well as boost their global operations. In some monopolistic industries like the oil and chemical industries, redundancy is still a dire problem restricting the development of their businesses. Compared with their foreign counterparts, their productivity is just a mere one tenth if not lower, leading to lower inputs in R&D. As the government removes administrative approval procedures for projects in the oil and chemical industries, allowing entry of private companies into the market will encourage healthy competition between state-owned and private enterprises, which in turn could bring about rapid improvements in productivity and global competitiveness within these sectors. Heavy reliance on petrochemicals imports will also change, and the price of declining products will fall, thereby enabling Chinese citizens to enjoy the fruits of the reforms, such as low oil prices. State-owned enterprises in these industries should hence be fully prepared, as they cannot entirely rely on protection from the government any longer. Therefore they should not hesitate to undertake reforms that have similarly and successfully been time-tested in other industries, and helped increase efficiency through employee downsizing, and helped them fiercely compete against other companies in the private sector as well as the foreign multinationals.

11.3 Resolve to Innovate, Target Policies and Finish the New Round of the SOE Reform

The *Guideline* on deepening SOE reform issued by the Party Central Committee and the State Council is a highly necessary plan. We must thoroughly study it before carefully implementing it. We must formulate specific reform plans for each enterprise according to the unique settings of various industries and enterprises, and submit them to relevant departments for approval immediately after expert consultations and third-party assessments. We should strive to plan first before we act, to avoid haste. Therefore we cannot act until the reform plan has been perfected.

The state-owned assets management system is the first to undergo reformation because it is required that all state-owned asset management institutions at all levels truly change their functions from "asset management at the core" to "capital management at the core" and from managing physical matter to managing value. We need to do away with some outdated management functions and establish some new innovative ones. When assessing enterprises, we should focus more on their capacities for profit, capital appreciation, technical innovation and potential long-term development. We will inject capital into forward-looking emerging industries and innovative enterprises in accordance with the national development strategies and development policies. We will support mergers and acquisitions of enterprises, increase their research and development capabilities and boost capital investment for weak links. At the same time, we will draw up capital from industries and businesses that are withdrawing from the market. For wholly state-owned enterprises, controlling and participating state-owned enterprises, the government should perform its corresponding contributions according to the proportion of their capital contribution. For companies that are capable of operating directly as state-owned capital companies, we should give them a corresponding mandate to assist weak enterprises to grow into global corporations with cutting edge technology and strong internal capabilities. With regards to various competitive industries, public welfare industries and monopolistic industries, we will define the nature of existing SOEs and formulate differentiated reform plans. The transformation of state-owned asset management institutions sets them free from specific roles and allows them to solely focus on optimizing the allocation of state-owned capital. This is required for the autonomy of SOEs and turns them into true market players. It is also crucial to give a full play to the role of state asset management, to enhance the guiding force of a state-owned economy and amplify the significance of state-owned capital.

We should in fact highlight the establishment and improvement of modern corporate systems based on the shareholding mechanisms as the focus of these reforms. Meanwhile, the reform of state-owned enterprises has made great progress since the CPC decided at the Third Plenary Session of the 14th Central Committee to establish a modern corporate system featuring clear property rights, specific rights and responsibilities for a separate administrative group independent from the systematic management as well as proper management. However, the progress of the reform has yet to meet a point of equilibrium. Tasks for improving a modern corporate system, implementing diversified property rights and establishing a normative corporate governance structure are still a major challenge. A modern corporate system is a vital accomplishment in the race to a more modern civilization. It is a continuous summation and creation in the history of industrial development over the past two centuries, as well as for the communal wealth of the human society. In the modern corporate governance structure, the board of directors is at the core, which means it should be a highly intelligent and capable decision-making management body in that, members of the board shall be composed of individuals with rich managerial experiences and possess a broad knowledge of subjects in various fields. The board must also include a certain proportion of freelance directors, besides full-time directors. The board of directors shall set up a committee for strategy, investment, research and development, finance, remuneration, and law, and should discuss major issues that determine the day today running of businesses and shall be responsible for the board of shareholders. The board of shareholders is the highest authority of the enterprise and is responsible for the profits and losses of the company. Major investment decisions, profit distribution plans and the appointment and dismissal of the president shall be decided by the board of shareholders. Management members, which are appointed or dismissed by the board of directors, are responsible for organizing routine production and operation activities, and are answerable to the board of directors. This type of a scientific governance structure, featuring labor distribution, coordination, checks and balances, is the key to running successful enterprises. We must therefore establish such a system if we want to cultivate our own multinational companies and "century-old shops." Only in this way can we effectively avoid problems such as insider control, bribery, loss of state-owned assets and redundancy from arising. Only after the establishment of a standardized corporate system on the basis of property rights diversification, can the employee shareholding system be implemented. Members at the core and those in support roles as well as veteran staff members should hold appropriate proportions of shares in order to establish a sense of community with a shared future. Only in this way can enterprises remain prosperous for a long time. Since the previous reforms, some enterprises have implemented the employee shareholding system or even long-term incentive mechanisms. These systems have enhanced cohesion within the companies and enabled them to grow rapidly, creating successful outcomes. It's however crucial to note that, employee ownership does not necessarily mean that everyone owns equal shares neither should it become the new version of equal distribution regardless of one's contribution. Some enterprises can annually select high performing employees and reward them with stock options while some can opt to adopt a stock option system for executives. Both of which are effective incentives.

The *Guideline* was proposed to "clarify the legal status of Party memberships within the corporate governance structure of state-owned enterprises, and to innovate the way and means to highlight their role. This is our political edge. In the past, we were able to seize power using this strength, and so we could also apply the same model to run SEOs. The Party's core political role are mainly embodied in ensuring the implementation of its policies, boosting the morale of the labor force, promoting corporate innovation and development and helping businesses fulfill their social, economic, and ecological responsibilities. The Party's function therefore is mainly manifested through its exemplary and vanguard role of its members. This also explains why our military ultimately won the fight to establish the People's Republic of China because the Party was well represented in the army. In this age where we are tirelessly striving to advance our country, we should therefore continue to play the roles of the Party committee, the Party's grassroots organizations and Party members, in order to consolidate its strengths while at the same time building a modern corporate system. This way, we can surely build world-class conglomerates. That said, it's important to note that Party building and strengthening within various enterprises is not dispensable. Instead, we must uphold and encourage its growth, because it champions good values, and guarantees the building of a strong, prosperous, democratic, culturally advanced and harmonious modern socialist country.

Chapter 12
Exploring Building of New-Type Think Tanks with Chinese Characteristics

The document issued by the Third Plenary Session of the 18th Central Committee of the Communist Party of China, *Decision on Certain Major Issues concerning Comprehensively Deepening Reform* (hereinafter referred to as the *Decision*) includes the decisions to "strengthen the building of new-type think tanks with Chinese characteristics, and establish a sound decision-making consultation system." This important decision by the Party represents the first time that the development of think tanks has been elevated to the level of improving socialist democracy. The *Decision* puts forward the important task of strengthening the organization of think tanks, and clarifies the direction of work. These steps have provided a huge boost for the vast majority of people working in think tanks.

The China International Economic Exchange Center was established in March 2009 as a non-governmental think tank. From inception to overall development, the center has aimed to build itself into a world-class think tank. Driven by the principle of promoting the fundamental interests of the Chinese people, the center is committed to providing services relating to decision-making in macro economy and enterprise operations. It adheres to new ideas and systems. Relying on market mechanisms, it has made unremitting explorations in building a management system and operation model based on independent operation and financing, and has accumulated experience in building new types of think tanks with Chinese characteristics.

With a view to implementing the plan on the reform and development of think tanks from the 18th Central Committee's Third Plenary Session, and drawing on the experience of the China International Economic Exchange Center, this article aims to further the discussion on how to build a new type of think tank with Chinese characteristics.

This article originally appeared in *Globalization*, no. 3, 2014.

X. Zheng, *China's 40 Years of Economic Reform and Development*,
https://doi.org/10.1007/978-981-13-2727-8_12

12.1 The Significance of the Decision Made at the 18th Central Committee's Third Plenary Session to Build New Types of Think Tanks with Chinese Characteristics

It was in 2013 that President Xi Jinping first issued important instructions on building new types of think tanks with Chinese characteristics. These were met with an enthusiastic response from Party and government departments, especially those engaged in both policy and theoretical research. Everyone is now examining how best to implement these instructions and develop new types of Chinese think tanks. The organization of think tanks was then included in the *Decision* of the 18th Party Central Committee's Third Plenary Session, thus making the building of new types of think tanks with Chinese characteristics a major measure for comprehensively deepening reform and improving the democratic decision-making mechanism. Both President Xi Jinping's instructions and the *Decision* point to the necessity and importance of strengthening the development of think tanks in the current context.

Enhancing the development of think tanks is an essential part of modernizing the national governance system and governance capacity. This modernization effort constitutes an overall goal set by the Third Plenary Session, into which the task of building new types of think tanks is incorporated into. By changing the national management system to a national governance system, the *Decision* points out the Party's new development direction for national governance. In addition to playing the role of government, another important aspect of national governance for the Party is tapping the power of the whole of society to promote harmony, stability, civilization and progress in society. Because think tanks bring together a large amount of talent, their research in fields such as economy, politics, culture and society and suggestions on improving the quality of national governance are imbued with the wisdom of the people. Giving full play to think tanks will help to promote the modernization of the national governance system and governance capacity.

Strengthening the organization of think tanks is an objective necessary to realize scientific decision-making in complex contexts. With the acceleration of economic globalization, the economies of the world are converging and interacting with each other. Countries that want to gain an advantage amid international competition and fully grasp and get the most out of information on global economic, political and military changes in a comprehensive and timely manner, need to be able to approach changes in the international situation from the perspective of the people's interests in order to ensure the correct response. Such a task is too difficult to be accomplished by Party and government departments alone. Therefore, strengthening the organization of think tanks is an important guarantee to making timely and correct decisions and avoiding mistakes, and ensures the central government can rely on think tanks across all fields. These think tanks collect relevant information, make timely analysis and scientific judgments and provide intellectual support for the central government in decision-making.

Strengthening the organization of think tanks is an objective necessary to push forward reform, opening up and modernization in China. The Third Plenary Session set out plans to comprehensively deepen reform to address systematic problems in economics, politics, culture, society, ecology and other fields. If these tasks are to be completed within the next 7 years, we need to make a series of reform implementation plans, and manage the top-level design of reform. Making these plans will require the wisdom of think tanks. Think tanks in all fields can provide suggestions and advice on the basis of comprehensive surveys and research. Only with access to the innovative work of these think tanks, can government departments compare proposals and choose the pragmatic and viable ones, which ensures reform is implemented smoothly and delivers the expected results.

Strengthening the organization of think tanks is an important measure for improving the socialist democratic system. In the *Decision* the CPC decided to improve the socialist democratic system with Chinese characteristics. Promoting democracy is about bringing together the wisdom of people, and drawing on the suggestions and advice of experts, especially of think tanks, in order to further improve the decision-making process. Generally speaking, the opinions of experts are more representative of the long-term interests and fundamental interests of the people, and experts tend to see the true nature of issues rather than just their appearance. Therefore, paying close attention to the opinions of think tanks is a critical to improving the efficiency of democracy and the level of decision-making.

Strengthening the development of think tanks is also an objective requirement for improving the quality of Chinese think tanks. Since reform began, Party and government departments at all levels have been paying increasing attention to policy research, and have by in large all established policy research institutions. These institutions maintain close relationships with non-governmental think tanks in all fields, absorbing opinions from all aspects of society, and, in doing so, serve an important role in making decision-making more scientific. However, one of their main defects is that they are attached to Party and government organizations. As professionals who serve Party and governments leaders, their ability to think independently is severely weakened. These policy research institutions usually hold back their opinions if they believe that their conjectures are contradictory with those of leaders. They, therefore, cannot provide suggestions and advice in the same way that independent think tanks can.

12.2 Building New Types of Think Tanks with Chinese Characteristics Requires the Experiences of Developed Countries

Building new types of think tanks with Chinese characteristics is a new task for us. We should, therefore, draw on the experience of developed countries. They have already accumulated rich experience through the long-term practice of national governance.

In the United States, for example, there are more than 2800 think tanks distributed across economic, political, cultural, ecological and other fields. None of them is financially supported by the government, and they all participate in competition. Think tanks offer different solutions to major problems in national economic, social development and security. When the government is making a decision, it only needs to compare various proposals and select the best one. In this way, blind decisions and decision-making errors can be avoided. Most think tanks represent the interests of various parties, and reflect the views and demands of that party. However, there are also some that transcend partisan interests and put forward proposals that are more suitable and objective. It is the experience of these types of think tanks that we should look to learn from in building new types of think tanks with Chinese characteristics.

The Brookings Institution is a 100-year-old think tank funded by a well-known entrepreneur, who made improving the welfare of the American people its governing principle. He suggested that there are three elements to running a good think tank over the long term. The first element is to improve the quality of research results. The Brookings Institution has more than 80 researchers, each with two or three assistants. These researchers, being regarded as the institution's most valuable assets, are provided with a good working environment. The Brookings Institution is so successful because of the quality of its research, and this strategy was one of the key reasons why it was ranked first ahead of all its American counterparts in 2012. The second element is independence. Researchers need to be able to independently analyze and study problems. It is not easy for think tanks to maintain independence and objectivity in the partisan political environment of the United States. One can have insights, hold on to one's own opinions and improve the quality of research results through independent thinking. The third element is influence, which includes influence on the decision-making of governments and enterprises and public opinion. The influence of think tanks' research results is primarily reflected in the decision-making of governments. Seeing their research results from the main basis for government decision-making, or translating these results into government policies, is the most important target for think tanks in executing their functions and competing. Think tanks can also influence, guide or change public opinion through publication of their research results. While some research results are classified and only offered to certain institutions, some may be made public, and the wider these are spread, the better. In terms of evaluating American think tanks, the number of studies that are adopted by the government, the number of the studies that are quoted by in other sectors and the influence of studies on the media are the main evaluation criteria, thus encouraging think tanks to improve the level of their research and fulfill their functions.

A large number of think tanks in the United States provide consultation services to enterprises. They offer customized intelligence services for enterprises' decision-making based on forecasts of macro-economy trends and global market demands, as well as studies of the management experiences of successful enterprises. The best time for an American think tank to develop is when the United States is in economic trouble. Because this is when enterprises are seeking solutions, it provides opportunities for think tanks. An important element of the professional ethics of American companies is that they respect the work of think tanks. They do not dump them after they have learned what they want to know. When American companies go overseas for investment surveys and contract negotiations, they usually bring people from consultation firms to assist. These American companies usually advise Chinese companies that the best way to successfully invest in the US is to hire a qualified consultation firm. Spending a little money on consultation will generate much greater commercial interest. In the late 1990s, I brought a group to the United States to explore the consultation industry there. We visited all the most famous US consultation firms, after this I also wrote a book about the industry. This has made me realize that, if China's companies are to go global and become multinational, the first thing they must do is develop the consultation industry, and never pretend to understand something they do not.

Many companies in the consultation industry in developed countries tend to tie their own development to the development of enterprises. Nomura, for example, is a well-known Japanese company that specializes in providing services to help enterprises go global. The strategy that they put forward is the "double-headed eagle" strategy, which involves supporting consultation through research and driving research through consultation, and working to create symbiosis with Japanese enterprises to produce mutual benefits. In the 1970s, Nomura played an important role in promoting Japanese companies' overseas investment. Nomura not only analyzes foreign investment environments and investment opportunities and provides consulting services for enterprises making investment decisions, but also offers market trading and financing services for Japanese companies engaging in international mergers and acquisitions. Nomura has maintained close ties with global Japanese companies and has formed a community of interests with these enterprises. Nomura's "double-headed eagle" strategy is worthy of study; it can serve as a point of reference for China's consultation enterprises that are committed to providing enterprises with decision-making services.

As think tanks provide services to society in the form of intellectual work, the selection and cultivation of consultants is a matter that determines their survival. McKinsey & Company, a famous American think tank, is where Japan's famous "master of management," Mr. Ohmae Kenichi, has worked for a long time. In the 1990s, he introduced me to how talent is cultivated at the company. Its recruits are talented students from famous universities. After entering the company, new talent is trained in the same way that masters train their apprentices. After at least 7 years of teaching, assistance and instruction, they are finally able to work independently. Those working in think tanks need not only professional expertise in a certain field, but also interdisciplinary knowledge. Those in highest demand are experts who understand the needs of clients and can compile opinions from all sectors to put together a plan that best satisfies their clients.

Without financial support from the government, think tanks in developed countries need to provide high-quality research on their own merits and win the trust of their clients to earn revenue. Therefore, competition becomes the crucial law for their development. They must improve their competitiveness if they want to develop. Those that underperform will be weeded out in competition, while high-quality think tanks and researchers will stand out. Unlike China, think tanks in developed countries do not have "iron rice bowls" (fixed jobs that are financially supported by the government), but it is precisely because of this that they are able to make "golden rice bowls." As think tanks generally pay well, it is a decent job to be a think-tank researcher. The "iron rice bowl" formula that relies on financial support from the government will not give rise to a group of high-level think tanks.

12.3 Main Problems in the Development of Chinese Think Tanks

Most of the existing 3000 think tanks in China are financially supported by the government and are under no pressure for survival. The government provides a good environment and conditions for their research, but the most serious defect of these think tanks is lack of competition, which leaves little vitality for them to develop. I have been engaged in policy research for over 30 years. I worked in the research office of CPC Central Committee in 1981, and then worked in policy research offices in the State Information Center and National Planning Commission, before going to the Central Policy Research Office of the CPC Central Committee. From my own experience, the level of policy research must first be improved to strengthen competition mechanisms. Competition mechanisms should not only exist inside institutions, but also among research institutions. Therefore, it is recommended that the number of personnel affiliated to the Party and government institutions be reduced by as much as possible in order to encourage the development of non-governmental think tanks which are not financially supported by the government and rely on the market to determine their existence. The establishment of the China International Economic Exchange Center five years ago was an attempt to build a new and non-governmental think tank that wasn't supported by the government. For five years, the China International Economic Exchange Center has been exploring this path. By providing paid consultation services to the government and enterprises, establishing research funds, seeking social support for funding for research and projects and advising the government to buy services, the Center has been able to establish a virtuous cycle. Many brilliant young researchers have thrown away their "iron rice bowls" and joined the China International Economic Exchange Center consultation team, and have helped to improve the scope of research, improve the quality of research results and expand the social influence of the Center. We firmly believe that by following this path, we can contribute to the establishment of world-class think tanks.

The second serious problem for Chinese think tanks is the low recognition of IPR. Because people in China think that the outcomes of intellectual work should be provided to the government and society for free, they are not used to paying for consulting services. Therefore, the consultation market is severely underdeveloped, and the development of new types of think tanks with Chinese characteristics, especially those of non-governmental think tanks, has been hindered. We must uphold the proposals of the Third Plenary Session of the 18th Central Committee of the Communist Party of China regarding the decisive role of the market in the allocation of resources to strengthen the perception that the outcomes of intellectual work have the commercial value for exchange and recognize that the inputs of intellectual work should get reasonable returns. In this way, we can establish value compensation mechanisms for intellectual work outcomes. Put simply, we should respect the important role of consultation in improving enterprise operation capabilities and in government decision-making. We should recognize that outcomes in this regard need to be paid for, and people should be willing to pay in accordance with the value of this kind of work. This is especially true when the economy is at a crucial stage of industrial upgrading and economic transformation. Enterprises have just started to go global and make overseas investments, so giving play to think tanks including consultation in the decision-making process is a fundamental means for enterprises and governments to improve their level of decision-making. By fully developing the consultation market and strengthening competition among consultation companies, we can ensure there is a motivation to produce high-quality research results and attract more talented people to join the research consultation teams.

The third existing problem in the development of Chinese think tanks is that the degree of openness and internationalization is low. This is the result of the traditional planning system that has long been in place. The level of the research results of think tanks depends largely on their ability to absorb comprehensive global information for systematic analysis. Chinese think tanks should strengthen cooperation and personnel exchanges with famous foreign think tanks and learn from world-class think tanks. We should encourage Chinese think-tank researchers to take up positions in foreign think tanks as visiting scholars and engage in academic exchanges. At the same time, we should invite researchers of foreign think tanks to come to China for cooperation and research and absorb foreign scholars into Chinese think tanks. For issues of common concern, we can cooperate to undertake research projects and share results. We should expand the international vision of our researchers by making China's think tanks more open. The China International Economic Exchange Center has hosted the Global Think Tank Summit three times, to which famous scholars and experts from famous think tanks were invited to hold discussions with each other. This exchange of ideas has proven to be an inspiration. Mr. Henry Kissinger, the prominent expert on think tanks, delivered speeches at each of the three Global Think Tank Summits, and has helped to raise its profile. Mr. Kissinger said that all national economies are moving in the direction of globalization, but that decision-making is still dispersed. Solving this problem requires full exchange and communication among think tanks. Many colleagues proposed to build a global alliance of think tanks based on the Global Think Tank Summit and to provide intellectual support for intergovernmental cooperation through the exchange and cooperation of global think tanks. I think this is a visionary proposal.

The fourth problem for Chinese think tanks is that Party and government institutions at all levels attach differing degrees of importance to them. Some Party and government officials see their role as being of great importance and believe they can develop rapidly. Many at local level, however, still do not recognize their role and are not yet in the habit of applying the outcomes they produce to improve their work. Think tanks in their regions and institutions are far from being tapped into. Therefore, Party and government departments at all levels and enterprise administrative departments should carefully study the *Decision* and relevant plans, pay a high level of attention to the building of new types of think tanks with Chinese characteristics and give full play to them in the consultation and decision-making process. Policy research institutions set up within Party and government departments and think tanks financed by fiscal support should establish close relationships with non-governmental think tanks. Researchers in these institutions should not fall victim to the scholars' habit of scorning each other. They should provide services for government, enterprises and society through equal competition and exchange of researchers. There should be a revolving door for researchers in think tanks, non-governmental think tanks in particular, and civil servants. Excellent researchers should be employed as civil servants in Party and governmental institutions, and civil servants in these institutions should regularly engage in periods of work in think tanks to "recharge."

12.4 Building New Types of Think Tanks with Chinese Characteristics Must Include a Firm Grasp of the Right Direction

In developing new types of think tanks with Chinese characteristics, socialism with Chinese characteristics must be upheld. The theory of socialism with Chinese characteristics is a major innovation of the Communist Party of China that has been made according China's realities. It is the guiding theory of China's modernization, and the theoretical principle that must be adhered to in building new types of think tanks with Chinese characteristics. It is the fundamental guarantee for organizing successful new types of think tanks. Any left or right departure would have an adverse effect on socialism with Chinese characteristics. In the field of social science, upholding Chinese socialism is of vital importance.

In developing new types of think tanks with Chinese characteristics, we must be committed to the principle of ensuring the welfare of Chinese people. We need to study the economic, political and military issues of China and the world according to the long-term and fundamental interests of Chinese people. Think tanks across the globe all take servicing the interests of their own people and country as their primary objective. And Chinese think tanks must do the same. Sometimes, some short-term and partial interests are sacrificed for long-term and overall interests. Think tanks should aim to maximize the interests of all Chinese people and make correct judgments and provide correct advice after weighing the positives and negatives of any issue.

In organizing a new type of think tank with Chinese characteristics, we should strive to improve the ability of researchers to independently analyze and solve problems. In particular, we should focus on practical and pragmatic solutions to problems. Such proposals are more likely to be adopted by the relevant decision-making departments so that the results could be brought into effect as soon as possible. Mr. Zeng Peiyan, the president of the China International Economic Exchange Center, required that the Center set giving play to the "last kick" as its main function. This means considering all the research results of various aspects, translating these results into optional plans for decision-making in accordance with the needs of the reform and development of the economy, and submitting them to the central leadership and central departments so that they can refer to them in decision-making. The adoption of the recommendations and the degree of impact on decision-making are important measures for assessing the effects of the research. Success in these areas has enabled the China Center for International Economic Exchanges to fulfill its unique role in a very short space of time. On issues such as establishing free trade parks and ports, mobilizing the enthusiasm of commercial banks in foreign exchange lending, establishing the Asian Infrastructure Investment Bank, developing the Huai River Economic Belt and the Yellow River Ji-Chinese Character-Type Bend Economic Belt, the Center has made great contributions to decision-making.

In organizing new types of think tanks with Chinese characteristics, we must have a strong sense of social responsibility. Publishing and disseminating the results of think tanks or researchers will cause different degrees of impact on public opinion. Think tanks and researchers should have a high sense of responsibility toward society, and should work to increase positive energy instead of negative energy. Think tanks should properly guide social and international public opinion by writing important and influential articles and publishing vital research results to help the government. As think tanks provide paid service to enterprises and governments, it is normal for governments to buy the service of think tanks by paying research fees. However, a think tank cannot lose its ethics in pursuit for profit; this is something a socially responsible think tank will never do. If a think tank loses its sense of social responsibility, it will lose both the trust of people and its source of life.

Organizing new types of think tanks with Chinese characteristics is a new undertaking. It will require all kinds of think tanks to work together, to keep exploring, to improve their research and services in cooperation and competition, and to play an even more important role in China's modernization in the future.

Chapter 13
Enhancing the Systematicness, Integrality, and Cooperativity of Reforms

The CPC Central Committee's Decision on Certain Major Issues concerning Comprehensively Deepening Reform stated, "The overall objective of comprehensively deepening reforms is to develop a sound socialist system with Chinese characteristics and to promote the modernization of our governance system and governing capability. We must therefore improve the systematicness, integrality, and cooperativity of these reforms." We must also speed up "the economic, political, cultural, social, ecological civilization reforms as well as the Party building system." At this point, giving prominence to a coordinated support and systematic integration of various transformations has become a major and urgent task to amplify their effectiveness and to achieve the set goal on time.

13.1 One General Objective for These Six Major Reforms

The initiative to comprehensively deepen the reforms comprises of six key areas, i.e. the economy, politics, culture, society, ecological civilization and a Party building system. Although each reform is mandated with its own different tasks and requirements, they all have one general objective. Therefore in the process of formulating every reform plan and pushing it forward, we ought to set our eyes on the overall goal of developing a sound socialist system with Chinese characteristics, realizing a state governing system and modernizing our governance capacity. The establishment of such a general objective must therefore be defined at the starting point and follow the fundamental purpose of these reforms.

This socialist system with Chinese characteristics chosen by the CPC is the right path to be followed in its quest to achieve its long-term practices of the industrial revolution and development. This is also in the common interest of 1.3 billion people

---

This article originally appeared abridged in *People's Daily*, February 2, 2018.

X. Zheng, *China's 40 Years of Economic Reform and Development*,
https://doi.org/10.1007/978-981-13-2727-8_13

all across the country. A large number of facts both at home and abroad have proven that it is only by taking the socialist path with Chinese characteristics that China can quickly lift itself out of poverty and enable its citizens to lead a moderately prosperous life.

The system design of socialism with Chinese characteristics begins firstly with the fact that China is still in the primary stages of achieving this range of economic and social systems, in order to be able to mobilize all the elements that develop productivity and accelerate the building of the material base of socialism while establishing relationships of production. Meanwhile, these relationships must also be aligned with this material base of socialism in combination with a superstructure that is in sync with such relationships of production. Therefore, these reforms inevitably involve economic, political, cultural and social issues. The all-around deployment made by the Third Plenary Session of the 18th CPC Central Committee on six major reforms revolves around the goal of perfecting and developing a socialist system with Chinese characteristics. Our reform practices should, under no circumstances, deviate from this overall goal. Over the past 39 years of reform and opening up, China has created an economic miracle that caught the attention of the world, fully proved the vitality of a socialist system with Chinese characteristics and improved our confidence in the path and theory that we have chosen. By comprehensively deepening the reforms and developing a well-structured, efficiently-regulated and effectively-run institutional system, our institutional infrastructure will soon become more mature and more solid to further stimulate vitality and growth. Making it possible for a moderately prosperous society to take shape by 2020 and GDP per capita to reach the level of the medium-developed countries by mid this century. With the Chinese Dream becoming a reality, the advantages of a socialist system with Chinese characteristics will soon get better understood and appreciated by the outside world.

Promoting modernization of the governance system and capacity is also needed to transform the institutional advantages into competencies within the national administration, social administration, economic development and international competition. Therefore this is an opportunity for all to excel and create a legislative environment supporting education, social security, health and employment. It would also make China a prosperous, democratic, culturally advanced, harmonious and beautiful country. This however can only be true if the socialist system with Chinese characteristics is integrated into the process of modernizing the country's governance system and governing capacity so that the institutional advantages can be brought into full play. Governance can be in the form of national administration, the rule of law, virtue, regional autonomy, community-based autonomy and shared governance, etc., enabling a universal-covering, diversified, multi-tiered governance system that is comprehensive and efficient. To achieve this, the country's governance efficiency and governing capacity should be improved through the marketization of China's economy, the legalization of society, the democratization of politics, the transparency of power and the mechanism of supervision and restriction. In terms of the governing bodies, we should give full play to the role of the government, people's congresses, political consultative conferences, democratic parties, mass organizations, social groups, enterprises and institutions, and think tanks at all levels while upholding CPC's leadership, engaging with the general public in running the country to form a concerted effort of governance. In terms of governance methods, it is necessary to make an extensive use of information networks and intelligent platforms in order to establish a unified command, monitoring and early warning systems that can respond to requests for information as well as handle emergency situations. The modernization of the country's governance system and governing capacity should also be at the heart of these major reforms, which requires that tangible systems be established and integrated to form a sophisticated, comprehensive, efficient and highly functional governance infrastructure together with mechanisms for running the country and ensuring peace, stability and wellbeing.

13.2 Six Major Reforms as One Enormous and Structured Social Project

These six reforms, as one huge project with complex-structured and interrelated components, cover all aspects of the country's governance system and constitute a complete social framework. All reforms are mutually reinforcing and counterbalance each other. It's only through coordinated and concerted efforts can the effectiveness of the system and results be achieved. It therefore is imperative to follow the ideology of managing state affairs and the administration created by Xi Jinping to maintain the big-picture, carefully deploy and effectively coordinate in order to make these reforms successful.

The transformation of the economic system is the focus of the overall reforms. All other reforms, after all, are just about improving productivity and providing a strong foundation. In accordance with historical materialism, where productive forces determine relations of production and the economic base determines the superstructure, it's important that while designing political, cultural, social, ecological and Party building systems, the level of productivity should be taken into account and these systems be aligned with the economic reforms to resolve issues that cannot be solved by the economic system alone and boost productivity. For example, market competition is an important driving force behind productivity. However, the market can be blind, resulting in widened income gaps and a lack of social justice. This is where the political, social and cultural systems step in and restore order, balance efficiency and fairness, and raise the moral standards and quality of the nation. Economic development is like swimming against the tide. In the initial stages of socialism, we must always adhere to the principle that economic development is the main goal and stick to it using development as the key to solving all problems. An unswerving and unremitting commitment to economic development should therefore be maintained. The core issue of the economic reform is to address the relationship between the government and the market. By deepening this reform, a comprehensive set of systems should be established to allow the market to play a decisive role in allocating resources and enable the government to function effectively. In addition, the mechanisms for motivating and balancing economic development should be in place to ensure the economy continues to grow in a sustainable and healthy manner.

Political reforms are critical to where society is headed. Things go wrong when the country is going in the wrong direction. We must therefore ensure that reforms and development stay on the right track of socialism with Chinese characteristics through the transformation of the political system. A strong commitment to, the people's congress system, CPC-led multiparty cooperation and political consultation, regional ethnic autonomy system and grassroots self-governance system is a must. We should also stick to the idea of running the country and managing administrative affairs according to the law. We should also strengthen our socialist democratic system to allow different forms of democracies and promote public engagements at all levels. With regards to major policy decisions and reform programs concerning the interests of the general public, the voice of the masses should be heard, to ensure democratic rights of our people.

Culture is the spiritual pillar of the Chinese nation that underpins national cohesion and provides a powerful driving force for reform and development. We should therefore upgrade our cultural management and production systems. In addition to carrying forward our traditional culture, we should also nourish a socialist culture with the characteristics of the times and ethos rooted in the core values of our people and create literary and artworks that reflect the great practices of the reforms and opening up. Needless to say, fixing such problems as money worshipping and extravagance that market behaviors tend to breed with a positive energy of culture and morality is also integral to this goal. A modern public cultural service system and modern cultural market systems should therefore be developed. Cultural exchanges and trade with foreign countries should be promoted to learn from the cultural achievements of the outside world. Our soft power in foreign economic cooperation should also be bolstered by building up a cultural influence and awareness around the world.

Social development is the ultimate goal of economic development and the social management system is the stabilizer of a country and its society. Therefore the vitality of social development will be boosted by the reform of the social system if we fix the issue of social development lagging behind economic development. By reforming the distribution system, income inequality—a problem that the capitalist system has failed to fix—will be tackled and we will be able to allow our people to benefit from these transformations and developmental achievements. We should hence focus on improving our social management capabilities in modernizing the country's governance system and governing capacity. The equal access to public services between urban and rural areas and between different regions can also be achieved through fiscal equalization and solving the problem of inequality for basic rights affecting all citizens. Therefore transforming the medical, education and social security systems and encouraging the role of private investment will ensure that these mechanisms meet the growing needs of our people amidst the potential population shift. Educational equity could also improve employment and national quality standards, which will, in turn, contribute to social equity.

It is a common desire among Chinese people to make their country more attractive. The ecological reform will thus result in the right concepts, systems, laws and market mechanisms for ecological management and environmental protection that can deliver on the promises of our government on clean air and water. The perception that environmental management will hold back economic development should be ignored and green businesses promoted to facilitate an ecological management system.

Reforming the Party building system and maintaining the Party's advanced nature and purity are the political guarantees for reform and opening up. Democratic centralism, party leadership and the ruling paradigm should be improved in accordance with the law in a more rational and democratic manner. The CPC's leadership in comprehensively deepening the reforms will be strengthened and promoted, with the party committees at all levels—providing guidance and playing a key role in coordinating our efforts. We must strengthen our leading bodies and grassroots Party organizations, deepen the reforms of the personnel system, maximize the consensus on reforms, mobilize all positive factors, and form a synergy of reforms.

These six major reforms are therefore the key components of the overall project, with each taking a unique position and playing a unique role. When formulating the reform program, in addition to the unique nature of each reform, the correlation with other key transformations must be taken into account to make sure all efforts are coordinated, complemented and integrated. The success of deepening these reforms will thus only be possible through a systematic integration and joint efforts.

13.3 Challenges Facing the Six Major Reforms

These reforms are now in a critical stage with each of them facing some tough issues. We must therefore rise to the challenge, instead of running away from our problems. This requires us to look into each problem closely and come up with a range of possible solutions. After careful comparison, we will then select the best possible solution with maximum benefits and minimum costs before acting decisively.

The biggest difficulty of reform is handling the relationship between equity and efficiency. Since the policy of reform and opening up was introduced, we have placed slightly more emphasis on efficiency. But, from now on, we need to place more emphasis on equity. The main reason for the widening income gap is not income from labor but from property. It has been calculated that property income accounts for 60% of the disparity in individual incomes. Indeed, one of the main reasons for the large disparity in urban and rural incomes is the commercialization of urban housing, which has had a prominent wealth effect, whereas rural housing is regulated so that it can only be sold to people who live locally. It has, therefore, not been properly commercialized. General Secretary Xi Jinping stated the Party's intention to "equalize the basic rights and interests of urban and rural residents." As the current system has led to unequal housing rights and interests between urban and rural residents, it is in need of reform. In addition to this, developing joint-stock cooperative enterprises and allowing employees of mixed-ownership enterprises to hold shares have become major sources of property income, so restructuring and development should be encouraged. Huawei, for example, has 170,000 employees, of which more than 70,000 hold shares. The ratio of shares allotted to labor and those allotted to capital is 3:1. This shareholding structure and allotment ratio has boosted the enthusiasm of the workforce, as employees with shares have become the real owners of the company and increased their property income. The trailblazing significance of Huawei's approach lies in the fact that it has made its employees equity stakeholders as well as its optimal allotment ratio, which resolves the basic contradiction of capitalism identified by Marx in *Das Kapital* concerning the extraction of surplus value from labor. This breakthrough was only possible under socialism with Chinese characteristics. In accordance with the Decision of the Third Plenary Session on deepening enterprise reform, more employees will be allowed to become capital owners, which will become an important way to achieve greater efficiency and focus on equity.

Handling the relationship between government and the market is another difficulty when comprehensively advancing reform. The biggest obstacle to deciding whether to let the market play the decisive role in allocating resources is the difference in developmental levels between urban and rural areas. Urban factors of production have become market-based, but rural factors of production have not, or at least not fully. According to the rules of commodity profitability, it always flows toward places that are highly market-based and with high prices. As such, there is a siphon effect from rural to urban markets, with rural labor, capital, land and other factors of production flooding cities. There is no flow of factors of production from cities to the countryside, however, which is a fundamental reason for the widening urban-rural development gap.

For the market to play a decisive role in allocating resources, the first step is to break down barriers between urban and rural markets to allow idle capital to flow from cities to the countryside. The Third Plenary Session clearly proposed that rural property should be able to be mortgaged, secured or transferred, but this is yet to be implemented. Allowing the movement of urban capital to rural areas is critical to comprehensively advance reform. Other issues that need to be addressed to comprehensively advance reform include handling the relationships between public welfare and for-profit cultural products and between decision-making by businesses and the leadership of the Party. We should summarize the successful experiences of relevant parties at the community level, boldly explore innovations and have the courage to tackle prominent issues in order to take a significant step forward in our reform efforts.

13.4 Six Major Reforms to Tap Huge Development Potential

Although China's total economic output ranks second in the world, its per capita GDP ranks only 89th, indicating huge potential for further economic development. The most important thing is to release that growth potential through further reform. Moreover, it is hard to overcome the difficulties in reform by one means alone, so adopting six major reforms will help us to overcome any issues.

First, it is necessary to use a combination of urban and rural reforms to tap the huge development potential of rural areas. Accelerating agricultural modernization, building a new countryside, giving migrant workers urban residency permits and constructing characterful small towns will provide powerful new momentum for long-term sustainable economic growth. We must utilize the political advantages of the CPC and the institutional advantages of our social system, rouse the public to pay attention to and support rural reform and development, and show solicitude for the vital interests of migrant workers so as to create a powerful cohesive force for promoting integrated urban and rural reforms.

Reform of the economic system should focus on establishing an integrated development system for urban and rural areas. The cultural system should place more emphasis on the basic rights and interests of people in rural areas and encourage them to lift themselves out of poverty. A central task of our social system should be to achieve parity of public services for urban and rural residents. We need our ecological system to identify effective methods of controlling non-point source pollution on rural land and to solve issues relating to rural garbage disposal and environmental sanitation. The system for Party building should pay particular attention to developing rural community-level Party branches and training rural Party members to become experts and experts to become Party members. The combination of these various reforms will help achieve major breakthroughs in the integrated reform and development of urban and rural areas.

We need to focus on reforming the investment system to make up for deficiencies in the supply of public goods. There is a supply shortage of public products in such areas as the environment, education, health, social security, pensions, transport, IT and culture, and there is a lack of suitable investment projects for available funds. We should, therefore, encourage public-private partnerships to guide non-governmental capital and bank financing toward causes that increase the supply of public goods.

We also need to focus on reforming the education system for science and technology to stimulate technological innovation. Reforms in this area have yielded pleasing results, but we need greater effort, with an emphasis on solving the imbalance in the degree of attention. In particular, cities, state-owned enterprises and universities where scientific and technological innovations are concentrated need to adopt reforms to create incentive mechanisms, cultural atmospheres and social environments conducive to technological innovation so as to make it a genuine new driving force of development.

Part II
The Development Pattern

Chapter 14
Transforming the Development Pattern Is the Fundamental Approach for Dealing with the Crisis

To deal with the international financial crisis, the central government has decisively taken a series of measures, which have achieved initial success. With central-budgeted investment playing an important role in driving bank loans, social investment and resident consumption, the continued decline of economic growth since the second half of 2008 has essentially been arrested. However, the situation remains daunting. In recent years, China's gross export volume has approached that of domestic gross retail sales of consumer goods. Under such circumstances, exports have plummeted drastically from annual growth rates of about 20% over the past few years to a point where it has become tremendously difficult to reach annual growth targets. It is expected that the economies of developed countries will find it very difficult to recover this year, and that China's export volume for the year will drop by a further 5–10%. Therefore, in addition to stabilizing exports, the other key to achieving this year's goals lies in ensuring an expansion in domestic demand offsets the negative impact of the decrease in exports. Moreover, whether changes in the development pattern can be achieved will determine if domestic demand expansion policies will have a role to play over both the short and long term and if financial support and policies will be able to sustain their efficiency. In other words, only by making breakthroughs in the policy of transforming our development pattern, can we translate pressure into impetus and challenges into opportunities, and fundamentally respond to the international financial crisis to maintain the momentum of steady and rapid economic growth in 2009 and for years to come.

This article originally appeared in *People's Daily*, June 15, 2009.

X. Zheng, *China's 40 Years of Economic Reform and Development*,
https://doi.org/10.1007/978-981-13-2727-8_14

14.1 Adjust the Demand Structure by Enhancing the Role of Consumption in Boosting Economic Growth

To Transform the development pattern was a major strategy put forward at the 17th CPC National Congress, and it represents a fundamental approach for implementing the Theory of Balanced and Sustainable Development. This transformation primarily involves adjusting the demand structure, implementing domestic demand expansion policies, especially those related to consumption, and transforming the economic development pattern from being mainly investment and export driven to being driven by consumption, investment and export in a coordinated fashion. The idea is to address the severe imbalance between consumption and investment and between domestic demand and demand for imports. The dramatic drop in exports due to the international financial crisis has been the source of the great urgency for this transformation.

Excessively low consumption rates and excessively high investment rates have been the salient features of imbalanced economic growth in China. In 2007, the consumption rate stood at 35.4%, which is a 17% decrease from the record high of 52% in 1985, and about 30% lower than that of developed countries. In contrast to the low consumption rates, the investment rate from 2003 to 2007 reached 42.4% on an average annual basis, the highest in history. In particular, industries like steel, cement, electrolytic aluminum and real estate saw excessively fast growth, which led to overcapacity. If the consumption market is not expanded accordingly, then we will face a pattern of increasing ineffective investment and bad debt, which will make sustained, steady and relatively fast growth difficult to achieve. Intensifying trade conflicts, a growing trade surplus and disequilibrium in the balance of payments resulting from years of soaring exports have also influenced macroeconomic stability. Overreliance on investment and exports, low consumption contribution rates and mass idle production capacity have become major constraints hindering fast and sustainable growth.

Therefore, the current tasks of macro regulation are to increase consumption rates, lower investment rates and enhance the effect of consumption in boosting growth. First, we should adjust the income distribution structure and focus on increasing the incomes of those in the low- and middle-income groups, especially farmers. Second, we need to expand the scope of consumption, transform consumption from being survival-oriented to development- and utility-oriented. We need to actively cultivate new areas of consumption and meet various levels of demand. Third, we need to expand consumption credit and improve the social security system. We should establish and improve the credit investigation system for individual consumption and optimize the consumption credit market, expedite education and health system reform to alleviate education and medical care burdens, increase the coverage of pension insurance, employment injury insurance and unemployment insurance, and expedite a resolution for the transfer and continuation of rural migrant workers' insurance accounts. Fourth, we must adjust the investment structure so it moves in line with the requirements for upgrading the consumption structure, and improve the consumption environment. We should accelerate construction of a modern comprehensive transportation system with railways as the primary focus, strengthen cultural and tourism infrastructure, move faster to roll out new-generation Internet and facilitate tri-network integration (telecoms, radio and TV, and Internet networks); increase the prevalence of tap water, improve power grids and accelerate road construction in rural areas and provide a greater variety of fiscal subsidies for rural home appliances. Fifth, we should develop the housing, automobile and stock markets as joint strategic priorities for consumption expansion. The housing and car markets are to a certain extent influenced by the stock market. To maintain stable and healthy development of the stock market, gross supply and demand should be adjusted to avoid severe fluctuations, while fundamental systems should be strengthened. Likewise, just as a stable and prosperous capital market can underpin the sustained prosperity of the housing and car markets, the housing and car industries can also become pillars for long-term economic growth. If multiple measures are taken to increase the resident income/GDP ratio and consumption rate by 10 and 15% to 55 and 50%, respectively, within three years (with the highest levels approaching 56 and 52% in 1985), then over 5 trillion yuan worth of commodities would be converted annually from investment and export to consumption, which would improve the economic structure and markedly elevate living standards. These are critical measures and fundamental objectives for carrying out human-oriented and balanced and sustainable development.

14.2 Adjust the Industrial Structure by Developing the Tertiary Industry

The second transformation is to bring an end to over-reliance on the secondary industry for economic growth. To do this we need to accelerate development of the tertiary industry and achieve coordination between the primary, secondary and tertiary industries. An underdeveloped tertiary industry is a pronounced problem in the industrial structure. In 2008, the share of value added of the tertiary industry in GDP was only 40.1%, and the share of total employees was 33.2%. Both figures are lower than those of developed countries and are even lower than the average levels in developing countries. An underdeveloped tertiary industry has led to severe conflicts in employment and has impeded economic growth.

The tertiary industry is lagging behind in three areas: The first is in production service industries such as R&D and logistics. In developed countries, technological R&D is made up of technical advancement service systems, including IPR, human resources, information, venture capital and technology training markets which provide comprehensive services for corporate R&D. Despite the relatively fast development of the technology market in China, there is still a large gap in meeting the demands of enterprises, and we have a long way to go in building an innovative country. The backwardness of the logistics industry is marked by a low degree of specialization and low participation of social sectors, problems which have resulted in high costs. In developed countries, circulation costs generally account for less than 10% of GDP, while in China this figure is as high as 18%. Transporting the same goods from Chengdu in Southwest China to Shanghai in East China is more expensive than transporting them from Hamburg, Germany to Shanghai. Urgent tasks for the government include providing support to strengthen the logistics industry, setting up cross-border and cross-regional modern logistic systems, establishing a group of logistics hubs and developing logistics enterprises. Second, China lags behind in the modern service industry. Developed countries boast well-established intermediary service organizations in accounting, auditing, law, consulting, supervision, credit investigation, certification, price evaluation, and bidding & tendering with large numbers of employees. These organizations have taking on government functions in many areas and play a critical role in building orderly markets and ensuring fair competition. The sudden shut-down of Lehman Brothers, which had an A+ credit score, was a major event that exacerbated the financial crisis in the US, and was the result of an absence of supervision and professional ethics among credit rating agencies. Taking this as an example of what not to do, we should break our delusions regarding overseas intermediary agencies, accelerate the building of a modern market intermediary service system and provide quality services to customers both at home and abroad. Third, China lags behind in the community service industry. In developed countries, community service provision represents an important sector for absorbing labor, as it covers a wide range of areas, including education, health care, housekeeping, sports, exercising and psychological counseling. The community service industry in China is just getting off the ground, and many services are still not available to residents. By developing this sector, we can overcome the difficulties brought on by surplus labor resources. At present, a number of cities have built well-developed communities with outstanding community workers, which have contributed greatly to solving the unemployment issue and building a harmonious society.

14.3 Optimize Structures for Key Factors by Promoting Industrial Enhancements Based on Self-innovation

The third transformation is to shift the economic growth mode from relying mainly on resource consumption to relying on S&T progress, workforce quality improvements and management innovation. Some regions and enterprises have are still experiencing a boom in business in spite of the negative impact of the international financial crisis. The secret to this has been the value they have placed on technological R&D inputs, their development of proprietary IPR and brands, and their greater market competitiveness and share both at home and abroad. One example of this is Shenzhen, which has maintained strong momentum in development despite a nationwide slowdown in economic growth. It has been able to do so because it has spent many years establishing an environment that incentivizes technological R&D, cultivating a group of high-tech enterprises, and transforming from overseas-funded enterprises to domestically-funded high-tech enterprises being dominant and from processing to general trade being dominant. Shenzhen has on the basis of innovation blazed a trail in industrial upgrading. Another example is Huawei, whose annual R&D input accounted for 10% of sales revenue and its R&D staff account for about half of total employees. In 2008 its international patent applications ranked first among global enterprises, and its contract sales jumped by over 40%. Many Chinese cities enjoy even higher-quality S&T resources than Shenzhen and many enterprises, especially large SOEs, boast even greater S&T resources than Huawei. As long as mechanisms for technological advancement similar to those of Shenzhen and Huawei are employed, and the knowledge of technicians is fully utilized, then new development space can be opened up.

To advance innovation, there must a high degree of emphasis given to cultivating management and innovation talent. Management and technology represent the engines of economic growth. According to the requirements of international business operations and competition, we should work to improve operations and management, and develop new management systems and mechanisms. Universities should attach more importance to developing innovative talent and enterprises should set up teams for technical innovation, so as to build sound platforms for invention and creation.

14.4 Create Export Demand and Strive to Curb Export Decline

To respond to the economic downturn and declining export demand in developed countries, we need to adopt effective measures, stabilize and expand export demand through multiple channels, work to reverse the downward trend in exports as soon as possible, and relieve the pressure on economic growth and employment.

Because of our advantages resulting from adequate foreign exchange reserves and overcapacity, we can create export demand by exporting capital. The first thing we need to do is to drive equipment and service exports by expanding overseas energy and resource investments. We should encourage large enterprises and SMEs to "go global" to obtain more energy and resource exploitation and development rights. By boosting overseas investment, China can increase its geological prospecting equipment, resource development equipment and technical service exports. This will also help to meet our demand for more energy and resources. Second, we need to increase the export of related goods and labor services by expanding governmental foreign aid loans. Infrastructure is underdeveloped, and energy supplies inefficient in some developing countries, especially those in Asia, Africa and Latin America. If greater loan assistance could be properly provided to these countries and bilateral currency swaps could be increased, our exports would be greatly boosted. Third, we should promote the export of domestic components and raw materials by encouraging processing trade enterprises to go global. Our manufacturing industry, especially the light, textile, and auto industries, are capable of setting up factories in other countries. We can effectively boost exports through overseas investment just as foreign investors have been developing processing trade in our country through the "three processing and one compensation" method. Fourth, we should expand foreign dealers' imports of Chinese products by offering RMB loans. The international financial crisis has hit foreign financial institutions hard, and many dealers in Chinese products have reduced imports due to a lack of liquid capital. Encouraging Chinese banks to offer RMB loans to those dealers while controlling risks would help to support our exports. Finally, we must expand exports of mechanical and electrical products such as power equipment, engineering machinery, machine tools, ship and textile equipment by increasing credit for buyers. Although they are internationally competitive and hold comparative advantages, our mechanical and electrical industries are to a certain extent under pressure from overcapacity. This provides enterprises with an incentive to expand exports. Supporting expanded exports through buyers' credit can help curb the decline in exports.

Chapter 15
Taking Measures to Increase the Share of Resident Income in GDP

The political report to the 17th CPC National Congress report aims to transform the development pattern by shifting China's growth model from reliance on investments and exports to consumption, investments, and exports. In the context of the global economic crisis and a slowdown in export growth, China has been implementing policies to expand domestic demand, with an emphasis on consumption, to turn crisis into opportunity and sustain steady and rapid growth.

The excessively low consumption rate is very unfavorable in the economy. In 2007, the country's consumption rate stood at 35.4%, the lowest it has been since the start of reform and opening up three decades ago, and 17% lower than the historical high of 52% in 1985, and about 30% lower than developed economies. The low consumption rate will have a serious negative impact on the health of the economy. First, the standard of living for most people cannot rise along with the rapid economic growth, which reduces the macro benefits of the economy. Second, excessive reliance on investments and exports has resulted in overcapacity. China's investment rate reached an annual average of 42.4% between the years of 2003 and 2007, the highest in history. From 2001 to 2007, the contribution rates of three types of demands of consumption, investments, and net exports to the nation's economic growth reached on average 40.6, 48.4, and 11.1%, respectively. The consumption contribution rate was markedly low and a great deal of industrial production capacity has remained underutilized. Consumption had severely constrained economic growth. Third, the continual increase in the proportion of government expenditures has led to extravagance and waste of resources. In the last consumption expenditure, government expenditures increased from 21.6% in the 1980s to 27.3% in 2007.

There are two main reasons behind the excessively low consumption rate.

First, increases in urban and rural resident income have long lagged behind the growth rate, thus resulting in the constant decrease of its share in GDP. Over the three

---

This article originally appeared in the *Journal of the Chinese People's Political Consultative Conference,* July 27, 2009.

X. Zheng, *China's 40 Years of Economic Reform and Development*,
https://doi.org/10.1007/978-981-13-2727-8_15

decades from 1978 to 2007, the annual average increase of GDP reached 9.8% and that of resident income reached 7%. In 2007, the share of urban and rural resident income in GDP decreased to a historical low of 45, 11% lower than the highest level of 56% in 1985.

Second, the growing income gap between urban and rural areas, between regions and between some individuals has constrained the purchasing power of low- and middle-income people. The ratio of urban to rural income expanded from its lowest of 1.9:1 in 1985 to 3.3:1 in 2007. Consumer good retail sales at or below county levels in the gross amount dropped from 67.6% in 1978 to 32.3% in 2007. In 2005, the urban resident income ratio of the eastern, middle, western, and northeastern regions was 1: 0.64: 0.65: 0.64, respectively, and that of rural residents reached 1: 0.65: 0.59: 0.93, respectively. The share of employee salaries in GDP at the national level decreased from its highest of 17% in 1980 to 11% in 2007, and 65% of employee salaries were lower than the national average. The social income distribution, the Gini coefficient, exceeded 0.43, propelling China into the ranks of countries with a relatively large income disparity.

In order to enhance the role of consumption in boosting economic growth and reverse the internal trend toward imbalance between consumption and investments, China has to adopt major measures to increase the share of resident income in GDP as well as increase the consumption rate.

It was suggested that a special project of "double increase" be put in place, namely increasing the share of resident income in GDP from 10 to 55% and increasing the consumption rate from 15 to 50% within three years, respectively approaching the highest levels of 56 and 52% in 1985 since China's reform and opening up. If that goal can be achieved, then each year over 5 trillion yuan worth of products will be available for consumption rather than investments and exports. As a result, living standards will increase dramatically, the human-oriented Theory of Balanced and Sustainable Development can be implemented, and the development pattern transformation of expanding domestic demand, especially consumption, can be truly realized.

To this end, the following policy measures are adopted:

(1) Adjust the income distribution structure, increase the income of low- and middle-income people, especially that of farmers, increase the remuneration for labor, and lower capital income through such adjustment leverages as budget and taxation in the initial distribution; increase resident income and decrease state revenue in the redistribution; and reduce the tax burden on low- and middle-income people, and allocate a certain proportion of SOEs' profits for the social security fund.
(2) Broaden the scope of consumption and facilitate upgrades in the consumption structure; and transform consumption from being survival-oriented to being development- and utility-oriented.
(3) Expand consumer credit and improve social security systems; accelerate education and health care reform, increase government input and encourage investment from social sectors; and expand coverage of insurance schemes, such as pension, occupational injury, and unemployment.

(4) Adjust the investment structure and improve the consumption environment.
(5) Regulate the market order and protect consumers' rights.
6) Reasonably guide consumption expectations and advocate healthy consumption.
(7) Facilitate the sustained and healthy development of the housing, auto, and stock markets.

Chapter 16
Enhancing the Role of Consumption in Boosting Economic Growth

Consumption is associated with ensuring the 8% growth rate in 2009, the steady and rapid development in the period to come, the transformation of the development pattern adopted at the 17th CPC National Congress, and the realization of the Theory of Balanced and Sustainable Development.

Consumption is the goal of production and the ending and starting points for the social production process. People have a strong desire to develop productivity, so as to constantly improve their consumption levels. Nowadays, scientific and technological progress has greatly increased labor productivity, which helps translate the desire for consumption into reality. During the planned economy period in an agricultural society, consumption was constrained mainly by supply capacity. However, since learning to manufacture various products through developing modern industry and establishing a socialist market economy system, a major constraint on consumption growth has been the consumption demand of people with the capacity to pay.

Over the past 30 years, China's reform and opening up has greatly aroused people's enthusiasm for labor, thus bringing about strong modern production capacity. However, the inadequate consumption demands of residents are seriously impeding economic growth. Among the three transformations of the development pattern adopted at the 17th CPC National Congress, the first is to enhance the role of consumption in boosting economic growth and realize the transformation from reliance on investments and exports to greater coordination among consumption, investments, and exports. In the context of the global economic crisis and stalled export growth in China, the expansion of domestic demand, especially resident consumption, is of great significance in transforming crisis into opportunity and sustaining steady and rapid economic growth.

This article originally appeared in *Money China*, no. 9, 2009.

X. Zheng, *China's 40 Years of Economic Reform and Development*,
https://doi.org/10.1007/978-981-13-2727-8_16

16.1 The Excessively Low Resident Consumption Rate Is Very Unfavorable in the Current Economy

In 2007, the resident consumption rate in China dropped to 35.4%, and the rate in 2008 was even lower than the 2007 level of 35.4%, the lowest point in the past 30 years since reform and opening up began. In 2007, China's GDP stood at 30 trillion yuan, among which, civilian consumption accounted for slightly over 30%. This low proportion was 17% lower than its level of 52% in 1985 and 30% lower than developed countries. This is such an unfavorable parameter among all macroeconomic parameters that China will need to attach greater importance to it.

1. *The low resident consumption rate will create a serious negative impact on the operations of the economy*

First, the living standards of the vast resident population cannot rise with the rapid economic growth, which reduces the macro benefits of the economy. Consumption is an important indicator of macroeconomic benefits. Because the nation was anxious for quick economic success and understanding of the theory of giving top priority to the growth of the means of production during the 30 years prior to the nation's reform and opening up was lopsided, people's living standards failed to improve for quite a long period of time. During the early 1980s, China changed its policies, established the "six priorities" policy in the light and textile industries, and lowered the excessively high investment rate. As a result, the 1980s saw the greatest economic return, and 1985 saw the resident consumption rate reach 52%, which is the highest level since the nation's reform and opening up. However, following the rapid development of heavy industry in 2003, both the final consumption rate and resident consumption rate have witnessed consecutive years of decline, and decreased by 13 and 14%, respectively, in 2007 compared to the level at the beginning of the nation's reform and opening up in 1978.

Second, over-reliance on investments and exports for economic growth has resulted in overcapacity. Along with the low consumption rates came excessively high investment rates and saving rates, and thus economic growth is too reliant on investments and exports. In particular, industries such as steel, cement, and real estate have seen rapid growth in recent years. China's steel production capacity now stands at 650 million tons. How does that compare with the world? The total world capacity is 1.3 billion tons, and China accounts for just half of the world's steel production capacity. In 2007, China produced 500 million tons of steel, and 150 million tons of production capacity remains un-utilized. Moreover, a great deal of manufacturing capacity has not been utilized and the operation rate is still low. All these factors have reduced the efficiency of the economy.

Third, the constantly increasing share of government expenditures has led to extravagance and waste of resources. In the last consumption expenditure, Government expenditures reached 21.6% in the 1980s, 24.2% in the 1990s, 26.8% between 2001 and 2006, and 27.3% in 2007, which is the highest level since the nation's reform and opening up. The large share of government expenditures further curbed resident consumption demand.

2. *Owing to the many reasons for the low resident consumption rate, China needs to analyze from a holistic perspective to discover the root causes*

First, the growth of urban and rural resident income cannot keep up with that of the economy, which is the fundamental constraint on the consumption increase. Over the past 30 years, urban and rural resident incomes have not been growing along with the economic growth; therefore, the consumption demand of those able to pay cannot increase with the economic growth. This is one of the fundamental reasons for the excessively low resident consumption rate. To put it simply, people do not have the money to buy what they want.

Second, the income gap between urban and rural areas, between regions, and between residents has enlarged, curbing the purchasing power of low- and middle-income people. The share of resident income in GDP has continually decreased over the past three decades. Rural net income accounted for only 30% of urban income. The decrease in the rural population over the past 30 years is due to the over 200 million people who have moved out of rural areas. However, there is still a rural population of 700 million people who buy one fifth of the commodities, while the urban population buys the other four fifths of them. In terms of the urban rural resident income ratio, eastern China is the highest, followed by the northeastern region, the middle region, and the western region. The ratio between the rural per capita income in the west and that in the east is 0.59:1.

Third, calculations show that overseas-funded enterprises have used various means to transfer the majority of their profits, resulting in low employee income and state tax revenue. Foreign capital has contributed a great deal to China's economic growth, accounting for 30% of industrial added value, 58% of exports, and 88% of high-tech exports. Take Huawei and a overseas-funded one for instance. Regarding sales volume, Huawei reached 70 billion yuan, while the other reached 140 billion yuan; for annual tax paid, Huawei accounted for 5 billion yuan, while the other accounted for only 100 million yuan; regarding employee numbers, Huawei had 60,000 employees, while the other had 200,000 employees; for the salaries of new college graduates, the Huawei employees received about 6000 yuan per month., while the other employees earned about 1000 yuan (it is hard enough for them to get 4-5000 yuan per month within a year). It can, therefore, be noted that overseas-funded enterprises have contributed much to China's economy. Their exports are counted as China's and their performance are counted in the country's GDP, but the bulk of the profits end up in the pockets of foreign businesspersons.

Fourth, China is currently in the industrialization stage of development, with the characteristics of heavy-chemical industry and accelerated infrastructure construction, and so a relatively high investment rate is required at this stage. The urbanization rate has been constantly increasing, having reached 45% in 2008. As a large number of the population has moved from the countryside to cities, a relatively high investment rate has been needed to satisfy the requirement for infrastructure. This is an analysis of the negative impacts and causes of the excessively low resident consumption rate.

16.2 Increasing the Resident Consumption Rate Is a Major Task of Macro Regulation

In order to increase the resident consumption rate, the first thing to do is to increase the income of the residents, especially that of low- and middle-income people and farmers. In order to make major adjustments to the income distribution structure, China needs to increase the share of labor remuneration and lower the share of capital income in the primary distribution, thus shifting the situation of too much capital income and low labor income in the primary distribution.

In redistribution, China needs to increase the share of resident income, lower the excess share of the government and enterprises, focus on increasing the income of the low- and middle-income people, expand the share of middle-income people, and gradually put an "olive-shaped" income distribution structure in place. The National Bureau of Statistics defines households with an annual income of 60,000–200,000 yuan as middle-income, and those earning over 200,000 yuan as high-income, and the combination of middle- and high-income people will account for over 50% of the urban and rural residents by 2020, thus initially forming the "olive-shaped" income distribution structure. When the middle-income people account for the majority, consumption growth will be boosted.

Here is an option: If it is possible for China to take comprehensive measures within approximately three years to increase the share of resident income in GDP and the resident consumption rate by 10 percentage points and 15 percentage points to 55 and 50%, respectively, approaching 56 and 52% of the highest level since reform and opening up in 1985. It is fair to say that China can realize this target if efforts are made through a major adjustment of the income distribution structure. If this goal is achieved, each year about five trillion yuan of goods could be used for consumption instead of for investments and exports, thus dramatically elevating the consumption level of residents nationwide. Some five trillion yuan of goods used for consumption will remarkably increase the living standards of the people. After this adjustment, China will achieve the first transformation of the development pattern and soundly implement a people-oriented Theory of Balanced and Sustainable Development.

The primary purpose of increasing resident income is to increase farmers' income. In the early years of reform and opening up, the per capita net income gap between urban and rural residents was not very big, but it has widened in recent years. The absolute volume of urban resident income is now more than three times that of the rural. If the incomes of urban and rural residents continue to grow at the same speed, the absolute gap will continue to widen. In other words, the absolute volume of the increase of 3.3 percentage points in rural income is equal to a 1 percentage point increase in urban income, and rural income growth is even slower than urban income growth. Therefore, faster rural income growth has become China's first priority. The Third Plenary Session of the 17th CPC Central Committee has identified how to increase rural income as soon as possible, namely accelerate the transfer of rural labor to secondary and tertiary industries and that of rural population to urban areas. At present, agricultural labor productivity accounts for only one sixth of the secondary and tertiary industries, rural labor accounts for 43% of the labor force, and agricultural added value accounts for just 10% of GDP. Low productivity, which failed to create wealth, has resulted in low rural income. China cannot achieve remarkable progress simply through payment transfers and by funding farmers. The fundamental approach is to increase the productivity of farmers, which is constrained by the scale of farming operations. For example, at present, a farmer takes care of 5 mu of land on average. Those in plain areas can afford to cultivate hundreds or even thousands of mu of land on the strength of mechanized farming, but there are not as many land resources for increases in productivity. How should this be dealt with? China needs to develop intensive agriculture, which increases per unit yield on the one hand and advances large-scale land operations under the precondition of labor transfer on the other hand.

The second measure is to expand the scope of consumption and facilitate the upgrading in the consumption structure. In 2005, the Engel Coefficient was 36.7%, which means that expenditures on housing, traveling, health, education, communication, and recreation account for more than 60% of resident consumption. The Engel Coefficient of rural consumption has also decreased to 45.5%. Generally speaking, resident consumption has been experiencing a transition from food and shelter-oriented consumption to development-oriented consumption. Marx said that there are three types of consumption: survival-, development-, and entertainment. During the transition to development-oriented consumption, expenditures on education, health, communication, and recreation, especially that on living and traveling, will witness rapid growth.

The third measure is to expand consumer credit and improve the social security system. Consumer credit now accounts for 15–20% of outstanding credit. According to the experience of developed economies, the share of consumer credit in total loans can be increased to about 30%, so there is still huge room for improvement. In terms of vehicle consumption, 80% of the vehicles in developed countries are financed through credit, while in China the figure is only 8%. When the concept of car loans was still relatively new, some people maliciously avoided repayment. Therefore, China is trying to establish systems to investigate and guarantee credit, which would be a huge boost to the development of consumer credit.

The fourth measure is to adjust the investment structure and improve the consumption environment. Compared with the Republic of Korea, Japan, and the US, food accounts for a larger share in China's consumption structure. In this stage of development, the hot spot, or growth point, lies in increasing expenditures on living and traveling, namely boosting consumption through prioritizing the improvement of living and traveling conditions.

The fifth measure is to regulate market order and protect consumers' rights and interests. Good order and high-quality services are preconditions for expanding consumption, so China needs to crack down on counterfeit and substandard products, wipe out price fraud, and ensure safe consumption. The "Sanlu" Milk Powder Incident has heavily influenced the milk industry. Up till now, milk production has recovered to only about 80% of its maximum level. It was recently learned that in certain places, dairy cows were slaughtered for meat. A great number of foreign milk products have been imported, especially from New Zealand, which has gained a big market share in China, as New Zealand has a free trade agreement with the country.

These sixth measures are meant to rationally guide consumption expectations and advocate healthy consumption. China needs to encourage fugal, non-damaging, development-oriented, and civilized consumption, and avoid conspicuous, blind-following, and luxurious consumption.

16.3 Facilitate Linked Development of the Housing, Auto, and Stock Markets, and Advance Sustained and Healthy Consumption Growth

The housing, auto, and stock markets are the three major engines driving China's economic growth. They are interconnected, interdependent, and mutually reinforcing. The stable and healthy development of these three markets holds the key to higher resident consumption rates, so China needs to study the internal rules of the markets, improve relevant favorable policies, and advance the linked development of these markets as a strategic priority for expanding domestic demand, especially consumption.

1. *Facilitate and sustain the prosperity of the housing market*

Better living conditions are urgently desired by the vast majority of urban and rural residents. In studies on consumption intentions in China, improving living conditions has always been the top priority. With a long industrial chain, the housing market is a huge boost to relevant industries. Since 2008, the price increase in urban housing has decreased as a result of the State Council's policies on stable housing prices, the majority of consumers, and requirements put in place to ensure the long-term, healthy development of the housing industry.

The main target for the development of the housing industry in China must meet the housing demands of the residents, especially low- and middle-income people. In order to implement the requirements for providing adequate housing according to the report of the 17th National Congress of the CPC, urban housing prices should be controlled at a reasonable level that is in line with the income of the vast majority of residents, and should not be raised through bubbles such as speculative activities. In many localities, about 50% of government expenditures comes from land lease approvals, meaning the higher the housing price, the greater the income from approving land leases. This method has already become the second greatest financial source for local governments, so as a result, many local governments tend to raise housing prices.

According to the document issued by the State Council in 2007, local governments' responsibility in stabilizing the urban housing prices should be strengthened. In this regard, China should learn from the housing bubbles created in Japan and Hong Kong. When the bubbles had been created, income increased in all areas, the economies grew fast, and all sectors were happy. However, the ensuing bursts brought a disastrous impact to their economies. In Japan, housing prices decreased to about half of their highest levels, while prices in Hong Kong also fell far lower than their highest levels. Therefore, when enterprises create housing bubbles to stimulate economic growth, it is like quenching thirst with poison.

China should learn from Singapore and Germany, which managed to stabilize their housing prices and meet the housing demand of the vast majority of their residents. While working in the Policy Research Office of the National Planning Commission, the author had the honor of joining the State Council's Leading Group for housing Reform to research this issue. Visits were paid to Japan, Singapore, Germany, and the Netherlands to study the development of the housing industry. Based on comparative studies, the author had a keen feeling that China should never follow Japan or the special administrative region of Hong Kong, but should learn from Germany and the Netherlands. The housing prices in Germany have been maintained at the same levels since the 1950s following the end of World War II. German established housing savings banks in the 1950s, a certain amount of money is deposited when a baby is born, and continues to be deposited annually at a fixed interest rate, and with government bonuses, until he or she needs a house when getting married. Besides returning all the money, an equal amount of loans is also offered, which jointly account for one third of the total funds for housing. By stabilizing housing prices, the Germans have maintained the stability of the whole market and the economy at large. According to German colleagues, their solution to the housing problem was the best across Europe, and the housing level is the highest in the continent. The Netherlands has had a well-established system of combining housing loans with house insurance for over 100 years, which has stabilized the housing market there. These countries have done well to solve these problems and maintain economic stability with stable housing prices. Therefore, the State Council is right in issuing the policy for a stable urban housing market.

When it comes to development of the housing market, the priority is to ensure government-subsidized housing by strengthening the supply of affordable and low-rental housing. In this round of the expansion of domestic demand, the Treasury bond will be used to build about 10 million government-subsidized houses within three years. This will play a significant role in developing the construction material industry and building a dynamic real estate market. Three decades have elapsed since reform and opening up, but the country still has some people living in shanty towns, their housing should be improved, and some nomads have a need to settle down. Therefore, the 10 million government-subsidized houses will help improve their living conditions, and will represent an important measure for all of China's people to share the fruits of reform and development.

Moreover, China needs to vitalize the secondhand housing market and expand the house leasing market. Since reform and opening up, houses have become private properties, but it can still hard for housing to enter the market. By vitalizing the second-hand housing market, young people can buy old houses at lower prices, and then upgrade with their increased income. To build a larger house leasing market, China needs to set up a housing market for urban-rural integration. Breakthroughs in this regard are yet to come, so the issue could be further studied. China may be the only country left in the world that allows rural residents to buy houses in cities but not urban residents to buy houses in rural areas. Years ago, the Republic of Korea even offered subsidies to encourage actors and high-income earners to buy houses in rural areas. Why? To allow those groups of people to bring civilization to the rural areas. In Germany, the rural labor force accounts for only 1–2% of the total, but 62% of Germans live in the countryside or in small towns. When moving to the countryside, urban residents also took their modern lifestyle and civilization with them. Moreover, wherever they went, they tried to improve local infrastructure, including roads, water, and power facilities. For instance, the highway and rail transport connecting urban areas made commuting faster. Meanwhile, those people moving to the countryside helped improve local living conditions tremendously.

The concept of urban-rural integration proposed in this paper deals with six fields: planning, industry development, infrastructure, public services, employment market, and social management. The idea is another integration of the housing market so that China can further study and discuss the issue. Many localities, in fact, have brought about breakthroughs in this regard.

2. *Boost car consumption*

In 2008, China's per capita GDP reached US$3200, marking the beginning of the era of mass car consumption. Owning cars on a family basis has been the dream of generations of the Chinese people. With the increase in the resident income and the development of the auto industry, China became the world's largest auto consumption market by January or February 2009. That year, both the annual production and sales of cars exceeded 10 million. China is delighted to see more and more Chinese realize their dreams of owning cars.

Due to the global financial crisis in the second half of 2008, domestic auto sales growth has been dampened, experiencing a short halt after consecutive years of dramatic growth. With the issuing of various favorable measures for auto loans, sales picked up. Profit from vehicle production accounted for only 10% of that of the whole auto industry, supply of parts and components accounted for 20%, sales accounted for 20%, and services (maintenance, oil changes, modifications, insurance, and loans) accounted for 50%. Automobiles play an important role in facilitating social development and employment. In developed countries, about one in six of the working population works in the auto industry. It is fair to say that without personal vehicles, there would be no modernization. Some used to claim that personal vehicles are not suitable for China, and that the Chinese should ride bicycles. But how could per capita GDP be raised to US$10,000 without personal vehicles?

For more auto consumption, the first is to expand auto loans. The stagnant and bad auto loans accumulated in the previous years have increased massively, so auto loans have declined. China needs to put in place a credit system for auto loans that makes use of satellite positioning systems to create better conditions for the development of auto loans.

The second is to improve the environment for vehicle use. In urban planning, car-owning households should be taken into consideration, and parking lots need to be built in new business districts. While parking lots have developed into an independent business in other countries, some of China's major cities should introduce related technologies and management experience as soon as possible. Foreign countries are already been quite advanced in building underground and multilevel stacked parking lots, so China needs to take into consideration all factors, including urban development, housing construction, and household car ownership. The unreasonable charge on owning a vehicle needs to be reduced and the cost of vehicle use needs to be lowered.

The third is to encourage the purchasing of electric vehicles, hybrid electric vehicles, and medium- and small-displacement vehicles. China's auto consumption policies have made clear stipulations. One positive is that China is quite advanced in terms of electric vehicle (EV) technologies. For example, BYD developed an lithium iron phosphate battery and applied for an international patent. The vehicle can travel up to 300 km on a single charge, while charging for 15 min allows it to reach over 80% of the range limit. Consumers can use such vehicles during the day and charge them at night with lower electricity prices. EVs that do not emit any pollutants and are zero-emission have a promising future in cities.

The fourth is to extend the auto industrial chain and give full play to the role of the auto industry in boosting employment and consumption. According to the experience of developed countries, China needs to develop upstream and downstream industries in all links such as sales, maintenance, finance, insurance, fuel, parts and components, parking, and car washing, so as to create favorable conditions for vehicle production and consumption and therefore bring about greater economic and social benefits.

3. *Facilitate the steady and healthy development of the capital market*

With the development of the securities market, more and more people have gained property income. The securities market, especially the stock market, is increasingly affecting the housing and auto markets, which is the same case with Hong Kong and Taiwan. In Taiwan, when the stock market goes up, consumption rises; and when the stock market goes down, consumption drops. Therefore, China needs to advance the steady and healthy development of the capital market. China's recently developed capital market is still suffering from the absence of well-established mechanisms and the lack of management experience, therefore big fluctuations in the stock market is inevitable.

In order to ensure the stable and healthy development of the stock market, China needs to strengthen the building of fundamental systems on the one hand, and improve macro regulation of the stock market on the other hand. In recent years, relevant government departments have made a great deal of progress, and have tried to further master the rules of macro regulation of the stock market to enhance the regulation capabilities. Generally speaking, regulations on the gross supply and demand of the stock market can help realize steady and healthy development and avoid big ups and downs in the stock market. China needs to properly increase supply to avoid overheating when the stock market goes up, and strengthen demand to avoid plummeting when the market goes down. Many economists have made a analysis on this big fluctuation—the supply and demand structure saw certain changes. As China's stock market is still in the development stage, China's needs to regulate gross volume. The argument that the government should neither manage nor intervene in the stock market is irresponsible. China needs to strengthen the monitoring of the stock market and distinguish regulation of gross volume from administrative intervention. The regulation of gross volume is not necessarily administrative intervention; instead, it should be treated as an important government mission. China also needs to crack down on various illegal activities in accordance with the law to facilitate its standardized development, and develop a multi-tiered capital market, establish the Growth Enterprise Market in a timely manner, and build stronger securities investment agencies.

Efforts should be made to improve the multi-tiered capital market, achieve expert financing and rational investment, and build stronger securities investment agencies, so that China's capital market can truly play its role in selecting excellent enterprises based on evaluation, produce internationally competitive enterprises, and enable the vast majority of investors to share the fruits of enterprise development and increase property income. The stability and prosperity of the capital market needs to underpin the sustained prosperity of the housing and auto markets, which should become enduring pillar industries for driving economic growth.

Chapter 17
Promoting Economic Growth by Improving People's Livelihood

The year 2009 was a time when China made remarkable achievements while withstanding severe tests. Impacted by the international financial crisis, China effectively made up for the negative impact of plummeting exports by implementing an economic stimulus package plan for expanding domestic demand. As a result, the economy recovered and maintained a sound momentum of steady and rapid growth. The proud achievement fully demonstrated China's capacity to resist risks, as well as the good decision-making by the CPC Central Committee and the State Council and their superb skills in regulation. In the upcoming year of 2010, China needs to act in accordance with the requirements and deployment of the Central Economic Work Conference, continue adherence to the guidelines on expanding domestic demand, make macro regulation more targeted and flexible, focus on the transformation of economic development patterns, boost economic growth through improving livelihoods, set up endogenous growth mechanisms, and sustain sound and rapid growth.

17.1 Maintain Continuity and Stability of Macro-economic Policies

As in 2009, China implemented the decisions and arrangements of the CPC Central Committee, enforced active fiscal policies, and moderately loosened monetary policies, leading the major economies in economic recovery. However, China should be clear-minded that the economic recovery is still unconsolidated, unstable, and inharmonious. As developed countries, which are China's major export destinations, remain sluggish in economic growth and import demand over the next two to three years, China's exports will not be able to recover their growth rate from years ago and will not contribute more to economic growth. The booming investment

This article originally appeared in *People's Daily*, December 28, 2009.

X. Zheng, *China's 40 Years of Economic Reform and Development*,
https://doi.org/10.1007/978-981-13-2727-8_17

in 2009 mainly relied on state-owned investments. Without remarkably accelerated non-state-owned investments and support from the national debt funds, the growth of state-owned investments will inevitably slow down, which will impede economic recovery. Resident consumption saw rapid growth in 2009, but the reliance on consumption cannot solely offset the influence of decreased exports. If the current pro-consumption policies are cancelled or weakened next year, the speed of consumption growth will undoubtedly decrease. Therefore, if the current economic stimulus policies are retracted or weakened, the economic recovery trend might reverse; and if the growth rate drops, China would have to shoulder the burden of a second launch and might pay a steeper price. Meanwhile, new construction projects have increased year-on-year by over 80% compared with 2009, so there might be a batch of uncompleted projects if funds are less in supply. Therefore, next year China will continue implementation of the active fiscal policy and moderately loosen monetary policy. This expansionary economic policy can only be stopped when endogenous impetus is created and an endogenous mechanism for steady and rapid economic growth is established.

Of course, the implementation of the active fiscal policy and moderately loose monetary policy in 2010 resulted from timely and appropriate adjustments, which were in line with economic operations instead of simply repeating the policies of 2009. Fiscal policies should focus on advancing resident consumption, social investments, and structural optimization of loans and exports, so as to accomplish greater achievements in transforming economic development patterns and economic structural optimization. Moreover, the moderately loose monetary policy should be constantly improved—maintaining a certain scale of loaning, optimizing the loan structure, increasing loans for small and low-profit enterprises and farmer households, sustaining support in construction projects, increasing consumer credit, and preventing the flow of credit funds into the stock market, the latter of which could lead to an excessively quick rise in asset prices.

17.2 Highlight Resident Consumption to Expand Domestic Demand

Increasing resident consumption levels represents both an important manifestation for implementing the Theory of Balanced and Sustainable Development and a fundamental impetus for economic growth. The political report of the 17th CPC National Congress put forward the transformation of the development pattern. In addition, the first transformation is to shift the main reliance on investments and exports to that on consumption, investments, and exports, which indicates a bigger role for consumption in boosting economic growth. That transformation deals with the greatest conflicts in China's economic structure, identifying the fundamental approach to long-term, sustained, and balanced economic development. Our investment rate stood at 42.5% on average from 2003 to 2008, which was the period with the highest investment rate. In 2008, that figure reached as high as 43.5%. The investment rate in 2009 is estimated to exceed the previous year, reaching a new high. In addition, the resident consumption rate decreased to 37.7% on average during that period, which was the lowest in history. In 2008, the figure dropped to as low as 35.3%. Compared with foreign countries, China is undergoing a more severe imbalance between consumption and investment. For developed economies, the resident consumption rate is generally about 70%, twice that of China's. The high investment rate and low resident consumption rate, which is inevitable to a certain extent amid fast industrialization and urbanization, resulted from many factors. However, the main reason is China's understanding of and adherence to the underlying rules of a socialist market economy system. The major conflicts for macroeconomic management under the conventional planned economic system include insufficient supply and expanded demand, while those under a market economic system include excessive supply and inadequate demand. Serving as just intermediate demand, investment means increasing demand in the short run but more supply in the long run. Enduring high investment rates will inevitably lead to overcapacity, which will become more severe in the context of impeded exports. That is why the 17th National Congress of the CPC was so visionary in deciding to transform the development pattern from the perspective of adjusting the demand structure. The international financial crisis made this transformation a more urgent task for China to fulfill.

To increase the resident consumption rate, China needs to take comprehensive measures. Most importantly, the income distribution structure should be adjusted by raising the share of resident income in national income and the earnings of low- and middle-income people. If China can increase the urban and rural resident income/GDP ratio from 43% in 2008 to 53% and the resident consumption rate from 35% in 2008 to 50% within three years, respectively approaching their highest levels of 56 and 52% in 1985, then the imbalance between consumption and investment will be utterly transformed. Over 5 trillion yuan of national income annually could be used to boost consumption instead of investments and exports, and the gross retail sales of consumer goods of the whole society would jump by 45–50%. That means the resident consumption level would greatly increase and China's economic growth will get on track for relying on domestic demand.

The Central Economic Work Conference has made specific deployments on increasing resident income, especially for low- and middle-income people and raising the resident consumption rate. As long as Chinas acts in line with the deployments, the demand structure will witness a sea of change.

17.3 Expand Public Services as a Strategic Priority of Livelihood Improvement

China still suffers from an outstanding weak link in public services, which includes health care, education, social security, information, culture, public transport, water, power and gas supply, and environmental protection. As China can hardly meet the demands of the vast majority of residents due to lagged development in the aforementioned areas, the expansion of demand and upgrading of the consumption structure are also constrained. From the perspective of the current development stage, China is still experiencing a transition from survival-oriented to development- and entertainment-oriented consumption. Particularly, development-oriented consumption is experiencing a period of fast growth, which indicates that there is huge demand in culture and health after enjoying adequate food and housing, but China stills need to step up its efforts to enhance supply capacity. This requires that China develop social undertakings and expand public services as strategic priorities for more consumption. The Central Economic Work Conference stressed that next year China will unwaveringly improve people's livelihood and develop social undertakings as the priorities to expand domestic demand and adjust the economic structure. In accordance with the requirements of urban-rural integration of economic and social development, greater efforts are needed in developing social undertakings and public services in rural areas, so as to make sure that urban and rural residents can gradually enjoy generally equal basic public services.

Developing social undertakings and offering more public services serve as the important foundation for realizing balanced and sustainable development and social harmony. When developing health care, China should work to ensure universal health care, especially in rural areas, and eliminate the shortage of doctors and medicine in remote rural areas. Efforts should be made to expand coverage of health insurance, ensure universal basic health services, and provide better and cheaper health services. When it comes to developing education, China needs to adjust and optimize its structure and produce talent oriented toward social demands. China should be standing ready to offer education services according to residents' needs, thus ensuring that the structure of education will be compatible with that of social demands. In the meantime, China needs to step up its efforts to develop vocational education. The improvement of the social security system should be a high priority on the agenda for expanding public services. As the social security system is not well established, people are inclined to save more money for unexpected incidents, which has influenced their current consumption. In accordance with the requirements for basic-level and extensive coverage, China should build up the universal social security system as soon as possible and form a social security network. Information and cultural services will be the new growth points of public services. China should take 3G communication facility construction as an opportunity, enrich the content of online services, realize tri-networks integration (the combination of telephone, cable television, and internet) as soon as possible, lower the cost of communication, and provide fast, convenient, and cost-effective information services to residents. With modern media tools such as carrier networks, China needs to expand health care services, spread and popularize scientific knowledge, and improve the cultural life of the people. Infrastructure services such as urban-rural transportation, water, power and gas supply, garbage treatment, and environmental protection are all subject to supply falling short of demand. China should allocate more funding in those areas, so that people can enjoy convenient traveling, drink clean water, breath fresh air, and work and live in a sound environment.

17.4 Expedite Reform of the Social Management System

Compared with the economic management system, the social management system is more complicated, as it covers more areas. In the past 30 years, China has made huge progress in reforming the economic management system, but the reform of the social management system is relatively lagging, which is the fundamental reason why the development of social undertakings fell short of economic growth. In accordance with the philosophy of the Central Conference on Economic Work, China should expedite reforms in social sectors and advance various social undertakings through reform.

The difference between the two systems is that economic entities run their businesses under the mechanisms of market competition and survival of the fittest, while social service entities are divided into non-profit, for-profit, and semi-non-profit and semi-for-profit types. Thus, different management systems and reform plans that take into consideration the different features of the various industries and service entities are needed. For instance, neither education nor health care can be totally categorized into non-profit or for-profit types. Basic education and basic health care, which are mainly funded by fiscal input, provide non-profit services; specialized and diversified education and health care services, which may be primarily funded by social resources, provide for-profit services; and various education and health care service entities may need to integrate fiscal and social inputs to provide both non-profit and for-profit services.

Achieving this goal will require case-by-case analysis and targeted, realistic reform plans. In terms of the social security system and urban and rural infrastructure construction, China should also establish concrete and feasible reform measures based on various financial conditions, so as to attract social input and accelerate the speed of construction. Many sectors are suffering from problems such as being in demand without sufficient funding or having excessive funding without an investment plan. The fundamental cause behind all this is the absence of reasonable investment mechanisms. China can draw upon the experience of developed countries in this regard. Governmental bodies of all levels and research agencies in all fields should intensify their efforts in their research and analysis of relevant reform proposals, and hasten implementation after reaching consensus among social sectors. This is how reform helps provide systemic and institutional guarantees for the development of social undertakings. The economic system reform has served as the source of growth for economic development over the past 30 years, while the reform of the social management system will undoubtedly underpin the development of social undertakings. The author is convinced that by 2020, when China meets the goal of building a moderately prosperous society in all aspects, social undertakings and economic sectors will develop in a simultaneous and coordinated manner, individual consumption will be boosted for the vast majority of residents, public service consumption will reach a relatively high level, and a better life will be created for the people.

Chapter 18
Transforming the Economic Development Pattern Is an Urgent Strategic Task

At the workshop on implementing the Theory of Balanced and Sustainable Development attended by provincial leaders in early 2010, President Hu Jintao stressed that transforming the economic development pattern is an urgent strategic task. This important decision, which was in line with domestic and international economic situations, has been urgently needed to deal with the international financial crisis and to sustain the sound momentum of economic recovery since the second half of 2009, and is a fundamental approach for implementing the Theory of Balanced and Sustainable Development and maintaining steady and fast growth for a relatively long period of time. China will further its understanding on the importance and urgency of transforming the development pattern, and pool its energy and resources to make breakthroughs in transforming the development pattern in the near term.

18.1 The Shift from Transforming the Economic Growth Model to that of Transforming the Economic Development Pattern Manifests the He Party's Deeper Understanding of Economic Development Rules

In 1995, the Recommendations of the CPC Central Committee on Formulating the Ninth Five-Year Plan for Economic and Social Development and 2010 Long-Term Goals were adopted at the 15th Plenary Session of the 14th Central Committee, in which the CPC decided to transform the economic growth model, stressed the transition from extensive economic growth to intensive economic growth, and called for advancing the transformation of the economic growth model through transforming the economic system.

This article originally appeared in *Study on Accelerating Transformation of Development Pattern (2010–2011),* Social Sciences Academic Press, Beijing, 2011).

X. Zheng, *China's 40 Years of Economic Reform and Development*,
https://doi.org/10.1007/978-981-13-2727-8_18

From 1995 to 2007, when the 17th National Congress of the CPC was convened, China made tremendous progress in transforming the economic growth pattern. Over that 12-year period, a landmark event was that the share of electronic machinery, the oil and chemical industry, auto manufacturing, and the construction industry in GDP increased from 12 to 20%. Those four industries have gradually become the pillar industries of the economy, playing a critical role in underpinning the fast economic growth during that period.

In 2007, the CPC decided at its 17th National Congress to transform the development pattern in accordance with the new situations and missions of the new development stage, which has become the fundamental approach to implementing the Theory of Balanced and Sustainable Development.

The transformation is minor in the literal sense, but its content has been greatly enriched, manifesting the Party's deeper understanding of economic development rules. Transforming the economic growth pattern mainly deals with adjusting the structure of the factors of production, facilitating transformation from extensive economic growth to intensive economic growth through technical progress, and entails better management and scaled operations and improving the quality and efficiency of economic growth.

Transforming the development pattern is conducted from three aspects. In terms of adjusting demand structure, China needs to transform from excessive reliance on investments and exports to reliance on consumption, investments, and exports, thus enhancing the role of consumption in boosting economic growth. In terms of adjusting the supply structure or industrial structure, China needs to transform from over-reliance on the secondary industry to coordinated development of the primary, secondary, and tertiary industries, and focus on the tertiary industry by increasing its share in GDP. In terms of adjusting the structure of the factors of production, China needs to stop over-reliance on resource consumption, and instead drive economic growth through technical progress, higher labor force quality, and management innovation. If those three transformations can be realized, China will be able to tackle the international financial crisis and create favorable conditions for sustained, steady, and rapid growth for a relatively long period of time.

If fast economic growth can be sustained under the traditional growth pattern before the financial crisis, then the transformation of the development pattern will become more urgent and necessary after the crisis. At its 17th National Congress the CPC was visionary to decide to transform the economic development pattern. After the Republic of Korea was hit hard by the global financial crisis in the second half of 2008, the Chinese economy suffered a setback in 2009. To overcome the crisis, China was only able to resort to transforming the economic development pattern. At the workshop on implementing the Theory of Balanced and Sustainable Development attended by provincial leaders in early 2010, General Secretary Hu Jintao, Premier Wen Jiabao, Vice President Xi Jinping, and Vice Premier Li Keqiang all made important remarks. The workshop discussed and made deployments on how to make tangible progress in the transformation of the economic development pattern in 2010. In a relevant 2000-plus-character report published by Xinhua News Agency, the word "accelerate" was used 56 times, which indicated the urgency of transforming the economic development pattern.

18.2 Transform from Mainly Relying on Investments and Exports to the Coordinated Development of Consumption, Investments, and Exports

1. *Highlight Expansion of Resident Consumption*

When it comes to transforming the economic development pattern, the first transformation is to adjust the demand structure. This idea was put forward to resolve the outstanding conflicts in the process of economic development. Over the three decades from 1978 to 2008, the changes of consumption, investments, and exports in gross demand have been exerting an increasingly large influence on the economy.

During those three decades, the final consumption rate gradually decreased from its highest level of 67% to about 48%. The final consumption rate includes government consumption and resident consumption. Government expenditures accounted for about 14%, staying at a basically stable level. The resident consumption rate and final consumption rate experienced synchronous changes. The resident consumption rate also gradually decreased from its highest level of 53% to less than 40% in recent years, even to its lowest level of 35.1% in 2009 (see Fig. 18.1).

China's GDP in 2009 stood at 34 trillion yuan, among which only slightly over one third was consumed by the public. China has spent a great deal of energy and resources to make products, but only a very small portion of them are consumed by the people. The US resident consumption rate once reached as high as 72%, while China has not yet reached even half of that. In developed European countries and

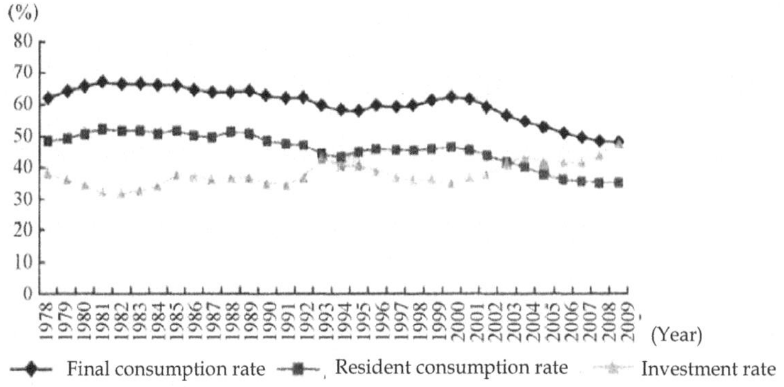

Fig. 18.1 Final consumption rate, resident consumption rate and investment rate from 1978 to 2009. *Source* China Statistical Yearbook 2010

Japan, the resident consumption rate stood at around 60%, over 20 percentage points higher than that of China.

The consumption rate gradually decreased while the investment rate gradually increased. On the one hand, the economy has re-accelerated its growth since 2003. Thanks to infrastructure construction and real estate industry development, the heavy-chemical industry has grown faster, and the steel, cement, electrolytic aluminum, and technology equipment industries have all witnessed rapid growth, which resulted in high investment rates for a long time. In 2008, the investment rate rose to 43.5%. The direct impact of the excessively high investment rate and low consumption rate resulted in the resident consumption level being unable to increase along with economic growth. On the other hand, a large number of products have been used for investments and exports, which resulted in underutilized production capacity and more trade disputes. The home appliance industry started only at an average rate of around 60% while the production capacity of steel and mechanics were not fully exploited, which led to a huge waste of investment.

If China fails to develop production capacity, then it will be difficult to reap the benefits of investments, non-performing loans might increase, and finally inflation may be triggered. Over the decades, China's economy has been experiencing these periodic ups and downs, and it was not until 2003 that the country was able to eliminate such a concern. The period following 2003 has been a time of the most rapid, steady, and fruitful economic growth in China's history. However, as the traditional development pattern has resulted in an increasing amount of conflicts in economic operations, China's reliance on investments and exports has reached its limit, and thus the traditional development pattern cannot be implemented any more.

In previous years, China has suffered from anti-dumping and trade disputes targeted at exports to many different countries, and has become the top country to be sued for anti-dumping in the world. The US has been adopting trade protectionism policies, forcing the RMB to appreciate. The financial crisis has led the market to drop in developed countries. It is estimated that within the past three to five years, those markets will not grow as fast as they used to before the crisis and will absorb fewer Chinese products. As a result, the role of exports in boosting economic growth will become less prominent. In order to make up for the negative impact that plummeting exports has had on China's growth, domestic demand had to be expanded in 2009. Consumption has been accelerating, but consumption alone could not make up for the negative impact of declining exports—only dramatically increasing investments could help. In 2009, investments rose by over 30% and gross investments reached 22 trillion yuan. This is what China had to do. The high investment rate and investment growth rate could not be sustained. In that year, investments mainly went to livelihood projects and infrastructure construction. This was highly necessary, as it would exert significant impact on future economic development. However, if the momentum of investment growth cannot be constrained, there might be excessive infrastructure construction in the years to come.

Over-reliance on exports and investments can no longer be sustained, which is an important reason why the CPC Central Committee decided to transform the development pattern earlier this year.

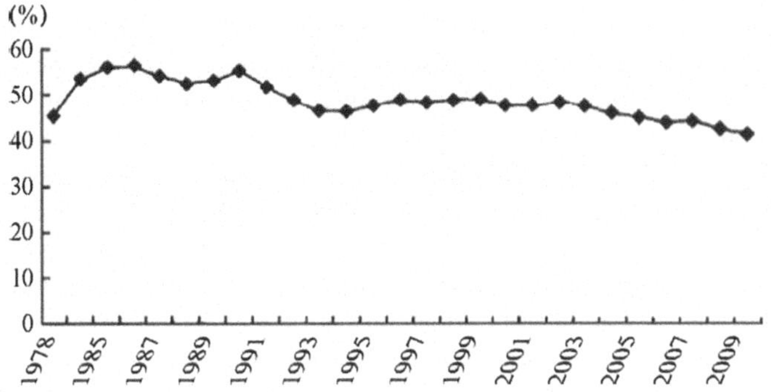

Fig. 18.2 Share of urban and rural resident income in gross national income. *Source* China Statistical Yearbook (various years)

2. *Adjust the Structure of Income Distribution*

The most important cause of the low resident consumption rate is the unreasonable income distribution structure.

First, the share of urban and rural resident income in gross national income is gradually decreasing. In 1985 that share stood at 56%. However, it gradually dropped from its relatively high level in the early 1990s to a historical low of 42% in 2009 (see Fig. 18.2). Over the 30 years since reform and opening up, urban and rural resident income has seen an annual average growth of around 7%, and GDP has seen an annual average growth of 9.8%. The over 2 percentage points' gap between these two figures is the fundamental reason for the decreasing share of urban and rural resident income in gross national income and the reason for the decreasing resident consumption rate.

Second, the income structure is unreasonable and the income gap is widening. The income gap among individuals, industries, and regions, especially between urban and rural residents, is constantly enlarging. In the early phase of reform and opening up, the urban and rural resident income ratio was 2:1, but it has enlarged to 3.3:1. As rural income did not rise, the share of consumption by farmers (the majority of the population) in gross social consumption gradually decreased. In the early phase of reform and opening up, the gross retail sales of consumer goods at and below the county level and at the municipal level accounted for one half, respectively. However, the former dropped to 30% in 2009, which meant that the 700 million-plus people in the rural population consumed less than one third of the commodities, while the 600 million people in the urban population consumed the remaining two thirds. The urban market of industrial consumer goods has become saturated, but rural residents are still unable to afford goods. The income gap between urban and rural residents has been widening, therefore the huge potential of the rural consumption market has not been tapped. This is an important reason behind the low resident consumption rate.

During the annual sessions of the NPC and the CPPCC National Committee in 2008, I put forward a "double increase" proposal in accordance with the philosophy of the 17th National Congress of the CPC, namely increasing the share of urban and rural resident income in gross national income and increasing the resident consumption rate. If within three to five years the share of urban and rural resident income in gross national income can be increased from 43 to 53% (2 percentage points lower than the historical high of 55%) and the resident consumption rate can be increased from 35 to 50% (3 percentage points lower than the historical high of 53%), the demand structure will change significantly, which means a huge increase in the incomes and consumption and a greater role of consumption in boosting economic growth. If the resident consumption rate can be elevated to 50%, each year about five trillion yuan of products will be used for consumption instead of investments and exports. Nowadays, the gross retail sales of consumer goods each year stands at only 12 trillion yuan. If another five trillion yuan can be added, the standard of living will be changed dramatically. This is absolutely feasible. Once this goal is achieved, macroeconomic benefits will be greatly enhanced, the vast majority of people will enjoy more tangible benefits from economic development, and the people-oriented Theory of Balanced and Sustainable Development will be truly implemented. In order to deal with the supply shortage in the 1970s, Japan formulated an "income doubling plan," which doubled income within 10 years. If China can, during the 12th Five-Year Plan period, bring about a relatively fast income increase for urban and rural residents, especially that of the low- and middle-income people and farmers, the "engine" of consumption will drive economic growth with greater power.

In order to adjust the structure of income distribution, the most important tasks are as follows:

(1) Increase Farmers' Income

Greater fiscal input should be allocated for agriculture, so as to boost farmers' income through facilitating agricultural growth. An important approach to increasing farmers' income is to reduce the rural population. The share of the rural labor force in the entire labor force is 43%, while that of the developed countries is 2–3%. Among all the provinces, municipalities and autonomous regions, that share in Zhejiang decreased to 18.2% in 2009 in a most rapid manner, making it the first province to lower the share to less than 20%. In Suzhou and Wuxi, the share has also dropped to less than 10%. The share of the rural labor force in the entire labor force is the most direct indicator of economic and social development in a country or a region. China has 1.8 billion mu of arable land and 480 million rural laborers, which means that the land ownership for each laborer is no more than 4 mu. According to current mechanical conditions, each laborer can cultivate 500–1000 mu of land in plain areas. Each household now takes care of 7 mu of land on average, which has resulted in surplus labor time. Low labor productivity is one determinant of the low rural resident income. Government subsidies and developing agricultural industries are important, but they cannot solve the determinant of low productivity and low income.

At the Third Plenary Session of the 17th Central Committee, the CPC decided to carry out two transformations for the fundamental operating system in rural areas.

One is the transformation to intensive farmer household operations, and the other is transforming the service system to involve social sectors and specialized development. Intensive operations of farmer households will free the majority of the rural labor force from farming, so that they can engage in cultivating the industry, start businesses, or find employment in urban areas. Farmers' income, while working in cities plus that from land subletting, will bring another 30,000–40,000 yuan to each household each year. When that happens, the earnings between urban and rural residents will be almost equal, and the rural areas will become moderately prosperous. Moreover, agricultural modernization will lead to huge demand for large-scale agricultural machines, which will boost the development of the agricultural machinery industry.

(2) Break Monopolies and Narrow the Income Gap Between Industries

Unlike developed countries, the income gap between different industries is huge in China. In developed countries, labor and funds can flow freely between industries. The funds will flow to industries with high capital profits, and the labor force to industries with high-income levels. In 2005, the State Council issued the *Guidelines on Encouraging, Supporting and Guiding the Development of Individual, Private and Non-public Ownership Businesses*. The 36 guidelines decided to introduce the market competition mechanism in areas like the power industry, telecommunications, railway, civil aviation, and petroleum; and supporting non-public capital in participating in investments, construction, and the operations of municipal public utilities and infrastructure, such as urban water, gas and heat supply, public transport, and sewage and garbage treatment. However, as all of these industries have monopolies, the threshold is too high for social funds to go in. Breaking industrial monopolies, therefore, is the most important approach to narrowing the income gap between different industries.

(3) China Will Gradually Provide Equal Public Services.

The lagged public service development resulted from limited investments in public services. China's supply has already exceeded demand in individual consumers' goods, but supply remains inadequate in the areas of education, health care, social security, urban transport, water and power supply, and garbage and sewage treatment. The reason behind the insufficient supply is that the system reform lagged behind. Those areas have been underpinned by government investments for a long time, making it difficult for social funds to be involved. All this has impeded the development of those industries, and consequently the demand for public services cannot be met. China's need to develop education as a method for consumption, and work to meet the demand for educating the people. Society should provide learning opportunities for those willing to learn and enable them to learn what they want. The problem that new college graduates discover is that getting a job is not that simple. The gross enrollment rate in the Republic of Korea stands at around 50%, that in Japan around 70%, and that in China only 24%. Having received college education, the students had their quality improved, which helped improve the quality of the people as a whole.

China will advance public service through reforming the social system. In the US, the share of service consumption in resident consumption has reached 70%, and commodity consumption has reached 30%, while in China those numbers are 30 and 70%, respectively. Some say that Chinese people prefer eating while Americans prefer playing, so US consumption for services is higher, whereas Chinese commodity consumption is higher. This is wrong. With income increases, Chinese residents will be more inclined to consume high-quality services, including education, health care, tourism, and culture. To solve the outstanding problem of a low share in resident service consumption, China needs to increase supply and meet the demands in this regard. More supply will require reform. Premier Wen Jiabao stated in the 2010 government report that this year but also in the next three years the administration would focus on advancing social undertakings, expanding public service consumption, and meeting the demands of the vast majority of the people for a higher standard of living through encouraging consumption of education, health care, and social security. The planning proposals on reforming the science and technology (S&T) system and social security system have been made. In 2010, the planning for education reform was approved, which has had a profound impact on education advancement.

(4) Improve the Personal Income Tax System

China will narrow the personal income gap by adjusting personal income tax. To do so, China will need to implement the comprehensive personal income tax system, increase the standards of personal income tax deductions, and transition from a tax system that is dominated by indirect taxes to one that is dominated by direct taxes. With personal income increases and tax system reform, China will lower the tax burden on enterprises, increase the share of personal income tax in the entire tax system, and adjust the personal income gap through tax system reform.

3. *Expand Public Services as Priority for Increasing Consumption*

Public services include such things as education, health care, social security, information, culture, public transport, water, power and gas supply, and environmental protection. Public services are suffering from insufficient supply and are becoming an outstanding weak link. Developing social undertakings and increasing the supply of public services represent the requirement of implementing balanced and sustainable development and building a harmonious society. By setting up a public financial system, China will gradually realize generally equal per capita expenditures on public services and provide equal basic public services. Remarkably, narrowing the gap of income and consumption in the short run is very difficult, but increasing public financial expenditures, especially realizing the equalization of public financial expenditures, will ensure generally equal public services be provided to each Chinese citizen, no matter whether they live in cities or in the countryside, in coastal areas or border regions. Ultimately, they will gain access to generally equal services in health care, education, and social security. The priority for narrowing the consumption gap will be public services. This is also a very important goal for building a harmonious society in the future.

4. *Accelerating Urbanization Offers the Greatest Potential for Expanding Domestic Demand, Especially Consumption*

In the next 20 years leading to 2030, the demand for investments and consumption resulting from urbanization will be the greatest potential for driving economic growth. It is estimated that each addition to the urban population will bring about a five-fold increase in consumption expenditure and about 100,000 yuan of potential investment demand for urban infrastructure and public services. From 1997 to 2007, the annual average urbanization rate increased by 1.4 percentage points, and 200 million people were added, with 20 million being added each year. Due to the impact of the financial crisis in 2008 and 2009, the urbanization growth rate slowed, standing at only 0.9 percentage points in 2009. Over the next 10 years, the urbanization growth rate is expected to return to the average level from 1997 to 2007. If the rate can be sustained and each year 20 million people move to cities, the potential investment demand for infrastructure each year alone will reach approximately 20 trillion yuan. The urbanization rate now stands at 46.6%. If it rises to 60% in 2020 and 70% in 2030, the tasks of industrialization and urbanization will be generally fulfilled.

China has maintained rapid economic growth for 30 years, Japan for 20 years, and the Republic of Korea for 30 years. In the next 10–20 years, China could still maintain its momentum of fast economic growth. Increasing China's low urbanization level will create huge demand for investments and consumption, which will be large enough to sustain a relatively fast growth rate over the next 10–20 years.

Allowing rural migrant workers to become urban residents should be an important approach to facilitating urbanization. An important problem for urbanization is how to allow those rural migrant workers find stable incomes and jobs like urban residents. This is a quite significant task. China will need to offer necessary services to them, such as low-rent housing in urban government-subsidized housing, as well as nurseries and schools as public services.

China will enhance the comprehensive carrying capacity of large and medium-sized cities and small towns. Between developing major cities or enhancing the carrying capacity of large and medium-sized cities and small towns, which one should be the priority of advancing urbanization in China? Major cities have more job opportunities but a higher cost of living, while large and medium-sized cities and small towns have a lower cost of living but fewer job opportunities. How can China resolve this conflict? Developing clusters of cities may be the solution. That is, to build a 1.5-h living-circle by integrating one mega city and its surrounding large and medium-sized cities and small towns. However, China will need to learn from the satellite towns built by Paris. People with varied levels of income should live together within an integrated region instead of being separated from each other, so as to create a harmonious social atmosphere. Urbanization is an issue of long-term development. China needs to learn from the lessons of developed countries and properly deal with the job opportunity and living cost conflict that exists between major cities and small towns, and create favorable conditions for realizing social harmony.

18.3 Transition from Major Reliance on Secondary Industry to Reliance on the Linked Development of Primary, Secondary, and Tertiary Industries

As early as the 1990s, the State Council promulgated a document on encouraging the development of the tertiary industry. More than a decade has elapsed since then, but China has yet to make breakthroughs in developing the tertiary industry. For the tertiary industry, value added now accounts for only 43% of GDP and employees account for only 34% of all public employees, both around 10 percentage points lower than the global average, 20–30 percentage points lower than developed countries, and even 10 percentage points lower than India. The per capita GDP in India is only half of China's, but its value added from the tertiary industry accounts for almost 50% of its GDP. In developed countries, 70–80% of the people are employed by the tertiary industry. The lagged development has made it difficult for the industry to develop its strength in absorbing a large number of employees.

There are several reasons for its slow development in China. The first is the heavy tax burden. Since the reform of the tax system in 1994, taxation on the secondary industry was changed to value-added tax and that on the tertiary industry became business tax, making the latter heavier than the former. The second is the absence of a financial system for small-sized enterprises and individually-owned businesses in the tertiary industry. The tertiary industry mainly consists of small-sized enterprises and individually-owned businesses that need a relatively small scale of funding. In the current banking system, a financial system providing petty loans has not been put in place. The state-owned commercial banks tend to offer loans to big enterprises and big projects, so the small enterprises and individually-owned businesses cannot gain access to loaning support. Third is the lack of experience in developing emerging service industries for production activities. The lagged development of the tertiary industry has severely constrained the development of the primary and secondary industries.

The priority is to accelerate the development of the tertiary industry. In recent years, the ratio of primary to secondary to tertiary industry was 11:47:42, while that of the US was 1:22:77. In terms of output value, the overall size of the primary and secondary industries has approached and even surpassed that of the US, but the tertiary industry is still about nine trillion yuan less than that of the US. Therefore, the major reason for the smaller GDP than the US is the lag in development of the tertiary industry. Accelerating development of the tertiary industry has become an important component for adjusting the industrial structure. Specifically, China is not lagging behind in the traditional essential service industries, but in the emerging industries of production activities, including technology, accounting, auditing, consulting, finance, insurance, logistics, and intermediary services. For example, logistics costs in developed countries account for around 10% of GDP, but nearly 20% in China. This is because a specialized modern logistics system involving social sectors has not been put in place. Technical innovation, which includes evaluation and trading technology, has become an important component of the tertiary industry. In China, production services usually stay within an enterprise.

To expedite development of the tertiary industry, China must formulate effective policies for facilitating development of the secondary and tertiary industries. China will strive to make breakthroughs in advancing the tertiary industry during the 12th Five-Year Plan period.

18.4 Transform the Economic Growth Mode from Relying Mainly on Resource Consumption to Relying on S&T Progress, Workforce Quality Improvement, and Management Innovation

1. *Enterprises Should Become Major Players in Facilitating Innovation*

The Third Plenary Session of the 16th CPC Central Committee approved the *Resolution of the CPC Central Committee on Improving Socialist Market Economy*, confirming the central role of enterprises in advancing corporate technical progress and S&T input. At the Fifth Plenary Session of its 16th Central Committee, the CPC approved *The Recommendations of CPC Central Committee for Formulating the 11th Five-Year Plan*, further stressing innovation capacity as the central link to realizing industrial upgrading. The political report to the 17th National Congress of the CPC pointed out that enhancing innovation capacity and building an innovative country represent the core of the national development strategy. The CPC Central Committee has been giving increasingly great prominence to innovation. As innovation has won the attention of all social sectors, the R&D input from all levels of government and from enterprises has constantly increased, and an increasing amount of research findings have been published. However, there is still a huge gap in technical innovation in comparison with developed countries, which can be indicated by the number of international patent applications. In 2009, the US applied for about 50,000 international patents, while China applied for 8000, about one sixth that of the US; and US GDP totaled 14 trillion dollars, while China approached 5 trillion dollars, about one third that of the US. All these objectively measure the gap in science, technology, and innovation (STI) capacity between the two countries. In the 8000 international patent applications, the owners of the patents were very unevenly distributed. Huawei solely applied for over 1600 patents, ranking No. 1, and ZTE ranked No. 2. The two companies in Shenzhen jointly applied for 27% of the country's international patent applications.

The state-owned enterprises (SOEs) have not become major innovators, mainly because the indicators for their performance are about value preservation and increasing tangible assets instead of increasing intangible assets. With greater social progress, intangible assets have become more important. A system for transforming the development pattern and innovation should be put in place. If systems remain unchanged, the development pattern will be hard to transform and enterprises will be reluctant to increase their R&D input. China needs to set up a mechanism for encouraging R&D input through SOEs. Huawei is able to apply for over 1000 patents, but actually, most SOEs are capable of achieving that much as well. If China could produce 30 companies as competitive as Huawei, the S&T strengths would be markedly enhanced.

2. *Improve Pro-innovation Policies and the Social Environment*

China needs to set up a policy ecosystem where innovation drives high-tech industry development. Why are Huawei and ZTE based in Shenzhen? When reviewing their experience over the 30 years since reform and opening up, it was discovered that Shenzhen is the only major Chinese city blazing the trail of advancing industrial upgrading through innovation. Since the mid-1990s, Shenzhen has explicitly proposed two transformations: Transforming from enterprises dominated by foreign funds to that of domestically-funded high-tech enterprises, and transforming from trade dominated by processing to general trade. Having proposed that, the municipal government started to formulate relevant policies. In order to align efforts to support domestic-funded high-tech enterprises, the Shenzhen municipal government helped run two companies respectively dedicated to venture capital and loan guarantees. Over 90% of the enterprises thriving in Shenzhen were supported by those two companies when they were in their stages of crucial development.

3. *Fully Exploit S&T Resources in the International Market*

The economic crisis has caused certain enterprises in developed countries to suffer from operation difficulties and even border bankruptcy. Through international mergers and acquisitions, China could buy overseas companies with operational difficulties yet with quality S&T resources, so as to raise the nation's innovation capacity to a higher level.

Thanks to innovation in talent introduction, China will be able to attract more outstanding overseas talents. In the past, China paid over one million dollars annually to host overseas senior engineers, but in the wake of the crisis, only hundreds of thousands of dollars was needed. The invited overseas engineers and the country's own research personnel will jointly form an excellent team for joint research, and the technology achievements will belong 100% to the Chinese side. As S&T resources abound in the international market, China should utilize them instead of working behind closed doors for research. It would be an excellent option for China to utilize S&T resources in the international market for stronger innovation capacity.

18.5 Accelerate the Transformation of the Agricultural Development Pattern

At the Third Plenary Session of the 17th Central Committee, the CPC adopted the Central Committee's Decision on Facilitating Reform and Development, which required improvement of the fundamental operating system in rural areas. This identified the direction of future rural reform. It was particularly stressed that six rural systems be established or improved, namely stabilizing and improving the fundamental operating system in rural areas; making the land management system stricter and more standardized; refining the support and protection system for agriculture; establishing a modern rural financial system; setting up an urban-rural integration system; and improving the rural democratic management system. The six systems jointly form the comprehensive deployment for advancing rural reform in the next period to come. Establishing and improving those systems will be conducive to agricultural modernization and rural harmony and stability.

Setting up an urban-rural integration system is of vital importance to rural development. Urban-rural integration consists of the following six areas:

One, integration of urban-rural planning. The development of cities and rural areas needs to be planned in an integrated manner. A comprehensive city plan should be made, and a clear and scientific distribution of work should be put in place regarding the location of residential areas, industrial zones, protected croplands, ecological conservation areas, and trading areas. China will strive to bring about a general urban-rural development layout within five to ten years featuring a beautiful environment by making constant efforts.

Two, integration of industrial layout. Industries in urban and rural areas need to be integrated with each other. In China, farmers care only about planting crops, while processors and retailers are concerned about the profit of processing and sales. It is very hard for farmers to get rich. Farmers could sell their products through cooperatives in supermarkets opened by themselves in cities. And cities could set up agricultural service companies for fertilizer, irrigation, and reaping, so as to provide commercialized services to farmers.

Three, integration of infrastructure. Urban roads, water and power supply, and sewage and garbage treatment need to be extended to rural areas, so that farmers can also enjoy modern life. In particular, farmers need to gain access to tap water. Having accessed tap water, rural residents could buy home appliances such as washing machines. Therefore, access to tap water is an important part of improving rural living standards.

Four, integration of public services. Education, health care, and social security need to extend their presence in rural areas. Premier Wen Jiabao has explicitly proposed missions such as realizing a basic-level and a full-coverage urban-rural social security system, thus gradually elevating the level of social security.

Five, integration of factor markets. China should facilitate the free and two-way flow of production factors between urban and rural areas. Chongqing and Chengdu have done an excellent job in this area. Chengdu has worked ceaselessly in the recent decade to realize urban-rural integration. In Chengdu, urban residents rent farmers' houses in the outskirts to encourage farmhouse tourism, while farmers use the rental income to sell their farm produce in rented buildings in the city. Harmony between urban and rural areas and the people has prevailed. The urban-rural integration has helped solve many problems.

Six, integration of social management. Chengdu has carried out integration of social management and has merged the urban-rural household registration systems. Both urban and rural residents are residents of Chengdu. The city has established a democratic management system. The rural areas and cities used to set up management agencies separately, but now they are under unified management. For example, any division of the Civil Affairs Bureau governs relevant businesses in both cities and rural areas. Chengdu has also explored much on the integration of administrative management. Guided by the Third Plenary Session of the 17th CPC Central Committee, the explorations turned out to be very meaningful.

18.6 Open Wider to Facilitate the Transformation of the Development Pattern

Opening ourselves wider to facilitate reform and development has been an important experience over the past 30 years since reform and opening up. After being impacted by the financial crisis, opening wider became an important approach to transforming the development pattern. In September 2010, the country's foreign exchange reserve reached 2.65 trillion dollars. In addition, China had great surplus industrial production capacity. Those two problems were burdens if treated separately, but a strength if combined, because commodity and labor service exports could be driven through capital exports using foreign exchange reserves and by giving play to the surplus production capacity. Expanding overseas technical resources is conducive to creating export demand, breaking resource bottlenecks, making foreign exchange reserves safer, and advancing the internationalization of the RMB, as well as other goals.

In 2009, China's exports decreased by 16%. It remained a daunting task to return to the level of 2008. Under current circumstances, China can create export demand through overseas investments. There are at least five approaches. First is to facilitate the exports of the country's exploitation and development equipment through expanded overseas investments in energy and resources, which could also meet the country's demand for energy and resources. Second is to allow the country's manufacturing industry to "go global" through expanded overseas processing trade, which could drive parts and components exports. Third is to facilitate equipment and labor service exports through offering greater economic assistance to developing countries. Fourth is to expand exports of mechanical and electrical products by offering more buyer credit for mechanical and electrical product exports. Fifth is to expand bilateral RMB swaps so that countries willing but unable to afford Chinese products can buy them with RMB and pay the loans with energy and resources.

By expanding overseas investments, China can meet economic development demand for resources such as iron ore, aluminum oxide, copper, petroleum, and natural gas, establish stable channels of overseas supply, and change foreign exchange reserves into resource reserves. All these approaches would not only help make the nation's foreign exchange reserves safer, but also advance internationalization of the RMB.

18.7 Set up Systems and Mechanisms for Transforming the Development Pattern

China needs to put in place systems and mechanisms for transforming the development pattern, so that the operations and decision-making of enterprises can be conducted in line with the requirements of the transformation of the development pattern.

1. *Activate the Basic Role of the Market in Resource Allocation by Building up Systems*

China needs to improve the factor market by integrating commodities, capital, human resources, land, and natural resources. Resource prices should reflect not only the cost of mining, but also the cost of environment and degree of rarity. Nowadays, the resource price does not reflect the rarity of the resources, which has resulted in excessively low resource prices. Consequently, China needs to protect the resources and activate the efficiency of resources by adjusting resource prices.

2. *Reform the Fiscal and Taxation Systems*

After the substitution of tax payment for profit delivery in 1994, a tax sharing system between the central authority and localities was put in place. The reform turned out to be very successful. Since then, China has seen a remarkable increase in both the share of central finance in total fiscal revenue and that of fiscal revenue in GDP. However, local financial power has failed to match government duties. Local fiscal revenue increased slowly, so some local governments resorted to land finance, trying to use land-transferring fees as a way to make up for insufficient local government expenditures. In certain coastal cities, the land-transferring fees equaled half of government fiscal revenue. This is unsustainable. A stable taxation source is needed for local governments.

3. *Reform the Financial System*

At present, China's financial system is generally functioning in a healthy manner, and the quality of banking assets is relatively good. Three of the world's top ten banks in 2009 were from China. The non-performing asset ratio of Chinese banks is gradually decreasing. The problem is the absence of a petty loan system for small-sized enterprises, individual households, and farmer households. Therefore, the priority of the reform should be building a financial system for small- and micro-sized economic entities. The US has over 8000 banks, among which 90% are regional community banks. Community banks accept deposits and offer loans within their area. The banks are familiar with local customers, making them important pillars for local economic development. The current financial system is functioning only with a few dozen "main artery" big banks, and without "blood capillary" small banks. The consequence is that the "blood" of finance cannot flow to the small- and micro-sized economic entities. Therefore, China needs to support public entrepreneurial activities and the industrialization of technical innovation through reform and through improving financial service systems.

4. *Reform the System of Administrative Management*

The Chinese government should not intervene in the affairs that the market can deal with. Instead, the government should serve as a good referee, focusing on the formulation of systems and policies. The reform of public institutions affiliated with the government should be put on the agenda. The reform will be more complicated than that of enterprises, because public institutions are non-profit, for-profit, semi-non-profit, and semi-for-profit. China needs to confirm how much financial support is offered according to their nature and missions, so as to arouse their initiative for further development. The reform of those institutions will be a priority in China's future reform.

Chapter 19
Promoting the Concept of Innovative, Coordinated, Green, Open and Shared Development

One salient feature of the Program for the 13th Five-Year Plan is the emphasis it gives to the concept of innovative, coordinated, green, open and shared development. This is in accordance with the Suggestions of the 5th Plenary Session of the 18th CPC Central Committee. As a profound reform vital to our development in a macro sense, promoting this concept represents a fundamental guarantee for building a moderately prosperous society in all respects by 2020, and has far-reaching significance for ensuring the sustained, long-term economic development.

19.1 Stick to Innovative Development by Giving Play to the Leading Role of STI

The Suggestions of the 5th Plenary Session of the 18th CPC Central Committee state, "Innovation represents the primary engine for driving development." This means we must put innovation at the core of national development, constantly facilitate innovation in our theories, systems, S&T and culture, and ensure that innovation prevails not only in all work of the Party and the country but also throughout society. This statement has elevated the importance of innovation, enriched its meaning, and raised the overall requirements for acting on the concept of innovation-driven development.

Theory comes from and guides practice, and is superior to practice. If practices stand up, then the tree of theories will ever remain green. With 1.3 billion people and over 80 million CPC members, it is important that China use the right theories to advance its socialist undertaking. Our remarkable achievements over the 38 years since the reform and opening up began have resulted primarily from Deng Xiaoping Theory, Three Representatives, and Theory of Balanced and Sustainable Develop-

---

This article originally appeared in *Qiushi*, Chinese edition, no. 11, 2016.

X. Zheng, *China's 40 Years of Economic Reform and Development*,
https://doi.org/10.1007/978-981-13-2727-8_19

ment being put forward at the right time and providing the right guidance. We also need to constantly summarize and develop our theories on the basis of practice in order to advance the great undertaking of reform and opening up. In addition to innovating socialist theory with Chinese characteristics, we also need to summarize and develop new theories in reform and opening up, economic development, social progress, Party building, state governance and international cooperation, elevate perceptual knowledge to rational cognition, and allow reform and development to become more voluntary, forward-looking and effective.

In accordance with the requirements of the Third Plenary Session of the 18th CPC Central Committee on furthering comprehensive reform, we need to proactively undertake systemic innovation. Through systemic innovation, we can adopt reform measures proven effective by practice and gradually build a relatively mature system that meets the requirements for developing a socialist market economy system.

Enhancing science, technology and innovation capacity and building an innovative country comprise both the fundamental approach for pursuing economic transformation and upgrading and the core of advancing supply-side structural reform. We must carry out the specific deployments regarding innovation and entrepreneurship stipulated in the government work report. When it comes to reform of S&T and education systems, we should learn from the US. Why has the US been a world leader in S&T for such a long period of time? First, it has a market mechanism that upholds competition. If they don't innovate, US enterprises cannot survive. Moreover, there is fierce competition among universities. Technological universities in the US serve as the source and foundation of science technology and innovation and are important technology patent makers. An important criterion for evaluating a university is its impact on industrial development, namely, to what extent it facilitates technical progress in relevant industries. In relying on Stanford University and UC Berkeley, Silicon Valley has emerged as a driver of global development in the electronics and information industry. Second, the US is able to attract global talent with preferential treatment and global top students with generous scholarships. Of those employed in new start-up companies that set up each year in Silicon Valley, over 50% are Asians, and most of this figure are Chinese and Indian. Third, the US government began innovative engineering projects at different stages to drive economic and social development and worked with enterprises to help them overcome their difficulties, thus driving global science and technological progress. For example, the Manhattan Project drove nuclear industry development, the Star Wars Program facilitated space and aeronautics industry development, the information superhighway pushed development of the Internet, and the new energy program and manufacturing sector resurgence plan currently underway are also delivering breakthroughs. Fourth, the US has advanced venture capital systems. The US provides whole-chain financial services, including angel investment, seed money, venture capital fund, private equity investment fund and Growth Enterprise Market etc. for STI activities throughout the stages of initiation, improvement, and engineering and industrialization. Where Stanford University is located, there is also a small town with a concentration of a large number of venture capital firms. These companies maintain close contact with professors and students from Stanford. Those who with research findings or even just an idea can attract many venture capitalists that help them analyze market prospects and translate innovative ideas into tangible benefits as quickly as possible. Almost every professor and student in the electronic engineering department of Stanford University has owned patents or companies. Fifth, military technologies are put to civil use free of charge, which helps drive development of the civil high-tech industry. Each year, the US Department of Defense has over 300 billion dollars of military R&D expenditure and product orders. Entrusted enterprises can put these military technologies to civil use without being charged. Integration between the military and civilian sectors pushes forward the development of cutting-edge technologies. In aiming to close the gap in S&T between China and the rest of the world, we should draw lessons from these practices.

We need to facilitate cultural innovation and build a prosperous cultural industry by fully utilizing our enduring and rich cultural resources, and strive to provide the general public with pleasant cultural products that can prevail in the world.

The Suggestions state that STI should play a leading role in facilitating innovation across the board. Science and technology constitute primary productivity, which sees productivity playing a decisive role in the relations of production, and the economic base plying a similar role in relation to the superstructure. This means that economic and social development that is STI driven will inevitably play a decisive and leading role in boosting theoretical, institutional and cultural innovation. Thinking modes and behavior patterns related to STI and resulting social customs that uphold innovation can exert a significant all-round influence on innovation, thus helping to build an innovative country.

19.2 Pursue Coordinated Development with a Focus on Rural Areas and the Central and Western Regions and on Social Development

The growing gap between urban and rural development is the outstanding problem in China's economy today. The development gap between the central and western regions and the eastern region is primarily manifest in the disparity in rural areas, thus making the regional gap an essentially urban-rural divide. One of the highlights of recent years has been that the incomes of rural residents have grown at a faster rate than urban residents. That said, the urban-rural resident income ratio is still high at 2.7:1. We have to increase the incomes of farmers, especially those in the middle and western parts of China, as soon as possible. And this is a problem that must be resolved during the 13th Five-Year Plan period.

The key to narrowing the gap between urban and rural areas is to facilitate reform and development lies in terms of urban-rural integration. This includes promoting agricultural modernization, building a new countryside and granting urban residency to rural migrant workers. This approach offers the greatest potential for China's development today. During a group study session for members of the CPC Political Bureau on April 30 last year, President Xi Jinping delivered an important speech on urban-rural integration. He remarked: "The most difficult and complicated part of building a moderately prosperous society in all respects is the development of rural areas, especially rural poverty-stricken areas." "We must step up our efforts and increase investment to secure major breakthroughs in coordinating urban and rural development, especially on the issues of breaking the urban-rural dual structure, promoting equal exchange of urban and rural factors and ensuring balanced allocation of public resources. This will help inject new impetus into rural development and involve farmers in the reform and development process in an equitable way, so that they can share the fruits of the reform and development." He further argued, "Our goals are to ensure equal basic rights for urban and rural residents, equal public services in urban and rural areas, a balance between urban and rural incomes, reasonable allocation of urban rural factors and integration of urban and rural industries." This speech pointed out the direction for urban-rural integration reforms and identified the key goals for realizing urban-rural coordinated development. The whole Party should place great importance on this speech and act in line with its philosophies in all respects.

Ensuring equal basic rights for urban and rural residents is a precondition for urban-rural integration. At present, the inequality in basic rights between urban and rural residents is manifested primarily in two aspects. The first is the inequality in property rights. Urban means of production and consumption have both been totally commercialized. All land, factory buildings, equipment and residences owned by the state, collectively or individually have all been allowed to move freely in the market. However, the situation relating to rural land and residence property rights remains unclear. Rural households' legal person property rights to land and houses are yet to be implemented, which means farmers' most important means of production and consumption have yet to be commercialized. As a result, unlike urban residents, those in rural areas cannot enjoy the benefits brought by real estate during the course of urbanization. Herein lies the greatest inequality in terms of the basic rights of urban and rural residents and the most important reason for the widening income gap between the two. Second is the inequality in the household registration system. Despite making a huge contribution to the development of cities, 280 million rural migrant workers cannot enjoy the various social security and public service benefits on offers to those with urban household registration because they hold rural household registration. Moreover, for the majority, their family members do not live with them. The Decision of the Third Plenary Session of the 18th CPC Central Committee states that "Farmers are entitled to owning, using, earning, and transferring mortgage contract management rights and warranty rights regarding contracted land." It also states, "The usufruct of farmer household homesteads should be protected, the system of rural homesteads be reformed, a number of pilot areas be selected, mortgaged, and guaranteed, and transfer of rural property rights be facilitated in a careful and steady manner, and ultimately a path to increased rural property income be found." "Under the precondition of compliance with planning and usage regulations, the transfer, leasing and pooling of profitable collective land for construction in rural areas should be permitted, so that it is on a level footing equal with state-owned land in entering the market in terms of rights and prices." As important breakthroughs in the rural land system and residence system, the three aforementioned reforms will see rural land and houses becoming commodities, and they confirm farmer households' ownership of their houses and the legal person property rights of contracted land and homesteads. They will also activate the decisive role of market in rural land resource allocation, facilitate the economic and intensive utilization of land resources, provide an institutional guarantee for farmers in voluntarily choosing whether their residence and household registration is urban or rural, and open the door for them to earn property income through transferring houses and land usage rights including homesteads. If during the 13th Five-Year Plan period a change was made to allow the usufruct of rural land to be mortgaged, it would lead to a 20 trillion yuan of banking loans and social investment for agricultural modernization, which would allow for us to build a new countryside and grant urban residency to rural migrant workers. This would ensure social capital is put to better use. In this were to be the case, we would witness dramatic changes in rural areas and the income gap between urban and rural areas would be narrowed greatly. Tapping into this huge demand potential would be decisive in stabilizing growth. Chongqing is a city that has been facilitating reform on urban-rural integration for seven consecutive years, and the rate at which it is granting urban residency is one of the fastest in China. This has created strong impetus for growth and turned it into the fastest growing city nationwide.

Social development lagging behind economic development is another manifestation of structural distortion. In particular, the demand for public services of most people cannot be met, especially in the areas of education, health care, social security, municipal administration, culture, sports and information. The reason behind the insufficient supply of public services is because of a major reliance on fiscal input. When fiscal input is inadequate, development slows down. Reform of the investment system and public-private partnership can ensure reasonable economic returns from public service investment and attract social investment and banking loans for developing public services, which will play a significant role in expanding domestic demand and stabilizing growth.

19.3 Uphold Green Development by Developing the Environmental Protection Industry into a Pillar Industry

The government work report states that we should develop environmental protection so it becomes a pillar industry. This is the fundamental approach to achieving green development. Building a beautiful China and ensuring clean air and water and a comfortable living environment represent the ardent aspirations and solemn commitment of China's administration. The key to reaching these goals is to set up effective mechanisms and systems, so as to attract social funds and bank loans for environmental governance and make the environmental protection industry a new investment hot spot and economic growth point. At the Third Plenary Session of the 18th Central Committee, the CPC decided to accelerate the building an ecological progress system, which includes system of paid resource usage, an ecological compensation system, a polluter payment system and third-party treatment system centered on the public goods value compensation mechanism. In doing so, we can put the reasonable returns they provide toward environmental governance investment and R&D for environmental protection technologies. In the meantime, we also need to improve the standards for pollutant emissions and set up a strict supervision and inspection system. This will ensure that the business operations of all enterprises begin at the same starting line, that no enterprise conscientiously implementing the standards will suffer losses and that no enterprise practicing fraud and continuing to release stealth emissions will reap benefits. As a matter of fact, when it comes to environmental governance, what we lack is neither technology nor funding, but mechanisms. The government work report focused on the establishment of the pollution treatment system and mechanism, a move which has boosted the confidence of the people that environmental improvements are being made. As we improve the environment by developing the environmental protection industry, those who, up to now, have thought that more investment in environmental governance will inevitably slow down economic growth will change their outlook. We will see a huge leap in our thinking as we work to cultivate the environmental protection industry into a pillar industry and add the shared commodities of clean air and water and a beautiful environment into our GDP calculations. All this will necessarily help eradicate smog, bring about clear skies, clean water, and improve the ecological environment as soon as possible.

19.4 Adhere to Open Development by Undertaking a Higher Level of Economic Opening up

The 13th Five-Year Plan set the goal of undertaking a higher level of economic opening up. The goal was proposed to adapt the trend of China's in-depth economic integration into the global economy and represents a requirement for further opening the country. To achieve a higher level of economic opening up, we need to, first and foremost, achieve sound coordination between what is going on at home and abroad, ensure a balance between imports and exports, give equal prominence to "bringing in" and "going global," introduce capital, technology and talent simultaneously and better utilize both domestic and international markets and resources. We need to optimize export structures, improve the value added and technology content of export products, and work for a gradual transition from labor- and resource-intensive products being our main exports to mainly technology-, capital- and knowledge-intensive products being our main exports. We will expand service exports and get rid of the service trade deficit. Efforts will also be made to increase the share of general trade exports. In light of global market sluggishness, we will create export demand by expanding overseas investments to drive commodity and labor service exports through capital exports. We will utilize technology resources and international marketing networks from overseas enterprises and enhance the technical innovation and international business operation capacity of domestic enterprises by promoting international mergers and acquisitions; break the energy and resource bottlenecks impeding our economic development by purchasing exploitation rights to overseas energy resources; facilitate the export of domestic parts and components by conducting processing trade abroad; and drive exports of domestic construction materials and engineering equipment by undertaking engineering projects in other countries. In terms of import commodities such as petroleum, iron ore, soybean, cotton and palm oil, we will establish stable overseas bases for production and supply, and ports, storage, and transport facilities through overseas investments. Guided by the Belt and Road initiative, we will boost economic cooperation with participating countries to create a new picture of opening to the outside world. Third, we will facilitate two-way opening in the financial industry. With the focus on the internationalization of the RMB, we will enhance overseas circulation of the RMB as a settlement instrument for international trade and technology resources and reserve currency, and expand the scale of bilateral RMB swaps with other countries. While opening domestic financial markets, we should encourage domestic commercial banks to set up overseas branches. Ensuring a generally stable RMB interest rate is an important condition of its internationalization. Fourth, we will be actively involved in global economic governance and public goods supply and ensure we have a greater say in formulating international economic rules. Efforts will be made to strengthen the international coordination of macro-economic policies, so as to contribute to world economic stability.

19.5 Stick to Shared Development by Building a Moderately Prosperous Society for the People

The Recommendations adopted at the Fifth Plenary Session uphold the principle of the major role of the people and emphasize a people-oriented development philosophy. Improving livelihoods and facilitating people's all-round development represent the starting point and ultimate goal of China's development. In the 38 years since the reform and opening up began, living standards have greatly increased. That's said, we cannot ignore the widening income gap between individuals and China's high Gini coefficient. Deng Xiaoping proposed that a certain group of people and some regions be allowed to get rich first, and that they would then in turn help others to achieve common prosperity. It is now time to highlight common prosperity. The strategic priorities in the 13th Five-Year Plan period will be poverty alleviation and the building of a moderately prosperous society. Focusing on promoting self-reliance instead of reliance on others, we will work to enhance the employability of those on low-incomes to boost their take-home pay. Coastal cities in all regions are having difficulties in recruiting workers. Endowing each worker with one labor skill through vocational training and encouraging them to seek employment outside their hometowns is a shortcut to poverty eradication. For poor families unable to secure a living from work, we should utilize social security systems to ensure they have decent lives. This is a manifestation of the superiority of the socialist system.

The concept of innovative, coordinated, green, open and shared development is well-established. Innovative development plays a leading role in overall development, coordinated development acts as the mechanism for balanced development, green development reflects the quality requirements of development, open development facilitates exchange of resources, culture and value between China and other countries, and shared development is the engine for further development. If this development concept is carried forward, the economy will always develop in the right direction under the leadership of innovation, fluctuations will be avoided through the institutional guarantee of balanced development, more ecological, economic and social benefits will be brought about in accordance with green economy standards, the product exchange and complementarity in strengths needed to build an open economy of a higher level will be developed, and common prosperity will be achieved by sharing development outcomes. In doing so, we will unleash the enthusiasm for labor and creativity of all people. The new development concept marks a higher level of understanding about the development of rules underlying the socialist market economy with Chinese characteristics. Under its guidance, our economy can come to resemble a hi-speed train speeding toward its destination in a steady, secure and timely manner.

Chapter 20
China Has Great Potential to Join the Ranks of High-Income Countries

In 2015, China's per capita GDP reached US$8000, but there is still a long way to go before reaching high-income status with at least US$12,000 of per capita income. According to the experience of other countries, this is a difficult task. Many countries have failed to join that rank regardless of years of hard work. For China, it is a test on the socialist market economy system with Chinese characteristics as well as on the CPC's governance capability. In accordance with the requirements of the Third Plenary Session of the 18th CPC Central Committee, China should focus on the "Three Reforms," unleash the huge potential from the three aspects of reform, and put in place three engines of economic growth, which would be enough to drive China to become a high-income country by around 2022.

20.1 Facilitate Urban-Rural Integration and Eliminate Misunderstandings

If the positive and negative experiences of development are analyzed, it is clear that all the countries that joined the ranks of high-income countries did so after basically eliminating the gap between the urban and rural development, while all those falling into the middle-income trap had a huge gap between urban and rural development. Over the 40 years of industrialization in the Republic of Korea, the urban-rural income ratio always stood at around 1:0.9. There are two main reasons behind this: First, the country has successfully implemented a campaign for building a new countryside since the 1970s. Second, farmers transferred their land to generate income from land appreciation during the course of urbanization. The urban-rural income ratio in China now stands at 2.7:1, which indicates a salient feature of the urban-rural dual economic structure. This is not only a major obstacle to joining the

---

This article originally appeared in *Reference News*, April 7, 2016.

X. Zheng, *China's 40 Years of Economic Reform and Development*,
https://doi.org/10.1007/978-981-13-2727-8_20

ranks of high-income countries, but also a major potential opportunity for current economic growth. There are three reasons for the large gap between urban and rural development.

First, the inequality in property rights and household registration rights between urban and rural residents is hampering farmers' income. The houses of urban residents have already been commodified, while those of farmers have not, which made it impossible for farmers to share the benefits of real estate appreciation during the course of urbanization. This is the major reason for the widened income gap between urban and rural residents. Rural migrant workers have contributed a great deal to the cities they worked in, but their status as rural residents made it impossible for them to share in the various public services associated with urban residents.

Second, there are still policy barriers between urban and rural markets, which severely constrained the two-way free flow of production factors and increase of agricultural productivity. The rural labor force, funds, and land can constantly flow into cities, while the capital, talent, and technology from urban areas cannot flow to the rural areas.

Third, the government invested in public services and infrastructure concentrated in cities, so the better the cities are built, the bigger the contrast there will be between urban and rural areas.

The *Decision* of the Third Plenary Session of the 18th CPC Central Committee made important breakthroughs in the management system of rural contracted land, homestead, and profitable collective land for construction by allowing mortgages, guarantees, and transfers of usufruct. According to rough estimates, the transfer fees of the right to contract and use land exceeded 1 trillion yuan per year; and the total value of homesteads reached over 50 trillion yuan. If the three lands can be used as pledges, 20 trillion yuan of banking loans and social funds will be pooled during the 13th Five-Year Plan period, which will be invested in agricultural modernization, building of a new countryside, and making sure rural migrant workers enjoy the same rights as urban residents. Moreover, it will help make better use of social capital. The circulation of land management rights can help develop intensive farming and modern agriculture, raise more demand for means of production, such as agricultural machinery, and attract a high-quality agricultural labor force, so as to greatly increase agricultural productivity and make farming a truly decent profession. The building of a new countryside will change rural living conditions and eco-systems, make rural areas more livable and more beautiful, and create new huge markets for construction materials, home appliances, and vehicles. Ensuring rural migrant workers enjoy the same rights as urban residents will fulfill the family reunion dream of 413 million citizens (over 200 million rural migrant workers, 60 million children stay behind in rural areas when their parents work in cities, 43 million women, and 40 million senior citizens), and create huge demand for city construction and service industry development. China must conscientiously implement General Secretary Xi Jinping's requirements to "gradually let rural residents have equal basic rights and interests and the same public services as urban residents, balance the income of rural and urban residents, optimize the distribution of essential factors," facilitate reform and development of urban-rural integration, completely change the appearance of rural areas, narrow the income gap between urban and rural residents in a quick manner, and finish the building of a moderately prosperous society in all respects by 2020.

The reform on urban-rural integration holds the key to eliminating misunderstandings. Separating rural land ownership from usufruct and allowing mortgages, guarantees, and transfers of usufruct are not negations of public land ownership, but are improvements of the realization of collective land ownership. Only by separating ownership from usufruct and making land production factors that can be exchanged and integrated, can China match the market economy and activate the decisive role of the market in the allocation of land. Of course, land transfers will be subject to usage regulations. The transfer of rural land into non-rural land has to comply with laws and regulations. In February, the State Council issued the Guidelines of Facilitating New Urbanization, which requires that the policy on matching urban construction land increase and rural construction land decrease be thoroughly implemented. This represents the specific implementation of carrying forward the philosophies of the Third Plenary Session. In fact, China drew upon the experience of the state-owned asset management system reform before launching rural land system reform. The Third Plenary Session of the 14th Central Committee made it a requirement that SOEs be endowed with legal person property rights to their state-owned assets, so as to effectively match the market economy with the economy under the ownership of the whole people. The Second Plenary Session of the 18th Central Committee further required the transformation from asset management to capital management, so as to bring about closer integration between the market economy and the economy under the ownership of the whole people. For a long time, the absence of rural land commodification has severely constrained the integration between the rural economy and market economy, and has constrained the development of rural productivity too. The direction of rural land system reform proposed by the Third Plenary Session should be strictly implemented.

Last year, Chongqing's GDP saw a year-on-year increase of 11%, ranking it first among Chinese provinces as well as autonomous regions and municipalities. How is it that Chongqing, which is located in the underdeveloped mountainous western part of the country, can lead the whole country? The major reason is that the urban-rural integration reform implemented for seven consecutive years has unleashed huge potential for growth. In recent years, Chongqing's rate of transforming migrants into urban residents has been faster than all the cities in China. Thanks to the municipality's unified land ticket market, farmers who withdraw from homestead can share the differential rent and generate considerable property income. The market mechanism and government support are equivalent to providing each farmer becoming an urban resident with 100,000 yuan of "settlement allowance" and five "new clothes"; namely, health care, pension fund, housing security, children's education, and all the public services for urban residents. Chongqing's experience, if promoted, is bound to inject huge impetus into the whole economy, becoming a fundamental approach to overcoming the middle-income trap.

20.2 Improve the Investment System and Increase the Public Goods

At present, our means of production and consumption are almost totally subject to overcapacity, while only public goods and services suffer from insufficient supply. Environment, transportation, municipal administration, education, health care, elderly care, information, and culture can hardly meet the demands of the vast majority of residents. What resulted in the insufficient supply of public goods was the enduring major reliance on fiscal investments. Inadequate funding has led to lagged development, and rural development is lagging behind urban development. To solve this problem, China must accelerate reform of the investment system, advance the model of government-enterprise cooperation, ensure reasonable return on public goods investment through policy formulation, and select qualified enterprises for construction and operation missions through open tendering. Specifically, there are several options, including Build-Operate-Transfer (BOT) and Build-Transfer (BT). This model would make it easy to solve urban traffic jams as well as parking, medical treatment, kindergarten enrollment, nursing home, and garbage and sewage treatment problems. Moreover, China should quicken its pace to build high-speed railway networks covering the whole country and rail transit networks within city clusters and between downtown and on the outskirts, and put in place new-generation networks covering urban and rural areas, so as to lay a solid foundation for future development. Making energy efficiency and environmental protection a pillar industry represents an important mission put forward by the government work report this year. This requires that China get rid of the stereotype that environmental governance impedes economic development and treat environmental governance as a new investment hot spot and economic growth point. To this end, China needs to implement the make polluters pay for waste treatment scheme and the third-party management system put forward by the Third Plenary Session. The government needs to map out unified standards of pollutant discharge and practice strict supervision and inspection. As a result, all enterprises can conduct their businesses at the same starting line, no enterprise conscientiously treating pollution will suffer losses, and no enterprise practicing fraud will reap benefits. It should be noted that existing technologies and equipment used against various pollutants are mature, so most of the problems could be properly resolved with domestic technologies. As long as the country is willing to conscientiously fight pollution with an adequate amount of resources, China will be able to overcome smog and bring about a clear sky at an early date. Thanks to the aforementioned supply-side reform, investment will be vitalized and the investment structure will optimized. This will not only manifest the nation's people-oriented development objective, but also play a critical role in overcoming the "middle-income trap" by stabilizing near-term growth and sustaining long-term growth.

The prevalence of the public-private partnership (PPP) model requires coordination of multiple departments. The planning and supervisory authorities should bear the responsibility of selecting the best construction projects, the finance departments should offer and guide funding, and banking credit funds should be followed up on. Only through inter-departmental coordination can the country attain greater achievements. Otherwise, any single department will find it difficult to accomplish the mission. When choosing investment entities, China should uphold competition by treating state-owned enterprises (SOEs) and private enterprises equally. The country will encourage enterprises of all ownerships to establish project companies with shareholding systems, put in place strong leadership agencies, and bear the risks of investment. China will adhere to the project owner responsibility system, bidding and tendering system, and construction supervision system that have been proven effective, so as to ensure the quality of engineering projects. Efforts need to be made to strengthen the entire management process, from construction and operations and to the capital pay-off of the PPP projects, while also averting the risks of breach of contracts and other liability problems.

20.3 Draw upon the US Experience and Focus on Science, Technology, and Innovation

To transcend the middle-income trap, China must realize the industrial structure transition from the mainly labor-intensive and resource-intensive structure to the mainly capital-intensive, technology-intensive, and knowledge-intensive structure. This requires that China increase technology research and development (R&D) input, and improve industrial structure and product structure through technologies with proprietary intellectual property rights. Relying on technologies brought by overseas-funded enterprises will not make China a high-income country, because whoever masters these technologies has the right to allocate the profits In order to enrich the people and build a stronger country, improving technology R&D capacity and international competitiveness is the only way forward.

Comparatively speaking, the US has long been leading the world in science and technology, so it has accumulated rich and successful experience. In 2015, the US applied for 57,000 international patents, down by 6.7% compared with the previous year; China applied for 30,000, up by 16.8% compared with the previous year. US applications were 1.9 times those of China. However, in 2011, US international patent applications were six times higher than China's. China is rapidly narrowing its gap with the US in terms of international patent applications. For domestic patent applications, China has outperformed the US to rank first in the world since 2006. To catch up with and surpass the US in science, technology, and innovation (STI) capacity, China needs to learn from the US in at least five aspects.

First, the US boasts a fully competitive market. Without innovation, enterprises will soon border on bankruptcy. Therefore, US companies all treat innovation as the way to survive. US universities also compete with each other fiercely. Only good universities can attract high-quality students and pay faculties with higher salaries. The quality of a university is determined mainly by its impact on relevant industries, namely to what extent a school or department is driving the technological progress of relevant industries. Silicon Valley thrived mainly by relying on Stanford University and the University of California, Berkeley. All professors and students majoring in technology at those two schools conduct scientific research and own their own patents or even enterprises. Universities are the origins of science and technology (S&T) progress and the bases of technology patent creation. The students are innovative thinkers, and the professors who produce them are standing at the very forefront of S&T.

Second, the US government started major innovative science and technology projects at different stages and works with enterprises to overcome difficulties, thus driving global technology progress. For example, the Manhattan Project drove the nuclear industry development; the Star Wars Program facilitated space and aeronautics industry development; the information superhighway pushed the development of the Internet; and the newly proposed new energy program and reindustrialization plan are also making progress.

Third, the US has a well-established venture capital system, including Angel Investment, Seed Money, venture capital funds, private equity funds, and NASDAQ. Besides Stanford University, there is also a small town pooling a large number of venture capital firms. Once professors and students in the university have any innovative idea, a large number of venture capitalists will come and help analyze methods for further research and prospects for technology engineering, commercialization, and industrialization, and provide the funding for them. Many innovations may fail in the end, but the benefits of the small amount of the successful innovations have made up for the losses of the failures.

Fourth, the US pools global talents. The US is attracting global innovative talents with generous pay and sound research conditions. Among the new start-up companies in Silicon Valley each year, about 50% are made by Asians, mainly Chinese and Indian. US universities pool global top students for further studies with generous scholarships. The best graduates will be chosen to stay to work. While China has proposed the idea of selecting talents worldwide for development, the US has long been practicing the same idea.

Fifth, the US boasts an industrial system featuring military-civil integration. Each year, the US Department of Defense funds over US$300 billion of military research programs and military product orders. Besides meeting the military demand, the entrusted enterprises can transfer their research outcomes for civil use, which drives the development of the high-tech industry for civilian use. As China is still catching up with the US in terms of STI, it is absolutely necessary that the country draws upon its experience by being a modest student.

China needs to further strengthen the role of enterprises as the major players in innovation. What is delightful is that Huawei and ZTE have been ranking globally among the top three for several years in a row in terms of international patent applications. Among the top 10, about half are Chinese-funded enterprises. China should encourage enterprises to put more of profits into R&D investment. Particularly, SOEs should play a leading role in driving innovation. For high-tech products that are highly reliant on imports, such as chips, engines, and carbon fiber, the country should build industrial clusters, work together to deal with difficulties, and share the benefits.

The low rate of research finding translations is an outstanding issue for China. The reasons are as follows: Some technologies are not mature enough; attention paid to and investment in engineering and industrialization of technology outcomes are inadequate; and as the bulk of the benefits of technology transfer for on-duty inventions has to go to the finance department, the inventors are not enthusiastic to translate their research findings. Effective measures should be adopted to solve these problems. By rallying efforts of various stakeholders, China can accelerate the translation of R&D outcomes into actual productivity.

Reforming the education system, establishing high-level and innovative universities, and cultivating a large number of innovative talents represent the basic strategic project for enhancing innovation capacity and implementing innovation-driven development. Over the three decades or so since reform and opening up, China has worked to make enterprises the major innovation players and to solve the enduring problem of the separation of S&T and the economy through reforming the S&T system. However, S&T remains separate from education. The universities are still weak in innovation capacity and exert little impact on industrial technological progress. Patent applications from universities are few among global universities. There is an extremely severe shortage of innovative professors, and outdated textbooks are imparting backward technologies and knowledge to the students. The competition mechanism is absent among and within universities, and top talents are hard to produce due to an uncompetitive mechanism. The universities have failed to set up mechanisms for close cooperation with the venture capital system and with enterprises, resulting in the separation between talent cultivation and market demand.

Reforming the education system requires, first and foremost, the establishment of a competition mechanism among and within universities. The country should put in place a third-party evaluation system for the quality of universities and a system for appointing professors. Social-funded and Sino-foreign cooperative schools should be encouraged. The California Institute of Technology (Caltech), which helped China select and produce Qian Xuesen, has been ranked first among technology universities for five consecutive years. One of its features is that its undergraduates are not allowed to apply for graduate programs at Caltech, and its graduates are not allowed to assume teaching posts in Caltech, so as to avoid easy entry into the institute without competition. China can learn from this mechanism.

Second, Caltech selects innovative professors globally and gives them preferential treatment. Stanford University and Caltech are both extremely strict in professor selection. Only top scholars widely recognized around the world can be recruited, so as to select the best of the best and avoid choosing too many. If the mechanism is hard to implement on a large scale, it can be implemented in some schools first and then its coverage can be expanded gradually.

Third, a matching mechanism for universities and venture capital should be set up. The country needs to improve the venture capital system from angel investment to the Growth Enterprise Market, and provide follow-up services for the entire innovation process. University professors and students should be encouraged to create patents and other technology outcomes and establish high- and new-tech enterprises with their outcomes.

Fourth, from basic education to college education, cramming and exam-oriented education should be replaced by inspirational and innovative education, so as to make students ambitious about changing the world and to encourage innovative thinking. China should increase the share of vocational education and stress practical skill training for students. Universities should be given autonomy in selecting disciplines, professor enrollment, and teaching content and methods for student cultivation.

Part III
Macro Regulation

Chapter 21
The Macro Regulatory System of China's Market Economy

21.1 Macro Regulation of Decentralized and Coordinated Market Economies

At present, major Western countries with market economies are using different macro regulatory systems according to their own situations, forming various market economy models. Generally, these models can be divided into two categories: decentralized market economies and coordinated market economies.

The decentralized market economy, represented by the United States and the United Kingdom, has the following three features: (1) Rather than formulating a programmatic plan for economic development, the states only make routine fiscal budget plans; (2) The states do not formulate industrial policies, but implement protective tariff policies for certain industries at different times; (3) Direct financing is the main source of enterprise funds, while indirect financing plays a subsidiary role.

The main features of the coordinated market economy, which is represented by Germany, Japan, and South Korea are: (1) The states formulate programmatic plans for economic development, including mid- and long-term plans, annual plans, and special plans; (2) The states formulate industrial policies and provide support through fiscal and economic policies for different tasks at different stages of economic development: (3) Indirect financing is the main source of enterprise funds, while direct financing plays a subsidiary role.

Obviously, the biggest difference between the two economic models is the degree to which the government intervenes in the economy. Although economists are still debating the merits of the two models, one fact is undeniable: The coordinated market economy would create a more favorable environment for the country's economy, and thus enable the economy to develop faster in the long run. This can be proven from the

---

This article originally appeared in *China Industrial Economics*, no. 9, 1993.

X. Zheng, *China's 40 Years of Economic Reform and Development*,
https://doi.org/10.1007/978-981-13-2727-8_21

American people's accusation of the government during the presidential election of 1992 and the strengthened intervention in the market by the Clinton administration.

In countries with coordinated market economies, the three regulating leverages; namely, planning, fiscal regulation, and financial regulation, play different roles in macro regulation.

Germany's financial regulations are its core means for regulating the economy. Independent of government, the central bank is fully and exclusively responsible for money issuance and price stabilization in the market. The independent banking system is the most significant feature of the former Federal Republic of Germany's economic management system. Because of this system, the former Federal Republic of Germany has maintained price stability since the late 1950s, which provides the conditions for the German economy to maintain stable growth over a long period of time.

The central focus of macro regulation in Japan is actually fiscal regulation. In particular, during the rapid-growth stage of the 1960s and 1970s, the government accumulated a large amount of construction funds, including the fiscal budget, national debt, postal savings, and insurance funds of what was known as special accounting, which was used for policy-based investment and lending. The government also directed and diverted commercial bank loans, which ensured the implementation of industrial policies and the realization of the national economic development plan. It was the fiscal investment and financing that stimulated exports and helped Japan to achieve the industrialization of heavy industry and the chemical industry. Fiscal investment and financing can be regarded as Japan's most successful macro regulation, and one of the most important explanations for Japan's rapid economic growth since the 1950s.

South Korea takes planning as the centerpiece of its macro regulation. The Economic Planning Board (EPB) created by South Korea in the early 1960s had four major functions: designing plans, coordinating policies, budgeting, and maintaining market order. As a super ministry, the EPB is the center of the market economy system dominated by the government. It is a significant feature for South Korea's macroeconomic management system to integrate a fiscal budget with an economic development plan and to support the plan with a budget and credit program. In 1962, South Korea was a backward agricultural country with per capita GNP of US$87. Now, this number has reached nearly US$7000 and the country has become an emerging industrialized country producing sound industrial products, including steel, automobiles, ships, petroleum, and electronics, which rank in the world's top 10 product rankings. South Korea's first five-year plan was compiled in 1962, and six five-year plans have been completed so far. The national economic development of South Korea has basically followed its planned path.

Although Germany, Japan, and South Korea adopted different macroeconomic management systems, their practice has proven that all these systems are successful. This is because their systems not only fit the countries' economic and technological levels, the competitiveness of their enterprises, and their national cultural and social context, but also because they adapt to the different requirements of important tasks at different stages of their economic development. Although the present macroeconomic systems of Japan and South Korea are very different from their rapid growth stages, their experience and the experience of other emerging industrialized countries and regions have proven that if the latecomers are to implement a catch-up strategy and reach the development level in a short period of time, which took two or three centuries for developed countries to attain, the government must play the leading role so that the defects of market regulation can be offset by the government and the resources can be concentrated in the places with the best economic returns. Without the powerful macro regulation of the government, industrial development would have to rely on the spontaneous regulation of the market—a lengthy process, which means quite lot of inefficient and redundant construction while the concentrations of technology and production are gradually improved through competition. The "latecomer advantage" cannot be leveraged in this way.

21.2 The Main Tasks for Macro Regulation

At present, productivity in China is relatively low and the productivity structure is still a dual-sector model, which means the Chinese economy still faces the dual tasks of industrialization and modernization. Playing catch-up is essential for achieving the level of per capita GNP as in medium-developed countries by the middle of the 21st century. China should establish a socialist market economy system to unleash the enormous potential of the Chinese economy and, at the same time, build the macroeconomic regulatory system. The main tasks for macro regulation are:

1. *Maintaining balance in economic aggregate*

The balance between gross demand and gross supply is the fundamental balance in various economic relationships. Only when the economic aggregate is balanced can China stabilize price levels and achieve steady economic growth. Maintaining balance in economic aggregate should take both demand and supply into consideration. Regulating demand involves moderate investment controls and the growth speed of consumption. The trickiest problem at present is that the past administrative regulation, which regulates by issuing investment plans, is not effective anymore, but the new risk-restraint mechanism has yet to be established; therefore, the investment regulatory system, which mainly relies on indirect means, cannot function effectively. The investment inflation that began in 1993 has come into being, resulting in a sharp increase of investment prices and a drop in the RMB exchange rate because of the increasing reliance on exports. If this situation cannot be changed immediately, then there might be a risk of inflation. The fundamental cause of this situation is the lagging financial system reform and the present double-track currency price system, which together cause a large amount of money to circulate outside the banking system. Local governments at all levels and enterprises manage to raise funds, issue stocks and bonds, or use bank and non-bank lenders, and use cash flow lending so as to bypass the restraints of the credit system and expand fixed asset investments.

The development of the economic situation fully demonstrates that it is necessary to strengthen financial regulations and restrain the expansion of gross demand.

2. *Optimizing the industrial structure and regional productivity distribution*

Under the market economy, the market mechanism will play a basic role in the allocation of resources. But the market is not a panacea. Experience in many countries has shown that the government should play an important role in adjusting the industrial structure and the regional productivity distribution. Therefore, an important function of macro regulation is to use various economic leverages to guide the flow of funds so that the funds can meet the requirements of economic development strategies and structural adjustment. Government regulation is compatible with the market mechanism, and acts as a supplement to market regulation. The structural adjustment is confronted with three main tasks: (1) Attracting funds for infrastructure construction and basic industries so as to overcome the restraints of transportation, telecommunication, and energy; (2) Overcoming the inappropriate investment structure and constructing and building in accordance with the required economic scale; (3) Solving the problem of the aggravated imbalance of regional economic development due to the large flow of funds into coastal areas from inland areas. Obviously, these problems can't be solved by the market alone, so powerful government regulations are essential.

3. *Developing enterprise groups that are globally competitive*

The development of contemporary industrial production has the characteristics of internationalization, centralization, and socialization. Large transnational enterprise groups are very critical to production, research, and trade. Internationalization means the production of product accessories can be distributed across the world according to the principle of comparative advantages. Concentration means that some industries are increasingly concentrated in a few enterprises; and the larger the enterprise is, the stronger its capability for technological development and competitiveness. Socialization means that as production becomes increasingly dissected, the market share of an enterprise's product becomes higher. In this case, only by integrating Chinas industrial production into the world production system can the nation learn production technology and management experience. China cannot have business relations with foreign transnational companies without large enterprise groups. Large foreign enterprise groups are formed gradually through long-term competition. China should actively develop enterprise groups and strive to create a group of internationally famous and competitive enterprises in a relatively short period of time.

4. *Protecting the interests of the country and its enterprises in international communication*

With the expansion of the opening up of China, Chinese enterprises have more contacts with foreign countries. In foreign trade and exchanges, the government represents the nation's interests, and should use regulations, tariffs, and other means to adjust relations and negotiate with foreign governments. In particular, the restoration of China's status as a contracting party for the General Agreement on Tariffs and

Trade requires the country to reform the existing foreign trade system in accordance with international practices, which means that Chinese enterprises will directly face international competition. This situation makes it more necessary for the government to flexibly apply tax policies and to adjust import and export structures according to the requirements of structural adjustments and industrial upgrading so as to protect domestic infant industries and expand exports.

21.3 Coordination and Cooperation of Planning, Fiscal Policy, and Financial Regulations in Macroeconomic Regulation

Establishing an effective and flexible macroeconomic regulatory system is a prerequisite for a modern market economy to perform well. Departments that employ the means of regulations should cooperate closely with each other, and there should be checks and balances for rights and limitations within these departments. The most important thing is the coordination and cooperation of the three regulatory means; namely, planning, fiscal policy, and financial regulations.

Planning is the foundation of macro regulation. The economy and social development plan should include not only development goals, development priorities, and strategic principles, but also the means to guarantee the achievement of development goals (i.e. the employment of various leverages for economic regulation). Publishing various economic policies through planning can help direct micro-economic activities. The planning of the market economy is fundamentally different from a planned economy, for it is no longer plans consisting of mandatory plans and plans oriented toward indexing. Rather, the planning is orientation, predictions, and policy prescriptions. The plan stipulates that the state shall order goods and a few products that are vital to the economic life of the state and the economy. National plans are mainly mid- and long-term ones, while annual plans focus on balancing government finance, credit, and foreign currencies, as well as adjustments to the economic structure. For products whose supply and demand are volatile in the market, the annual plan will predict their production, construction, and demand in the domestic and foreign markets.

Fiscal policy is the principal means of macro regulation. Currently, government revenue takes up a relatively small part of national revenue, and the proportion of the Central Government's revenue to the government's overall revenue is also relatively small. Most of the country's finances are used to maintain the expenditures of current accounts, leaving little financial resources for construction. Thus, national finances are reduced to "payroll finances," and fail to play a crucial role in macro regulation. In the future, China will implement the multilevel budget system with reform of the fiscal and tax systems, in which case, government construction finances will increase over time. At the same time, China will issue national financial construction bonds to raise funds for national debt issued for economic construction. Government finance plays a more important role in the adjustment of the structure of the economy.

Financial regulations become increasingly important as reforms continue to deepen. Currently, banks account for over 80% of all enterprise financial resources. Therefore, financial regulation has played a crucial role not only in controlling the economic aggregate, but also in adjusting the economic structure. Countries with market-economies centered on financial regulation usually have a very powerful monetary regulation committee responsible for controlling the issuance of currency, so as to stabilize the economies of their countries. In China, it is essential to establish an independent Central Bank and a national monetary regulation committee. Likewise, China should correspondingly establish supervisory institutions to strengthen the supervision of banks, such as a banking supervision bureau (Note: In China, the supervisory institution is the China Banking Regulatory Commission). China should establish a risk-restraint mechanism inside the banking system and achieve a unified currency pricing system, from the dual exchange rate system to a floating exchange rate, which will strengthen the supervision of the Central Bank over commercial banks and other non-bank financial institutions. Based on the experiences of various countries, in order to have stable financial resources for key national infrastructure and basic industry construction projects, China needs to separate policy-backed financial institutions from commercial financial institutions and establish a long-term national development bank. Considering the fact that public ownership is the main theme of China's economic system, the country should establish a national investment corporation to operate the investments of state-owned capital funds. This investment corporation will be responsible for preserving and increasing the value of state-owned funds and will coordinate with the long-term national development bank to form a national investment policy and finance system.

The coordination and cooperation of planning, fiscal policies, and banks will generally be realized through the formulation and implementation of the yearly plan. When formulating the next annual plan, China should rely on the task of economic development to put forward fiscal policy and financial regulation proposals and draft plans after rounds of consultations and negotiations, submit the draft to the State Council for approval, and implement the plan after the approval of the National People's Congress.

During the implementation of the plan, China will encounter abrupt problems from time to time, in which case it will be necessary to regulate and coordinate in a timely manner. The specific measures to take and how forceful these measures will be must be determined by the regulation plan put forward by relevant departments after consultation and negotiation, then the regulation plan will be submitted to the State Council for a final decision. The contradictions that occur while coordinating and applying the economic levers and within departments will generally be solved through negotiations between relevant departments. Therefore, China should establish regular systems for the coordination of meetings and establish institutions within planning, economy and trade, monetary, and finance departments.

21.4 Establishing A Macroeconomic Regulatory System Requires Transformation of the Government Functions

The key reason why the market economy is able to be so energetic and dynamic is that it can enable every producer and operator to take full initiative and tap their creativity through material benefits and market competition. It allows producers and operators to choose the direction and approach of their businesses based on market demands and on the principle of benefits, in which case various production factors can flow to where there is the highest demand and profitability according to their prices.

Macro regulation must be carried out to accommodate this kind of initiative and free choice, and must be conducive to the smooth operation of the market system. The government's regulation of the market should follow the law of value, and therefore should never interrupt the market. Government regulation would be counterproductive if it crossed this line. For a long time, it has seemed that China's planning and regulations have been running counter to that law, which has impeded the development of productivity. Macro regulations have changed fundamentally under the market economy compared with that under the planned economy.

Enterprises are market entities, and the energy and power of economic development comes from the initiatives and free choices of enterprises. At present, part of the power that ought to belong to SOEs is still in the hands of the government, hindering the transformation of the operation system of SOEs. Thus the government should continue to transform its functions and truly regulate and manage the macroeconomy, and relax and liberalize the microeconomy. SOEs cannot make their own management decisions and take full responsibility for their profits and losses until they are no longer reliant on the government. Reforming existing SOEs into limited liability companies is common in market-economy countries, and could cause the state to shed its never-ending liability of enterprises. It would help separate the government from enterprises and enable the government to separate its regulations on state-owned assets from its macro regulation function, which not only facilitates the implementation of the autonomous operational rights of SOEs, but also helps the government to concentrate on macro regulation.

Maintaining market order and protecting reasonable competition are also major functions of macro regulation. All the developed countries with market-economies have anti-monopoly laws and fair competition laws as a way to regularize and standardize the economy. China is just getting started in this respect, so it is inevitable that the nation encounter some disorder and illegal activities, which nonetheless should be taken seriously. China needs to learn from other countries and accelerate economic legislation so as to build rules-based economic operations and macro regulations.

Chapter 22
Ensuring 8 Percent Economic Growth This Year

As one of the three main factors supporting economic growth this year, domestic consumption demand will continue to grow steadily. It is estimated that the gross retail sales of consumer goods this year will grow by 10%, and consumption demand will take up approximately 3 percentage points of the 8% of economic growth this year. However, there remain uncertainties in the promoting function of investments in fixed assets and exports for economic growth.

After July 1997, following the drastic depreciation of the Thai Baht (THB), currencies of some Southeast Asian countries and regions likewise plunged one after another, and the value of these currencies in the US stock market and HK market fell below records. In order to respond to the impact of the Asian financial crisis on China's economy, in April 2018 I wrote the article Problems and Advice for Ensuring the 8% Growth Rate for This Year, and proposed to expand domestic demand by issuing national debt. This article was submitted to the State Council by Mr. Zeng Peiyan, the then Minister of the National Planning Commission, after which the then Premier Zhu Rongji wrote: "Li Lanqing, Wu Bangguo, Wen Jiabao, and Wu Yi, please read this article" on April 18, 1998. Wu Bangguo, Vice Premier of the State Council, wrote on April 23 that "we might be able to initiate some city building projects, such as upgrading low voltage power grids, urban transportation (rail transit in cities that have the need and resources), and city environmental protection; of course, we should avoid herd mentality, and take demand and feasibility into consideration. This is my advice for further consideration." Li Lanqing, the then Vice Premier of the State Council, wrote on April 27, "I agree with the advice of comrade Wu Bangguo." Wen Jiabao, the then Vice Premier of the State Council, read and noted on this article on April 22. Wu Yi, the then State Councilor, wrote on April 20 that "we must spare no effort to achieve the growth rate of 10% in export growth." In April, the State Council decided to issue an additional 100 billion yuan of the 10 long-term construction bonds. In practice, the bonds were designed to be worth 125 billion yuan, and the bank-supported loans were 100 billion yuan. The loans were used in construction projects of transportation and communication, irrigation and water conservancy, urban infrastructure and environmental protection, the upgrading of urban and rural power grids, and economically affordable housing. National debts were issued for five years in a row. This policy greatly reversed the trend of deflation, supported economic growth, laid a strong foundation for rapid economic growth over the next decade, and successfully transformed the challenges of the Asian financial crisis into an opportunity for development.

X. Zheng, *China's 40 Years of Economic Reform and Development*,
https://doi.org/10.1007/978-981-13-2727-8_22

From the perspective of fixed asset investments, in order to ensure the 8% of economic growth this year, the *Notice of the Central Committee of the Communist Party of China on Sending the Guidelines of the National Planning Commission on Dealing with the Southeast Asian Financial Crisis and Maintaining the Continuous, Rapid and Sound Economic Development* clearly states the intention to expand domestic demand, accelerate infrastructure construction, and invest an additional 205 billion yuan is based on the original scale of fixed asset investments. Problems reflected by various aspects during the implementation are as follows: First, commercial banks are commonly reluctant and afraid to issue loans. In particular, commercial banks clearly declare that they do not want to lend money for projects in irrigation and water conservancy, ecological construction, and other projects with low capital ratios. In order to implement the additional investment, the National Planning Commission has recommended project loans worth 140 billion yuan and expects commercial banks to issue 98 billion yuan of the loans. For now, the banks have only confirmed 17.5 billion yuan, which leaves 36.1 billion yuan of loans for further evaluation. Other than the 53.6 billion yuan of loans accepted by the banks, there are still 44.4 billion yuan of loans that failed to get lending from banks. The amount of investment to be finished this year will be affected if the evaluation of the loans cannot be finished this year. Second, although there should be US$40 billion of foreign direct investment in the originally confirmed 2785 billion yuan of fixed asset investments, as prescribed in the regulation target, and it is estimated by the Ministry of Foreign Trade and Economic Cooperation (MOFTEC) that the maximum foreign direct investment can only reach US$35 billion, which is US$5 billion less than the target. This means that 40 billion yuan of foreign direct investment will need to be covered by additional domestic investment. Third, it is very difficult to accomplish technological upgrading project investment goals. Last year, the investment for technological upgrading projects was scheduled to be 430 billion yuan, but the actual investment completed was only 387 billion yuan. This year, the scheduled investment for technological upgrading is 470 billion yuan. In the additional investment of 205 billion yuan, the additional investment for technological upgrading projects is 20 billion yuan, in which case the technological upgrading investment goal reaches 490 billion yuan. However, it is very difficult to choose projects that are commercially in demand and profitable because of the strengthening restraint of the market, the shortage of funds of enterprises, and inadequate technological reserves. Some banks take the approach of "getting new loans after repayment" and "repayment with new loans," making it even harder for transformation and renovation loans to be issued in full.

From the perspective of exports, momentum weakened owning to the impact of the Southeast Asian financial crisis. According to the target put forward by the MOFTEC, the total volume of exports and imports this year will increase by 10%, with exports at US$201 billion, and the imports at US$156.6 billion. The trade surplus is US$44.4 billion, which is US$4 billion more than that of last year. Net exports will drive 0.3–0.4 percentage points of economic growth. This is an optimistic estimation.

Based on this estimation, the total investment of the year will add 4.7 percentage points in the 8% of economic growth, which means the fixed asset investment will total 2.98 trillion yuan and grow by approximately 17.8%. Thus, adding the 205 billion yuan of fixed asset investment can basically guarantee the growth target of 8%. However, according to the export orders of East China Fair and Tianjin Fair (in March), as well as recent research, it is difficult to accomplish the targeted export growth of 10%. If export growth is 5% and import growth is still 10%, then the trade surplus is US$32 billion, which is US$8.3 billion less than that of last year. The effect of net exports will be negative 0.7 percentage points. Compared with the estimation of the US$44.4 billion of trade surplus, there is 1 to 1.1 percentage points needed to be offset by domestic investment, and the total investment needs to increase economic growth by 5.7%. Correspondingly, fixed asset investment needs to reach 3.08 trillion yuan, with an increase of 21.8%. In that case, China would need to add 100 billion yuan to the additional 205 billion yuan of fixed asset investment.[1]

In conclusion, setting aside other factors, the reduction of foreign direct investment and net exports alone would entail an additional 140 billion yuan of domestic investment over the year to ensure the targeted 8% economic growth. If the 140 billion yuan cannot be available for the additional investment in a timely manner, then economic growth would decrease this year by 1.5 percentage points, in which case the economic growth speed this year would be only 6.5%.

In order to provide a stable and reliable basis for this year's growth target, a number of additional infrastructure construction projects will need to be launched. Several cities with sufficient financial resources and favorable conditions to initiate a number of utility projects in water, heating, electricity, sewage treatment, and rail transportation need to be selected. Local cities are fully prepared for these projects, and many have submitted these projects for approval, thus the situation is now ripe for ramping up construction. A number of projects for small and medium-sized irrigation and water conservancy projects as well as ecological construction can also be selected.

In order to meet the demand for additional investment funds, China should allow local governments to appropriately use their future financial resources in advance, which means that local branches of the China Investment Corporation would need to issue 25 billion yuan of bonds, which would be repaid with budgetary and extra-budgetary funds. The term of the suggested additional 25 billion yuan of national bonds should be 8 to 10 years, and the proportion of institutional investors to bond holders should be higher. Currently, China's national debt takes up only 4.93% of its GDP, which is far below the 40–50% in developed countries. The scale of national debt accounts for only 6.73% of personal savings deposits, which is also small

[1]In April 1998, the State Council decided to issue an additional 100 billion yuan of 10 long-term construction bonds. In practice, the bonds were designed to be worth 125 billion yuan, and the bank-supported loans were 100 billion yuan. The loans were used in the transportation and communication, irrigation and water conservancy, urban infrastructure and environmental protection, the upgrading of urban and rural power grids, and economically affordable housing. This decision played a crucial role in reversing deflation trends, expanding domestic demand, and maintaining rapid yet steady economic development. At the same time, this policy fostered a number of high-quality assets, and increased the momentum of economic development.

compared with that of developed countries. Therefore, there remains considerable space to issue additional national bonds. In addition, the 5 billion yuan of central government finances, which has been confirmed for additional allocation, should be made available as soon as possible.

Chapter 23
New Situations and Missions After a Soft Landing

Since 1993, macro regulation focusing on curbing inflation has made great achievements. While the economy is now in a favorable situation of "high growth and low inflation," new problems emerged, such as growth speed and employment. Having a proper understanding of the new tasks in the new situation and taking timely and effective measures are important guarantees for maintaining the current momentum for a long time to come.

23.1 Whether or not China Can Maintain Economic Growth Over 8 Percent Has Become the Focus of Domestic and International Attention

In 1992, encouraged and inspired by Deng Xiaoping's important talks in the south of China and by the guiding principles from the 14th National Congress of the CPC, people throughout the country committed themselves to reform and opening up as well as modernization. GDP growth in 1992 reached 14.2%. In the second half of 1993, targeting the problems arising in the economy, including indiscriminate collecting funds, disorderly inter-bank lending, unapproved establishment of financial institutions, and the favoring of real estate and development zones, the Central Committee of the CPC and the State Council made resolute decisions to rectify the financial order through the implementation of moderately tight fiscal and monetary policies. Economic growth declined to 13.5% in 1993. In the following four years, China moderately restrained the scale of social fixed asset investment so as to curb inflation, and economic growth was 12.6, 10.5, 9.7, and 8.8%, respectively, with a decline of one percentage point each year. Meanwhile, price inflation dropped largely

---

This article originally appeared in *Study, Research and Reference*, no. 5, 1998.

X. Zheng, *China's 40 Years of Economic Reform and Development*,
https://doi.org/10.1007/978-981-13-2727-8_23

year by year, and the rise in retail prices dropped from its high at 21.4% in 1994 to 0.8% in 1997. In January 1998, overall prices were down to negative 1.5% compared with the same period of the previous year. The country has fully accomplished a soft landing so far. According to the requirements for maintaining good momentum in the macroeconomy, the ideal scenario is to stop the decline of economic growth and maintain the present appropriate growth rate over a long time. However, the growth rate decline over five consecutive years has formed enormous inertia. One percentage point of decline would cause the economic growth of 1998 to be well below 8%. To stop this decline and maintain rapid economic growth, China must promptly and resolutely adjust the demand and maintain the necessary driving forces of demand for economic growth.

Promoting reform and opening up as well as maintaining economic and social stability entails continuous yet rapid economic growth. If the reform of SOEs is strengthened in 1998, then their reform and reorganization will be greater, demand will be bigger, and production will be in full motion, and China will realize a rapidly growing economy. Likewise, the country cannot ease the employment pressure unless rapid economic growth can be maintained. Experience from recent years demonstrates that each percentage point of GDP growth generally creates over 800,000 jobs. But the average of the newly added urban workforce on a yearly basis is 7 million. Thus, economic growth has to reach 9% in order to meet the demands of the employment for the newly added urban workforce. The problem of unemployment is extremely pressing when economic growth falls below 8%. In the global context of the slowed economic growth that followed the Asian financial crisis, China made great contributions to the world economy and maintained its rapid economic growth, which helped China strengthen its international position.

It is possible to realize rapid economic growth.

First, China's national saving rate is relatively high. The average saving rate has reached 40% since reform and opening up and could support the investment rate of 33% or more.

Second, China's market demand is big. At present, the per capita GDP is only over US$700, which puts China is in the low-income bracket. China can maintain large consumption demand by adjusting the income distribution so as to drive economic growth.

Third, China has an abundant supply of energy and raw materials and a great surplus of production capacity. Meanwhile, there is large potential for resource conservation and therefore resources are sufficient to support rapid economic growth.

Fourth, although China's economy has undergone ups and downs over the past two decades of reform and opening up, its economy has still maintained an average annual growth rate of 9.8%, which demonstrates that China has the potential of maintaining such growth.

Fifth, compared with the cases of Japan maintaining its rapid economic growth for 20 years and South Korea maintaining its rapid economic growth for 29 years, China is bigger, does not have an economic basis as good as these two foreign countries, and has unbalanced economic development in different regions. Therefore, China has greater growth potential and the period for China's economic growth will be longer.

Currently, not only are people all over China concerned about the economic growth of 1998, the whole world is also paying attention to China. Some predict that China will, in the end, fail to avoid the impact of this financial crisis, in which case economic growth would slow and the RMB would undergo depreciation. This kind of opinion is popular among some people. Influenced by this pessimistic view, they do not have enough confidence in the development of China's economy, and take a wait-and-see attitude toward foreign investment in China. Maintaining economic growth above 8% can refute this opinion through facts and bring in more foreign investment. The year 1998 is the first year following the 15th National Congress of the CPC. This year is a crucial link for the accomplishment of the Ninth Five-Year-Plan, and is also the first year of governance of the newly-selected leaders following the Ninth National People's Congress of the People's Republic of China (PRC). Therefore, maintaining the momentum of economic development is not only of economic significance, but also has great political significance.

23.2 Expanding Domestic Demand and Cultivating New Growth Areas Is the Key to Maintaining Rapid Economic Growth

The major difference between the socialist market economy and the traditional planned economy is that, under the planned economy, economic growth is mainly limited by supply. However, with the appearance of the buyer's market in China and the deepening of reform, the market mechanism has played a decisive role in regulating economic activities. Therefore, macroeconomic management should transform from the supply management system under the planned economy to one of demand management, so as to adapt to the requirements of developing the socialist market economy.

The so-called demand management is mainly the management of three factors driving the economic growth; namely, final consumption, total investment, and net exports. China should maintain a necessary balanced growth of the gross demand through the regulation of various macro-economic policies, thereby maintaining the necessary driving forces for economic growth. When gross demand grows too fast, although economic growth will gain momentum in the short term, the dramatic growth of gross demand will inevitably result in inflation, causing marked ups and downs. When gross demand grows too slowly, its driving force of economic growth is weak, in which case economic growth will slow and the economy's growth potential will not be brought into full play.

Regarding the three major factors driving economic growth, according to statistics from 1991 to 1997, the pull effect of final consumption was 54.5%, total investment was 40.7%, and net exports was 5.2%. It can be seen that consumption and investment played an important role in driving economic growth.

In 1998, the financial crisis in Southeast Asia and East Asia brought an adverse impact on China's economic growth. The currency depreciation in neighboring countries and regions caused a tough situation for China's exports. Exports in 1998 were estimated to be lower than that of 1997; therefore, the pull effect of export-led growth was obviously weaker. In 1997, net exports totaled US$40.3 billion, 2.3 times as much as that of 1996. Exports contributed 2.87 percentage points to the 8.8% of GDP growth, or 32.6% of GDP. Whereas in 1998, it is estimated that net exports will be US$15.5 billion less than that of the previous year and the corresponding contribution of net exports to economic growth will be negative 1.21 percentage points. So compared with 1997, the pull effect of exports alone in 1998, if quantified, will be reduced by 4 percentage points. That reduction will be offset by expanding consumption and investment demand.

Consumption is the final end of production, and is the original driving force for economic growth. China cannot provide lasting power for economic growth unless continuous growth of consumption can be maintained. Since the Eighth Five-Year-Plan period, there have been three years when consumption contributed to over 60% of economic growth, of which two years were over 50%. In 1993, because of the extraordinary increase of investment, fixed asset investment increased by 61.8% compared with the previous year. Investment contributed to 62.1% of economic growth, thus causing the contribution of consumption to economic growth to be reduced to 49%. In 1997, however, consumption only contributed to 34.4% of economic growth, which made the country pay higher attention to consumption. The weakening pull effect of consumption-led economic growth was caused by the following:

First, the pattern of consumption is still in the stage of welfare consumption, supply consumption, and group consumption. Some commodities that should be categorized into individual consumption are still kept out of the field of individual consumption, while the consumption policies for some products are hindering the expansion of consumption and dampening the circulation between production and consumption, such as the consumption policies for urban housing.

Second, there are still wide gaps in the income and consumption levels between urban and rural residents. The consumer goods that are saturated in the urban market cannot serve as alternatives for or be absorbed in the rural market, which is especially true in the country's vast rural areas in the central and western regions.

Third, as unemployed and laid-off workers flow to urban areas, residents would rather deposit their money into banks in case of unexpected incidents than spend their money. Some low-income residents lack purchasing power for the goods they need to purchase.

Fourth, the product mix is not adaptable to the changes of market demand and multi-tiered consumption demand, in which case the selling prices of some products become unaffordable because the intermediate links of these products cost too much.

Fifth, consumption is still too limited and new areas of consumption, including health, culture, tourism, and services are still underdeveloped. Currently, excessive inventory and spare production capacity are growing. According to estimates, there are more than 3 billion men's shirts, over 4 billion pairs of leather shoes, and tens of millions of motorcycles that remain as unsold inventory. While the existing production capacity cannot be fully tapped, new production lines are being set in motion one after another. China is now saddled with more than 70 million square meters of commodity housing inventory throughout the country, and there is overcapacity in sectors such as steel and cement and construction teams that are left idle. These commodities are excessive not because people do not need them or cannot afford them. The key reason is that the production is detached from demand, and the policies for consumption and distribution are not suitable to the requirements of economic development.

When analyzing the contradictions of capitalism, Marx and Engels pointed out that the contradiction between the socialization of production and the private ownership of production is the basic contradiction of the capitalist society. When reflected in the fields of production and circulation, this basic contradiction is the contradiction between the unlimited expansion of production capacity and the social demand people can afford, which will inevitably lead to periodic economic crises. One of the major differences between the socialist market economy and the capitalism economy is that the political power is in the hands of the broad working people. The government represents the benefits of the people, and the purpose for production is to meet the rising demand of people's material and cultural life. Therefore, China is completely capable of adjusting the income levels of people, or their ability to consume, to the development level of productivity, and steer production to adapt to market demand through implementing reasonable policies for the distribution of national income. Thus, China can fundamentally resolve the contradiction between the development of productivity and the demand people can afford, and avoid the crisis of overproduction. In particular, the level of per capita income and the level of consumption in China are both relatively low, so there remains huge potential for consumption demand. If the country can maintain reasonable consumption growth by adjusting consumption and income policies, China can provide huge driving forces for continuous economic growth, and create essential conditions for the continuous, rapid, and sound development of the economy.

When expanding the field of consumption and improving consumption levels, China should focus on meeting the requirements of the people to improve the level of their housing and transportation under the premise of improving food, clothing, and other daily necessities. It can be said that since reform and opening up, China has maintained long-term and rapid development of agriculture, textile, and other light industries mainly by satisfying the requirements of people's food, clothing, and other daily necessities. But in the next two decades, industries aimed at satisfying the requirements of people's living and traveling, including industries such as urban housing and transportation, as well as other relevant industries, will gain opportunities for rapid development and become new economic growth points. Compared with the spending on food, clothing, and other necessities, the spending on commodities and services in housing and transportation will increase to the tens of thousands in yuan from thousands of yuan, which means that the proportion of consumption and services for housing and transportation will gradually surpass the proportion of the consumption for food, clothing, and other daily necessities. Therefore, the consumption and services for housing and transportation will have a greater and more lasting pull effect on economic growth. In developed countries where the per capita GDP exceeds US$10,000, industries related to the improvement of living and traveling are major industries driving economic growth. Some countries even put more than half of their investments into housing and infrastructure. To support the expansion of consumption for living and traveling, China needs to promote new selling methods in the distribution industries, such as installment payment plans and mortgage loans. People work hard to improve their living and traveling conditions, which creates great driving forces for economic growth and is conducive to social security.

It is impossible to make breakthroughs in consumption demand considering the decline of export growth in 1998. So, relying on the expansion of investment to drive economic growth will be of decisive significance for the economic situation. It is estimated that in the planned 8% economic growth in 1998, investment will contribute 6 percentage points, in which case the contribution of investment to economic growth in 1998 will be over 60%. Without investment, it is impossible for China to reverse the trend of declining economic growth. Investment expansion priorities include construction of railways, highways, telecommunications, environmental protection, small and medium-sized irrigation and water conservancy projects, urban housing and infrastructure, technological upgrading, and industrialization of high and new technology.

Right now is the golden period for the construction of railways and highways. This is because consumption is transitioning, residential saving rates are high, and the young workforce accounts for a large proportion of the whole population. China should seize the opportunity, enhance investment, and establish a highly-advanced comprehensive transportation system before the population ages. China should accelerate infrastructure construction of urban roads, water, electricity, heating and gas utilities, and deal with serious traffic jams and pollution in urban areas. China should prioritize the development of small and medium-sized cities as well as rural towns, and make the technological, educational, commercial, transport, and information centers of these small and medium-sized towns drive the development of the local economy, thus driving the economic development of rural areas.

23.3 Achieve Rapid Economic Growth Based on Structural Optimization and the Transformation of the Growth Model

Accelerating economic growth does not entail returning to the old way of high input and low output, and high consumption and low profits. China should implement intensive management and rely on new technology to reduce the consumption of energy and raw materials and increase the production and sophistication of products. China should vigorously develop technology-intensive and capital-intensive industries while continuing to develop labor-intensive industries. During the financial crisis in Southeast Asia and East Asia, some countries were seriously hit and suffered great losses, but other countries and regions resisted the impact of the crisis. The reason for this lies in the technological level of industries and industrial structures. At present, China is at a crucial stage of industrial upgrading. Labor-intensive products have been saturated in the domestic market while exports cannot increase significantly because of the protection of foreign markets, and two thirds of the domestic technology equipment market is made up of imported products. Accelerating the development of technology-intensive industries and capital-intensive industries is vital for the development and fate of China's industry. The import and export of China's mechanical and electronic products struck a balance for the first time in 1997. The value of exports reached US$60 billion, thus mechanical and electronic products replaced textiles to become the largest export commodity. However, it is obvious that the country stills has a lot to do to catch up with developed countries. For example, 80% of the exported products of the United States are high-tech products, and this figure in Japan and Germany is 95 and 85%, respectively. Annually, China spends more than US$6 billion of its foreign reserves to import over 4 million tons of ethylene and around 1.73 million tons of ethylene downstream products, including synthetic fiber, and the annual expenditure on imported cars and relevant accessories reaches US$9.4 billion. If China is to catch up with developed countries, it must enhance its support for the mechanical and electronic industries, and realize the revitalization of the pillar industries, including the mechanical and auto industries as well as the petroleum and chemical industries through exports and import substitution.

China should accelerate the industrialization of high and new technology. The competition in modern global markets is ultimately the competition of technology. Whoever commands new and high technology will stay ahead of the curve in economic development, take the initiative in the market, and occupy an advantageous position in competition. The United States has invested huge efforts in developing high technology, through which the US has maintained its leading role in the field of technology, drove the economic growth of the country, and consolidated its supremacy. Japan is also promoting creative science and technology as its administrative core and as the focus of its administrative reform for the 21st century, and has conducted a joint study to assess the combination of industry, academia, and government. European Union members are also dedicating more efforts to scientific and technological research. If China is to realize its cross-century development objectives specified at the 15th National Congress of the CPC and accomplish the second and third steps of the strategic arrangements for the development of the economy, the country must dedicate more efforts to the research of high technology. The strength and advantage of the socialist system is that it enables resources to be pooled to solve major problems. China should give play to this strength and advantage, set finite targets, and concentrate human, material, and financial resources to tackle these difficulties. Particularly, in the fields of large-scale integrated circuits, nuclear power, aerospace and aviation, bio-engineering, new materials, and high-speed railway equipment, China should pool its resources and enhance investment in scientific research, accelerate development, and drive the modernization of the economy.

23.4 Improve Investment and Financing Mechanisms and Direct Personal Savings Deposits to Investment Priorities

The financial source for expanding domestic demand and increasing fixed asset investment should be based on domestic financing. Personal savings deposits in China's banks have reached over 4 trillion yuan so far. Since the proportion of direct financing is relatively small, investment risks are concentrated in bank loans. In 1997, China's fixed asset investment reached 2530.1 billion yuan, an increase of 10.1% over the previous year. After being adjusted for inflation, the actual increase is about 9%, marking the smallest growth since the Eighth Five-Year Plan. Other than stringent macro regulation, enterprises and banks enhanced their risk management, which is also an important reason for the slowing growth of investment. This is good for the reform of the investment and financing mechanism, as it shows that long-term investment hunger has been relieved to some extent. In 1998, China will accelerate financial system reform, in which banks will independently evaluate, review, and decide on loan projects for fixed asset investment. Since the acceleration of the reform, enterprises have strengthened responsibilities for preventing investment risks, and it will be more prudent for them to make decisions on investments with bank loans. Therefore, by deepening the reform of enterprises and the financial system, actions of enterprises and banks will undergo major changes this year. It is very likely that loans will not be issued because of the lack of good investment projects, which makes it difficult for investment to grow rapidly. This would make it risky to accomplish the target of increasing investment through macro regulation.

To solve this problem, China needs to adopt new measures, which mainly include increasing the proportion of directly financing enterprises and investment projects by expanding investment and financing channels. China should adopt foreign approaches in this regard, such as issuing project construction bonds, and establish industrial investment funds and other types of funds and methods common in foreign countries. China should accelerate pilot programs and promotions through BOT, the transfer of management rights, and so on to raise funds, thereby accelerating the building of infrastructure and basic industries. Promoting these new investments and financing approaches can reduce the pressure on loan risks for commercial banks, find new channels of financial resources for investment, strengthen investors' responsibility to prevent risks, and help reduce investment mistakes and increase investment profits.

China should actively support the development of SMEs and rural township enterprises. Foreign experience demonstrates that SMEs play an important role in attracting the workforce for employment and driving the progress of technology. Even in countries where big enterprises have absolute advantages, like the United States and Japan, SMEs still attract over 70% of the workforce and create more than half of the total industrial output of scientific research. China is now at the stage of accelerating industrialization and modernization and faces great employment pressure; therefore, the country should do more to protect and support the development of SMEs. China should satisfy the SME demands for loans as much as possible, and set up funds for small and medium-sized enterprises (SMEs) to support the development of SMEs through fiscal and policy loans, similar to the United States and Japan.

China should further utilize foreign investment. In the Asian financial crisis, China maintained rapid economic growth and stabilized the RMB exchange rate, which demonstrates good prospects for the development of China's economy and its stable investment environment. China should seize this opportunity and enhance the work of attracting foreign investment, and particularly attract multinational companies to invest in technology and capital-intensive projects, and give part of the domestic market to foreign investment when necessary. China should steadily expand this field using foreign investment, and attract more foreign investment for the development of resources in central and western parts of China and for infrastructure construction.

Chapter 24
Macroeconomic Management Reform in China

24.1 The Basic Direction of the Macroeconomic Management System Reform

1. *Break the highly-centralized management system and streamline administration and delegation of power*

The highly-centralized management system is one of the major characteristics of the traditional economic system. The principal theoretical basis for the formation of this management system is that China has transferred the means of production to public ownership, in which case the government serves as the management center of the social economy, directly allocates social labor according to the demands of society, and thus strikes a balance between the supply and demand of social products. Considering this characteristic, China regards the whole society as one big factory, in which the state assigns plans in a unified manner and implements state monopolies for purchasing and marketing products, and where the state has control over revenues and expenditures and plans the allocation of workforce labor. The country's leaders believe that, by doing this, China can overcome the capitalist contradiction between the socialization of production and the private ownership of production means as well as the contradiction between unlimited production capacity expansion and limited affordability of social demand, thereby avoiding periodic economic crises, and realizing long-term and stable economic development.

During the primary stage of development since the establishment of the PRC, this kind of highly-centralized management system played an important role in pooling the nation's resources to build a number of industrial and transport projects and consolidating the foundation of industrialization. Thanks to the highly-centralized management system, although China was weak during the First Five-Year Plan period,

This article originally appeared in *China's Economic Transformation over the Past 20 Years*, Beijing: Foreign Languages Press, 1999.

X. Zheng, *China's 40 Years of Economic Reform and Development*,
https://doi.org/10.1007/978-981-13-2727-8_24

the country still managed to carry out 156 major projects at the same time. The successful development of China's atomic bombs, hydrogen bombs, and satellites in the 1960s, and the great achievements in the three decades preceding reform and opening up, especially during the rapid development of China's heavy industries, all can be attributed to the highly-centralized management system in which China gave play to socialism's strength of pooling resources to solve major problems.

However, with the development of the economic scale and productivity of China, this highly-centralized management system showed an increasing amount of defects that were mainly reflected in the following problems: Local economic management authorities were too limited; and enterprises were like an abacus, which the government kept fiddling with. Problems like this severely restricted the enthusiasm and energy of local places and enterprises. Likewise, satisfying the ever-changing and diversifying social demand entails continuous adjustments to production. However, it is impossible to accurately predict and calculate this kind of ever-changing and diversifying demand; therefore, it is impracticable to accommodate the enormous and ever-shifting social production into a unified plan. If the country insists on doing impracticable or impossible things, China will find ourselves wasting energy and achieving nothing. Then it will become common for nothing to go as planned. The highly-centralized management system limited product variety, hindered technological advances, and twisted industrial structure, which, together with the influence of political factors, put the economy into continuous fluctuations. The target for economic development fell through. Practice demonstrated that this kind of highly-centralized management system hinders the development of productivity.

The Third Plenary Session of the 11th CPC Central Committee held in 1978 returned to the ideological line of materialism held by the Party, analyzed the defects of China's economic system, and clearly stated that the "four modernizations" (modernization of agriculture, industry, national defense, and science and technology) demand a significant improvement in social productivity. Therefore, China must comprehensively change the relations of production and the superstructure that are out of pace with the development of productivity, as well as all inappropriate management, activities, and thoughts. Therefore, the realization of the four modernizations is a profound reform. The Plenary Session pointed out the direction, principle, and major tasks of the reform. Since then, China's macro-management system reform has entered a glorious stage where understanding and practice have promoted each other and achieved new breakthroughs. China has carried out the following reform measures in the streamlining of administration and delegation of power:

(1) Giving farmers autonomous rights in the production and operation of their land

Reform started with rural areas. As rural areas have a large population with relatively little arable land and most the work of farmers is done by manual labor, the yield of farm products often depended on farmers' enthusiasm toward production. Therefore, changing land management rights and the situation in which production is conducted according to decentralization plans is the first step of the rural economic system reform. China abolished the system of people's commune and changed the three-level ownership system: commune, production brigade, and production team. China used production teams as the basic operations management system, implemented the household contract responsibility system, and integrated individual farmer households' management system with the unified collective management system. China handed over the rights of agricultural production and management to farmer households. Prior to 1979, the Chinese government released mandatory plans for the yields of 25 categories of major farm products, and assigned different plans for sowing areas and for the yields of the 25 kinds of farm products for different areas. By 1985, the mandatory plans for agricultural production had been cancelled, and guidance plans and market regulation was separately implemented for the yields of major farm products. At present, the government primarily implements the policy of purchasing grain without limitations at protective prices to encourage farmers' enthusiasm for growing crops and to guide farmers to adjust the mix of crops they grow. The handover of autonomous land operation rights significantly motivated farmers' production. From 1978 to 1984, total grain output in China reached 407.3 million tons from 304.8 million tons, with an average annual growth of 4.95%. Per capita grain possession increased from 318.7 to 395.5 kg, with an annual average growth of 3.66%, which ensured adequate food for the Chinese people. By 1996, total grain output had reached 504.5 million tons and per capita grain possession had amounted to 414.4 kg, thereby realizing that there is surplus grain in good harvest.

(2) Expanding autonomous rights of enterprises

In 1984, the Third Plenary Session of the 12th CPC Central Committee adopted the *Decision on Economic System Reform*, marking the shift of the reform from rural areas to cities. Centering on expanding the autonomous operational rights of SOEs, China carried out comprehensive reform measures in macroeconomic fields, including planning, goods and materials, labor wages, finance, business and trade, commodity prices, and fiscal taxation. These reforms made important breakthroughs in changing the old management system, where management authority was too centralized. In 1978, the State Council issued the *Regulations on Enhancing the Autonomy of State-owned Industrial Enterprise Management*, and the *Law of Industrial Enterprises Owned by the Whole People* later. In 1992, the State Council issued the *Regulations on the Management System Transformation of Industrial Enterprises Owned by the Whole People*. The autonomous operational rights of enterprises were gradually expanded and implemented at different levels. These autonomous rights include the right to make production and operation decisions, the right to price products and labor services, the right to sell products, the right to purchase materials, the right to import and export, the right to make investment decisions, the right to dispose self-retained funds, the right to dispose the assets of enterprises, the right to distribute salaries and bonuses, the right to set up internal organizations, and the right to refuse apportionment. These rights have helped enterprises gradually develop in making management decisions independently, taking responsibility for profits and losses, and assuming risks and developing themselves independently, thus enhancing their vitality. At the same time, the handing over of the rights has created favorable conditions for the transformation of the government's managerial function.

(3) Anything that can be managed by the market should be left to the market

In the traditional economic system, the government undertook many things that should have been handled through the market. For example, commodity prices should be formed through market competition, which can enable prices to function as an indication of market demand and as means of competition and give play to the basic role of the market in allocating resources. However, before the reform, most commodities were priced by the government. Among the total retail sales, total sales revenue by means of production, and the total value of purchased agricultural and sideline products, government pricing took up 97, 100, and 92%, respectively. Currently, the market-based pricing mechanism is established. Now the market pricing accounts for 92.5% of total retail sales, 82.1% of total sales revenue by means of production, and 79% of the total value of purchased agricultural and side-line products. Some affairs that can be managed through market intermediary institutions are left with those institutions.

(4) Expanding local economic management authorities

China is a country with a large population and vast territory. The population and size of a province of China is often comparable to that of a country in Europe. Developing economies with local advantages and characteristics under the guidance of unified national planning and policies is a major component of reform, which gives full play to local governments to organize economic construction and exploit different conditions in different areas. Local economic management authorities were relatively limited before reform. With the advancement of the reform, however, those authorities expanded gradually.

In fields such as production, investment, distribution, price, foreign trade, foreign exchange, labor wages, technology, and social development, much of the management authority that used to belong to the central government was delegated to local governments. Regarding the approval of fixed asset investment projects, China separated them according to the scale of investment, in which case the National Planning Commission approves large and medium-sized projects and relevant departments and local governments approve the small projects. The scale of these investment projects depends on the minimum standard of investment funds. The floor of investment projects to be approved by the National Planning Commission was 10 million yuan before 1985 and 30 million yuan in 1985. In 1987, the floor of investment projects in energy, transportation, raw materials, and other industrial fields was raised to 50 million yuan. In order to meet the requirements of reform and opening up, China also gradually delegated authority for approving investment projects in some open coastal areas. In 1985, the State Council decided that the governments of Guangdong and Fujian provinces could approve the large and medium-sized infrastructure construction projects with investment of less than 200 million yuan, as long as the construction did not require state facilitation. In 1988, the State Council decided that construction projects with total investment of less than 200 million yuan in Hainan Province could be approved independently by the province as long as it was able to moderate the conditions for construction, production, sales, foreign exchange, and so on, and had the ability to pay. That same year, the State Council also decided that export-oriented projects with export products accounting for over 70% of their products having no quota restrictions should be approved independently by provinces. In 1992, the State Council decided that non-productive project proposals for Pudong, Shanghai, with total investment over the floor funds should be approved first by the National Planning Commission or the State Council, after which the feasibility study and the report on construction commencement should be approved independently by the Shanghai government and submitted to the National Planning Commission on record for reference. For large and medium-sized projects with total investment under 200 million yuan, as long as these projects complied with the state's industrial policies and did not need the state to help solve relevant conditions, the proposal for the project could be first submitted to the National Planning Commission for approval, after which the feasibility study and the report on construction commencement would be approved by the Shanghai government independently.

In adapting to the requirements of reform and opening up, China adopted a series of special policies for some areas. In 1985, the State Council stipulated that all non-productive projects in Guangdong and Fujian provinces that were supported by foreign investment could be approved independently by the provincial governments, regardless of the scale of these projects. In addition, the provincial governments could also approve technology-introduction projects that were arranged by the two provinces with self-raised, self-retained foreign exchanges independently if the investment of the project is no more than US$10 million. Since 1988, joint ventures using Chinese and foreign investment and Chinese-foreign co-operative enterprises in Tianjin, Shanghai, Guangdong, Fujian, Beijing, Liaoning, Hebei, Shandong, Jiangsu, Zhejiang, Guangxi, and special economic zones in China can all be approved independently by local authorities if the projects are productive, fit the state's industrial policies, do not need the state to solve problems of conditions for construction, production and operations, and foreign exchange receipt and payment, and if total investment is less than US$30 million. Foreign investment projects in Hainan Province concerning energy, transportation, telecommunication, and other infrastructure and tourist facilities can be approved independently by the provincial government, regardless of the scale, as long as they do not need the state to help solve issues regarding the conditions for construction, production, and operations. Other foreign investment projects and foreign loan projects that borrow and pay money on their own can also be approved independently by the relevant provincial government if investment is no more than US$30 million and the construction, production, and operation could all be dealt with independently and do not include state quotas. The same kind of projects mentioned above in inland provinces, autonomous regions, municipalities with independent planning status, and special economic zones whose investment is less than US$10 million can be approved by those governments themselves.

Because central cities play a special role in economic development, China has given independent planning status to 14 central cities and open coastal cities successively. From February 1983 to February 1989, the State Council successively approved the independent planning status of cities including Chongqing, Wuhan,

Shenyang, Dalian, Harbin, Guangzhou, Xi'an, Qingdao, Ningbo, Xiamen, Shenzhen, Nanjing, Chengdu, and Changchun, and gave these cities provincial status for economic management, which means their economic and social development plans can be directly submitted to the National Planning Commission as cities specifically designated in the state plans. In order to further reasonably divide responsibilities and clearly define the relationship between the central government, provinces, and autonomous regions, between cities and counties, as well as between municipalities directly under the central government and districts and counties, the central government decided in July 1993 that only Chongqing, Shenzhen, Dalian, Qingdao, Ningbo, and Xiamen would still be subject to independent planning, while other provincial capitals will no longer be subject to independent planning but could continue to enjoy preferential policies for coastal open cities.

In order to motivate enthusiasm toward local governments at all levels to manage their property and break the rigid system in which the fiscal budget management was too centralized and over-controlled, including unified state control over income and expenditures, since 1980, China has successively implemented various financial contracting systems on local finance, including systems with categorized revenue and expenditures as well as multilevel contracting, and systems with categorized tax and designated scope of revenue and expenditure as well as multilevel contracting. Areas inhabited by minorities, underdeveloped areas, parts of the coastal open areas, and municipalities with independent planning status implemented special budget management systems. China has also established and improved the fiscal budget management system in villages and towns.

In March 1985, the State Council issued the *Regulations on Implementing the Financial Management System of Categorized Tax, Designated Scope of Revenue and Expenditure and Multilevel Contracting,* which categorized taxes as the basis for categorizing the fiscal revenue of governments at all levels. With this, the country started to change its approach of categorizing revenues according to the administrative subordination relationships between enterprises and public institutions, thereby making a significant step toward finally implementing the complete tax sharing system.

In July 1988, the State Council issued the *Decision on Local-Level Financial Contracting Methods,* which stipulated the implementation of various contracting methods, including revenue increments, total revenue shares, total revenue shares plus increment shares, increments of revenue turned over to the state, specific amounts of revenue turned over to the state, and specific amounts of subsidy, respectively, in 37 regions. These methods were adapted to different situations in different regions, which is conducive to a relative balance in these regions. Maintaining a contracting base and method to specify revenue shares for several years was beneficial for expanding local autonomy and motivating local governments to increase revenue and reduce expenditures. However, this contracting system reform was not set up according to reasonably designed taxes, but primarily to the administrative subordination of enterprises. The categorization of expenditures was not in accordance with their factors, but rather the expenditure base. The increments of revenue were basically in line with local finance, which, with the development of the economy, lessens the proportion of the central finance.

The reform measures mentioned above were certainly beneficial for breaking from the highly-centralized financial system, increasing financial resources of local areas, and motivating the enthusiasm of local authorities, but problems also emerged during implementation. First, the fiscal system was not standardized enough to comply with the principles of efficiency and equity. Second, the contracting fiscal system might encourage regional barriers and protection, which would hinder the formation of a national uniform market. Third, the fiscal system and the tax system could not support each other well, so some local governments reduced or remitted taxes without the consent of the central government, causing serious loss of national fiscal revenue. Fourth, this contracting system could not reverse the trend in which the proportion of fiscal revenue in GNP and the proportion of central fiscal revenue in the national fiscal revenue were both shrinking, which would inevitably weaken the financial base of the country in terms of macro regulation. All these measures can only be solved through the tax sharing system.

There are two major purposes of the tax sharing system. One is to establish the standard relations of distribution between the central and local governments to ensure the unification of financial and administrative powers in governments at all levels, and to realize the efficient combination of responsibility, authority, and profits, and eliminate the arbitrary distribution of financial resources among governments. The second is to gradually increase the proportion of fiscal revenue in GDP and moderately increase the proportion of central fiscal revenue in the national fiscal revenue to enhance the strength of the central government in terms of macro regulation.

The implementation of the tax sharing system can be generally divided into five steps.

(i) Categorizing all levels of government expenditure in accordance with specific definitions of central and local administrative powers

Central financial expenditures include investment in capital constructions managed by the central government, expenses for pilot production of new products, the costs of technological upgrading of enterprises directly under central management, and expenditures for geological prospecting and so on. The expenditures arranged by central finance mainly include national defense, armed police officers, foreign affairs and foreign aid, central administration, repayment of capital and interest of domestic and foreign debts that should be undertook by central finance, public security, and social undertakings such as culture, education, health, science, and others. Local financial expenditures and categories mainly include: investment in capital construction managed by local governments, pilot production of new products and costs of technological upgrading of local enterprises, support for agriculture, city maintenance and construction, local administrative management and social undertakings such as culture, education, health, science, and others, public security, part of the expenditure of armed police officers and militias, price subsidies, and other relevant expenditures.

(ii) The scope of government administrative and financial powers at all levels defines central and local revenues under the principle that financial power shall be commensurate with administrative power and that revenue be commensurate with expenditures

The central government's fixed revenue includes but is not limited to: tariffs, excise tax and value-added tax (VAT) on imported goods, excise tax, central enterprise corporate income tax, non-bank financial enterprises corporate income tax, income collectively paid by railway departments, bank head offices, insurance company heads and other relevant departments (including business tax, income tax, profits and urban maintenance, and construction tax), as well as the profits of central enterprises turned over to the state. For export refunds of foreign trade enterprises, except for the 20% of the export rebates that have been undertaken by local governments, the export refund thereafter would all be undertaken by local government finances.

Local government fixed revenue includes but is not limited to: business tax (excluding business tax of bank head offices, railway departments, and insurance company head offices), local enterprise corporate income tax (excluding the non-bank financial institutions corporate income tax mentioned above), the profits of local enterprises turned over to local governments, individual income tax, urban and township land use tax, fixed assets investment orientation regulation tax, farmland occupation tax, contract tax, inheritance tax and gift tax, land appreciation tax, and the income from compensated assignment of rights to use state-owned land.

Local and central governments shared finance revenue includes value-added tax, resource tax, and securities transaction tax. The central government takes 75% of the value-added tax, and local government takes the remaining 25%. Resource taxes are categorized by different resources. Resource tax of offshore petroleum resources is a revenue source for the central government, while other resource taxes are revenue for local governments. The central government and local government both take 50% of the securities transaction tax.

(iii) Setting a reasonable basis for local finance revenue and expenditures

The reform in 1994 set 1993 as the base year for calculating the fiscal and tax system, and allowed local governments to keep the financial resources they retained in 1993.

(iv) Appraising and setting reasonable revenue amounts that local governments should turn over to the state and the amount of subsidy local governments should receive

The central government implements a rebates system or transfer payment system for local governments on the basis that most of the revenue is centralized by the central government.

(v) Corresponding to the tax sharing system, china separately sets central and local tax authorities. central taxes and shared taxes are collected by the central tax authority, and the shared revenue is returned proportionately to local authorities. local tax authorities collect local taxes

This measure achieved the expected results from the perspective of implementing the tax sharing system reform measures. The national fiscal revenue realized continuous significant increases, and the proportion of central fiscal revenue began to rise. With the development of the administrative management system reform, the scope of the administrative powers of central and local government was further specified and the fiscal distribution relations among governments at all levels were gradually standardized, which set a consolidated basis for establishing a stable relationship between the central government and local governments and fully motivating local governments under the unified leadership of the state.

2. *Break equal distribution regardless of contribution and form a competition mechanism*

It is a major characteristic of the old system that SOEs rely on and benefit from equal distribution regardless of contribution implemented by the state. Therefore, breaking this system to form a competition mechanism among SOEs and thereby motivating these enterprises to engage themselves in production, operations, and technological development with material benefits is a starting point to make breakthroughs in reforming the macro-management system.

The biggest difficulty in promoting this reform is people's traditional way of thinking and the power of habits, which can be explained by the fact that SOEs have been accustomed to relying on the arrangements of the government for decades. Enterprise production and output all followed the plans of the state, in which the products were allocated by the state, enterprise profits were turned over to the state, enterprise activities were funded by the government, and enterprise staff was also arranged by the state. Enterprise management was limited to the management of the process of production. As time passed, SOEs became like caged tigers that lost their ability to compete and survive. They did not know how to adapt to market demands, lacked the ability for product and technological development, and were burdened with backward management and redundant workers. The competition of three types of overseas-funded enterprises; namely, Chinese-overseas equity joint ventures, Chinese-overseas contractual joint ventures, and wholly foreign-owned enterprises, as well as rural township enterprises, put SOEs in a very passive situation, and some foreign economists even believed that there were no real enterprises in China after assessing the SOE management system. At the same time, governments at all levels established many departments to regulate enterprises and covered the businesses of the enterprises, which not only shackled enterprises, but also made it impossible for the government to focus on researching and resolving major affairs in the macroeconomy and the development of public utilities, thereby causing a mismatch of functions between the government and SOEs.

In order to break the system of equal distribution regardless of contribution of enterprises and gradually introduce SOEs into the market, the State Council in 1979 issued the *Regulations for State-owned Enterprises to Retain Part of the Profit at the Disposal of Enterprises*, which allowed enterprises to establish production development funds, welfare funds, and bonus funds for workers and staff. In 1981, China started to implement various methods of profit retaining and contracting responsibility for profits and losses, which linked the performance of enterprises in terms of production and operations with the interests of enterprises and staff. This measure made enterprises and staffs care about the performance of the enterprises regarding material benefits, thus taking the first step to break the system of equal distribution regardless of contribution.

In order to stabilize the relation of profits distribution between the state and enterprises, and to resolve those defects existing in the system of turning over profits to the state, China began to explore the approach of introducing income tax into the distribution of profits. In 1983, the State Council approved and forwarded the *Tentative Methods on Profit Replacement by Tax of State-owned Enterprises*, and started to levy income tax comprehensively beginning in June that year. Large and medium-sized SOEs with profits paid income tax at the rate of 55%. Part of the profits AT (after-tax) was turned over to the state, and the remainder could be kept by enterprises. This was the first step in reforming substitution of tax payment for profit delivery.

The second step of the reform happened in September 1984. In addition to categorizing the original industrial and commercial tax into some new taxes according to different objects of taxation, large and medium-sized profitable enterprises had to pay income tax at the fixed rate of 55%, profitable SOEs had to pay income tax according to the calculation of the new progressive rates levied on income in excess of specific amounts with eight grades, and the rates of adjustable tax were adjusted according to the different situations of the enterprises. At the same time, profitable enterprises became responsible for profits and losses after paying income tax, and the state stopped allocating funds for enterprises. The state moderately reduced some standards for small enterprises, and continued to implement loan repayment before tax and extraction for two kinds of funds; namely, welfare funds and bonus funds for workers and staff.

The second step of the substitution of tax payment for profit delivery increased the financial resources retained by enterprises, enhanced their vitality, improved their abilities for self-development, and consolidated the national fiscal revenue. However, the overly-high income tax rates and the adjustable tax rate set for individual enterprises harmed the best performing enterprises. In addition, the stipulation of loan repayment before tax and the extraction of welfare funds and bonus funds for workers and staff also complicated the relations between the state and enterprises.

When implementing the substitution of tax payment for profit delivery, the state continued to implement a distribution method that made some enterprises and departments contract responsibilities for profits and losses, including contracting the responsibility for incremental profits turned over to the state and for input and output. Unprofitable enterprises and enterprises with low profit took contracting responsibility for profits and losses. The civil aviation and posts and telecommunications departments shared profits with the state. Petroleum and oil companies took on overall responsibility for input and output. Metallurgical departments took on contracting responsibility for input and output. And China Non-Ferrous Metal Corporation took on contracting responsibility for output.

During the reform of the fiscal and tax systems in 1994, China cancelled the adjustable tax and the welfare funds and bonus funds for workers and staff and for various contracting methods, and unified the corporation income tax of domestic enterprises at the flat rate of 33%. For some enterprises with low profitability, the state added two preferential tax rates at 27 and 18% for a period. This reform was a significant step forward for standardizing the relations between enterprises and the state, breaking from the system of equal distribution regardless of contribution completely, and establishing a fair competition mechanism among enterprises.

3. *Establish and improve the macro regulatory system*

Reforming the macro-economic management system entails the combination of breaking and building, which means China needs to break first and then build, or build first and then break, or break and build at the same time. If streamlining administration and delegating power and equal distribution regardless of contribution mentioned above is considered to be the breaking of the traditional economic system, then establishing and improving a new macro regulatory system that can adapt to the demand of the socialist market economy is extremely essential.

(1) The market economy needs macro regulation

The 14th National Congress of the CPC proposed the reform goal of establishing the socialist market economic system and making an entry into a new stage of reform. The Third Plenary Session of the 14th CPC Central Committee held in 1993 adopted the *Decision of the CPC Central Committee on Establishing the Socialist Market Economy* (hereinafter referred to as the Decision), and comprehensively planned the architecture of the socialist market economy, proposed the requirements for transforming government functions and establishing a sound macro regulatory system, and pointed out that the socialist market economy must have a sound macro regulatory system. The major tasks of macro regulation are maintaining a general balance in the economic aggregate, promoting the prioritization of the economic structure, leading the continuous, rapid, and healthy development of the economy, and driving comprehensive social progress. Mainly, with the economic approaches, macro regulation will make important strides in reforming the fiscal and tax system, financial system, investment system, and planning system, and in establishing a mechanism where planning, financial, and fiscal systems coordinate and restrict each other as well as in enhancing the comprehensive coordination of economic operations. Specifically, regarding planning, the government proposed targets and tasks for developing the economy and for social development, and for supporting economic policies. In finance, the Central Bank established stabilizing the value of the RMB as the main task, adjusted the total supply of currencies, and maintained the balance of international payments. In the fiscal system, the fiscal departments will apply budget and fiscal approaches, and stress the moderation of the economic structure and social distribution. The monetary and fiscal policies will help adjust the basic balance between social gross demand and gross supply, and promote the coordinated development of the economy and society with the coordination of industrial policies.

The fact that the market economy needs macro regulation is determined by the objective laws of the market economy itself. In a market economy, the law of value is the principle that must be followed by various economic activities. The allocation of production factors is mainly powered by the moving of value, which, compared with resource allocation through the administrative approach in the traditional system, is more efficient and profitable. However, the market is a panacea. It has spontaneity and blindness defects. Problems in macro-economic aggregate, economic structure, distribution of income, and social security cannot be solved by the market. Rather, the market needs macro regulation to supplement where the market cannot function well, thereby offsetting the defects of the market itself. At the same time, the smooth regulation of the market relies on stable economic and social environments. If the economy and commodity prices change radically, then the leverage of value would malfunction. China is a developing country, so the macroeconomic policy of the government is of vital importance for implementing the strategy of catching up with and surpassing developed countries. Without effective macro regulation, China cannot implement the correct development strategy or formulate economic policies that can promote the continuous, rapid, and healthy development of the economy. The experience of countries with developed markets and emerging industrialized countries has also proven that macro regulation is essential. Countries with developed markets all have unique macro regulations. This is especially true with emerging industrialized countries and regions. The important factor for an economy taking off is that a country formulates and implements the right development strategies while tapping into the vitality of the microeconomy. China is a country with a large population, weak economic foundation, and unbalanced development. Only macro regulatory policies can enable China to correctly tap into the vitality of market competition, coordinate various contradictory relations in economic development, stabilize the macroeconomy, and create a sound macroeconomic environment for realizing the development target of modernization.

(2) Improving the macro regulatory system in practice

Transitioning from the traditional planning economic system to the socialist market economy involves the establishment of a new macro regulatory system. Since the proposal of the reform target for establishing the socialist market economy in 1992, China has been exploring approaches for practicing macro regulation in curbing inflation and expanding domestic demand as a way to help establish and improve the macro regulatory system and greatly push forward reform and development.

In 1992, under the guidance of the series of speeches in the southern tours of Deng Xiaoping and the 14th National Congress of the CPC, economic development and reform and opening up noticeably improved. In the first half of 1993, China's GDP increased by 13.9% over the same period last year, total industrial output value increased by 25.1%, fixed asset investments increased by 61%, and gross retail sales of consumer goods increased by 21.6%. The dramatic increase shows that the economy is overheating. The first problem in this situation is that the economic aggregate is out of control, in which case gross demand has been growing so fast that it has gone beyond the gross supply. The second problem is the imbalanced structure. Stocks, futures, and real estate have been expanding fast, but the development of infrastructure and basic industries is lagging behind. The contradiction of the transportation industry being a bottleneck that restrains economic development is particularly pressing. The third problem is the financial disorder. Indiscriminate collection of funds, disorderly interbank lending, unapproved establishment of financial institutions, and the real estate boom and development zone fever have been pressing and pushing each other, worsening the imbalance between gross demand and gross supply and further distorting the economic structure. At the same time, various unreasonable tax reductions and exemptions as well as tax evasion greatly eroded the normality of fiscal revenue. The fifth problem is the imbalance between domestic and foreign economies. Exports increased by only 4.4% while imports increased by 23.2%, which indicates that the RMB has depreciated greatly and the pressure on the balance between international revenue and expenditures is growing.

In order to solve these problems and stop the overall economic situation from worsening, in the late part of the June 1993, the Central Committee of the CPC issued the *Notice of the CPC Central Committee on Strengthening and Improving Macro Regulatory Measures* and adopted a series of macroeconomic regulatory measures.

In finance, China forbade all forms of fund collections that violated the regulations of China, strictly limited the scale of the yearly issuance of various securities, strictly controlled the issuance of securities of local governments, set deadlines for the cancellation of financial institutions set up without national permission or set deadlines for these financial institutions to incorporate into approved financial institutions, and banned black market negotiable securities transactions. China strictly controlled the issuance of currency, called off loans for non-bank financial institutions from the People's Bank of China (PBC), set deadlines to take back inter-bank lending funds that violated relevant regulations, increased deposit and loan interest rates twice, cancelled the regulation right to adjust 7% of the loans at provincial bank branches, required that the interest rates of all fund collections were not higher than that of the treasury bonds of the same period, and prioritized the issuance of treasury bonds and the Priority Construction Treasury.

In fiscal and tax management, China strengthened tax collection and management, removed tax reductions and exemptions with unauthorized approval, abrogated policies to reduce funds for energy and transportation and budget adjustment, curbed the rapid expansion of purchasing power of social groupings, cut 20% of the budget for conference fees, and strictly limited activities that required going abroad as well as various exhibition activities for investment attraction.

In foreign exchange management, China improved methods for foreign exchange payment, strictly examined foreign investments and other outflows of foreign exchange capital, carried out large-scale exchange rate intervention by underselling hundreds of millions of US dollars in the domestic foreign exchange market, strictly limited the circulation of foreign currencies in the domestic market, and banned speculation on foreign currencies and other speculative acts.

In controlling fixed asset investments, China strictly limited the scale of investments, cleared projects under construction, strictly controlled new projects, and enhanced the management of the real estate market.

In curbing price inflation, China strictly controlled the rising of commodity and service prices that were regulated by the state, stopped publishing price adjustment measures by local management, and established the grain risk fund and non-staple food regulation fund. The implementation of the macro regulatory policies mentioned above gained noticeable achievements. The economic overheat cooled down, the financial order improved markedly, the disorderly phenomenon of indiscriminate fund collection, disorderly inter-bank lending, unapproved establishment of financial institutions were basically curbed, and over half of the disorderly inter-bank lending funds were taken back. Clearing and rectifying real estate and development zones effectively restrained speculation and bubbles, stabilizing the stock market and cooling down the real estate fever.

In order to consolidate the achievements of macro regulation and adapt macroeconomic management to the requirements of the socialist market economy, the Central Committee of the CPC and the State Council in 1994 resolutely put forward significant reforms for the macro-economic regulatory system, including the fiscal and tax system, financial system, foreign exchange system, and price system. Despite the comprehensive coverage of these fields, the big difficulty, and the risks, these reforms went smoothly, because China fully prepared the reform plans, carried out supporting measures, and coped with problems that arose in the implementation process. The timely and smooth functioning of new systems consolidated and brought about the achievements of macro regulation. In 1995, the country further made curbing inflation the major task of macro regulation and adopted a series of responding measures centering on this task. These measures mainly included implementing appropriately tight fiscal monetary policies; continuing to strictly control the scale of fixed asset investments and new investment projects, limiting loans for fixed asset investment according to plans, and clearing projects under construction; restraining the overheated growth of funds focusing on consumption, stopping and correcting the practices of randomly raising salaries and giving bonuses and allowances; ensuring order in the distribution sector and strengthen the management and regulation of market prices; letting state-owned businesses and rural supply and marketing cooperatives play the main role in stabilizing the market and prices; establishing and improving the system for reserving important commodities and the price risk fund at both the central and local levels to enhance the economic strength of the state to regulate the market; taking all-round measures to strengthen agriculture reform, carrying out a system where provincial governors take responsibility for the "rice bag" (grain supply) program, the system of city mayors taking responsibility for the "vegetable basket" (non-grain food supply) program and the responsibility system for controlling prices, and carrying out the "vegetable basket" program with the major goal of establishing the supply base for urban non-staple foods; using imports to enhance regulation of the domestic market; and improving market regulations and rules, regulating market pricing activities, and enhancing the regulation of prices.

After years of macro regulation, China not only vigorously promoted the continuous, rapid, and healthy development of the economy, but also effectively resolved a series of pressing problems and contradictions arising in the great stride forward, including the excessively rapid growth of investment and consumption, financial disorder, the issuance of excessive currency, and the overly-high increase of prices, thereby avoiding radical changes in the economy and basically achieving a soft landing. The whole economy started to enter the development track at a moderately rapid and relatively steady pace. The success of macro regulation guaranteed the accomplishment of the 8th Five-Year Plan during which China achieved the fastest economic growth and smallest fluctuations compared with other five-year plans since the PRC, which got the Ninth Five-Year Plan off to a great start.

However, with the success of the soft landing, the contradiction of inadequate demand arose in economic life. The outbreak of the Asian financial crisis in the second half of 1997 caused the currencies of China's neighboring countries and regions to plunge dramatically and impacted exports and imports, which in turn seriously impacted the development of China's economy. In order to maintain continuous yet rapid growth, the central government resolutely in the spring of 1998 decided to adopt policies to expand domestic demand. In the second half of the same year, China issued 100 billion yuan of national debts and attracted 100 billion yuan of bank loans. The money was mainly used in agriculture and forestry, water conservancy, transportation, telecommunications, urban and rural power grids, national grain reserves, affordable urban housing, ecological environment, and urban infrastructure building. In 1999, China further enhanced and expanded domestic demand, continued to adopt proactive fiscal policies, and issued additional national debts for projects including infrastructure projects under construction, technological upgrading of enterprises, ecological environment, and the infrastructure needed by expanding the enrollment of students at colleges and universities. The banks took a series of measures to increase the supply of currencies. From 1998 to the first half of 1999, the Central Bank slashed interest rates four times, removed limits on the scale of commercial bank loans, delivered many guiding opinions on loans, increased re-lending for rural cooperatives, and extended the floating range of interest rates on loans for SMEs. In order to increase the supply of base money, the PBC improved the system for the required reserve ratio, broadened the open market operation of national debts and financial bonds, and strengthened the Central Bank to manage the money market. As a result, China maintained relatively rapid economic growth despite commodity prices having registered negative growth for more than 20 months in a row.

From curbing inflation to expanding domestic demand, the macro regulatory system is being improved in practice. The three regulation methods; namely, planning, fiscal regulation, and financial regulation, achieved cooperation and coordination with each other, improving the efficiency of macro regulation. The characteristics of the macro regulatory system and operational mechanism in recent years are summarized as follows.

(i) Establishing a reasonable and efficient system of macro regulatory targets through annual plans

Macro regulation must first have specific targets. Various regulation methods must center on these targets to form a highly-effective synergy. The Central Economic Work Conference at the end of each year will analyze the economic situation, propose the targets and policy measures for economic development in the next year, and formulate a draft annual plan and submit it to the National People's Congress for further discussion. The centerpiece to the annual plan is the eight major targets of macro regulation; namely, economic growth, fixed asset investment of the whole society, price inflation, total imports and exports, fiscal revenue and expenditures, the issuance of currency, the registered urban unemployment rate, and natural population growth rate. These eight indexes influence and restrain each other, which fully reflect economic operations. In order to reasonably set these eight primary targets, China must carry out deep analysis and well-founded predication of economic operation trends and think over the strength and results of macro-economic policies. Generally, the eight targets are finalized by the State Council after rounds of consultations with the National Planning Commission, fiscal departments, banks, and other relevant departments, and after studying and taking the opinions of experts into consideration. These targets should have legal effect after approval by the National People's Congress, and departments of the government will spare no effort to realize these targets. Therefore, in this sense, planning is the basis for macro regulation and the foundation for the coordination of various regulation methods.

(ii) Adopting timely regulatory measures to respond to new circumstances in economic operations

There will be unexpected situations from time to time in economic operations. The macro regulatory system must be capable of finding and tracing these unexpected situations in a timely manner and adjusting the direction and the strength of relevant policies to realize the macro regulatory targets. When China encounters factors that have a relatively large influence on the economy that make it difficult to realize regulatory targets, the regulatory targets will need to be modified with the approval of the NPC Standing Committee. Whether or not China can take correct and timely measures in response to emergent situations is a test to the validity of the macro regulatory system.

The Southeast Asian financial crisis in the second half of 1997 seriously affected China's exports. Since 1998, China has taken a series of macro regulatory measures to remedy the economy, which has been hit by the international financial crisis. These measures include implementing positive fiscal policies, issuing national debts, and enhancing infrastructure; formulating policies that encourage private investment and improving financial services for SMEs; adjusting income distribution policies, increasing salaries, and raising standards for subsistence allowances for laid-off workers, the unemployment security fund, and the urban minimum subsistence level; modifying prices, eliminating unreasonable fees, and setting up consumer credit to boost consumption; accelerating urban housing system reform and cultivating the urban housing industry as a new economic growth point; expanding enrollment at colleges and universities; increasing the rate of export refunds and enhancing support for export credits; and allowing foreign capital to be invested in more fields and adopting more positive policies to attract foreign capital, among other things. The timely publication and application of these regulatory policies played an important role in solving the contradiction of inadequate demand and in supporting the continuous, rapid, and sound development of the economy. China has found effective methods for curbing inflation and realizing an economic soft landing to date, but the country is still in search for effective approaches to expand demand; in particular, to increase private investment and encourage consumption, which entails further exploration in practice.

(iii) Tight fiscal, monetary, investment, consumption, export, and distribution policies coordination

The macro regulation system is a unified system in which various economic leverages are interlinked, thus these leverages should coordinate with each other and work together while centering on the common regulatory targets. With regard to the coordination of fiscal and monetary policies, it can be said that monetary policies played a significant role in curbing inflation from 1993 to 1996, while fiscal policies were of vital importance in boosting the economy and expanding domestic demand in recent years. However, judging from the situation that commodity prices are declining and the trend of deflation has become increasingly obvious in recent years, currency policies should play a greater role.

The purpose of the positive fiscal policies is not only to promote the construction of some key projects with fiscal bonds; more importantly, these policies could increase bank loans and private investment, thereby driving the expansion of consumption. Obviously, the positive fiscal policies implemented in recent years did not bring this driving effect into play, which greatly weakened the effect of the policies in expanding domestic demand. For this problem, China needs to continue exploring the practice of expanding domestic demand.

(iv) It is possible that macro regulatory policies will turn out to be ineffective

Not all macro regulatory policies can achieve the expected targets. Sometimes the policies are highly effective, and sometimes they are not very successful. Generally speaking, in regards to the implementation of macro regulatory policies in recent years, the policies for curbing demand are relatively effective, but the policies for expanding demand and increasing effective supply are only successful in times of shortage, whereas in a buyer's market, it is difficult for the policies to play their roles. Specifically, the PBC lowered deposit interest rates seven consecutive times to try to boost consumption and investment, but the rate of household savings still increased greatly, market sales were still low, and demand for investment was weak. The bank hoped to increase the supply of currencies to increase loans, but inadequate effective demand limited the speed of increasing money supply and loans. This is a problem that has not been resolved in the past 50 years since the establishment of the PRC. This suggests that the implementation of macro regulatory policies entails supporting policies in relevant perspectives, favorable economic and social environments, and in policy transmission mechanisms. Otherwise, it is difficult for these policies to receive social responses. This is the new problem that macro regulation is now facing, and China needs to explore and study it thoroughly.

24.2 The Planning System Reform

The planning system reform has made great progress for over two decades. Generally, this period consists of two stages. The first stage was the planning management system period from 1978 to 1993, during which reform of the management system was highly centralized. The second stage is the systematical innovation period from 1993 to present, during which the new-type planning system, the content, and the methods of the planning were made to adapt to the requirements of the socialist market economy.

1. ***Major content of China's planning system reform before 1993***

Before 1993, China's planning system reform was mainly reflected in the vigorous reduction and improvement of mandatory plans, in which case mandatory plans gradually became the primary form of planning and played a significant role in developing market mechanisms in many fields.

(1) Production

The field of agricultural production. Before 1979, the Chinese government implemented mandatory planning and management regarding the yields of 25 kinds of major farm products, and assigned different plans for sowing areas and yields for the 25 kinds of farm products in different areas. Since the Third Plenary Session of the 11th CPC Central Committee, the Chinese government gradually reduced the mandatory plans, and cancelled all of them by 1985. By the end of 1993, the state only guided planning and management for nine major farm products; namely, grain, cotton, oil seeds, sugar crops, flue-cured tobacco, total output of meat, marine products, afforestation areas, and natural rubber.

The field of industrial production. The products under the mandatory planning and management by the National Planning Commission are shown in the chart below, in which product types decrease year by year.

Industrial products under the National Planning Commission mandatory planning management (%)

Year	Product variety	The proportion of products in gross industrial output value
1980	120	40.0
1985	60	20.0
1992	59	11.7
1993	36	6.8

Source National Bureau of Statistics

The fields of transportation, post, and telecommunications. Since 1985, the state has implemented mandatory planning and management for railway freight volume, waterway freight volume, and handled cargo volume at major coastal ports for some key products. At the same time, for these products, the state guided the planning and management for highway freight volume in transport departments, cargo handled volume at ports, steamship and barge freight volume, total civil aviation transportation turnover, and total post and transportation business volume.

(2) Commodity distribution

There were 256 kinds of materials allocated by the state in 1979, and this number was reduced to just over 20 in 1985 and to 19 in 1990. Although there were still 19 kinds of materials allocated by the state in 1992, the proportion of state allocation dropped noticeably. In 1993, this number decreased to 12.

Changes in the proportion of the main materials allocated by the state in the total volume of domestic production (%)

Year	Steel	Timber	Cement	Coal
1979	77.1	85.0	35.7	58.9
1984	62.3	44.3	24.1	49.0
1990	41.6	30.7	13.1	50.4
1991	40.7	25.9	11.0	52.5
1992	34.3	19.5	6.9	49.5
1993	19.9	9.9	4.5	49.2

Source National Bureau of Statistics

In 1979, there were 65 kinds of commodities collected and allocated by the state (the No. 1 category of goods), and this number was reduced to 23 and 15 in 1987 and 1993, respectively. Out of the 15 kinds of commodities that were collected and allocated by the state in 1993, 13 were under mandatory planning and management, and the remaining two were guided by planning and management.

(3) Price controls

Giving play to the role of the market in pricing.

In 1992, the National Bureau of Price liberalized the prices of 571 kinds of products, and delegated the pricing power of 22 kinds of products to the provincial level. By the end of 1992, the number of industrial production means directly regulated by the Bureau and relevant central departments had been reduced from 737 in 1991 to 89. And only 33 of the 89 kinds of industrial production means were priced by the state. In 1993, the state also liberalized the prices of major parts of steel and around 200 million tons of coal allocated by the state. In agricultural products, there were nine kinds of products that had their prices regulated by the Bureau and other relevant departments by the end of 1992, of which, five kinds of products were priced by the state and the remaining four were set at state-guided prices. The purchasing prices and selling prices of grain were basically liberalized nationwide in 1993. By the end of 1992, the proportion of the sales priced by the government in total retail sales was 5.9%, and this number was 12.5% in total farmer agricultural product sales and 18.7% in the total industrial enterprise production means sales.

(4) Foreign trade

Export commodities.

In 1980, there were over 900 kinds of supplying export commodities coordinated by the National Planning Commission, and this number was reduced to 31 in 1985 and 29 in 1991. China started implementing the *Interim Measures for the Administration of the Export Commodities* in 1993, in which the state confirmed 138 kinds of export commodities administered by quota licenses, of which, 38 were under planning quota administration, 54 under voluntary quota administration, 22 under general license administration, and 24 under passive quota administration. The proportion of commodities under export quota administration decreased from 66% in the past to the present 30.5%.

(5) Social development

Labor wages. In the past, the National Planning Commission was responsible for setting the total number of planned labor wages for the whole country as well as for issuing national labor wage plans in different departments and regions, in which, the Commission separately presented indicators for the wages of government offices, public institutions, and enterprises, and qualitatively controlled the wages of these institutions. Since 1993, the state added some indicators for the whole society to the original labor wage reform indicators, thus combining the number of staff, the total number of wages and GNP, and indicators for economic benefits together. At the same time, the state broadened the scope of planning from ownership by all the people to all the workers and the sum of their wages. Besides the increase in the proportion of total wages under the ownership of all the people, which could not be exceeded, other indicators were administered only as supervising and directing indicators at a macro level, thus these indicators needed not be assigned and specifically implemented by lower-level institutions. The plans for the Change from Rural Residents to Urban Residents would be submitted to the National Planning Commission by the planning departments at provincial and city levels for comprehensive balance, after which these plans would be listed as state plans, whereby the National Planning Commission would assign different plans for regions and implement these plans as mandatory planning and management.

In education, the combination of mandatory plans and guiding plans was the practice that the state-planned enrollment was directed through mandatory plans, while the enrollment of entrusted training and self-supporting students was directed through guiding plans.

The state included complete plans in the fields of health, culture, radio, television, film, sports, and social security into the plans for economy and social development as the guiding plans.

When the scope of direct state administration was drastically reduced, the direct administration by local governments was also reduced noticeably.

2. ***Major contents of China's planning system reform after 1993***

With the deepening of economic system reform, and in accordance with the spirit of the 14th National Congress of the CPC and the Third Plenary Session of the 14th CPC Central Committee, after the Eighth Five-Year Plan period, and especially since 1993, reform of the planning system entered a period of systematical innovation with the establishment of the socialist market economy and a new planning system as its major content. During this period, the planning system reform achieved the following progress:

1. Continued reduction of the scope of the mandatory planning and management

(i) Production

In the field of agricultural production, and on the basis of all mandatory plans being cancelled in 1985, the state only guided planning and management for the production of nine major farm products; namely, grain, cotton, oil seeds, sugar crops, flue-cured tobacco, total output of meat, marine products, qualified afforestation areas, and natural rubber. In the field of industrial production, the kinds of products under the National Planning Commission's mandatory planning and management were reduced from 36 in 1993 to 12 in 1998, and the proportion of these products in total industrial output was only 4.1%.

(ii) Commodity distribution

The materials allocated and coordinated by the National Planning Commission were further reduced based on the reduction to 12 kinds of materials in 1993. In 1998, the National Planning Commission only implemented unified allocation of some of the products in five production means; namely, crude oil, refined oil, coal, natural gas, and automobiles.

(iii) Price controls

The establishment of the market-based pricing mechanism. Currently, besides there being several monopolistic public utilities and some important commodities that relate to the economy and the people's livelihood, which are unfit for competition and still need to be priced by the government, most commodities and services are priced by the market. In 1996, the proportion of commodities priced by the market adjustment in the total retail sales reached 92.5%, and the proportion of commodities of government-directed prices was 1.2%, while the proportion of commodities priced by the government was only 6.3%. Production means, besides several important commodities, including petroleum, electricity, and fertilizers, were still priced by the government, while other commodities were all market-adjusted prices. The proportion of commodities of market-adjusted prices in the total sales revenue of production means was 81.1%, and the proportion of government-directed commodity prices was 4.9%, while the proportion of commodities priced by the market was only 14%. In the total value of the purchase of agricultural and side line products, the proportions of commodities of market-adjusted prices, government-directed prices, and government-set prices were 79, 4.1 and 16.9%, respectively.

(iv) Fixed asset investments

The decision-making power for enterprises and local government investment was further expanded. Currently, the investment funds arranged by the state account for as little as 20% in fixed asset investments.

(v) Foreign trade and foreign exchange

Since 1994, the state cancelled all mandatory plans for total imports and exports. At the same time, the state further expanded autonomous rights for the foreign trade of enterprises, reduced the types of commodities under quota and license management, and liberalized the scope of import and export businesses with the exception of several important and special commodities. The state adjusted and modified foreign trade mainly by comprehensively taking advantage of the exchange rate, tariffs, interest rates, export credits, and other economic leverages. The tariff level was reduced from 43.2% in the beginning of 1992 to the present 17%. In 1994, China successfully unified exchange rates and established the unified inter-bank foreign exchange market and the managed RMB floating exchange rate system based on market supply and demand. Based on this, China began undertaking the obligations of Article VIII of the IMF Articles of Agreement from December 1, 1996—three years earlier than the realization of RMB current account convertibility that China promised to the world.

2. Improvement of balancing and coordination methods for annual macro-economic aggregate and major structures

In the formulation and implementation of the annual plan, China needs to improve the value and magnitude of balancing calculations, and improve the coordination and balance of social funds. Meanwhile, China needs to continue to maintain balance in other production factors and all basic commodity markets in China. The balance and coordination of China's economic aggregate and major structures should be carried out at the following levels: The first level is the balance between social gross demand and gross supply. The second level is the balance between the total volume of social funds and major structures. The third level is the calculation of the balance between the resources and use of the disposable monetary income of residents. The fourth level is the calculation of the balance of the sources and uses of fixed asset investments. The fifth level is the calculation of the balance between supply and demand for important agricultural products, energy and basic raw materials, and the main means of agricultural production. The sixth level is the calculation of the balance of the social workforce. And the seventh level is the calculation between the level of overall market prices and major pricing structures. While working to improve the balance between macro-economic aggregate and major structures, the planning departments have enhanced their connections and coordination with departments responsible for economic adjustment, which has played an important role in macro regulation.

3. Planning indicator system reform

In 1995, in accordance with the nature and function of planning indicators, China generally divided planning indicators into three categories; namely, macro regulation indicators, expectation indicators, and national public fund and resources allocation indicators. As a special method of national-level macro regulation and public resources allocation, several planning indicators are still mandated by the state, which is especially necessary in the transformation from the old system to the new one.

4. The gradual establishment and improvement of the national order system

China began to establish the national order system in 1994. In 1995, the country continued to make national orders for rubber, cars, tires, and pig iron. Based on the experience of tentative national orders, China standardized the national order system gradually, and initially established the unified national order system, which includes important agricultural products, agricultural production means, and basic industrial products.

5. The establishment and improvement of the national planning report and information release system

China formulated the tentative annual planning report in 1993, which reflected the transformation of the planning functions and the policy-enhancing nature of the planning work. In 1995, China further standardized the nature, variety, content, form, formulation, publication, and implementation of planning reports, thereby forming a relatively complete series of the annual planning reports. In addition, China also proposed some planning reports for special subjects regarding pressing contradictions and important problems in the economic development of each year. In addition, China also established the planning report publication system in 1995.

The improvement of the macro-economic information release system. In 1997, in order to direct the investment of micro-economic entities, the National Planning Commission released a sequence of economic information, including production and construction, market demand, and major problems existing in the development of electricity, coal, oil refining, ethylene, transportation, steel and non-ferrous metal, and other industries, as well as in national policy orientation.

6. Managing immediate regulations during the implementation of the plans

The state carries out timely and moderate immediate regulations based on macroeconomy improvements and market operation tracing, monitoring, predictions, and early warnings. The focuses of the immediate regulations are modifying the volume and direction of social funds to ensure that demand for key-project funds can be met; managing the dynamic balance of the market supply of sensitive commodities and coping with problems that demand comprehensive coordination of planning departments in production, construction, transportation, domestic trade, and foreign economy and trade; and dealing with the work to implement disaster prevention and relief and other emergency situations.

7. Increasing the importance of industrial-directed economic structure adjustment and enhancement

The National Planning Commission and other relevant departments have been improving studies of comprehensive and special industrial policies since 1994. The *Outline of State Industry Policies for the 1990s* and the *Industrial Policies of the Auto Industry* has been approved by the State Council for implementation. In December 1997, the National Planning Commission released the *Catalogue of Industries, Products and Technology China Prioritizes for Development*, and at the same time, released the newly revised *Catalogue for the Guidance of Foreign Investment Industries* and *Water Conservancy Industrial Policies*, the first industrial policy in China's basic industries.

8. Further improvements of medium and long-term planning methods

In adapting to the requirements of the development of the socialist market economy, China's planning system gradually transformed into one in which the medium-and long-term plans play a leading role. This is conducive to taking advantage of the market in terms of short-term resource allocation, and will help give play to the planning for long-term resource allocation, which can facilitate mutual complements between planning and the market. In order to reasonably formulate the Ninth Five-Year Plan for Economic and Social Development and Long-Range Objectives to the Year 2010, China further reformed the content and methods for formulating plans. (1) Strengthening the study of medium and long-term development strategies to make the Ninth Five-Year Plan a strategic plan that can lay a good foundation for China in the 21st century. (2) Improving forecasting of the medium and long-term market operation environment, the development momentum for world economics, technological progresses, and other perspectives; fully implementing a sustainable development strategy; and promoting the transformation of the economic growth model from an extensive model to an intensive model. (3) Plan comprehensively and have clear priorities. China will seize the key areas and major issues that will have significant influence over the overall picture for which China will deepen studies and focus on planning. China will pay more attention to development planning for social undertakings that reflect government functions, especially the formulation of plans for education, health, population, technology, environmental protection, city utilities, poverty alleviation, social security, and other undertakings. (4) China will ensure that balance calculations and connections, as well as the coordination of major macroeconomic indicators, are well-managed, and that the speed of economic growth and the scale of investment are reasonably set for the 9th Five-Year Plan. (5) China will further explore new ways to facilitate the combination of planning and the market while formulating medium and long-term plans. (6) China will ensure that the medium and long-term plans and industrial policies and land management, medium and long-term plans and annual plans, as well as comprehensive plans and other various special plans and policies are well connected, so that China can form an implementation system for national medium and long-term strategies and plans.

24.3 Reform of the Fiscal and Tax Systems

China's fiscal and tax system reform started with the decentralization and interest concessions of local governments and enterprises. In the primary stage of reform and opening up, through decentralization and interest concessions in the reform of the fiscal and tax systems, China broke the system of state control over revenue and expenditures that was tailored to the planned economic system, gradually corrected the defects of over-control, and greatly energized the enthusiasm and creativity of local governments and enterprises to develop the economy. In particular, since the 14th National Congress of the CPC, China has, in light of its goal to establish the socialist market economy, made breakthroughs in the reform of the fiscal and tax systems. The country defined some basic relations in the fiscal distribution and basically established a framework of fiscal and tax systems tailored to the socialist market economy. In the fiscal system, China broke the state's former highly-centralized control over the revenue and expenditure management model, and successfully transformed the financial contracting system into a tax sharing system, thereby basically establishing the multilevel fiscal system with the tax sharing system as its basis. In the tax system, China broke the monotonous tax system under the planned economy, broadened the range of tax adjustments, and established a new turnover tax system featuring value-added tax as the main body and excise and income taxes as supplements. Meanwhile, the country also established and improved the income tax system. In budget formulation, China reformed the traditional single budget system and preliminarily implemented the multiple budget system consisting of a regular budget and a constructive budget.

1. *The transformation from the compound fiscal and taxation system to the tax sharing system featuring value-added tax as the main body*

After the two-step substitutions of tax payment for profit delivery from 1983 to 1984, the original industrial and commercial tax was divided into product tax, value-added tax, business tax, and salt tax. China also levied resource taxes on some extraction enterprises. In addition, China started to levy local taxes, including urban maintenance and construction tax, real estate tax, vehicle and vessel use tax, and urban and township land use tax. In order to meet the requirements of the economic system reform, China also levied some new taxes. By 1993, there were 32 tax categories, and the compound taxation system, in which the turnover tax and income tax served as main body and in which other supplementary taxes complemented each other, has basically taken shape.

Following financial contracting and two-step substitution of tax payment for profit delivery, the fiscal and tax system reform has made great breakthroughs. However, in some respects, the fiscal and tax systems still cannot meet the demands of the socialist market economy. The first problem is that the uneven tax burden is detrimental to fair competition among enterprises. The corporation income tax is categorized into different tax categories according to different enterprise ownership, thus the tax rates are inconsistent. The turnover tax is designed to deal with the problem of adjusting unreasonable planning prices, but there are excessive levels in turnover tax rates and the gaps between levels are too big. The second problem is that the distribution relations between the state and enterprises are too complicated and are not standardized; therefore, national fiscal revenue cannot guarantee stable financial resources. The third problem is that the proportion of central fiscal revenue in national fiscal revenue becomes lower and lower, which leads to the mismatch between central financial resources and the responsibilities undertaken by the central government. Therefore, the state's capability to regulate the economy is weakened. The fourth problem is that neither the scope nor the strength of the tax adjustments is enough, and the adjustments in the land and capital markets are far from effective. The fifth problem is that domestic and foreign enterprises implement different tax systems, which leads to pressing contradictions. There are also some chaotic operations within the fiscal and tax operation systems.

To solve these problems, the central government decided to deepen reform of the fiscal and tax systems. The guiding thoughts of the fiscal and tax system reform in 1994 were to unify tax laws, even tax burdens, simplify the tax system, separate powers in a reasonable way, define distribution relations, guarantee fiscal revenues, and establish fiscal and tax systems that meet the requirements of establishing the socialist market economy.

Basically, the reform of turnover tax changed the traditional method for categorizing tax items according to products and setting different tax rates with specific tax items, and established the system in which the value-added tax was collected in the production link and the distribution link. The reform target was to establish a turnover tax system featuring the value-added tax as the main body, with the excise tax and business tax as supplements. In practice, the reform was intended to abolish the industrial and commercial consolidated tax, and to transform the industrial and commercial consolidated tax of 1993 into value-added tax, business tax, and excise tax in the proportion of 55, 35, and 10%, respectively. The new turnover tax consisted of value-added tax, excise tax, and business tax. The value-added tax was generally collected in the production sector and links of wholesale and retail, while the excise tax was levied on several consumer goods. For taxable services that do not pay value-added tax and sales of real estate, China would collect business tax. The value-added tax was on the newly added value created by the tax payer's production or operations, as well as the additional value of commodities. The scope of value-added tax covered the links of production, wholesale, retail, importing, processing, and repairing. The basic tax rate of the value-added tax was 17%, and the low-level tax rate was 13%. The scope of the low-level tax rate mainly covered basic food and agricultural production means. Export products should generally enjoy a value-added tax rate of zero. In the management of taxation, China established the system where the value-added tax was excluded from the price and the tax deduction was noted on the invoice. For small-scale taxpayers whose yearly sales were relatively low or whose financial accounting was incomplete, China used a simple taxation method in which the VAT was collected with specific collection rates based on the full amount of sales revenue.

VAT taxation system reform. China specifically established a tax registration system for VAT taxpayers, used a special VAT invoice, and audited VAT taxpayers in terms of selling and buying parties, which established an effective auditing system.

There were 11 new excise tax items, including tobacco, alcohol, cosmetics, expensive jewelry, motorcycles, automobiles, diesel, and kerosene, as well as other items. China adopted a per a unit tax and an ad valorem tax to collect the excise tax. For ad valorem items, China collected the excise tax with specific rates on the price that excluded VAT but included the amount of excise tax. In accordance with the general taxation of VAT, China levied a business tax on a portion of business activities. The scope of the business tax extended from provision of labor services and transferring assets to selling immovable property. Units and individuals engaged in taxable businesses, transferring, and selling would pay the business tax with specific tax rates on the volume of their sales. The business tax rate was 3% in industries such as transportation, construction, post and telecommunications, culture, and sports, 5% in the service industry, assets transferring, and immovable property sales, 8% in the financial insurance industry, and 5–20% in the entertainment industry.

The new turnover tax system was uniformly applied to all domestic and foreign enterprises, and the industrial and commercial consolidated taxes for foreign enterprises were cancelled. In order to maintain the continuity and stability of tax policies concerning foreigners, China kept preferential tax policies in the transition period, and adopted a method of tax returns to cope with the rising tax burden of some foreigner-concerned taxpayers. If the tax collected using the method after the reform is more than that before the reform, China will return the difference after review and approval by the competent tax authority.

The basic content of the income tax system reform was to adopt an income tax rate of 33% as the unified tax rate for domestic enterprises nationwide beginning in 1994. China adopted a two low-level buffering tax rate for some enterprises with low profitability. The income tax rate in the financial insurance industry was not changed in the initial stage of the reform, but starting from 1997, the financial insurance industry had to implement 33% of the unified income tax rate. For SOEs, China canceled the adjustable tax and stopped collecting the construction fund for key energy and transportation projects and the adjustable fund for the national budget. China also unified the original individual income tax, individual income adjustable tax, and income tax of urban and rural individual businesses, thereby adjusting taxable items. The new income tax rate was set to at the progressive rates of 5—45% for wages or salaries. Meanwhile, China also levied land appreciation taxes, reformed resource taxes, including extending the range of resource taxes, and reformed and adjusted other taxes, which made the tax structure more reasonable.

After the fiscal and tax system reform in 1994, China basically established a tax system with turnover tax as the main component. The characteristic of this tax system is that it boasted stable financial resources, which played an important role in stabilizing fiscal revenue and supporting economic growth. With the deepening of economic reform and development, China's income distribution structure changed greatly, in which some people became wealthy before others. However, the present tax system is far from adequate to maintain equal and fair income distribution. In order to cope with the widening gap in income distribution, China will need to rely on the fiscal and tax system reform so income tax can play its important role in adjusting income distribution, by which China can create a favorable environment for shaping a relatively stable middle-income class nationwide to stabilize the foundation for the development of the economy.

2. *Multi-budget: national budget system reform*

The national budget was changed from a single budget to a multi-budget in 1992. The multi-budget can be divided into two parts: recurrent budget and constructive budget. The recurrent budget does not include deficits. While the funds for part of the central constructive budget can be raised by borrowing at home or abroad on condition that the scale and structure of the borrowing are both reasonable, the local constructive budget is formulated according to the principle of balancing revenue and expenditures. The multi-budget enhances the budget balancing mechanism, which helps implement the principle of acting in accordance with one's ability. The implementation of the tax sharing system in 1994 changed the way the central authority formulated local budgets, thereby strengthening budget restraints.

In the past, China's national fiscal and tax budget system was formed in the highly-centralized planning system. Under the system of state control over revenue and expenditures, it was natural and logical that the single budget serve as the basic form of the national budget system. Similarly, the establishment of the socialist market system means that reform of the national budget system is essential. Now that the economic activities and connections in the market economy have changed from the single model to a diversified, multi model, and the channels for the flow of funds are varied, the present model can no longer meet the requirements of the national budget management and effectively supervise various fiscal funds. Reforms of the central and provincial budget management system were therefore put on the agenda.

The multi-budget system in China follows the following principles: The first principle is that reform of the multi-budget system must be conducive to the general targets of the socialist market economy. With the deepening of reform, many economic components in China achieved remarkable development. Accordingly, the macro regulatory system for SOEs has been transforming from direct regulation to indirect regulation, and regulation approaches have been changing from administrative means to economic and legal means. As an important macro regulation method, the national budget must adapt to these changes. The second principle is that multi-budget system reform must be conducive to the embodiment of the double functions of the socialist state. China is a socialist state with public ownership serving as the main body of its economic system. The state is both the regulator of the economy and the owner of state-owned assets. State finances should not only ensure the smooth functioning of the state apparatus, but also guarantee the preservation and increase the value of state-owned assets. Therefore, the multi-budget must serve dual functions. The third principle is that reform of the multi-budget system must be conducive to the clear definition of the distribution relations between fiscal departments and other departments. China's extra-budgetary funds are relatively large, in which case the multi-budget should include such funds into the scope of budget management. The fourth principle is that multi-budget system reform must be conducive to the enhancement of the fiscal budget restraints mechanism. It should be reasonable and concise, and should truthfully reflect the direction and volume of fiscal funds. The fifth principle is that multi-budget system reform must be conducive to the progress of reform in relevant fields. The sixth principle is that multi-budget system reform must be conducive to the legal system in building national finance.

3. *Fee-to-tax: the critical step for fiscal and tax system reform*

For a long time after reform and opening up, the centerpiece of the fiscal and tax system reform was decentralization and interest concessions. During the reform, China successively implemented the financial contracting system applied by the Central Government over local governments, and the contracting system the state applied to manage enterprises. This was beneficial for bringing the enthusiasm of local governments and enterprises into play. However, as financial power was decentralized, government departments became redundant, and the pressure on government expenditures continued to grow. Local governments at all levels found it more and more difficult to maintain expenditures for staff and economic building. In recent years, the problem of some local governments or departments asking for ultra vires charges and extorting people's wealth under all sorts of pretexts is becoming increasingly serious. According to statistics, the various charges and funds of the state was 360 billion yuan (excluding social security funds) in 1996, accounting for 46% of the fiscal revenue that year. And around 80% of these charges and funds were ultra vires. According to studies of typical examples and relevant estimations, the ratio of the total volume of practical charges and funds to fiscal revenue is 1:1.

These charges and funds are products of China's transition from the old system to the new one. They played a positive role to some extent in helping governments at all levels to raise funds and accelerating the economic building and the development of social undertakings. But now these charges and funds have developed well-beyond their original purposes, resulting in series of problems. The first problem is that it aggravated the burdens on enterprises. According to the investigation by the State Economic and Trade Commission into 300 key enterprises in China, unreasonable burdens on SOEs take up approximately 20% of earned profits and taxes, a proportion equivalent to earned profits. The second problem is that it seriously erodes the tax base. The tax base was narrowed after the charges and collection of funds, thereby directly reducing national fiscal revenue. The third problem is that it requires people to collect the fees and funds, which increases the cost and causes redundancy in departments. It has been discovered that about 30–40% of the current charges and funds are used for supporting staff, and this percentage can be as high as almost 100% for some charges. It not only increases the cost of collection, but also causes overstaffing and redundancy in departments. The fourth problem is that it causes indiscriminate investments in some places. A large amount of the charges and funds is used for "small but all-inclusive" and "big and all-inclusive" construction projects that are inefficient and redundant, making economic structures even more unbalanced. The fifth problem is that these charges and funds provide breeding grounds for corruption. The large amounts of charges and funds are under the radar of fiscal supervision and become an important resource for the unit-owned exchequer set up by local governments and departments, which upsets distribution orders and facilitates corruption. Therefore, on the basis of deepening reform of the fiscal and tax systems, China must carry out the fee-to-tax reform according to the requirements of developing the socialist market economy.

The general target of the fee-to-tax reform is to establish a government income distribution system featuring taxation as the main component and small fees as supplements. Implementing the fee-to-tax reform means taking several years to reduce the proportion of non-tax revenue in the fiscal revenue to the general level of the majority of countries in the world, and to increase the proportion of national fiscal revenue in GDP to approximately 20%.

The implementation of the fee-to-tax reform is of significant importance for promoting the economy and social development. First, the fee-to-tax reform helps increase the proportion of fiscal revenue in GDP and thus enhances the ability of government finance in macro regulation. Owning to the large amounts of existing charges and funds, the increasing financial resources that can be disposed by government finance has been very limited in recent years. Implementing the fee-to-tax reform can help incorporate large amounts of government finance dispersed in local governments and departments into fiscal revenue, which would enable the state to concentrate necessary financial resources to support the development of economic and social programs in accordance with the general target and requirements of macro regulation. Second, the fee-to-tax reform is conducive to tax administration by law and the standard distribution of fiscal revenue. A considerable part of the existing charges and funds has taxation characteristics. Implementing the fee-to-tax reform can lawfully absorb the variously non-standard charges and funds into the tax administration system, further define distribution relations between government, enterprises and institutions, and individuals, and completely put this kind of distribution on the radar of social supervision to implement legalized and standardized management. Third, the fee-to-tax reform is conducive to cracking down on corruption and establishing an efficient and clean government. Under the conditions of developing the socialist market economy, the main source of government revenue should be taxation instead of charges and funds. Implementing the fee-to-tax reform is the only way to prevent off-the-books income, eliminate the breeding ground for corruption in the system, and create favorable conditions for the establishment of an efficient and clean government.

The first measure of the fee-to-tax reform is to include the charges and funds that have taxation characteristics into the scope of the fee-to-tax reform. For example, replacing road maintenance fees and surcharges on vehicle purchases, waterway passenger transportation, and highway construction funds with a fuel tax; including a compensation fee for mineral resources, a radio management fee, and a water resources fee into the scope of resource tax; replacing surcharges on education, rural education undertakings, and local education and local education funds with education tax; and including surcharges on city public utilities, city drainage facility usage fees, and fees for supporting municipal facilities into urban maintenance tax.

In 1999, China needs to first make breakthroughs in the reform of road and vehicle fees, which entails setting standard examples and accumulating experience, and then extend the reform into other fields. The second is to transform those charges that do not reflect government functions but the nature of market operations into operating fees and to levy taxes on these fees according to the law. China should fully separate government fees from operating fees, and encourage those public institutions that are self-sufficient or have completed fiscal deficiency payment to gradually transform into enterprises or intermediary institutions, thereby letting them get operating fees through the market. The third measure is to keep several necessary charging items while formulating relevant methods to improve and standardize these charges. China will carry out the two-line management of fiscal revenue and expenditures for fees that are kept and cannot be included into the scope of taxation, and is determined to cancel unreasonable charges and funds. For those charges and funds that must be finished during the transition period, China will schedule their cancellation. During the clean-up and rectification period, China will suspend the approval process for all charges and funds. China will cancel those unreasonable charges under various sorts of pretexts.

Although China's fiscal and tax system reform achieved considerable progress, the country still has a lot to do to meet the requirements of economic and social development. The current fiscal and tax systems and the current fiscal situation cannot meet the requirements for further development of the economy and society, so reform of the fiscal and tax systems faces many new challenges, especially when there are many changes in the domestic and international economic environments. Reform is extremely difficult under such circumstance. However, it is believed that under the great leadership of the Central Committee of the CPC with Comrade Jiang Zemin at its core, China's fiscal and tax system reform will achieve greater progress. With the deepening of reform, China's fiscal situation will be improved fundamentally and provide more powerful support for the development of the economy.

24.4 The Reform of the Financial System

The guiding thought of China's financial system reform is to meet the requirements of establishing the socialist market economy, to adapt to the basic economic system with public ownership serving as its main component while allowing for the development of all types of ownership, to be suitable for China's situation of multilevel economic development and uneven development in different regions, to allow finance to play its role in macro regulation and optimization of resource allocation in the economy, to be conducive to preventing financial risks and stabilizing financial order, and to be conducive to adapting to the trend of financial globalization and promoting the continuous, rapid, and sound development of the economy. The targets of financial system reform are to establish the macro regulatory system of the central bank, which implements monetary policies independently under the leadership of the State Council, to set up a financial system whereby policy-backed and commercial financial institutions are separate from each other as well as whereby state-owned commercial banks serve as the main body and various financial institutions coexist, and to establish a financial market system featuring unified, open, order, competitive, and strict management.

1. *Ensure a powerful central bank regulation system and enhance financial regulation*

The primary task of deepening reform of financial system is to build the PBC into a true state Central Bank and establish a powerful central bank regulation system. There are four main parts of the reform. The first is to confirm the responsibilities of the central bank. The PBC is China's central bank and it holds a monopoly on the issuance of currency, which means the PBC is the issuing bank of China. The PBC regulates financial institutions and activities across the country on behalf of the Chinese government and manages the national treasury. According to the Law on the People's Bank of China, the PBC has eleven items of responsibilities that can be summarized into six categories: Formulating and implementing monetary policies and maintaining a stable currency value; regulating financial institutions according to law and protecting the legal and sound operations of the financial sector; maintaining the smooth running of payment and clearing systems; holding, managing, and operating national foreign exchange reserves and gold reserves; engaging in agent services of the national treasury and other international services; and representing the Chinese government to engage in relevant global financial activities. The businesses of PBC offices at all levels are administered in a centralized and uniform way. There are seven functions of PBC affiliates: Financial regulation, investigation and statistics analysis, lateral position adjustment, national treasury management, cash allocation, foreign exchanges management, and inter-bank settlement.

Reforming and improving the monetary policy system. The *Decision of the CPC Central Committee on Establishing the Socialist Market Economy* stated that the central bank should regulate the money supply mainly through monetary policy instruments such as a deposit reserve ratio, re-lending rates of the central bank, and open market operations, instead of mainly doing it through credit scale as in the past. The final target of the monetary policies is maintaining the stable value of the RMB, preventing inflation, and thereby boosting economic development.

Improving the state-owned commercial bank management of loans is an important step for China's financial macro regulation to meet the requirements of the socialist market economy. Approved by the State Council, the PBC decided to cancel limits on the scale of loans issued by state-owned commercial banks since the beginning of 1998 and gradually promote asset-liability management and risk management. This was an important measure in putting the spirit of the National Meeting of Financial Work into practice and accelerating and deepening financial reform, as well as a significant transformation of China's financial macro regulation approaches.

Strengthening financial regulation is a requirement for maintaining the smooth operations of the financial system and the foundation for the effective implementation of monetary policies. The main purposes of financial regulation are ensuring the security and liquidity of assets in financial institutions, maintaining moderate solvency to protect the interests of depositors, maintaining financial order and securing the financial system, and ensuring fair and efficient competition within the financial system.

Reforming the regulatory system of the PBC is a significant step in strengthening financial regulation. The Central Committee of the CPC and the State Council decided to carry out the reform of the PBC's regulatory system in October 1997. The main content of the reform included dismantling 31 PBC branches in provinces, municipalities directly under the Central Government and autonomous regions, establishing nine trans-provincial branches, setting up financial regulation offices in provincial capitals that did not have branches, dismantling redundant affiliates in the same city, defining the rights and obligations in financial regulation for the head office, branches, central sub-branches, and sub-branches, and enhancing the financial regulatory responsibilities of PBC affiliates. This reform is conducive to enhancing the authority of the PBC to carry out monetary policies and is beneficial for strengthening the independence and impartiality of the PBC to regulate finance and improving the management of the employees of the PBC.

2. *Establish a diversified banking system and guide the sound development of non-bank financial institutions*

Since reform and opening up, China's banking system has developed from a single banking system into a diversified one led by the central bank and with wholly state-owned commercial banks as the main body together with joint-stock and regional commercial banks and various financial institutions. China will improve the economic performance and services of banks through diversifying financial institutions and introducing a system of competition.

(1) Building the national policy bank

Policy-backed finance is essential in the development of a country. It is actually a financial approach where government and finance penetrate and take advantage of each other. On the one hand, policy-backed finance is a way to transform fiscal distribution. On the other hand, fiscal distribution uses financial approaches to operate fiscal funds. Policy-backed financial institutions are an important instrument for the government to carry out macro regulation and economic intervention. These institutions are also the main bodies of macro regulation that implement and undertake the function of government macro regulation as well as the main bodies of the micro market engaged in the currency operating businesses. Building an independent policy bank helps form different interest subjects, which can form a better restraint mechanism.

According to the relevant documents of the State Council, China's policy bank is the "independent legal person," and carries out "independent accounting, independent and break-even operations, and enterprise-style management." This stipulation indicates that the policy bank is also a financial enterprise. On the one hand, the policy bank is a financial enterprise, because it has the same intermediary function as commercial financial institutions. On the other hand, the policy bank is different because of its close relationship with the government. The policy bank is after all a bank, no matter how powerful its policy-backed functions are, because it retains the nature of a financial enterprise. Therefore, to become a true bank, it must implement government economic policies in the fashion of a bank, instead of government finance, aid, or allotment.

Policy-backed finance keeps certain characteristics under the traditional planning financial system; for example, asset allocation and operation regulation of policy-backed finance are both plan-based, but it operates on the premise of not disturbing market mechanisms, and it is oriented toward supplementing the commercial finance banks and overcoming the defects and the negative nature of the market. The operation mechanism of policy-backed financial institutions is not the same mechanism for planning the financial system, and these institutions are not affiliates or administrative instruments subject to the government. Rather, these policy-backed financial institutions are the financial boosters tailored to macro regulation. Supported by relevant laws, policy-backed financial institutions will operate and develop side by side with commercial financial institutions. In the whole financial system, commercial finance is the main component, while policy-backed finance serves as a supplement.

(2) The transformation from professional banks to true commercial banks

After separating policy businesses, the original professional banks, including the Industrial and Commercial Bank of China, Agricultural Bank of China, Bank of China, and China Construction Bank, are transformed into state-owned commercial banks, in which case these banks will, according to the requirements of the establishment of modern commercial banks, strengthen internal management, prevent financial risks, and strengthen the unified legal system and unified management and strict supervision through the head offices of affiliate businesses. This is an important step toward intensive management.

The centerpiece of commercial bank reform is to establish an operation mechanism featuring independent management, sole responsibility for profits and losses, self-development, and self-discipline. The wholly state-owned commercial banks are the main body of China's commercial banks. Since 1994, the State Council has demonstrated many times that the wholly state-owned commercial banks would no longer issue policy-backed loans, which provided the environment for the reform of the wholly state-owned commercial banks. The requirements of the reform for wholly state-owned commercial banks are as follows: Improve their ability to make profits by running businesses according to law, increase revenue, and reduce expenditures; focus on large and medium cities (excluding the Agricultural Bank of China); dismantle or merge affiliates with small proportions of businesses or chronic losses to streamline the institution and cut expenditures; strengthen first-class legal person regulations, improve internal control mechanisms, increase capital through various channels to raise, and maintain the capital adequacy ratio; verify and write off bad debts one by one, separate and transfer a part of nonperforming loans formed in the past for professional institution management, establish a strict loan quality management system, and strive to make the quality of assets reach the levels of moderately developed countries.

(3) Reforming the rural cooperative management system in accordance with the principles of the cooperative system

Rural cooperatives are the foundation of China's rural finance, therefore, reforming the rural cooperative management system is vital for the overall development of China's agriculture. Currently, among the various problems of the rural cooperative, the core issue is that the guidelines of its businesses deviate from the principles of the cooperative system. The cooperative system is suitable not only for the long-term household contracting system in China's rural areas, but also for the requirements of modernized commodity production in rural areas. At present, it is still difficult for China to increase the income of farmers by increasing the prices of agricultural products, and the contradiction between the rural production of small commodities and domestic big markets is increasingly pressing. Thus, China needs a cooperative form that closely connects the production, processing, and sales of agricultural and side-line products with financial services to deal with the contradiction between rural household production and operations and the big domestic market. China needs to return profits from agricultural product processing and sales to farmers according to the sales of agricultural and side-line products, which could improve the outcome of farmers and enhance their purchasing power for industrial products. Regarding all the problems and measures mentioned above, in order to boost the development of the rural cooperative economy, China should insist on building rural cooperatives into the cooperative financial organizations where farmers become voluntary shareholders, and where members of the cooperatives implement democratic management and mainly offer services for members of the cooperative.

(4) Developing various non-bank financial institutions step by step

Insurance companies, securities companies, trust and investment companies, and finance companies of enterprise groups are important components of China's financial system, especially the securities companies and trust and investment companies, which have played an important role in the development of China's capital market. China developed the capital market from scratch and increased securities funds each year, which was a great achievement of China's financial reform. The proportion of a country's direct financing depends mainly on the credit status, business performance, and the abilities of social financing for enterprises. The moderate and lawful expansion of direct financing will not reduce the total volume of social funds; instead, it could relieve the pressure of bank credit and reduce risks for banks. The central bank needs to continue cooperating with relevant departments to deepen enterprise shareholding system reform, accelerate the development of the capital market moderately, and gradually expand the proportion of direct finance. Reform of trust and investment companies must be based on credit, separate management, scale of operations, and have strict supervision. In the primary stage of the 1980s, fund increases were disposable to local finance and enterprises, which required responding financial institutions to manage the funds on behalf of them to increase returns on assets. In reference to foreign practice, China established trust and investment companies, a kind of non-bank financial institution. However, because of the overestimation of the demand for trust businesses, there were too many trust and investment companies that invested the short-term trust deposits into real estate, which, worsened by the weak regulation over these companies, and put many trust and investment companies into their current predicaments. Trust and investment institutions must follow the operation principles of "managing others' money as entrusted," fully separate trust businesses and securities businesses, improve scale management, and carry out strict supervision. Enterprise group finance companies need to be based on raising the idle funds of groups' members, upgrade the technology of the enterprise groups, and avoid turning finance companies into short-term finance-based commercial banks.

(5) Improving the opening up level of the financial sector

Foreign financial institutions in China are an essential part of China's financial sector. The first principle for the expansion of the opening up of China's financial sector is fair competition and mutual benefit. China will introduce foreign financial institutions to promote the reform and development of the financial sector. At the same time, domestic financial institutions will be supported to expand their businesses overseas, which could enhance the ability of China's financial sector for international competition and expand China's economic and trade cooperation with other countries. The second principle is that China's trade and economic cooperation with other countries and regions is the foundation of the financial opening up, thus the opening up of the financial sector should be compatible with the development level of economic cooperation. The third principle is that the opening up of the financial sector should be compatible with the level of China's financial regulations. China will control market access conditions vigorously, and introduce financial institutions with good credit status, strong performance, and high management levels. The fourth principle is to achieve national treatment for foreign financial institutions in China in the areas of taxation, services, and regulation. Since the Long-Term Credit Bank of Japan set up its representative office in China, the first foreign financial institution in Beijing in 1979, there have been 175 foreign banks in China with a total current asset value of US$35.4 billion. The total value of foreign exchange loans hit US$27.0 billion, with foreign bank exchange taking up a quarter of total domestic foreign exchange loans. Nine insurance companies from eight countries set up 12 commercial institutions in China, among which 10 have started their businesses.

3. *Improving and standardizing the financial market and reform the foreign exchange management system*

Practice has proven that the establishment and development of the financial market is significant for optimizing resource allocation, invigorating financial circulation, improving the efficiency of funds usage, raising long-term funds, and establishing the modern corporate system.

The financial market generally consists of a currency market and capital market. The capital market is actually the financial market for securities finance and mid-to-long-term capital loans operated for more than a year, including the stock market, bond market, fund market, and mid-to-long term credit market. As funds in these markets are mainly used to expand reproduction, they are called the capital market. As an important component of the capital market, the security market has the power to attract mid-to-long-term funds by issuing stocks and bonds. The stocks and bonds publicly issued by the security market are very flexible, because they are also capable of trading freely and circulating in the secondary market. The currency market is the financial market for short-term funds operated for less than a year, including the inter-bank lending market, bill discount market, repo market, and short-term credit market. The capital market and currency market are both places for trade through supplying and demanding, thus they are the reservoir and diverting station that pool and distribute funds. The capital market and currency market have their own functions. Those who demand funds can raise long-term funds in the capital market and short-term funds in the currency market. After continuous expansion and diversification, the currency market with the inter-bank lending market and foreign exchange market as the main body as well as the security market consisting of stocks and national debt trade have taken shape gradually in China's financial market.

The purpose of China's financial market reform is to establish a financial market system with unification, openness, orderly competition, and strict regulation. The new financial market has the following characteristics: it is unified, yet it operates at multiple levels; namely, the high-level financial market allocates resources nationwide, and the middle and low-level financial markets allocate resources within regions. The new financial market system has increased the capacity of currency and capital markets, and the traditional flat allocation was replaced by market financial instruments to pool funds. Under the vigorous regulation of the central bank, entities in the market must be defined clearly to regulate their qualifications and activities. The coexistence of the two-way flow of funds in markets of the same level and the one-way flow of funds between markets at different levels enables the country to control the direction of the flows, which could strike a general balance in the currency market. Under the regulations of the central bank, the capital market maintains a general balance between the first market and the secondary market by strictly controlling the first market and moderately liberalizing the secondary market.

Developing the security market is inevitable for establishing the socialist market economy. Establishing a security market with sound development, good order, and secure operations is significant for China to optimize the allocation of resources, adjust the economic structure, raise more social funds, and boost the development of the economy. Therefore, strong regulation and standardized operations are guarantees for the sound development of the security market. The decision of the central government to establish a unified regulation system for securities and futures and to let the China Securities Regulatory Commission be responsible for regulating the securities sector and futures sector is the great reform of the securities regulation system.

The implementation of the Securities Law of the People's Republic of China is a significant milestone in the building of China's securities market legal system. The code of conduct confirmed by the Securities Law reflects the will of the country, and is in the common interests of investors, operators, and issuers; and has binding force for all participants in the securities market. China should particularly stress and insist the following principles in the code of conduct: All activities in the securities market must be transparent, fair, and equitable; all issuance and trade must comply with the law and be carried out according to the requirements of the law; China must protect the legal interests of investors in accordance with the law while letting investors be aware of risks; China must forbid insider trading, defrauding clients, and manipulating market activities; strengthening the regulation of the securities market according to the law while making sure the regulators themselves comply with the law and are more transparent and subject to supervision; ensuring all the links and relevant departments in the securities market take their responsibilities endowed by the law and that issuance and trade information are true, accurate, and complete; and China must punish illegal activities without leniency to protect market order and public interests. Implementing these principles in the securities market is essential for maintaining the standards and order of the securities market and promoting the steady and sound development of the market.

Deepening reform of the foreign exchange system is necessary for economic development in the context of accelerating development and reform. The target of China's foreign exchange system reform is to maintain a stable exchange rate of the RMB and steadily make the RMB a convertible currency. In November of 1993, the *Decision of the CPC Central Committee on Establishing the Socialist Market Economy* adopted by the Central Committee of the CPC proposed to establish the market-based and managed floating exchange rate regime and the unified and standard foreign exchange market, and to gradually make the RMB a convertible currency. China adheres to the managed, floating exchange rate regime based on market supply and demand, and ensures the steady weighted average exchange rate of the RMB against major currencies in the world. In 1994, China carried out significant reform of the foreign exchange management system, during which China accomplished the unification of exchange rates. And in December 1996, China achieved the convertibility of the RMB current account ahead of schedule. China established the inter-bank foreign exchange market, implemented a system of banking exchange settlement and sales, cancelled foreign exchange retention and payment, and cancelled mandatory plans for foreign exchange revenue and expenditures. The macro regulation of international payments was realized through economic and legal means. China stopped issuing and using foreign exchange certificates and exercised strict regulation of foreign exchange payment of capital accounts at the same time. Gradually liberalizing control over foreign exchanges of capital accounts and finally realizing free RMB convertibility that included capital account convertibility is the final target of the foreign exchange system reform, which will take a relatively long time to accomplish. Practice has proven that the reform measures help China control the total volume and structure of foreign debts and is conducive to protecting the interests of foreign investors, thus the reform is highly recognized by the international community.

Since the start of reform and opening up but especially in recent years, China's financial system reform has made significant progress. The opening up of the financial sector has continued to expand, and the enhancement of financial regulation and the improvement of financial services has attained remarkable achievements, which has played an important role in strengthening and improving macro regulation, curbing inflation, promoting economic development, and maintaining social stability. Nonetheless, China should know clearly that there are still many contradictions and problems in the financial sector at present. China has gained precious experience and has attained remarkable achievements in curbing inflation, but with new changes in domestic and foreign environments, the development of China's economy still faces a relatively complicated foreign environment, and the current financial system is not capable of meeting the requirements of the new developmental situation of the socialist market economy. At present, financial austerity is the fundamental reason for the continuous decline of commodity prices and financial constraints in various sectors, and is the reason for slow growth in social investment and inadequate demand for consumption. China needs to take positive and prudent measures to enhance the boosting effect of monetary policy on economic growth and establish a credit incentive mechanism while strengthening efforts to prevent and resolve financial risks. China should urge state-owned commercial banks to not only prioritize inspecting the security and reliability of loans, but also stress market prospects and the feasibility of credit projects, thereby raising the efficiency and profits of bank funds and accelerating capital turnover.

Chapter 25
Expanding Domestic Demand: A Vital Strategic Guideline

25.1 Expanding Domestic Demand Plays a Critical Role in Maintaining a Rapid Economic Growth

The pressing problem for China's economy in 1998 was that China's export growth was greatly weakened by the Asian financial crisis. The estimated export growth stood at 10% earlier that year, but registered a negative growth in May, in which case the pull effect of exports on economic growth was weakened. Serious floods also led to loss of lives, property and livelihoods for people in disaster stricken areas which also affected production and transportation. As China's economic growth had been slowing down for five consecutive years, reversing this trend and rallying economic growth entailed huge efforts. In addition, with the emergence of the comprehensive buyer's market, it was even more difficult to energize the market and promote economic development. In the face of these challenges, the central government put forward a series of policies and measures to stimulate and expand domestic demand and adjusted them to suit the existing economic environment. The first measure was to remodel investment plans and expand the scale of investment. As a result, the total social fixed assets investment was raised to over 15% up from 10% in order to redirect more capital toward agriculture and forestry, water conservancy, railways, highways, telecommunications, environmental protection and urban infrastructure projects. The second measure was to expand investment fields and increase funding. A month later while enhancing construction projects in these sectors, the State Council also decided to increase investment in the national grain reserves depot, urban and rural power grids, urban affordable housing and ecological construction. The third measure was to implement positive fiscal and monetary policies and to ensure that construction projects were fully funded. In this regard, the central government issued 100 billion yuan for ten-year long-term national bonds to supplement and increase

This article originally appeared in *People's Daily*, January 12, 1999.

X. Zheng, *China's 40 Years of Economic Reform and Development*,
https://doi.org/10.1007/978-981-13-2727-8_25

the capital for infrastructure construction projects, attracting 100 billion yuan in commercial bank loans. The fourth measure was to combat floods, deliver disaster relief, and engage in post-disaster reconstruction. To manage that, China vigorously launched a wide ranging green projects, cordoned off mountains to plant forests, stopped deforestation, converted hill slopes into terraced fields, and built drainage basins for major streams and tributaries within the upper and middle reaches of the Yangtze and the Yellow rivers. In the middle and lower reaches of the Yangtze River, farmlands were turned into lakes and dams broken to form flood discharge outlets. High-standard dikes were also built to control and hold back water. In order to give full play to the advancement of infrastructure and pull economic growth, that year the amount of construction was heavily increased. State Council departments, local governments and units, banks and construction units all worked around the clock to ensure that funds were put in place and their projects ready for launching within the shortest time possible. By the second half of 1998, investment growth had gained momentum month-on-month. Between the months of January and November, state-owned institutions had attracted a staggering 1503.5 billion yuan in investments, a 22.3% year-on-year increase, or a 10% increase from that of the same period the previous year. The complete list of fixed assets investment was approximately 2868.0 billion yuan, an increase of 15% more than the previous year. On the other hand, construction of key national projects was enhanced and the completion status was better than that of previous years. By the end of October, 76% of the 118 key projects had been accomplished. The growth of investment significantly boosted economic growth, which meant that policies put in place to stimulate and expand domestic demand had attained remarkable results. Meanwhile by August, the growth of industrial production had started to rally, with a growth of 7.9%, a higher percentage than that of the previous year and 0.3 percentage points more than that of the month of July. The GDP of the third quarter stood at 7.6% higher than that of the previous year and a 0.8 percentage point higher than that of the second quarter, which meant that GDP had reached a turning point from a potential decline to rising for the first time in more than five years. The momentum of the economic rallying was also greater in the fourth quarter, and the annual target previously set at 7.8% of GDP growth was finally achieved.

Policies for expanding domestic demand had become of vital importance by 1998 and for that reason China overcame the unexpected difficulties and maintained a steady and rapid economic growth. The newly-added 100 billion yuan of national debts investment plus bank loans it brought about and other various investments all contributed to pulling the economic growth by about 2 percentage points, keeping in mind that at least 60% of the work was completed that year. After experiencing a soft landing, China then started to explore new effective approaches to kick-start the economy. Experience had proven once again that the Central Committee of the CPC with Comrade Jiang Zemin at its core had the ability to resolutely make correct decisions when faced by complex situations.

Although the measures for expanding domestic demand achieved expected results, it's crucial to note that the expansion of domestic demand in 1998 was only based on expanding investment as the growth of consumption was still relatively low.

Meanwhile the growth of state-owned institutions had gained momentum, but the expected growth of investment for private institutions stood at zero and below. The priority of the new investments was infrastructure building, which was considered a great choice given that the upgrading of the industrial structure was still slow. The growth of investment funds relied mainly on fiscal approaches, which was necessary as a short-term strategy. However a further expansion of investment needed the support of monetary policies and of course, these problems could be solved during a further expansion of domestic demand in the future.

25.2 Expanding Domestic Demand as the Basis Standpoint for China's Economic Development

As a critical step to realize long-term, continuous, rapid and sound economic development, expanding domestic demand should be the fundamental principle and the basic standpoint for China's economic development.

We cannot exploit the huge potential hidden within China's economic growth unless we insist on expanding domestic demand. As a large developing country, China has stepped into the ranks of low- and middle-income countries due to its GDP per capita that stands at just over US$800. As wide as the gap between China and the developed countries is, it still poses the potential for China's fast development. Foreign investors invest in China because they see these developmental prospects. The question to us however is how to exploit this opportunity. From the very start, China's economic development has been hampered by low market demands a low level of development, brought about by obstinate policies and consumption systems. Therefore, we should adjust consumption to maintain the pull effect for economic development. To achieve that, we ought to understand that under the traditionally planned economy, the challenge of expanded demand has been bothering us for decades due to lack of market restraints. Whereas under a market economy, restraint mechanisms for investment and consumption naturally take shape. Therefore the new tasks that China faces in macro regulation and consumption management are: expanding demand in due time and exploring new niche sectors relative to the growth of supply capacity.

China's high saving rate provides favorable conditions for increasing domestic demand. Thriftiness is a long-running tradition of the Chinese people, in which saving rates in China are relatively high. In particular, since 1992, personal savings deposits of urban and rural residents have increased by 800 billion yuan annually on average, reaching more than five trillion yuan from 1.15 trillion yuan today. Personal financial assets have exceeded eight trillion yuan if the various financial securities are taken into account. We should make good use of this considerable asset and reasonably employ it in investment and consumption so as to transform the potential and long-term demand into realistic and immediate demand. This in turn would prove to be a powerful pulling force for the current economic growth. The key is to take effective measures and make good use of the savings, accelerate its circulation and raise the efficiency of funds. In the meantime, we should actively utilize foreign capital as it is also an important way to increase domestic investment demand.

We cannot improve people's lives unless we insist on expanding domestic consumption because increasing exports and expanding foreign demand will boost domestic demand, improve domestic production capacity, and satisfy the requirements of raising domestic consumption levels. This form of expansion in particular will therefore directly benefit our people. Raising people's consumption levels is conducive for the virtuous circle between production and consumption as well as for boosting morale of the workforce, which can become a powerful force for economic growth. Currently, the level of China's consumption per capita is still relatively low, hence we need to focus on increasing the size of the social wealth pie in order to elevate people's lives. There are 900 million people currently living in rural areas, and it is expected that China's economic aggregate will triple or even quadruple if we raise the consumption level of these people to the present level of urban dwellers.

We need to insist on increasing domestic demand to maintain steady economic growth in the constantly changing international environment. There are now many new changes and characteristics in the development of the global economy. The impact of the Asian financial crisis still lingers on, weakening the growth of the global economy, especially that of trade. The re-organization of the global economic structure had accelerated with the rapid development of knowledge-based economies and general overcapacity of traditional products. Trade protectionism is also growing, and trade barriers have notably been increasing. With the acceleration of the international capital circulation, there are more uncertainties in the development of the global economy. China's predicted economic situation is even more serious, particularly against the backdrop that currency manipulation in some Asian countries has enhanced their export competitiveness, leaving China to face even more pressure in exports. We should hence take the expansion of domestic demand as a fundamental position for dealing with the adverse effects caused by setbacks in export growth and take the initiative in economic development.

25.3 Priorities and Major Tasks for Expanding Domestic Demand in 1999

We need to continue increasing investment and guarantee the quality of our infrastructure building. We will continue to implement policies for expanding domestic demand, further increasing the scale of fixed assets investment and maintaining a relatively rapid growth of investment. In addition to increasing investment of state-owned institutions, we will vigorously increase the investment of non-state-owned institutions. Two decades after the reform and opening up, the annual growth of investment in these private institutions increased by 28.6%, 10.2 percentage points higher than that of state-owned institutions, which played an important role in boosting economic growth. Investment growth of non-state-owned institutions however slowed down in 1998, a trend that was considered abnormal. We therefore, need to take effective measures to tackle and change this and similar situations. To do that, it is important to create a favorable environment for the investment growth of non-state-owned institutions in respect to loans, direct investment and investment orientation, etc.

For infrastructure construction, the priority should be on enhancing project management and guaranteeing the quality of construction. We will enhance administrative leadership, by which we can strictly implement the legal person responsibility system for projects, promote a standard competitive-bidding and supervision system, and guarantee construction quality through public supervision and other measures.

We will accelerate structural adjustment and actively cultivate new economic growth points. Structural adjustment is a pressing task for the current economic work, which requires more effort to promote the upgrading of the industrial structure and increase the quality and profits of economic growth. First, we should actively take advantage of advanced technology to upgrade and improve traditional industries, phase out backward industrial technology and production equipment, and reduce the surplus of production capacity. Second, we should invest a great deal in kick-starting the equipment manufacturing industry. We need to accelerate infrastructure construction, take national key construction projects as our platform for focusing on introducing foreign advanced technology, design and manufacturing cooperation, improve our ability to develop products and technology by ourselves, promote the independent production of key equipment, and advance the technology of equipment manufacturing. Third, we should develop emerging industries and high-tech industries, and increase the weight of technology-intensive industries within the economy. We need to explore high-tech venture capital mechanisms, pilot finance programs for high-tech industrial projects, support the construction of high-tech industrial demonstration projects, and accelerate the development of the electronic information industry.

We also need to encourage local consumption as a major measure for expanding domestic demand, and kick-start investment and consumption bi-directionally. As an intermediate demand, investment must match consumption levels to boost a continuous growth of demand. Only in this way can we achieve the expected profits and realize the virtuous cycle of social reproduction. Increasing consumer demand entails further improvement of the income distribution structure and distribution system as well as enhancing the purchasing power of urban and rural dwellers, especially of those within the low- and middle-income bracket. We therefore need to reasonably direct people's expectations regarding future needs and encourage individuals at different income levels to increase consumption, which will energize the market.

Food, clothing, housing, transportation and other daily necessities are the basic needs for human survival. Currently, urban residents need for food and clothing has basically been met. According to the general rule of the structural hierarchy of needs, consumption patterns have moved from thousands of yuan spent on purchasing home appliances to the tens-of-thousands of yuan in houses and automobiles and other high-value products. And as consumer demand for housing and transportation continues to increase, there will be a high-growth period for industries whose products and services meet housing and transportation demands, which will become the newest economic growth point. However, in the fields of urban housing and transport consumption, the welfare-, supply- and group-oriented consumption models still remain as obstacles because of the existing mechanical systems, policies and other factors. Consumer goods and activities for housing and transportation are also still not included into the field of individual commodity consumption, thus suppressing the development of consumer demand in housing and transportation and dampening the development of industries relevant to these two sectors.

Therefore, we need to improve people's overall living and transportation situations. At present, the overly high price of real estate in big cities is also as a result of lack of sophisticated yet efficient transportation systems. Meanwhile, overpopulation in urban centers has induced the overly high land prices. If we can build residential districts with complete supporting facilities in urban places where the environment is great, and link these districts with cities by light rails or highways, then people will spontaneously choose to live in suburban areas with provide better air quality and tranquility. This measure can effectively curb the skyrocketing costs of land in downtown areas, and facilitate a sound and mutually supported development of various industries relevant to housing and transportation.

We should also vigorously expand the rural market. We need to take the acceleration of the rural power grid's upgrading as a great opportunity to increase the penetration rate of home appliances. We need to enhance infrastructure construction of water facilities, roads, and telecommunication and improve the rural consumption environment. We need to vigorously develop and produce agricultural machinery and various production means that are marketable, for example, equipment that are highly water-efficient for irrigation, grain drying, field operation, agricultural products processing and transportation. We need to develop small towns step by step, boost the development and the process of agricultural industrialization in secondary and tertiary industries in the countryside, and campaign for the structural adjustments for the rural economy.

We need to further expand the area of consumption and promote the industrialization of non-compulsory education, medical and health care services as well as community services. On the premise of no additional national investment, we need to encourage setting up of private schools and developing various levels of education, so that all those who want to study can have access to education. Community service is another industry that is in urgent need of development. In developed countries for example, social workers in communities account for about 30% of all workers in the entire society. In terms of this proportion, China is just getting started in community services. Recreational tourism consumption is quietly thriving. Domestic tourism revenue reached 211.2 billion yuan in 1997. In fact according to a sample survey, 80% of urban residents have traveled outside their cities. Therefore, we need to create a more favorable policy environment for the development of the tertiary industry.

When continuing to implement positive fiscal policies, we must have appropriate monetary policies to support and supplement the former. Fiscal policies are effective and easy to operate when kick-starting the economy. They also have a significant pull effect on economic growth. We therefore need to continue applying fiscal policies, expand investment and consumption demands, and promote the optimization of supply composition. We need to moderately expand the scale of government debt financing in due time, apply interest subsidies and other financial means to allow fiscal leveraging of lead social funds. The fiscal deficit accounted for 2.2% of GDP in 1998, lower than the global recommended line of 3%. The debt balance at the end of 1998 took up approximately 10.3% of GDP, which was far much smaller than the proportion of developed countries, thus there remains room for additional issuance of national debts. Currently, there is no need to worry about inflation as commodity prices have registered a negative growth for 15 consecutive months. In the meantime, we need to moderately increase the supply of currency on the premise that loans can be paid back in good time and according to the terms and conditions for expanding domestic demand to realize an effective combination of preventing financial risks and expanding credit investment, as well as to guarantee safety, profitability and liquidity at the same time. Ultimately, we need to improve financial services, expand credit channels, improve the quality of project evaluation, and formulate specific measures in order to increase loans for small and medium-sized Enterprises (SMEs).

Chapter 26
Translating Inflation Pressure into Impetus for Industrial Upgrading

In 2010, we accomplished a transformation in China's economy from a slowdown to steady and relatively rapid growth. However, with this transformation came increasing inflation pressure. The year 2011 marks the beginning of the 12th Five-Year Plan. For the next five to ten years, we need to make progress in transforming the economic growth model, maintain the trend of sound and rapid economic development, and lay a strong foundation for steady and rapid economic development by promoting strategic structural adjustments to the economy. To accomplish these goals, we must follow the principles of the Central Economic Work Conference held at the end of last year, implement positive fiscal policies and prudent monetary policies, make macro regulation more targeted, flexible and effective, and maintain general stability in commodity prices. At the same time, we should also strive to direct social funds to serve the transformation of the growth model, and transform inflation pressure into a driving force for industrial upgrading.

26.1 An Analysis of Current Inflation Pressure

In 2010, consumer prices in China saw an increase of 3.3% year on year. As the increase followed a 0.7% decrease in the previous year, consumer prices generally remained within the normal range. Further, the central government adopted various measures to promptly curb commodity price rises in the second half of 2010, which caused the growth rate of the Consumer Price Index (CPI) to slow. The turning point came in December, when the year-on-year increase of the CPI fell from 5.1 to 4.6%. An analysis tells us that structural factors and import increases are two of the primary characteristics reflected in the price changes of 2010. In November, when CPI growth was greatest, food and house price increases accounted for 74 and 18%

This article originally appeared in *People's Daily*, February 23, 2011.

X. Zheng, *China's 40 Years of Economic Reform and Development*,
https://doi.org/10.1007/978-981-13-2727-8_26

respectively of the upward pressure on commodity prices, or taken together 92%. Therefore, if we are to keep commodity prices generally stable in 2011, we need to focus on suppressing prices increases in food items and housing. Increases in the price of imported minerals contributed to significant upward pressure on the factory price increase of domestic industrial products. Purchasing prices for raw materials, fuel and power have risen by 9.5% compared with last year, pushing up factory prices for industrial products by 5.5% year on year.

Suppressing increases in the price of food items is a top priority in maintaining overall price stability in 2011 and, as part of this priority, controlling vegetable prices in cities is the most important task. Therefore, it is necessary to refocus on the program that makes city mayors responsible for the "vegetable basket" (non-grain food supply). When inflation was extremely serious in the mid-1990s, big cities vigorously implemented the Non-Staple Food Project, which played an important role in curbing inflation. As many vegetable-planting fields have since given way to high-rise real estate, vegetable supplies in cities now mainly come from other areas via long-distance transport. This not only causes huge waste in terms of energy and goods, but drives up vegetable prices. For this reason, some experts have proposed an extension of the "vegetable basket" program to make city mayors responsible for the "vegetable garden." Such a move makes sense.

The second priority in stabilizing commodity prices is to curb rising house prices in urban areas. The provision of adequate housing, a notion put forward at the 17th CPC National Congress, should be the objective in developing the housing industry. While houses are commodities, they also retain the characteristics of a public product, which means they must not be used for speculation. We should learn from the lessons of Japan's real estate bubble burst. To a certain extent, the stability of the real estate market affects overall market stability, which in turn has an impact on social stability as a whole. If we are to ensure stable social and economic development over the long term, we must prevent a bubble from forming in real estate. Since 2010, the central government has issued three documents putting forward policies and measures to stabilize house prices, which have achieved initial progress. At present, the key is to enhance the responsibilities of local governments, control the price of land, and significantly increase the supply of government-subsidized housing. As long as we implement the central government's decisions, we will without doubt realize the establishment of an urban housing system with Chinese characteristics that can ensure development and prosperity in the real estate sector on the basis of stable housing prices.

In recent years, the price of imported iron ore, as well as other minerals, has continued to rise, placing an unbearable burden on many domestic steel enterprises. One important way to address this problem is to expand the scale of outward investment. We can use this to obtain more energy resource exploration and development rights, establish overseas stable supply sources, and finally break the pricing monopoly of transnational enterprises. In the process, we should not only encourage large enterprises to go global but also SMEs. We should also increase foreign exchange support for enterprises, especially SMEs, to go global. On obtaining energy resource exploration and development rights, SMEs can join with large enterprises to create synergy in going global with the help of government aid loans. We should leverage this synergy to sustain our hard work and efforts over the coming years and change the situation where prices of imported resources are controlled by foreign countries.

26.2 Directing Surplus Funds Toward Structural Adjustment and Industrial Upgrading

Over the past two years, China has implemented easing monetary policies to deal with the impact of the international financial crisis. The increase of foreign exchange reserves has forced the central bank to issue more base money, which has boosted the liquidity surplus of banks. These monetary policies and the surplus liquidity have intensified inflation pressure. We should take proactive measures to solve this problem, striving to turn negative factors into favorable ones. This will require strong steps that would see surplus funds being channeled toward structural adjustment and industrial upgrading efforts. Specifically, we need to direct funds into the following fields.

Social funds should be invested in the capital market to develop it as quickly as possible. China's capital market has been under development for just a short period, so it still represents a weak link compared to the banking financial market. We need to grasp the opportunity presented by surplus liquidity and move quickly to develop this market. We should accelerate reforms concerning the enterprise listing mechanism, to further increase the number of listed enterprises, encourage Chinese enterprises listed overseas to return to the A-share market, gradually relax access for foreign enterprises, lower the threshold for listing on the SME board and growth enterprise board, establish an OTC market and transfer-board mechanism between the OTC market and the growth enterprise board, and improve the multi-tiered capital market system. We should prioritize the development of qualified institutional investors, standardize market-trading activities, and strengthen the appeal of the capital market for investors. We should take full advantage of its functions in selecting good enterprises, allocating capital and adjust distribution, and let it serve as an engine for industrial upgrading and a pool of funding.

Social funds should be invested in strategic emerging industries to drive industrial upgrading through innovation. We should strengthen fiscal and taxation support, let fiscal funds channel and spur people's enthusiasm for investment, encourage banks and enterprises to invest in strategic emerging industries, such as new generation IT, energy-saving and environmental protection technologies, new energy, biotechnology, high-end equipment manufacturing, new materials and new energy vehicles. We should set up special funds to develop strategic emerging industries and focus financial resources on supporting major industrial innovation development projects and major application and demonstration projects. We should improve and implement the various national policies that promote technological innovation, and encourage enterprises to invest more money in scientific R&D to boost the amount of Chinese held intellectual property and proprietary brands. We should actively develop venture capital firms and equity investment funds, and support the translation of technological breakthroughs into engineering projects and industrialized production. The government should set up funds to encourage investment in venture capital and support its growth for entrepreneurs. The scale of SMEs composite bond issuance should be expanded, and key enterprises in strategic emerging industries should be allowed to issue corporate bonds. We also should promote credit innovation as well as intellectual property secured financing and industrial chain financing.

Social funds should be invested in public services and infrastructure to accelerate social development and urbanization. Education, medical care and some other social programs along with infrastructure have long been lacking in cities, which holds back efforts to improve living standards and increase urbanization. The major reason for this problem is that these domains mainly rely on investment from government, which has limited financial resources. Therefore, we need to explore new channels to source funding for public services, establishing investment funds and adopting BOT (build, operate, transfer) and other mature investment and operation approaches to direct social funds toward public services and infrastructure. We should encourage the development of private schools and non-state hospitals to meet diverse consumer demand. We should accelerate the construction of high-speed railways and improve the modern and comprehensive transportation system. In terms of subways, there is much to learn from the construction model applied in Hong Kong, which sets aside part of the land around subway stations to be used for commercial operation by subway companies. This approach offsets the losses of subway companies by providing them with a source of commercial profit and avoids situations that see government overburdened with transportation subsidies. We can also apply new building and operational models such as implementing market- and enterprise-oriented management to garbage disposal and sewage treatment. It is estimated that for each person newly settled in an urban area an extra 100,000 yuan of additional investment in public services is required. Every 1% increase in the rate of urbanization is equivalent to more than 10 million people or over 10 trillion yuan of additional public service investment. Increasing investment in public services can not only see idle funds being put to use, but also expand consumption and push forward urbanization.

Social funds should be invested in tertiary industry to accelerate the development of production services. Development of China's tertiary industry has been lagging far behind for a long time. In 2009, the added value of the tertiary industry accounted for only 43% of GDP, while it accounted for only 34% of employment. Both of these figures are ten percentage points below the international average. A lagging tertiary industry has not only resulted in employment pressure, but also hindered the development of the primary and secondary industries. Therefore, boosting development in this sector is crucial if we are to transform our economic development model. We should prioritize the development of production service industries, including marketing, logistics, consultation, legal services, accounting, auditing, technology market, price evaluation, and trade in services. We should encourage the general public in particular to start their own businesses, and establish a micro-finance system for small- and micro-sized operating entities to support the many small and individual businesses in the tertiary industry. We need to see full implementation of the State

Council regulations and rules issued last year on encouraging private investment and the introduction of implementation rules to allow private funds to set up small-scale financial institutions. Tax reduction and exemption policies should also be introduced for individual businesses and entrepreneurs. According to calculations, if the tax threshold for individual businesses were to be raised from the current monthly turnover of 5000 yuan to 10,000 yuan, then 20 million people would stand to benefit. This would greatly improve the climate for entrepreneurs. Further, such a measure would lessen the tax intake by no more than one billion yuan. We should also encourage the development of new-type commercial activities, such as chain delivery and online trading, to significantly boost the development of the tertiary industry.

Social funds should be invested in agricultural modernization to cultivate new kinds of agricultural operating entities. Currently, China has the conditions in place to undertake agricultural modernization and holds great opportunities that can make this happen: (1) It has abundant financial resources, as a large amount of funds await investment; (2) Its farmers possess strengths which would allow them to transfer to the many other sectors that are desperate for labor; (3) Agricultural development is supported by the market because of strong consumer demand for high-quality green agricultural products. Agricultural modernization requires a large amount of financial investment, so farmers' savings and government investment alone are far from adequate. We should innovate relevant systems to promote much greater investment of social funds in agricultural modernization. This will involve cultivating new forms of agricultural investment as well as operating entities, including family farms, rural cooperatives, agricultural companies, developing intensive and modern agriculture, issuing certificates to confirm farmers' rights for contracting land and homesteads, legally protecting farmers' land use rights and promoting the orderly transfer of land contracts and management rights. We should establish a new system for urban-rural integration that lets cities lead rural development. Agricultural modernization will not only significantly boost agricultural productivity, but will also spur the development of relevant industries. It will serve to free up a large amount of labor engaged in farm work, drive the development of secondary and tertiary industries, facilitate the flow of rural residents into cities and finally help to mold a new landscape in coordinated urban-rural coordinated development.

Social funds should be invested overseas to transform foreign exchange reserves into reserves of material resources. China has huge foreign exchange reserves and has been saddled with overcapacity in industrial production. Expanding overseas investment can help achieve to four things: (1) Develop overseas processing trade and create new demand for exports; (2) Promote mergers and acquisitions with overseas enterprises that hold good technological resources, which will help to quickly improve China's innovation capacity; (3) Gain more energy resource exploration rights and development rights abroad, which will break the bottlenecks in energy and resources that limit long-term economic development; (4) Convert currencies and bonds of foreign exchange reserves into material resource reserves, thus effectively preventing the risk of foreign currency devaluation. From this it is clear that we need to take effective measures to see enterprises' need for foreign currencies satisfied, so that they are able go global.

Chapter 27
Improving Coordination of Economic Growth, Structural Adjustment and Commodity Prices

The 12th Five-Year Plan period is crucial for building a moderately prosperous society in all respects, deepening reform and opening up, and speeding up the transformation of the economic development pattern. The year 2011 is the first year of the 12th Five-Year Plan period, so maintaining the momentum of development is critical for accomplishing the targets in the Plan. We need to correctly and clearly understand the economic problems emerging at present, keep macro-economic policies consistent and flexible, and make policies more targeted, flexible and effective. In particular, we need to strike a balance between ensuring steady and rapid economic development, making adjustments to the economic structure and maintaining the overall stability of commodity prices, so that we can make substantial progress in transforming China's economic development model.

27.1 Achieving Steady and Robust Economic Development While Keeping Commodity Prices Stable and Making Structural Adjustments

During the 11th Five-Year Plan period, China registered an average annual economic growth rate of 11.2% despite the international financial crisis. However, there emerged some contradictions and problems in the country's economic life after this new round of rapid economic growth began. Among these, the most pressing are rising inflationary pressure, an imbalance between investment and consumption, a seriously lagging tertiary industry, an over-dependence on the consumption of material resources for economic growth, an imbalance between economic and social development, a widening gap between urban and rural development and an ecological environment that has been seriously damaged and needs to be saved. If we cannot

---

This article originally appeared in *Qiushi*, Chinese edition, no. 9. 2011.

X. Zheng, *China's 40 Years of Economic Reform and Development*,
https://doi.org/10.1007/978-981-13-2727-8_27

get a handle on these problems quickly, then not only short-term economic stability, but also long-term sustainable development, will be affected. Therefore, in economic work this year, we must ensure synergy in how we address current contradictions and solve long-term developmental problems, and strengthen the consistency of and coordination between economic growth, structural adjustments and commodity price stability, so that we can attain steady yet rapid economic development while stabilizing commodity prices and making structural adjustments.

Maintaining steady and rapid economic development is the basic task in economic work this year, and it is also the key to solving various problems and contradictions. To suppress excessive price growth for a number of commodities, we must realize a rapid increase in production growth and ensure sufficient supply of products. Adjusting the economic structure also entails modifying production growth, which is especially important when it comes to the task of expanding resident consumption. This in part requires us to increase individual incomes by creating more jobs, which can only be achieved if relatively rapid economic growth is maintained. We should be clear that the task of maintaining a fairly rapid rate of economic growth this year will be difficult, with the main problems we main encounter centering on the issue of inadequate demand. The specific worries in terms of inadequate demand are as follows: (1) Despite the relatively rapid growth of private investment, as the four-trillion-yuan investment plan initiated by the government in previous years basically finished this year, whether the growth of private investment can offset the negative impact of the exiting of government policies that stimulated investment remains a question; (2) Automobile and house trading, two popular consumption sectors, have cooled off for various reasons with sales growth declining, hence the stimulatory effect of consumption in these two sectors has weakened; (3) The central bank increased interest rates several times to control the scale of credit and ultimately curb inflation, which has hindered the growth of investment and consumption to some extent; (4) There has been great difficulty in stimulating import demand in developed countries as their economies undergo a very slow recovery, which, along with the negative effects of trade protectionism, have made it very hard for China's export levels to quickly recover to what they before the financial crisis. For all these reasons, the task that requires high attention and appropriate handling in macro regulation this year is to maintain the steady growth of gross demand, which ultimately needs to provide enough driving force for steady yet rapid economic growth.

Carrying out strategic structural adjustments on the economy is the fundamental way to ensure commodity prices remain stable and economic growth maintains speed and sustainability. It also represents a major step in transforming the economic development pattern. Only by taking into account both immediate and long-term interests, can we remove immediate worries. The decision of the 17th National Congress of the CPC to transform the economic development pattern is exactly the kind of major strategic decision that considers long-term interests. According to the requirements for transforming the economic development pattern, we are to realize transformations in six major areas over the next five years. First, we need to adjust the structure of demand to transform the economic growth model from investment- and export-driven model to a coordinated consumption-, investment- and export-driven model, which will boost the stimulatory effect of consumption on economic growth. Second, we need to adjust the structure of supply to transform from a secondary industry-driven model to a model that is driven in a coordinated fashion by the primary, secondary and tertiary industries, and that puts emphasis on the development of the tertiary industry. Third, we need to adjust the structure of production factors to transition from a model that mainly relies on material resource consumption to one that relies on technological progress, and improvements of management and labor quality, and which allows innovation to drive industrial upgrading. Fourth, we need to adjust the economic and social development structure to change the situation where social development lags far behind economic growth, and we need to vigorously develop social programs. Fifth, we need to adjust the urban-rural structure to reverse the trend of a widening urban-rural gap, and to establish a new development picture for urban-rural integration. Sixth, we need to adjust domestic and import production economy structures to transform the developmental structure from mainly relying on bringing into stressing both bringing in and going global. These six transformations guarantee that we will enhance our ability to withstand economic shocks, confidently face the changes in income resulting from rising costs, and effectively cope with the pressure of inflation. The most important thing is to ensure that we ultimately make substantial breakthroughs in these six areas as it is critical not only for ensuring steady yet rapid economic development over the next five years, but also for China's development over the next decade or even two decades, and it is also vital to China's overcoming the middle-income trap and stepping into the ranks of high-income countries.

Maintaining the overall stability of commodity prices is the primary task for the macro regulation this year, and is also an important condition in maintaining economic growth and making structural adjustments to the economy. Currently, the momentum of rising commodity prices is noticeable, as consumer prices, on the basis of the increase of 3.3% last year, rose by 4.9% in January and February compared the same period last year, and in March, growth exceeded 5%, figures which suggest a strong possibility of inflation. The stability of commodity prices is important for the stability of the economy. We must maintain the overall stability in this area to create a favorable market environment for investment and consumption, and bring about the necessary market pressure to make structural adjustments. Therefore, the stability of commodity prices to a certain extent affects the accomplishment of the strategic tasks, namely, the task of transforming the pattern of economic development. To maintain the stability of commodity prices, we have to moderately control gross demand by adjusting the economic aggregate, which means that we will need to make some sacrifices in terms of the rate of economic growth. After full consideration of the situation, the target growth rate for the economy this year was set at about 8% and the increase of consumer prices at around 4%.

27.2 Channeling Investment in Accordance with the Requirements for Accelerating the Transformation of the Economic Development Pattern

In 2008, to deal with the onslaught from the international financial crisis, China moved to implement a relatively loose monetary policy. The increase in foreign exchange reserves also forced the central bank to issue an increased amount of base money. It was these two measures that led to current surplus liquidity and an increase in inflationary pressure. Furthermore, a large amount of funds are required to make the strategic adjustments planned for during the 12th Five-Year Plan. Against this background, we need to optimize the credit structure, develop the capital market, and direct surplus liquid assets into the fields where structural adjustments need to be made. Only in this way, can we support industrial upgrading and transform the economic development pattern, while also effectively relieve inflationary pressure at the same time. Specifically, we need to guide the flow of social funds into the following fields.

Social funds should be directed into the capital market. Compared with the banking and finance market, China's capital market lags behind. In terms of the sources of corporate funds, the ratio of funds from the capital market to those from bank loans is 3:7; this ratio is about 7:3 in developed countries. In the capital market, the ratio of bond market financing to stock market financing can be as high as 7:3 in developed countries; in China bond market financing is just getting off the ground. These imbalances have increased financing costs for enterprises, and caused financial risks to become overly concentrated in banks, while viable financing channels are difficult to find for many non-listed enterprises. To address these issues, we should seize the current surplus liquidity as an opportunity and move as quickly as possible to develop the capital market. We should accelerate the reform of the enterprise listing mechanism, further increase the number of listed enterprises, encourage Chinese enterprises listed overseas to return to the A-share market, gradually relax access for listing on the SME board and growth enterprise board, establish an OTC market and a transfer-board mechanism between the OTC market and growth enterprise board, and improve the multi-tiered capital market system. We should regulate trading activities in the market, enhance the appeal of the capital market for investors, and take full take advantage of the capital market's functions in identifying good enterprises, allocating capital, and adjusting distribution so that it can become the engine for industrial upgrading and the pooling of funds.

Social funds should be directed to strategic emerging industries. We should boost fiscal and taxation policy support for innovation and strategic emerging industries, let fiscal funds direct and motivate people's enthusiasm for investment, and encourage banks and enterprises to invest in strategic emerging industries, including new-generation IT, energy-saving and environmental protection technology, new energy, biological technology, high-end equipment manufacturing, new materials and new energy vehicles. We should set up funds for the development of strategic emerging industries and support major industrial innovation development projects and major application demonstration projects. We should improve and implement various national policies that promote innovation, and encourage enterprises to increase investment in scientific research and development, so that China can create more proprietary IPR and brands. We should vigorously develop venture capital firms and private equity funds, and provide more support to see technological results being translated into engineering projects and industrialized production. We should set up government funds to encourage investment in venture capital and support the growth of venture capital for entrepreneurs. We should expand the scale of SMEs' composite bond issuance, and allow key enterprises in strategic emerging industries to issue corporate bonds. We should promote credit innovation and carry out IPR pledge financing and industrial chain financing.

Social funds should be directed toward the development of public services. It is estimated that each newly registered individual in an urban area brings an additional 100,000 yuan of investment in public services. That means an urban population increase of 20 million each year would bring about an increase of about two trillion yuan of additional investment in public services. China lacks in terms of services in education, medical care and other social programs as well as city infrastructure. This is preventing us from realizing improvements in people's lives and hindering the urbanization rate. Increasing investment in public services can not only expand consumption and push forward the process of urbanization, but also direct idle funds to many uses. But for quite some time, such fields have been supported mainly by government investment. When government financial resources are insufficient, these areas have had to rely on revenue from the transfer of land use rights and on financing platforms guaranteed by local governments. However, revenue from the transfer of land use rights has become a major reason for the steep rises in housing prices, while financing platforms also hold many dormant risks; both of these situations are unsustainable. Therefore, we need to explore new financial sources for investment in public services. We should establish investment funds for public services, adopt the build-operate-transfer (BOT) and build-transfer-operate (BTO) models for franchise rights and other investment and operation approaches to direct social funds into public services and infrastructure. We should encourage the establishment of private schools and hospitals. We should accelerate the construction of high-speed railways and improve the modern and comprehensive transportation system. We should accelerate the construction of inter-city railways to meet the requirements in developing city clusters. We can also adopt new building and operational models in subways, garbage disposal and sewage treatment in cities, and implement the market- and enterprise-oriented management.

Social funds should be directed toward the tertiary industry. In 2009, the value added of China's tertiary industry accounted for only 43% of GDP; the proportion of jobs created by the sector was just 34%. Both of these figures are more than ten percentage points below the international average. The long-time lag in the tertiary industry has not only increased employment pressure, but also hindered the development of the primary and the secondary industries. We should attach great importance to developing production service industries, such as marketing, logistics, consultation, legal services, accounting, auditing, technology market, price evaluation and trade in services. We should establish a micro-finance system targeted at small- and micro-sized operating entities to support the many small and individual businesses in the tertiary industry. We should take the implementation of rules and regulations issued by the State Council as an opportunity to encourage private investment and formulate specific implementation rules to allow private funds set up small financial institutions. And we should implement tax reduction and exemption policies for individual businesses and entrepreneurs. According to calculations, if we raise the threshold of taxation for individual businesses from the current monthly turnover of 5000 yuan to 10,000, about 20 million people will stand to benefit. This would greatly improve the climate for entrepreneurs, with an overall reduction in taxes of up to one billion yuan. In the meantime, we should encourage the development of new-type commercial activities, such as chain delivery and online trading. In conclusion, we need employ multiple approaches and great efforts to considerably boost the development of the tertiary industry.

Social funds should be directed toward agricultural modernization. At present, China is facing greater opportunities than ever before to accelerate agricultural modernization. The first of these is that the country possesses abundant financial resources with a large amount of social funds seeking investment opportunities. The second is that there are opportunities for the agricultural workforce to transfer to sectors with labor shortages. The third is that agricultural modernization has the support of the market, as consumer demand for high-quality agricultural products is high. Agricultural modernization requires a significant amount of financial investment, so farmers' savings and government funds alone will be far from adequate. We must upgrade relevant systems. Only by making such improvements will we be able to see a substantial amount of social funds being pumped into the cause of agricultural modernization in the right way. In line with this, we need to cultivate new-type agricultural investment and operating entities, including family farms, rural cooperatives and agricultural companies, so that farmers can become shareholders through their land contract and management rights and develop large-scale and intensified agriculture. We should issue certificates to confirm farmers' rights for contracting land and homesteads, protect farmers' usufruct by the law and promote the orderly transfer of land contract and management rights. We should establish a new system for urban-rural integration, one that would see cities leading rural development. Agricultural modernization will not only provide a boost to agri-industry, it will also free up a large proportion of the agricultural workforce, helping to drive the development of the secondary and tertiary industries, facilitating the transfer of the rural population from rural areas to cities and ultimately stimulating coordinated urban-rural development. It will also increase agricultural productivity and land yields, thereby bringing about a new round in the release of productive forces and playing a decisive role in reducing the urban-rural gap.

Social funds should be directed into investments in overseas energy and resources as well as international mergers and acquisitions. China has huge foreign exchange reserves and overcapacity in industrial production. Expanding overseas investment can achieve four results:

(1) Developing overseas processing trade will create new demand for exports
(2) Mergers and acquisitions with overseas enterprises that have good technological resources will help to more quickly improve our ability for innovation
(3) Obtaining more energy resources exploration rights and development rights abroad will help to break energy and resource bottlenecks that limit long-term economic development
(4) Converting currencies and bonds of foreign exchange reserves into material resource reserves will effectively guard against the risks posed by devaluations in foreign currencies and exchanges.

Therefore, it is suggested that the central bank transfer part of its foreign exchange reserves into commercial banks, which would enable them to lend foreign exchange to enterprises to meet their foreign exchange needs as they go global.

27.3 Start by Increasing the Supply of Products in Short Supply to Relieve Inflationary Pressure

Currently, price changes are mainly reflected in structural and imported inflation. In the month when CPI increased at the fastest rate for a number of years, the increase in food and housing prices accounted for 74 and 18% respectively of the upward pressure on commodity prices. The total proportion of the increases in food and housing prices in the CPI was as high as 92%. We need to focus on limiting price increases in these two areas if we are to maintain the overall stability of commodity prices in 2011. The imported inflation of commodity prices is also very noticeable. In particular, the increase in the volume of imported minerals constitutes the source of considerable upward pressure on the factory prices of domestic industrial products. Purchasing prices for raw materials, fuel and power have risen 9.5% compared with that of last year, pushing up the price of industrial products by 5.5% in the process.

Suppressing rising food prices is the top priority in maintaining overall price stability this year, with the rising price of vegetables in cities as the main concern. Thus, it is necessary to once again promote the program in which city mayors take responsibility for the "vegetable basket" (non-grain food supply). When inflation was very serious in the mid-1990s, many cities proactively implemented the Non-Staple Food Project, which played an important role in curbing inflation. More than a decade on, what were once vegetable-planting fields have become high-rise real estate, and over 70% of the vegetable supply in cities is brought in through long-distance transport, which not only causes huge energy and goods waste, but also drives up vegetable prices. For this reason, some experts have suggested extending the "vegetable basket" responsibility program to see city mayors taking responsibility for the "vegetable garden." Such a move makes sense. Generally speaking, it is economical and acceptable that 50–60% of vegetable supply in big- and medium-sized cities is grown in local areas; this proportion is also appropriate for building green cities.

The second priority in stabilizing commodity prices is to curb the rise of urban housing prices. Adequate housing, a policy put forward by the 17th National Congress of the CPC, should be the target in developing the housing industry. It is true that houses are a kind of commodity and hence have economic functions, but they are also property that concerns people's lives and thus has social functions. This means that houses must not become commodities for speculation. We should draw lessons from the real estate bubble burst in Japan. The stability of the real estate market affects and even decides the stability of the overall market to some extent, while the stability of the market affects and dictates social stability. If we are to achieve the long-term stable development of the economy and society, we must prevent real estate bubbles from occurring. Since last year, the State Council has issued documents on three occasions putting forward policies and measures to stabilize house prices, steps which have achieved initial progress. The key now is to improve the responsibility system for local governments, control the price of land, and significantly increase the supply of government-subsidized housing. At present, we need to ensure that construction funds for affordable housing are in place and make sure that the planned construction of 10 million affordable houses can be commenced and completed in time. We also need to pay attention to the establishment of the distribution and exit mechanisms for affordable housing.

In recent years, because of the monopoly of transnational companies, the prices of China's imported iron ores and other minerals have increased for several consecutive years. It was calculated by relevant institutions that in the last year alone, China paid as much as US$23 billion of iron ore monopoly excess profit to foreign companies, an unbearable burden for many domestic steel enterprises. For China, aside from acquiring a greater say in setting the prices of imported products through unified negotiation with foreign companies, the fundamental way to solve this problem is to expand the scale of overseas investment. This would involve China acquiring more overseas energy resource exploration and development rights, establishing stable overseas supply sources and ultimately breaking the price-fixing monopoly of transnational enterprises. Therefore, we should encourage not only large enterprises but also SMEs to go global. SMEs can often accomplish things that big enterprises cannot. After acquiring exploration and development rights for energy resources, SMEs can unite with large enterprises to form a synergy in going global with the help of government aid loans, thereby, after years of relentless efforts, finally bringing about a change in the situation which sees the prices of imported resources being controlled by others.

While we cannot prevent the international price of petroleum from rising, we can deal with the problem in two ways. On the one hand, we can expand overseas investment, and on the other hand, we can focus on utilizing domestic resources, especially our abundant coal resources. For now, China has the technology for direct and indirect coal liquefaction, and it has built several demonstration production lines and found appropriate pollutant treatment methods. The cost of domestic petroleum production is far less than the price of imported petroleum, thus enabling us to carry out large-scale production. We should research strategic policies to replace imported petroleum with liquefied coal, as it represents the fundamental way to significantly reduce our reliance on imported petroleum.

Chapter 28
Properly Handling Dialectical Relationships in Economic Work

The recent Central Economic Work Conference looked at the current economic situation, adopted the basic principle of seeking progress while maintaining stability, and reflected on the uniform understanding of the Communist Party of China. The Chinese government will follow the guidance of the Conference and realize its economic growth target, despite the difficult economic environment in China, and across the world. This requires an understanding of how to deal with the five types of dialectical relationships in practice, and China should be able to distinguish the main contradictions as well as reasons for these contradictions and ultimately be able to turn things around.

28.1 Gain a Strong Understanding of the Dialectical Relationship Between Supply and Demand

Supply and demand are opposing forces that depend on each other. Demand cannot exist without supply, while supply is useless without demand. When studying supply, it is important to consider the aggregate and structure of demand, and production should be based on anticipated demand. Only in this way can the value of products be realized through the market mechanism, which enables the expansion of social reproduction. Similarly, when studying demand, China must consider the capability to supply as well as adjust demand in proportion to this capability to prevent inflation caused by demand being greater than supply or deflation caused by falling demand.

During the planned economy period, there was a shortage of production factors because of the lack of an effective restraint mechanism. The restraining effect of demand on economic growth started to improve after the shortage problem was solved and the market economy was established. By expanding domestic demand,

---

This article originally appeared in *Qiushi*, Chinese edition, no. 4, 2017.

X. Zheng, *China's 40 Years of Economic Reform and Development*,
https://doi.org/10.1007/978-981-13-2727-8_28

China was able to boost economic growth. This was also the key to years of double-digit growth since the late 1990s, especially in the first decade of the 21st century. Currently, the country's problem of overcapacity indicates that there is a problem with the supply-side structure. Specifically, there is serious overcapacity in labor and resource-intensive industries, while technology and knowledge-intensive industries are facing insufficient supply.

Meanwhile, the problem of inadequate demand cannot be ignored. In *Capital*, Karl Marx analyzed the causes of the periodic crises of overproduction in the capitalist market economy. He pointed out that the contradiction between the continuous increase in production capacity and what people can afford is the fundamental contradiction of capitalism, and argued that this will inevitably result in a crisis of overproduction. The economic law is the fundamental law of the market economy, and with a market economy in place, China must accept this law. During the 37 years since reform, China's average annual growth rate rose from 33.9% in the 6th Five-Year Plan period to 44.7% in the 11th Five-Year Plan period, an increase of 10.8 percentage points. In addition, the final consumption rate fell by 17.6 percentage points during the corresponding period, from 66.4 to 48.8%. Although investment and consumption were improved during the 12th Five-Year Plan period, they remained unbalanced. As the growth of investment has greatly outpaced personal income growth, consumption growth has lagged far behind the expansion of production capacity.

The facts tell us that China has, either voluntarily or unconsciously, expanded production capacity so much that it has decoupled from the demand for affordable goods. This is the fundamental reason for the overcapacity problem. If there is anything wrong with the ratio of investment to consumption in the economy, then the overall economic picture will be affected and sustainable economic development will be impeded. Therefore, in the current macro-level regulatory framework, it is important to understand the dialectical relationship between supply and demand and continue promoting supply-side reform. Accelerating changes in the industrial structure and production mix, which can strengthen supply, requires cutting overcapacity, reducing inventory, and reducing supply problems. At the same time, aggregate demand needs to be expanded to some extent, especially with regard to affordable goods and services. Doing so will drive economic growth. It will also stabilize economic growth during a period of restructure. The focus should be on expanding domestic demand when dealing with the relationships between domestic and external demand factors. This is because the two factors are somewhat dependent on each other, and so they have to be coordinated with domestic demand. In the first half of 2016, overseas investment was 67% higher than that of last year, while domestic investment increased by only 8%, which, given that domestic investment growth slowed down and private investment was particularly sluggish, is abnormal for such a dramatic rise in overseas investment. Hence, expanding domestic demand is the only way to directly stabilize economic growth, benefit the people, and provide financial support for expanding external demand.

28.2 Gain a Strong Understanding of the Dialectical Relationship Between Short-Term and Long-Term Economic Development

As the saying goes, a journey of a thousand miles begins with a single step. Maintaining long-term, steady, and sound economic development involves the synergy of long-term strategic targets and short-term action plans. Hence, it is necessary to have clear medium and long-term targets and short-term goals for economic development and the corresponding long-term strategic measures and short-term regulatory moves. In order to realize the medium and long-term development targets, it is essential to implement a long-term development strategy. This means the country should increase aggregate supply and optimize the supply structure through fiscal policies, and ultimately increase total-factor productivity.

As for short-term regulation, aggregate demand needs to be regulated through monetary policies, and there needs to be an overall balance between aggregate supply and demand to realize steady economic growth. While regulation is carried out at the macro level, it is important to achieve a synergy between a long-term development strategy and short-term regulation through planning. By formulating a development plan that is middle to long term, an annual plan, and a special plan, the Chinese government will be able to propose different development targets, strategies, principles, and policies in different planning periods. This in turn will provide a basis for applying fiscal, monetary, and other means to regulate the economy and ensure the coordination and cooperation of the three regulating leverages; namely, planning, fiscal policy, and financial regulation. When formulating the annual regulation plan, the focus should be on balancing and coordinating the eight indexes; namely, economic growth, resident income, commodity prices, employment, public finance, monetary policy, and international payments. By taking all these factors into consideration, China has shown that it is committed to maintaining continuous and steady economic growth and preventing radical economic changes.

As investment demand is an intermediate demand, investment growth and the investment structure are important for whether supply adapts to demand growth and structural changes, but also for industrial structure upgrades and long-term economic growth. China needs to apply relevant policies, such as fiscal policies and land supply policies, to guide social and credit funds for investment to meet the demand for medium and long-term development plans. Years of experience in regulation at the macro level has proven that short-term goals and long-term targets are a unity of opposites. Overemphasis on either side will cause a lopsided relationship and bring about huge losses for economic development. Overemphasis on short-term goals will lead to the unpractical pursuit of high-speed economic growth, whereas seeking instant success will bring about potential dangers for long-term development. The final result would be quite the opposite of what was expected. On the other hand, overemphasizing long-term strategic targets makes for another problem: unpractical ambitions to quickly accomplish such targets, which, as another irrational form of pursuit for quick success, comes at the cost of short-term economic growth, and could even cripple development, thus giving rise to systematic risks.

Imagine for a moment that the economy was a car. When the car is overheated, we need to apply the brakes quickly. Similarly, when the car is losing speed, we need to step on the gas. China's experience has proven that it is sometimes necessary to smooth the periodic fluctuations in the economy. This is also the art of macro-level regulation. China will need to apply this successful experience to its economic development for a long time to come. In the past 67 years of development, the most likely mistake has been the impractical pursuit for instant success. China should clearly understand that for now, emphasizing transformation of the economic growth model and economic structure is a mid to long-term target. This is especially true when it comes to the transformation of the industrial structure, as it is impossible to transform the structure from a resource and labor-intensive model to a technology and knowledge-intensive one in three to five years or within a single five-year plan. Industrial structure is intimately connected with different phases of economic development, so the country must strive to accomplish this goal while keeping to the laws of economic development.

In China's macro-level regulation, feasible and practicable short-term goals must be clearly distinguished from the targets that entail long-term efforts. An eye should be kept on the direction of long-term development in short-term moves, so as to make sure the economy is upgrading rather than downgrading. To be more specific, China should guide funds for investment to transform the economic development model. In this way, the investment will not only satisfy the current demand for economic growth, but also facilitate structural optimization.

28.3 Gain a Strong Understanding of the Dialectical Relationship Between Urban and Rural Development

The widening gap between urban and rural development is a major problem in China's economy. China's GDP per capita is now in the middle to high-income bracket, but there is still a sizeable gap between the current level and the US$12,000 threshold for the ranks of high-income countries. Many countries have hovered around this threshold but, in the end, failed to avoid the middle-income trap. Whether or not China can step into the high-income ranks is a test for the governance capability of the Communist Party of China and the effectiveness of the socialist market economy. Judging from international experience, it is clear that those countries that have stepped into the ranks of high-income countries all have one thing in common: they successfully dealt with the urban-rural dual economic structure problem, thereby attaining roughly equal labor productivity in the primary, secondary, and tertiary industries; and narrowing the rural-urban income gap. Failing to narrow this gap is the reason why the other countries got bogged down in the middle-income trap. Currently, China's labor productivity in the primary industry is less than one third of overall labor productivity, thus the income of urban residents to that of rural residents is 2.7:1. In the face of such a huge gap, it is difficult for China to step into the ranks of high-income countries.

President Xi Jinping has called for the country to ensure equal basic rights for urban and rural residents, equal public services in urban and rural areas, balanced urban and rural incomes, reasonable allocation of urban rural factors, and integration of urban and rural industries. This is clearly targeted at the main problem in the current economic situation, and it is meant to be the direction and the goal for the reform and development of urban-rural integration. The government should continue to attach great importance to the "three engines" of urban-rural integration: agricultural modernization, building a new countryside, and transforming rural residents into urban residents.

Adjusting the urban-rural structure involves reform. As President Xi Jinping pointed out recently, the reform must target development, satisfy basic demands, and fulfill the desires of the Chinese people. Promoting urban-rural integration reform is exactly the kind of significant reform measure that meets the above demands and will give the biggest new impetus to boost economic growth. According to the *Decision of the Central Committee of the Communist Party of China on Certain Major Issues concerning Comprehensively Deepening Reform* (hereinafter referred to as the *Decision*) adopted by the Third Plenary Session of the 18th CPC Central Committee, the top priority of the current reform is to confirm farmers' land rights. How public-owned rural land can be harmonized with the market economy is a major question to be answered for establishing the socialist market economy. Giving farmer households' property rights to their contracted land and homesteads are two ways to further realize public-owned rural land. Land becomes a commodity that can be transferred or merged, which will allow the market to play a more decisive role in allocating land resources. Hence, certificates should be issued to confirm farmers' rights for contracting land and homesteads, and the regulation system for changing land usage should be improved, too.

The second focus is the establishment of a construction-land market that unifies urban and rural areas. China is now in the process of urbanization—the largest ever in the history of mankind. It is inevitable that land available for construction in cities will grow while that in rural areas is reduced. The high demand for land use in urban areas will inevitably increase the economic importance of land for construction purposes and the amount of arable land. China's policies for the increase or reduction of construction land in urban and rural areas must comply with this rule of change. As labor transfers are nationwide, a construction-land market that unifies urban and rural areas must be established. Immovable properties must be allowed to move along with population transfers in the form of property value, as it is necessary to promote rather than impede the process of urbanization. Thus, the relations of production can conform with, rather than limit, the development of productivity.

The third focus is to narrow the gap between urban and rural capital markets. Production factors in cities have long been market-oriented, but this is not the case in rural areas. The long-term difference caused a "siphon" where urban markets pulled the production factors in rural markets, and thus formed a "barrier lake" between the two markets, which is the fundamental reason for the widening gap between urban and rural development. If farmers' usufruct property rights to homestead land can be pledged, then it would motivate 20 trillion yuan worth of bank loans and social investment during the period of 13th Five-Year Plan. Once that amount is invested in agricultural modernization, the new countryside is built, and rural migrant workers become urban residents, the urban-rural gap will narrow quickly, thereby providing a solid guarantee for the building of a society that is moderately prosperous in all respects by 2020.

The fourth focus is to provide China's newest urban residents with public services equal to that of established urban residents. In recent years, more than three million rural people have registered as permanent urban residents in Chongqing Municipality. The municipal government gave them a settling-in allowance, which is compensation for leaving their homestead as well as rights to five urban services; namely, elderly care, medical care, housing, entry into urban kindergarten, and entry into urban schools. All coastal cities should follow the successful example of Chongqing.

The fifth focus is to regard characteristic towns as the breakthrough points for urban-rural integration. A variety of characteristic towns should be developed in the one-hour radius around central cities, which not only helps solve the problem of rising house prices in central cities, traffic jams, and air pollution, but also facilitates urban and rural development. Currently, the National Development and Reform Commission and five other five relevant ministries support maximizing synergy between enterprises and the building of beautiful and characteristic towns, which literally covers thousands of enterprises and towns, so as to facilitate city-industry integration. This measure will play an important role in optimizing the structure and pattern of urban areas and in promoting the process of new urbanization.

28.4 Gain a Strong Understanding of the Dialectical Relationship Between the Real Economy and the Virtual Economy

The real economy and the virtual economy depend on each other, transform with each other, facilitate each other, and check each other. As China's economy is becoming more market-oriented, gaining a strong understanding of the relationship between the virtual economy and the real economy is vital to preventing economic fluctuations and realizing continuous and steady economic growth.

International experience has demonstrated that the main reason for the Asian financial crisis in 1997 was that the heavy burden of foreign debt was beyond the debt-bearing capacity of certain countries. Once debt repayment became a problem, foreign capital would rush out of the country, which eventually led to the financial crisis. As for the international financial crisis that occurred in the United States in 2008, the main reasons were: derivatives had gotten out of control, and the virtual economy had over expanded. Once a financial institution became insolvent, the debt chain would break, creating a systematic crisis.

International experience has also shown that the virtual economy is intimately linked with real estate bubbles. In the 1980s, Japan saw real estate loans inflate so much that the real estate bubble finally burst, causing the Japanese economy to collapse and making it difficult to recover. In China's virtual economy, there are currently two serious problems in need of attention.

The first problem is that corporate debt levels are too high, and debt repayment pressure is intense. The main reason for this problem is that China's financial system is based on indirect financing, which means that corporate financing relies mainly on bank loans. Hence, the government should accelerate the development of the capital market, and reduce corporate debt rates by expanding equity financing, so as to prevent debt risks.

The second problem is that house prices in several central cities are too high, giving rise to a real estate bubble, that is, at least to some extent. Thus, the government should increase the supply of residential land, allow functions to disperse out of cities and into rural areas, and develop characteristic towns so as to cool down the housing market.

28.5 Gain a Strong Understanding of the Dialectical Relationship Between the Government and the Market

Dealing with the relationship between the government and the market has been a core issue since the start of reform. The *Decision* adopted at the Third Plenary Session of the 18th CPC Central Committee points out that the market should play a decisive role in allocating resources, and the government should be allowed to perform its due functions. This is a breakthrough for the Party's understanding of the relationship between the government and the market. Allowing the market to play a decisive role in the allocation of resources is to observe the law of value. The movement of value inside an industry enables advanced enterprises to quickly pool resources and fully develop, and phases out backward industries. This movement of value allows weak industries to attract a large amount of resources by offering a relatively high return on investment, and thus quickly develop. On the other side, as this movement of value lowers the cost of capital, it becomes more difficult for industries with overcapacity to expand. Hence, the reasonable allocation of resources among different industries is achieved as the movement of value allocates resources according to consumer demand. The due functions of the government are executing macro-level regulation and market regulation, providing public services, and external coordination. The whole reform process consists of the government transforming its functions, and the market enhancing its role in the allocation of resources.

For now, the focus should be on the following perspectives, so as to coordinate the relationship between the government and the market.

The first perspective is to improve the total-factor market system that unifies urban and rural areas. Letting the market play its decisive role in allocating resources entails a mature market system. Thus, it is important to accelerate the establishment of a total-factor market system at the national level, especially one which allows the mutual flow of factors between urban and rural areas. By doing this, the government can "activate" resources in rural areas and bring the market mechanism into full play in boosting rural development. In addition, administrative barriers separating different regions should be removed so as to accelerate the flow of production factors from China's coastal areas to the central and western areas as well as from central cities to their surrounding areas. The environmental protection system needs to be improved, a mechanism of compensation for the value of the environment in economic terms should be established, and a market mechanism that facilitates the development of the environmental protection industry is needed.

China must do its best to promote the transformation and upgrading of the economy. Realizing this goal requires the nation to realize the following three transformations:

1. Demand structure transformation, which means the main driving force for economic growth should be shifted from investment and exports to consumption.
2. Industrial structure transformation, which means the focus on the secondary industry should be shifted to the coordinated development of the primary, secondary, and tertiary industries, and development of the tertiary industry should be accelerated.
3. Factor structure transformation, which means that the main support for economic growth should be shifted from consumption of material resources to technological progress, perfection of management, and improvement of labor quality.

These transformations are comprehensive and strategic. China will not attain success unless it fully taps into the synergy of the market mechanism and government guidance. Industrial policies should be transformed from selective policies to functional ones, which means that the government needs to change the practice of promoting key developmental industries and giving these industries special support, and begin to implement balanced incentive policies that are focused on economic transformation and upgrading. For example, technological progress and energy conservation and emission reduction should be encouraged and supported, along with economic activities that are helpful to the realization of these policies, regardless of industry type or enterprise nature.

The income distribution structure needs to be adjusted to realize shared development. Coordinating the relationship between efficiency and equity is always a major issue for the government. The Fifth Plenary Session of the 18th CPC Central Committee put forward a new concept of development, of which shared development is an integral part of it. This concept was put forward in response to the widening income gap, with the aim of narrowing that gap by stressing shared development. China should enhance the adjustment of income distribution without negatively affecting efficiency so as to increase the income of low and middle-income people, especially that of farmers, faster. The best way to do this is to improve the labor capacity of low and middle-income people by enhancing their skill sets, and encouraging them to pursue innovation and start businesses by providing them with more high-paid job opportunities. China should provide assistance for vulnerable groups and realize equality in distribution through equality in education.

Part IV
Balanced Urban-Rural Development

Chapter 29
Facilitating Coordinated Agricultural Modernization, Industrialization and Urbanization

Coordinating agricultural modernization, industrialization and urbanization is critical to economic development during the 12th Five-Year Plan period. The theme for economic development in this period is centered on the Theory of Balanced and Sustainable Development, and transformation of the economic growth mode is the main task. Within this transformation, the recasting of the agricultural development pattern is not only a key component but a precondition for achieving a series of strategic changes. For example, we are now on the path toward consumption-driven economic growth; but the goal of driving growth by expanding consumption can hardly be realized if rural incomes don't increase. To see the tertiary industry growing more quickly, the agricultural services system has to be improved. If we are to rely on technical innovation for industrial upgrading, quality improvements in the labor force and better management, then science and technology from an agricultural standpoint must be developed, and the quality of the rural labor force raised. Therefore, an overall transformation of our economic growth model must incorporate a similar transformation in the agricultural development pattern.

29.1 Agricultural Modernization Is Clearly Lagging Behind Industrialization and Urbanization

There are four prominent symptoms of lagging agricultural modernization.

First, there is an extremely large disparity in productivity between the primary industry and the secondary and tertiary industries. In 2010, the added value of agriculture accounted for workers. It can, therefore, be estimated that the productivity ratio of agriculture and the secondary and tertiary industries is 1:5.3. That is to say, the goods and service value created by 5.3 agricultural workers annually is

This article originally appeared in *Newsletter on Rural Work*, no. 17, 2011.

X. Zheng, *China's 40 Years of Economic Reform and Development*,
https://doi.org/10.1007/978-981-13-2727-8_29

equivalent to that created by one worker in the secondary or tertiary industries. That ratio has since risen to 1:6, about 1% higher than a decade ago. The modernization of a country must also involve a process of increasing productivity in the primary industry so that it approaches secondary and tertiary industry productivity. Creating more value through increased agricultural productivity is the only way to increase rural incomes and to see per capita income in agriculture catch up with that of the secondary and tertiary industries. This has been proven by the development of all provinces, autonomous regions and municipalities over the past 30 years of reform and opening up. In Zhejiang Province, the proportion of the agricultural labor force has decreased to now account for just 17% of the total non-government labor force. In Jiangsu that figure is to 19%. As a result, the ratio of rural to urban income has fallen to 1:1.9, much lower than the national average of 1:3.23. However, what is worrying is that in major agricultural provinces in central China the figures are still around 50%. Herein lies concrete proof that agricultural modernization is lagging behind industrialization and urbanization.

Second, the disparity in technological equipment between China and advanced countries in primary industry is much wider than in secondary industry. Although a gap remains between the levels of industrial technological equipment in China and internationally advanced levels, we have already developed some high-tech industries that approach international standards. Moreover, some enterprises and sectors in traditional industry already lead the world. Comparatively speaking, however, the gap in agricultural between China and advanced countries in the world is much greater. Be it mechanization, chemical application, water conservancy or promotion of good breeds, agricultural technologies, as a whole, are less developed than industrial ones.

Third, standardized large-scale agriculture involving various social sectors has yet to be developed. The key to achieving a transformation in the agricultural development pattern is to make the leap from traditional agriculture to modern agriculture. Traditional agriculture is based on a self-sufficient natural economy with a very low commoditization rate. Agricultural products should, however, serve all of society. A balanced relationship should be developed between production capacity and market demand, one that can adapt to demand changes. We should make products according to what society needs and how much. Unfortunately, that is a long way from being realized when it comes to agriculture. This is evidenced by large fluctuations in the prices of certain products such as pork and garlic in recent years. This has resulted from low marketization rates and an enduring failure to match production with demand. Limited in scale, Chinese agriculture still relies on small-scale production, meaning that it retains the features of the natural economy to a certain extent. A low rate of standardization is reflected in our failure to put in place a guarantee system for the quality of farm produce. This has directly resulted in a series of food safety incidents. The melamine incident alone brought disastrous consequences to our milk industry. It also presented producers abroad with development opportunities. France and Germany are considering restricting the export of domestic milk powder, claiming that excessive quantities being sold into China is pushing up prices domestically and undermining the interests of consumers at home. What about our dairy farmers? The destruction of eco-systems has severely damaged the dairy processing industry.

Therefore, how we build a quality guarantee system represents a major issue that must be resolved during agricultural modernization.

Fourth, the quality of the agricultural labor force does not meet the requirements of agricultural modernization. Although there are still 400 million workers engaged in agriculture, there are very few young people in their twenties or those of middle age. It is predominantly the elderly that are engaged in farming. If this is the case, how can we realize agricultural modernization? Many worry that no one is committed to farming any more. This reflects the weakness of the agricultural industry. The only way to maintain a high-quality labor force in rural areas is to improve intensive agricultural development and make it so that those working in rural planting and cultivation industries earn more than those employed in urban areas. We need to seize opportunities presented by rapid industrialization and urbanization over the next ten to fifteen years to accelerate agricultural modernization and change the current prevailing situation which see it lagging behind industrialization and urbanization. Last year, China's per capita GDP exceeded US$4000. The key to successfully building a moderately prosperous society in all respects by 2020 is to ensure the 600–700 million people living in rural areas can enjoy moderately prosperous lives. It is projected that by 2025 our GDP will have surpassed the US to lead the world, and per capita GDP will have more than doubled to reach 12,000 dollars, making us a high-income country. If this is to be the case, agriculture has to be modernized so it doesn't hold back industrialization and urbanization. Examining the development experiences and lessons of Latin American countries, we found that they have been stuck in the middle-income trap for as long as 30, 40, or even 50 years, and per capita GDP has remained in the thousands of dollars. That is largely because of the dual structure between urban and rural areas has not been dealt with properly. Latin American countries mostly have large rural populations with low productivity that are difficult to integrate into the processes of industrialization, modernization and urbanization. Asian countries, such as the Philippines, Malaysia, Thailand, Myanmar and Cambodia are beset by similar problems. Japan and the four Asian tigers have managed to evade the middle-income trap, because they have successfully solved the urban-rural dual structure problem, and in doing so, have seen per capita GDP jump to over 10,000 dollars. Therefore, whether, over the next ten to fifteen years, China can build a moderately prosperous society in all respects, avoid falling into the middle-income trap, join the rank of high-income countries, and outperform the US in the economic aggregate all hinges on rural development and agricultural modernization. As these processes unfold, more and more rural residents should become engaged in the secondary and tertiary industries, and come to enjoy the results of modernization and share in the outcomes of reform and opening up. We must seize the opportunities at hand, take a holistic standpoint in relation to agriculture and focus driving its modernization.

29.2 Seizing Rare Historic Opportunities to Modernize Agricultural

First opportunity: There are more than adequate social funds available for investment, which means agricultural modernization can be underpinned by sufficient funding. Annual revenue from land transfers has already reached over two trillion yuan. And due to excess liquidity, banks are under pressure because of a failure to find entities to provide with loans. In addition, those with extra cash to spare can invest in modernization projects with higher rates of return. Therefore, what China needs in advancing agricultural modernization is not money, but approaches for putting mechanisms in place that attract social funds.

Second opportunity: There are destinations for laborers transferring out of agriculture. These are not just limited to the Pearl River Delta and Yangtze River Delta, there also cities in central and western China that have encountered difficulties in labor recruitment. No one need bother asking about jobs with monthly incomes of 1000 yuan or less; basic salaries have now reached 1500–2000 yuan. We need to seize this opportunity to move part of the rural population to urban areas by transferring a portion of the labor force out of agricultural and into the secondary and tertiary industries. This would help to see the creation of favorable conditions for agricultural modernization.

Third opportunity: The market for high-quality farm produce enjoys sound prospects thanks to the huge demand for high-quality green products. With improved living standards, people are demanding better quality agricultural products. As long as those products are green and trustworthy, people will be happy to pay more for them.

Fourth opportunity: Chinese industry can provide the equipment needed for agricultural modernization so that it is underpinned by strong technology and production capacity. Agricultural modernization creates huge demand for machinery, which provides development opportunities in the agricultural machinery industry. Once the demand is there for such machinery, industry production capacity will soon be enhanced and the ability to manufacture large-scale and whole-process agricultural machinery will increase.

These four opportunities, if seized, will help create a sound environment and mechanism for agricultural modernization. These are real rare opportunities. Agricultural modernization has a history of thousands of years in China. Developed countries have already become post-industrialized societies, while we are still going through the transition from an agricultural society to an industrial one. Though many localities are now in the mid- and late phase of industrialization, a considerable amount of areas in central and western regions are only in the initial or mid-phases. Under such circumstances, we need to seize sound opportunities and study how we can use them to accelerate agricultural modernization.

29.3 Cultivating New Agricultural Investment and Operation Entities

Modernized big agriculture based on intensive development and social sector involvement cannot be established on the basis of hundreds of millions of small-scale households. We must build and cultivate new agricultural investment and operating entities. We need to pool funds in rural areas and, more importantly, work on cultivating three specific types of investment and operation entities.

First, family farms. As a single basic production and operation unit, families have great adaptability. Even in the US and some developed European countries, family farms are still major entities in agriculture and play a crucial role. One family farm in the US can take care of hundreds of acres of land, and in Europe anything up to a hundred acres. Drawing on this experience, we need to further stimulate the family operation entities initiative. An example of a success story of this initiative comes from Keshan County in Heilongjiang Province, where an elderly farmer, together with his four sons and their wives, farm almost a thousand acres, earning an annual net income of 700,000 yuan.

Second, rural cooperatives. Based on clearly established ownership and the pooling of land as shares, cooperatives need to now become standardized companies that integrate capital with labor. This is fundamentally different from the usual practice of equal distribution regardless of contribution. In developed countries like France and the Netherlands, cooperatives play a critical role in agricultural production. In France, farm produce sold through cooperatives accounts for 80% of total farm produce. Agricultural brands, including red wine brands, are all owned by cooperatives, and agricultural subsidies from the French Ministry of Agriculture are allocated directly to the cooperatives while private enterprises are ineligible for subsidies. Capitalist countries set great store by rural cooperatives, and as a socialist country, we should be working harder to see their development by encouraging new investment in rural areas and cultivating new operation entities.

Third, agricultural companies. By now, the heads of some rural township enterprises have accumulated some wealth. As previous farmers who love and know agriculture, they are willing to invest their hard-earned money in this area. Instead of refusing and fearing such investors, the government should embrace them and allow them to put their money into developing agricultural entities. New types of investment and operation entities need to be set up to pool social funds in rural areas.

29.4 Summarizing and Promoting Successful Experiences of Various Localities in Agricultural Modernization

Over the past 30 years of reform and opening up, various localities have created practical and innovative models for modern agricultural. Such experiences are as valuable as the contract operation practices that came out of Xiaogang Village in

Anhui Province. We should conscientiously summarize and spread these kinds of helpful experiences. Examples include: (1) Land transfers in Keshan County, Heilongjiang Province; (2) Large-scale operations in Korla City, Bayingol Mongolian Autonomous Prefecture, Xinjiang Uygur Autonomous Region; (3) Urban-rural integration in Chengdu; (4) Urban-rural integration in Xinxiang, Henan Province; (5) Urban-rural integration in Kunshan, Jiangsu Province; (6) Cooperatives pooling land as shares in Shunyi District, Beijing; (7) Making land a source of income for farmers in Chongqing; (8) Pooling land as shares to develop agricultural cultivation in Laiyang, Shandong Province.

These examples are all models of agricultural and industrial modernization, and represent the way forward for the development of agriculture in China. They hold valuable lessons and are an inspiration for agricultural modernization in other localities.

Chapter 30
Sticking to New Urbanization with Chinese Characteristics

Urbanization is an inevitable outcome in social development following industrialization, and stands in sharp contrast to the dispersed populations of agricultural societies. Over the past 35 years since reform and opening up began, an accelerated rate of industrialization has seen urbanization also advancing in a rapid manner. The huge supply capacity and consumption demand arising from industrialization and urbanization have made a concrete contribution to economic development. Over the next 20 years, urbanization will continue to serve as the most powerful driver of economic development. In China, with its vast territory and imbalanced development, urbanization will unfold in multiple layers and forms. Further reform of the rural land system and explorations on how to effectively realize collective rural land ownership are core issues in ensuring its advance. We should work toward advancing new urbanization with Chinese characteristics based on our actual conditions.

30.1 Urbanization Will Be the Most Fundamental Driver of China's Economic Development Over the Next Two Decades

Urbanization results from the development and clustering of industry and commerce, thus providing strong impetus for economic development. This implies that industrialization and urbanization should be developed in a coordinated and simultaneous fashion. However, due to systematic hurdles, urbanization has so far, in the first 35 years of reform and opening, been lagging behind industrialization. One glaring symptom of this is that over 200 million rural migrant workers employed in the urban secondary and tertiary industries are not fully covered under the urban household registration and social security systems, and rural contracted land continues to be

---

This article originally appeared in *Globalization*, no. 12, 2013.

X. Zheng, *China's 40 Years of Economic Reform and Development*,
https://doi.org/10.1007/978-981-13-2727-8_30

cultivated by either rural migrant workers themselves or their friends or relatives. This situation has given rise three severe consequences.

First, we have failed to cultivate stable and high-quality industrial workers. In particular, it is a pity that some technical female workers return to their hometowns for marriage after they have become familiar with their industry. Teams of workers are generally not stable, so effective professional technical training is difficult to provide. At present, ordinary skilled workers are easy to find, but technical workers are rare. This is hampering progress in manufacturing and improvements in product quality.

Second, agriculture has long been a weak industry lacking international competitiveness. Agricultural modernization and urbanization are two sides of the same coin. The massive outflow of young workers from the rural labor force has resulted in agriculture becoming "an old man's game," while policies supporting the circulation and concentration of land having been slow coming into operation. Consequently, rural areas have failed to maintain a high-quality labor force, progress in intensive agricultural development and modernization has been seriously hindered, and some localities have even witnessed the abandonment of farmland. A lagging urbanization process has also slowed down the pace of agricultural modernization.

Third, the role of industrialization and urbanization in boosting economic and social development has in a general sense been weakened. Industrialization creates supply, and urbanization demand. While urbanization has greatly boosted supply capacity throughout the process of modernizing big industry, the fact that it is lagging behind has resulted in inadequate consumption demand, aggravating overcapacity and slowing down social progress. In particular, the separation of husbands and wives due to work and the fact that tens of millions of children have been left behind in rural areas have brought about new conflicts for society as a whole as well as enduring psychological pain for the affected families.

Over the next 20 years, urbanization will remain the primary engine for economic development. Urbanization creates huge investment and consumption demand. It is estimated that each addition to the urban population adds 100,000 yuan of investment in urban infrastructure. This means an increase of 10 million in the urban population would bring one trillion yuan of investment. When a rural resident becomes an urban resident, his or her commodity consumption jumps threefold. Therefore, urbanization can unleash huge potential for driving economic development.

In 2012, China's urban population came to account for 52% of the total population. In line with the experience of developed countries, the urbanization rate stabilizes when the urban population reaches 70%. Over the next 20 years, the urban population will annually increase by around 1%, or 13 million people. The 18th National Party Congress set the goal of granting urban residency to rural migrant workers, which means that they will be equally entitled to public services like education, health care and social security. This will attract more and more rural residents to cities. Moreover, faster development of the service industry will also facilitate the urbanization process. The tax reform of replacing business tax with value-added tax in the tertiary industry will create a favorable climate for developing the services sector. With the tertiary industry flourishing, more job opportunities will become available in cities. In line with these trends, it is likely that the annual rate of urbanization will be about 1% over the next 20 years. The mission of industrialization and urbanization will be basically accomplished by 2030 when the urbanization rate is projected to be around 70% and per capita income will have exceeded US$17,000. At that time, the stage of rapid growth will come to an end. In accordance with the requirements of urban-rural integration, we should work continuously to eliminate the obstacles impeding the free mobility of production factors between urban and rural areas, in order to unleash potential for economic development during the course of urbanization.

30.2 Three City Clusters as the Engines Driving Economic Growth

Due to a large population and imbalanced development, the models of urbanization in China are bound to differ in nature. One salient feature however will be the simultaneous facilitation and coordination of the three city clusters, which include Beijing, Shanghai and Guangzhou as centers, sub-regional city clusters with provincial capitals as centers and local urbanization with counties as centers.

Over the past 35 years of development, we have managed to initially establish the Pearl River Delta city cluster with Guangzhou as the center, the Yangtze River Delta city cluster with Shanghai as the center and the Bohai Rim city cluster with Beijing as the center. In 2012, the economic aggregate of these three city clusters all topped one trillion dollars, with the Yangtze River Delta, which includes Shanghai, Jiangsu and Zhejiang, reaching a GDP of US$1.7 trillion, the Bohai Rim, which includes Beijing, Tianjin, Hebei and Liaoning, reaching a GDP of 1.3 trillion dollars and the Pearl River Delta, including Guangdong and HK, registering a GDP of 1.1 trillion dollars. The combined GDP of these regions accounted for 47.8% of total GDP in China. By 2020, the economic aggregate of each city cluster will have exceeded two trillion dollars, surpassing city clusters such as New York and Tokyo. These are two of the largest clusters in the world in terms of GDP, and are critical components of the American and Japanese economies and even the global economy. China's three clusters have become centers for science and technology, finance, manufacturing, trade, communication and information and constitute growth poles and engines for national economic growth. Moreover, they, too, will come to exert a significant influence on the global economy.

Faster development of the three city clusters must be based on the elimination of administration barriers and market segregation and the establishment of mechanisms for integrated development. Within these regions, we should allow free mobility of production factors and optimize resource allocation. We need to act in line with objective economic laws and reduce administrative interference as much as possible. At present, administrative barriers and market segregation are the biggest obstacles to the development of the three city clusters. For example, houses in major cities and the downtown areas of cities may be priced as high as tens of thousands of yuan per square meter, while those in the outskirts within half an hour's drive or surrounding regions may be as low as thousands of yuan per square meter. If there was fast transit to connect downtown areas with the outskirts, to link urban areas with surrounding regions and to facilitate industrial development and reasonable population mobility, then the rise of urban housing prices would be effectively curbed, traffic jams would be alleviated and outskirts and surrounding regions could thrive. To achieve these goals, we need to urgently reduce administration levels and activate market mechanisms.

30.3 Sub-regional City Clusters with Provincial Capitals as Centers

In the vast regions of central and western China, most provincial capitals have become economic centers in their own provinces and play a critical role in provincial economic development. Regional city clusters can be developed if provincial capitals serve as centers and are connected to neighboring prefecture-level cities by inter-city high-speed railways. Second tier city clusters differ from the three national-level city clusters in that they represent the drivers of provincial economic growth. At present, with relevant plans confirmed and strong impetus for development in existence, these city clusters have completed the initial stage of development, and are starting to play an increasingly important role in leading central and western regions in catching up with coastal areas.

With Zhengzhou at the center, other clusters of cities in central China, which include Luoyang, Kaifeng, Xuchang, Luohe, Xinxiang and Anyang, have been connected by the Beijing-Guangzhou and Lanzhou-Lianyungang railways, which has helped to establish a half-hour commute radius for residents. Regional integrated development has made a substantial contribution to the emergence of central China's economic zone. The development of Zhengzhou into an international aviation hub has further strengthened its role as a national logistics hub. The high-speed rail line between Zhengzhou and Chongqing will soon be in operation and will see stronger economic engagement between Nanyang and cities in central China. The cluster of cities in central China is helping Henan to simultaneously advance industrialization, urbanization and agricultural modernization without sacrificing crop production. This trend signals a new approach to modernization in central China.

Wuhan is at the center of a cluster of cities which includes Yichang, Huangshi, Ezhou, Xiaogan, Huanggang and Xiangyang. Connected by Beijing-Guangzhou railway and the Yangtze River for water transport, this cluster is catching up economically. Home to companies such as BAOWU, Dongfeng Motor Company Limited and Wuhan Optics Valley, this region boasts a solid industrial foundation, and serves as central China's manufacturing center. With fertile soil, large rainfall and a large area of rivers and lakes, Hubei Province has always been a land of abundance. The development of the Wuhan city cluster constitutes an important pillar of central China's economic emergence.

The city cluster of Changsha, Zhuzhou and Xiangtan represents the economic center of Hunan Province. Engineering equipment, rolling stock and animation have become pillar industries here. Hunan boasts a plentiful supply of talent, rich resources and advantageous geography. Faster growth of the city cluster of Changsha, Zhuzhou and Xiangtan is bound to see Hunan's economy thriving as a whole. Hunan will come to outperform coastal areas in terms of development.

The city cluster centered on Chengdu includes cities such as Deyang, Mianyang, Leshan, Yibin, Nanchong and Zigong. A land of plenty, the Chengdu plain enjoys rich science and technology resources, strong manufacturing capacity and advanced agricultural production. Guided by the national west development strategy over the past decade, the western regions have become destinations of industrial transfers from coastal regions and overseas, which has sparked rapid growth in the electronics, auto, airplane, pharmacy and power generation equipment industries. Chengdu, in particular, has explored an urban-rural development coordination system. It has made bold innovations in advancing the integration of markets for production factors as well as the integration of social management between urban and rural areas, and just may well rank among the first in the western region to successfully pursue a path of urban-rural integration while at the same time realizing modernization.

The emergence and rapid development of the aforementioned four regional city clusters have helped the provinces involved to accumulate experience in modernizing agriculture through industrialization and urbanization and have displayed the huge potential for development in central and western China as well as the right path to tapping into that potential. The central and western provinces that have traditionally been agricultural strongholds all have dense populations, advanced transportation and rich cultural backgrounds. The landmass and population of just one of these provinces are equivalent to those of a large European country. It could be said that the coastal regions have been on the path to modernization for the last 35 years. If, over the next 20 years, these big agricultural provinces can catch up with coastal areas on the basis of accelerated industrialization and urbanization, we will see a solid foundation being set for China's modernization drive, which will ensure success in the great undertaking of Chinese rejuvenation.

City cluster development is an important trend in urbanization. Both the three first-tier city clusters and the second-tier regional city clusters reflect that trend. The reason why this trend is so important in urbanization is because of the complementary relationship between central cities and satellite cities, which can help realize the distribution of specialized functions to various cities and improve overall efficiency. A manifestation of this distribution is the way in which individual cities in these clusters have come to specialize in port transportation, processing and manufacturing, commercial markets, R&D, education and training, recreation and tourism and living.

30.4 Urbanization at Local Level with Counties at the Center

The third tier of urbanization with Chinese characteristics is a local-level model which puts counties at the center and incorporates county seats, small towns and new-type rural communities. This model will ensure modern living and urban public services for people living in counties, small towns and new-type communities who are employed in the secondary and tertiary industries. A precondition of this, though, is that county economies should be developed enough to offer sufficient job opportunities in these industries. This will require an advanced transport network covering whole counties so that a commuter radius of half an hour's drive from the center can be put in place. In county-level cities in southern Jiangsu and Zhejiang, such as Kunshan, Jiangyin, Wujiang, Wujin, Anji, Yuyao, Shangyu and Cixi, most rural residents have started working in local industrial and commercial sectors and a large amount of laborers from outside these provinces have been attracted and accommodated in these places thanks to thriving rural township enterprises. The local people work where they live. Some live by rivers and mountains, some in bamboo forests, and some in well-arranged villas. This has made for a beautiful, clean, convenient and comfortable living environment for residents. They no longer yearn for the big cities and are even reluctant to transfer their household registration to cities where universities are located. A higher quality of urbanization can be achieved with this model than those in place in medium-sized and big cities with larger populations. Any region that has the conditions to implement such a model should do so.

In the relatively economically developed areas of Henan Province like Changyuan, Huixian County and Wuyang in Xinxiang, initiatives to build a new type of rural countryside have been launched and, for the last few years, public services have been improving. Farmers were not forced but incentivized to buy properties in housing communities at cost price on the condition that they gave up their homesteads. If the area of those homesteads was larger than that of the newly occupied dwelling, the surplus would be given over to real estate developers for commercial development. The profits generated therein were used to subsidize the construction of the housing communities. This helped integrate farming households' needs for better living conditions and developers' interests with the government's development plans, thus creating a self-circulating mechanism. The majority of the residents who moved into these new communities took up employment in the secondary and tertiary industries, while a minority continued farming. Building new-type rural communities at the same time as developing industrial and agricultural parks has helped to integrate industrialization, urbanization and agricultural modernization, thus putting in place systems for urban-rural integration. These new-type rural communities should be incorporated into urban community planning and brought under the coverage of unified public services systems, so as to create a stronger momentum for the joint development of industrialization, urbanization and agricultural modernization and gradually narrow the disparity between urban and rural areas.

There are examples in developed countries of local urbanization at county level. For example, in Germany, a country with a high level of urbanization, 67% of the urban population lives in small towns. These towns are integrated into a developed transportation system and are beautifully and elegantly laid out. There is usually only one factory or bank per town. But commuting is convenient for residents and living standards are higher when compared with major cities, so people are more inclined to settle down here.

The average population of Chinese counties stands at around 800,000. If a county can accommodate 200,000–400,000 people, with two small towns accommodating around 200,000 people and new-type rural communities another 200,000, all counties would be basically able to realize urbanization. In counties with developed industrial and commercial industries as well as tourism, this approach to local urbanization should be adopted.

30.5 Major Reasons Behind the Rapid Development of City Clusters

City cluster development based on a distribution of labor has resulted from two factors. First is the need for the development of industrial clusters. Due to international trade development and greater global competition, enterprises need to increase the proportion of locally purchased supporting raw materials and parts and components in order to lower costs, boost competitiveness, and extend the industrial chain to upper and lower streams. This has brought about opportunities for the development of surrounding cities. City clusters that were bonded by industrial clusters have in turn facilitated the boom of those same industrial clusters. This mutual reinforcement has led to unparalleled competitiveness nationwide and powerful internal impetus for city cluster development. This has been particularly true in the Yangtze River Delta and Pearl River Delta. For example, in Heqiao Town, the development of the chemical fabric textile printing and dyeing industry has driven the emergence of chemical fiber materials, which has transformed this region into the world's largest and most competitive textile industry cluster and city cluster underpinned by work distribution. Furthermore, the emergence of the electronics industry in Shenzhen has led to the development of processing trade development with electronic products at the core in Dongguan. Their complementary parts and components supply, R&D, marketing network, technical talent and a mobile skilled labor force has enhanced overall competitiveness and forged a strong momentum for the development of both industry and city clusters. The rapid development of city clusters has not just been a story of big and medium-sized clusters, but also of small ones. Since the inception of reform and opening up, we have witnessed the emergence of small-scale city clusters which have been labeled the "massive economy," which refers to the establishment of internationally competitive industrial clusters focused on the production and marketing of certain products within a single county or town, on the basis of specialized labor distribution. This is a trend that has been conducive to the advancement of industrialization and urbanization. For instance, the emergence and constant development of small commodity cities, such as Yiwu, has led to a boom in neighboring small towns. Numerous sectors have thrived under the "massive economy," including ties in Diezhou, Zhejiang, cranes in Changyuan, Henan, and socks in Datang, Zhejiang, cotton spinning in Weiqiao, Shandong, wool spinning in Xinqiao, Jiangsu, printing in Longgang, Zhejiang and clothes in Shishi, Fujian.

The second factor behind the rapid development of city clusters is modern means of transportation. The emergence of expressways, and especially inter-city high-speed railways, has substantially shortened transportation times, increased the mobility of people and goods, provided more job opportunities and changed people's mindset toward urbanization. Embodying this mindset is the TOD model (transit, orientation and development). Broadly speaking, this means transport guides urban and productivity distribution and economic development. In keeping with this trend, we need to speed up the construction of high-speed railways, establish high-speed railway networks within and between all city clusters around the country, and give full play to their role in facilitating economic and social development and in contributing to the advancement of new urbanization with Chinese characteristics.

30.6 Rural Land Reform Is the Key to Unleashing the Potential of Urbanization

Reforming the rural land system and finding effective ways to achieve collective ownership of rural land represent critical means for unleashing the great potential of urbanization. At present, there are four obstacles still impeding the urbanization process, obstacles whose resolution hinges upon effective reform of the rural land system.

First, to become urban residents, rural migrant workers will need to transfer usufruct of their original land in order to obtain funding support. The primary issue to be addressed in urbanization is the need to grant residency to more than 200 million rural migrant workers. The quality of employment and level of income of rural migrant workers are still low. To allow rural migrant workers to settle down in cities and enjoy decent lives, in addition to providing public rental housing for them in the form of subsidized housing and enabling them to enjoy public services such as social security, the government also needs to allow them to be able commercially transfer contracted land and private houses in rural areas so they can use the money they earn to settle down in cities. To this end, we need to establish a compensation mechanism for farmers' contracted land, homesteads and houses. Such an institutional arrangement is reasonable; and attempts to block it should no longer continue.

Second, increases in the amount of construction land needed for urbanization can be supplemented by reducing rural construction land. The movement of hundreds of millions from the rural population will inevitably lead to more land being required for construction in urban areas. The increase in construction land can be fully offset through rural land compensation. The rural per capita homestead ownership is now 3.5 times that of urban regions. Experience has proven that policy adjustments which allow homesteads to be exchanged for urban land for residence can reduce the amount of land occupied in an area by over 50%. This would not only meet the demand for construction land in cities, but also add new arable land. While we advance this work, we must also facilitate reform of the rural land system.

Third, developing intensive modern agriculture requires the establishment of a concentrated land transfer system. There are now 280 million people in the rural labor force taking care of 1.8 billion mu of land. Each person in the labor force cultivates only 6.4 mu on average. In light of current mechanization levels, each person has potential to take care of hundreds or even thousands of mu. Large-scale intensive land management is essential if we are to improve rural productivity and land yields and turn what has been a weak sector into a competitive one. To this end, we must set up the system for land contractual management rights, recognize the value of rights exchanges, issue certificates to rural households and encourage the rural residents to pool land in agricultural cooperatives, family farms and agricultural companies either voluntarily or with compensation. Moreover, we should allow banks to provide stronger credit support to agriculture by permitting the mortgaging of land management rights and homestead usage rights. This also requires acknowledging the value of exchanging those rights and issuing certificates to farmer households for usufruct ownership.

Fourth, establishing new-type rural communities requires commoditization of rural houses including homesteads. Because natural villages have developed over thousands of years, rural areas have been characterized by scattered populations, large occupation of land and costly supporting public infrastructure. Establishing new-type rural communities is an important task in building a new socialist countryside. As adjustment of the rural residential layout will necessarily involve the exchange of original houses for new ones, we must acknowledge rural homesteads and real estate as commodities, and allow ownership of the dwellings of rural households to be transferred on the market, setting up a rural real estate market and utilizing market mechanisms instead of administrative approaches to adjust the rural residential layout. In some localities, homesteads have been exchanged for residential houses. These exchanges were basically realized through administrative approaches and are easy to promote in financially strong places. If market mechanisms could be introduced and developers were to deal with operations under the guidance of government planning, such practices could prevail once farmers' interests are safeguarded. The establishment of new-type rural communities will create huge demand, and play a significant role in building a clean and beautiful countryside and driving economic growth.

Chapter 31
Exploring Methods for Realizing Public Rural Land Ownership

At present, China is experiencing rapid industrialization, urbanization and agricultural modernization. Industrialization requires a constant stream of high-quality labor from rural areas. How should we handle the contracted land of rural residents as they take up employment in the secondary and tertiary industries? Urbanization should ensure housing and public services for these new residents. How can we enable them to swap their rural houses for urban ones and turn the remaining rural homesteads into urban construction land? Agricultural modernization requires the development of non-government big agriculture. How can we turn small-scale household land management into large-scale intensive operations? These are the urgent questions that the Decision of the Central Committee of the CPC on Certain Major Issues concerning Comprehensively Deepening Reform (hereinafter referred to as the Decision) adopted at the 18th CPC Central Committee's Third Plenary Session, has provided definite answers. In the Decision, there are three breakthroughs concerning the reform and implementation of the rural land system, which once they have been carefully studied and fully understood, will provide strong impetus for the simultaneous development of industrialization, urbanization and agricultural modernization, thus helping us reach the goal of building a moderately prosperous society in all respects by 2020 as set at the 18th National Party Congress.

31.1 Allow Mortgages, Guarantees and Circulation of Contracted Land Management Rights for Farmers

Since reform began, over 200 million farmers have left the land to become rural migrant workers. The large majority cultivated their contracted land when they returned to their hometowns during busy farming seasons, or this work was carried

---

This article originally appeared in *Newsletter on Rural Work*, no. 22, 2014.

X. Zheng, *China's 40 Years of Economic Reform and Development*,
https://doi.org/10.1007/978-981-13-2727-8_31

out by relatives and friends. This has brought about two negative consequences. First, an extensive cultivation mode reduced land yields and many localities saw farmland being abandoned. Second, high-quality industrial workers were hard to come by as their jobs were unstable, which impeded the process of industrial upgrading. The only solution to these conflicts is to encourage rural migrant workers to transfer their contracted land so that it is concentrated under large-scale operators. Many localities have already been doing this, but national policy support has been inadequate. The *Decision* clearly states that farmers will be endowed with the rights to contracted land tenure, use, earning and transfer, mortgage and guarantee of contracted land management rights, and that they will be allowed to become shareholders in industrialized operations through their contracted land management rights. It also stated that the Party will encourage the transfer of contracted land management rights to households specializing in large-scale farming, to other family farms, and to rural cooperatives and agricultural firms, so as to develop multiple forms of large-scale operations. This represents a major breakthrough in the rural land management system and an important reform based on rural realities. In line with the *Decision*, the public ownership system of rural land will see ownership, contracting rights and management rights being separated. Ownership will belong to the rural collective, contracting rights to rural households and management rights will be open to all. We will maintain the ownership of land, implement contracting rights and lift restrictions on management rights. Ownership is not allowed to be freely traded, so land annexation can be avoided. After contracting rights have been mortgaged by rural households, creditors can only obtain the land usufruct if the collaterals are lost. As the contracting right belongs to rural households, they will enjoy legal person property rights and usufruct contracted land and therefore can obtain earnings from land transfers or property income. With contracting rights having exchange value, farmers moving into cities will have greater initiative to transfer these rights. Loosening management rights and encouraging big farming households, agricultural companies and cooperatives to expand the scale of land management will play an important role in boosting agricultural productivity and land yield. We have seen from past experience that revenue from land transfers for some farmers can even outweigh the net income they earn from cultivating the land themselves. Some localities have made annual transfer fees for each mu of land equivalent to the market price of 500 kg of wheat. Funds can be invested in intensive agricultural operations, and the removal of ridges can increase arable land by 5%, while unified management to ensure sound varieties, deep sloughing, irrigation, fertilizer application and pest control can ensure higher per unit yields and increase the rate of return by over 30%. We need to move swiftly and effectively to issue certificates confirming land rights, so as to create favorable conditions for transferring land contracting rights.

At present, there are a number of opportunities for agricultural modernization. First, those exiting the agricultural labor force have destinations to transfer into; second, a large amount of social funds are urgently seeking investment opportunities; third, there is huge market demand for quality green farm produce; fourth, the agri-industry can meet agricultural modernization's demand for technology equipment. These four opportunities, if integrated with policies that support the transfer of contracted land management rights, can dramatically speed up agricultural modernization.

Land contract rights transfers will enable farmers to earn more by enhancing efficiency. Based on the annual transfer fees of 700 yuan for each mu of land, each household can earn 7000 yuan from 10 mu of land. A rural couple employed in urban areas can earn around 60,000 yuan annually. If the money they earn from subletting land is included, such couple could join the ranks of middle-income families. As farmers will possess larger areas of land to be cultivated and managed, their income can also increase markedly. From experience, we know that in single cropping regions a farmer can cultivate 100–120 mu of land. In double cropping regions that figure is 50–60 mu of land, which would bring agricultural productivity in touching distance with the average levels of the secondary and tertiary industries and make farming a decent profession. In light of current mechanization levels, each person in the labor force can take care of thousands of mu of land in plains and hill regions. In the rice producing areas of southern China, a farmer can cultivate hundreds of mu of paddy fields. With an increase in labor productivity, farmer's incomes will exceed urban incomes, which will be conducive to cultivating highly-skilled farmers. As large-scale land operations greatly promote agricultural modernization, our agricultural sector will evolve from a weak industry to an internationally competitive one.

31.2 Facilitate Mortgages, Guarantees and Transfers of Rural Housing Properties in a Steady and Prudent Manner

This year's government work report sets the goal of expediting the granting of urban residency to 100 million rural migrant workers. One basic condition for urban residency is ensuring housing for rural migrant workers. They will hardly be able to afford a house if solely relying on their income. However, if their houses in rural areas could be sold, they could earn a considerable sum of money, which would make renting or buying a house in a city affordable. The *Decision* also states that the usufruct of farmer household homesteads should be protected, the system of rural homesteads should be reformed and improved, a number of areas should be selected to conduct pilot schemes, and the mortgage, warranty and transfer of rural property rights should be facilitated in a prudent and steady manner, with a view to ultimately identifying a path for increasing rural property incomes. As an important breakthrough in the rural housing and homestead system reform, this will provide a policy guarantee for the commoditization of rural houses. Apart from helping increase farmers' incomes and narrowing the income gap between urban and rural areas, advancing the reform set out in the *Decision* will not only reduce the total area of rural housing and meet the requirement of urbanization to bring new land for construction on stream, but also facilitate the process of granting rural migrant workers residency. At present there are 280 million rural migrant workers and 60 million children, 46 million women and 40 million elderly men left behind in rural areas. A total of 400 million people are not living with their family members. In mass education, we must emphasize a concern for people's way of living and work to help 400 million people reunite with their families. What a great undertaking! Our work on this should be carried out in line with the realities of different localities.

Based on the experiences of all countries in the world, construction land is reduced and arable land increased during the urbanization process. This is because urbanization results in more intensive use of land. In China, the per capita construction land in rural areas is 3.5 times more than that of urban areas. National urban and rural construction land has reached an area of 220,000 km^2, of which rural construction land accounts for 170,000 km^2, or 255 million mu. At present, the greatest potential in terms of land resources lies in rural homesteads. Acknowledging the commodity value of houses including homesteads in rural areas and allowing them to be exchanged on the market are objective requirements of ensuring intensive and conservational land use. Advancing the reform will not lead us encroach on the limit of 1.8 billion mu below which arable land cannot fall. On the contrary, it will increase arable land. As homesteads usually stand on good land, their per unit yield will certainly be higher than ordinary arable land after reclamation.

Acknowledging the commodity property of rural residents reflects the requirement for realizing two-way free production factor mobility between urban and rural areas and the objective requirement of activating the decisive role of the market in resource allocation. The socialist market economy system has been in implementation for over 20 years, but we are still not recognizing farmers' houses as commodities. This has seriously undermined their interests and resulted in a constantly widening income gap between urban and rural areas. More than 80% of urban residents own their private houses, so their property will keep rising as housing prices increase. However, farmers have been losing out on property price increases as their houses are not commodities. Restricting farmers from trading their houses on the market is nothing more than depriving them of the right to earn property income. Herein lies the greatest inequality between urban and rural residents. In allowing for the mortgage, warranty and transfer of farmers' homesteads including houses, the *Decision* represents a major breakthrough in the rural real estate system. It also stands as an important manifestation of the market determining resource allocation. According to rough estimates, if each mu of land is valued at 200,000 yuan, then the 170,000 km^2 of homesteads in rural areas will have a market value of over 51 trillion yuan. This huge fortune would be the most valuable *hongbao* (traditional Chinese envelope containing money as a gift) received by farmers as a result of the *Decision*. It will effectively narrow the income gap between urban and rural residents and become an important pillar in building a moderately prosperous countryside in all respects and advancing the granting of urban residency to rural migrant workers.

Some may worry what rural migrant workers will do if they become unemployed and cannot return to their rural homes. Such worry is unnecessary. Former rural residents under the urban household registration system will have access to urban unemployment insurance. What's more, the historical process of industrialization and urbanization in China is irreversible. The generations that follow rural migrant workers, having received better education in cities, will have stronger survivability. After gradually integrating themselves into cities, they will not go back to the countryside.

In line with international experience, farmers being able to enjoy land value-added revenue during the process of urbanization is the key to avoiding the middle-income trap and joining the ranks of high-income countries. Japan and the Republic of Korea on one hand and India, Brazil and Mexico on the other hand, have respectively provided positive and negative experiences in this regard. While we are experiencing a critical stage on the way to becoming a high-income country, enabling farmers to share the benefits of land appreciation will help ensure that we change the urban-rural dual structure and join the ranks of high-income countries.

31.3 Rural Collectively-Owned Construction Land Should Be Subject to the Same Rights and Prices as State-Owned Land

The *Decision* points out that under the precondition of compliance with planning and usage regulations, we will allow the transferring and leasing and share pooling of profitable collective land for construction in rural areas, and will ensure market entry with rights and prices that are equal to those of state-owned land. For a long time, new urban construction land has been turned into state-owned land after its acquisition from farmers by the government. After improving the infrastructure of roads, water and power supply, the land would be opened to bidding, be auctioned off or become open for transfer. The bulk of the land appreciation earnings went to the government, while the rights and interests of the farmers offering the land often could not be safeguarded. According to the Decision, farmers will enjoy higher compensation from profitable construction land, including favorable treatment in employment, social security and housing. This is an important reform of the land acquisition system that ensures farmers' interests are safeguarded. It is particularly stressed that we should set up a distribution mechanism for revenue from land appreciation, take the nation, the collective and the individual into account, and increase individual income in a reasonable manner. This demonstrates a strong attention to the interests of farmers.

The three reforms of the rural land system will bring about major changes in the realization of public land ownership and will see it effectively integrated into the market economy.

Establishing one integrated urban-rural market for construction land is an important approach to exploiting the decisive role of the market in land resource allocation. For too long, we have not been able to realize two-way free mobility between urban and rural areas. The labor force, funds and land of rural areas have been flowing endlessly into cities, while funds, technology and talent from urban areas have not moved in the opposite direction. The blockade between urban and rural markets has been the fundamental reason for the constantly widening gap between urban and rural areas. Building an integrated urban-rural factor market, including a land market, is a fundamental approach to accelerating rural development.

Non-profit construction land still needs to be acquired by the government. As our country is now experiencing a stage of fast growth in infrastructure construction, the building of railways, roads, pipelines and airports will inevitably occupy a portion of arable land. Local Party committees and governments at all levels need to engage well with the people, persuade them to consider these types of situations from a holistic perspective, facilitate smooth infrastructure construction and effectively control costs. Good infrastructure construction will be conducive not only to local economic development but also to increasing farmers' incomes.

The three reforms of the rural land system will bring about major changes in the realization of public ownership of land and effectively integrate it with the market economy. By separating ownership from management rights in SOE reform, we have achieved integration between the state-owned sector and the market economy. According to the decision adopted at the Third Plenary Session of the 14th CPC Central Committee, SOEs have legal person property rights to state-owned assets and can use them for mortgages, warranties, transfers and earning revenue. According to the Third Plenary Session of the 18th CPC Central Committee, SOE management should move from a predominant focus on asset management to concentrate on capital management. Now we are replicating that successful experience in the rural land system. Given this, there should not be any difficulty from the perspectives of theory and practice. The one slight difference is that rural land is subject to usage regulations, so the transfer of arable land must be conducted without altering its use. Converting arable land into construction land must conform to construction planning and go through the procedures of land acquisition. The Third Plenary Session of the 17th CPC Central Committee also decided that the land rural land compensation should be carried out within the provincial regions. This would enable the reclamation of distributed construction land in rural areas. Land market trading and unified adjustment through planning departments will help meet investors' demand for construction land. By developing the land ticket market, Chongqing has explored how to distribute construction land in rural areas. This approach helps to meet the three goals at the same time—it satisfies the demand for construction land from industrialization and urbanization, increases the amount of arable land and raises the incomes of farmers.

Chapter 32
Focusing on Rural Reform, Breaking Demand Bottlenecks

Our economy is now facing downward pressure, more difficulties in business production and operation and the emergence of economic risks. Further, inadequate demand represents a major contradiction in the economy. We must focus on dealing with this problem by adopting major reform measures. The fundamental way to tackle this issue is to refocus on rural reform, substantially adjust the relations between urban and rural areas and unleash the huge potential of rural demand and urban-rural integration. If within 10 to 15 years, agricultural labor productivity can be increased to the levels of average social labor productivity, the income of farmers can rise parallel to that of urban citizens and the development gap between urban and rural areas can be basically eliminated. Moreover, we can not only sustain 7.5-plus percent economic growth rate until 2030, but also showcase the superiority of the socialist system with Chinese characteristics.

32.1 Inadequate Demand Is the Major Problem Currently Affecting the Economy

What is the major contradiction in current economic operations? Inadequate final demand. Overcapacity and inadequate demand are two different ways of expressing the same problem. Our macroeconomic countermeasures must be adapted to tackle this major contradiction.

Rome was not built in a day. Looking at the past 30-plus years of development, the high growth we achieved was basically based on high investment, high resource consumption and high pollution—an extensive development path. However, we cannot simply blame the contributors, because at that time the major contradiction lay in the extremely short supply of commodities. We spent 20 years dealing with this problem.

This article originally appeared in *Guangming Daily*, January 28, 2015.

X. Zheng, *China's 40 Years of Economic Reform and Development*,
https://doi.org/10.1007/978-981-13-2727-8_32

And resolving it was an extraordinary achievement. That said, we were relatively slow to become aware of the severe consequences of high investment rates and low consumption rates; we failed to take effective measures in a timely manner, and were still happy to rely on investment. Consequently, over the past years, investment has continued to soar, while final consumption, or resident consumption, has continued to fall, thus leading to an extreme disparity between the two. These are the fundamental reasons for the downward economic development pressure, the inadequate demand and the sluggish growth we are currently experiencing. From 1981 to 2013, the rate of investment rose from 32.5 to 47.8%, while the final consumption rate slumped from 67.1 to 49.8% and the resident consumption rate dropped from 52.5 to 36.2%. Respectively that is an increase of 15.3%, and decreases of 17.3 and 16.3%. At present, about half of GDP created each year is used for greater production, while only slightly more than one third is goes toward consumption by over 1.3 billion people. The resident consumption rate of the US stands at 70%. China's investment and consumption structure, unique in the world, is wholly unsustainable.

Quite clearly, our economic development is now constrained by demand instead of supply. If the problem of inadequate demand is not resolved, it will be hard to make progress in other measures. The major purpose of carrying out structural adjustments is to create and unleash new demand. Macroeconomic management departments and research institutes should focus on dealing with the constraints imposed by bottlenecks in demand.

Karl Marx, who spent his whole life studying market economy rules, drew the conclusion that the contradiction between ever-increasing production capacity and the demand people can afford is the fundamental contradiction of capitalism, and that this contradiction will inevitably result in periodic crisis of production surplus. In the wake of World War II, developed economies, needing to avoid an overcapacity crisis, strengthened their economic predictions and macro regulation and worked on building welfare societies, thus managing to escape out from under the burden of overcapacity.

In china, however, we proposed the establishment of a socialist market economy system a mere 20 years ago. We still do not have effective solutions due to limited understanding and research of the objective rules of the market economy. While the problem of inadequate supply under the planned economy system is something we have already resolved. Overcapacity is a problem we not yet effectively dealt with.

32.2 Releasing Rural Demand Potential Is the Key to Resolving Inadequate Demand

According to statistics for 2013, out of a rural population of 630 million, 240 million people were part of the rural labor force. The rural labor force accounted for 31.4% of China's total employees. Rural labor productivity was only one third of average social productivity, while farmers' per capita income was only one third of the income of urban residents. It is time to raise rural productivity to the social average level, so that rural residents can attain parity in income with urban residents. Unleashing the consumption potential of the 630 million people in the rural population can help realize a 7.5-plus percent economic growth rate through 2030. Experience in reform and development over the past over 30 years has shown that, no matter the commodity, as long as rural residents learn how to make it, it will see a rapid shift from demand exceeding supply to supply exceeding demand; no matter the commodity, as long as rural residents can afford it, it will see a rapid shift from supply exceeding demand to demand exceeding supply. To unleash the huge potential of rural demand, the first thing we must do is enhance the purchasing power of farmers. Many cities have already imposed restrictions on car purchases due to traffic jams, but there is no such thing as a traffic jam in rural areas. In 2013, there were 127 million civilian cars, which means less than 10% of the population own cars. The world average is over 30%, and in developed countries it has reached 80% or more. If cars were affordable for rural residents, they could underpin the high-speed growth of the auto-industry for the next decade or more and bring about profound changes in the urban-rural structure.

Developing modernized and specialized large-scale big agriculture by means of a faster transformation in the agricultural development pattern is the fundamental approach to increasing rural labor productivity and farmer's incomes. At the National Agricultural Economic Work Conference, President Xi Jinping stated that if each person in the labor force could plant 100–120 mu of land in the northern single-cropping regions, and 50–60 mu of land in the southern double-cropping regions, then the primary-industry labor productivity rate would reach or exceed secondary and tertiary industry levels, and farming would become an attractive occupation. It is already possible to meet these requirements in the vast plain and hill regions. Agricultural modernization is faced with unprecedented opportunities for development. First, there are jobs available for those in the rural labor force transferring out of agriculture as labor recruitment has been difficult everywhere; second, agri-industry can provide adequate means for agricultural production including agricultural machinery and equipment; third, there is strong market demand for quality farm produce; fourth, various levels of government have invested over 5 trillion yuan in the development of agriculture, farmers, and the countryside, and this is set to further increase. It is high time that we capitalize on these favorable conditions to bring about a marked increase in rural labor productivity and narrow or even close the income gap between urban and rural residents. In reality, this gap has already been closed in coastal areas, where farmers enjoy wealthier lives than urban residents and the rural living environment is better than in cities. We should work to see that this is the case throughout the country so that more and more farmers are content to continue farming.

In late December last year, I visited rural areas in Heihe City, where over 85% of the land was transferred at a price of around 700 yuan per mu per year and is now cultivated by cooperatives, agricultural companies or large farming households. In one village, more than 20,000 mu of arable land was previously cultivated by more than 220 farmers. However, since the establishment of the cooperatives, only about a dozen farmers are taking care of the same area of land, while the rest have found employment in cities. Thanks to the introduction of the educated youth from Shanghai who used to work in rural areas, women in rural areas can earn a monthly income of over 5,000 yuan in Shanghai. If a couple works in the city, they have the potential to earn a yearly income of 100,000 yuan. With land transfer fees of over 10,000 yuan, the family income would top 110,000 yuan, two to three times what they would earn from farming. Standardized large-scale management by cooperatives has helped increase per unit yield by over 30%. Of the three management models (cooperative, agricultural company, and major planting households) the joint stock cooperative system was more popular for farmers in Heihe. That was because the land, agricultural machinery and farm use materials could all be pooled as shares, so that farmers could share profits according to contributions. The cooperatives paid salaries to the managing staff and agricultural machinery operators. The staff in cooperatives were usually members who could also receive dividends on top of their salary, which was just slightly lower than the wages of rural migrant workers. However, as they were able to stay at home, they could still take care of their families.

The Central Economic Work Conference identified the transformation of the agricultural development pattern as third in the list of priorities for this year. As long as policy guidance and encouragement is strengthened, land transfer can be accelerated. The natural economic model with families as the main units which has lasted for thousands of years will gradually withdraw from the historical stage as the tide of industrialization and urbanization takes precedent.

32.3 Encouraging Rural Migrant Workers to Buy Houses in Cities After They Are Paid to Give up Their Homesteads

There are now 280 million rural migrant workers and 60 million children, 43 million women and 40 million elderly men left behind in rural areas. A total of 413 million people are eager to unite with their family members. A large number of children cannot live with their parents, and suffer from psychological pain as a result. Accelerating family reunions for rural migrant workers will increase the huge demand for urban construction, which will quickly ensure growth is stable. At its Third Plenary Session, the 17th CPC Central Committee decided that rural land compensation can be paid only within provincial regions. At its Third Plenary Session, the 18th CPC Central Committee decided that we should allow the mortgage, warranty and transfer of farmer households' rights for land use, and endow homesteads with commodity properties for the first time. Thanks to land use rights, namely, legal person property rights, farmers can enjoy the benefits of land appreciation in the process of urbanization just as urban residents do. The benefits from differential land rent farmers can enjoy after quitting their homesteads is dependent on the scope of the market. In visits to rural areas in Xinxiang in Henan in early January, I learned that when farmer households withdrew from their homesteads, they earned only around 50,000 yuan for each mu of land in the county-level land market and 200,000 yuan for each mu in the city-level land market in Xinxiang. According to the estimates of land departments, if the provincial land market in Zhengzhou were opened, each mu of land would be sold for around 500,000 yuan. For rural migrant workers buying houses in cities, this would be a considerable sum. To attract more rural migrant workers to cities, we should build welfare houses for them. Urban residents used to enjoy welfare houses, but wealth has increased along with soaring housing prices. The critical part of the policy is to increase housing construction land as rural migrant workers withdraw from their homesteads, so that lower-priced, affordable houses can be built for them.

There are many advantages to granting urban residency to rural migrant workers. First, this represents a major action of the Party and government in caring about people's lives. It will exert a profound impact on the relationship between the Party and rural residents. Second, rural migrant workers, having settled down in cities, can take part in technical training courses of various kinds and remain in enterprises once becoming skilled in the labor force, which will be conducive to building stable high-quality industrial personnel teams. Third, it will be conducive to conserving land resources, and rural migrant workers won't need to build unused houses in rural areas with their hard-earned money. Fourth, building houses for 400 million people in cities will create huge demand, and increase consumption demand among newcomers, which would provide a fundamental solution to the conflict of inadequate demand.

32.4 Correcting Misunderstandings

In order to refocus on rural reform and unleash the huge potential of rural development, we must eliminate obstructive mindsets and correct some misunderstandings.

First, some believe that reform of the rural land system is bound to push arable land near or below the minimum of 1.8 billion mu and undermine national food security. Developing modern agriculture will transform our agriculture from a weak industry to an internationally competitive industry. This is the fundamental guarantee to food security. The precondition to the transfer of land management rights is that the use of the land does not change. Of course, we should avail of the opportunity of land management right transfers to promote the coordinated development of spatial food planting structures, economic crops and animal feed and increase the share of animal husbandry in agriculture. In doing so, the same area of land may be able generate other food in addition to crops. Rural residents withdrawing from homesteads can not only help to meet the requirement for construction land, but also save over 50% of land for cultivation. This has already been proven through experiences in pilot regions. International experience also shows that in all countries arable land increases during the urbanization process. Currently, rural homesteads nationwide occupy 170,000 km^2 or 255 million mu. The land of each rural resident is more than three times that

of urban residents. It is essential that we build a construction land market based on urban-rural integration and facilitate economical and intensive use of land resources. Second, what should we do when rural migrant workers can't return to their rural homes if unemployed? Having become urban residents, they will be able to avail of urban social security coverage, including insurance covering elderly care, health care, unemployment and occupational injury. Therefore, there will no longer a need for them to worry about unemployment.
Third, some worry that the excessive issuing of currency and inflation may occur after farmers gain legal person property rights to their land. Since reform began, we have always worried that farmers' incomes might not rise, but have never thought about what to do when they become rich. Farmers should be able to enjoy the profits from land value appreciation as urban residents do in the process of urbanization, and be able participate in differential land renting in major cities by trading their homesteads which are far away from cities in regional land transaction markets. Those are the rights of the farmers. We ought to be delighted in seeing rural migrant workers earning property income out of the homesteads from which they withdrew and using it to buy houses and cars in cities. The purchasing power enhanced by rural migrant workers can only help to alleviate austerity. Claiming there will be an outbreak of inflation is wholly irrelevant.

Ever since reform and opening up began, each and every major breakthrough has originated from the countryside. We must shoulder the urgent historical mission of refocusing on rural reform and work to ensure that rural labor productivity exceeds average social productivity and that per capita rural income catches up with per capita urban income, thus basically eliminating the development gap between urban and rural areas.

Chapter 33
Accelerating Urban-Rural Integration to Build a Moderately Prosperous Society in All Respects

How can we stimulate an enormous potential for economic development and relieve the pressure driving economic growth downwards? The fundamental approach is to speed up the reform and development processes for urban-rural integration. In this regard, the *Decision* of the Third Plenary Session of the 18th CPC Central Committee designed important plans for the establishment of a new system for this integration. Therefore much emphasis should be placed on the reforms and facilitation of urban-rural coordinated development projects and be regarded as the major urgent tasks for building a moderately prosperous society in all respects by 2020 while also ensuring a sustainable and healthy economic development.

Last year on April 30th during a collective learning meeting for members of the CPC Political Bureau, General Secretary Xi Jinping delivered an important systemic speech on the improvement of urban-rural integration system. In his remarks, he noted that the most difficult and complicated part of building a moderately prosperous society in all respects is developing rural areas, especially those stricken by poverty. We must therefore step up efforts and increase our input if we must achieve major breakthroughs in coordinating urban and rural development, especially if we want to break the urban-rural dual structure, promote equal exchange of urban and rural factors, and allocate public resources in a balanced manner. All of this will help stimulate momentum in the process of developing rural areas and involve farmers in the reform and development process in an equitable way, so that they can also share the fruits of this campaign He further stressed that our goals are to ensure equal fundamental rights for urban and rural dwellers, equal public services in urban and rural areas, balanced urban and rural wages, reasonable allocation of urban-rural factors and the integration of urban and rural industries. Therefore this speech identified the direction and specific measures for reforms to facilitate urban-rural integration. As a result, the Party, as a whole, should also pay attention to this goal and act in line with its philosophies across all fields.

This article originally appeared in *Reform*, no. 1, 2016.

X. Zheng, *China's 40 Years of Economic Reform and Development*,
https://doi.org/10.1007/978-981-13-2727-8_33

33.1 Ensuring Equal Fundamental Rights for Urban and Rural Residents Is the Precondition for Urban-Rural Integration

To accomplish our mission for industrialization, we have had to adopt the price scissors method to highlight the difference between industrial products and agricultural products, while underpinning industrial growth through agriculture. In the meantime, the management system of separating urban areas from rural areas should be adopted to prevent mass migration of rural dwellers to cities, which might result in a shortage in agricultural produce in urban areas. Unfortunately as current systems have been in existence for more than 60 years, some fixed beliefs and practices may already have been adopted. Those systems involving fundamental rights and interests of urban and rural residents seem so inappropriate in today's China where we are striving to build a moderately prosperous society in all respects.

Currently, fundamental rights for urban and rural residents are not equal mainly within two respects.

First, inequality in property rights. The urban means of production and consumption are almost totally based on commercialization. Land, factory buildings, equipment and residences owned by the state, collective and individual properties have all been allowed to move freely in the market. However, property rights for rural land and residences remain unclear, because the legalities of property rights for those living in rural areas are yet to be implemented. Additionally, as the most important means of agricultural production and consumption in rural areas, land and homes still have to be commercialized and marketized. As a result, farmers cannot enjoy benefits resulting from real estate improvement in the course of urbanization in the same way their urban counterparts do. This is the greatest inequality within the fundamental rights of urban and rural residents and the most important reason for the widening gap in income for urban and rural residents.

Second, inequality in the household registration system. The 280 million rural migrant workers have contributed a great deal to the construction of cities, and in fact some of them have even been working in cities for twenty or thirty years. However, due to their rural household registration, they cannot benefit from various social security and public services under the urban household registration system. Moreover, most of their family members still live elsewhere. This therefore is very unreasonable when it comes to the necessity of ensuring the fundamental rights and interests of farmers are taken care of. The *Decision* of the Third Plenary Session of the 18th CPC Central Committee stressed the need for farmers to have a right to own, use, make earnings and transfer through the mortgage land contract their management rights. It also stated that the usufruct of homesteads for farmers should be protected, the system of rural homesteads be reformed, a number of pilot places be selected, mortgage, warranty and transfer of rural property rights be facilitated in a discreet and steady manner, and ultimately a path to increased rural property income be found. The *Decision* also stated that under the precondition of compliance with planning and use regulation, transfer, leasing and shares pooling be allowed for profitable collective pieces of land meant for construction in rural areas, and ensure market entry with equal rights and prices compared with state-owned land. These three measures were the major breakthroughs in the realization of rural public land ownership and the reform of the farmer residence system. It, for the first time, turned rural land and rural housing into commodities, confirmed house ownership for farmers and gave them legal person property rights for contracted land and homesteads, gave full play to the pivotal role played by market forces in rural land resource allocation. Additionally, it also facilitated the economical and intensive usage of land resources, provided a precondition for farmers to voluntarily choose residence and household registration in either urban or rural areas, and opened the door for gaining property income attained from house transfers and having the right to use land, including the establishing of a homestead.

Meanwhile, acknowledging farmers' legal property rights became a totally different matter compared with the privatization of land, as the former solved the issue of effective balancing between public land ownership and the market economy. This was the masterpiece of the Communist Party of China. Hitherto if we can carry forward the philosophy of the Third Plenary Session, we might ensure that all citizens regardless of place of residence have access to equal rights and interests; including property rights to land and housing. We should therefore be content and happy for farmers gaining access to these rights.

33.2 Ensuring Equal Access to Public Services for Both Urban and Rural Areas Is a Key Step Toward the Intended Urban-Rural Integration

The public service gap between urban and rural areas is a major manifestation of the disparity between urban and rural development. Rural areas appear to be lagging behind cities in multiple areas, including those in elderly care, education, healthcare, transport, water and power supply and the general physical environment. That is perhaps due to public services being concentrated in cities, which in turn makes urban centers seem more attractive to rural dwellers. That is also because access to basic public services in rural areas, especially those located in central and western regions of the country, are particularly poor. It's therefore due to this lack of access that has constrained rural economic development and hampered improvements that would otherwise elevate the quality of life for the farming community.

In order to improve the situation in these areas and especially in those within the central and western regions of China, respective local governments should focus on advancing public services. They also ought to equalize the urban and rural per capita public financial expenditure, and make up for the development of public services in these areas as soon as possible. Education, health care, transport, environmental protection and elderly care should be regarded as priorities. In contrast, access to public services in the country's coastal rural areas has seen a fast development by amassing wealth through township enterprise schemes. Hence these types of richer rural areas have dramatically improved their public services mainly due to their own added input with support for their local governments. Therefore, those still struggling to advance must also seek to adopt this approach if they want to boost growth and development in their regions.

The other hand, the PPP model should prevail in developing rural tertiary industries and an effective approach devised to attract social funding for rural development. This would require rural homes and contracted lands to be pledged for bank loans. Commercial development on residential land based on rural land conservation could help attract social funding and pull urban capital and urban dwellers toward the countryside. But we should first consider trying to build farm villages in city outskirts and tourism areas for urban residents then gradually increase their popularity. China's rural areas would witness a sea of change, if the 20 trillion yuan in bank loans and social funding can be geared toward agricultural modernization, developing the countryside and integrating rural migrant workers during the 13th Five-Year Plan period. With a substantial increase in wages for farmers, China can avoid falling into the middle-income trap and underpin a sustainable and healthy economic development.

33.3 Income Balance Between Urban and Rural Residents Is the Fundamental Objective of Urban-Rural Integration

The wide income gap between urban and rural residents is a major manifestation of the gap between urban-rural development. Achieving a balance between urban and rural residents is the key to establishing a mechanism of integrated urban-rural development. The per capita income growth rate for farmers has exceeded that of urban residents. It thus is great news that the income gap between urban and rural dwellers has been narrowed down from 3.3:1 in 2009 to 2.8:1 in 2014. Sustaining this sound momentum hence relies fundamentally on increasing agricultural productivity, which in turn requires expanded operation scale for lands. At present, one rural labor force can cultivate only seven mu of land on average. Therefore, if within the monocropping regions a farmer can cultivate up to 100–120 mu and 50–60 mu of land within the double cropping regions, agricultural productivity could reach the social average levels, and farming would become a decent trade. Under the precondition that rural areas are collectively entitled to ownership of land, we could hence allow households to consent to paid transfer for management rights with contractual rights. In doing so, rural households can gain property income and the management of large pieces of land can be advanced. It is necessary to encourage the development of various types of cooperative economies, especially those pooling land contracting rights of shares. We should encourage rural migrant workers to return to their hometowns to take part in entrepreneurial activities while developing, modern methods of agriculture, farm produce processing, commercial circulation and rural tourism. Meanwhile, only the surplus rural labor force should be encouraged to find job opportunities elsewhere in urban centers. Especially today where most coastal regions and cities are facing challenges in the recruitment of personnel. Currently the thinking for rural dwellers is for example, as the household service industry suffers from labor shortage, a maternity matron earns a monthly income of between 5000 and 6000 yuan in the rural areas; but if a couple goes to the city to find jobs, their annual income substantially increases and can reach 80,000–90,000 yuan. If they sublet their land, their household annual income could reach around 100,000 yuan, which enables them to catch up with or surpass that average income of urban residents. Evidently, as long as an urban-rural integrated system and policy ecosystem is created, it will give full play to all regions and industries to advance hence encourage the development of rural area. This might also help boost the agricultural industry and help realize the wage balance between urban and rural dwellers.

To give another example, during the past 40 years of industrialization and urbanization for the Republic of Korea, urban and rural income has been increasing simultaneously, with the income ratio staying at around 1:0.9. There are two main reasons behind this trend. First, the country launched a campaign of building the countryside. Then in the early 1970s the government funded all rural development projects. Second, farmers were allowed to share all benefits emanating from land appreciation during the course of urbanization. As a socialist country led by the Communist Party, China should therefore also be more capable of realizing similar simultaneous income growths for both urban and rural residents.

33.4 Reasonable Allocation of Urban and Rural Factors Is the Inevitable Requirement of Urban-Rural Integration

Facilitating reasonable allocation of urban and rural resources means realizing coordinated development between urban and rural areas. The key to that is to allow two-way free mobility of various types of production factors between urban and rural areas and activate the vital role of market forces in resource allocation. For a long period of time, many man-made obstacles have forced the work force, funds and land belonging to rural areas to constantly flow into cities, while little of the funds, technology and talent from urban areas moved to rural areas. This has been the underlying reason for the constantly widening gap between urban and rural areas. To end this, these obstacles as the impeding factors must be eliminated in order to carry on the primary mission for integration reforms while keeping in mind the goal of the *Decision* released during the Third Plenary Session of the 18th CPC Central Committee.

As land is an important production factor, we should also allow market forces to play their role in the process of allocating land resources. Different from other factors, land is associated with another issue of use regulation. Turning arable land into construction land must conform to construction planning and go through relevant legal procedures. The *Decision* of the Third Plenary Session of the 17th CPC Central Committee also stated explicitly that rural land compensation can be carried out only within the provincial regions. However, up until now this has only gone through the pilot phase in a few counties. Based on the implementation opinion on rural reforms issued by the General Office of the CPC Central Committee last year, "we should improve and expand the land compensation for urban and rural construction lands as well as the pilot project for "land ticket." We should also exemplify Chongqing's experience in developing a "land ticket" market. In Chongqing farmers are allowed to share the differential rent of urban land by giving up their homesteads faraway from cities in the municipal land ticket market. Moreover, we can properly deal with the potential problem of compensation by establishing third-party land quality evaluation agencies for land quality supervision. If we can set up a system of free and equal exchange of urban and rural factors for their reasonable allocation, it will be completely possible to ensure that the per capita income of farmers within central China and those within the plains and hilly regions of western China catch up with that of those in coastal areas within 5–10 years.

33.5 Three Approaches to Accelerate Reform and Development of Urban-Rural Integration

To accelerate this development process of urban-rural integration, we must facilitate agricultural modernization, build a new countryside and integrate rural migrant workers in a consolidated and simultaneous manner. The State Council requires that focus be set on three pressing tasks that affect 100 million people by helping rural migrants enjoy resident status in cities and towns all across eastern China, elevate he lifestyles of 100 million rural migrant workers in their hometowns within the central and western Chinese cities and provide 100 million people living in rundown areas in cities with decent housing. The three matters are mutually containing and influencing. Agricultural modernization can therefore further unleash the potential of the rural workforce, improve industrial agricultural development and boost water conservancy. A new countryside can improve the environment for production and local lifestyle and the development of the construction material industry. The integration of migrant workers can thus help more than 400 million people fulfill the dream of family reunions. Handling matters properly requires reformation of the rural land system. By issuing certificates of rights for rural land, we will encourage the concentration of contracted land management rights in cooperatives, agricultural companies and family farms, thus creating favorable conditions for expanding the scale of land management and advancing intensive and modernized agricultural development. If farmers covered by the urban household registration system leave their homesteads, it will not only meet the cities' demand for more construction land but also add some arable land, thus facilitating the building of new countryside and integration of rural migrant workers. Some wonder whether the rural land system reform would challenge the arable land minimum of 1.8 billion mu. According to the history of all countries in the world, arable land has all been expanding during the process of urbanization. Rural homesteads nationwide occupy an area of 170,000 km^2, about 250 million mu. The construction land for each rural resident is more than three times that for each urban resident. With a decrease in the rural population and an increase in the urban population, we can implement a policy that governs the rural land compensation for urban and rural construction lands. In doing so, the area of our arable land will likely increase by over 100 mu. Promoting such reforms in a systemic and holistic manner will therefore stimulate an enormous demand potential, give a strong boost to our economic growth in the next decade and beyond, as a result narrowing the gap between urban and rural development. Eventually, China will transcend the middle-income trap and join the ranks of high-income countries by realizing over 12,000 dollar of per capita GDP come 2022. Meanwhile, the year 2021 marks the centenary of the founding of the CPC. It is therefore our Party's greatest contribution to humanity having spent a century turning a semi-feudal and semi-colonial country into a high-income one.

Chapter 34
Drawing upon the Experience and Lessons of the Netherlands and Japan to Accelerate Agricultural Modernization

There is an urgent need to build a moderately prosperous society in all respects by 2020 and create necessary conditions for overcoming a potential middle-income trap. This will help us establish labor intensive and modernized industries across all sectors and turn agriculture into an internationally competitive industry, while increasing productivity in order to boost the country's social progress index and elevate rural per capita income to equal that of urban centers. Thanks to China's rapid industrialization and urbanization that began in 1978, all the necessary material conditions have been put in place to accelerate agricultural modernization. As a result, our economic and social development is able to provide better job opportunities for the surplus agricultural labor and redeploy them to other sectors. What's more, we have a strong supply of agricultural capacity to increase production and boost our capital sum. Therefore what we really need is a clear management system. To expedite this process, it is therefore necessary to put into consideration realities of China and draw upon the experiences from other countries. The Netherlands and Japan for example, have adopted different paths that have led to positive and negative outcomes respectively. It therefore is crucial that we draw upon their respective experiences when making comparisons, considerations and references.

Speech at a Workshop on Accelerating Agricultural Modernization sponsored by the China Moderately Prosperous Society Association on April 23, 2016.

X. Zheng, *China's 40 Years of Economic Reform and Development*,
https://doi.org/10.1007/978-981-13-2727-8_34

34.1 The Dutch Agriculture for Instance Focuses on Large-Scale Production Incorporating Various Social Sectors with Cooperatives as Major Players, While the Japanese Agriculture Prioritizes Small Production, with Farming Households as the Major Players

It's important to note that even though the Netherlands is a global agricultural giant, the country does not have favorable conditions for agricultural development. Its climate is gloomy, cold and humid with limited lighting hours. The per capita arable land is only 1.3 mu and its arable land covers just 27%. Meanwhile 60% of its population lives below sea level. The survival of their arable land is only thanks to a concrete 2400 km-dam built by the country's forefathers. As a result, Dutch people highly cherish their land and focus on increasing yields. Among the 1.9 million hectares of farmland, 57% is used for agriculture and horticulture while 40% is covered by grasslands.

The 250,000-person agricultural labor force runs 73,000 farms, of which 18,900 are dairy cattle farms, 16,800 livestock farms and 11,100 cultivation farms. The country also put in place a management system integrating plantation, livestock breeding, processing and sales. Families are the major players in planting and breeding stages, while cooperatives are more involved in the processing and sale. Each family can choose to participate in one or more cooperatives depending on their plant or breed varieties. Globally, Dutch dairy products are well renowned. Families play a major role in raising dairy cattle and participate in cooperatives for dairy products. In addition to purchasing milk from family owned dairy farms, cooperatives also distribute dividends to their members in line with individual shares and management level. With a common goal, cooperatives and their members share the same commercial brands and safeguard the quality and credit of the products. Meanwhile most farmers opt for tulips as their core product probably because Floriculture is considered very lucrative; and because this type of farming also deals with work distribution, some families have stuck to planting the same variety for decades. Flower cooperatives composed of over 3000 farmers have also established the biggest flower wholesale market in the world, which covers a total area of about 12 football pitches. Every day at the markets, products start to be auctioned off at 5 a.m. and by 9 a.m. they are already being sold at retail stores all across Europe. Flower sales account for 80% of the total European market. It is therefore due to agriculture integrating labor distribution and natural processes and having a highly organized industry that has become the major driving force behind the Netherland's global competitiveness.

Japan on the other hand has over two million major players in agricultural management whereby basically, rural households independently conduct production activities in a scattered and small-scale manner. Rural households also form funding cooperation with each other, although generally speaking, Japan's agriculture has been suffering from an inadequate workforce and relatively low level of organization. Consequently, this has led to Japan losing its agricultural competitiveness in the global arena. For instance, a kilo of local Japanese rice costs a staggering 100 yuan which screams premium price for its citizens and that's one of the reasons why the country is considered the largest importer of farm produce in the world.

34.2 Back to the Netherlands, That's Why the Country's Agricultural Industry Is Considered Highly Lucrative Whereas that of Japan Can Barely Survive Minus Government Subsidies

Large-scale agriculture involving various social sectors based on the distribution of labor has thus increased productivity and economic benefits for the Netherlands. The rural labor force accounts for 2% of the total social workforce, while the agricultural added value stands at 4% of the total GDP and agriculture makes up 25% of the total exports. As the per capita agricultural output value of the labor force has exceeded 40,000 € and exports per labor force reached 33,000 $, labor productivity and farmers' income within the primary industry have both outperformed those within the secondary and tertiary Industries. In the Netherlands, farming is considered a truly decent job; hence agriculture has become a pillar industry for the economy.

In Japan, however, agriculture has become a heavy burden for the economy. In 2014, the agricultural added value stood at 6 trillion yen, while government subsidies also accounted for 6 trillion yen, meaning no profits were made from the over 2 million major agricultural players in the entire year. Luckily, Japan has a strong industrial profitability and a small rural population; otherwise the government would be unable to afford the subsidization.

34.3 While the Netherlands Demands High Quality from Its Agricultural Workforce, Japan's Agriculture Has Been Reduced to an Aging Industry

As a resource-, knowledge- and technology-intensive industry, the Dutch agriculture boasts cutting edge technologies in the breeding and cultivation of flowers and vegetables, breeding and reproduction of dairy and meat cattle varieties, as well as in food processing equipment. High standards in the quality of labor for agricultural production and management have also been formulated. Only those individuals with certificates otherwise known as "green certificates" from a recognized agricultural university are permitted to engage in farming activities. Meanwhile those without green certificates will be denied the right of management and the right to inherit family-owned private land. The national agricultural education system is therefore divided into three tiers. First is the junior level aimed at producing technical workers, then the secondary level for agronomists and finally the senior level for researchers. Farm operations and management are two basic skills that all agricultural employees must learn. The improved education system and the strict qualification management system have enabled farmers to be highly skilled and provided human resource a guarantee for agriculture to become an industry that holds a global competitive edge.

In 2015, the Japanese agricultural sector employed 2.09 million people at an average age of 65.8. Unfortunately As the population gets older and the elderly retire, the younger generation has been reluctant to take over farming. Consequently, the agricultural workforce has reduced by 20% over the past half decade. The country's rural work force only accounted for 4%, while that of the agricultural added value in GDP was only 1%. Due to this labor shortage in the agricultural industry, 424,000 hectares of arable land have since been abandoned. The decline in Japan's agricultural activities has thus been in sharp contrast with that of the Netherlands'.

34.4 While the Netherlands Is Devoted to Developing High Value-Added Exports, Japan Is Trying Its Utmost to Protect Its Farm Produce Market

With a small territory, the Netherlands has only 1.6% of our arable land and 0.1% of our agricultural workforce. In 2015, Dutch agricultural exports reached a value of US$82.4 billion and since 1989, the country's net export volume has been ranked second globally, only behind the US even though it imports some foods and feeds to meet demands for the developing domestic food and livestock industries. Based on its basic national conditions for scarce per capita land resources, the Netherlands only imports agricultural products that require significant land masses and water resources. These resources are then turned into those that are labor-, technology- and knowledge-intensive for exporting, after their transformation and appreciation. In doing so, the economic benefit has been enhanced. To achieve this felt presence for the country's agricultural products in the international markets, the Netherlands invited American and European quality supervision experts to help set up its own quality standards. With much stricter standards than those set for international markets, the country has kept practicing strict supervision and management, which has helped gain the trust of foreign consumers.

In contrast, due to a lack of international agricultural competitiveness, Japan has erected various kinds of barriers for farm produce imports in order to protect its domestic agricultural products. Closing the market has thus led to backwardness. At present, Japan's food self-sufficiency rate stands at only 39%. Due to the basic demand for agricultural products, the country therefore still has to rely on imports whose imports share keeps increasing. According to the evaluation of agricultural competitiveness by relevant international institutions, the index for the Netherlands was 0.261, while that for Japan was −0.914. Therefore it's safe to say Japan's agriculture has turned out to be a classic representation of failure.

What inspirations can we acquire from the lessons of the Netherlands and Japan? First, it is necessary to adopt the path of large-scale production involving all social sectors with cooperatives as the main management entities based on household land contracting because from this Dutch experience, a rural cooperative development strategy is vital to achieving what one single family cannot do. From integrating production, processing and selling and enabling farmers to share the benefits out of three links of planting and breeding, deep processing and process marketing; increasing production efficiency by adopting advanced S&T and large agricultural machinery; establishing and protecting farm produce brands and improving credibility and market share; to incorporating small-scale rural households into specialized production systems involving all social sectors for shared benefits and cooperatives can also have various forms. Therefore, joint stock partnerships, land pooling as well as business operations could equally benefit Chinese farmers. Meanwhile by setting up a modern property rights system and a contribution-based distribution system, cooperatives can also avoid egalitarianism. Second, it is necessary to attract a high-quality labor force for agricultural management. This means developing intensive and highly efficient agricultural systems through transfer of land management rights. In doing so, those dedicated to agricultural management can earn a much better income compared with those seeking jobs in cities. Currently, our rural workforce is facing an aging population trend, similar to that of Japan hence the need to pay high attention to that. Third, it is necessary to strengthen agricultural research and technical training systems, cultivate new varieties of agricultural products and work to ensure that the rural labor force masters advanced, farming technologies, feeding and processing. Simply relying on the guidance of agricultural technicians is not enough; instead, we must ensure that farmers are equipped with cutting edge technologies and relevant skill sets. Fourth, it is necessary to proactively expand agricultural exports and establish open agriculture initiatives. Our agricultural workforce used to be 900 times more than that of the Netherlands but in 2015, China's imports and exports from agriculture stood at US$187. 56 billion, of which exports accounted for US$70.68 billion, US$11.7 billion less than the Netherlands, and imports US$116.88 billion with a deficit of US$46.2 billion. Therefore while we try to learn from the Netherlands, we should also take advantage of our rich labor resources and endeavor to expand our exports. By exporting labor-, technology- and knowledge-intensive agricultural products and importing some resource-intensive ones, and tapping the full potential of our rich labor resources to offset the effects of our land can in return force us to increase agricultural productivity and gain comparative benefits from foreign trade.

Chapter 35
Urban-Rural Integration Is the Greatest New Driver for Growth

Having experienced over 30 years of rapid growth, China's economy has been plagued by new challenges, of which the most outstanding ones are overcapacity, a downward economic growth and a lack of momentum. Therefore, how to form new growth engines with a sustainable and healthy development through further reforms is the most pressing issue in both theoretical and policy terms.

35.1 Economic Restructuring Is the Driver of New Development

Over the long course of economic development, the inevitable economic restructuring could constantly trigger a new momentum for economic growth. If the ossified system impeding the much needed restructuring cannot induce a new development momentum, economic growth could potentially slow down and even stagnate. The key to economic miracles since the previous reforms has been three major restructuring campaigns of continuous transformation.

The first restructuring was the household contract responsibility system and the ensuing rural township enterprise emergence which drove the economic expansion in the 1980s. As the reform stimulated an enormous potential for hundreds of millions of farmers in developing the economy and eradicating poverty, rural productivity and agricultural yields increased dramatically. Not forgetting the extreme lack of industrial consumer goods that forced us to spend more than ten years putting an end to the shortage economy that was haunting us for decades by developing rural township enterprises and meeting market demands. The restructuring was characterized by the markedly increased supply of products within the agricultural sector. Meanwhile the light and textile industry also rapidly increased the share of its final

This article originally appeared in *Study Times*, December 15, 2016.

X. Zheng, *China's 40 Years of Economic Reform and Development*,
https://doi.org/10.1007/978-981-13-2727-8_35

consumption goods in gross social products, which changed the long-term distortion of emphasizing heavy industry and despising light industries while lagging agricultural development and unleashing enormous development potential.

This has since not only met market demands, but also driven a fast economic growth.

The second restructuring was about the macro management system reforms and revitalization of four pillar industries, with SOE reform at the core, leading to an economic expansion in the 1990s. In 1993, the 14th NPC put forward its goal for reformations in establishing a socialist market economy system while the Third Plenary Session of the 14th NPC formulated specific plans. The reforms for building this type of a system with enterprises as major players stimulated the vitality of the economy. Meanwhile, the Ninth Five-Year Plan stipulated that we revitalize four pillar industries that included electronic machineries, oil and chemical industries, auto making and construction industries to quickly up their shares in the economy from 8% to over 25%. This in turn improved living standards, and lowered the level of reliance on, electronic machinery exports and oil and chemical industry products. In the end, shares for heavy industries in the industrial structure increased from around 50% to more than 70%, and the fast development of this sector became a major engine behind the country's economic growth.

The third restructuring was about the economy that was experiencing a golden decade with a double-digit growth, and issuing long-term construction bonds for infrastructure building within the first ten years of the new century. Within a short period of time within the first decade of this century, China's expressway and hi-speed railway mileage both took the No. 1 spot globally. Higher education enrolment increased by more than ten times, and the country's global economic aggregate rose from sixth to second place, laying a solid foundation for a sustained economic growth.

Since then, practice has proven that we face different missions and needs for restructuring at different stages of our economic development. Therefore the only way to sustain a healthy economic development is to, act in line with set rules and intrinsic requirements for economic development, break through conventional thinking and obstacles, create a sound policy ecosystem for restructuring and direct all social capital toward restructuring.

35.2 How Urban-Rural Integration Can Gain Momentum

In 2015, China's per capita GDP reached US$8,000. That is to say that there is still a large disparity before the country can join the ranks of high-income countries that boast 12,000 $ of per capita income keeping in mind that many countries have hovered around this threshold, but still failed to avoid the middle-income trap. Whether China can join the ranks of the developed nations is a test to the governance of the CPC and the vitality of the socialist market economy system with Chinese characteristics. Judging from an international experience, we can see that those countries that have stepped into the ranks of high-income countries have one thing in common; their successes in dealing with the problem of urban-rural dual structure thereby attaining a roughly equal labor productivity within the primary, secondary and tertiary industries and drawing close the income between urban and rural dwellers. The reason why those countries were bogged down in the middle-income trap was that for a long time, they were not able to narrow the urban-rural gap. At present, there are many conflicts facing our economic and social development, among which the large urban-rural development disparity is the most outstanding. In turn this challenge determines and affects other conflicts. Moreover, the nature of regional gaps is a manifestation of a developmental disparity between the urban and rural areas. For example, there is almost no gap between urban areas in the central, western and eastern China but there is indeed a conspicuous gap between rural areas within these three regions. The income ratio for urban residents to rural residents in the country is 2.7:1, and that in Zhejiang for example stands at 1.7:1. In the face of such an enormous urban-rural development gap nationwide, it is therefore difficult for China to step into the ranks of high-income countries.

On April 30, 2015, in a significant urban-rural integration speech delivered during the collective learning held at the Political Bureau of the CPC Central Committee, General Secretary, Xi Jinping, encouraged leaders to strive and realize, equal fundamental rights and interests, equal basic public services and balanced income between urban and rural residents, reasonable allocation of urban and rural factors and the integration of industrial development in all regions of the country. This speech should serve as an important reminder and be a guiding principle in facilitating the much talked about urban-rural integration. To promote the reforms for this integration, we should focus on agricultural modernization, building of a new countryside and integrating rural migrant workers.

At the same time, it is crucial to point out that low labor productivity and the lack of international competitiveness are the most outstanding issues facing our agricultural sector. One of the most pressing tasks for modernizing this industry calls for increasing supply efficiency by developing large-scale intensive and specialized big agriculture, incorporating all social sectors. The resulting strong demand for agricultural means of production and service industry will thereby drive the development of the service industry including those dealing in agricultural machinery and chemical engineering. Moreover, modernization can lead to a strong demand for the development of water conservancy, which could in turn pull investment toward such projects.

So far we have made tremendous achievements in building a new countryside, but there is still a big gap between urban and rural areas that remain, especially in areas of infrastructure and public service. In light of village renovations and new-type community constructions, greater input in rural infrastructure building can stimulate a strong demand for the construction material industry and gradually turn the countryside into a more attractive, more livable and more desirable place for all people.

Nationwide, there are an estimated 280 million rural migrant workers, 60 million left-behind children, 43 million left-behind women, and 40 million old people. Sadly, some 413 million people are not living with their family members. That's why a family reunion is not only a rural migrant worker's dream, it is also a requirement that can boost their morale and nurture them into becoming high-quality teams of industrial workers. Therefore providing rural migrant workers with government-subsidized housing plus giving them access to public services and increasing the urbanization rate of populations under household registration systems will reduce the pressure on demand for urban housing, infrastructure and public service and become a strong engine in boosting economic growth.

In addition to urban-rural integration, China still needs to show some new momentum. The country suffers from a supply shortage of public goods. By promoting, the PPP model, adopting fiscal investments and loans, policy-backed financial institutions and guide bank loans and social investment, we can have massive space in the developing of transport, communication, environmental protection, education, health care, municipal administration, old age care, culture and tourism, and so on. It's only by encouraging the development of a third industry through a comprehensive advanced tax system for replacing business tax with value-added tax, can we be able to sustain a sound momentum for fast development of the industry. We are working on facilitating an industrial upgrading through innovation methods by implementing mass entrepreneurship and innovation policies. Comparatively speaking, urban-rural integration is no doubt the greatest new momentum, while urban-rural restructuring is a historic requirement for the new stage of economic development. While the previous three rounds of restructuring since the reforms have injected new momentum into economic development in a timely manner, the upcoming round with urban-rural restructuring at its core will provide a much anticipated momentum for a sustained and healthy economic development within the next decade.

35.3 Focusing on Reforms for Urban-Rural Integration Is the Only Way by Which to Release a Great New Momentum

Urban-rural restructuring requires reforms for further advancement. As President Xi Jinping recently noted, the reform process "must be specifically targeted to meet the requirements of development, satisfy the demands of the basic levels, and fulfill the desires of the Chinese people." Promoting reforms for urban-rural integration is exactly the most significant measure that will satisfy the needs of economic development and help accommodate the concerns of the public. According to a *Decision* adopted by the Third Plenary Session of the 18th Central Committee of the Communist Party of China, priorities for promoting the reform on urban-rural integration should include the following:

The first focus is to confirm rural households' legal person property rights for their land. However, how public ownership for rural land can be harmonized with the market economy is a major question to be answered before establishing a socialist market economy. The Third Plenary Session of the 14th CPC Central Committee also required that SOEs be endowed with legal personal property rights to their state-owned assets and become independently managed entities, which has helped realize the integration between the national and market economies. Similarly, if the rural households can also be endowed with the same rights for contracted land and homesteads, the usufruct of land will become commodities that can be transferred and integrated without changing the public land ownership, which in turn can pave way for activating the decisive role of market forces in land resource allocation. Therefore, we should issue certificates to confirm rural households' rights for contracted lands and homesteads. Once entitled, rural households can then gain property income from transferring those rights and can choose to either manage their lands themselves or transfer their management rights as per the opportunity costs. This would create proper conditions for the concentration of land management rights for cooperatives, agricultural companies and farming professionals. It will also aid in developing large-scale operations. In addition to this, rural migrant workers can attain property income from their idle homesteads and houses in rural areas through market trading. This in turn would enable an effective market mechanism for, an intensive and economical use of lands designated for construction purposes and optimized land allocation processes.

The second focus for the reforms is the establishment of a market of land for construction purposes that unifies both urban and rural areas. This year, the State Council issued Document No. 8, titled *Guidelines on Facilitating New Urbanization*, which required a thorough implementation the top policy when matching the urban construction land increase and rural construction land decrease. This is a clear specification for carrying forward philosophies of the Third Plenary Session of the 18th NPC when reforming the land system in rural areas. As a significant proportion of the labor force is set to transition from simply agriculture to second and tertiary industries in the course of industrialization and urbanization, a large population will move from rural areas to cities. This will inevitably be followed by an increase in urban construction land and a decrease of rural construction land. In the meantime, due to the more intensive use of land in urban areas, the population per unit of construction land in urban areas is more than three times that of rural areas. This will then result in an economical use of construction land and increase of arable land. According to estimates, homesteads sit on a 250 million mu of land, nationwide. Therefore if these homesteads and houses can become commodities, more than 50% of rural construction land will be reduced. The experience of all developed countries has proven that arable land expands due to urbanization. Thus policy regarding the adjustment of urban and rural construction land should be compatible with the greatest urbanization process in human history that China is experiencing. Meanwhile over the course of the past 30 years, the country's workforce has been flowing all across the country with coastal areas absorbing the majority of the rural surplus labor force from middle and western China. Therefore it is only through establishing a unified national urban-rural market of land for construction purposes, and adjusting such land among all the urban and rural areas in the country, can the idle land resulting from the rural population decrease to meet the demands of the new urban land for construction purposes, and curb the skyrocketing prices for real estate. If property revenue from rural land for construction purposes is used for purchasing houses in cities, real state will realize a transfer in space and form of value, alongside the population flow. Only in doing so can the adjustment of production relations meet the demands of productivity development and avoid impeding this process. It is, therefore, inevitable and urgent that we build a market of land for construction purposes featuring urban-rural integration. What Chongqing tried in developing the land ticket market is commendable. If its experience can be copied all across the country, enormous macroeconomic and social benefits are bound to be made.

The third focus of the reform is to remove existing barriers between the urban and rural capital markets. As various production factors in cities have long been market-oriented while the production factors in rural areas especially those regarding land and houses have not been fully liberalized, marketized or even half-marketized, the long-term difference has as a result caused a siphon where rural land, its labor force and capital have constantly been flowing into cities. Meanwhile urban resources have failed to equally enter rural areas. As a result, this long-term mono-directional capital market has been the fundamental reason for the constantly widening gap between urban and rural development. One salient phenomenon is the growth for big surplus urban capital and the rising urban real estate prices on one hand, and the severe rural capital shortage and unimaginably low rural real estate prices on the other hand. If contracting, right to land, the right to use homesteads and the right to management of the profitable collective land for construction can be pledged, and 20 trillion yuan in bank loans and social capital be leveraged for agricultural modernization, building of a new countryside and the integration of rural migrant workers achieved within the 13th Five-Year Plan period, rural areas could experience dramatic changes. This however will not only guarantee the building of a moderately prosperous society in all respects by 2020, but will also help avoid falling into the middle-income trap and join the ranks of high-income countries by 2022.

The fourth focus of the reform is to provide farmers granted urban residency with access to public services equal to those for urban residents. In recent years, more than three million farmers have been registered as permanent urban residents in Chongqing. How was this achieved? The city government awarded these rural dwellers a settling-in allowance, as a compensation for handing over their homesteads, on top of other five "gifts," namely, the urban public services for elderly care, medical care, housing, the entry to urban kindergartens and schools, and so on. Chongqing has thus worked so fruitfully on the integration of its rural migrant workers, even though it is a very mountainous city in western China and not so rich. Meanwhile in coastal cities; considered to be much wealthier than those located in the western region, rural migrant workers have contributed a great deal to the local economic development. It therefore makes sense for the latter to allocate funds for the integration of its rural migrant workers instead of leaving the burden of providing them with housing and social security services to their hometowns. To gain competitiveness, coastal cities must also have a high-quality stable team of industrial workers by retaining these migrant workers as a requirement for a sustainable local economic development.

35.4 Correcting Misunderstandings to Accelerate Urban-Rural Integration

The Third Plenary Session of the 18th CPC Central Committee put forward the theories and deployment on the reform and development of urban-rural integration. The key was to ensure consistency in the thinking of officials at various levels keeping in mind the philosophies of the *Decision* and its full implementation. At present, it is therefore necessary to correct some misunderstandings.

We must eliminate the misconception that the separation of two rights in rural areas is land privatization. On the contrary, we have established an effective way to implement public land ownership, which can be integrated within the market economy to better adhere to ownership of rural land. By, confirming rural households' legal personal property rights to land and separating ownership, contracting rights and management rights to arable land, rural households can gain property income from transferring their management rights with contracting right to land. Some rural areas in central China have in fact been quite creative in making the annual transfer fees for each mu of land by equating the transaction to the market price of 500 kg of wheat. The right to use homesteads could therefore be transferred at a cost of around 200,000 yuan per mu, which was the trading price in Chongqing. In this case, it thus is the usufruct instead of the ownership that will be transferred, so public ownership of land remains unchanged.

We must eliminate any misunderstandings that urban capital flowing into rural areas is looting of rural resources; because it's only by confirming the marketization status of the rural resources that farmers can share the property income from real estate in the course of urbanization. In line with market economy rules, production factors always concentrate in the most profitable areas. It is therefore only after having the value of exchange can rural production factors attract capital. Capital is the pioneer of factor flow. Once capital starts to flow into rural areas, other production factors will subsequently flock into rural areas as well, in turn facilitating rural economic and social progress.

We must also eliminate the misunderstandings that the urban-rural integration will challenge the minimum 1.8 billion mu of arable land. On the contrary, implementing the policy of linking urban construction land increase to the rural construction land decrease can reduce wastage of rural homesteads. From experience, at least 40% of vacated homesteads can be used to increase arable land. As for the issue of rural land compensation, we could easily solve it by establishing a system of arable land quality supervision.

We must finally eliminate the misconception that the process of resolving issues affecting agriculture, rural areas and farmers mainly relies on fiscal input. On the contrary, it's only by setting up a market mechanism of urban-rural integration and attracting a great deal of social capital and bank loans, can we rapidly change the underdeveloped rural and agricultural landscape. The national finance has already made its utmost in dealing with issues of agriculture, rural areas and farmers, as the expenditure in those areas accounts for over 10% of total fiscal expenditures. We therefore should change the fiscal funding for these areas from depending on subsidies to that of guidance in order to leverage and direct more social funds and bank loans toward agriculture and rural development.

Chapter 36
Regarding Attractive Towns as the Breakthrough for Urban-Rural Integration

On December 12 last year, the National Development and Reform Commission, China Development Bank, China Everbright Bank, China Enterprise Confederation, China Enterprise Directors Association, and China Urban-townization Promotion Council jointly issued the *Notice on Advancing Characteristic Towns through Implementing the Enterprise-Township Cooperation Project*. In line with President Xi Jinping's important instructions on the development of characteristic towns, the notice calls upon enterprises, public institutions, and local governments to work together to create attractive towns and stresses that the market play a guiding role and encourages social organizations and capital to get involved. The healthy expansion of attractive towns in line with the notice is needed to promote new urbanization and make a breakthrough in the realization of urban-rural integration. Building charming and livable small attractive towns that possess industries and the functions of cities is of great strategic significance to optimizing urban planning and structure, driving rural development, improving specialization and involvement of social sectors, enhancing international competitiveness, and building a moderately prosperous society in all respects by 2020.

China is currently experiencing rapid industrialization and urbanization. Urbanization is a major driving force of economic growth. With rapid industrialization, the urbanization level has been elevated markedly over the 38 years since the start of reform. In 2015, the urbanization rate stood at 56.1%. The mushrooming of cities of all sizes has played a critical role in pooling production factors and forming modern productivity, becoming an important driver of development. Urbanization, to a large extent, forms naturally in the course of development. However, this course has brought about some new issues that need to be addressed:

First, some fast growing big cities and megacities suffer from traffic problems, air pollution, and high home prices, which constrain the sustainable development of cities.

This article originally appeared in *Economic Daily*, November 10, 2016.

X. Zheng, *China's 40 Years of Economic Reform and Development*,
https://doi.org/10.1007/978-981-13-2727-8_36

Second, a dual structure between the permanent population and the registered population has formed. Its formation has been detrimental to cultivating a stable and skilled industrial workforce and has led to inequalities between the two groups of residents.

Third, urban structure is unreasonable. There is not enough cities in total and big and mega cities attract the bulk of enterprises and talent at the expense of small and medium-sized cities and especially small towns, which struggle to attract and retain talent. This is especially true in central and western China. Within city clusters, administrative divisions often distort resource allocation. In addition, bustling cities are usually surrounded by backward villages, creating an enormous economic development gap.

Building attractive towns can deal with the disadvantages of urbanization. Compared with big cities, towns have the following advantages:

First, towns push forward urban-rural integration. The development of attractive towns on the outskirts can drive the development of rural infrastructure and public services in surrounding areas, provide jobs, facilitate the integration between urban and rural industries, and spread urban civilization. This will ultimately narrow the development gap and coordinate the development between urban and rural areas.

Second, towns improve the quality of life for citizens. China wants towns to provide a charming and comfortable living environment as well as quality education and health care services. China also wants them to be a place where people can breathe clean air without noise pollution. Being able to provide more job opportunities is top on the agenda of small towns, where most people can live closer to their homes. In addition, housing is relatively cheaper. The end result is that people living and working in towns can enjoy higher living quality than in cities.

Third, towns put in place complete and efficient industrial chains. By focusing on one type of product or service, attractive towns can form complete industrial chains that bring together R&D, production, logistics, and marketing. This highly specialized distribution of work lowers costs, improves efficiency, and enhances international competitiveness. Furthermore, a well-established service system and sound development environment only need to rely on a single enterprise, university, hospital, research institute, or bank.

Fourth, towns enhance the overall competitiveness of city clusters. A development model featuring coordination between cities of all sizes can be put in place. With major cities as the centers, the complementarily between cities can improve the overall innovation capacity and development vitality of the city clusters, which in turn can drive S&T growth and cultural progress for the country and the world at large.

Fifth, towns improve economic momentum. A number of enterprises and public institutions in downtown areas can seek development opportunities in attractive towns, which will not only allow them to expand their space of development but also boost the demand for infrastructure, public services, and factories. This will drive economic growth.

In light of the experience of developed countries, this model of development has become an important part of urbanization. And living in these towns has become the pursuit of many people. In Germany, the urbanization rate is over 90%, but 70% of its population live in small towns. The famous Volkswagen, Mercedes-Benz, and Housing Deposit Bank brands are all separately located in small towns. In the US, people and industries first concentrated in cities and then started to spread to the surrounding areas. In the outskirts of mega cities like New York, there are many attractive towns, such as the hedge fund town in Greenwich, CT, and the concentration of venture capital companies near Stanford University. These towns not only create a unique environment, but also play an important role in global economic growth. In countries like France and Switzerland, attractive towns have also become beautiful sceneries.

China has also achieved some successes in developing attractive towns. Over the 30-plus years since reform, China's textile industry has gradually moved from major cities to small towns, mainly three towns: Heqiao Town in Shaoxing, Zhejiang, which specializes in chemical fiber textile printing and dyeing; Xinqiao Town in Jiangyin, Jiangsu, which specializes in wool textile; and Weiqiao Town in Zouping, Shandong, which specializes in cotton textile. Their production scale, technical level, and product variety are unmatched in the world. Datang Town in Zhuji, Zhejiang, for instance, produces more than half of the world's socks. And a number of small towns specializing in tourism, S&T, finance, commerce, industry, and culture have emerged and are thriving. Various specialized production factors are concentrated in these small towns, making them competitive across the nation and even the world. Since reform, Zhejiang has constructed 78 attractive towns for the incubation of research findings, finance, online stores, silk, and fashion. The towns are bound to further enhance the quality and international competitiveness of Zhejiang's massive economy.

Thanks to years of effort, China has built the largest highway network, high-speed railway network, and communication network in the world. This has allowed personnel and materials to flow rapidly on a massive scale between urban and rural areas and among cities. The modern urban clusters that have emerged in the Yangtze River Delta and Pearl River Delta are playing a critical role in the global economy. New development space needs to be opened for advancing mass entrepreneurship and innovation. Having built strong capacity in manufacturing, China must act fast to open up new market opportunities. From a holistic perspective, China has mature conditions for adjusting the structure and layout of urbanization and accelerating the development of attractive towns.

There are several areas to which China should pay attention:

One, layout and overall planning should be meticulous. Attractive towns should be located within a one-hour radius of major urban areas, so as to take advantage of the booming development of secondary and tertiary industries in those cities. All this will be conducive to forming clusters and their surrounding areas. Situated far away from major cities, these small towns must first improve their infrastructure, including transport, and feasibility studies and overall planning need to be done well for their development. Moreover, China needs to avoid "blind development", which means the plan outlines need to be reviewed by experts and third parties.

Two, it is important to highlight the uniqueness and advantages of small towns. It is necessary to ground their development in reality and attract enterprises and research institutes, and it is important that the small towns strive to be the best in their specialization through work distribution and coordination, technical innovation, and management innovation. Each town must develop in its own unique way and according to its own strengths. Industries, products, and enterprises need to be chosen according to their own strengths. Attractive towns should get the support and space needed to create new competitive advantages.

Three, China should consider urban-rural integration and a flexible approach to land management. As urban and rural areas integrate, residents in small towns will be given equal access to various fundamental rights and interests and public services. To meet the demand of labor mobility nationwide, China will need to establish a nationally unified land ticket system similar to the one in Chongqing, comprehensively address the tensions between increases in urban construction and decreases in rural construction, deepen reform of the rural land system, and allow farmers under the urban household registration system to transfer their land-use rights in order to gain property income. In other words, the allocation of land resources should be determined by the market.

Four, guidance and funding based on the public-private partnership (PPP) model are important. Using this model, China can attract private capital for the development of small towns. China will need to also support their development by encouraging policy-based finance, commercial loans, and various foundations and bonds. The property rights of individual persons should be allowed to be mortgaged to leverage bank loans and social capital for the development of the towns.

Five, finding the right town for the right enterprise or vice versa and demonstration projects for cooperation, including the implementation of the Enterprise-Township Cooperation Project and the development of attractive towns, require the support and involvement of enterprises and local governments. It is a shared hope that such projects will encourage more enterprises, universities, hospitals, banks, and research institutes to exit expensive and crowded cities and create their own beautiful environment and development space in small towns. In driving the development of towns and surrounding areas, China will need to alter the current trend of excessive concentration of resources in major cities and steer the country's urbanization in a new direction.

Part V
Innovation

Chapter 37
Innovation: The Key to Transforming the Growth Pattern

At present, China's economy is experiencing fast and steady growth. In order to maintain good development momentum, the country must transform its economic growth pattern and optimize and upgrade its industrial structure. Enhancing innovation capacity is the key. China must get various sectors on board and work toward breakthroughs in innovation.

37.1 Innovation Is the Key to Transforming the Economic Growth Pattern

Since 2003, China's economy has grown rapidly and has experienced high growth, low inflation, and high efficiency. In 2003, 2004, and the first half of this year, the GDP growth rate was maintained at a high level of 9.5%. During the same period, consumer prices increased by only 1.2, 3.9, and 2.3%, respectively, and China's fiscal revenue increased by 4.9, 21.4, and 14.6%, respectively. The profits of industrial enterprises above the designated size (annual sales over 5 million yuan) saw an increase of 44.1, 36.0, and 19.1%, respectively. Crop yields stopped falling and started rising and farmers' income increased markedly. Good sustainable macroeconomic development is a hard-won achievement.

However, there are some issues. The accelerated economic growth rate over the past two-plus years was, to a certain extent, a result of the excessively rapid growth of the steel, cement, electrolytic aluminum, and real estate. In other words, these industries contributed to the extensive growth pattern characterized by high input, high consumption, and high pollution. In the past two years, the total energy consumption increased by 15.3 and 15.2%, respectively, and the elasticity coefficient of energy demand has increased from the annual average of 0.21 from 1996 to 2002 to

---

This article originally appeared in *Qiushi*, Chinese edition, no. 8, 2005.

X. Zheng, *China's 40 Years of Economic Reform and Development*,
https://doi.org/10.1007/978-981-13-2727-8_37

1.61 and 1.60, respectively. The investment elasticity coefficient, namely the ratio of fixed-asset investment growth to GDP growth, increased from 1.44 times from 1996 to 2002 to 2.92 times and 2.72 times, respectively.

This shows that to realize the same level off rapid economic growth, greater energy and investment is needed. In 2004, China's GDP accounted for 4% of global GDP, but primary energy consumption accounted for 12%, fresh water 15%, aluminum oxide 25%, steel 28%, and cement 50%. The demand for important resources under that structure, especially iron ore and aluminum oxide, has far outstripped domestic supply, while excessive reliance on imports has been limited by the supply and transport capacity of the international market. Therefore, the unsustainability of extensive growth has become the most outstanding issue for the country.

When formulating the Ninth Five-Year Plan in 1995, the CPC Central Committee identified the transformation from an extensive growth pattern to an intensive one. Over the years, China has made progress but no breakthroughs in transforming its growth pattern. In particular, the extensive growth pattern has apparently returned in the recent past two years. The main reason is a lack of innovation in technological development. China has everything it needs for technology-intensive industries and products, including a market, funds, and labor, but due to a lack of technologies, the country is unable to start working on highly profitable investment projects. This means China can only rely on imports over the long run. However, domestically mature technologies at the low end of the industrial chain have become investment hot spots, thus a large number of low-level duplicates. Therefore, the lack of proprietary technologies and products is a major constraint for transforming the growth pattern and restructuring the economy.

To eliminate economic growth challenges and realize steady and rapid long-term growth, China must transform its growth pattern. The only way to totally get rid of the extensive growth pattern is to enhance innovation capacity, increase investments in Chinese technologies, the information industry, and other industries featuring high technology, good economic benefits, low material consumption, and low levels of pollution, and make full use of the labor force and encourage new industrialization. All in all, enhancing innovation capacity is the key to realizing steady and rapid economic growth and avoiding economic fluctuations.

37.2 Preparations for Realizing Innovation Are Done

China has already laid the groundwork for implementing the strategy of innovation, adding high-tech R&D inputs, and making technological progress contribute more to economic growth.

First, after over 20 years of economic reform, China's economic strength has been markedly enhanced. GDP has risen to seventh in the world and China ranks third in terms of the volume of imports and exports. Last year, central government revenue stood at 2.6 trillion yuan and total fixed-asset investments exceeded seven trillion yuan, adding to the inputs in technological development.

Second, over the past two-plus decades of reform, China has introduced a lot of advanced technologies and equipment. This has greatly narrowed the gap with advanced technologies from overseas. In each industry, Chin has technical equipment that is at least on par with international equipment of the same type.

Third, over the years China has cultivated a large number of talents. In state-owned enterprises and public institutions alone, there are 21.7 million technicians and 2.26 million scientists and engineers. And they have formed great research teams in all fields. Each year, S&T expenditures exceed 350 billion yuan.

Fourth, a number of outstanding enterprises that developed rapidly through innovation have emerged, proving that China is fully capable of carrying out technological innovation. Their successful experiences have enhanced Chinese enterprises' confidence in seeking development through innovation. For example:

From 1983 to present, the sales revenue of Haier Group has grown 70% annually on average. It went from being a small collectively-owned factory to a multinational home appliance maker with an annual sales volume of over 100 billion yuan. Technological development is an important reason behind the success of Haier. With 5% of sales revenue going into technological development, Haier boasts a strong S&T development team and owns over 3000 patents. Nowadays, the company creates more than two patents each day on average.

Huawei is leading global technological development in the communications industry, mainly as a result of technological innovation. This year, its sales revenue exceeded 70 billion yuan, of which US$5 billion were in export volume. Among the company's 23,000 employees, 13,000 of them are dedicated to technological development. Last year, the company invested 4.5 billion yuan in technological development, accounting for 10% of its sales volume.

Chery Holdings is a latecomer in the auto industry. The first car it sent to the market was developed by itself. However, it has not only occupied its market share in the fiercely competitive domestic market, but also set up two assembly plants in foreign countries. Moreover, over 10% of its sales revenue went to technological development, and the number of employees devoted to technological development account for 60% of the national auto industry.

There are numerous other examples. All successful enterprises and visionary entrepreneurs attach great importance to technological development and are willing to increase input in this area. If there could be 1000 such enterprises in China, the bottlenecks impeding resource utilization would be removed and the country would achieve stable, rapid growth.

37.3 Build an Innovation System Featuring Collaboration Between Academia and Industry

The lack of technology resources is currently the biggest bottleneck impeding economic development. Breaking requires investment in technology. According to the National Bureau of Statistics, 71% of the nation's big and medium-sized enterprises have not yet set up technological development departments, and two thirds of them have not launched relevant activities. In 2003, the enterprises' S&T expenditures accounted for only 1.52% of sales revenue, of which only 0.66% of that amount was spent on new product developments. Enterprises' technology R&D should not be lower than 3% of their sales revenue, at least according to international experience; otherwise, they will lose their competitive edge. In high-technology enterprises, the proportion should be even more—greater than 10%. Innovation based on the absorption and adaptation of foreign technologies is a shortcut to technological progress. Take for instance Japan and the Republic of Korea, both of which were introducing European and American technologies. The ratio of input for introducing technologies to that of absorbing and adapting innovation in those two countries was 1:5, while that for China was 1:0.07. Consequently, China continued the practice of introducing foreign technologies, but it took a long for the country to create proprietary technologies and products.

Chinese companies generally lacked the initiative to develop technologies because of institutional reasons. To change this situation, China needs to set up a diversified shareholding system as well as a modern corporate system and corresponding corporate governance structure. It is especially important to set up a system under which a board of directors is elected to represent shareholders and makes management decisions on behalf of the investors. Only in this way can managers increase inputs in technological development and keep an eye on the long-term development of the enterprise. At present, the technological development input of enterprises accounts for more than 50% of the nation's total input, but even this is still far from sufficient. Foreign experience has shown that enterprises' technological development input and staff should account for over 70%. All the big and medium-sized enterprises need to establish their own departments for technological development. There should be products under production that area waiting to enter the market and the R&D phase. S&T should be put on the top of enterprises' agendas, as it will determine their rise and fall.

China needs to allocate its research forces through collaboration between academia and industry in a reasonable manner. The research departments of science academies and universities are mainly devoted to basic and applied research, while enterprises are generally focused on the development of new products, techniques, and technologies. Once the market gets involved, technological development and applied research should shorten engineering application times as well as industrialization and technical outcomes, thus bridging the relationship between S&T and the economy.

Big enterprises should become the base of technological progress in their respective industries, but SMEs should play their roles in technological innovation, too. China needs to encourage application-oriented research institutes to partner with big enterprises. This will not only be conducive to enhancing the research capacity of the latter, but also to developing the former. At present, such institutes have made some achievements in providing technology services to enterprises, but their role in major industry-related R&D projects is minor. If this trend continues, those institutes could be driven out of the market. China should continue to reform ministry-affiliated research institutes and recognize the promise of big enterprises. China needs to leverage the strength of SMEs; that being their quick market response, and adopt favorable policies to encourage the development of tech-based SMEs, especially in the areas of software and parts and components. There needs to be a large number of specialized SMEs to make progress in technology, and many large enterprises have grown out of small enterprises.

In order to implement the nation's innovation strategy, China should incorporate original innovation, systemic integration, and innovation based on the assimilation and absorption of imported technologies. Recently, China has paid close attention to innovation based on introduced technologies. Experience has shown that compared with original innovation and systemic integration, innovation based on the assimilation and absorption of imported technologies can save a lot of time and money. For major equipment and engineering projects, China needs to adopt systemic integration for innovation and organize technicians for joint research projects in various fields. China also needs to encourage original innovation, get rid of impetuous attitudes and eagerness for instant benefits, uphold debate among different schools of thought, and create a good atmosphere for innovation.

37.4 Set the Stage for Innovation

Enhancing awareness of innovation and building an innovative country requires close coordination between government and enterprises. Efforts should be made to expedite the establishment and improvement of institutions for and policies and regulations on technological development input and innovation, which will guide enterprises in voluntarily seeking development through technological progress.

China needs to tax policies that encourage enterprises to spend more money pioneering technologies. In fact, China already has such policies, but efforts are inadequate, thresholds are high, and coverage is limited. The country's preferential tax policies mainly relate to direct tax reductions. In other words, they do not target R&D deductions, depreciation, investment allowance, tax deferral, and tax exemptions for fixed-asset investments in high-tech and new technology industries. The favorable taxation policies are targeted at enterprises and not at R&D activities. This may lead to abuse.

Once an enterprise is accredited as a high-tech or new technology enterprise, non-S&T benefits may also enjoy favorable treatment. Moreover, this may actually lead to a lack of favorable treatment. The reason for this is that a great deal of S&T activities in regular enterprises cannot easily enjoy favorable tax policies. Only the annual added 10% of the R&D input can, which is a very strict requirement. Consequently, only less than 14% of backbone enterprises can meet the requirement, and those that do enjoy favorable funding only enjoy 5.8% of what they should enjoy. The imported key parts and components enterprises' need for new technological development and domestic equipment manufacturing do not fully enjoy the favorable tariff and import value-added tax (VAT) policies, and therefore the competitiveness of domestic equipment is decreased, which has a dampening effect on the initiative for self-directed R&D. Compared with developed countries, China is still lagging behind in terms of the concreteness and coverage of favorable tax policies for self-directed R&D. Therefore, tax reform needs to be stepped up in order to put in place a system for innovation.

Efforts should be made to establish and improve entrepreneurship funds, risk investment, and the Growth Enterprise Market. A venture capital mechanism conducive to STI and the translation of research results into productivity is needed, and the country should try to attract a great deal of social funding for R&D and the translation of research findings. This work is still in the initial stages and the pace needs to be quickened. Drawing upon the experience of developed countries, China needs to attract foreign venture capital firms, cultivate talent devoted to risky investments, and gradually create an atmosphere for risky investments.

Efforts should also be made to encourage the application of new products and equipment through government purchasing. In the initial phase, the government should support and help Chinese products and equipment gradually development in terms of design and quality throughout the course of application. Government purchasing is an important policy in supporting new products and equipment, one which is widely adopted in the US for instance. According to the *Buy American Act*, taxpayer money should be used to support domestic enterprises whenever possible. China should learn from this American experience.

Major projects can serve as a way to transfer market technologies. China's huge market demand is an important resource. The country needs to attract foreign and domestic enterprises for joint design and joint production by using the nation's market resources and encourage the transferring of technologies to domestic enterprises. This approach has been adopted in the Ertan Hydropower Plant and Three Gorges Dam international bidding invitations for power equipment. The foreign enterprises coming to bid must align with domestic equipment manufacturers in the bidding and transferring of technologies to domestic enterprises. If domestic enterprises are sufficiently capable, they can be the major bidding entity in alliance with foreign enterprises that serve as technology supporters. This not only opens the Chinese market to foreign enterprises, but also improves domestic manufacturing technologies.

China needs to set up an S&T system to promote military-civil integration, so that technology can meet both military and civilian needs. Promoting integration between the two sectors is a successful approach to supporting industrial technology progress in the US for instance. The US high-tech industries leading the world today are mostly military technologies funded by the US government that have made their way to the civilian sector. For a long period of time, China has been copying the former USSR's research system, which separates military and civilian technologies and cuts ties with military technologies to advance civil ones. China needs to completely get rid of this remnant of old the planned economy and establish a new S&T system that promotes military-civil integration and military technology for civil purposes.

China should give full play to key labs, engineering centers, and other technology incubators. A series of links are needed if the outcomes from research institutes and universities are to be quickly translated into products needed by the market. Labs and engineering centers should be built at both the central and local levels. With preferential policies, China can attract the research outcomes of talents and use the technology transfers related to engineering application and industrialization. In China, a large number of S&T outcomes have not been developed, patent utilization rates are relatively low, and the link between research outcomes and technology transfers is weak. In particular, some old industrial bases are undergoing industrial transformation, so it is highly necessary to do a good job in the aforementioned areas for establishing new industries. The Ruhr region in Germany has successfully made the switch from coal and iron industries to electronic and biological industries. And engineering centers have played a critical role in that process.

Chapter 38
Multiple Approaches to Greater Innovation Capacity

Since the Fifth Plenary Session of the 16th CPC Central Committee—when the innovation strategy was first put forward, the concept of innovation has attracted global attention, especially from various levels of government and enterprises. For the current stage and for some time to come, enhancing this capacity will be of strategic importance for China's economic development.

First, enhancing innovation capacity is the key to transforming the nation's growth pattern. The need to transform the growth pattern was raised as early as the Ninth Five-Year Plan period, but the country has made limited progress in the past decade. The reason is that China lacks proprietary products and technologies. Only by enhancing innovation capacity and having proprietary products and technologies can China truly realize the transformation from extensive growth to sustainable growth.

Second, enhancing innovation capacity is necessary to maintain steady, rapid, and sustained economic growth. In the mid-1990s, the economy entered a new stage of steady and rapid growth for a period of 10 years. During that decade, the economy stabilized. Annual economic growth had a gap of no greater than two percentage points. The steady growth was a hard-won achievement. The CPC Central Committee and the State Council aim to maintain that momentum to the "11th Five-Year Plan" period and for another 15 years till 2020, with an average annual growth rate of between 8 and 9%. But in order to reach that goal, China will need to enhance its innovation capacity and become less reliant on investments and exports. Particularly, China will need to stop relying on the rapid growth of high consumption, high pollution, and high input industries, and develop high-tech industries and industries that are energy and resource efficient and in which added value is high and the advantages of labor resources are fully utilized. This can help create investment hot spots and economic growth points. Only through innovation can the country maintain steady and rapid long-term economic growth.

This article originally appeared in *Party Building in Enterprises*, no. 2, 2007.

X. Zheng, *China's 40 Years of Economic Reform and Development*,
https://doi.org/10.1007/978-981-13-2727-8_38

Third, enhancing innovation capacity is also needed to realize the simultaneous growth of people's incomes and economic growth. Even though the country's GDP has been growing at 9–10% on average annually over the past years, people's incomes are not keeping up with the rapid GDP growth. The wealth of the nation is growing, but not quickly. This is mainly because the most profitable industries are often forged through foreign investors or processing trade and quite a large portion of export products are original equipment manufacturer (OEM) products intended for export. For example, China has exported US$100 billion worth of textile products since 2005, making it the world's largest textile exporter. However, for textile product exports and especially clothes, 80% of them were OEM products intended for export.

Thus, China works hard throughout the entire production process, while foreign companies just label their brands in the last link. Some 80% of the profits go to the foreign enterprises, while only a small portion finds its way to Chinese pockets—and in spite of all the hard work.

This result applies to all domestic enterprises. If the vast majority of profits all go to foreign businesses or imported products, then one must ask: when will the Chinese people get rich? This is why enhancing innovation capacity is so central to transforming the growth pattern. Steady and rapid long-term economic growth cannot be achieved unless people's incomes can keep up with growth.

The goal of innovation is to develop proprietary products and technologies, and there are multiple approaches to reaching that goal. Recently, while summarizing the experience of innovation of domestic enterprises, I found nine approaches. Below, I share my research outcomes regarding how to enhance China's innovation capacity.

The first approach is innovation after the assimilation and absorption of imported technologies. This approach was put forward by the Fifth Plenary Session. For some time to come, China should adopt this approach in industries that can introduce technologies. This approach to innovation is a proven shortcut to technological innovation, because it saves time and reduces costs. When introducing European and American technologies, Japan and the Republic of Korea quickly created competitive products through this approach. Consequently, they highly value innovation based on the assimilation and absorption of imported technologies.

The second approach is to innovate through systemic integration. This approach mainly applies to equipment and products that are large in scale and complex, such as technology equipment. Technology equipment research covers technologies in various technical fields and various links. By pooling technologies in all fields, great technologies can be developed to handle complex missions.

The third approach is original innovation. Original innovation is mainly dependent on research institutes and university professors, but is also possible in enterprises. Two enterprises in Shenzhen have accomplished two world-class innovation achievements. Below are the two cases:

The first case was a way to treat cancer through genetic engineering. This breakthrough has helped cure many patients. Coming from military medical universities, the researchers succeeded after returning to China for research after pursuing studies in the US and Japan.

The second case was made by technicians at Netac Shenzhen. They graduated from the Chinese Academy of Sciences (CAS) and came up with some innovative ideas while working overseas. They returned to China and began research in data storage technologies. Their invention was a direct connection between flash memory and whole-system persistence (WSP), and it was unique in not only the IT industry but also across the world. Major foreign companies including Sony and Panasonic all lined up to license it.

Both achievements were the result of original innovation made by small enterprises, so the role of enterprises in original innovation should not be underestimated. Original innovation is possible as long as research can be conducted.

The fourth approach is the integration of technology with trade and international bidding. A typical example is the manufacturing of power units under the Three Gorges Dam model. The approach of integrating technology with trade and international bidding has been practiced for the 14 power units of the Zuo'an Power Plant. All the bid winners were foreign multinationals. However, they were required to choose one Chinese manufacturer as a partner, transfer technologies to China, and entrust domestic enterprises to manufacture at least one power unit. Thanks to the bidding system for the Zuo'an Power Plant construction project, domestic enterprises enhanced their design and manufacturing capacities. When the bidding for 12 power units at the You'an Power Plant opened, eight Chinese enterprises won, including Harbin Power Corporation. The power units manufactured by them were also innovative, at least according to the enterprises. Thus, government purchasing programs and international bidding can be applied in all major projects to enhance the innovation capacity of domestic enterprises.

The fifth approach is to acquire intellectual property assets through international acquisitions. Some foreign enterprises have technologies and have achieved S&T outcomes, but they have no market, while domestic enterprises desire technology. Their cooperation will bring about win-win outcomes. Some domestic enterprises acquire foreign enterprises that are bordering on bankruptcy or with operational challenges in order to acquire intellectual property assets and technology resources, including technology outcomes and the talents that produced them. Such acquisitions enhance their innovation capacity, and there are many successful cases in places like Shanghai and Zhejiang.

The sixth approach is to entrust foreign institutes to with proprietary technologies. Some technologies are urgently needed for national economic and social development, but domestic research capacity is insufficient to develop them. Under such circumstances, China can launch international bids and entrust foreign research institutes to help with R&D. The direct liquefaction technology of Shenhua Group is a successful case.

The seventh approach is joint R&D and sharing of outcomes through international cooperation. Foreign enterprises and research institutes are willing to cooperate with China. The president of the Weizmann Institute of Science once remarked that he stood ready to work with China on scientific research. He further said that China can propose projects for bilateral cooperation and suggested that the two sides respectively cover their own research expenses and share the research outcomes with each other. This approach can also be promoted. China has been involved in the Galileo satellite navigation system and international research on thermonuclear fusion. These technologies can be developed through international cooperation. China can make use of foreign research forces by setting up overseas R&D institutes. Huawei and ZTE are both success cases. They established overseas research branches, hired local researchers, and owned the research outcomes.

The eighth approach is domestic design and foreign manufacturing, or domestic manufacturing of imported key parts and components. Take Huawei for example. When the company set off to design program-controlled switches, Huawei had to manufacture them abroad or purchase them directly from abroad. The switches could be manufactured in other countries, and the key parts and components could be purchased for domestic manufacturing. China can design many products, but is unable to manufacture them at home; that is, at least, at the same level of quality. Therefore, China can design them at home and manufacture them abroad.

Another option is making the majority of products overseas and purchasing the rest for domestic manufacturing. This can also enhance innovation capacity. Going back to the example of Huawei, the company stands at the frontier of international technological development in the area of telecommunications equipment. In 2005, Huawei had over 30,000 employees, of which 20,000 of them were dedicated to research. The technological development input stood at over five billion yuan, accounting for 10% of its sales revenue, while the Department of High-Tech Industry of the National Development and Reform Commission (NDRC) was in charge of allocating just over one billion yuan each year. The Huawei example is an example of great R&D input intensity!

This intensity has led to results. In 2005, Huawei applied for over 240 international technology patents. Cisco, a leading international high-tech company, applied for over 220 international patents in that year, some 20 fewer than Huawei. In 2005, the nation as a whole applied for over 2000 international patents. Huawei accounted for one tenth of the total. China has many enterprises. If one hundred of them could become more like Huawei, then the nation's innovation capacity would be greatly enhanced.

Lastly, the ninth approach is collaboration between academia and industry. Chinese enterprises are generally weak in R&D. Some technical issues may be difficult for enterprises to solve, but easy for research institutes and universities. China should take advantage of this old yet effective approach.

There are multiple approaches to innovation, all of which require constant attention. Where there is input, there is return. It is unacceptable that the innovation input in China's large and medium-sized SOEs is lower than the national average, as they boast the best technology, the highest profits, and the most outstanding technicians. They should become the mainstay of innovation, pioneers in technology, and leaders in the technology industries.

Thanks to this workshop, friends from enterprises and the media can jointly call for innovation, and encourage China's enterprises to spend money on technological development and adopt appropriate approaches to technological innovations in light of their own conditions. There should be little doubt that after 5 or 10 years of effort, China will be able to create a large number of proprietary products and technologies, attract investment for these technological outcomes, form new investment hot spots and economic growth points, advance the upgrading of the industrial structure, and realize steady and rapid long-term economic growth for the next decade and beyond.

Chapter 39
Huawei: The Secret to Its Success

According to the statistics recently issued by WIPO, Huawei applied for 1737 (Patent Cooperation Treaty) PCTs in 2008, becoming the biggest filer of international patent applications in the world. Huawei has ranked first among Chinese enterprises in terms of patent applications for six consecutive years, and first in China for three consecutive years. By the end of December 2008, Huawei had applied for a total of 35,773 domestic and international patents.

Impacted by the current international financial crisis, global telecommunication giants including Vodaphone and Ericsson all saw a drop in business. However, Huawei's total contract revenue was US$23.3 billion in 2008, a year-on-year growth of 46%.

Huawei quickly developed from a small company without its own products and technologies to an international telecommunication giant within a short span of 21 years. How?

The answer to that question is innovation. Indigenous innovation grew the great telecommunication company and crowned it king of international patent applications.

39.1 Market Orientation

Basic principles of technical innovation

Whether it is development of core technologies or product design, market orientation is Huawei's basic model of technological innovation. Huawei makes R&D staff responsible for the market success of its products. Their efforts are tested not only by outcomes of R&D projects, but also by procedures and assessment mechanisms.

This article originally appeared in *People's Daily*, April 27, 2009, and was coauthored with Xu Zhuwu.

X. Zheng, *China's 40 Years of Economic Reform and Development*,
https://doi.org/10.1007/978-981-13-2727-8_39

The market-oriented approach to technological innovation has helped Huawei win not only consumers, but also market.

In 1998, through a market survey, and especially in-depth exchanges with telecommunication operators, Huawei figured out that there is huge demand for network access servers and that the current ones lacked telecommunication functions. Therefore, Huawei rapidly developed the A8010, an innovative access server, which quickly became popular and accounted for 70% of the market in 2000.

While developing the 3G market in Europe, Huawei found that European operators wanted base stations that took up less space, were easy to install, more environmentally friendly and energy efficient, and had better coverage. Therefore, Huawei proposed the concept of distributed base stations, and took the lead to industrialize them. By completely changing the design of conventional base stations, Huawei greatly decreased the cost of machine room construction and renting, made it easier and cheaper for equipment installation, and reduced operation costs by more than 30%. The distributed base station has become the priority plan of global mobile operators in deploying mobile networks. A large number of operators have seen great improvements in network quality and performance by adopting Huawei's solutions. According to Businessweek, Huawei succeeded because it provides customers with top-quality products and the greatest cost-effectiveness.

39.2 High Input

Gain the right to survive

Huawei's constant progress would not be possible without highly intensive input in material and human resources.

At the time when Huawei was founded, it used all the profits it gained from selling foreign products, which were not that much, for developing small-scale switcher technology. It concentrated its efforts on dealing with major technical issues and gradually took on a leading role and created greater space for profits. Later on, it gradually thrived by constantly using profits for R&D and product upgrades.

Now, Huawei insists on using no less than 10% of its sales revenue and 43% of its staff for R&D as well as 10% of the R&D input to research on frontier technologies, core technologies, and basic technologies. In order to accumulate strong technical talent, Huawei has been recruiting 3000–4000 people annually from prominent universities in China for several consecutive years. Even today, it still insists on recruiting thousands of outstanding technicians at home and abroad. In terms of sales revenue and staff increases, Huawei has invested at least one billion dollars annually in R&D over the past two years, with its research personnel reaching 40,000. Its research input intensity has always ranked top among the nation's information industry enterprises and the company is on level with international renowned enterprises in the high-tech industry.

Apart from driving innovation in technology, Huawei also attaches importance to protecting technological innovations. As early as 1995, Huawei took the lead among domestic enterprises in establishing a department for intellectual property, which is in charge of the company's IP affairs. Protecting technologies and increasing patent ownerships have become the basics of its IP work. This is also a major reason for the constant increase in patent applications and its top position at home and abroad.

Technological innovation carries huge risk, and there is no guarantee that massive input will pay off in the end. However, Huawei has always placed high importance on technological innovation. Huawei's successes in developing telecommunication technologies have shown that overcoming risk will bring rewards.

"The biggest risk Huawei faces is failure to innovate," Ren Zhengfei, President of Huawei, remarked. "Without innovation, survival in the high-tech industry becomes almost impossible. If we continue to stay in the second or third class without daring to take risks and following others, we will never be able to compete with multinationals and gain the right to survive. Being conservative will not lead to rapid development," he said.

39.3 Incentive Mechanisms

Fertile soil for producing R&D talents

In the words of the president of Huawei, China does not lack the seed of innovation. What China lacks is the soil of innovation. People in Huawei believe that R&D is at the heart of enterprises, so there is support for well-established incentive mechanisms. To this end, Huawei has put in place multiple incentives for its R&D staff. Incentives such as salary, bonus, pension, health care, equity, and other favorable treatments.

With regard to material incentives, there are various kinds of favorable treatment available to the R&D staff. And in terms of payment mechanisms, Huawei arranges salaries according to responsibility and competence, bonuses according to performance, and equity according to potential. As long as a promising employee is willing to work hard, Huawei will provide with sufficient development opportunities and development space. Among other things, the company sets goals and challenges for its various R&D staff. Each project development team is fully autonomous, while the leaders of development departments mainly deal with development orientation instead of project details. Moreover, the company highly values moral encouragement, recognizes and praises staff through various approaches, and openly awards employees with medals, trophies, and corporate culture honors.

39.4 Joint Struggle

Secret to overcoming major technological issues

There is a huge picture hanging inside the headquarters of Huawei in Wanpan, Shenzhen. It is a picture of 10 young people standing in a group with their hands gripping closely. The picture conveys a clear message: In the hearts and minds of the people of Huawei, every victory is the result of unity, cooperation, and joint struggle.

Each new employee in Huawei receives a letter telling them that Huawei is a high-tech enterprise focusing on big markets, big systems, and big structures. It goes on to say that those without a sense of responsibility and a spirit of cooperation and who are unwilling to join the struggle will lose the opportunity to forge ahead with Huawei.

Frequent interdepartmental endeavors to overcome technical difficulties are a great "landscape" in Huawei. The successful outcomes of R&D on large complex product systems, such as the C&C08 switcher, GSM, data communication, and intelligent network, were all made by thousands of R&D staff in different regions within a period of two to three years.

In order to realize innovation breakthroughs at an early date and narrow the gap with foreign telecommunication giants, Huawei's R&D staff often work extra hours and sleep on the their mattresses in offices when they get tired. This "mattress culture" is carried forward even today.

A graduate student from Tsinghua University said that, "At Huawei, we can achieve what one single person cannot. The outcomes of the joint struggle of hundreds of people are the products of national pride and honor. This is why the R&D staff has always been so enthusiastic about their work."

39.5 Global Resources

Guarantee to outperform frontier technologies

In core technologies, Huawei acknowledges itself as a latecomer and acknowledges the leadership role of Western enterprises. It is therefore explicitly stated in the *Huawei Basic Law* that the company needs to widely absorb the latest research outcomes in electronic and information technology around the world, learn from excellent enterprises at home and abroad, cooperate with others, and independently develop leading core technologies. This is how Huawei approaches the development of core technologies.

In order to integrate global innovation resources in a timely manner, Huawei has set up 14 R&D centers in China and around the world. They are located in Stockholm, Sweden; Dallas and Silicon Valley in the US; Europe; Bangalore, India; and Shenzhen, Shanghai, Beijing, Nanjing, Xi'an, Chengdu, and Wuhan in China. The centers form a well-established global R&D system, which helps absorb international talents and helps the company keep up with global developments in technology. Through technology collaboration with 36 of the world's top 50 operators, Huawei has established nearly 20 joint innovation centers.

In terms of technological innovation, Huawei is a good case study. The company went from being a follower in the field to a major player on the international stage. Furthermore, the company conducts advanced R&D activities with international research institutes. In 3G patents, Huawei ranks among the top five in the world in ownership of patents; and in LTE (long-term 4G evolution) patents, Huawei ranks in the world's top three. In the global patent competition, Huawei has grown from a follower in the 2G era to a parallel runner in global 3G and now the company is poised to become a leading runner in 4G.

Chapter 40
Innovation Is Central to Realizing Industrial Upgrading

Innovation was stressed at the Central Conference on Economic Work. This is not only an important summary by the CPC Central Committee regarding experience in achieving good and fast economic and social development. It is also the key to achieving industrial upgrading and transforming the economic development pattern. Looking across the modern history of the world, each severe economic crisis was accompanied by an adjustment in the global industrial structure and technological revolution. The global financial crisis, which broke out in 2008, will substantially stimulate global S&T progress and the emergence of new technology-based industries, and provide a historic opportunity to develop the green economy. If China is to overcome the crisis and turn challenges into opportunities, strong emphasize must be put on innovation, industrial upgrading has to be advanced through innovation, and steps should be taken to enhance international competitiveness.

40.1 The Urgency of Highlighting Innovation in the Post-crisis Era

The global financial crisis has had a negative impact on developed economies, such as the United States. The financial bubble burst has reduced market demand, slowed global trade, and impacted the economies of developed countries. As all countries have adopted economic stimulus policies and financial assistance programs, and an economic collapse, such as the great crisis of the 1930s, was averted and the global economy began to recover in the second half of 2009. However, since it takes time to fully resolve such an issue, residential consumption, which accounts for the bulk of total demand, is unlikely to recover within a short period of time. In addition, since S&T development has not yet witnessed any major breakthroughs, the global

---

This article originally appeared in *Qiushi,* Chinese edition, no. 2, 2010.

X. Zheng, *China's 40 Years of Economic Reform and Development*,
https://doi.org/10.1007/978-981-13-2727-8_40

economy will likely continue to grow at a low rate for some time. According to the historical record, walking out of the shadow of the crisis and turning recovery into prosperity requires new STI policies, which will create new economic growth points for advancing industrial structure upgrading.

In the agreement signed at the recently concluded UN Climate Change Conference in Copenhagen, agreement was reached on long-term goals, funding, technology, and transparency. Major projects concerning S&T research and industry development were also proposed. Governments of all countries, scientists, economists, and entrepreneurs are all seeking solutions and exploring cleaner production strategies and the possibilities of a low-carbon economy. Who will win in the next round of global competition will be determined by high-tech R&D and the speed at which new technologies are turned into new products and services. US President Barack Obama proposed a 10-year program on new energy and low-carbon technologies, adding some three trillion dollars in new value. He expressed hope for leading the next round of industrial structure adjustments and continuing global economic, scientific, and technological leadership by occupying the commanding height of innovation. Developed powers, such as the EU and Japan, have also formulated plans and increased R&D inputs. High-tech R&D is a major project and economic development strategy, and it will have a profound impact on the global landscape and on human society.

China is currently undergoing rapid industrialization and urbanization. To catch up with the advanced countries in terms of economic development, China is optimizing and upgrading its industrial structure, transforming its economic development pattern, shifting away from reliance on material consumption to reliance on S&T progress, management perfection, and labor quality improvement, and putting more emphasis on the tertiary industry. In the 11th Five-Year Plan, China committed itself to reducing emissions per unit GDP energy use by 20% by 2010; namely, reducing CO_2 emissions by 1.5 billion tons, so as to make great contributions to tackling global climate change. Recently, the government proposed lowering emissions per unit of GDP by 40–45% by 2020, compared with 2005 levels. These actions fully demonstrate China's image as a responsible major country.

According to the requirements of the Theory of Balanced and Sustainable Development, China also set the development goals of building a resource-conserving and environmentally-friendly society. Furthermore, China has endeavored to move away from resource-intensive industries and toward capital, technology, and knowledge-intensive industries, lowered the share of resource-based industries featuring high energy consumption and high pollution in the economy, made better use of technology in this regard, and added more value to products. Accomplishing these goals requires integrating industrial technology improvements and industrial structure upgrading with a new round of adjustments to the global industrial structure. In other words, China should not only narrow the industrial technology and industrial structure gaps with developed countries as soon as possible, but also keep up with the pace of progress and adjustment. Doing so will bring about a more arduous task of facilitating S&T progress and structural adjustment. Currently, Chinese exports are dropping, while newer high-technology products can be exported. This proves that innovation is an effective measure against the crisis at hand.

Introducing technology and foreign capital is a shortcut for making progress in industrial technology and industrial upgrading. However, as a large economy, China's economic development must be based on proprietary technologies. This is the fundamental approach to creating greater wealth for the Chinese people. Moreover, core technologies cannot be accessed through purchases. The only way to access them is to enhance China's innovation capacity. According to a suggestion in the 11th Five-Year Plan formulated by the 5th Plenary Session of the 16th CPC Central Committee, China should deepen its implementation of rejuvenating the nation through science and education as well as its implementation of revitalizing the nation through talent, and should regard enhancing innovation capacity as the strategic foundation of S&T development and central to adjusting the industrial structure and transforming the growth pattern. The report to the 17th CPC National Congress highlighted enhancing China's innovation capacity and building an innovative country. This is the main feature of the national development strategy and the key to greater comprehensive national strength. These arguments fully embody the high attention given by the CPC Central Committee to this major issue of national vicissitude. The breakout of the global financial crisis showcases the committee's vision and the sense of urgency in China for enhancing innovation capacity and building an innovative country.

40.2 Innovation: A Core Strategy of Development for Enterprises

Enterprises hold the key to translating S&T into productivity and facilitating industrial upgrading through innovation. China should enhance their innovation capacity and establish a technological innovation system featuring a dominant role for enterprises, an orientation toward the market, and industry-academia-research partnerships. As enterprises are most familiar with the market, they can develop new products according to demand and quickly get them into the market and attain quick returns from R&D investment. As enterprises are most familiar with the latest trends in industrial technologies, they can rapidly transform outcomes of basic and applied research into new products. Those serving as major players of technological innovation can fundamentally resolve the institutional problem of separation between S&T and the economy. In developed countries, 70% of research staff and funding are concentrated in enterprises. It was decided at the 17th CPC National Congress that innovation elements would be concentrated in enterprises. This is crucial for the development of China's S&T system and will increase the innovation capacity of Chinese enterprises.

In recent years, Chinese enterprises have grown their R&D spending rapidly. From 2004 to 2008, the R&D expenditure of industrial enterprises above the designated scale grew 29.2% per year on average. However, there is still a large gap compared with the requirement of the report to the 17th CPC National Congress. In 2008, only 57.6% of scientists and engineers dedicated to S&T activities in China came from enterprises. Only 6.5% of the industrial enterprises above the designated scale conducted R&D activities, and R&D expenditure accounted for only 0.61% their turnover. In medium and large-sized industrial enterprises, the two aforementioned figures were 24.9 and 0.84%, respectively. The ratio of expenditures on technology introduction to absorbing and spending was 3.8:1 in industrial enterprises above the designated scale and 4.1:1 for large and medium-sized enterprises. New product sales accounted for only 6.7% of major business turnover in large and medium-sized enterprises. This shows that although industrial enterprises have given greater attention to industrial R&D, they have yet to start seeking development through technological progress. Instead, they remain more focused on introduction and less on innovating on the technologies. This is very inappropriate in the context of fiercer international competition and new challenges for S&T progress in the post-crisis era.

Practice has proven that in high-tech R&D, every penny of investment will lead to its due return. The more you invest, the greater the return. In recent years, many of China's enterprises have already pursued rapid growth through innovation, ranking among the top performers in domestic and international markets. For example, Huawei's annual R&D input is expected to account for 10% of its sales revenue. If this target cannot be met, it will be a major issue that the company will have to deal with at the end of each year. Last year, its seven billion yuan of R&D investment and 1600-plus international applications both ranked first among global enterprises. Even with the decline in the global telecommunication equipment market, Huawei still increased its sales revenue by over 30%, as innovation enhanced its competitiveness. The average age of its staff is only 27, and the research teams are all formed by new graduates from domestic universities. As Huawei's success has proven, Chinese enterprises enjoy huge potential for technological innovation—the key being a development strategy with innovation as the core, are more willing than ever to increase R&D spending and are good at forming teams to tackle difficult technical issues. As long as the nation persists, success is guaranteed. The Chinese nation can create satisfactory technologies, regardless of the situation in foreign countries.

SOEs, especially those under central management, boast substantial funding and numerous talents. Standing at the frontier of all technological fields, they should become the major force in innovation. To this end, the government should raise compliance exams to a higher standard, establish a system to evaluate technological results, and include intangible asset betterment in the scope of examination to stimulate high-tech R&D input and increase the formation of natural assets. If the 100-plus SOEs in China could all give as much attention to high-tech R&D as Huawei, the problem of technological backwardness would be eliminated. This is especially true for the lack of core technologies, and more attention in this area would help the nation reach the strategic goals of driving industrial upgrading and transforming the development pattern through technical innovation.

40.3 Improving the Establishment of Innovation Policies and the Social Environment

In 2006, the State Council issued the program for medium and long-term S&T development, which identified the goals, missions, and strategic priorities of S&T development up till the year 2020. With regard to the implementation of the program, all relevant departments have put in place over 70 supporting policies, which have played an important role in encouraging innovation; however, many problems remain. As surveyed by the departments, some policies have been difficult to implement. With regard to the policy that reduces taxes on technological developments by 150%, only 38% of enterprises enjoyed the tax deduction, while 19% failed to enjoy it due to inadequate interdepartmental coordination and another 19% did not know the policy existed. A comprehensive review and summary of policy implementation is needed to make necessary improvements and adjustments. For policies less used by enterprises, the government should explore the reasons and refine the implementation methods so as to increase the effects of the policies. As for the high-tech R&D of strategic emerging industries, the government should implement special policies and achieve breakthroughs as soon as possible, so as to occupy the commanding heights of global S&T and industry development.

China should further improve its policies for innovation and improve the social environment; the key being to improve the mechanism for venture capital investment in high-tech industries. Local governments should use their funds to encourage investment and provide loan guarantees and interest subsidies for high-tech enterprises, so as to create a sound policy system for technological innovation and the industrialization of technology breakthroughs. The city of Shenzhen offers its experience in this respect. Since China's economic reform, its economic development has transformed greatly—from overseas-funded enterprises playing the major role to that of Chinese-funded high-tech enterprises, and from the dominance of processing trade to that of general trade.

The key to that was the establishment of a policy for innovation and a sound social ecosystem. A venture capital firm and a loan guarantee company funded and run by the municipal government are devoted to supporting start-ups and rising high-tech enterprises. To a certain extent, more than 90% of the high-tech enterprises that have developed in Shenzhen have been supported by these two companies in their critical phase of development. Thanks to their support, the two companies have expanded the economies of scale, increased efforts in supporting other companies, and have driven the development of companies that specialize in private investment risk and loan guarantee. The city has over 200 companies that specialize in investment risk, which account for over 70% of the national total. It is this pro-innovation environment that facilitates the development of the high-tech industry and creates the miracle of Shenzhen. This successful practice has inspired the nation. In terms of STI resources, Shenzhen is not the best. Many major cities in China are now home to a larger number of research institutes, universities, and scientific personnel—even more than Shenzhen. If major Chinese cities can adopt the Shenzhen model in creating an environment that encourages innovation, then dozens of creative cities like Shenzhen can be created in a short period of time. If all the cities rely on their own strengths and lead the world in one or two technological fields, then they will be reliable enough to meet the strategic goal of building an innovative country as proposed by the 17th CPC National Congress.

In 2009, the launch of the Growth Enterprise Market (GEM) provided a new financing approach to the development of high-tech enterprises. NASDAQ has produced a large number of high-tech enterprises for the United States. Global software industry leaders such as Microsoft grew and thrived relying on NASDAQ. At present, they are focusing on China for attracting listed enterprises. It is China's hope that GEM can draw upon the experience of NASDAQ in serving as a trading platform to select and support the development of high-tech enterprises in China.

China also needs to integrate support for innovation with that of entrepreneurship. In recent years, some local governments have issued a series of policies for encouraging entrepreneurship and advancing employment through entrepreneurial activities. This has played a remarkable role in creating more major market players. Thanks to the rapidly increasing number of start-ups and privately-owned businesses, unemployment has been greatly reduced, thus boosting the local economy. Particularly in the central and western regions, any locality that conscientiously implements policies for entrepreneurship has seen faster residential income growth. China should strive to realize organic integration between encouraging innovation and supporting entrepreneurship, encourage entrepreneurial activities by technicians and college graduates, and push forward entrepreneurship by boosting innovation.

40.4 Give Full Play to S&T Resources in the International Market to Enhance Innovation Capacity

The global financial crisis has brought about great difficulties for enterprises in developed countries. A number of enterprises with sound S&T resources have been suffering greatly due to market demand and the supply of funds. For Chinese enterprises, it is a rare opportunity in history to enhance innovation capacity by purchasing international S&T resources. The huge sum of foreign exchange reserves held by China provides adequate funding for international M&A. China's enterprises should be choosy about which enterprises to merge with after acquiring relevant international information and conducting in-depth surveys. Generally speaking, during the crisis, merging with or holding the shares of companies facing difficulties in order to avoid closings and layoffs will not only be embraced by those enterprises, but also supported by local governments. China's overseas branches and various think tanks should provide relevant information and consultation services for international M&A to reduce investment mistakes.

As the country searches for talent and pursues innovation, foreign S&T talents should be introduced and integrated with domestic ones, so as to jointly solve research and technical difficulties. Practice has proven that introduction is a shortcut to innovation. In the wake of the international financial crisis, some scientists and engineers overseas are unable to find satisfactory results, and some newly retired ones want to contribute more. This presents an opportunity for China to attract international talents. To this end, China should make the introduction of talent for innovation a strategy for innovation capacity enhancement. In addition, all levels of the government need to offer support to attract overseas talent through enterprises.

Enterprises should set up R&D branches abroad, attract local talents, and learn about the latest trends in S&T. Thanks to joint R&D efforts between domestic and overseas branches based on modern information and communication technology and different time zones, research can be carried out nonstop, around the clock. Many domestic enterprises have already set up such branches, which has played a critical role in boosting the development of technology in enterprises.

China needs to make better use of foreign investments and encourage the establishment of R&D branches through multinationals. At the same time, the technology spillover effects of overseas-funded enterprises should be utilized in a proactive manner in order to drive innovation by Chinese enterprises. Processing trade items should be gradually transformed into general trade products with proprietary IPRs and brands through absorption, greater support mechanisms, reverse takeovers, and other methods.

There is a saying that first-class enterprises sell standards, second-class do patents, third-class do products, and fourth-class do cheap labor. This is a vivid description of the positions of different types of enterprises in market competition, and is the market standard for evaluating enterprises' innovation capacity. China is ranked first in the world in terms of having sales for more than 100 products. China is, therefore, indeed a big manufacturing country, but far from being a manufacturing powerhouse. OEM products still account for the bulk of the country's exports. Due to the lack of standards, patents, and brands owned by China, domestic enterprises can only share a very small portion of total profits. This situation needs to change as soon as possible, and the best way to do that is by implementing an innovation strategy. Doing so will increase the benefits from economic activities and help boost residential incomes in the country.

Chapter 41
Why Shenzhen's Patent Application Leads the World

In the political report to the 17th CPC National Congress in 2007, it was decided to put improving the capacity of innovation and building an innovative country at the core of the national development strategy. The seven years since then has seen a period when R&D expenditure saw its fastest growth and S&T outcomes substantially increased. In 2013, China's national R&D input accounted for 2.09% of the total GDP, while the number of domestic invention patent authorizations reached 144,000, while that of international patent applications stood at 21,516. Our international patent application accounted for 10.5% of the global total. Meanwhile, the gap with the US was significantly narrowed. In the four years from 2010 to 2013, the US's international patent application was 6.0, 3.6, 2.8 and 2.5 times respectively that of China. If this trend continues, our application for international patents could catch up with or even outperform the US within a couple of years.

However, we should note that China's patent application policy is quite imbalanced. Geographically, patent applications have traditionally been more concentrated in the coastal cities with a few in the central and western regions. In terms of industry, patent applications have been more concentrated within the ICT, oil and chemical industries as well as in the electric vehicle sector and only a few originate from the bio-engineering, machinery manufacturing, animal husbandry and aquaculture areas. In terms of applicants, private enterprises submitted the most applications, while a few came from SOEs, research institutes and universities.

In particular, last year Shenzhen had a total of 10,049 international patent applications, a year-on-year increase of 25.3%, accounting for 48.1% of the total international patent applications by domestic enterprises and individuals. In the global enterprises' ranking of international patent applications, four of China's enterprises joined the top 50. ZTE, Huawei, CSOT and Tencent respectively accounted for 2nd, 3rd, 17th and 48th positions with 2309, 2094, 916 and 365 applications respectively. All four enterprises are headquartered in Shenzhen.

This article originally appeared in *Economic Daily*, July 21, 2014.

X. Zheng, *China's 40 Years of Economic Reform and Development*,
https://doi.org/10.1007/978-981-13-2727-8_41

I am convinced that anyone who notes these figures will be shocked and amazed. On one hand, we are proud of Shenzhen's innovation capacity; but on the other hand, we are ashamed by this gap between Shenzhen and other regions of the country. It's crucial to note that as a city, Shenzhen does not enjoy the best STI resources compared to other major Chinese cities, as it is only characterized by a limited number of well-known research institutes, universities, CAS & CAE members, professors and tutors to doctors. So how can such a city generate so many S&T outcomes? What gaps can we identify in comparison with Beijing, Shanghai, Wuhan, Xi'an, Chengdu and Shenyang where S&T resources are concentrated? What valuable experiences can we learn from Shenzhen?

First, The Cultural Atmosphere that Upholds Innovation

Since the early 1980s, Shenzhen has constantly attracted ambitious young people from all across the country. They come to Shenzhen for neither government titles nor cozy living. Instead, they are determined to start their own businesses through innovation. In terms of institution, they want to steer a new path and create the latest technologies in modern times. Those who dare to act innovatively are well respected in Shenzhen, where new thinking, modes and technologies are inclined to be adopted. They are able to endure any hardships just to conquer any technical difficulties faced. For instance, Huawei owns a total of 18,881 effective invention patents, the most among Chinese enterprises and its corporate culture has been dubbed, the "mattress culture" where each new staff member is given a mattress when they first report for duty. This mattress is then to be placed in their office. Once entrusted by the leadership, the staff will start working during the day and only use the mattress for taking a nap before getting back to work again upon waking up. Notably, the average age of employees at Huawei stands at 27 years old and it is their death-defying spirit that has enabled Huawei to lead the global communication equipment industry from scratch within 25 years. A large number of companies such as ZTE, Tencent, Ocean's King Lighting, HONGFUJIN and BYD all have also progressed due to innovation. Thus innovation has become the soul of Shenzhen and its innovative culture has become one of the most salient features of this city compared with others.

Second, The Pro-innovation Competition Mechanism

Survival of the fittest is an important role in market competition. In Shenzhen, people respect the rules of market competition, so the vitality for corporate development and the creativity of the staff is always aroused. Meanwhile, in almost every industry, there are at least two companies competing with each other. For example, Huawei and ZTE are both devoted to communication equipment manufacturing therefore they compete with each other. On the international market, wherever one of them goes to seek new business, evidently the other would follow. In 2010, Huawei's international patent applications ranked No. 1 in the world. Two years later, ZTE ranked No. 1 among all the world's enterprises. In the course of competing with each other, both companies have since become leading runners of innovation and international operations among Chinese enterprises.

Third, The Social Environment that Tolerates Failures and Where Technological Innovation is Highly Risky and New Products or Technologies are Usually Created after Many Failures

Establishing a social environment that encourages innovation and tolerates failure is therefore of utmost importance for an enterprise and the nation as a whole. Those who have failed in innovation must be comforted and encouraged. Leaders must voluntarily shoulder the responsibilities and remember not to condemn or punish those who fail. We need to promote the first set of policies and encourage the application of innovative equipment and products. For those who encounter accidents when applying the first set, we need to help find the root causes, improve technical equipment, refine the insurance system, set up economic compensation mechanisms and continue with the encouragement. Only by setting up a social environment of failure tolerance can we form a pro-innovation atmosphere.

Fourth, An Inclusive Talent Strategy

Talent is the foundation of innovation. It is rare to meet talent that can create new technologies, so we must attract expertise from all across the globe. Shenzhen's success in innovation is mainly reliant on attracting talent not only from every corner of the country but also from all over the world. In Shenzhen, there are many companies thriving after engineering and industrializing, based on technical outcomes from various parts of the country. Some are the result of entrepreneurial successes are from overseas scholars bringing their technical expertise to China. BGI is ranked among the top in the world in research force and outcome of genetic studies. The firm was founded by a number of overseas Chinese scholars returning to China. One important reason behind US leadership in STI is that they attract global talent. Among new start-up companies based in Silicon Valley, each year about 50% are made by Asians—mainly Chinese and Indian. Unfortunately, we still are lagging far behind in this area. Particularly in terms of attracting foreign talent, therefore we need to learn from the US.

Fifth, Venture Capital with Insightful Judgments

Technical innovation and engineering and industrializing of technical outcomes must be supported by venture capital mechanisms. Previously, the Shenzhen municipal government funded a venture capital firm and a loan guarantee company specializing in engineering and industrializing technical outcomes. Among the mature high-tech enterprises in Shenzhen, a vast majority have been supported by the two companies in their early or key developmental phases. Thanks to the leadership of the two state-owned venture capital firms, over 200 private venture capital firms were pooled in the 1990s, two thirds of such firms being in the country. For an enterprise or project worthy of investment, usually a venture capital firm affiliated with the government will invest a portion and then private ones will follow. Nowadays, venture capital firms in Shenzhen have huge funding. Stationed in Shenzhen, they have also made their presence felt in other cities with intensive S&T resources giving play to a spillover effect.

Sixth, An Open Global Vision

S&T respects no national boundaries and is the common wealth of mankind. In an enclosed city or country, S&T must surely be backwards. Opening up to the outside world has been the vision since the establishment of the city of Shenzhen. During the process of expanding foreign trade, Shenzhen became familiar with the foreign markets, learned about global technology trends and gradually owned technologies with proprietary IPR through introduction, digestion and innovation. Previously, high-tech parts and components were processed abroad, the products were then sold to foreign markets and the designs were done at home. Gradually, R&D agencies were set up in other countries and foreign intelligence used. As a result a path to foreign-oriented economic and technical development had been steered.

Seventh, A Support Policy Featuring Equal Treatment

A government support policy is highly necessary for enhancing innovation capacities and developing a high and new technology industry. This is of utmost importance for countries trying to catch up with their advanced counterparts. The government should thus adopt tax reduction, interest subsidies and capital subsidies to encourage more R&D inputs by enterprises and also adopt engineering and industrializing of technical outcomes. Favorable treatment should be offered to innovative enterprises in the areas of bank loans, company listings and bond issuing. The government should also efficiently run high-tech zones and innovative enterprises and establish technology R&D centers and technology incubation centers in line with the requirements of local dominant industry development. Equal treatment should be offered to SOEs and private enterprises. We should pay more attention to giving play to the role of small enterprises in technical innovation and offer support to small and micro enterprises. The government budget should spend more on technical innovation and less on other areas. Practice has proven that in technical innovation, each penny worth investing will lead to its due return.

Chapter 42
Expediting Setting Up an Economic System and Development Pattern Centered on Innovation

At a workshop attended by officials from the CPC committees of seven provinces and municipalities in East China on May 27, General Secretary Xi Jinping remarked that achieving national strength is closely related to innovation. To implement an innovation-driven development strategy, the government will need to facilitate innovation in various areas, including S&T, industries, enterprises, markets, products, and business models, so as to expedite the setting up of an economic system and development pattern centered on innovation. In the words of Xi, China has entered a new normal. China will need to overcome many difficulties, including downward pressure on the economy, excess capacity, and lack of internal driving forces for growth. Thus, it is important for the country to turn President Xi's words into action and allow innovation to arouse the wisdom of China's 1.3 billion people and unleash new driving forces for economic growth.

42.1 China Has Entered a New Phase of Innovation-Driven Sustainable Growth

China's rapid economic growth has been sustained for 37 years, with the nation's GDP per capita reaching the level of medium high-income countries. Looking across the history of global economic development, it is obvious that without leadership and support for technological and institutional innovations, economic growth would stagnate. Innovation-driven development has become the key to economic development in the new phase.

Reducing overcapacity will be dependent on innovation. More than 200 industrial products rank top in the world. The production of new energy, raw materials, consumer goods, and investment products in China account for a third to two thirds of

This article originally appeared in *Qiushi*, Chinese edition, no. 21, 2015.

X. Zheng, *China's 40 Years of Economic Reform and Development*,
https://doi.org/10.1007/978-981-13-2727-8_42

the global total. This is the result of long-term investment-driven economic growth. However, the constantly expanding production capacity has outweighed market demand, resulting in overcapacity. As a result, the utilization rate of equipment stands at only around 70%. Against this backdrop of excess backward production capacity, high-tech products are forced to rely on exports. For example, the annual importation of chips and precision industrial products both exceed US$200 billion. China is the world's biggest car producer and consumer, but the key parts and components with high added value are mostly imported. Thus, as we can see, the underlying overcapacity problem is insufficient supply of high-tech products and weak technological innovation capacity.

Breaking the tech monopolies that corner the international market requires innovation. Since the start of China's economic reform, the country has been importing large amounts of advanced technology and management expertise. In addition, China has been improving its industrial technology and corporate management by re-innovating on advanced technologies and methods. Up until recently, China has bought almost all of its general technologies, but it is impossible to buy core technologies in the international market. The problem for China is that it is not investing enough to build on imported technologies. The ratio of such investment in Japan and the Republic of Korea is 1:5, while in China, it less than 1:1. China must rely on innovation for breaking the tech monopoly in the international market.

Transcending the middle-income trap relies on innovation. One major difference between high-income countries and countries that have been trapped at middle income for a long time is whether the income between urban and rural residents is generally equal and the urban-rural development gap has been essentially eliminated. In order to narrow the development gap between urban and rural areas, the key is to mobilize various production factors, advance urban-rural integration, and increase the average level of agricultural productivity by accelerating the transfer of agricultural productivity to nonagricultural sectors and developing intensive farming. Nowadays, the income equality between urban and rural residents has increased more than three times. The reason for this is that agricultural productivity accounts for less than a third of the overall level of productivity. It is basically impossible to join the ranks of high-income countries when the rural population of a country accounts for nearly half of the total and there is still a large income gap between urban and rural residents. Therefore, in order to avoid falling into the trap, China must conduct institutional innovation, establish a new system of urban-rural integration, facilitate the flow of urban technologies, capital, and talent to rural areas, and accelerate agricultural modernization.

Advancing innovation-driven development is already an important goal for China. The report of the 17th CPC National Congress makes improving innovation capacity and building an innovative country core features of the national development strategy. The eight years since then has been a period of fast R&D growth and frequent S&T outcomes. Now, China's annual R&D input ranks second in the world, and first in number of R&D staff. These enterprises have become major players in the world of R&D input and innovation and number of innovative enterprises, such as Huawei and ZTE, have emerged. Huawei's and ZTE's annual patent applications have jumped to the top in the world. The number of China's domestic applications also ranks first in the world. China has narrowed the gap with the US in terms of international patent applications filed by enterprises. This is because the various reform measures proposed by the Third Plenary Session of the 18th CPC Central Committee have been gradually implemented, institutional innovation has further unleashed the potential of innovation and entrepreneurship, and the initiative of the vast majority of scientists and engineers has been aroused. It is fair to say that innovation development is inspiring the nation and an economic system and development model led and supported by innovation are taking shape.

42.2 How to Build an Economic System Led and Supported by Innovation

An economic system led and supported by innovation is completely different from that based on conventional technologies. It requires that the high and new technology industry be the dominant industry of the economy. New technologies and products must account for a certain share in economic value added each year, so as to realize expanded reproduction, in which a part of the surplus value is turned into capital. Even in conventional industries, China must adopt the latest modern technologies in order to transform. This includes realizing integration between industrialization and IT applications, widely adopting bio-engineering technologies in agriculture, widely applying modern logistics and transport technologies in the tertiary industry, and constantly increasing the share of clean and renewable energy in the energy industry. Compared with the traditional economic system, the new economic system is poised to greatly enhance economic, social, and ecological effects.

In order to set up an economic system led and supported by innovation, it is important to advance innovation in various areas, including S&T, industries, enterprises, markets, products, and business models.

STI has a strong effect on innovation. S&T represents the primary productive force. It prevails in every aspect and link of production, including technology equipment, production techniques, and operational technology. Technological progress is the driver of economic development. STI includes innovation in basic science, applied science, and specialized technology. Thus, China must establish a reasonable layout for human resources, funding, and material resources in those areas, and realize their mutual coordination and reinforcement. At present, China should put more resources in basic research, the breakthroughs of which would advance progress in applied and specialized technologies.

Industrial innovation is the standpoint of technological progress. The only way to translate S&T into productivity and bring tangible benefits to people is to transform the outcomes of basic and applied research into industrial technologies. Modern technology has led to a series of new industries, such as the internet, remote controls, genetic engineering, new energy, lasers, graphene, terahertz radiation, and 3D printing to name a few. A strong effort to catch up in these areas should be made, since there is still a large gap with such advanced technology at the international level. There is also a large gap with developed countries in terms of upgrading and transforming traditional industry technologies. In the oil and chemical industry, for instance, some US$200 billion worth of crude oil and precision instruments and chemical products were respectively imported on a yearly basis, which shows that China is still lagging far behind developed countries in traditional industrial technologies. If China could develop the coal chemical industry by utilizing the nation's rich coal resources as well as its leading coal chemical technologies, then China could surely end its heavy reliance on the importation of oil and chemical products. Each year, the nation imports over US$200 billion's worth of electronic chips. If the government could organize joint efforts in chip development, then the nation could kick start its domestic chip industry.

Corporate innovation is a key driving force behind technological innovation. At present, R&D input, the research force, and research outcomes account for over 70% of the total in society, which is up to speed with developed countries. This is huge progress. However, there is an imbalance between enterprise interest in technological R&D and actual investment in the field. Among the industrial enterprises above the designated scale, in 2013, only 14.8% of the enterprises conducted R&D and related activities, and R&D intensity stood at only 0.8%. Generally speaking, in conventional industries, R&D expenditure should account for over 3% of sales revenue; in high-tech industries, the proportion should exceed 10%. Most of China's enterprises have not yet reached those standards. Therefore, China should implement the instructions of General Secretary Xi to expedite the establishment of an economic system led and supported by innovation. China must start with enterprises and try to make more enterprises innovation-based.

Market innovation is the precondition for realizing the value of enterprises' products. In the context of overcapacity and stricter requirements, if enterprises want to seek constant development, then they must put consumers first and satisfy market demand and expand into new markets. Most importantly, China needs to be proficient at tapping the market. For example, as environmental pollution worsens, the environmental protection industry will become a new growth point; with the advent of an aging population, elderly care services and the fitness industry will become more important; and with more and more enterprises going global, new industries will be born, as a range of overseas investment services, such as consulting, financing, and insurance have to be provided for them. Not only should the domestic market be studied and developed, but that same level of attention should also be given to the international market. Only through market innovation can economic growth be boosted through diversified large-scale markets.

Product innovation is the necessary requirement for adapting to the constantly changing market. With the increase in people's incomes, consumption is on the rise, and S&T progress will lead to more new products and services to deal with the changes. By regarding product development as the foundation of survival, enterprises will not only meet existing demand, but also create new demand by developing their own products. Product innovation should focus on function and appearance, but also quality and safety, and always with the aim of creating famous trademarks.

Business model innovation is operational innovation, and is based on the requirements of new technologies and standards. New business models emerge, firstly and mostly, in commercial areas, with chain stores, supermarkets, warehouses, fast delivery, and fast food as representatives. Their convenience, speed, and efficiency make them strong competitors to traditional businesses. With the emergence of the Internet, production, circulation, and living have all changed, as can be seen with the emergence of online shops, Internet finance, mobile payment, crowd funding, online education, digital design and manufacturing, 3D printing, cultural creativity, tourism, reserving and renting, online entertainment, and so on. In almost all economic fields, whoever is first to take action is the first to gain opportunities and bring about great achievements.

Management innovation is the main driving force and foundation of various types of innovations. Management innovation refers to the innovation of systems, institutions, and mechanisms. A good system can result in common aspirations, such as a peaceful co-existence, care for the elderly, and education for the young. A good institution can stimulate the wisdom of the people and motivate them to work together. A good operational mechanism can increase the efficiency of enterprises, universities, research institutes, and even the whole country. Flexible and highly efficient operations maximize human capital, material resources, and funding. Management and S&T are the "two wheels" that drive modernization. Thus, STI must be supported by management innovation. It is in China's interest to draw upon advanced management experience in the modern world, constantly innovate management, and manage the country and its institutes and industries with efficiency.

42.3 How to Build an Innovation-Driven Development Model

The establishment of an innovation-driven development model concerns the entire process, from STI to economic development. China must reform and restructure each link.

First, it is important to stimulate key drivers of innovation. Enterprises, universities, and research institutes play an important role in advancing STI. At present, private enterprises are the major technology innovators, and the technology patents applied for each year by them account for around two thirds of the total national applications. SOEs have huge potential for innovation. By implementing the reform measures of the Third Plenary Session of the 18th CPC Central Committee, the orientation can be transformed from asset management to that of capital management, a system of mixed ownership can be developed, an employee share ownership system can be set up, and market competition can be strengthened. This will allow China to ultimately boost its innovation capability. In developed countries, universities serve as

STI bases, and major innovations often originate in universities. Some estimate that in modern times, nearly 70% of all STI outcomes come from universities. China should learn from developed countries in this regard and nurture highly innovative universities. This should be the priority of education and S&T system reforms. By introducing top professors and faculty members, domestic universities will be able to build world-class disciplines and make more S&T achievements. Based on the reform of the management systems in research institutes, full play will be given to the role of science academies and various STI research institutes, whose focus is on basic research. Since reform, research institutes affiliated with various departments have played a weaker role in the research of major industrial technologies. Therefore, they should organize industry alliances with the help of industrial associations and governments to implement joint innovation projects and overcome technical difficulties impeding industry development as soon as possible.

Second, effective approaches are needed to translate S&T outcomes into production. For a long time, engineering applications and industrialization have been the weak links in China's S&T system. In developed countries, the rate of translating S&T outcomes usually stands at around 60%, while in China, it stands at less than 20%. Besides the inferior quality of research findings, another reason behind the low rate is that it the nation lacks a mechanism for connecting users, technology owners, and the government. As enterprises are worried about the maturity of new technologies, they are not very willing to invest in engineering applications and pilot technologies, and are usually unwilling to take the risk of being the first. Technology owners lack funding for engineering applications and pilot programs. Particularly, the benefits of government-funded research outcomes are different for the researchers. Therefore, there is little incentive for researchers to do in-depth research or to care much about the S&T outcomes. Regarding these problems, government departments should strengthen the translation of S&T outcomes by deepening reform of the S&T system. More funding should be allocated for establishing a special fund for engineering applications and pilot programs, so as to subsidize the link. For the financial support that goes into producing technical outcomes and the inventions made by employees, later earnings should mostly go to the organizations or individuals who own the outcomes.

Third, there is need to improve the venture capital system for innovation and entrepreneurship. STI is fruitless without financial support. Thus, it is important to establish a good venture capital system, including seed money, venture capital funds, private equity funds, and GEM funds. This is the only way to activate the supporting role of finance for STI and high and new technology development. Seed money is a venture capital fund for investing in the R&D phase of start-ups. Venture capital funds only invest in companies with development potential and rapid growth. Entities funded under those two circumstances are all small high-tech enterprises at the early phase of entrepreneurship. Private equity funds are for non-listed companies. Most of the funded enterprises have a positive cash flow. Seed money is a type of early-phase investment tool, while the latter is intended for late-phase investment. China should improve GEM, so as to set up an exit mechanism for venture capital funds. High-tech enterprises in the US for instance grew mainly by relying on venture capital funds. As a latecomer, China should learn from foreign countries in cultivating and developing various types of venture capital funding, with an eye on supporting promising high-tech enterprises based on market-based valuation, optimization, and investment mechanisms.

Fourth, the government should play a role in supporting innovation and entrepreneurship. The vitality of innovation comes from the market, but the role of the government should not be ignored. The reasonable role of the government is an important reason why the US is able to maintain its leadership role in global S&T development. In terms of boosting innovation and entrepreneurship, the US government plays four main roles.

First, the US government launches national major engineering projects to drive S&T progress in different phases and mobilizes all kinds of resources for their implementation. For example, the Manhattan Project drove the development of the nuclear industry; the "Star Wars" program facilitated the development of the space and aeronautics industry; the information superhighway drove the development of the internet; and the new energy and manufacturing resurgence programs underway right now are playing a critical role in the development of the energy and manufacturing industries.

Second, the US government allows government-funded military technologies to be transferred to civilian industries, which helps facilitate the progress of civilian technology.

Third, the US government formulates intellectual property laws, improves the competition environment, and supports the development of small enterprises. The government also has a special bureau for small enterprises that allocates funding for the transformation of their S&T outcomes.

Fourth, the US government strives to attract global talent. It attracts outstanding global talent to study and work in America by providing scholarships and offering a path to American citizenship. In the current stage, China is only able to catch up quickly by way of formulating correct policies, laws, regulations, and development strategies based on China's own realities and drawing upon the management experience of developed countries, such as the US.

Lastly, the US government produces and attracts innovative talent at home and abroad. Talented people hold the key to establishing an economic system and development model led and supported by innovation. While stepping up efforts to produce innovative talent at home, the Chinese government should also select and use talent from all across the world, as called for by the Third Plenary Session of the 18th CPC Central Committee. China should care about children when they are young, cultivate their innovation capacity, and produce leaders based on further reform of the nation's education systems. Thus, overseas students should be encouraged to return upon completion of their studies, strategies and policies should be mapped out for attracting global talent, and enterprises should be encouraged to use local human resources by establishing overseas R&D branches.

Part VI
Industrial Revitalization

Chapter 43
The Cultivation and Development of Pillar Industries in the 1990s

43.1 The New Stage and Major Tasks of Economic Growth

Fifteen years of reform and opening up have greatly boosted China's economic growth and changed the country's economic outlook, ushering the country's economic growth into a new stage. The principal indications of this new stage are as follows: (1) agriculture has been developed enough to meet the basic food requirements of most Chinese people; (2) the supply for industrial consumer goods has been changed from shortage to low-level surplus; (3) energy and raw materials output has gained a spot on the world's top list. The industrialization of many countries has proved that there would be a leap for economic development when agriculture and labor-intensive industries meet people's demands for subsistence, or in other words, when per capita GDP stand at between 300 and US$400. The aim of this economic leap is to meet consumer demands at the higher level, focus on the development of capital-intensive and technology-intensive industries, which can steer economic growth to the stage of an accelerated industrialization process. Based on all these indications, it is clear that China has already stepped into a new stage of accelerated industrialization.

Considering the development stage of consumer demands, it has been included in the agenda that China will soon solve the problem of housing and transport as the country sets its targets on reaching the level of a moderately prosperous society in the 20th century. According to sample surveys and opinion polls, the biggest wish for urban dwellers is to improve their housing environment, and have telephones and automobiles as tools for information passage and transport. Without the development of these new fields, it would be impossible for per capita GDP to leap from the level of US$300–US$1000.

This article originally appeared in *Reform and Opening Up Forum*, no. 2, 1993.

X. Zheng, *China's 40 Years of Economic Reform and Development*,
https://doi.org/10.1007/978-981-13-2727-8_43

Considering the current industrial development, globally China's level of gross production for coal, cement and agricultural products is ranked at number one while power generation is ranked fourth and steel production takes the third spot. In agricultural and industrial production, China has been the leading provider of labor resource and power for the processing industry. Nonetheless, the added value of the industry is ranked 11th in the world, lower than Brazil. The reason for this is that the processing intensity and technology of Chinese products, as well as China's industrial structure and product mix are at the low end of the international industrial chain. We can only produce 1/6–1/4 of the production value of developed countries with the same amount of energy and raw materials consumption. Considering that a combined added value of the manufacturing industries of China, the US and Japan in 1990 were US$94 billion, US$868.2 billion and US$689.3 billion respectively, this meant that China's added value of the industry accounted for only one ninth and one seventh that of the US and Japan. Hence, in the new stage of economic growth, the direction of China's industrial development must transform from an extensive model to intensive model. The development focus should also be shifted from coal, steel and other primary energy and raw materials to energy-saving, material-saving high-value-added products. The processing industry should also transform from an ordinary processing industry to a processing industry with higher processing intensity and high technology.

43.2 The New Economic Growth Areas in the 1990s

In the 1980s, the development of China's economy was driven mainly by a rapid growth of agriculture, textile and other light industries as well as building the materials industry. As the economy needed to step into a new growth stage in the 1990s, we had to seek out new economic growth points. Therefore leading industries that boost the development of the economy, new growth points should have the following features:

(1) the industry must have a significant pull effect on production and consumption, and have a high degree of industrial relevance and good market prospects;
(2) products of the industry must have high added value and technology and be highly capable of withdrawing currency from circulation;
(3) the industry must have an appeal for investment and should be capable of rapid development with enough resources;
(4) the industry must also have promising economic benefits to help increase fiscal revenue.

In the industrial field, cultivation and establishment of new leading industries must comply with the requirements of the 14th National Congress of the CPC. It would therefore be beneficial to revitalize the machinery and electronic industry, oil and chemical industry, automobile and construction industry that have the features mentioned above, and make them the pillars of the economy.

China's electronic industry did not start very late, and we invested a good amount of human and financial resources in it, but it grew too slowly that it was lagging behind the developed electronic industries in foreign countries. In 1990, China's net output value for its electronic industry was about US$14.5 billion, and this number in the US stood at US$226.3 billion whereas Japan's was at US$158.7 billion and even South Korea attained US$26 billion of the net output value from its electronic industry. The electronic industry alone has made China's GDP US$210 billion and US$140 billion less than that of the US and Japan respectively. It also was 2.2 times and 1.5 times of China's added value of the industry. This gap cannot be offset solely by developing the textile and other light industry, as well as other regular processing industries. The most important thing is that a lagging electronic industry will lower the overall competitiveness of China's machinery products, hinder the development of information industry, and ultimately affect the technical level of the whole industry and all sectors of the society. As Mr. Jiang Zemin said, the electronic industry is the multiplier of the economy. This is very visionary. As a result, focusing our resources on developing the electronic industry and making it the pillar industry in the 1990s shall be at the top of our list of industrial development. In the machinery industry, we should regard the production of large sets of equipment, including transportation and telecommunications equipment, energy equipment, and chemical industrial equipment, as the priority of development. It would be beneficial to develop the production of mechanical and electrical products according to the requirements of mechatronics. As the shipbuilding industry is a technology-intensive and labor-intensive industry, China has an edge to developing a shipbuilding industry. Accelerating the development of the shipbuilding industry will not only revitalize the shipping cause, but also help earn foreign exchange through export.

The oil and chemical industry is also an important sector, and therefore developed countries generally regard it as the pillar industry and give priority to its development. From 1950 to 1990, while the world's steel production increased three folds, production of ethylene and plastic increased by 60 times. This was due to the cost of producing plastics being only half of that for producing steel. At present, the proportion of plastics to substitute steel is as high as 50% in foreign countries, while the proportion is no more than 10% in China. China's Ethylene production lags far behind that in developed countries like the US and Japan. It in fact cannot even catch up with that of South Korea. In 1991, South Korea's ethylene production reached 2.55 million tons while that of China was only 1.76 million tons. Therefore the backward ethylene industry pushed up demand for steel consumption, but the rapid development of the industry brought huge pressure on energy consumption and transportation, which is very uneconomical in the perspective of a macro-economy. As for the oil and chemical industry, the production of fine chemical products accounted for a small proportion of the whole industry, which was also a reflection of the fact that China's oil and chemical enterprises were lagging behind. If we are to develop the oil and chemical industry, we need to therefore put the production of fine chemical products at a prominent position; a crucial approach to increasing economic benefits of the oil and chemical industry.

Meanwhile, China's auto industry was rather the weakest link within the industrial structure, so we had to use the invaluable foreign exchange to import our automobiles. US$2.5 billion was also spent on imported parts and components to produce one million cars in 1992. The expenditure on each imported car was equal to an investment needed to produce a car in a domestic automobile factory. Today, imported automobiles now take up around one third of the total number of vehicles in the country while China's automobile production only accounts for one eighteenth that of Japan. Also, it's important to note that China started to develop its auto industry 10 years earlier than South Korea which began developing its auto industry in the 1960s. Despite that head start, China's automobile production is still two times less than that of South Korea. Additionally, automobile has become Korea's flagship product for export, and 70% of South Korean families own cars. More notably, South Korea's territory is only one per cent that of China, but cars South Koreans own total more than five million, only two million less than the cars owned by Chinese citizens. A car is a typical kind of a high-value-added product, and an automobile civilization is an important symbol of the modern industrial civilization. Currently, the development of China's steel industry, chemical industry, machinery industry and petroleum industry has laid the foundation for a great development of the auto industry. We therefore cannot translate the more than one trillion yuan of deposits of Chinese people unless we exchange them with high involvement products, such as cars. Foreign experience has demonstrated that households cannot own cars until the per capita GDP reaches US$1000. The per capita GDP in China's Pearl River Delta region, southern Jiangsu, the Hangzhou-Jiaxing-Huzhou area and some suburban areas is more than US$1000. The steadily growing presence of cars in families will play a crucially integral role in stabilizing commodity prices in the market. Clearly the time is ripe for a strong development of the auto industry in China.

Additionally as a labor-intensive sector, the construction industry should be a powerful pillar for China. In foreign countries, the construction industry takes up more than 20% of GDP, but in China, that figure is only 5%. The biggest hindrance to the development of the construction industry has been the welfare of urban housing and its decommercialization. Which means that the production, circulation, distribution and consumption cannot enter into a virtuous cycle. As a result, we should, through the reform of housing commercialization, promote the development of the construction industry while complying with the law of value. Improving people's housing conditions is an integral strategy that would help us reach the level of a moderately prosperous society by the end of the 20th century. While accelerating the reforms aimed at the housing commercialization, we need to also engage in transforming the country's income distribution system. It would also be beneficial to translate welfare subsidies for housing into salaries, in order to regulate the supply and demand by modulating house prices. By doing this, we can tackle the unfair distribution of housing and transform part of people's income into an investment for the construction of new property, which will in turn support the development of the housing sector. The construction industry, including infrastructure construction, should also adopt social fund raising and value compensation. During the 1980s, China built more than 1000 bridges in the Pearl Delta region, ending a history of auto ferrying in that region at one stroke. This was one method of building more bridges and generating profits from them—a measure worth promoting.

Since then, the four pillar industries mentioned above have become leading industries driving industrial development in the new stage of China's economic growth and are also viewed as the new economic growth points. As they have a high market demand and degree of industrial relevance, developing them undoubtedly encouraged a rapid development in Chinese industries and boosted the whole economy in the 1990s.

43.3 The Development of Pillar Industries Requires Powerful Industry Organizational Policies

Apart from the new materials sector within the electronic and chemical industries, the four pillar industries are viewed as the traditional sectors that boast mature production technologies. Therefore In order to tap the latecomer advantages, we need to formulate clear industrial policies, make use of macro regulation and policy guidance, and apply administrative approaches when necessary to accelerate the cultivation and development of these pillar industries. Of course, all the macro regulatory and administrative approaches by the government should be carried out without interfering with the normal functions of market mechanisms. It would therefore be beneficial to enable this mechanism to fully play its mandated role in the allocation of resources, and pool the various kinds of production factors within enterprises that boast advanced technologies, high management level, good product quality and low production costs through market competition. By supporting advanced enterprises, we can also help increase their market share, and phase out backward enterprises and products of low quality. This is the only effective way to overcome the current problem facing construction projects that are too miniaturized and dispersed, as well as the regression of technology.

Another helpful strategy is to organize the building of pillar industries using the principle of economies of scale. The four pillar industries are all typical with remarkable economies of scale benefits. For example, we cannot achieve a specialized and socialized production of auto parts and components, unless we significantly lower costs, and make cars that are more competitive in the international markets until our annual production within the auto industry reaches 300,000 plus. For the chemical industry on the other hand, the economic scale of ethylene production should be 300,000 tons per year compared to the current largest scale of ethylene production which has exceeded 700,000 tons in foreign countries; because those construction projects failing to meet the standards of economic scale cannot survive when China restores the status of contracting party of the General Agreement on Tariffs and Trade that allows the import of foreign products. Hence, the principles of economies of scale should be vital for the development of these pillar industries.

Reorganizing existing enterprises according to the requirements of specialized and socialized production is another crucial measure of their development. The four industries have already had considerable production capacities, so the foundation for their reorganization is good, and the layout for this process has also been laid. The problem however, is that the productions are too dispersed as all enterprises are only either keen on "large and all-inclusive" or "small but all-inclusive" productions. In the meantime, their products slowly become outdated, their equipment too old and these enterprises get saddled with over-staffing. That's why the focus must now be on producing new products with promising market potentials and uniting production-related enterprises in order to break the barriers within the industry and develop a horizontal union. This is especially true for the electronic, mechanical and auto industries whereby these sectors are made up of a multitude of production factories, whereas those enterprises capable of large-scale, specialized and high-level productions are scarce. Therefore, according to economic laws and principles of sharing benefits and risks at the same time, we should unite enterprises of the same type through the coordination of governments at all levels. Also in order to remove the restrictions on local financial contracting systems, we also ought to reform the tax system; which means that we have to transform the current turnover tax collected in accordance with the place of production, and then turn it into income tax collected in accordance with the place of operators and investors. This would encourage local governments to give support based on the benefits as per the horizontal investment and union within enterprises.

With regards to R&D for important new technologies and products, we should unify talent resources in the industry to tackle problems facing the development process. For example, we need to consolidate our talents, material and financial resources to make achievements in the manufacturing technology of integrated circuits and other key components, and have achievements shared by all. While we should also actively introduce foreign technologies to speed up our domestic technological progress, foreign countries are generally not willing to sell their truly competitive and advanced technologies. Therefore, we need to depend on ourselves to develop similar important technologies, such as those in the electronic industry. At the same time, we could invite foreign experts, especially foreign experts of Chinese origin, to cooperate in R&D.

The time frame for implementing projects should be as short as possible, so that investment could reach a relatively high level. Once we start the projects, we should work around the clock to implement them, because the earlier the implementation process, the sooner the return on investment will be. If the time frame is too long, the debt of loan interests would be correspondingly higher. Some foreign countries spent only one year to construct a mini-sized car factory with an annual production of 240,000 cars. Such a short time frame can be attributed to full preparation, where they did not waste any second when the projects were started. This is therefore one important experience.

43.4 Establishing Effective and Flexible Investment and Financing Mechanisms

Most of the pillar industries are capital-intensive. As a result, to develop these types of industries, we must invigorate the capital market, establish sound investment and financing systems, so that enterprises and investors can get the funds needed in time.

The shareholding system is an important fundraising form. It would be beneficial to select some projects with relatively high expected rates of returns on investment in the key construction projects determined in the Eighth Five-Year Plan and 10-year planning, and provide these projects with a joint investment from the central government, local governments and enterprises. Profits and assignment of jobs can be distributed in proportion with the amount of investment. We can adopt the bidding method of choosing enterprises. We need to increase pilot stock markets to change the situation where the demand for stock markets considerably exceeds supply. Nonetheless, considering China's situation, for the foreseeable future, financial resources of these enterprises would mainly come from indirect financing, and the direct financing will remain at a low level. Even in Japan, a country with a developed stock market, direct financing only accounts for around 30% of all the financial resources for enterprises, and the rest of it comes from bank loans and other financial institutions. Enterprises with a higher proportion of indirect financing have a stronger competitive edge. Considering China's actual situation, currently it is necessary to moderately develop the stock financing of enterprises in order to enable the society to supervise these enterprises and explore new financing channels. Nevertheless, in the long run, we should make indirect financing from banks as the major financing channel for enterprises, and rigorously develop this financing method.

It would be beneficial to establish state policy investment banks, because some enterprises and construction projects have good social benefits but their investment recovery period is long and the rate of return on investment is low. For these enterprises, we should provide a moderate proportion of fiscal funds as an interest subsidy to support these industries. As with regards to other regular construction projects, loans from commercial banks should play the leading role.

Tapping foreign investment is another channel of financial resources to develop pillar industries. This is especially true for the auto, construction, oil and chemical industries, among others. These sectors have become sunset industries, so we need to attract them into China or buy their second-hand equipment, while we strive to get a buyer's credit. In conclusion, to develop China's pillar industries rapidly we should take advantage of foreign resources and their production capacity.

Chapter 44
On the Strategy of Big Enterprises and Groups of China

44.1 Assurance that the Large Enterprise Group Strategy Is Principal in China's Economic Development and Institutional Transformation in the Near Future

During the 46 years since the establishment of the People's Republic of China, we have established a relatively complete industrial system with high technological levels and overall scale—plus huge state-owned assets. However, those enterprises and organizations formed in a planned economy often face problems to do with simplistic businesses, small scale decentralized structures and lack of technological development capabilities. In addition, state-owned asset structures taking shape in the planned economy can also be plagued by dispersed arrangements, languidness and low efficiency. Therefore it is clear that that these enterprises, organizations and assets structures cannot meet the requirements for developing a successful socialist market economy. However, even with the reorganization and adjustments slightly improving, these structures still pose as a serious problem. As a result, the major task in front of us is to more quickly form a new economic pattern featuring higher levels of competition, more grouped organizational structures and higher scale profits that can fit within the Ninth Five-Year Plan period and even beyond that. It is our belief that we should be steadfast and quick to build enterprise groups that integrate technology, factory (production) and trade. An enterprise group can be the backbone of the economy and become a leading force for progressing various industries, which will then drive the optimization and upgrade of the whole economic structure. This therefore is our most pressing issue for us to tackle.

Other pressing problems affecting the Chinese economy are low industrial concentration and minor scale merits, which directly restrict our capability for economic

---

This article originally appeared in *China Industrial Economics*, no. 11, 1995, and was coauthored with Li Liang.

X. Zheng, *China's 40 Years of Economic Reform and Development*,
https://doi.org/10.1007/978-981-13-2727-8_44

competition and economic efficiency because key industries in developed market-economies are supposed to be highly centralized. Take the US as an example. In 1972, the top four American enterprises dealing with automobile, plate glass, turbine and turbine engines, refrigeration and freezers as well as those producing television tubes, together accounted for 99, 92, 90, 85 and 83% respectively. And the top eight US enterprises (groups) together took up 100, 96, 98 and 97%. Therefore, it can be regarded that in Western countries, large enterprises always play a leading role in almost all important industries. China once tried to build an industrial trust in the 1960s, but soon this organization was criticized as being of a capitalist nature. In the absence of market competition and barriers between sectors and blocks therefore, the structure of enterprise organization grew more like a short tree—which is small but divergent, and demonstrated a dispersed pattern. In China's 431 biggest enterprises, there are only 27 of them with over one billion yuan of fixed asset of core enterprises, 144 with 100 million yuan to one billion yuan, 83 with 50 million yuan to 100 million yuan and 177 with no more than 50 million yuan. So far, China is yet to make it to the list of world-class enterprises.

The socialist market economy should therefore not only be an economic system with simple and redundant low-level competition, but rather, it should be a modern market economy that suits a socialized mass production of a higher level. Similarly, the modern corporate system should not just a corporate system with proprietorships and partnerships as the principal form in the early stages of capitalism. Rather, it must be a corporate system in which large enterprises are the principal force, and a limited liability system is the mainstream. Since the mid-19th century, western countries have gradually established such an economic pattern where large enterprises or groups with large absolute scale and large market shares dominate the lifeblood and future of the various industries and even the whole economy. Looking at the history of the development of capitalism, we can see that it is precisely during the process of capital concentration and economic collectivization that technological and industrial reforms occurred. The reforms facilitated the development of specialization and coordination, and fostered the corporate legal person systems, legal person governance structures (corporate governance) and the divisional organization systems that decentralized the force of large enterprises. The occurrence and development of these systems therefore enhanced the stability, order and efficiency of the capitalist market system. Just like many Western economists have said, we are now in an economic age when large enterprises are the hub of the whole economy. As a result, it is reasonable to say that China's socialist market economy is a market economy where state-owned enterprises (groups) are the principal bodies while SMEs still fully develop.

In order to establish a socialist market system, it is therefore our belief that we should not only liberalize the market, but also innovate organizational structures in order to cultivate large enterprise groups under the visible hand that is government regulations. Keeping in mind that the Chinese market is not yet mature enough, large enterprise groups can also fundamentally change market structures, form the mechanisms for profits that would benefit the society as a whole and improve the level of competitions in the market economy and ultimately form a true market mechanism for allocating social labor according to corresponding shares. The market competition should not be a race for SMEs in dealing with commodity pricing and sales. Instead, it should be an organized competition of large enterprises and groups with a market vision, courage, strategies and operating capabilities. In China's industrial economic structure in the future, sectors like textile, clothing, shoes, hats, and toys manufacturing would be regulated mainly by the market. However, for sectors featuring intensive capital, batch production and high levels of asset specialization, we must cultivate large enterprise groups and ensure organized and orderly competition. Sectors of this kind include the auto industry, steel production, telecommunications, glass production, electronic and electrical products manufacturing, chemical industry, aerospace and aircraft manufacturing industry.

44.2 Fully Understanding the Economies of Scale of Enterprise Groups and Its Role in Stabilizing and Coordinating the Economy

Economics tells us that transformation from dispersion to concentration and from small to large scale may lead to a progressive increase of return to scale. In order to moderately step up the industrial and economic concentration, we can lower the production cost per unit and thus increase labor productivity, that which is referred to as the economies of scale. The advantages of economies of scale are mainly reflected in economies of production scale, economies of investment scale, economies of technological innovation scale, economies of management scale and economies of structural upgrading and so on. Enterprise groups led by large enterprises can also have the combination effect of production factors, amplification effect of unit equity capital and the synergy of capital operation.

In a modern market economy, the development of enterprise groups and the concentration of operations are complementary to a socialized mass production and development of a specialized and coordinated production. Big enterprises and SMEs are linked through a network among them, within which these enterprises integrate various businesses through a variety of purchase and sale relations and through organizing a peripheral cooperation and the signing of contracts. As a result, stable internal structures for industries and markets take shape. In Japan, there are many SMEs centering around large enterprises, but such a huge amount of SMEs are not operating in their own way, rather, these companies take the large enterprises as their core reflection and develop in a small and smart, small and specialized, small and flexible as well as small and profitable fashion. The growth of large enterprise groups will automatically improve industrial and economic qualities, prevent risks and reduce resistance for the operation of a macro-economy, enhance economic stability and lessen cyclical fluctuations in the economy.

Big enterprise groups generally are the, foundation for technological progress in modern industries, major innovator for industrial application technologies and the principal body driving science and technology development. These roles therefore cannot simply be substituted by any other scientific and research organizations. In the history of a capitalist economy, it was the capital monopoly and concentration that formed syndicates, which made for an industrial revolution and technological revolution following World War II and facilitated great developments in computer technologies, laser, aerospace, nuclear energy and synthetic chemicals. Meanwhile, the investment needed in modern R&D is too much for both a single SME and the government. Hence, the function of large enterprise groups in organizing R&D on the basis of product innovation is precisely the principal force for a modern technological revolution. Historically, the scientific prowess of these enterprises is what has made many western governments entrust some of their planning projects to large enterprises. Some governments even provide the entrusted enterprises with fiscal funds. Also, in some countries, almost all large enterprises have several scientific research centers. In fact, some enterprises even have more R&D staff compared to their production personnel. Thus investment in R&D generally accounts for over 10% of their revenue, and the proportion can reach as high as 20% in some enterprises. In this perspective, China has still got a lot to do. In order to promote China's scientific and technological progress, and drive science and technology into productive forces, we must therefore rely on large enterprise groups and tap their function as the hub connecting technology and technological innovation amongst production organizations.

For China, large enterprise groups are not only the principal force in international competition, but also the foundation for international cooperation. Today, the circulation of international capital, technology and commodities generally occurs amongst large multinational companies. Large enterprises also play a leading role in high-level international cooperation. As China's economy is increasingly integrated into the global economy, it at the same time is facing stiff competition internationally. At present, China's existing enterprise groups are hardly powerful enough to be able to compete with foreign multinational companies. As a result China opts to restrain while at the same time implementing further reform and opening up as well as expanding its presence in the international market. With that in mind, we must therefore cultivate a number of large powerful and competitive enterprise groups to confront their foreign counterparts plugging their products into China. This would enable us to effectively cooperate with them while introducing high technology and foreign capital into our market in turn helping Chinese enterprises really go global. Right now however, China is still in urgent need for such large enterprise groups.

In the modern market economy, the conglomeration of enterprises with groups as the principal form is also capable of macro conduction and coordination. Big enterprise groups can use their influence in their industries and economic sectors to motivate SMEs, which means that large enterprises can play the role of a coordinator for the industrial development and market order, while influencing and guiding SMEs through their production scales, market shares, broad connection, good credit and product quality and even their enterprise culture. Governments alone are not capable of playing such a significant role or cannot perform better than large enterprise groups. Therefore, through parent enterprise groups, public interests and government wills can be sent to basic levels more effectively. Furthermore, governments can collect micro economic information through the parent company in order to improve their decision-making ability and enhance their regulations. The direct regulation of enterprises by the government is characteristic of its old system. However, the new system does not mean that governments will be detached from enterprises. The key to this relationship is to form an intermediary that can be a bridge between the government and SMEs, as well as between the macro-economy and the micro-economy. In this way, the government and key industrial organizations can have a mutual dependence. Apart from industrial associations, large enterprise groups are also an important part of this kind of key industrial organizations. As the government commits itself to formulating policies and macroeconomic guidance, the social intermediary force engages in policy implementation and its role as the backbone of the economy. Hence this trend is fast becoming the basic structure for modern market economies.

Big enterprise groups so far have played a special role in the building of China's new state-owned assets management system. In the traditional system, the government's involvement in enterprises and capital seriously constrained business operations, lowering the efficacy of state-owned assets. At the same time, state-owned assets were distributed in various industries and sectors, so the decentralized management caused a scarce organization of scale. Since reform, however, despite enterprises gaining vitality after their decentralization and interest concessions of the government, the unnecessary distribution of state-owned assets remained as a problem, and the contradiction between government administrative management and capital management was not solved either. What's more, problems like disorderly regulations, losses of state-owned assets and the serious infringement of property interests were also rampant. As a result, to further deepen the reform process, we must now clarify property rights and straighten up the state-owned assets management systems. In the future therefore, state-owned assets must be relatively concentrated in certain key and strategic industries, where the government cannot directly be responsible for their management, at least for those within a single enterprise. This therefore requires us to carry out important strategic adjustments to the structure of these assets in order to gradually focus on large enterprise groups of strategic interests.

44.3 Lessons China Can Learn from the Western Market Economy in Promoting Economic Collectivization and Large Enterprise Policies

The modern market economies and so-called modern legal person systems in Western countries are built within the growth of large enterprises. All countries with developed industries have at some point experienced this process when the scale of enterprises expanded rapidly and the whole industrial production became more and more concentrated within large enterprises. Just as Karl Marx said when analyzing the mode of production of capitalism, "The world would still be without railways if it had had to wait until accumulation had got a few individual capitals far enough to be adequate for the construction of a railway. Centralization, on the contrary, accomplished this in the twinkling of an eye, by means of joint-stock companies."[1] The concentration and the share holding companies Marx said are precisely the mode of production that large enterprises need.

In the 1870s, the success of the DuPont Company was because the three young du Pont cousins—T. Coleman, Pierre S. and Alfred I., graduated from Massachusetts Institute of Technology, then joined and reorganized the DuPont brand. They integrated all the DuPont businesses and some other companies in relevant industries into a unified company, which in turn increased the company's production capacity to 60% of that of the whole industry. And in the initial stages of the 20th century, when the General Motors Corporation (GM) was on the verge of bankruptcy, Pierre S., one of the three du Pont cousins, entered the company and bought the Buick brand as well as the control of a number of enterprises dealing with the production of car components. He then reorganized the structure of the GM and brought it back to life. The economic concentration would inevitably cause a system of innovation, so Pierre and Alfred Pritchard Sloan, the iconic entrepreneur, cooperated and initiated a decentralization model in coordination with a uniform plan for the company and established independent operations for the business division at GM.

Since then, there have been two well-known waves of enterprise mergers in the history of the US. The first wave was an acquisition featuring a horizontal integration from 1897 to 1903, which gave birth to cartels such as the US Steel and the DuPont Company, and so on. The second wave was mainly the horizontal and vertical integration that occurred between 1925 and 1930. This one formed a number of enterprise groups and transnational conglomerates. The United Kingdom, Germany, Japan and France also had many Trust and Konzern monopolistic organizations through syndication at the end of the 19th century and at the beginning of the 20th century, rapidly realizing industrialization and modernization. Of course, capital concentration and enterprise collectivization can also lead to excessive monopoly, which can dampen fair competition. The modern capitalistic economy has meanwhile been caught up in an intertwined development of monopoly and competition. Today more than ever, the world economy keeps seeing concentrated, grouped, transnational and integrated productions and operations, which meet the requirements of economies of scale and coexist within a dispersed, miniaturized, competitive and varied production and operations process that meet the requirements of a specialized labor division. Governments of capitalist countries are also riding along with this trend and regulating their industrial order and market structures through anti-trust and pro-competition policies. Lenin called the capitalist governments the "national commission of billionaires," because the governance of these governments was based on these large syndicates and, they voluntarily or unconsciously, implemented a series of policies supporting large syndicates. Hence, the implemented large group policies can be categorized as follows:

[1] https://www.marxists.org/archive/marx/works/1867-c1/ch25.htm.

First, the governments of Japan, South Korea and some other countries attach great importance to developing large enterprise groups through industrial policies, and these governments pay high attention to the cultivation of enterprise groups in industries that enjoy government support.
Second, the capitalist economic planning promoted by the Western countries after World War II is also in favor of large enterprises.
Third, the preferential tax policies for large enterprises are not only conducive to the accumulation of national monopoly capital, but also beneficial for the redistribution of private monopoly capital.
Fourth, Western governments support large syndicates through credit policies, which means that financial institutions controlled by governments give priority to syndicates in loans and offer them low interest rates. Some governments even offer subsidies to monopolistic enterprises through fiscal spending or offer them interest repayments.
Fifth, these western countries use public spending and national orders for goods to support large enterprise groups. For example, during World War II, the US government provided 70% of armament orders worth a huge amount of money to one hundred large companies, which significantly facilitated the development of these enterprises.
Sixth, some countries also offer a huge amount of research funds for scientific research institutions of large enterprises, or allow monopolistic enterprises to take advantage of their scientific results.
Seventh, these governments promote structural adjustments to facilitate the development of large enterprises. When privatizing state-owned enterprises, some Western countries often sell some lucrative state-owned enterprises to individual monopoly capitalists with a price much lower than the value of the assets, or simply entrust these assets to some private syndicates for operation. Russia and various other eastern European countries generally adopted this measure of cultivating large enterprise groups during the privatization, and organized syndication of industrial enterprises as well as the association of industrial sectors and financial enterprises.

44.4 The Implementation of China's Large Group Strategy Must Be Promoted with a Coordination of Structural Adjustments in Existing State-Owned Assets and the Revitalization of Pillar Industries

A large group strategy cannot be realized by a single capital; therefore centralization through syndicates is a must. Looking at the history of the development of a market economy, we find that syndication and acquisition are the basic ways to adjust the structure of assets in a market. They can also accelerate capital concentration and expansion. While syndication may rapidly realize a collectivization of existing enterprises, acquisition can in fact rapidly turn many SMEs into large enterprises and transform large enterprises into mega-corporations or conglomerates. Characterized by the enterprise consolidation, both syndication and acquisition actually belong to the horizontal and vertical integrations. A horizontal integration applies to the syndication, acquisition or merger of industries that produce similar kinds of products. Vertical integration on the other hand applies to the syndication, acquisition or merger of units or departments that are relevant with the supply, production, sales and scientific research of their principal products. For China, the transition from the planned economy to the market economy and the marketization of state-owned assets will require a long process of structural shifts. It is therefore necessary and inevitable to engage in syndication and acquisition, as these measures are beneficial for the country's national development strategies as well as industrial policies. This is thus a historic opportunity for China.

Since the spontaneous structural adjustments of the market are extremely slow, the Chinese government should plan and guide these adjustments plus their reorganization. The first thing we should do is to plan the enterprise structure, industrial structure and regional structure for state-owned assets, and moderately scale down the covering industries of state-owned assets in order to reshape the distribution of state-owned assets in industries and enterprise organizations. The structural reorganization should be a unique choice for China's reforms on public ownership, which essentially are distinguished from the privatization measures adopted by the Soviet Union and some eastern European countries. China's various regions should also change and be in pursuit of an extensive, inclusive and systematic development concept, and actively adjust local industrial structures by organizing regional economic integrations and ultimately solve the problem that make its regional industrial structures seem too similar to each other.

The first task for structural reorganization is to remove barriers between regions and those between departments. Establish and give priority to a number of large enterprise groups that are interlinked through property rights of state-owned assets. At the present time, existing SOEs should all be included in the scope for structural reorganization. Apart from the various wholly state-owned enterprises that have monopolistic control in some special industries, the majority of SOEs should undergo integration that will enable enterprise centralization or face a merger and acquisition that will enable large-scale enterprise concentrations. For those small and medium-sized enterprises (SMEs), faced with challenges in collectivization or centralization, if they belong to non-essential industries, we could gradually denationalize them through reforms.

Structural reorganization should reflect the principle of stressing efficiency and highlighting priorities. During the Ninth Five-Year Plan period, China will extensively implement the industrial policies of the 1990s, spare no effort in revitalizing pillar industries and support leading industries in order to accomplish a strategic step by step target aimed at achieving high-level industrial structure. In order to reach the target, it is suggested that the reorganization of state-owned assets be combined with the strategic planning for large groups. That is to say, we should, on the condition of uniform planning, moderately invest in operational state-owned assets and increase the volumes of our national and private investments injected into the electronic industry, auto industry, petroleum and chemical industry, machinery industry and construction industry. This should be a process for building large enterprise groups and supporting the collectivization of key enterprises.

At present, we should particularly place high premium on the large enterprise groups included in the national pilot program in order to help them play their important role in the structural reorganization. It would be beneficial to rigorously encourage pilot groups to engage in business integration or acquisition to improve the level of their production scales and overall performance. It would also be meaningful to encourage parent companies to participate in the market's property rights in order to integrate or merge with production enterprises dealing with similar products and with enterprises and public institutions that are relevant with regards to supply chains, scientific research, sales, foreign trade, and so on. Enabling the parent company to coordinate and direct the integration, acquisition, separation and merger within the enterprise and major structural shifts such as foreign investment, capital increase or reduction, and so on would also be instrumental. For the pilot SOEs whose parent companies need integration or acquisition, the government should provide them with, administrative policy support, special credits and prominent debt reduction for enterprises subject to integration or acquisition.

In order to better accommodate this strategy, we should therefore reform the management system of state-owned assets. On the basis of promoting the parent-subsidiary company system, characterized by connected property rights as the principal bond, those in charge shall therefore develop part of the company of these large enterprise groups and make them owners of state-owned property rights for the existing assets. The government will also authorize these parent companies to operate and manage these property rights, play the role of investors on behalf of the government and be responsible for the preservation and increase of the value of state-owned assets. It would therefore be beneficial to rigorously push forward the separation of government and business and standardize regulations that govern enterprise groups. In order to do this, we must therefore abolish the affiliation between regulating departments of the government and its subsidiary companies that are part of these pilot enterprise groups while at the same time entrusting the corresponding parent companies to manage their subsidiary companies. The central and local governments must not interfere with these property rights and the handling of the parent companies or try to arbitrarily influence the legal person property rights of member enterprises. In short, administrative departments should not regulate certain individual member enterprises within these enterprise groups. Rather, these departments shall independently carry out their industrial planning and management through the established enterprise groups in order to implement standards set for product quality and safe production as well as put in place relevant policies and regulations to govern relevant industries. In this way, we will not only realize the enterprise-oriented operation and scientific management of state-owned assets through large enterprise groups, but also significantly boost their growth.

44.5 The Key to Implementing a Large Enterprise Group Strategy Is to Establish a Policy Guarantee System

For now, various parties have reached a broad consensus on the significance of developing large enterprise groups. The *Decision of the CPC Central Committee on Certain Issues of Establishing the Socialist Market Economy* adopted at the Third Plenary Session of the 14th CPC Central Committee also clearly pointed out that we should "develop a number of trans-regional and trans-industrial large enterprises with public ownership as the principal body and the connection of property rights as the principal bond, and encourage these enterprises to play its role in facilitating structural adjustment, improving economies of scale, accelerating the development of new technologies and new products, and enhancing the international competitiveness of China's enterprises." Now, the crucial point is how to establish an effective policy guarantee system.

First, we should implement industrial and supporting investment policies that are conducive to the development of large enterprise groups. It would be beneficial to continue exerting more authority to qualified enterprise groups for investment. When arranging investment projects, the government should give priority to planned projects proposed by large enterprise groups, but only those that meet the requirements stipulated in the industrial policies on condition that the value of projects is no more than the total investment of fixed asset investments. The government could entrust some key projects to capable large groups for investment and construction, which will make these large groups play an important role in the adjusting of the industrial structure and in the increasing of returns on investment (ROI). In addition, entrusted groups can thereby build their business scales and enhance their competitiveness in both the domestic and foreign markets. With regards to major projects from the state, the government could learn from countries like France and broadly adopt contracts for economic plans and form a stable relationship with a number of large enterprise groups.

Second, we should implement financial policies that benefit large enterprise groups. The measures for research and consideration can be categorized as follows:

(1) upon the foundation of complying with the national industrial policies, national banks shall provide priority to large enterprise groups in issuing credits for production and business operations;
(2) for part of policy construction projects undertaken by large enterprise groups, the national policy banks shall provide them with relative preferential policy loans as support;
(3) for loans from commercial banks applied by large enterprise groups undertaking key state construction projects, the fiscal departments shall provide a certain number of interest repayments on merits;
(4) as for the national direct financing plan and policy, the government shall especially consider production and construction financing demand from large

enterprise groups and provide priority to them as per the planned stock and bond issuance;

(5) the government could also select part of commercial banks or non-bank financial institutions to hold shares in the new construction projects of pilot enterprises, in order to facilitate a direct combination of financial capital and industrial capital;

(6) the government shall also provide more authority to large enterprise groups for overseas investments, allow qualified groups to directly use international commercial loans with approval, and pilot a balanced management for large enterprise groups on foreign debt;

(7) the qualified parent companies of enterprise groups have priority over foreign financing with approval, including direct issuance of bonds and stocks overseas.

Third, we should implement state-owned capital profit distribution policies that benefit large enterprise groups. It would also be beneficial to learn from Japanese enterprising ways of attaching importance to retaining profit. Under the guidance of the national industrial policies and sector plans, the government can allow large groups to retain a moderate part of the return on equity of state-owned assets from the parent companies' capital reserves. These retained profits can be directed toward construction projects approved or entrusted by the state, or be kept to boost capital of parent companies, or be put to use as circulating funds for these enterprise groups. These measures will ensure that large enterprise groups can develop their capital-operating ability to continuously increase the value of their capital.

Fourth, we should build a tax policy system that benefit large enterprise groups. The top priority now is to make a breakthrough in the existing rigid enterprise tax payment system. That entails changing the current practice that enterprise groups pay income tax through central or local fiscal and tax departments as individual enterprises. It would also be instrumental to consolidate the tax payment sources of large enterprise groups and allow the parent companies to set up a unified mechanism on the basis of consolidated financial statements that pay taxes to the central or local tax departments. China also ought to advance its research on the improvement of the sharing system of corporate income tax through central and local tax departments. In addition, the government should work out a series of preferential tax policies that benefit group-oriented operations and boost the development of economies of scale.

Fifth, we should have a national order system that benefits large enterprise groups and helps improve the government's production planning management for enterprises. In general, the government should design production assignments for parent companies of large enterprise groups in the form of national orders for goods. Through national orders, the government can direct and support the production and operation of enterprise groups, and arrange resources to help enterprises in their demand for crucial energies, raw materials and transportation. In addition, the government can also help solve problems that hinder enterprise groups from accomplishing their production assignments.

Sixth, we should rigorously encourage pilot enterprise groups to engage in international businesses in order to form a foreign trade policy system that facilitates the development of enterprise groups. It would be beneficial therefore to guide enterprise groups in building a sense of international competition, and urge these groups to formulate or improve their strategies for overseas development. On this basis, the government should continue to grant large enterprise groups more autonomy to venture into foreign trade. Enterprise groups can moderately expand their export and import businesses to meet their actual demands. These groups are also encouraged to contract foreign projects, increase overseas export of labor, and engage in international cooperation and communication. It would also be integral to encourage these large enterprise groups to also cooperate with foreign trade enterprises and carry out overseas investment and business in order to enhance the export competitiveness and develop the group according to the standard operational model of transnational enterprises. Also instrumental would be supporting a number of parent companies and help them to directly open accounts in the Export-Import Bank of China and the Bank of China for foreign exchange settlement and application for foreign exchange loans. It would also be beneficial to beef up the export of large mechanical and electrical products produced by large enterprise groups. The Bank of China could launch trial seller's credit for large enterprise groups. Overseas branches of the Bank of China should play a positive role in servicing large enterprise groups in fields such as those in export information, credit guarantee and other services relevant with credit loans. Guided by the national industrial policies and coordinated by the parent companies, qualified member companies for enterprise groups could reorganize themselves by cooperating or establishing joint venture enterprises with foreign companies. In addition, member companies could set up new liability limited companies in order to seek opportunities for overseas development.

Seventh, we ought to enhance information exchange and communication between the government and large enterprise groups. The departments in charge of extensive economic management and industrial administration should regularly publish macroeconomic information to direct the production and operation of enterprise groups. As required by the government, enterprise groups have the obligation to report their production and operation situations and any challenges being faced. Ultimately, various forms of communication, information exchanges, negotiations and dialogues should be established between government departments and large enterprise groups.

Chapter 45
Mobilizing Various Sectors to Develop the Tertiary Industry

The development level of the tertiary industry is an important indicator of a country's economic and social development. In the 20-plus years after the establishment of China, China's tertiary industry made progress but did not receive enough attention. It was not until the Third Plenary Session of the 11th CPC Central Committee that the industry experienced remarkable development. From 1979 to 1991, the tertiary industry grew annually by 10%, which was even faster than the growth of GDP during the same period. The industry's rapid development has improved people's lives by boosting production development and providing jobs. However, China's tertiary industry is still in its early stages and it must adapt to the new situation of greater reform and opening up and stronger economic growth. To this end, the Central Committee of the CPC and the State Council decided to put greater emphasis on the development of the tertiary industry. In the report to the 14th National Congress of the Communist Party of China, Jiang Zemin made the major strategic decision to rigorously develop the tertiary industry.

To turn that decision into action, China must gain a better understanding of the tertiary industry. For a long time, China has defined modernization to mean building more factories and producing more goods. However, this approach to modernization fails to see the tertiary industry as a producing sector. As a result, development of the tertiary industry is being held back by strict regulations and limited access to the industry as well as by industry practices that have a dampening effect on the natural development of the tertiary industry. It should be recognized that labor in the tertiary industry is also a form of human labor in general, because value is created in much the same way.

However, there is also difference, which is important to point out. In the tertiary industry, the products created by the primary and secondary industries serve as the foundation for the production of non-material goods. The non-material goods provided by the tertiary industry also satisfy various demands of life. Thus, as science

This article originally appeared in *People's Daily*, March 5, 1992.

X. Zheng, *China's 40 Years of Economic Reform and Development*,
https://doi.org/10.1007/978-981-13-2727-8_45

and technology step closer toward becoming the primary productive forces, the intellectual elements in production are playing a more and more decisive role. Serving as both a "lubricant" and "multiplier" in the economy, the tertiary industry penetrates the primary and secondary industries and materializes in various goods and services. In addition, it provides a strong impetus for the development of the primary and secondary industries.

In order to develop the tertiary industry, China also needs to change the view that labor in the tertiary industry and commercial businesses and in the service industry in particular is inferior. The traditional view that plays up agriculture and industry but downplays commercial businesses has hindered the development of China's goods and services. As an open country, China should reject that old notion, think about labor differently, and regard occupations in the tertiary industry with great respect.

The development target of the tertiary industry proposed by the Central Committee of the CPC and the State Council aims to gradually establish a unified market that is socialist in nature, a social service system for urban and rural residents, and a social security system that is suitable to conditions in about ten years' time. In addition, growth of the tertiary industry is expected to be higher than that of the primary and secondary industries. Not only that, but the proportion of the value added and the percentage of the jobs created by the tertiary industry in the total labor force in China should reach or at least draw close to the average proportion of developing countries.

For now, China should focus on building the socialist market economy. Once that task is complete, China should start building a unified market that is socialist in nature, asocial service system for urban and rural residents, and a social security system that is suitable to China's conditions, and speed up the development of various industries, including industries that do not require major investments, provide quick returns, provide benefits, and employ many people and play an important role in economic growth and quality of life, as well as emerging industries that drive scientific advances and technological change, and basic industries that play an important role in the development of the economy.

Policy easing is the prerequisite for accelerating the development of the tertiary industry. In most sectors of the industry, distribution is spread over a wide area, liquidity is high, investment is small in scale, and labor is the principal force. This makes the tertiary industry suitable for investment from collectively owned enterprises, private businesses, and individuals. Sectors such as railway, highway, key ports, airports, post and telecommunications, scientific research, education, and urban public services and facilities should continue to rely on the state investment and operations as well as social power for building. As for service, entertainment, and for-benefit sectors, which include commercial business, catering, preschool and kindergarten, cleaning and hairdressing, repairing, porterage, taxi services, consulting, and family services, the goal should be to broadly encourage social power, including SOEs, urban and rural organizations for economic development, and individuals to fully engage in the development of these sectors.

To that end, it would be beneficial to do the following:

Always encourage the government, collectively owned enterprises, and individuals to engage in the development of the tertiary industry together, and continue to follow the principle that ownership and benefits belong to investors, so that all forces will be motivated to engage in the development of the tertiary industry.
Streamline the registration procedures for starting enterprises in the tertiary industry.
Break industry monopolies and remove local blockades in the tertiary industry and ensure fair competition. At the same time, formulate and improve relevant laws and regulations, with special emphasis placed on market regulation, improve the rules for market competition, and maintain market order in order to ensure the healthy development of the tertiary industry.
Establish a development mechanism for the industry—one which gradually improves itself and is orientated toward enterprises and society. This is also a vital step in the development of the tertiary industry.
Change the current practices of some sectors in the tertiary industry to prevent them from running through fiscal funds and subsidies. This includes the welfare, public benefit, and utility industries, as well as others.
Provide SOEs in the tertiary industry with operational autonomy and allow them to apply a variety of flexible operational approaches and expand their scope of business.
Create an environment that encourages enterprises, public institutions, logistic services of state organs, and welfare facilities to become more society and market-oriented.
Encourage staff, funds, and facilities of the primary and the secondary industries to enter the tertiary industry. On the one hand, the government should encourage the staff of the secondary industry and administrative organs to be separated from factories and their departments. This is so they can provide services for production and daily life. However, on the other hand, enterprises in the tertiary industry should be encouraged to carry out acquisitions of industrial enterprises that are on the verge of shut down, suspended, merged, or switched to other production.
Create favorable conditions for the regulation systems involved in the transfer of property and personnel management.
Encourage graduates of universities and colleges and demobilized military personnel to work in the tertiary industry.
Attach special importance to the development of the tertiary industry in rural areas and strive to establish a rural social service system.
Guide township enterprises and farmers to develop the tertiary industry in small towns and build markets and infrastructure in small towns to encourage agricultural laborers to take on non-agricultural jobs. And make sure farmers have government support to develop the tertiary industry in rural areas.
Take advantage of overseas funds, technology, and sales channels to develop the tertiary industry. To do this, however, China needs to attract foreign investment in the construction of transport facilities, and direct foreign investment in the education sector of some cities by providing courses on nature, science, business management,

and other educational courses, as well as vocational training. In the meantime, enterprises in the tertiary industry should be encouraged to expand overseas and engage in international business.

Developing the tertiary industry is important. The industry directly benefits people and is vital for the accomplishment of the second and third targets of China's economic development strategy. The nation should stick to the guiding principles from the 14th National Congress of the CPC and grasp the historic opportunities to boost the development of the tertiary industry with all resources at hand, and ultimately work for new progress in the development of China's economy.

Chapter 46
Adjusting the Investment Structure for New Industrialization

China has maintained steady yet rapid economic growth for 12 consecutive years. Since 2003, however, too much investment in some industries has created a number of problems including shortages of energy, raw materials, and transport capacity, as well as price increases, which could have an adverse effect on economic growth. As a result, adjusting the investment structure for a new of industrialization has become fundamental to resolving the pressing conflict in the current economy and preventing radical economic changes.

46.1 The Departure of the Investment Structure from the Development Strategy Is a Pressing Issue

In the four decades since the establishment of the People's Republic of China to the 1980s, China's economic development was plagued by cyclical inflation and serious economic fluctuations. When China's economy was performing well, investors flocked to various sectors. The result was that the scale of construction grew greater than China's financial resources, ultimately causing inflation. In order to curb inflation, the government had to adopt stringent measures to rectify the disorderly construction, and suspended many projects under construction. This caused serious fluctuations in the economy and led to huge losses. Since the Ninth Five-Year Plan period, China has learned its lesson and got down to finding a way to prevent serious economic fluctuations in the future.

For example, China set out to transform its economic growth model to make growth more heavily weighted toward consumption over investment, and proposed pushing forward with the transformation of the economic growth model. The 10th

---

Speech at the Forum for Coordinated Industrial and Environmental Development which first appeared in *China Economic Times*, June 7, 2004.

X. Zheng, *China's 40 Years of Economic Reform and Development*,
https://doi.org/10.1007/978-981-13-2727-8_46

Five-Year Plan further set out to strategically adjust the national economic structure and optimize and upgrade the industrial structure, and proposed strategies for how to accelerate industrialization and urbanization. In 2002, the 16th National Congress of the CPC said that China would pursue new industrialization, a concept that means that information technology should be applied to the process of industrialization, so that industrialization is defined by high technology and economic growth, low levels of resource consumption and environmental pollution, and the full application of human resources.

In 2003, following the proposal for pursuing new industrialization, at the Third Plenary Session of its 16th Central Committee, the CPC formulated the Theory of Balanced and Sustainable Development, which stresses putting people first and aims to promote extensive, coordinated, and sustainable development to advance individuals' development in all respects. The concept of new industrialization effectively combines industrialization and the transformation of growth model, while the Theory of Balanced and Sustainable Development coordinates economic development and social development with an eye on individuals' universal development. The strategic proposals reflect the Party's deepening understanding on how to foster economic development. The earnest implementation of these development strategies is essential for maintaining continuous, rapid, and healthy economic development.

We should recognize that it was China's proactive efforts to transform the growth model, make structural adjustments, and put in place regulations to deal with economic problems that enabled the country to curb inflation, overcome the challenges of inadequate supply, lessen the impact of the Asian financial crisis, and ward off the SARS epidemic. Those proactive efforts ultimately led to the longest period of steady yet rapid development since the establishment of the People's Republic of China. This is especially true during the period from 1997 to 2001, when China managed to maintain at least 7.1% of economic growth while consuming little-to-no energy–strong proof that the transformation of the growth model achieved some effective results.

Since 2003, the investment structure has changed remarkably. Investment in steel, cement, and electrolytic aluminum production as well as real estate has increased by 80% to even 100%. From the months of January to April in 2004, investment in these sectors continued to increase by 35–93% compared with the same period a year earlier. In comparison, the growth pace of investment for new industrialization was weak.

For example, China's electronic and information technology industry is leading the way in the new industrialization push, but 80% of the investment in this industry is from foreign investors, while only 10% is from SOEs and state-holding enterprises. The remaining 10% comes from private investment. The software sector, which is an import part of the information industry, contributed 16.7% to India's GDP, but this proportion was no more than one percent for China. In the domestic market, China's huge demand for software was mostly satisfied by foreign imports. Developing this sector would not cost much in terms of energy resources and pollution. On the contrary, its development would help bring out China's human resource advantage.

Unfortunately, investment in this sector has not increased, at least by a significant amount. It is also hard for some strategic industries key to the optimization and upgrading of the industrial structure to receive investment. For example, this is the case in industries such as large-scale equipment manufacturing, aircraft manufacturing, shipbuilding, fine chemicals, traditional Chinese medicine, and new energy. Last year, China imported more than US$200 billion of electronic machinery. If this electronic machinery could be manufactured domestically, then the country would half the cost with little energy consumption and pollution.

In 2003, China's investments in fixed assets increased by 26.7%. Of that amount, investments in capital construction and real estate increased by 28.7 and 29.7%, respectively, while investment in modernization and information–more essential sectors, only increased by 25.1%. The tertiary industry, which is a weak link in economy, also did not see a lot of investment growth, which means the growth of the tertiary industry will lag behind that of GDP for a long time to come. And investment in the primary industry was only 1.6% higher, which was in contrast with the emphasis of the CPC Central Committee on dealing with challenges in agriculture, rural areas, and farming.

In general, in the year 2003, investments in industries featuring high amounts of energy consumption, investment, and pollution grew quickly, while investments in industries that fit the requirements of new industrialization did not. This imbalance shows that the country is—either consciously or unconsciously, returning to the old, long path of extensive growth from more than a decade ago. If China continues to remain at the low end of the international industrial chain and rely on foreign imports for high-end goods, then the country will be more vulnerable to outside forces and it will be even more difficult to modernize the country. China's successes and failures should inform that the extensive growth model will result in inflation and serious economic fluctuations. Thus, the nation must never step on that old path again.

46.2 The Main Reasons for the Resurgence of the Extensive Growth Model

The departure of the investment structure from China's development strategies in 2003 has its reasons. At the same time, effective solutions cannot be found unless the root reasons for the departure are studied and researched.

The mains reasons are as follows:

First, China was restricted by the bottleneck of technology. The concept of new industrialization involves accelerating the development of the high-tech industry and other strategic industries. But the development of these industries are sometimes held back by the lack of technological resources, which means that, in spite of high demand and adequate funding, it is still difficult for the investment in these industries to grow. Technology has become a bottleneck, which is holding back advancement of the concept.

The reason for the bottleneck, however, is that a mechanism that encourages technological innovation has yet to be established. As a result, enterprises lack the enthusiasm to innovate and invest. According to the National Bureau of Statistics of China, in 2003, only 30% of the large and medium-sized enterprises in China were doing research and development studies, and only 25% had set up technology development institutions. In addition, R&D investment accounted for only 0.75% of sales revenue.

In foreign countries, R&D investment by enterprises is at least three percent of sales revenue. Any less than that and an enterprise would find it very difficult to develop over the long run. If the proportion is lower than two percent, an enterprise will be knocked out of the market. In addition, this proportion cannot be lower than 10% of sales revenue for enterprises engaged in the high and new-technology industries. China's Haier Group, for instance, ranks 95th on the list of the world's top 100 brands. It is the first Chinese brand to be included on the top 100 list. The key for Haier's success is investment in R&D. The Chinese company invests more than five% of its sales revenue in R&D.

Introducing technology and then innovating on the introduced technology is a fast way for enterprises to make technological progress. Compared with Japan and South Korea, China has not very successful so far. For Japan and South Korea, the ratio of investment for technology introduction to that for turning the introduced technology into an innovation is 1:5, while this ratio for China is 1:0.07. Benefiting from this, Japan and South Korea managed to make their own proprietary products and export a large volume of them after introducing European and American technologies. In contrast, China has long been emphasizing technology introduction but neglecting the innovation part of the equation. As a result, China cannot help but continue introducing technology, which has made it harder for China to engage in independent R&D and produce proprietary products.

The belief used to be that enterprises do not have enough funds to develop technology, while the truth of the matter is that even profitable enterprises have been reluctant to invest their money in technology development. Take the auto industry as an example. Key auto enterprises with annual profits ranging from five billion yuan to eight billion yuan are still not confident enough about developing new products. By contrast, the non-key ones that earned far less in comparison have shown greater enthusiasm about developing technology, and have gained some remarkable achievements. This fact shines a light on the problems of China's mechanism for technological progress.

Under the current mechanism, the current leaders of enterprises have to shoulder the potential risks of technology development, even though the benefits may not materialize in full during their tenures. The result is a lack of enthusiasm for technology development. In addition, domestic enterprises have a government safety net and can easily make profits through the cooperation with foreign enterprises, which makes them even more reluctant to take the tough path of independent technology development.

Thus, if China is to develop in line with the requirements of new industrialization, increase investment in technology-intensive industries, reduce dependence on energy and raw material consumption for economic growth, and reduce environmental impact, China has no choice but to deepen the reform of enterprises, establish a mechanism for technology innovation, and increase investment in technology development. This work will no doubt take time and will not address the immediate difficulties, but the country must remain determined to solve the fundamental problems, so that breakthroughs can be made after three to five years of relentless efforts.

Second, market demand is likely the cause of the investment imbalance. In recent years, there has been significant growth of investment in housing, automotive, and infrastructure as a result of improving housing conditions and upgrading of transport–a natural and inevitable outcome. However, China should also rationally direct the waves of consumption enthusiasm. The formation of more areas of consumption should be further encouraged, but the government must also do its best to avoid having an adverse effect on consumption, which could result in greater consumption but with less development of relevant industries.

At present, China's capacity for steel production is 230 million tons, but if the 130 million tons of steel under construction is added to the mix, the overall capacity for steel production reaches 360 million tons. That is higher than the amount of that of the US, Japan, Russia and members of the EU combined. Moving on to cement, China's capacity for cement production is 800 million tons and over one billion tons if the cement being used in construction projects is added, which is more than half of the world's capacity for cement production. Taking into consideration the development of other high-consumption industries as well, China will likely face a severe shortage of energy, raw materials, and transport capacity. The consequent rising prices of the goods, both inside and outside of China, would be terrible for the supply of resources and for the environment. The solution to this problem also lies in science and technology. China needs to introduce and independently develop new technologies to push forward the development of renewable energy, new materials, high-capacity transport, and affordable housing. With an eye to China's situation for resources and reserves, it is important to develop the coal liquefaction and bio-fuel industries, reduce petroleum imports, substitute metal materials with new synthetic materials, recover resources from waste, and develop a circular economy.

Third, the imbalance is also the result of Chinese politics. Developing the economy is the centerpiece for governments at all levels. This is especially true for governments after a leadership transition. New leaders seek quick political victories, so construction projects with instant benefits are the natural choice. They even sacrifice farmers' benefits by leasing land for construction funds and pledging land for loans. They also carry out redundant construction projects at the expense of the environment. Pursuing economic growth for political gain is also an important reason for the problem of too much investment in certain industries.

Last, the imbalance is the result of ineffective government efforts to direct resource allocation. Governments should use various economic policies to rationally direct the allocation of resources while enabling the market to play its basic role in allocating resources.

At the present stage, rapidly growing the economy and upgrading the industrial structure are both of vital importance. This is especially true where foreign investment is flowing into China. The government should adopt effective measures to support the development of domestic enterprises, and help the development of weak links and strategic industries in order to enhance the competitiveness of domestic enterprises. China should take full advantage of the nation's powerful economic leverages to direct the investment of enterprise funds and bank loans in line with the requirements of the concept of new industrialization and the Theory of Balanced and Sustainable Development. China should also use the law to protect land and other resources in serious shortage.

It is notable that the government is going to replace the role of enterprises in investment, and the measures taken to date are do not mean that the government is distorting market prices. More precisely, the government should regulate the economy and provide public services, ensure the implementation of national strategies for economic development, and ultimately achieve continuous, steady, and rapid national economic growth.

46.3 The Directions and Tasks for Adjustment of the Investment Structure

Since the second half of 2003, China has adopted a series of macro regulations, including limiting land requisitions, raising the proportion of funds set aside by enterprises for investment, surveying and rectifying development areas, and optimizing the credit structure according to industrial policies. The aim is to prevent too much investment from going into steel, cement, and electrolytic aluminum production; real estate; and other industries. During this period, corresponding policies should be formulated to encourage social funds to be invested in industries that meet the requirements of the concept of new industrialization and the Theory of Balanced and Sustainable Development, so that these funds can find new investment areas.

These new investment areas include the following industries: electronic and information technology, large-scale equipment manufacturing, transport equipment manufacturing, biotechnology and Traditional Chinese Medicine, new material, and renewable energy.

1. *China must rigorously develop the electronic and information technology industry*

In the past decade, the electronic and information technology industry has been developing with a speed that is two to three times faster than the country's GDP growth, making it the largest industry in China. China's electronic and information technology industry is the world's third most valuable and the total value of its exports is US$141 billion. With regards to the production of stored program control (SPC) telecommunications technology, mobile phones, color televisions, color monitors, laser discs, and radio-cassette recorders, China ranks first among all countries in the world. However, compared with developed countries, the information technology industry of China is large but not strong, and innovation capability is weak.

For example, core technologies are out of date, and there is an imbalance between software and hardware. The software and hardware that involve key technology are all imported. In 2003, China imported more than US$40 billion worth of integrated circuits and other electronic parts and components. In addition, the technological value and the added value of products are low. The added value of China's electronic and information technology products was only 18.3% in 2003, which is far lower than the 58% of the US in the same year. More investment is needed to accelerate the development of this industry in China. Thus, the country must expand the application of this industry, build supporting infrastructure and networks, let core technology innovations drive the deepening of reforms, improve the quality of enterprises, encourage indigenous development, and move forward by leaps and bounds.

2. *China must accelerate development of the large-scale equipment manufacturing industry*

The manufacturing of key equipment is the core of equipment manufacturing. It is important to improve mechanical science, manufacturing technology, information processing and control technologies, system integration, material technology, and other technologies, as well as to combine their strengths. Accelerating the development of key manufacturing technology is significant for promoting the upgrading of China's industrial structure and making technological progress, being able to carry out modernization projects, enhancing China's international competitiveness, and maintaining national security. It is in the country's interest to rely on major construction projects and push for indigenous equipment manufacturing. Doing so will allow breakthroughs to be made in key technologies and equipment in large-scale, efficient industries. This includes those industries with highly efficient power transmission and transfer systems, high-speed railway transportation, and numerically-controlled machines tools, as well as the various other industries, including: petrochemical, metallurgical, extractive, light, textile, and other important industries and sectors. This will allow China to essentially replace imports with domestic goods by the end of 2010.

3. *China must accelerate the development of transport equipment manufacturing industry*

The continuous improvement of China's transport infrastructure provides a great opportunity for the development of the transport equipment manufacturing industry. Industries such as automotive manufacturing, shipbuilding, aircraft manufacturing, and high-speed railway equipment manufacturing should all be developed at a rapid rate. At present, China has the capability to manufacture some equipment in these industries, and the nation boasts a large number of highly advanced teams with advanced technical skills. By developing this industry, China can improve machine manufacturing and ultimately wean itself from its reliance on the imports of key goods.

4. *China must rigorously develop biotechnology and Traditional Chinese Medicine*

Biotechnology is the leading high-tech industry. The rapidly developing industry has great potential and wields great influence around the world. Moreover, it an industry that China can catch up with developed countries in a relatively short time, as the gap is relatively small. Thus, accelerating the development of the biotechnology industry is of great importance for the transformation of the growth model and improving the quality of people's lives. China should continue to beef up its support for the industry and highlight the research of industries in biochips, functional genomics, genetically modified animals and plants, genetically engineered drugs and vaccines, conservation biology, new biological materials, breeding, biological fertilizer, biological pesticides, and biological medicines.

China should also development Traditional Chinese Medicine (TCM). As a national industry with a long history, TCM is the crystallization of the wisdom of the Chinese nation. People's growing fondness for nature has created interest in and a huge market for TCM. At present, however, the industry is underdeveloped in China. With only US$20 billion of annual international trade, the market share of TCM in China is just one percent. In some cases, the imports of foreign produced TCM medicines are greater than the exports of domestically produced TCM medicines. As a result, the country must accelerate the development of TCM, apply modern science and technology to its production, and take steps to modernize the industry. It is in China's interest to formulate and improve the standards and rules for domestically produced TCM medicines, develop a number of important products that have clear effectiveness, and tackle the development of a number of TCM medicines and key technologies for industrialization. In the meantime, support should be given to a number of competitive enterprises with proprietary technologies in order to continue China's advantage in TCM technology, realize the transition to a modern TCM industry, and ultimately make more contribution to people's welfare.

5. *China must rigorously develop the new material industry*

The new material industry, which is characteristic of high technology, products with high added-value, and the wide scope of relevant technology, is the main industry driving technological progress and structural adjustment. Compared with traditional materials, new materials have advantages in terms of performance, cost, and impact on energy and the environment. Thus, new materials are promising. Accelerating the development of this industry will provide raw materials to support the industrial upgrading of China's heavy chemical industry and the transformation of equipment manufacturing from a large industry into a strong one. The country should prioritize development of rare earth materials, high-temperature materials, superconducting materials, ceramic materials, laser materials, biological materials, and other high-performance new materials as strategic fields.

6. *China must accelerate the development of the renewable energy industry*

The renewable energy industry covers things like sustainable energies and resources, including wind energy, solar energy, nuclear energy, wave energy, geothermal energy, biological energy, marine energy, hydrogen energy and fuel cell technology, and biological fuels. It does not cover fossil fuels and large-scale hydropower. China has abundant renewable energy resources. The resources are almost inexhaustible and cause less damage to the environment. Thus, the vigorous development and application of renewable energy is conducive to sustainable development, which is of strategic significance for reducing the energy bottlenecks limiting China's economic development as well as for maintaining China's energy security. China should enhance support for the development of renewable energy, expand the use of renewable energy, and optimize the energy structure.

46.4 Carrying Out Economic Approaches in a Coordinated Manner to Direct the Allocation of Resources

The governments of developed countries took a lot of effective measures to support the development of their strategic industries, which has provided some valuable experience.

Below are some examples:

First, the US government uses fiscal funds to support the R&D of important strategies. For example, the US government provided more than US$280 billion of research funds for military industrial projects through the Department of Defense. These military-industrial projects are assigned to enterprises, research institutions, and universities and colleges. Usually, the research results are directly applied to civilian technologies, but in some cases, the results are used in the military industry. It is the application and commercialization of military-industrial technology that has allowed the US to gain a dominant position in high and new technology.

Second, the US government boosts the development of strategic industries by directly developing key technological projects. For example, the US government drove the development of the nuclear industry by engaging in the Manhattan Project, facilitated the growth of the aerospace engineering industry by formulating and implementing the "Star Wars" program, and pushed forward the development of the electronic and information technology industry by inventing the information superhighway. At present, large-scale implementation of the National Missile Defense (NMD) and Theater Missile Defense (TMD) programs are expected to have a large impact on the development of the military and information industries.

Third, the US government uses procurement to support the development of strategic industries. The *Buying American Act* was issued by the US government over 70 years ago, but it is still applicable now. The act stipulates that the US government give preference to goods produced with taxpayer dollars if the US government uses taxpayer funds. The procurement of imported products is allowed only when domestic enterprises are unable to meet the US government's demands. The US government has a department known as the Office of Procurement, which is responsible for the procurement of goods. A full 80% of the goods are military-industrial ones.

Fourth, various foreign government support their strategic industries by reducing interest rates and granting capital subsidies. The governments will allocate funds to support priority industries.

For example, the government of Japan conducted the "window guidance" policy to reduce interest rates on bank loans in order to support the development of strategic industries. For another example, in the early 1980s, the government of France formulated a plan for industrial modernization, which gave priority to aircraft, high-speed railway, nuclear energy, and biological engineering. The government funded these industries, and used the planning contracts to clarify the responsibilities of the government and enterprises. Supported by this plan, the prioritized industries gradually grew into internationally competitive French enterprises. Lastly, in order to support the development of its domestic industries, the government of Italy in the 1970s prioritized the textile, leather, automotive, and other advantageous industries. In addition to providing financial support to facilitate the growth of key enterprises, the government also organized professional panels to evaluate and provide advice for these enterprises, which enhanced the international competitiveness of these prioritized industries.

China is now in a crucial stage of industrialization and modernization, which makes it extremely necessary for the government to carry out long-term supply-side policies, direct the allocation of production factors, and set the path of new industrialization. The thinking that establishing the socialist market economy means to leave the market at the helm in the allocation of resources while the government should do nothing is bad for the economy. After all, it was the so-called "Washington Consensus" that caused some Latin American countries to miss the opportunity to develop their national industries and incur inflation and economic turbulence. The GDP per capita of these countries has long been low—ranging from US$1000 to US$2000. In contract, some Asian countries effectively combined market mechanisms with government guidance and developed proprietary products and competitive domestic industries. This enabled these Asian countries to increase GDP per capita to US$10,000 from a range of US$1000–US$3000. At this stage, China should take actions to enhance the guidance for investment.

First, the market competition mechanism should be brought into full play. Adjusting the investment structure for new industrialization means allocating resources through market competition. Competition is also necessary for preventing the concentration of investment in some industries. Only competition can phase out backward capacity, raise labor productivity, and strengthen the competitiveness of China's enterprises and products. Thus, China should establish a unified national market, remove regional barriers, break up monopolies, expand market access, and create an environment for fair competition.

Second, China needs a macro regulatory system that is coordinated with industrial, fiscal, financial, and land use policies. It would be beneficial to clarify the priorities for the development of strategic industries. It would also be beneficial to substitute the fiscal funds for infrastructure building with other sources of funding in order to earmark funding for guiding funds, which will be used to reduce interest rates on loans to support prioritized industries and construction projects. The reason for this is so that fiscal funds can serve as a lever to direct investment and optimize the industrial structure. Optimizing the debt structure so that it lines with industrial policies is not only conducive to the prosperity of strategic industries, but also beneficial for reducing loan risk.

Third, government procurement and other approaches can be used to support independent equipment manufacturing. China would benefit from preferential policies adopted to encourage the use of domestically produced equipment. Such preferential policies have already been implemented for equipment manufacturing in the rail industry and in environmental protection. However, these policies should be expanded to other sectors. When constructing the Three Gorges Hydropower Station, for instance, the government of China used international bidding to acquire technology for construction, which further improved the equipment manufacturing capabilities of domestic enterprises. Thus, China should learn from and promote this successful practice, broadly carry out the government procurement system, and accelerate the production of domestic equipment.

Fourth, enterprises need to increase their investment in technology R&D. The government should provide greater support to enterprises with R&D centers orientated toward technology and those that engage themselves in the development of science technology. This means financially supporting research and studies. In addition, financial support should be provided to key R&D projects on engineering and industrial technology. It would be beneficial to establish the Growth Enterprise Market, set up national venture capital funds, and encourage enterprises to invest more in equipment and technology upgrading.

Fifth, SOEs, collective enterprises, and non-public enterprises should be treated as equals when it comes to the application of policies. It is especially important to support the development of SMEs and high-tech enterprises, as well as enterprises that have promising exports and potential future performance. At present, the private economy is becoming less reliant on labor-intensive industries and more reliant on capital and technology-intensive industries. Private funds should participate in the reorganization of SOEs and the country should establish a mixed-ownership economy with a shareholding structure in order to incentivize SOEs and establish a modern corporate system and property rights.

Setting up the investment structure for new industrialization likewise entails the coordination of various departments in fields of planning, science and technology, taxation, finance, customs, environmental protection, resource management, business administration, and quality regulation. If the government and enterprises can find ways to work together, the country will have no problem applying the Theory of Balanced and Sustainable Development, pursuing new industrialization with Chinese characteristics, and accomplishing the target of building a moderately prosperous society in all respects.

Chapter 47
Solving Major Problems to Advance Supply-Side Structural Reform

The recently held Central Economic Work Conference shifted the focus to supply-side structural reform. To facilitate structural change, China needs to deepen reform, tap the potential of economic development, improve the quality of supply, and better satisfy people's increasing demands. Thus, importance should be attached to tackling the problems that could have a significant impact on the economy. In addition, the country must focus on structural reform and ensure that there is a strong foundation for steady, sound economic development.

47.1 Focus on Rural Reforms and Boost the Development of Urban-Rural Integration

The growing urban-rural development gap is the most prominent problem in the current economic structure. At present, China has more than 600 million people living in rural areas, and the income ratio of urban and rural residents is 2.7:1. High-income countries did not earn their status until they essentially eliminated the income gap between urban and rural residents. For China, if the urban-rural income gap cannot be narrowed significantly soon, the huge demand potential of the rural market cannot be tapped, making it more likely that the country will be bogged down in the middle-income trap and less likely that China will become a high-income country.

To avoid this unfavorable outcome, China must once again focus its efforts on rural reform, just like in the early stage of China's reform. This means that China must unleash rural productive forces and increasing farmers' income must become the top priority for the supply-side structural reform in the current stage of development. The reasons for the huge income gap between urban and rural residents boils down to the

This article originally appeared in *People's Daily*, February 16, 2017.

X. Zheng, *China's 40 Years of Economic Reform and Development*,
https://doi.org/10.1007/978-981-13-2727-8_47

fact that agricultural productivity is too low. Agricultural productivity accounts for no more than a third of the average productivity as a whole. Improving agricultural productivity is a systemic project, one which requires the continued movement of agricultural labor to the secondary and tertiary industries, as well as the transfer of the rural population from rural areas to cities and towns. As this process continues, the government should establish a new urban-rural integration system, so that the flows of capital, technology, and quality labor can be directed to rural areas.

On April 30, 2015, in his speech on urban-rural integration delivered to the collective learning group in the Political Bureau of the CPC Central Committee, Chinese President Xi Jinping stressed that urban and rural residents should have equal access to basic rights, equal access to basic public services in urban and rural areas, that there should be an equitable distribution of wealth, that the allocation of factors in urban and rural areas should be reasonable, and that there should be industrial integration in urban and rural areas.

Xi's speech clarified what works lies ahead to further strengthen urban-rural integration. The reason that the development of rural areas has long been lagging behind that of urban areas is the development difference between urban and rural markets. This is also why agricultural productivity is weak. While the production factors in cities are market-oriented, the production factors in rural areas are still not fully liberalized. The resulting imbalance pulls labor, land, capital, and other production factors away from rural areas, while the capital, technology, and quality labor in cities remains in place, thereby causing a severe capital surplus in cities and a severe capital shortage in rural areas.

In order to coordinate the development of urban and rural areas, a total-factor market system must be set up in rural areas and production factors must flow freely between urban and rural markets. The key to this is to reform the rural land system and to legally recognize rural land as a commodity.

The *Decision of the CPC Central Committee on Certain Major Issues concerning Comprehensively Deepening Reform* (hereinafter referred to as the *Decision*) adopted by the Third Plenary Session of the 18th CPC Central Committee pointed out a number of important points.

To accelerate the building of a new agricultural system, it pointed out that China must: "Endow farmers with the rights to land tenure, land use, land revenue, land transfer and mortgage and guarantee of contracted land use."

To endow farmers with more property rights, it pointed out that China must: "Ensure rural households' usufruct of their homestead, and improve the rural homestead system through reform. We will select several pilot areas to steadily and prudently push forward the mortgage, guarantee and transfer of farmers' residential property rights, and expand the channels for farmers to increase their property income."

According to the Chinese government, efforts should also be made to: "Form a unified construction land market for both urban and rural areas"; and "allow rural collectively owned profit-oriented construction land to be sold, leased and appraised as shares, and ensure that it can enter the market with the same rights and at the same prices as state-owned land."

China must earnestly implement these reform measures. Doing so will help ensure that land can enter the market and farmers are provided with property income. This will give rise to systems for the transfer of land use rights, the flow of labor, and the transformation of rural migrant workers into urbanites. The unoccupied homesteads can be used to increase land for urban construction and farming purposes, while the property income can help farmers buy houses in cities or towns, so that the whole household can be registered as urban. Compensating farmers for the use of their land is conducive to the development of large-scale operations involving land use, which, in turn, will raise agricultural productivity and provide the people leasing their land with a source of income. In addition, the reclamation of homesteads can be used to build villages and towns, which will change the backward infrastructure in rural areas, improve the environment for people living in rural areas, and make rural areas more beautiful and more pleasant places to live.

If the land owned by farmers can be leased during the 13th Five-Year Plan period, then 20 trillion yuan worth of bank loans and investment can be raised. Once that amount is invested in agricultural modernization, the building of new countryside and the transformation of rural migrant workers into urbanites can be realized. This will significantly narrow the development gap between urban and rural areas, thereby laying a strong foundation for building a society that is moderately prosperous in all respects by 2020. Developing characteristic towns will be the breakthrough for urban-rural integration.

The government should allocate special funds to support priority industries. The development of characteristic towns on the outskirts of cities can drive the development of the rural infrastructure and public services in the surrounding areas, provide jobs, facilitate the integrated development of the primary, secondary, and tertiary industries, and spread urban civilization. This effect is needed to realize the coordinated development of urban and rural areas.

Last year, on December 12, six ministries; namely, the National Development and Reform Commission, China Development Bank, China Enterprise Confederation, China Enterprise Directors Association, and China Urbanization Promotion Council, jointly issued a document to support the implementation of the program to implement the project of building charming, unique towns. That project is called the Industrial Urbanization Program (IUP), the aim of which is to encourage enterprises and public institutions in large cities to move out of the cities, which have some disadvantages including expensive land prices, traffic problems, and air pollution, and settle down in surrounding areas, in order to create a favorable environment and gain more development space. The hope is that more and more enterprises participate in this project.

47.2 Focus on the Reform of the Investment System and Increase the Supply of Public Goods

In the current supply structure, the means of production and consumer goods are already in excess supply; however, the supply of public services is insufficient. Issues that concern people the most, including the environment, transport, municipal administration, education, social security, culture, and information, and especially issues such as clean air and water, have become problems in urgent need of fixing. There is a systemic reason for this, which is explained below.

In the past, fiscal investment was the principal force supporting the supply of public goods, which meant that fiscal constraints would restrict supply. The best solution to this problem is to reform the investment system and resolve the contradiction through government-enterprise partnerships; namely, the public-private-partnership (PPP) model.

Under the PPP model, the government is required the government to carefully calculate the investment and profits in the public interest or semi-public interest and provide certain preferential policies for compensation, so that enterprises investing in these projects can have reasonable returns. Since such investments should be decided through open bidding, it is best to uphold fair competition by treating SOEs and private enterprises equally in the selection process. Last year, for example, there was a private enterprise that successively signed railway construction contracts and other infrastructure building contracts with Liangshan Yi Autonomous Prefecture of Sichuan province, Xiangxi Tujia and Miao Autonomous Prefecture of Hunan province, Enshi Tujia and Miao Autonomous Prefecture of Hubei Province, and Dali Bai Autonomous Prefecture of Yunnan Province. The total value of the investment was hundreds of billions of yuan. When accomplished, these projects will greatly improve the transport conditions in these regions. Thus, it is clear that the crux of the shortage of public goods is not related to money issues or technology and construction capability. The key to tackling the problem is to make sure that the government is proactive in its cooperation and coordination with and planning, fiscal, and financial departments.

For instance, when a project is under construction, the government and relevant enterprise should both comply with the contract and ensure the quality of construction. In addition, the policies and subsidies promised by the government to the investing enterprises should be in place in a timely manner. In 2016, M_2 slower growth than M_1. By the end of December 2016, M_1 growth was 21.4%, while M_2 growth was 11.3%. The difference was 10.1 percentage points. The reason for such a large imbalance can be contributed to years of economic downturn and the 54 consecutive months of negative producer prices. Enterprises did not have a lot of investment opportunities, so they invested less and deposited money in current accounts when they got loans from banks. In order to solve this problem, the government needs to promote PPP projects and fiscal funds should be used to direct bank loans. This will help save the dropping M_2, which has been falling for six years, and support the growth of investment in public goods.

The environment is another concern. For example, haze is a prominent problem of public concern. In order to deal with it, the government should implement the proposal that whoever harms the environment is responsible, which was raised in the *Decision* at the Third Plenary Session of the 18th Central Committee of the CPC, as well as promote a third-party management system. The government should set emission standards and charge emission fees, and strictly supervise the implementation of this system in order to attract investment and funding for improving the environment, and truly turn the environmental protection industry into a pillar industry.

47.3 Focus on Technology and Education Reform, and Increase the Supply of Technology and Talent

Technology and talent are the scarcest resources in the supply structure. The goal of supply-side structural reform is to improve the capability of innovation. Thus, China should put into practice its vision of innovative development and encourage technological innovation to realize industrial upgrading with proprietary technologies. This should be done so that the transition from resource and labor-intensive industries to technology and knowledge-intensive industries can be realized and so that the country can leap from the middle and low-end of the industrial chain to the middle and high-end.

The main obstacle is the lack of technological R&D and investment in technology. Some cities in China have established a good environment for innovation, and are starting to see some promising results. For example, the number of international patents originating from Shenzhen accounts for 47% of the total in China. Innovation has become the main driving force for Shenzhen's economic growth. In contrast, other cities in China have even better innovation resources than Shenzhen, but they have much less technological innovations than Shenzhen. This shows that the innovative potential of these cities has not been brought into full play. After years of relentless efforts, Shenzhen has built itself into an innovative city. The city has cultivated a cultural environment that values innovation, a market that encourages innovation, a society that tolerates failures in the process of innovation, a recruitment strategy that seeks the best talent, regardless of other factors, a venture capital system that recognizes potential, an awareness and willingness to open up to the world, and a system of preferential policies that treats and supports enterprises as equals.

Shenzhen is a model city. China's cities should learn from and promote the experience of Shenzhen, encourage enterprises to investment more in R&D, motivate the nation's scientists and engineers to innovate, and accelerate the engineering and commercialization of technological outcomes.

With regard to enterprises, China has had a number of innovative enterprises, and the number of China's international patents applications tops the world. For example, Huawei invested 59.6 billion yuan in R&D last year, and the company is one of the world's biggest filers of international patent applications. At present, five

Chinese enterprises are on the top 10 list of enterprises in the world for number of international patents. However, for most Chinese enterprises, R&D investment is not at the forefront of consideration—taking up no more than two percent of sales revenue. Some enterprises do not even have R&D activities or technological patents.

Part of the problem is that preferential policies for technological innovation are not yet highly utilized by enterprises. Enterprises have become the principal source of R&D investment and innovative outcomes, of which private enterprises are the principal force for technological innovation. Boasting a large number of talented personnel, SOEs are in urgent need to provide play to their potential for innovation. It would be beneficial, therefore, to establish an incentive mechanism for technological innovations in SOEs as soon as possible, so that SOEs can play a leading role and become the mainstay for innovation.

At the same time, colleges and universities should be more than just breeding grounds for innovative talents. Campuses should also be important bases for technological innovations. In order to accomplish the two tasks of breeding innovative talents and establishing bases for innovation, the government must first put in place a good educational system and have capable teachers. With regard to making technological innovations and becoming a leader in technology, China can learn from developed countries.

Let us take the US, for example.

First, the US is able to occupy the leading position in global technology because it has a market with full competition, which means that the survival of enterprises depends on their innovation capability. In addition, there are also fierce competitions among universities and colleges in the US. The quality of a university is determined mainly by its impact on relevant industries, or to what extent a school or department drives technological progress in their field or industry.

Second, the US government carries out innovative engineering projects and works with enterprises to overcome any difficulties. This process drives technological progress all around the world.

Third, the US has a mature venture capital system, including angel investment, seed money, venture capital, private equity, and the NASDAQ stock exchange.

Fourth, the US pools global talents. The government and schools attract great talent from across the world by providing good scholarships and payments.

Fifth, the US boasts an industrial system that combines military and civilian sectors. The US Department of Defense, for instance, invests over US$300 billion in military research programs and military product orders each year. Besides meeting the demands of the military, the entrusted enterprises adapt their research outcomes for civilian use, which drives the development of the high-tech industry. China should learn from the US experience in this regard and deepen technological and educational reform in light of China's situation.

However, certain steps must be taken.

First, China must build excellent and innovative universities. To do this, competitive mechanisms between and within universities need to be set up. To ensure the quality of education and appoint staff, a third-party assessment system should be established. Private schools and Sino-foreign cooperative schools should be also encouraged.
Second, it is important to select innovative professors from around the world based solely on their talents. If there is difficulty in implementing this system at the national level, it can first be tested in several schools and then expanded nationwide in a step by step fashion.
Third, a matching mechanism for universities and venture capital should be set up. We government needs to improve the venture capital system–from angel investment to Growth Enterprise Market, and provide follow-up services for the whole process of innovation. College professors and students should be encouraged to have patented inventions and other technological achievements, and they should also be encouraged to create their own high-tech companies.
Fourth, instead of spoon-feeding students and putting a lot of emphasis on exams, it is important that the country stress a holistic and innovative educational experience, so that schools can cultivate students' ambition to make a difference in the world and produce innovative thinkers. To this end, there should be more vocational education options available and it is important to develop students' practical skills. In addition, universities and colleges should be given autonomy in the selection of subjects, staff, teaching material, and teaching methods.

Part VII
Conclusion

Chapter 48
Exploring Methods of Reform Practically Suited to China's National Conditions

For the past 40 years, our country's policy of reform and opening up has followed the path of socialism with Chinese characteristics, which has greatly boosted economic and social development and led to remarkable achievements. The key to the success of reforms has been our adherence to the materialist ideological line of seeking truth from facts, connecting theory with practice and proceeding from reality in everything we do, as well as continually exploring methods of reform practically suited to China's national conditions. Once the objectives and direction of reforms have been decided, the correctness of reform methods is of decisive significance in their success. There have been many effective reform methods. The following is a summary of some of the most effective.

48.1 Using Economic Development as the Standard for Testing Reforms

In the early stages of the reform process, it was difficult for reforms to progress due to attacks on "leftist" thinking and fear of violating certain doctrine. It was an open discussion on the standards of truth that liberated people's thinking. This led to the understanding that the only test of whether a reform measure works is how it performs in practice. Reforms began in the countryside, starting with an innovation by the villagers of Xiaogang in Anhui Province. For a long time, egalitarianism and the "communal rice bowl" were the foundations of socialism in China. The system of people's communes had skipped the stage of developing the productive forces, thereby hindering development of the rural economy. The people of Xiaogang, however, secretly divided their land among households, which increased production and income. Although many people initially considered this to be a form capitalism,

This article originally appeared in *Qiushi*, Chinese edition, no. 12, 2018.

X. Zheng, *China's 40 Years of Economic Reform and Development*,
https://doi.org/10.1007/978-981-13-2727-8_48

based on the criteria of using practice to test truth, the experience of Xiaogang was rapidly promoted, causing national food production to increase significantly over subsequent years. In less than a decade, the once persistent problem of food shortages was solved and the thirty-year-old system for purchasing and selling food products was abolished. The merits of the household responsibility system were self-evident. The success of rural reforms stoked the enthusiasm of cadres and the masses for further reforms. As a result, reforms spread from the countryside to the cities, from agriculture to industry, and from the micro-economy to the macro-economy. Reforms became an irreversible trend. Looking back though, if leftist methods prior to the reforms had been adhered to and boundaries had not been pushed, then today's achievements might never have happened.

48.2 Always Keeping Reforms Market-Oriented

The planned economy essentially denies the commercial nature of social products and recognizes only the semi-commercial nature of personal consumer goods. It views the economy as a large factory and unifies product allocation, revenues and expenditures, deployment of personnel and wage increases. Under the planned economy, national investment was controlled by the State Planning Commission, with localities and enterprises having no investment rights. In the early days of the founding of the People's Republic, this system played a constructive role in concentrating efforts on industrialization. As the economy grew, however, its drawbacks became increasingly apparent and it hindered productivity. In a country such as China, which was dominated by a natural economy and small-scale agriculture for so long, the development of a commodity economy was a necessary historical stage for the rapid construction of a modern economic system. In the early days of reform, the emphasis was on developing the production and exchange of commodities. This was followed by supplementing the planned economy with market-based adjustments to create a planned commodity economy. Eventually, at the 14th National Party Congress, the decision was taken to establish a socialist market economic system. Both the Decision of the Third Plenary Session of the 14th CPC Central Committee to utilize the basic role of the market in allocating resources and the Decision of the Third Plenary Session of the 18th CPC Central Committee to utilize the decisive role of the market in allocating resources reflected the CPC's tireless exploration of a socialist economic system with Chinese characteristics and the constant refinement of its understanding of the laws of market economics. The entire 40-year reform process shows a clear transition toward market-oriented reforms. Emphasizing the role of the market shows respect for the role of the law of value, which cannot be altered simply by subjective will. The law of value dictates that, within the same industry, resources are allocated to the best company and the fittest companies survive. Between industries, it means that labor is allocated based on the needs of society to balance supply and demand for various commodities. This is impossible under a planned economy.

It is, of course, true that the market has blind spots. That is where the government must step in. The primary roles of the government are macro-control, market supervision and public services. By combining the roles of the market and the government, we can achieve sustained and healthy economic development.

48.3 Adhering to Gradual Reforms

The reform of China's economic system is a great unprecedented undertaking. In the course of advancing reforms, it is necessary not simply to avoid delaying economic development but to actually accelerate it in order to precipitate a rapid increase in people's incomes and win over people's support for reforms. As such, reforms cannot be initiated blindly out of eagerness for quick results. Rather, they must be implemented gradually and progressively. Situations must be weighed up properly before they are changed resolutely. Where uncertainty exists, it is better to wait. We must learn to nurture the new system within the old system, encourage its growth and gradually replace the old system. So-called reforms involving shock therapy are irresponsible to the people and they have always been forbidden in China's reform process.

The adjustment of the structure of ownership in China is an example of successful gradual reform. In the early days, there was no effective method of reforming SEOs and collective enterprises. The focus was on encouraging development of the private sector while continuing to explore methods for reforming the public sector. In the 1980s, six significant policies were implemented in China's textile industry, including prioritizing the provision of energy and raw materials to the industry, which helped township enterprises to thrive. As the private sector expanded, it placed competitive pressures on the public sector of the economy. Faced with the threat of closure if they failed to reform, the enthusiasm of SEOs toward reform increased markedly. At that time, tens of millions of employees were removed from SOEs, with most finding employment in private enterprises. If the private economy had not developed to create the conditions for the reform of SOEs, their reform would not have progressed so smoothly. In contrast to this, the failure of SOEs in the former Soviet Union and Eastern European countries to reform was due, in large part, to a lack of development in the private sector.

It was the proposal to establish a modern enterprise system at the Third Plenary Session of the 14th CPC Central Committee, however, that really set China's SOE reform on the right track. The establishment of a standardized corporate governance structure for a range of shareholding systems based on the requirements of clear property rights, clear responsibilities and authority, separation of government and enterprises, and management science allowed the gradual creation of a prosperous situation in which SOEs and private enterprises developed amid fair competition and brought out the best in each other.

48.4 Adhering to the System of Testing and then Expanding Reforms

It is difficult to determine whether a reform measure will develop productive forces without testing it in practice. Losses and passivity are inevitable without a full understanding of the validity of reform measures. As such, localities and enterprises have been encouraged to trial reforms first and then summarize their experiences so that successful reforms can be rolled out gradually across the country. This is an important approach adhered to in the reform of both micro- and macro-management systems that has ensured the success of reforms in China.

The Decision of the Third Plenary Session of the 18th CPC Central Committee stated that SOE reform should have capital management at its core, aim to develop a mixed economy and allow mixed ownership enterprises to implement employee stock ownership systems. These ideas were introduced from successful experiences in enterprise reform and development.

Central Huijin Investment Co., Ltd. is a good example of a company with sound capital management. The company manages several trillion yuan of capital and has shares in all the state-owned banks. It sends management personnel to meetings of the boards of directors and the shareholders' meetings of the banks to represent its interests. Huijin does not interfere in the operations of the banks, however, affording them sufficient operational autonomy. Huijin is a model of operational efficiency.

State-owned enterprises can absorb shares of private enterprises to develop the mixed-ownership economy, which is conducive to exerting respective advantages, improving international competitiveness, and avoiding insider control and tunneling. It is not about state-owned enterprises merging with private enterprises.

Allowing mixed-ownership enterprise employees (mainly those in management and technical positions) to hold shares helps to create a community of interests between employees and enterprises and encourages them to work together to run companies to the best of their ability. This is an advanced and typical experience that has emerged over four decades of reform and development. It has been tested in practice and should be implemented without compromise.

The replacement of business tax with VAT for service companies has proved to be a successful reform. It has reduced the tax burden of companies in the tertiary sector by an average of more than 30%, resulting in rapid development of the sector over successive years. This reform started as a trial in a few industries in certain localities but was rolled out nationwide and to the vast majority of industries following its success. A decline in tax revenues is expected in the initial stage of the reform, but the rapid development of the tertiary sector engendered by the change means total tax revenues will recover and surpass levels prior to the reform. Increasing the tax threshold for small and micro enterprises has had an even more significant effect. Due to the rapid increase in new enterprises and the accelerated development of companies, employment is up and the tax base has expanded, which will eventually result in higher tax revenues. Although the proportion of value added accounted for and number of people employed by the tertiary sector has clearly increased, there is still plenty of room for growth, and the reform still needs to be advanced and improved.

48.5 Adhering to Openness to Promote Reform and Development

The principle of promoting reform and development through openness has been consistently adhered to for 40 years. In the three decades prior to reform, due to the constraints of isolation imposed by the international environment, China had to be largely self-sufficient. Opening to the outside world in 1978 opened our eyes. We learned advanced foreign management techniques and technology, expanded exchanges of goods and personnel, changed traditional ways of thinking and greatly accelerated China's modernization process.

In terms of macro-management, in the 1980s we focused on studying the industrial policies, income doubling plan, fiscal investments, bank "window guidance" and import substitution strategy of Japan. In the 1990s, we focused on studying Germany's price stabilization and social policies, as well as the macroeconomic controls, coordinated fiscal and monetary policies, supervision of capital markets, science and technology progress policies, infrastructure financing methods, agricultural development policies and military-civilian integration of the US. We also humbly learned from some successful small and medium-sized countries and developing countries, such as South Korea's rapid industrialization, Holland's development of highly efficient agriculture, Finland's focus on science and technology and education, Ireland's establishment of export processing zones, Israel's focus on R&D and India's development of its software industry. In terms of legislating for a market economy, we proactively looked for examples and translated and learned from them. The experiences of foreign parties should not be learned from uncritically but should be applied flexibly based on China's national conditions. It was the lessons that we learned from those other countries that enabled us to form a macroeconomic management system with Chinese characteristics over time.

Large volumes of foreign capital and technology were brought in and joint ventures and overseas-funded enterprises were encouraged to rapidly improve the technological and operational capabilities of Chinese companies. By establishing special economic zones and opening up coastal and inland cities, China gradually opened to the outside world. Shenzhen is a prime example of promoting reform and development through openness. In just four decades, Shenzhen has grown from a small fishing village into an innovative metropolis with the largest economy in the Guangdong-Hong Kong-Macao Greater Bay Area. In 2017, China was the largest exporter and source of foreign direct investment in the world and the second largest importer and destination for foreign capital. As China implements the Belt and Road Initiative, the establishment of domestic pilot free trade zones and free trade ports will move ahead, creating a new model for fully opening to the outside world.

48.6 Coordinating and Promoting Reforms

Reforming an economic system requires both macroeconomic and microeconomic initiatives as well as reforms at different times to adhere to a master plan while being implemented steadily in order of importance. This master plan is the reform decisions issued at plenary session of the Central Committee every few years, which set out the strategy for the reform process. The following are some of the landmark Decisions that have guided reforms and achieved new successes: The Decision on Economic Structural Reform at the Third Plenary Session of the 12th Central Committee in 1984, the Decision on Certain Issues concerning Establishing a Socialist Market Economy at the Third Plenary Session of the 14th Central Committee in 1993, the Decision on Certain Major Issues concerning the Reform and Development of State-owned Enterprises at the Fourth Plenary Session of the 15th Central Committee in 1999, the Decision on Issues regarding the Improvement of the Socialist Market Economy at Third Plenary Session of the 16th Central Committee in 2003, the Decision on Certain Major Issues concerning Speeding Up the Reform and Development of Agriculture at the Third Plenary Session of the 17th Central Committee in 2008 and the Decision on Certain Major Issues concerning Comprehensively Deepening Reform at the Third Plenary Session of the 18th Central Committee in 2013. It is up to ministries and local governments to formulate detailed plans based on the Decisions of the Central Committee and to ensure reforms are focused and carried out in an orderly fashion.

Since the 18th National Congress of the Communist Party of China, reforms have shifted from the economic system to the political, cultural, social, environmental and Party building systems, and there has been greater emphasis on coordinating and integrating reforms. The 19th cpc National Congress viewed the pursuit of reform "in a more systematic, holistic, and coordinated way" as a significant experience for comprehensively deepening reform from the previous five-year period and even included it in the newly revised Party Constitution. The latest six major reforms focus on the major objectives of improving and developing the system of socialism with Chinese characteristics and modernizing China's system and capacity for governance. They contain sound overall decisions that need to be carefully executed and precisely coordinated, with an emphasis on practical results, in order to continuously generate new momentum in our development.

Appendix

Contents of the *Collected Works of Zheng Xinli*

Volume I
(1981–1990)

Finished Goods and Pricing of Finished Goods
Enhancing Centralized Management Is an Important Measure to Develop the Energy Industry
Keeping to the Path of Professional Cooperation: A Case Study of the Reorganization of the Beijing Machinery Bureau
Discussion on the Planned Economy and Regulation by the Market since the Issuance of the *Resolution*
Beijing First Machine Tool Factory's Study of the Theoretical and Political Work in Quotas
Controlling the Scale of Construction and Ensuring Robust Economic Development
Constraints to Greater Infrastructure Investment
Improving Quality of Life on the Basis of Developing Production
Funding Technological Progress
Technological Upgrading Entails a Long-Term Plan
Systematically Improving the Quality of Enterprises
Closing the Door on the Past and Exploring the Future: Review of Wang Mengkui's Book Titled *Exploration of China's Path of Building Socialism*
A Socialist Society Should Take a Proactive Approach to Reform
Successful Experience in Improving the Economic Accounting of Industrial Enterprises
On the Factory Director Responsibility System
The Responsibilities a Factory Director Should Undertake
An Urgent Task for Young and Middle-Aged Officials
The Second Revolution and Theoretical Development

X. Zheng, *China's 40 Years of Economic Reform and Development*,
https://doi.org/10.1007/978-981-13-2727-8

Improving Economic Performance
The Second Revolution and Theoretical Issues
Centering Economic Reform on China's Reality
Documents on Guiding Reform Based on China's Reality
The Problem of Food Security in Building a Moderately Prosperous Society
The Situation of Funds, Technology, and Labor Market in Foshan
Improving the Leasing Business in the Development Process
Strengthening Intra-Party Democracy and Political Activity within the Party
Preliminary Research on the System Control Model of the Socialist Market Economy
A Preliminary Analysis of the Economy in 1987
Changes and Problems in the Moderate-Scale Management of Agricultural Land in Shunyi County
Technology Goods and the Technology Market
Development of a Livestock Company with Annual Production Capacity of Millions of Peking Ducks: A Study of Qianlu Duck Farm in Shunyi County
Necessity of Developing Innovative Building Materials
Establishing a Macro Regulatory System to Coordinate Fiscal and Financial Policies
Adjustment of Fiscal Tightening
The Economy's Management Information System
Development of the Modern Information Industry and Accompanying Opportunities
Focusing on Market Competition to Kick-Start the Economy
Accelerating the Development of Educational Technology to Facilitate Economic Rejuvenation
On the Relationship between IT Application and Industrialization, Commercialization, and Socialization and Modernization

Volume II
(1990–1994)

Measures Taken to Achieve Robust Economic Development in the 1990s
The Auto Industry Should Become a Pillar Industry in the 20th Century
Macroeconomic Trends and Business Decisions of Enterprises
Year of 1991: The Market Is Rallying Fast But Is Unlikely to Make a Breakthrough
Preface to *The Book on Socialist Cultural and Ethical Progress*
Deepening Policy Studies: Excerpts from *The Book on Modern Policy Study*
Preface to *The Dictionary of the People's Republic of China*
Mobilizing Various Sectors to Develop the Tertiary Industry
The Maturing Market in the 1990s
Regulating the State-Enterprise Distribution Relationship According to a Modern Corporate System
The Reform of Ways to Realize Ownership by the Whole People
The Establishment of the Export-Import Bank of China
Expanding Enterprise Autonomy Will Not Cause Chaos and Confusion

The Auto Industry in the Face of Rejoining the General Agreement on Tariffs and Trade
Accelerating the Creation of the Socialist Market Economy
A Socialist Market Economy Must Have a Powerful Macro Regulatory System
Adapting to the Requirements of the Socialist Market Economy and Accelerating Reform of the Fixed-Asset Investment System
The Cultivation and Development of Pillar Industries in the 1990s
A Historic Mission of Chinese Entrepreneurs for the Next Decade and Beyond
Report on the Current Situation of China's Real Estate Market
Establishing an Incentive and Risk-Constraint Mechanism for Fixed-Asset Investments
China's New Stage of Economic Development and Long-Term Economic Growth Prospects
Report on the Real Estate Industries of Japan and Singapore
The Macro Regulatory System of China's Market Economy
Economic Thought of Deng Xiaoping regarding the Direction of the Reform of the Planning System
Reforming the Planning System and Transforming the Function of Planning
Upholding the Tasks of Reform, Development, and Stability

Volume III
(1994–1996)

An Analysis of Macroeconomic Policy (1993–1994)

Preface
Chapter I A Year of Continuous, Rapid, and Healthy Economic Development
Chapter II Financial Policy: Evaluation of 1993 and Trends in 1994
Chapter III Fiscal and Tax Policies: Evaluation of 1993 and Trends in 1994
Chapter IV Investment Policy: Evaluation of 1993 and Trends in 1994
Chapter V Pricing Policy: Evaluation of 1993 and Trends in 1994
Chapter VI Agricultural and Rural Development Policies: Evaluation of 1993 and Trends in 1994
Chapter VII Economic Foreign Policy: Evaluation of 1993 and Trends in 1994
Chapter VIII Macro-Level Real Estate Policy: Evaluation of 1993 and Trends in 1994

Establishing an Investment System for the Market Economy
Accelerating Reform, Promoting Development, and Maintaining Stability
Accelerating the Rejuvenation of the Economy around the Bohai Rim
Establishing and Improving the Socialist Market Economy
Macroeconomic Policies of the Republic of Korea
Accelerating the Development of Pillar Industries and Boosting the Economy
A Review of 90 Days of Comprehensive Reform
Improving Thoughts on Planning and Transforming the Functions of Planning
Focusing on the Key Links in the Rejuvenation of Pillar Industries
Long-Term Prospects for China's Economy

Pushing Forward Reforms of State-Owned Enterprises: In Commemoration of Jiang Yiwei
Curbing Inflation Is a Big-Picture Matter
Prospects and Expectations of China's Market in 1995
The Chinese Government's Development Strategy and Social Development
Transformation of the Growth Model Is the Centerpiece of the New Development Strategy
Great Guidelines for a New Century
On the Strategy of Big Enterprises and Groups of China
Maintaining Market Competition by Regulating Conduct
Keeping the Economy on Course for Robust Growth Is the Top Priority

Volume IV
(1995–1996)

Six Economic Reforms

Introduction
Chapter I Establishment of a Modern Corporate System
Chapter II Reform of the Fiscal and Taxation Systems
Chapter III Reform of the Financial System
Chapter IV Reform of Economic Foreign Policy
Chapter V Reform of the Planning System
Chapter VI Reform of the Fixed-Asset Investment System

References for Gaining a Better Understanding of the Report on the Work of the Government to the Fourth Session of Eighth National People's Congress

Chapter I Great Blueprint for the 21st Century
Chapter II Great Achievements of the 8th Five-Year Plan Period
Chapter III Targets and Guidelines for the Next 15 Years
Chapter IV Macro Regulatory Target for the Ninth Five-Year Plan
Chapter V Transforming the Economic Growth Model
Chapter VI Strengthening Agricultural Development
Chapter VII Strengthening the Development of Infrastructure and Basic Industries
Chapter VIII Rejuvenating Pillar Industries
Chapter IX Developing the Tertiary Industry
Chapter X Direction and Policies for Regional Economic Development
Chapter XI Establishing a Modern Corporate System
Chapter XII Developing and Improving the Market System
Chapter XIII Regulating and Improving the Systems of Primary Distribution and Secondary Distribution
Chapter XIV Accelerating Social Security Reform
Chapter XV Improving the Macro Regulatory System
Chapter XVI Developing an Open Economy
Chapter XVII Accelerating Economic Legislation
Chapter XVIII Developing Social Programs

Volume V
(1995–1996)

Strategies for the Rejuvenation of China's Pillar Industries

Preface
Chapter I Rejuvenating Pillar Industries Is the Strategic Task in the New Stage of Economic Development
Chapter II Objective Evidence for Determining the Four Pillar Industries
Chapter III Current Development Trends and Existing Problems of China's Pillar Industries
Chapter IV Suggestions for the Focuses, Targets, and Policies of Rejuvenating China's Pillar Industries
Chapter V China's Auto Industry Current Situation and Problems
Chapter VI Industrial Characteristics and Development Trends of the Auto Industry
Chapter VII Prospects and Expectations concerning China's Auto Market
Chapter VIII Development Strategy and Choices for China's Auto Industry
Chapter IX Measures to Rejuvenate China's Auto Industry

An Analysis of Macroeconomic Policy (1994–1995)

Preface
Chapter I A Year of Striking a Balance between Reform, Development, and Stability
Chapter II Financial Policy Evaluation of 1994 and Trends in 1995
Chapter III Fiscal and Tax Policies: Evaluation of 1994 and Trends in 1995
Chapter IV Investment Policy: Evaluation of 1994 and Trends in 1995
Chapter V Pricing Policy: Evaluation of 1994 and Trends in 1995
Chapter VI Agricultural and Rural Development Policies: Evaluation of 1994 and Trends in 1995
Chapter VII Policies for Foreign Trade and Foreign Exchange: Evaluation of 1994 and Trends in 1995
Chapter VIII Social Development Policy: Evaluation of 1994 and Trends in 1995

Economic Trends in 1996 and Macroeconomic Measures
Upholding the Scheme of Exchanging Market for Technology
Transforming the Growth Model
Moving from the Extensive Growth to an Intensive Growth Model
Letting Enterprise Groups Play the Leading Role as Soon as Possible
Stressing Industrial Safety While Enhancing Market Openness
Accelerating China's Economic Transformation
A Great Blueprint for the New Century

Volume VI
(1995–1997)

New Journey, New Guidelines: Gaining a Better Understanding of the Documents of the Fifth Plenary Session of the 14th CPC Central Committee
Industrial Development Policies: Comparing and Learning

Preface
New Stage of China's Economic Development and Industrial Policy
International Comparison of China's Industrial Development Policy
Hidden Government Intervention: Industrial Development Policy of the United States
Improving the Quality of Labor: Industrial Development Policy of Germany
Pushing Forward Industrial Modernization: Industrial Development Policy of France
Japan's Industrial Policy in the Period of High Economic Growth
Integrating Government Intervention and Export-Oriented Development Strategy: Industrial Development Policy of the Republic of Korea
International Experience and Lessons on Industrial Organization and Structures
Comparison of Foreign Trade Policy between China, Japan, the Republic of Korea, and Germany
Comparison of Technology Introduction Policy between China, Japan, and the Republic of Korea
Changes and Choices of China's Industrial Policy
Approaches and Measures to Improve Economies of Scale in China's Industrial Sector
New Understanding of China's Industrial Policy

Land Cultivation Should Be the Growth Area of China's Agricultural and Rural Development for the Next 15 Years
Accelerating Stock Adjustments to Encourage Acquisitions and Syndication: Answers to Questions of a Reporter with the *La Presse*
Revelations of the Zhongce Phenomenon
An Analysis of Economic Reform during the Period from 1996 to 1997
Rejuvenating Pillar Industries is the Strategic Task of Economic Development for the Next Decade and Beyond
Why It Is Difficult for the Urban Housing Industry to Become a Growth Point
Hong Kong's "Reunion" with China Will Bring New Opportunities for Economic Development of the Mainland: Answers to Questions of Hao Zehua, Reporter with *China Market News*
Creating a Stage of Long-Term, Continuous, and Healthy Development
Reforming the Investment and Financing Mechanisms, and Promoting Continuous and Robust Economic Growth
The Principal Breakthrough in Ideology and Theory
Historic Achievements

Volume VII
(1997–1999)

Technology Market and Information and Technology Consulting in the United States
Government Functions and the Development of the Legal System in China's Economic Transition
Gaining a Better Understanding of Deng Xiaoping Thought and Improving the Macro Regulatory System
Promoting the Two Transformations and Addressing the Two Challenges of Reform and Development
The Current Situation and Changing Trends of China's Industrial Structure
Striking a Balance between Infrastructure Building, Development of Basic Industries, and the Rejuvenation of Pillar Industries
Adjusting the Economic Structure, Expanding Markets, and Cultivating New Economic Growth Areas
A New Economic Growth Belt: Development Philosophy for the Regional Economies along the Beijing-Kowloon Railway
Maintaining the High-Growth and Low-Inflation Development Momentum
Seeking Progress While Maintaining Stability
Meeting the Requirements for Housing and Transport and Boosting Economic Growth: Answers to Questions of Hu Yuelong, Reporter with *China Economic Herald*
Ensuring 8 Percent Economic Growth This Year
The Focus Should Be on Implementation
New Situations and Missions after a Soft Landing
The Netherlands' Practice of Combining Home Mortgage Loans with Insurance and What China can Learn from It
Attending to Developing the Knowledge-Based Economy and Accelerating Modernization of the Economy
Expanding Domestic Demand: Explanation of China's New Economic Policies
Kick-Starting the Four Factors Driving the Consumer Market and Boosting Economic Growth: Answers to Questions of Li Anding, Reporter with *Xinhua News Agency*
Figuring Out Where China Should Start to Eliminate Redundant Construction
Information and Technology Industry Should Be a New Economic Growth Area
The Pulling Effect on Consumer Demand
The Responsibility for Quality Is of Paramount Importance
Improving Macroeconomic Regulation
Macroeconomic Management Reform in China
Expanding Domestic Demand: a Vital Strategic Guideline
Expanding Domestic Demand: What China Should Do This Year: Answers to Questions of Fei Weiwei, Reporter with *People's Daily*

A Good Start for the Economy But Still a Lot to Do to Expand Domestic Demand: Answers to Questions of Reporters in Regard to Sensitive Economic Issues
Industrial Upgrading and Adjustments to the Investment Structure
Giving Full Play to Hong Kong as a Free Port

Volume VIII
(1999)

Breaking Demand Bottlenecks and Promoting Economic Growth
Great Achievements and Promising Prospects: A Review of the Past Five Decades of China's Development and Prospects for the New Century
Proactively Kick-Starting the Consumer Market

A Case Study of Development Planning (I)
Introduction
Chapter I Basic Characteristics of China's Development Planning in the Current Period
Chapter II Main Tasks for Development Planning in the Current Period
Chapter III The Development Planning System and Planning Priorities
Chapter IV A New Form of Development Planning
Chapter V Formulation and Techniques of National Development Plans in the Socialist Market Economy
Chapter VI Reinvigorating the Country through Science and Education
Chapter VII Sustainable Development
Chapter VIII Total Supply and Demand Balance and Structural Optimization
Chapter IX Income Distribution and Consumption Adjustment
Chapter X Sources, Application, and Planned Management of Social Funds at the National Level
Chapter XI Planning and Management of Fixed-Asset Investment
Chapter XII Balance in International Payments and Foreign Economic Regulation
Chapter XIII Macro-Level Management and Regulation of Prices
Chapter XIV Application and Coordination of Macro Regulatory Approaches in Development Planning
Chapter XV Development Planning and the Building of a Legal System
Chapter XVI Development Planning and the New Economic Accounting System

Volume IX
(1999–2002)

A Case Study of Development Planning (II)

Chapter XVII Support System for Development Planning
Chapter XVIII Formation and Transformation of China's Planned Economy
Chapter XIX Overview of Development Planning in Foreign Countries
Chapter XX Formulation and Implementation of Each Five-Year Plan

Taking Proactive Measures and Encouraging Social Investment
Continuing to Expand Domestic Demand and Promoting Continuous and Rapid Economic Growth
Keeping to the Basic Policy of Expanding Domestic Demand and Promoting Continuous, Rapid, and Healthy Economic Growth
Current Priorities for Expanding Domestic Demand
Sticking to the Development Policy of Expanding Domestic Demand
Exploring New Ways to Use Foreign Capital to Facilitate Industrial Adjustment: A Report on the Joint Ventures and Cooperation between the Eastman Kodak Company and Chinese Photographic Materials Industries and Enterprises
Two Pillars for the Rejuvenation of the Chinese Nation
Support for China's Economic Growth over the Next Two Decades
Further Expanding Domestic Demand
The Three-Step Development Strategy and China's Modernization Process
Two Five Decades for China's Economic Development
The Role of Monetary Policy in the Falling Commodity Prices
China's Plan for Economic and Social Development and Its Agenda for Sustainable Development
Factors Holding Back Consumption Growth and Countermeasures
Expanding Domestic Demand Entails Expanding the Field of Consumption
Combine the Expansion of Domestic Demand with the Optimization of the Industrial Structure
Several Issues to Be Studied in the Formulation of the 10th Five-Year Plan
Systemic Impediments to Consumption Upgrading
Inadequate Demand: Principal Contradiction in the Current Economic Life
Targets and Tasks of Macro Regulation in 2000: Answers to Questions of Zhang Quanling, Reporter with *China Central Television*
A Review of the Past Five Decades of China's Development and Prospects by 2050
Prospects for China's Macroeconomy
New Plans for Government Investment
Expanding Domestic Demand: Top Priority of Macro Regulation
Seizing the Opportunities, Rise to the Occasion, and Proactively Confront the Challenges of Globalization
High Savings, High Investment, Low Income, and Low Consumption: Fundamental Causes for Inadequate Demand
Multiplying the Effect of the Holiday Economy
Developing High Technology, and Promoting Industrial Upgrading
Large-Scale Development in Western China Should Comply with Natural Laws and Economic Principles
Consolidating the Policy Effect of Expanding Domestic Demand and Maintain the Economic Upturn
The New Situation and New Tasks after the Development of a Full-Blown Buyer's Market
Problems for the Development of Real Estate Industry during the 10th Five-Year Plan Period

Accelerating the Strategic Adjustment of the Economic Structure
Policy and Strategy Are Vital to the Communist Party of China
A New Leg of the Journey and New Achievements in the Future: Gaining a Better Understanding of the *Recommendations for the 13th Five-Year Plan for Economic and Social Development* Adopted at the Fifth Plenary Session of the 15th CPC Central Committee
Seizing the Historic Opportunity and Accelerating National Rejuvenation
Hubei Province Will Enter a New Period of Rapid Development
Vehicles Facilitate Transport and Energize Cities
Principal Targets of Social and Economic Development for the Next Five Years
The Brand-Name Strategy Is the Path to Prosperity
Boosting the Development of E-Commerce
Researching the Formulation and Implementation of Economic Policies
Guidelines and Characteristics of the Outline of the 10th Five-Year Plan
Upholding Development as the Theme
Attracting Investment and Accelerating Development in Western China
Developing Famous Brands and Strengthening International Competitiveness
Opportunities and Challenges for Progressing by Leaps and Bounds
Increasing Investment Returns and the Investment Attractiveness of Western China
Problems to Be Studied in China's Current Rural Economic Development Situation
Seizing the Opportunities and Proactively Confronting the Challenges of Globalization
Looking at the Transformation of Rural Township Enterprises in Southern Jiangsu Province Based on the Market Performance of Jiangyin-Based Listed Companies
Trend and Approach of China's Industrial Upgrading amid Globalization
How Surrounding Areas Can Be Integrated into Beijing's Circle of Development: Answers to Questions of Reporters with *Farmers' Daily*
Sustainable Development Is the Sure Way to Grow Enterprises

Volume X
(2002–2005)

The Only Path to China's Rapid Agricultural Development and Industrialization
Learning from Foreign Countries and Promoting Industrial Agriculture
Problems to Be Studied and Solved in China's Current Macro Regulations
Gaining a Better Understanding of the Functions of Taxation
Implementing the Strategy of Exchanging Labor for Land, and Developing the Foreign Trade of Agricultural Products
Keeping the Birth of the 10-Thousand-Ton Metal Extrusion Machine in Perspective When Looking at China's Capacity for Equipment Manufacturing
Seizing the Opportunity, Going Global, and Developing Township and Village Enterprises
An Analysis of the Economy in the First Half of 2002 and Advice for Macro Regulatory Measures
Principal Breakthrough in Realization of Public Ownership: Investigation of the Public-Sector of the Economy and Development of Zhejiang Province

Securing Food Quality and Safety Is the Current Top Priority
Prospects for China's Economy by 2020
Problems and Measures in the Development of China's New Rural Cooperative Economic Organizations
Revitalizing Liaoning Province in Accelerating the Development of Strategic Industries
The Law of the People's Republic of China on Land Contract in Rural Areas Provides Legal Safeguards for Social Stability and Rural Development
Economic Theory Cannot Lag behind Practice
Policy Is Vital for China's Prosperity
Improving the Organization and Operation of Agricultural Industrialization
China's Macroeconomic Situation and Prospects
Development Entails New Thought
Relying on Regional Advantages and Strengthening Cities' Economic Prowess
Increasing the Revenue of Farmers of Principal Agricultural Products Is the Key to Solving the New Challenges Facing Agriculture, Countryside, and Farmers
Developing the Wheat Economy
Zhejiang Province's Answer to the Issue of Agriculture
Suggestions on the Reform of Shanxi Coal Transportation and Sales Group
Creating an Investment and Development Environment for the Building of Global Cities
Urbanization Cannot Lag behind Industrialization
Accelerating Reform, Adjusting the Economic Structure, Expanding Consumption, and Pursuing Coordinated Development: An Analysis of Economic Trends in 2003 and Suggestions for 2004
Developing the Capital Market Is the Priority to Improve the Market System
Improving the Guidelines of the Socialist Market Economy: Gaining a Better Understanding of the *Decision on Issues concerning Improving the Socialist Market Economy* adopted at the Third Plenary Session of the 16th CPC Central Committee
Increasing Vitality for the Development of the Economic Circle around Wuhan
The *Decision* Is the Guideline for Promoting Reform: Answers to Reporter with the *Study Times*
Deepening Reform of China's Labor and Employment Systems
The Mixed-Ownership Joint Stock System Is a Major Way to Realize Public Ownership
Two Innovations of the *Decision on Issues concerning Improving the Socialist Market Economy* Adopted at the Third Plenary Session of the 16th CPC Central Committee
A Historical Mission of the Top 100 Listed Chinese Companies
Accelerating Reforms of State-Owned Enterprises Is the Key to the Revitalization of the Northeast
Four Focuses of Macro Regulation in the Crucial Period
Developing Intellectual Properties and Strengthening Core Competency of Enterprises

Accelerating Reform of State-Owned Enterprises
Accelerating Social Sector Reforms
What Resources Can Be Tapped to Achieve the Rise of the Central Region?
Seizing the Opportunity of Opening Up and Accelerating the Development of Guangxi Province
Opinions on the Benefit the People Project and Industrial Development of Northern Jiangsu
Structural Problems Are More Harmful Than an Overheated Economy
Distorted Economic Relationships to Be Reversed during the 11th Five-Year Plan Period
Promoting Ways to Realize Public Ownership
Five Principal Strategies for Energy Security
Adjusting the Investment Structure for New Industrialization
The Economy Is at Another Juncture
Accelerating Rural Reform and Maintaining the Rapid Growth of Farmers' Income
Zhang Xiuji: An Entrepreneur Who Created the Glorious History of China's Machinery Industry
Exploring a New Path and Promoting New Development: Preface to *Bringing Out the Inner Dynamism for Development in Rural Areas: Investigation of Longmen County*
Macro Regulation: Focusing on Structural Adjustment, and Transform the Growth Model
Increasing Farmers' Income Should Start from Improving Rural Labor Productivity
Reviewing Experience, Increasing Investment, and Consolidating Achievements
Thoughts on Questions about the Rise of the Central Region
Current Economic Trends and Financial Regulations of China
Replacing Heavy and Chemical Industrialization with New Industrialization
Four Tasks for Economic Structural Adjustments
Current Priorities for Technological Innovation
Continuing to Explore Economic Principles and Sustain the Development Momentum over the Long Run
A Look at Large-Scale Development in Western China within the New Strategic Framework
Current Economic Situation and Principal Tasks in 2005
Key to the Transformation of the Economic Growth Model: Strengthening the Capacity for Innovation

Volume XI
(2003)

China: Industrialization in the 21st Century (I)
Chapter I A Historical Review of China's Growth Model
Chapter II Principal Tasks and Steps to Realize the Strategic Targets of Step Three
Chapter III Accelerating the Transformation of the Economic Growth Model

Chapter IV Transforming Several Kinds of Relationships in the Economic Growth Model
Chapter V Accelerating the Strategic Adjustments of the Economic Structure, Developing the Economy, and Improving Overall Quality
Chapter VI Promoting Technological Progress and Innovation, and Accelerating Industrial and Technological Upgrading
Chapter VII Raising the Level of Labor Quality and Fully Developing Human Resources
Chapter VIII Accelerating the Structural Adjustments of Enterprises to Increase the Efficiency of Production
Chapter IX Strengthening and Improving Enterprise Management, and Making the Management More Effective and Reasonable
Chapter X Accelerating the Transformation of the Economic Growth Model, and Continuing to Strengthen the Capacity for Sustainable Development
Chapter XI Transformation of China into a Knowledge-Based Economy
Chapter XII Improving the Economic System and Market Mechanisms, and Promoting the Transformation of the Economic Growth Model
Chapter XIII Developing an Open Economy and Promoting Economic Growth and Structural Adjustment as Part of Opening Up
Chapter XIV Encouraging a Policy Environment that Facilitates the Transformation of the Growth Model
Chapter XV Establishing an Indicator System to Facilitate the Transformation of the Growth Model
Chapter XVI Prioritizing the Development of the Information Industry and Driving the Process of Industrialization Through IT Application
Chapter XVII Consolidating and Strengthening Agriculture as the Basic Industry and Fully Developing the Rural Economy
Chapter XVIII Speeding Up Rural Industrialization and Promoting Agricultural Modernization and the Whole Industrialization Process
Chapter XIX Actively and Prudently Promoting Urbanization and Facilitating the Reasonable Concentration of Production Factors

Volume XII
(2006)

China: Industrialization in the 21st Century (II)
Chapter XX Cultivating and Consolidating Manufacturing Competitiveness, and Building a Powerful Pillar for the Economy
Chapter XXI Energy Industry
Chapter XXII Petrochemical Industry
Chapter XXIII Steel Industry
Chapter XXIV Auto Industry
Chapter XXV Shipping Industry
Chapter XXVI Machine Tool Industry

Volume XIII
(2006–2009)

Development: Precondition for a Harmonious Society
Promoting the Building of New Socialist Countryside, and Accelerating the Building of a Moderately Prosperous Society in All Respects in Rural Areas
Fully Deepening Rural Reform and Promoting the Building of a New Socialist Countryside
The Netherlands Way to Reverse the Agricultural Trade Deficit
Taking Ecological Civilization as a Starting Point for Making Breakthroughs, and Accelerating the Building of a New Socialist Countryside: Speech at Hainan at the Seminar on the Building of a New Socialist Countryside and Eco-Friendly Village
Placing a High Premium on Establishing Security Measures for Industrial Security
Focusing on New Trends in Mergers and Acquisitions of Foreign Assets
Supply and Demand Trends of China's Energy Sector for the Next 15 Years and Relevant Measures: Speech at the 12th China-France High-Level Economic and Financial Dialogue
Improving the Capacity for Innovation and Strengthening the Competitiveness of Enterprises
Industrialization and Urbanization Strategies to Boost the Development of Guangxi Province
Upholding All-Around, Balanced, and Coordinated Development to Build a Harmonious Society: Gaining a Better Understanding of the *Decision on Issues concerning Improving the Socialist Market Economy* Adopted at the Sixth Plenary Session of the 16th CPC Central Committee
Great Strategic Policies That Ensure National Security and Common Prosperity: Gaining a Better Understanding of the *Decision on Issues concerning Improving the Socialist Market Economy* Adopted at the Sixth Plenary Session of the 16th CPC Central Committee
Boosting Common Development in Regions
Opening Up of China's Financial Market and Risk Prevention Methods
Boosting the Development of the Auto Industry through Innovation
Development Trends in China's Rural Areas for the Next Five Years
Accelerating the Circulation of Production Factors and Developing the Yangtze River Economic Belt: Speech at the Forum on Productivity Development in the Yangtze River Economic Belt Held in Nanjing in 2006
An Analysis of the Progress of China's Work to Build a Moderately Prosperous Society in All Respects in Rural Areas
An Analysis and Predictions of China's Macro Economy for the Next 15 Years
Maintaining the Momentum of Robust and Rapid Economic Growth
The Prospect: The Path Directed by Quality in 2007: Policy Orientation of Macro Regulation
Development Trends in China's Manufacturing Industry amid Economic Globalization
Communicating with the Public on the Internet with Mainstream Voices in China

Multiple Approaches to Greater Innovation Capacity
Developing the Financial Industry: Principal Tasks for China's Economic Development in the Current Period: Speech at the 11th China Capital Market Forum
New Ideas and Opportunities for Cooperation with Transnational Companies
How to Build China's Own Brands: Speech at the Opening Ceremony of the 2006 Forum of National Leading Brand Enterprises
Social Harmony Is the Basic Requirement for Socialism with Chinese Characteristics
Deepening Reform
Focusing All Resources to Rejuvenate the Equipment Manufacturing Industry
Deepening Financial Reforms and Promoting Financial Industry Security
The Theory of Balanced and Sustainable Development Is the Principal Strategic Thought to Develop Socialism with Chinese Characteristics
Launching the Growth Enterprise Market and Supporting Technological Innovation and Entrepreneurship
Development Trends in China's Economy after the 17th CPC National Congress
Changes and Strategic Decision of China's Economic Growth: Speech at the Forum on Economic Situation and Macro Regulations Held in Beijing
Raising Chinese Residents' Consumption Rate Is the Principal Task of Macro Regulations
Finding the Right Starting Point for Financial System Reform
Improving People's Wellbeing, Confronting Challenges, and Tackling Difficult Problems: An Interpretation of *Decision of the CPC Central Committee on Some Principal Issues concerning Building a Harmonious Socialist Society*
Innovation is the Centerpiece of the National Development Strategy
Realizing the Sound and Rapid Development of the Economy: Gaining a Better Understanding of the Political Report to the 17th CPC National Congress
Focusing on Improving People's Lives, and Creating a Better Life for the Chinese People
Establishing the Income Distribution System that Embodies Social Equity: Gaining a Better Understanding the Political Report to the 17th CPC National Congress
Building an Country of Innovators through the Growth Enterprise Market: Speech at the 6th Forum on Finance for Small and Medium-Sized Enterprises
A Masterpiece of the Study of the Strategies for China's Economic Development
Improving the Modern Financial System and Preventing and Coping with Financial Risks
Rejuvenating the Domestic Equipment Manufacturing Industry Entails the Support of the Three Principal Policies
Three Tasks for Ensuring Rapid Economic Growth for the Next Five Years
The Direction that Must Be Upheld to Promote the Development of China's Economic and Social Development
Strengthen Agricultural Infrastructure and Promote a Moderately Prosperous Society in All Respects in Rural Areas
Three Focuses on Fully Deepening the Reform

New Opportunity for Deepening Administrative Reform
Further Improving the Basic Rural Management System: Speech at the Seminar on China's Rural Reform and Development
Realizing Agricultural Modernization in the Processes of Industrialization, Urbanization, IT Application, and Globalization
A Dramatic Economic Downturn Is Not a Risk Yet
Short-Term and Long-Term Measures to Curb Inflation
Now Is the Time to Make Development of the Liaoning Coastal Economic Zone a National Strategy
Commodity Prices, Structures, and Speed of Trade
Accelerating the Transformation and Upgrading of the Development of State-Owned Enterprises: Speech at the Seminar on the Promotion of Reform and Innovation of Sinotruck Group
Realizing Robust and Rapid Development While Curbing Inflation
Promoting Rural Reform through the Establishment of the Six Systems
Establishing the Sanxia Logistics Center to Facilitate Coordinated Regional Development
Pushing Rural Reform to a New Stage of Institutional Development
Human Resources Are a Core National Resource
Stabilizing and Improving the Basic Rural Management System: Implementing the *Decision* Adopted at the Third Plenary Session of the 17th CPC Central Committee
Establishing a System for the Integrated Development of the Economy and Society of Urban and Rural Areas
The Theory of Balanced and Sustainable Development: The Latest Socialist Theory with Chinese Characteristics: A Review of the Book Titled *Introducing Theory of Balanced and Sustainable Development*
Top Priority: Ensuring Robust and Rapid Economic Development
Striving to Reverse the Decline of Economic Growth

Volume XIV
(2009–2011)

Developing Cultural and Creative Industries Is a Principal Task
A Distinctive Textbook on Industrial Economics: A Review of *Industrial Economics* (Third Edition)
The Five Abolishments and Five Establishments of an Economic System That Has Significantly Emancipated the Productive Forces
Removing Institutional Impediments, and Tapping the Energy of Urban-Rural Integration
Strengthening the Pull Effect of Consumption on Economic Development
Huawei: The Secret to Its Success
Understanding the Government-Market Relationship in Response to the Global Financial Crisis
Transforming the Development Pattern Is the Fundamental Approach for Dealing with the Crisis
Six Questions for China's Top Think Tanks

Strengthening the Reform and Opening Up Initiative, and Raising the Awareness of Balanced and Sustainable Development

A Masterpiece Explaining China's Grain Market: A Review of *Development Report on China's Grain Market in 2009*

The 1st Global Think Tank Summit: *Beijing Initiative*

Solutions Are Always More Than the Relevant Problems: Speech at the 1st Global Think Tank Summit

Qingdao Port Has Its Own Traditions and Advantages, Which Cannot Be Borrowed by Foreign Enterprises

Implementing the Policy of Expanding Domestic Demand: Speech at the 1st China Center for International Economic Exchanges (CCIEE) "Monthly Economic Talk" on July 16, 2009

Expanding Domestic Demand Is the Fundamental Measure to Offset Export Decline: Answers to Questions of Reporters at the 1st China Center for International Economic Exchanges (CCIEE) "Monthly Economic Talk" on July 16, 2009

Principal Achievements of the 1st Global Think Tank Summit

Taking Measures to Increase the Share of Resident Income in GDP

Exploring the Path of Urban-Rural Integration: Preface to *Zhucheng Practice of Urban-Rural Integration at the County Level*

Speech at Northeast Asia Forest Ecosystem Conservation Forum (Yichun)

Promoting the Full Employment of Rural Labor Is the Fundamental Way to Narrow the Urban-Rural Gap

Promoting Harmony in East Asia through the Integration of Markets in China, Japan, and the Republic of Korea: Speech at the Seminar on the Pathway for Regional Economic Integration in East Asia in Tokyo

Transformation and Upgrading: Building Livable and Beautiful Cities: Summary of the Speech at the 2009 Happy Jiangyin Forum (Beijing)

Current Economic Trends and the Orientation of Macro Regulatory Policies in 2010: Opening Speech at the 15th Annual Meeting of the Chinese Association of Productivity Science (CAPS) and Seminar of Chinese Fellows of the World Academy of Productivity Science (WAPS)

The Party's Economic Development Strategies in the New Stage

Enhancing the Role of Consumption in Boosting Economic Growth

Modernization of China Entails Three Transformations

Promoting Economic Growth by Improving People's Livelihood

China's Economic Miracles in the Past Six Decades

Reforming and Innovating the Social Management System Is the Top Priority of Economic Work This Year

An Analysis of China's Economy in 2009 and Prospects for 2010

A Review of the Response to the Global Financial Crisis and Future Prospects: An Analysis of China's Economy and Macro Regulatory Policies in 2009

Innovation Is Central to Realizing Industrial Upgrading

Why Can the Revenue from the Transfer of Land-Use Rights Reach Trillions of Yuan?

Promoting the Transformation of the Development Model through Technology
Exemplars for Progressing by Leaps and Bounds: Preface to *Research of the Inner Mongolia Phenomenon: Strive to Take the Lead*
Strengthening Awareness, Initiative, and Creativity to Transform the Economic Development Model: A Review of the *Study of the Transformation of Economic Development Model*
Quickly Increasing the Wealth of Principal Agricultural Producers
Current Sensitive Issues of China's Economic Development
Ensuring Adequate Housing to Promote the Sound Development of China's Real Estate Industry
Economic Turnaround Momentum Is Strong, But Structural Upgrading Needs to Be Strengthened
China's Auto Industry Should Stand on the Shoulders of Giants to Seek Further Development
Global Economic Changes Present Opportunities and Challenges for China's Development
Establishing a Growth Mechanism in Asia
Suggestions for the Development Planning of the 12th Five-Year Plan Period in Henan Province
Accelerating the Transformation of the Development Model: Promoting Robust and Rapid Economic Growth: An Analysis of the Economy in the First Half of 2010 and the Prospects for the Second Half
Conservation in Distant Areas and Contracting in Near Places: The Practically of Yichun's Reform Model of State-Owned Forest Distribution: Speech at the Forum on the Reform of State-Owned Forest Tenure at the Fourth Anniversary of the Forest Tenure Pilot Reform Program of Yichun
The Establishment of the China Center for International Economic Exchanges (CCIEE) as Part of the Exploration on Building New Think Tanks
Establishing Leading Think Tanks: Speech at the Convention for the Establishment of the CCIEE Party Committee of the CPC
New Opportunities for Cooperation: The Beibu Gulf Economic Zone
Preventing Financial Risks in Common Development Projects
Maintaining Rapid Economic Development While Stabilizing Commodity Prices
The 11th Five-Year Plan: Translating Risks into Opportunities and Forge Ahead
Preface to *Cultural Construction and the National Soft Power*
Transformation of the Economic Development Model Is the Focus throughout the 12th Five-Year Plan Period
Four Historic Missions for Chinese Enterprises: Speech at the 10th China Annual Management Summit
Transforming the Economic Development Pattern Is an Urgent Strategic Task
Translating Inflation Pressure into Impetus for Industrial Upgrading
Enabling Emerging Economies to Play an Important Role in Driving Global Economic Recovery
Difficulties, Cooperation, and Needs for the BRICS Countries

Transforming the Development Model and Accelerating the Development of Central China
How State-Owned Enterprises Drive the Transformation of the Economic Development Model
Strategic Transformation of the Economic Development Model for the 12th Five-Year Plan: Speech at the Second China-Europe High-Level Political Parties Forum
Intangible Assets Should Also Be Taken into Consideration for SOE Assessments: Speech at the "Gold Prize Round Table" of Board of Directors of Chinese Listed Companies in May 2011
Improving Coordination of Economic Growth, Structural Adjustment and Commodity Prices
The Power of Urban-Rural Integration Is Reflected in Post-Disaster Recovery
Three Challenges for the Transformation of the Development Model of Private Enterprises
Establishing Leading Think Tanks in Study, Communication, and Consultation: Speech at the Second Global Think Tank Summit
Reform and Opening Up Is the Great Awakening of Members of the Communist Party of China
The Mainstay That Successfully Dealt with the International Financial Crisis
Three Transformations of the Development Model All Rely on Reform
Transformation of the Development Model Is Key for Solving Current and Long-Term Problems Affecting Economic and Social Development
Accelerating Development of the Logistics Industry Is the Strategic Priority for the Transformation of the Economic Development Model
Three Problems with the Goals to Rebalance the Global Economy: Preface to *Wages, Exchange Rates, and Trade Surplus*

Volume XV
(2011–2014)

The Double Targets of Curbing Inflation and Stabilizing Growth
Facilitating Coordinated Agricultural Modernization, Industrialization and Urbanization
China Is the Momentum behind the Global Economy
Accelerating the Establishment of a New Urban-Rural Integration System
Grasping the Opportunity of the Wi-Fi Era for Better Productivity
Essay for the Inaugural Issue of the *Journal of the Northeast Asia Studies*
Consolidating the Turning Point in Commodity Prices
Keeping Making Progress in Reform Is the Key for China's Path
How Economists Should Make Contributions to Prolong the Period of Rapid Economic Growth
Five Potential Outcomes for China's Economic Growth
New Tasks for Financial Reform

Strengthening Technological Innovation and Establishing Green Energy Bases: Speech at a Symposium on the Study of the Establishment of National Energy Base in Southern China by Guizhou Province
Adhering to the Strong Engine of the Expedited Innovation Reforms
Response to Major Natural Disasters and a Study of Food Security in China
Strengthening Economic Cooperation with Other BRICS Countries
Improving Livelihoods Is the Fundamental Purpose for the Transformation of the Economic Development Model
Focusing on Changes in Trends in Adjustments of the World Economic Pattern
Industrial Development Is the Way to Boost the Urban Economy
A Principal Reform to Implement Is the Concept of Exercising State Power for the Benefit of the People
Strengthening the Pull Effect of Demand on Economic Growth: Speech at a Symposium on the Economy in the First Half of 2012 held by the CPPCC Committee for Economic Affairs
Prioritizing the Stabilization of Economic Growth
The Institutional Safeguard for the Sustainable Development in Chins
Innovation Promotes the Integration of IT Application and Industrialization
Remarkable Achievements of Chinese Economic Theories
SOEs Should Take the Lead in Innovation: Speech at the 27th China Center for International Economic Exchanges (CCIEE) "Monthly Economic Talk" on September 20, 2012
Improving Land-Use Concentration through IT Application and Industrialization: Speech at the Symposium on Economical and Intensive Utilization of Land and Resources
Attracting Social Funds for Agricultural Modernization
Four Principal Challenges for Doubling Residents' Income
Seizing the New Opportunity for Promoting the Transformation of the Economic Development Model
Five Principal Opportunities for the Economic Development of China
Focusing on Key Aspects of Financial Reforms
Balancing the Government-Market Relationship Is Instrumental for Economic Structural Reform
Opportunities Brought by the International Financial Crisis for China's Economic Development
Sparing No Effort in Promoting Innovation
Raising the Bearing Capacity of County Towns for Industries and Population
Setting Transformation of the Development Model as the Target for Reform
Structural Reform and Adjustment Are the Approaches for the Target of Exploiting the Potential of Economic Growth
Building Consensus on Reform by Changing the Growth Model
Accelerating Agricultural Modernization Is the Inevitable Path for China to Become a High-Income Country
Suggestions on Building an Asian Infrastructure Investment and Financing Institution Led by China

What China Should Learn from Germany
Making Zhoushan the Gateway for China's Pacific Economic Circle
The Roadmap for the Reform of the Financial System
Focusing on the Transformation of the Development Model to Deepen Reform
Four Difficulties for Realizing the Target of Building a Moderately Prosperous Society in All Respects: Speech at the 2013 Annual Meeting of Board of Directors of the Chinese Association of Productivity Science (CAPS) and 2012 Seminar of Chinese Fellows of the World Academy of Productivity Science (WAPS)
Emerging Economies Should Strengthen Resistance to Financial Risks
Updating the Chinese Economy Should Be the Primary Measure to Stabilize Growth
Prospects of Challenges and Cooperation for Emerging Economies
Realizing Robust Growth in the Transformation of the Development Model
Four Explorations and the Inspiration for Urban-Rural Integration
My 13 Years on the National Planning Commission (1987–2000)
Building an Updated Version of the Chinese Economy: Views and Measures for Upgrading the Chinese Economy
Realizing Robust Growth by Expanding Domestic Demand and Adjusting the Economic Structure
Four Challenges for Building an Updated Version of the Chinese Economy
Responsibilities of the Chinese Auto Industry for the Next Decade
Transformation of the Growth Model and Expansion of Domestic Demand Entails Robust Economic Growth
Social Responsibilities of Enterprises: An Important Issue: Preface to Wang Tianren's *30 Talks on Social Responsibilities of Enterprises*
Upholding the Target of Establishing the Socialist Market Economy
Facts Prove that the Suggestions of the CPPCC Are Crucial
The Exploration of New and Diverse Models of Urbanization
Fully Grasping the Development Trends of China's Economy
Keeping Reform Oriented toward a Socialist Market Economy
Boosting Effective Demand
Sticking to New Urbanization with Chinese Characteristics
Three Principal Breakthroughs in Realizing the Public Ownership of Rural Land
The *Decision* Adopted at the Third Plenary Session of the 18th CPC Central Committee and the Future China
Problems for Deepening Economic Reforms
Stabilizing Economic Growth
Focusing on the Right Starting Point for Promoting Economic Transformation and Upgrading

Volume XVI
(2014–2016)

Exploring Building of New-Type Think Tanks with Chinese Characteristics
Removing Administrative Obstacles and Reforming the Governance System

A New Urbanization: Difficulties in Counties and Breakthroughs in City-Industry Integration
Accelerating the Development of the Huai River Economic Belt: An Important Strategic Step to Expand Domestic Demand
Improvement and Development of the Public Ownership System for Rural Land
Macro Regulation Should Transition from Aggregate Regulation to Structural Adjustment
Driving the Transformation of the Industrial Development Model through Innovation
Transforming the Traditional View of Development and Accelerating Economic Transformation and Upgrading: Dialogue between Executive Vice President Zheng Xinli and Professor Guan Yixin
A Comparative Study of the Beijing Government's Policy for Information and Technology Innovation
Optimizing the Macro Regulatory Structure
Learning from Foreign Countries, and Developing Agricultural Insurance: Speech at the 4th International Conference on Agricultural Insurance
Developing a Value-Based Compensation System for Public Goods and the Modern Fiscal System
Strengthening Macro regulation Capacity, and Accelerating Economic Transformation and Upgrading
Asia Is in Urgent Need of a Uniform Credit Rating System
Why Shenzhen's Patent Application Leads the World
Establishing an International Reserve Currency System with Checks and Balances
Making Cooperatives the Main Force for Ensuring Food Safety
Giving Play to New Development Engines through Reform and New Breakthroughs
Deepening Reform of the Financial System and Supporting the Development of the Real Economy
Reform of the Chinese Financial System and Its Influence on the International Currency System
How the Central Government Plans and Coordinates Reforms in Various Sectors at All Levels: Speech at the Party and the World Dialogue 2014
Letting the Market Decide the Allocation of Financial Resources
Exploring Methods for Realizing Public Rural Land Ownership
Facilitating the Mortgages, Guarantees, and Transfers of Rural Housing Properties in a Robust and Prudent Manner
Developing Outsourcing Service Models: An Important Approach to Solving the Employment Problem for College Students: Preface to *Report on China Outsourcing Development*
Upholding Balanced and Sustainable Development: Fundamental Approach for Small and Medium Cities to Develop
Focusing on Economic Reform and Tapping Growth Potential
Further Reforms of State-Owned Enterprises
The New Formal: New Understanding and Conclusion, Not a Package

Ensuring Robust Economic Growth
Stabilizing Growth Is the Top Priority of This Year's Economic Work
Tourism: Current Stage of China's Sunrise Industry
Focusing on Rural Reform, Breaking Demand Bottlenecks
The Key Is to Ensure the Balance between Stabilizing Growth and Adjusting the Economic Structure: Gaining a Better Understanding of and Implementing the Speech by Xi Jinping, General Secretary of the CPC Central Committee, at the Central Economic Work Conference
China's Overseas Investment Targets and Strategies
Focusing on New Bright Spots and Opportunities in the New Normal
New Conclusions on the Development Rules of China's Industrial Economy: A Review of *Industrial Economics* (Fourth Edition)
The Belt and Road Initiative Is the Principal Strategy to Improve the System for an Open Economy
What Hubei Province Should Do to Improve Its Level of Marketization
Accelerating Urban-Rural Integration to Build a Moderately Prosperous Society in All Aspects
Placing a High Premium on Tacking Downward Pressure on the Economy
Following the Historic Trend of Urban-Rural Integration: Preface to *Walking between Urban and Rural Areas*
Placing a High Premium on Systemic Risks Incurred by Economic Downturn
Building World-Famous Brands Is the Core to Building a Strong Nation
Learning Patriotism and Persistence from the Life of Cheng Siwei
Expediting Setting up an Economic System and Development Pattern Centered on Innovation
Three Focuses in the Starting Year of the 13th Five-Year Plan
Action Guide in the Decisive Stage in Completing a Moderately Prosperous Society in All Respects: Gaining a Better Understanding of the *Recommendations* Adopted at the Fifth Plenary Session of the 18th CPC Central Committee
Solving the Problem of Overcapacity Entails Marxist Theories of Politics and Economics
Figuring Out and Correcting the False Understanding of China's Development, and Focusing on Structural Reform
Promoting the Concept of Innovative, Coordinated, Green, Open and Shared Development
Getting Rid of Misconceptions on the Deepening of SOE Reform
China Has Great Potential to Join the Ranks of High-Income Countries
Drawing upon the Experience and Lessons of the Netherlands and Japan to Accelerate Agricultural Modernization
Conducting Targeted Poverty Alleviation to Realize a Moderately Prosperous Society in All Respects
Shenzhen's Efforts in Building High-Level and Innovative Universities

The manufacturer's authorised representative in the EU is Springer
Nature Customer Service Centre GmbH, Europaplatz 3, 69115 Heidelberg,
Germany. If you have any concerns regarding our products, please
contact ProductSafety@springernature.com

Printed and bound by CPI Group (UK) Ltd, Croydon, CR0 4YY
30/09/2026
02225448-0016